Bound for Beatitude

THOMISTIC RESSOURCEMENT SERIES

Volume 12

SERIES EDITORS

Matthew Levering, *Mundelein Seminary*

Thomas Joseph White, OP, *Pontifical University of St. Thomas Aquinas*

EDITORIAL BOARD

Serge-Thomas Bonino, OP, *Pontifical University of St. Thomas Aquinas*

Gilles Emery, OP, *University of Fribourg*

Reinhard Hütter, *The Catholic University of America*

Bruce Marshall, *Southern Methodist University*

Emmanuel Perrier, OP, *Dominican Studium, Toulouse*

Richard Schenk, OP, *University of Freiburg, Germany*

Kevin White, *The Catholic University of America*

Bound for Beatitude

A Thomistic Study in Eschatology and Ethics

REINHARD HÜTTER

The Catholic University of America Press
Washington, D.C.

Pope Paul VI, "Credo of the People of God" copyright © 1968
Libreria Editrice Vaticana

Copyright © 2019
The Catholic University of America Press
All rights reserved

Cataloging-in-Publication Data available from
the Library of Congress
ISBN 978-0-8132-3630-8

For
Father John
Confessor, Priest, Teacher,
and Friend

Contents

Preface	ix
Acknowledgments	xi
List of Abbreviations	xiii
Prologue: Beatitude—The Perfection of Being Human	1
1. Ordained for Beatitude—The Finality of the Created Intellect: Sacred Theology, Metaphysics, and the Natural Desire for the Vision of God	86
2. Equipped for Beatitude—To Be Good Is to Do the Truth: Eternal Law, Natural Law, Prudence, and Conscience	151
3. Liberated for Beatitude—Saved from Sin: Christ's Passion on the Cross, the Surpassing Act of Charity	175
4. The Beginning of Beatitude—The Substance of Things Hoped For: The Virtue of Faith	193
5. The Road to Beatitude—Divinization and Friendship with God: The Virtue of Charity	224
6. The Preparation for Beatitude—Justice toward God: The Virtue of Religion	253

7. Perseverance on the Journey to Beatitude—
Reclaiming Martyrdom: The Virtue
of Courage ... 297

8. Protecting the Journey to Beatitude—
Achieving Selfless Self-Control: The Virtue
of Chastity ... 329

9. The Exemplar of Beatitude—Hope for the
Wayfarer: The Blessed Virgin Mary's Bodily
Assumption into Heaven ... 367

Epilogue: God—Man's Beatitude ... 387

Selected Bibliography ... 447
Index of Names ... 479
General Index ... 485

Preface

This book has grown over the course of numerous years and in the context of countless conversations with friends, colleagues, and students. I will undoubtedly have forgotten some interlocutors, but I would like to record my thanks especially to Sr. Maria of the Angels, OP, and the Dominican nuns of the Monastery of Our Lady of Grace, North Guilford, Connecticut. I would also like to thank John F. Boyle, Fr. Romanus Cessario, OP, Thomas De Koninck, Archbishop Joseph Augustine Di Noia, OP, Fr. Kevin Flannery, SJ, Jennifer Frey, Fr. Simon Gaine, OP, Michael Gorman, Carlos A. Casanova Guerra, Francis Russell Hittinger, Nancy Heitzenrater Hütter, Warren Kinghorn, Angela McKay Knobel, Fr. Brian Kromholtz, OP, Fr. Matthew Lamb, Matthew Levering, Steven A. Long, Fr. Guy Mansini, OSB, Bruce D. Marshall, Anselm Mueller, John O'Callaghan, Michael Pakaluk, Thomas Pfau, Philip Rolnick, Miguel J. Romero, Fr. Richard Schenk, OP, Fr. Michael Sherwin, OP, Fr. Raymund Snyder, OP, Daria Spezzano, Fr. Ezra Sullivan, OP, Candace Vogler, Michael Maria Waldstein, Matthew Whelan, Fr. Thomas Joseph White, OP, and Matthias Zeindler.

The structure of the book has profited from the helpful advice offered by Fr. Thomas Joseph White, OP, and Matthew Levering. Several chapters are stronger because of the suggestions and criticisms offered by the academicians of the Pontifical Academy of St. Thomas Aquinas. I am very grateful for the astute criticisms and recommendations that two anonymous peer reviewers offered. Thanks to their collegial labor, I was able to improve the overall argument and to correct various mistakes.

Several chapters of this book benefited from the support of the John Templeton Foundation grant "Virtue, Happiness, and the Meaning of Life." I am grateful for the instructive interdisciplinary conversations with colleagues in philosophy, psychology, the social sciences, and neurobiology that the Templeton Foundation made possible. It has been a privilege to work with Paul Higgins in his judicious editing of the text. I am grateful to David Augustine, Meghan Duke, and Judith Heyhoe for their constructive comments and criticisms, as well as their editorial assistance. Special thanks go to David L. Augustine for compiling the indexes.

I thank the editors of *Espíritu*, *Nova et Vetera* (English edition), and *The Thomist* as well as the RIL editors (Santiago, Chile) for granting me permission to reprint material that is included here.

I dedicate this book in profound gratitude to Reverend Monsignor John Joseph Williams, PhD (University of Georgia, Athens), STD (Facultés Catholiques de Toulouse), to whom I am indebted in more ways than words can express.

Acknowledgments

Earlier versions of chapter 1 were presented as lectures on June 7, 2014, at the fourth Annual Philosophy Workshop, "Aquinas on God," at Mount Saint Mary College, Newburgh, New York, and on July 29, 2014, at the second International Conference on Thomistic Philosophy, "Gratia non tollit naturam, sed perficit cam," at the Center for Thomistic Studies, University of St. Thomas, Santiago, Chile, and published in the conference proceedings: "From God and Through God and for God Are All Things: Sacred Theology, Metaphysics, and Finality," in *Gratia non tollit naturam sed perficit eam: Sobre las relaciones y límites entre naturaleza y gracia: Actas del Segundo Congreso Internacional de Filosofía Tomista*, edited by Carlos A. Casanova, 119–76. Santiago: RIL Editores, 2016.

An earlier version of chapter 2 was delivered as a lecture at New York University, New York City, April 18, 2015, as part of the Thomistic Circles Symposium *Aquinas on Metaphysics and the Good* and was published in *Nova et Vetera* (English edition) 15, no. 1 (2017): 53–73.

An earlier version of chapter 3 was delivered as a lecture at the first *Nova et Vetera* Theological Conference, on Gary Anderson's *Sin: A History*, at the Augustine Institute, Denver, Colorado, in March 2010 and published subsequently in *Nova et Vetera* (English edition) 9, no. 1 (2011): 133–48.

An earlier version of chapter 4 was delivered on May 24, 2011, in Washington, D.C., as the presidential address at the Annual Conference of the Academy of Catholic Theology, whose topic was "Faith—Theologically and Philosophically Considered," and published subsequently in *Nova et Vetera* (English edition) 11, no. 2 (2013): 317–40.

An earlier version of chapter 5 was presented at the third international symposium of Thomistic Studies "Ser y Amar" (Being and Love) at Balmesiana, Barcelona, June 25–26, 2015, and subsequently published in *Espíritu* 65, no. 151 (2016): 173–99.

An earlier version of chapter 6 was presented as the keynote lecture at the Rev. Robert J. Randall Conference on Christianity and Culture at Providence College, Providence, Rhode Island, April 19–20, 2013. The theme of the conference was "The Virtue of Religion—Then and Now." A considerably abbreviated version of this chapter was presented at the plenary session of the Pontifical Academy of St. Thomas Aquinas, Casa Pio IV, Vatican, June 19–20, 2015, and subsequently published in *Nova et Vetera* (English edition) 14, no. 1 (2016): 15–60.

An earlier version of chapter 7 was presented on December 6, 2013, at the Thomistic Institute of the Pontifical Faculty of the Immaculate Conception, Dominican House of Studies, Washington, D.C., and previously, on June 22, 2013, at the XIII Plenary Session of the Pontifical Academy of St. Thomas Aquinas at the Casino Pio IV, Vatican City, and published subsequently in *The Thomist* 78, no. 4 (2014): 483–517.

An earlier version of chapter 8 was presented on October 21, 2011, at the Thomistic Circles Conference on "Christian Marriage: Nature and Sacrament" at the Thomistic Institute of the Dominican House of Studies, Washington, D.C., and published subsequently in *The Thomist* 77, no. 1 (2013): 1–39.

Earlier versions of chapter 9 were delivered as lectures on April 28, 2013, at the Monastery of Our Lady of Grace, North Guilford, Connecticut, and previously, on September 27, 2008, at a Symposium on Mariology at the University of Dallas in Dallas, Texas, and published subsequently in *Nova et Vetera* (English edition) 13, no. 2 (2015): 399–418.

Abbreviations

WORKS OF THOMAS AQUINAS

Comp. theol.	Compendium theologiae ad fratrem Reginaldum socium suum carissimum
De ente	De ente et essentia
De malo	Quaestiones disputatae de malo
De ver.	De veritate
De virt.	De virtutibus in communi
Expos. de Trin.	Expositio super librum Boethii de Trinitate
In de Div. Nom.	In librum beati Dionysii de divinis nominibus expositio
In Peri Hermeneias	Expositio libri Peryermenias
In Phys.	In octo libros Physicorum Aristotelis expositio
In Rom.	Super Epistolam ad Romanos
Q. de an.	Quaestiones de anima
Quod.	Quaestiones quodlibetales
Sent.	Scriptum super libros Sententiarum magistri Petri Lombardi episcopi Parisiensis
SCG	Summa contra Gentiles
ST	Summa Theologiae

OTHER WORKS

CCC — *Catechism of the Catholic Church*

Denzinger — *Compendium of Creeds, Definitions, and Declarations on Matters of Faith and Morals* (ed. Hünermann)

PG — *Patrologia Graeca* (ed. Migne)

PL — *Patrologia Latina* (ed. Migne)

Bound for Beatitude

Prologue

Beatitude—The Perfection of Being Human

———————

> Such as each one is, so does the end appear to him.
> —Thomas Aquinas, *Summa Theologiae*[1]

This book is about St. Thomas Aquinas's theology of beatitude and the journey thereto. In more contemporary terms, the book treats the meaning and purpose of human life embedded in that of the whole cosmos. This study is not an antiquarian exercise in the thought of a medieval thinker, but an exercise of *ressourcement* in the philosophical and theological wisdom of one of the most profound theologians of the Catholic church, one whom the church has canonized, granted the title "Doctor of the Church," and for a long time regarded as the common doctor. This exercise of *ressourcement* takes its methodological cues from the common doctor; hence, it is an integrated exercise of philosophical, dogmatic, and moral theology. Its specific theological topic—the ultimate human end, beatitude, and the journey thereto—stands at the very heart of St. Thomas's theology. Far from being passé, his theology of beatitude is of urgent pertinence as the crisis of

---

1. *Summa Theologiae* [hereafter "*ST*"] II-II, q. 24, a. 11: "Qualis unusquisque est, talis finis videtur ei." Aquinas is citing Aristotle, *Nicomachean Ethics* III.5. All English citations in this book from the *Summa Theologiae* are taken from the translation of the Fathers of the English Dominican Province (New York: Benziger Brothers, 1948). Alterations are indicated by brackets.

humanity and of creation and the exile of God seems to approach its apogee.

By way of a presentation, interpretation, and defense of Thomas Aquinas's doctrine of beatitude and the journey thereto, this book advances an argument based on four theses: (1) the loss of a theology of beatitude has greatly impoverished contemporary theology. In order to succeed and flourish, theology must recover a sound teleological orientation. (2) In order to recover a sound teleological orientation, theology must recover metaphysics as its privileged instrument. (3) Thomas Aquinas provides a still pertinent model for how theology might achieve these goals in a metaphysically profound theology of beatitude and the beatific vision. Finally, (4) Aquinas's rich and sophisticated account of the virtues charts the journey to beatitude in a way that still has analytic force and striking relevance in the early twenty-first century.

This book unfolds Aquinas's account of beatitude and its attainment in critical dialogue with certain hegemonic trends in modern and postmodern philosophy and theology, trends that converge in an unwavering insistence on a normative a-teleology and the uncritical acceptance of what Charles Taylor has aptly called "the immanent frame." The book intends to show how a *ressourcement* in Aquinas's thought will offer us ways to overcome the paralyzing theological imprisonment in the immanent frame and to recover the horizon of transcendence and with it the surpassing finality that encompasses humanity and all of creation.[2]

THE JOURNEY TO BEATITUDE:
MAPPING THE WAY

This prologue has four purposes: first, to adumbrate the biblical, theological, and philosophical contours of the notion of happiness; second, to introduce Thomas Aquinas's doctrine of divine happiness and the human participation therein, called the beatific vision; third,

---

2. In this book "finality" denotes the teleological structure of something ordered to an end proximately and ultimately to a final end. See chapter 1, pp. 109–34, for a more detailed discussion.

to offer an interpretation of Aquinas's pivotal treatise on happiness that opens, situates, and informs the whole moral theology of the *Summa Theologiae*; fourth and finally, to name and remove as far as possible four modern impediments that obstruct the understanding and reception of Aquinas's theology of beatitude for Catholics, Protestants, and seculars. At the conclusion of this prologue, I shall briefly offer reasons why such a *ressourcement* in Aquinas's thought is crucial for the full recovery of sacred theology and then lay out chapter by chapter the structure of the book.

The prologue ends with an appendix presenting a significant but largely forgotten recent profession of faith: Pope Paul VI's "Credo of the People of God." This profession of faith articulates authoritatively the material faith that Aquinas's teaching on the journey to beatitude undergirds, explicates, and defends, as well as the theological axiom on which Aquinas's teaching on beatitude rests.

The Biblical, Theological, and Philosophical Contours of Happiness

Everyone wants to be happy. This is a truism too obvious to even stop and think about. At least it seems so. But as soon as we begin to consider what appears at first to be evident, the inevitable question arises: what is happiness? The Psalter, the book of prayer common to Israel and the church, offers a timeless response. In its Latin translation, the Vulgate, Psalm 1 begins with the word "beatus," meaning happy or blessed. "Happy are those who do not follow the advice of the wicked, or take the path that sinners tread, or sit in the seat of scoffers; but their delight is in the law of the Lord, and on his law they meditate day and night" (Ps 1:1–2).[3] The longest psalm in the Bible, Psalm 119, a summary of the whole Psalter and indeed of the whole Bible, also opens with the word "beatus" in the Vulgate. "Happy are those whose way is blameless, who walk in the law of the Lord. Happy are those who keep his decrees, who seek him with their whole heart, who also do no wrong, but walk in his ways" (Ps 119:1–2). And finally, the Sermon on the Mount, Christ's proclamation of the law of the new covenant, in the Vulgate also begins with the word "beatus."

---

3. Biblical citations are drawn from the NRSV unless indicated otherwise.

"Blessed are the poor in spirit [*Beati pauperes spiritu*], for theirs is the kingdom of heaven" (Mt 5:3).

The Greek translation of the Hebrew scriptures, the Septuagint, uses in the opening of Psalms 1 and 119 for the Hebrew *aschrei* the same word that is found in the Greek New Testament at the beginning of the Sermon on the Mount: *makários*. Significantly, in classical Greek, *makariótēs* (beatitude) is reserved to denote the happiness of the gods.[4] While *makários* signifies specifically divine happiness, it is not, however, reserved only to God. In the Septuagint's rendition of the Psalter as well as in the New Testament's Sermon on the Mount, *makários* is used to signify a specific human relationship with God, actualized in distinct human dispositions and activities.[5] The end, or *telos*, as well as the content of this relationship with God is nothing less than the human participation—first inchoately, then perfectly—in divine happiness. The teaching of scripture is unequivocal: true and lasting happiness, beatitude, is found only when a person embraces the truth that God reveals, follows the path God thereby opens up to that person, and, through God's grace, begins to participate in the divine life.

Such a person is a sojourner or pilgrim (*viator*) journeying to the ultimate human end, the full and everlasting participation in God's own beatitude. In Psalm 1, these sojourners are called righteous. God knows their way (*via*) and watches over it because their way has God as its goal, its *telos*. Notably, in Psalm 1 of the Vulgate, the *via* the righteous person travels is contrasted with the way (*iter*) the wicked person chooses to forge for himself. *Via* is a road that leads to a specific destination. *Iter*, by contrast, is a pathway that may lead somewhere, but it might as well also lead nowhere and suddenly end in

---

4. A widely influential expression of this classical Greek view can be found in Aristotle's *Nicomachean Ethics*. There Aristotle differentiates sharply between *makariótes* as the highest form of happiness (*eudaimonía*), attainable only by the gods from the happiness available to mortals. See *Nicomachean Ethics* X.8, 1178b10, 21.

5. On this topic, see the biblical scholar Jonathan T. Pennington's important book, *The Sermon on the Mount and Human Flourishing: A Theological Commentary* (Grand Rapids, Mich.: Baker Academic, 2017) as well as the corresponding, greatly instructive treatment of the Sermon on the Mount from a virtue perspective by the moral theologian William C. Mattison III, *The Sermon on the Mount and Moral Theology: A Virtue Perspective* (Cambridge: Cambridge University Press, 2017).

the wilderness. Those who scoff at the righteous, those adversarial or indifferent to God, the impious (*impii*), choose a route "off the beaten path." Driven by their desires and guided by their own lights, they forge their own pathways. Psalm 1 describes the grave danger they are in thus: "The Lord watches over the way [*via*] of the righteous, but the way [*iter*] of the wicked will perish" (Ps 1:6).[6]

At the very heart of the Christian faith is the belief that the way (*via*) to, the truth (*veritas*) about, and the life (*vita*) of beatitude have become manifest in the person of Jesus Christ, God incarnate, who says, according to the Gospel of John: "I am the way, and the truth, and the life. No one comes to the Father except through me" (Jn 14:6).[7] The *viator* is one who, enabled by God's grace, chooses the way, embraces the truth, and inchoately participates in the life that is Christ. The *viator* is blessed (*beatus*) because of his incipient assimilation to the divine happiness (*beatitudo*) through his union with Christ in faith, hope, and charity. The *viator*'s nascent assimilation to beatitude finds a fitting expression in the famous statement attributed to St. Catherine of Siena: "All the way to heaven is heaven, because Christ is the way."[8]

This is what "coming to the Father" means, first inchoately in this life as a *viator*, and then perfectly in a way that radically transcends human imagination and understanding. According to the apostolic witness of St. Paul, human participation in divine happiness culminates in "what no eye has seen, nor ear heard, nor the human heart conceived, what God has prepared for those who love him" (1 Cor 2:9–10). What

---

6. For a profound and Thomistically inspired philosophical and theological reflection on this difficult and in recent times controversial topic, see Adrian J. Reimers, *Hell and the Mercy of God* (Washington, D.C.: The Catholic University of America Press, 2017).

7. I take the Gospel of John to be the work of an eyewitness of Christ's ministry, death, and resurrection. This view not only reflects the church's earliest tradition, but is also a perfectly defensible exegetical position, based on a rigorous line of historical-critical argumentation. I rely for the latter on the second edition of Richard Bauckham's groundbreaking study, *Jesus and the Eyewitnesses: The Gospels as Eyewitness Testimony*, 2nd ed. (Grand Rapids, Mich.: Eerdmans, 2017).

8. This saying is attributed to St. Catherine of Siena by Dorothy Day, *All the Way to Heaven: The Selected Letters of Dorothy Day*, ed. Robert Ellsberg (New York: Image Books, 2010), 328, and by Regis Martin, *The Last Things: Death, Judgment, Hell, and Heaven* (Charlotte, N.C.: TAN Books, 2014), 39.

God has prepared for those who are united with God through God's own love—charity—is an everlasting and perfect participation in divine happiness: "For now we see in a mirror, dimly, but then we will see face to face. Now I know only in part; then I will know fully, even as I have been fully known" (1 Cor 13:12). The *viator* sees in a mirror, dimly, and knows only in part by faith. The *comprehensor* will see face to face and will know fully. While not offering the explicit theological vocabulary, the New Testament witness suggests the distinction between the inchoate and imperfect beatitude of the *viator* and the perfect and everlasting beatitude of the *comprehensor* in what came to be called much later the "beatific vision." It is this divine revelation—explicated in the church's teaching and elucidated by the theologians of Christian antiquity—that Thomas Aquinas takes as his principal guide in order to conceive of beatitude, the human participation in divine happiness.

Correcting the Anthropocentric Misconception of Human Participation in Divine Happiness

The temptation to conceive of human participation in divine happiness along the lines of the predominant understanding of happiness in the Western Hemisphere is virtually irresistible. For better or worse, consumer capitalism has succeeded in shaping profoundly the dominant aspirations of contemporary Western societies. The ceaseless invention of new desires and the production and consumption of commodities that purportedly satisfy these desires encourages the unencumbered maximization of sensual pleasure, of subjective sovereignty over consumer choices (including choices concerning lifestyles, value systems, and body configurations). In this hegemonic socioeconomic environment, the dominant conception of happiness becomes synonymous with the attainment of a life of unimpeded preference satisfaction moving persistently toward the goal of comprehensive material, physical, and psychological well-being in concert with the combined increase in longevity, lifestyle choices, and the financial means to sustain both.

As an ideological outgrowth of this broad sociocultural trend, a new academic field has emerged: "Happiness studies" (or "wellness studies") attempts to integrate the empirical work of neurobiologists, psychologists, sociologists, and economists into a new discipline.[9] In his noteworthy *Ethics in the Conflicts of Modernity*, Alasdair MacIntyre advances an acute neo-Aristotelian critique of this currently dominant understanding of happiness and the science that purportedly investigates it. Consider his pithy characterization of this widespread notion of happiness:

> Happiness, thus understood, is a state of only positive feelings. It is therefore a state of freedom from unsatisfied desires and precludes grave apprehensions and fears. It comes in degrees, as does unhappiness, and everyone on this view wants to be happy in as many aspects of their life as possible. Different individuals in avowing or ascribing happiness may give more or less importance to this or that aspect. But they agree, and on this individual agents in their everyday lives and social scientific researchers are at one, in judging happiness so understood to be a very great good, perhaps the good.[10]

If we happen to be beholden to this understanding of happiness we might, unsurprisingly, come to think that participation in divine happiness must mean that God is the ultimate source of our preference satisfaction and thereby the guarantor of our comprehensive material, physical, and psychological well-being. God would thus come to serve as a religious instrument of personal convenience for the sake of achieving comprehensive "wellness" and prosperity. This line of thinking is not simply a hypothetical possibility but has found a distinct religious expression with global outreach in the so-called Prosperity Gospel.[11]

Yet the Psalter as well as the Sermon on the Mount clearly block what would be a detrimental reduction of divine happiness and human participation therein to the strictly anthropocentric measure characteristic of the immanent frame of contemporary consumer

---

9. For a thoughtful introduction to this new science that immediately pushes beyond its limits toward a deeper and more comprehensive account of happiness, see Richard Layard, *Happiness: Lessons from a New Science* (London: Penguin, 2005).

10. Alasdair MacIntyre, *Ethics in the Conflicts of Modernity: An Essay on Desire, Practical Reasoning, and Narrative* (Cambridge: Cambridge University Press, 2016), 196.

11. For an excellent account of this theologically and spiritually disconcerting phenomenon, see Kate Bowler, *Blessed: A History of the American Prosperity Gospel* (Oxford: Oxford University Press, 2013).

capitalism and the blatant as well as subtle forms of materialism it encourages. The life of the *viator* falls short of the happiness that happiness studies take as their ideal—which is simply the subjective appreciation of life, a state of the mind measurable by psychological parameters. But such a purported failure only makes plain that the notion of happiness that happiness studies presuppose is philosophically problematic and theologically erroneous. What then is divine happiness and the human participation therein?

DIVINE HAPPINESS AND HUMAN PARTICIPATION THEREIN

In 1 Timothy, God is designated as "he who is blessed [*beatus*] and only Sovereign [*solus potens*], the King of kings and the Lord of Lords" (1 Tm 5:18). Significantly, beatitude is attributed to God *before* sovereignty. Thomas Aquinas's consideration of divine happiness reflects the priority that 1 Timothy accords to beatitude, blessedness, as a divine attribute. Aquinas treats of divine happiness, *De divina beatitudine*, in a noteworthy and far from accidental place in question 26 of *Summa Theologiae* I. After completing a detailed consideration of the mystery of God under the aspect of the unity of the divine essence, God's oneness, and before turning to the consideration of the mystery of God under the aspect of the Trinity of divine persons, Aquinas considers divine happiness (*beatitudo divina*). He asks first what the essence of beatitude—happiness in general—is and offers this definition: "Nothing else is understood to be meant by the term beatitude than the perfect good of an intellectual nature" (*ST* I, q. 26, a. 1), which is, according to Aquinas, to understand all things. Beatitude is perfect possession of the consummate good by a perfect comprehension of it. Consequently, beatitude belongs to God in a very special manner. Because the divine essence has the perfections of intellect (*ST* I, q. 14) and will (*ST* I, q. 19) in an absolute actualization of both, God has interminable possession of the object of beatitude. Divine happiness is a state of surpassing intellectual and volitional fulfillment and hence most intensive life and simultaneously perfect rest—all of which belongs to God.

Furthermore, because divine happiness is absolutely perfect in and of itself, God's activity obviously cannot aim at any increase of God's own beatitude. God's activity *ad extra* rather aims at the communication of divine happiness to others. Crucially, the external communication of beatitude—what is usually called the divine economy (creation, providence, salvation, and deification)—reflects what is first and foremost characteristic of the divine life itself. At the core of the mystery of the Trinity of divine persons, we find the eternal communication, reception, and return of divine happiness. The mystery of the eternal generation of the Son by the Father and the eternal spiration of the Holy Spirit by the Father and the Son comprises in itself the eternal Trinitarian communication of the plenitude of divine happiness. To reiterate: because divine happiness is absolutely perfect in and of itself, as personally communicated, received, and returned *ad intra*, God's activity *ad extra* cannot increase divine beatitude, but rather communicates divine happiness exteriorly. The divine economy—creation, salvation (culminating in the incarnation), and deification—is nothing but the inclusion of rational creatures in the Trinitarian communication, reception, and return of divine happiness.

Salvation is absolutely central to Aquinas's account of the attainment of the supernatural ultimate human end. The mystery of iniquity, the root of which is the sin of pride, sits at heart of the all-too-real but ultimately vain attempt of the rational creature, angel and human, to attain perfect happiness not as the reception of the divine gift of participation in divine beatitude, but rather on the creature's own terms. Yet divine beatitude entails divine righteousness, that is, the identity in the divine essence of the goodness and holiness of God with God's will. Impenitent sin and entrenched evil, wickedness, are the manifestations of a will wounded by original and actual sin, and the consequent absence of the will's rectitude. Impenitent sin and the participation in the divine beatitude are mutually exclusive. This truth has crucial implications for the *viator*'s sojourn to beatitude: The healing and restoration of the will's rectitude is absolutely essential for the *viator*'s attainment of beatitude. Integral to the *viator*'s journey is therefore the acknowledgment of the *via-*

tor's own sinfulness and complete reliance upon Christ's righteousness and upon the ongoing aid of Christ's grace, for the course of the whole journey to beatitude. Integral to the healing and rectification of the *viator*'s will is also the consistent rejection of evil, sin, and wickedness not only in one's own heart but also in one's surroundings, both proximate and remote.[12] The divine life of beatitude entails the absolute rejection of evil, sin, and wickedness. The works of darkness (Eph 5:11) and divine beatitude are utterly incompatible, because "God is light and in him there is no darkness at all" (1 Jn 1:5). God loves sinners, but hates the sin such that sinners can only ever participate in the divine beatitude if they are saved from sin by an utterly surpassing act of divine love.[13] The Apostle John puts the matter thus: "In this is love, not that we loved God but that he loved us and sent his Son to be the atoning sacrifice for our sins" (1 Jn 4:10). Similarly, the Apostle Paul states: "God proves his love for us in that while we still were sinners Christ died for us" (Rom 5:8). The theological acolytes of modern humanism minimalize or deny outright the reality of human sin and the gravity of wickedness and thereby fail to appreciate one indispensable entailment of beatitude—the will's rectitude.

In sum, the blessed (*beati*) are called thus because they are assimilated to God's own beatitude. Participating in God's beatitude eternally is the divinely intended supernatural perfection of being human. It is for this perfection surpassing human nature that humans have been created, equipped, and saved; and in the extant order of divine providence it is this supernatural perfection that is the ultimate human end. The natural finality, proportionate to human nature, is subsumed in the latter's gratuitous extension, elevation, and surpassing supernatural perfection.

But how do creatures participate in divine happiness? After all, the human mind cannot intellectually grasp God's essence. God's es-

---

12. An insightful way of doing full justice to this central aspect of the *viator*'s journey is to read Aquinas's treatise on happiness in conjunction with one of the most profound and extraordinary late medieval poetic reflections on the quest for the true Christian life, William Langland's *Piers Plowman*: Sheryl Overmyer, *Two Guides for the Journey: Thomas Aquinas and William Langland on the Virtues* (Eugene, Ore.: Cascade, 2016).

13. Adrian J. Reimers makes an almost overdue case for this widely forgotten theological truth that is as clear as it is compelling in *Hell and the Mercy of God*.

sence and with it all the divine attributes identical with it, including divine happiness, transcend human comprehension and can therefore be grasped only analogically. In his analogical predication of the divine essence, Aquinas draws upon Aristotle's semantic triangle of thing, concept, and word (*res—ratio—nomen*). In a famous passage of his *On Interpretation* (*Peri Hermeneias*), Aristotle asserts that "spoken words are the symbols of mental experience and written words are the symbols of spoken words. Just as all [humans] have not the same writing, so all [humans] have not the same speech sounds, but the mental experiences, which these directly symbolize, are the same for all, as also are those things of which our experiences are the images."[14] Language manifests the structure of thought that in turn reflects reality (*res—ratio—nomen*). In the brief prologue to *Summa Theologiae* I, question 13, where Aquinas treats of human discourse about God, he states the crucial principle: "Everything is named by us according to our knowledge of it." All our knowing and naming occurs in the semantic triangle of thing, concept, and word.

Consider a brief example: the word (*nomen*) "cat" signifies a cat (*res*). *Res*, translated as "thing," is not, as one might initially think, a material object; rather, *res* is a transcendental and signifies all that can become the term of a knowing act. Justice is a *res*, as is Fermat's last theorem, and as is a cat. But what does the word "cat" mean? What is its intelligible character, its essence, its felinity? This is where the concept (*ratio*) comes into the picture. For a name—"cat"—always signifies a thing (*res*)—cat—under a certain concept (*ratio*), that is, the definition that states what the *res* signified by the name is: a four-legged meowing animal that people may keep as a pet.

Consider now the divine attributes: in questions 3–11 of *Summa Theologiae* I, Aquinas has shown that the divine attributes are identical with the divine essence and that we do not have any scientific,

---

14. Aristotle, *On Interpretation* I.1, 16a4–9, trans. Ella Mary Edghill in *The Works of Aristotle*, ed. W. D. Ross (Oxford: Clarendon Press, 1928). On Aristotle's semantic triangle, see Thomas Aquinas, *Expositio libri Peryermenias*, lib. 1, ii–iv, and John P. O'Callaghan, *Thomist Realism and the Linguistic Turn: Toward a More Perfect Form of Existence* (Notre Dame, Ind.: University of Notre Dame Press, 2003), 15–77; for an account of Aquinas's analogy of being and analogy of divine predication defended against two modern Protestant critics, see chapter 10 in my *Dust Bound for Heaven: Explorations in the Theology of Thomas Aquinas* (Grand Rapids, Mich.: Eerdmans, 2012), 349–86.

definitional knowledge of the divine essence. How can we name divine perfections—goodness or beatitude—without capitulating to a purely apophatic, negative discourse? Because we do not know the *ratio* of "divine goodness" we do not know the term's mode of signification, that is, how it is realized of God (*ST* I, q. 13, a. 3). The *ratio* of the name "goodness," as we understand it, does not represent adequately to the human mind the *res*, goodness, as it is in God. But, Aquinas argues, we still have access to the thing signified (*res significata*) because of the way we know God indirectly from creatures, "as their cause, by way of excellence and negation" (*ST* I, q. 13, a. 1). As every perfection is the effect of the creator and as the perfection of every effect must be present to a higher degree in its proper cause and in a surpassing way in the first cause, perfection names like "goodness" or "beatitude" are able to name God essentially (*substantialiter*).

Now, recall Aquinas's definition of beatitude: *the perfect good of an intellectual nature*. Given this definition, beatitude obviously denotes a divine perfection. But because we are unable to comprehend the divine essence, we do not understand the mode of signification of the name "beatitude" in reference to God. We are able to grasp the *ratio* and hence the mode of signification of the word "happy" in reference to a human, a dog, a lark, a day, or an hour. But we are unable to grasp it in the case of God. Nevertheless, the term "beatitude" does name God essentially. It signifies analogically the reality (*res*) of God's own beatitude. Certain entailments follow from this analogical predication, as Aquinas explains: "Beatitude is a certain perfection. But the divine perfection embraces [*complectitur*] all other perfections, as was shown above (q. 4, a. 2). Therefore the divine beatitude embraces [*complectitur*] all other beatitudes" (*ST* I, q. 26, a. 4, s.c.). It is true that God is eternally happy, even if we do not know what this happiness is in and of itself. Here is what Aquinas thinks can be stated with certainty, on account of the analogical predication of created perfections, about what is entailed in divine happiness:

As to contemplative happiness, God possesses a continual and most certain contemplation of Himself and of all things else; and as to that which is active, he has the governance of the whole universe. As to earthly happiness, which consists in delight, riches, power, dignity, and fame, according to Boethius (*De Consol.* iii. 10), He possesses joy in Himself and all things else for His delight; instead of riches he has that complete self-sufficiency, which is promised by riches; in place of power, He has omnipotence; for dignities, the government of all things; and in place of fame, He possesses the admiration of all creatures. (*ST* I, q. 26, a. 4)

Thus, the promise of a participation in the divine happiness entails for human beings the proper perfection of integral human happiness in a mode that surpasses our present understanding but includes the perfect realization of all true goods of body, soul, and conviviality (in short, of every mode of perfection characteristic of human nature) that humans desire in order to attain happiness. Every genuine created good (in contrast to a merely apparent good) the attainment of which is genuine happiness (in contrast to a merely apparent happiness) is entailed in divine happiness, the possession of the perfect good.

Do humans actually have the capacity to attain beatitude, to participate in the divine happiness? As finite, mortal, fallible, and indeed fallen creatures, humans might seem to be intrinsically incapable of attaining such perfect happiness. We might very well desire such beatitude—and even be unable not to desire it—but its attainment might be nothing but a fleeting dream beyond the grasp of our inescapable finitude and mortality, like a slug that dreams of soaring in the sky like an eagle.

It is an essential truth of divine revelation that humans are created in God's image. According to the church's constant teaching this means that humans are endowed by God with an immortal rational soul, the substantial form of an intellectual nature. It is this intellectual nature that makes humans capable of a formal (not entitative) union with the divine essence (*capax Dei*) and thus capable of attaining beatitude (*capax beatitudinis*). Aquinas, in concord with the Greek and Latin theologians of the early church, takes the rational soul with its higher faculties, intellect and will, as the surpassing principle that fundamentally distinguishes humans from all other animals. While animals, guided by instinct, exercise one kind of activity (*operatio*) that secures the survival and flourishing of each animal and its kind, humans have at their disposal two kinds of *operatio*.

The first kind, transitive action (*actio transiens*) aims at a *telos* exterior to the human agent. Its basic forms are political action (*praxis*), and the making of things in general (*poiesis*) and of art (*technē*) in particular. The second kind, intransitive action (*actio immanens*) is the kind of activity that is its own immanent *telos*. In its highest form, this kind of activity is realized in the knowledge of truth, in the knowledge of an object that is not merely practical or instrumental, but intrinsically meaningful. The ultimate end of the intransitive action, its perfection, is the unitive knowledge of God, the beatific vision. United with God, the knower desires nothing beyond the surpassing knowledge the beatific vision affords, for it unites the intellect with its proper end, unrestricted truth, and the will with its proper end, unrestricted good.

Intellect and will, the higher faculties of the human soul, make possible both kinds of operations, transitive as well as intransitive actions. They enable humans to be the very principle of transitive actions that are their own and therefore fall under their responsibility and control and, furthermore, enable humans to realize those immanent actions (faith, hope, and charity) that allow them to become *viatores*, pilgrims on the journey to beatitude, and eventually *comprehensores*, participators in the divine happiness through a surpassing union of vision and love. It is the very amplitude of the intellect that makes it capable of receiving this surpassing gratuitous gift. If God wanted to grant other animals the gift of beatitude, God would have to transform them first from nonrational into rational creatures and thereby do away with the very nature of the intended recipients of this gift. Rational creatures, by contrast, do not have to undergo any transformation of their nature in order to become capable of receiving the gift of union with God. On account of the rational soul, human nature is formally *capax Dei*. The satiation of intellect with the first truth and the will with the consummate good, which is God, in the beatific vision constitutes perfect human happiness, a state that issues in surpassing delight and joy. This is what Aquinas takes to be the contemplation characteristic of the beatific vision, the state of the *comprehensor*.[15]

---

[15]. For a closer consideration of the metaphysics and epistemology of the beatific vision, see the epilogue, pp. 389–409.

From a consideration of what divine happiness is, I have moved to a discussion of how human beings can participate in beatitude by intellect and will. I shall now enter into a consideration of how human beings are ordered to beatitude as their ultimate end.

The Singularity of the Final End

Due to their specific nature, human beings *qua* rational animals act in a specific way in order to attain their final end.[16] The determination to a specific proximate end is conceived by the intellect and effected by the rational appetite, the will. Aquinas argues that the order of ends to which the rational appetite, the will, is directed is an essential (*per se*) order rather than an accidental (*per accidens*) order. In an essential order of ends, each end is actually here and now ordered to another end in such a way that the whole order of ends is *actually here and now* ordered to a single final end. "For that which is first in the order of intention, is the principle, as it were, moving the appetite; consequently, if you remove this principle, there will be nothing to move the appetite" (*ST* I-II, q. 1, a. 4). Hence, in an essential, *per se* order, all other ends are subordinated to this single final end.

Why does Aquinas insist on the initially counterintuitive point that the order of ends to which the will is directed must be an essential, *per se* order? Consider this line of reasoning: if there were no single end to human life, the purposes of human agency would only accidentally interconnect. But such a merely accidental connection of purposes would immediately destroy the structure of an intelligible action that is the most basic unit of a human action (*actio humana*).[17] For every action receives its end (and thereby its intelligibility and, hence, desirability) from being embedded—not chronologically, but *actually here and now*—in a wider essential order of intelligible

---

16. On the twofold human finality, natural and supernatural, see below in this prologue, "Excursus: The Natural Desire for the Vision of God and the Ultimate Human End," pp. 35–40, and also chapter 1, pp. 134–50.

17. *ST* I-II, q. 1, a. 1. Following the original insight of Aristotle and Aquinas, G. E. M. Anscombe and Alasdair MacIntyre have made the case in the modern context that intelligible actions are the basic units of human moral agency in Anscombe's *Intention*, 2nd ed. (Ithaca, N.Y.: Cornell University Press, 1963), and MacIntyre's "The Intelligibility of Action," in *Rationality, Relativism, and Human Sciences*, ed. J. Margolis, M. Krausz, and R. M. Burian (Dordrecht: Nijhoff, 1986), 63–80.

purposes. Without the final end bearing *actually* (but not necessary consciously) *here and now* causally upon the proximate end, human actions would lack their constitutive intelligibility and hence their desirability for the rational appetite, the will. Aquinas puts it tersely: "That in which a [human being] rests as in his last end, is master of his affections, since he takes therefrom his entire rule of life" (*ST* I-II, q. 1, a. 5, s.c.). Bereft of the final end, human actions would receive their intelligibility (and hence their desirability) for the rational appetite exclusively from some proximate end. For absent an essential order of finality, the relationship between ends—or clusters of ends—becomes purely accidental, indeed arbitrary. When several ends are not ordained to one another by one last end, they become pointless and virtually indistinguishable from what Aquinas calls "acts of man" (*actiones hominis*; *ST* I-II, q. 1, a. 1), like scratching one's head—which is obviously absurd. Hence, all basic actions *qua* intelligible (and hence, desirable) are ordered *here and now* to a single final end in an essential order of finality. While human beings *actually* desire *here and now* everything that they in fact desire for the sake of one final end, they obviously do not always think of the final end when desiring or doing something particular. Nevertheless, it is the case that "the virtue of the first intention, which was in respect of the last end, remains in every desire directed to any object whatever, even though one's thoughts be not actually directed to the last end. Thus while walking along the road one needs not to be thinking of the end at every step" (*ST* I-II, q. 1, a. 6, ad 3).

The Formal and the Material Aspect of the Final End

While all humans agree that "happiness means the acquisition of the last end" (*ST* I-II, q. 1, a. 8), they differ widely about what this end consists in and, therefore, how happiness is achieved. Hence, Aquinas distinguishes between the *formal* aspect of the final end and its *material* aspect:

> We can speak of the last end in two ways: first, considering only the aspect of last end; secondly, considering the thing in which the aspect of last end is realized. So, then, as to the aspect of last end, all agree in desiring the last end: since all desire the fulfilment of their perfection, and it is precisely this

fulfilment in which the last end consists.... But as to the thing in which this aspect is realized, all [human beings] are not agreed as to their last end: since some desire riches, as their consummate good; some, pleasure; others, something else. (*ST* I-II, q. 1, a. 7)

Regarding the *formality* of the final end, there is necessarily universal agreement among human beings, for the formality of the final end corresponds to the formality of human nature in its teleological constitution. The confusion about the *material* aspect of the final end Aquinas understands to be a factual, perennial human phenomenon of fallen, post-paradisiacal life. This confusion is dispelled concretely but tenuously for the person who pursues the wisdom afforded by first philosophy or the metaphysics of being and thereby comes to understand God, the universal first cause and sovereign good, to be the ultimate end. Aquinas explains:

> It is impossible for any created good to constitute [human] happiness. For happiness is the perfect good, which lulls the appetite altogether; else it would not be the last end, if something yet remained to be desired. Now the object of the will [i.e., of the rational appetite], is the universal good; just as the object of the intellect is the universal true. Hence it is evident that [nothing] can lull [the human] will, save the universal good. This is to be found, not in any creature, but in God alone; because every creature has goodness by participation. Wherefore God alone can satisfy the [human] will, according to the words of Ps. cii. 5: *Who satisfieth thy desire with good things*. And consequently, God alone constitutes [human] happiness. (*ST* I-II, q. 2, a. 8)

A person thus enlightened by the wisdom of first philosophy will, however, remain profoundly uncertain about how to attain the ultimate end. Only persons who have faith, hope, and charity (some of whom might seek the wisdom afforded by sacred theology; others of whom might receive the surpassing wisdom of infused contemplation) will be endowed with the certainty that the theological virtue of hope affords, namely that, with the help of the omnipotent God, they will attain the ultimate end of surpassing beatitude permanently. For these persons—all of them *viatores*—the material aspect of the ultimate end is certain: God is indisputably and definitively the sole reality in which the aspect of the ultimate end is realized and in union with whom alone beatitude is attained.

The Objective and the Subjective Ultimate End

In addition to the material and formal aspects of the final end, Aquinas also distinguishes between the objective and subjective end. This distinction results from the ultimate ontological incommensurability between the transcendent first cause, who is subsistent being itself, and the contingent creature that receives its existence and its essence from another. Aquinas draws upon Aristotle's distinction between the *objective* and the *subjective* end, between the thing itself and its use.[18] Consider Aquinas's argument:

> As the philosopher says (*Phys.* ii.2), the end is twofold—the end *for which* [*cuius*] and the end *by which* [*quo*]; viz., the thing itself in which is found the aspect of good, and the use or acquisition of that thing.... If, therefore, we speak of [the human being's] last end as of the thing which is the end, thus all other things concur in [the human being's] last end, since God is the last end of [the human being] and of all other things.—If, however, we speak of [the human being's] last end, as of the acquisition of the end, then irrational creatures do not concur with [the human being] in this end. For [the human being] and other rational creatures attain to their last end by knowing and loving God: this is not possible to other creatures, which acquire their last end, in so far as they share in the Divine likeness, inasmuch as they are, or live, or even know.[19]

While God is indeed the *objective* ultimate end of the rational creature, the *subjective* ultimate end cannot be the uncreated absolute

---

18. Aristotle, *Magna Moralia* I.3, 1184b10–17, in *Metaphysics Books X–XIV. Oeconomica. Magna Moralia*, trans. Hugh Tredennick and C. Cyril Armstrong, Loeb Classical Library 28 (Cambridge, Mass.: Harvard University Press, 1935); *Physics* II.2, 194a35–36, in *Physics, or Natural Hearing*, trans. Glen Coughlin (South Bend, Ind.: St. Augustine's Press, 2004).

19. *ST* I-II, q. 1, a. 8. See also *ST* I-II, q. 2, a. 7: "As stated above [q. 1, a. 8], the end is twofold: namely, the thing itself, which we desire to attain, and the use, namely, the attainment or possession of that thing. If, then, we speak of [the human being's] last end, as to the thing itself which we desire as last end, it is impossible for [the human being's] last end to be the soul itself or something belonging to it.... But if we speak of [the human being's] last end, as to the attainment or possession thereof, or as to any use whatever of the thing itself desired as an end, thus does something of [the human being], in respect of his soul, belong to his last end: since [the human being] attains happiness through his soul. Therefore the thing itself which is desired as end is that which constitutes happiness, and makes [the human being] happy; but the attainment of this thing is called happiness. Consequently we must say that happiness is something belonging to the soul; but that which constitutes happiness is something outside the soul." See also *ST* I-II, q. 11, a. 3, ad 3.

beatitude of God, but must be a created participating beatitude, the fruition of the *objective* ultimate end in the human soul, in short, the beatific vision (*ST* I, q. 26, a. 3, ad 2).

The Two Ways of Arriving at Happiness

The two faculties of the rational creature that make this fruition possible are the intellect and its appetite, the will. Like the senses and the sense appetites, intellect and will are ordered to their respective proper objects, the intellect to unrestricted truth and the will to unrestricted good. The perfection of each faculty is the perfect union with its proper object: the intellect with the first truth, the will with the consummate good. Subjective union with the desired good, its attainment, satiates the will and constitutes happiness.

The human will is constitutively ordered to will happiness; the will is "hardwired" for happiness (*ST* I, q. 82, a. 1; I-II, q. 10, a. 2). It is the epitome of those things that "the will is incapable of not willing."[20] This being the case, Aquinas distinguishes two ways of arriving at happiness: by way of human natural powers and by way of sanctifying grace:

> Imperfect happiness that can be had in this life, can be acquired by [human beings] by [their] natural powers [*per sua naturalia*], *in the same way as virtue, in whose operation it consists*.... But [the human being's] perfect Happiness ... consists in the vision of the Divine Essence. Now the vision of God's Essence surpasses the nature not only of [the human being], but also of every creature.... Consequently, neither [the human being], nor any creature, can attain final Happiness [*beatitudinem ultimam*] by his natural powers [*per sua naturalia*]. (*ST* I-II, q. 5, a. 5; emphasis added)

The regular way of attaining imperfect happiness is by living the life of virtue in a full human life (Aristotle's *bios praktikos*). The extraordinary way of attaining imperfect but surpassing happiness is by living a life of virtue crowned by and focused on the pursuit of

---

20. Josef Pieper, *Happiness and Contemplation*, trans. Richard and Clara Winston (South Bend, Ind.: St. Augustine's Press, 1998), 21. *ST* I-II, q. 5, a. 4, ad 2, reads: "homo non potest non velle esse beatus." "[The human being] craves by nature happiness and bliss" (Pieper, *Happiness*, 20). Consider Pieper's felicitous rendition: "[The human being], as a reasoning being, desires his own happiness just as the falling stone 'seeks' the depths, as the flower turns to the light and the beast hunts its prey" (ibid., 21).

wisdom (Aristotle's *bios theoretikos*). The goal of this *bios* is the contemplation of the unchanging eternal truths and, ultimately, of the first principle of the creation and government of things. For the person pursuing such a life, the subjective attainment of the ultimate end will issue in a genuine, but transient, and therefore imperfect happiness of a natural contemplation of the first cause as mediated by its created effects. Only for the person elevated to the beatific vision, the intellectual and volitional union with the triune God, will the subjective attainment of the ultimate end issue in a surpassing fruition, in everlasting, unitive, and therefore perfect happiness: beatitude.

Short of the beatific vision, however, there is another more perfect way of attaining imperfect happiness for the person who has the theological virtues of faith, hope, and charity. The intellect of such a person is still bereft of the beatific vision, for the light of glory does not yet actualize the possible intellect so that the likeness of the divine essence is in the intellect (*ST* I, q. 12, a. 2). Recall that the intellect's act attains completion when the likeness of its object is in it. However, the will of such a person is united immediately to God. For the will's act attains perfection by being "inclined to the thing itself as existing in itself."[21] "Charity works formally ... by justifying the soul, it unites it to God" (*ST* II-II, q. 23, a. 2, ad 3). And for this reason "the charity [of the *viator*] adheres to God immediately."[22] Because of the inclination of the will in charity, the person who has faith formed by charity is already united with "the thing itself as existing in itself" (*ST* I, q. 82, a. 3) and, consequently, already attains inchoately its ultimate perfection. Such a person is, therefore, in a state of inchoate perfect happiness or beatitude, the immediate consequence of which is spiritual joy (*spirituale gaudium*). As Aquinas explains: "Charity is love of God, Whose good is unchangeable, since He is His goodness, and from the very fact that he is loved, He is in those who love Him by His most excellent effect, according to 1 John 4:16: 'He that abides in charity, abides in God and God in him.'

21. *ST* I, q. 82, a. 3: "ex eo quod voluntas inclinatur ad ipsam rem prout in se est." See also *ST* I-II, q. 27, a. 2, ad 2, and *ST* II-II, q. 27, a. 4.
22. *ST* II-II, q. 27, a. 4, s.c.: "Charity, by loving God, unites the soul immediately to Him with a chain of spiritual union."

Therefore, spiritual joy, which is about God, is caused by charity" (*ST* II-II, q. 28, a. 1).

The perfect happiness of the beatific vision that is achieved when the intellect receives in itself the likeness of the first truth is anticipated in the inchoative spiritual joy that issues from the spiritual union between God and the soul engendered by charity.[23] At the very moment the intellect's participation in the first truth becomes unmediated, "when by His grace God unites Himself to the created intellect, as an object made intelligible to it" (*ST* I, q. 12, a. 4), the *viator* becomes the *comprehensor*. The dawn of perfect happiness, experienced in the life of charity, of friendship with God, turns to the noonday of everlasting happiness—beatitude.

To summarize: according to Aquinas, the happiness of the human being is twofold. Genuine but transitory, and therefore imperfect, happiness is proportionate to the finality of human nature. Humans have the natural potency to arrive at this imperfect happiness. The everlasting, unitive, and therefore perfect happiness, beatitude, surpasses the capacity of human nature and can be obtained "by the power of God alone, by a kind of participation of the Godhead, about which it is written (2 Pt 1:4) that by Christ we are made partakers of the Divine nature" (*ST* I-II, q. 62, a. 1). Perfect human happiness is the subjective fruition resulting from the attainment of the objective ultimate end by way of an unmediated union of the intellect and will with God, who is the first cause of the rational soul's creation and enlightenment and who also is the rational soul's final end as the soul's universal good.[24] And insofar as the rational soul is

---

23. The transient but genuine happiness that the *bios theoretikos* affords, the contemplation of the eternal truths (metaphysics, mathematics, cosmology) is accessible only to a very small minority of intellectually gifted and exceedingly well-educated persons. The everlasting perfect beatitude that the beatific vision affords is, by contrast, open to every human being irrespective of natural disposition and cultural formation, as every created human soul has the natural capacity to be elevated to the beatific vision and to the concomitant everlasting perfect beatitude.

24. *ST* I-II, q. 3, a. 8: "Final and perfect happiness can consist in nothing else than the vision of the Divine Essence. To make this clear, two points must be observed: first, that [human beings are] not perfectly happy, so long as something remains for [them] to desire and seek; secondly, that the perfection of any power is determined by the nature of its object. Now the object of the intellect is *what a thing is*, i.e., the essence of a thing, according to *De Anima* iii. 6. Wherefore the intellect attains perfection, in so far as it knows

the substantial form of the body, it is the ultimate end of the whole human being, soul and body, to become a partaker of the divine nature, and thus a partaker of the unfathomable bliss of the divine life.[25]

After these preliminary clarifications, we have now reached the apposite point to turn directly to Aquinas's treatment of human happiness in his mature masterpiece, the *Summa Theologiae*. In the famous five opening questions of *Summa Theologiae* I-II, Aquinas considers all aspects of happiness in the context of inquiring into the ultimate human end and how this end might be attained or missed.[26]

---

the essence of a thing. If therefore an intellect know the essence of some effect, whereby it is not possible to know the essence of the cause, i.e., to know of the cause *what it is*, that intellect cannot be said to reach that cause simply, although it may be able to gather from the effect the knowledge that the cause is. Consequently, when [the human being] knows an effect, and knows that it has a cause, there naturally remains in [the human being] the desire to know about that cause, *what it is*. And this desire is one of wonder, and causes inquiry, as is stated in the beginning of the *Metaphysics* I, ch. 2.... If therefore the human intellect, knowing the essence of some created effect, knows no more of God than *that He is*, the perfection of that intellect does not yet reach simply the First Cause, but there remains in it the natural desire to seek the cause. Wherefore it is not yet perfectly happy. Consequently, for perfect happiness the intellect needs to reach the very Essence of the First Cause. And thus it will have its perfection through union with God as with that object, in which alone [human] happiness consists."

25. *ST* I, q, 26, a. 3. As one noted interpreter of Aquinas's thought rightly emphasizes, "[Human beings] cannot know that they are capable of attaining the vision of God except through faith based on divine teaching. That God actually does ordain [human beings] to Himself is a revealed truth known only by faith. Only the believer can hope and pray for this divine gift." Denis J. M. Bradley, *Aquinas on the Twofold Human Good: Reason and Human Happiness in Aquinas's Moral Science* (Washington, D.C.: The Catholic University of America Press, 1997), 524. Aquinas states explicitly: "The ultimate happiness [of the human being] consists in a supernatural vision of God: to which vision [the human being] cannot attain unless he be taught by God.... Hence, in order that a [human being] arrive at the perfect vision of heavenly happiness, he [or she] must first of all believe God, as a disciple believes the master who is teaching him" (*ST* II-II, q. 2, a. 3). For a close consideration of divine faith, see chapter 4.

26. A brief word on the medieval context and on Aquinas's sources: from the composition of Peter Lombard's *Four Books of Sentences* (written ca. 1150), which became the principal theological textbook for the next four hundred years, and due to the exceptional role Augustine's theology plays in this textbook, the topic of beatitude becomes the central theme of medieval theology in the Latin West right up until the Protestant Reformation. For greater detail, see Nikolaus Wicki, *Die Lehre von der himmlischen Seligkeit in der mittelalterlichen Scholastik von Petrus Lombardus bis Thomas von Aquin* (Fribourg: Universitätsverlag, 1954), and Roger Guindon, *Béatitude et théologie morale chez Saint Thomas d'Aquin: Origines, interprétation* (Ottawa: Éditions de l'Université, 1956). Next to Augustine, Aquinas's second major source is Aristotle. This aspect is instructively discussed by

AQUINAS'S TREATISE ON HAPPINESS
IN *SUMMA THEOLOGIAE* I-II

Aquinas's consideration of happiness (*beatitudo*) unfolds along the lines of five questions. (1) Is there an ultimate human end? (2) Which good makes the human being perfectly happy? (3) What does the human being do in order to obtain the good? (4) Which human dispositions and operations are part of happiness? (5) What do human beings have to do in order to become happy and what is only God able to do to make us perfectly happy?

Question 1: The Nature of the Ultimate End

Question 1 asks whether there is an ultimate human end at all. This question sets the stage for the whole inquiry; it treats happiness in general in conjunction with the teleology that characterizes human actions. At the very outset (a. 1), Aquinas introduces the central distinction between "human actions" (*actiones humanae*) and "actions of a human" (*actiones hominis*). "Human actions" are deliberately willed; one is in control—"lord" (*dominus*)—of these actions. "Actions of a human," by contrast, are not deliberately willed. They do not belong to the agent qua human (*inquantum est homo*); scratching one's head absentmindedly, for example, is an "action of a human."

As the will is the mental faculty whose object is the good-as-the-end, all human actions (*actiones humanae*) are for the sake of an end. It is not acting for an end, however, that makes deliberate action human. As Aquinas importantly shows, acting for an end is not reserved to rational beings alone (a. 2). Rather, all the efficient causes in the created universe produce determined effects—rational as

---

Andreas Speer, "Das Glück des Menschen," in *Thomas von Aquin: Die Summa theologiae*, ed. Speer (Berlin: de Gruyter, 2005), 141–66. In the *Nicomachean Ethics*, Aquinas encounters a fully developed and comprehensive eudaimonian ethics, that is, an ethics with happiness as its key concept of human flourishing in this life—without any eschatological perspective. Arguably, one of the lasting achievements of Aquinas is the full integration of the seminal insights of Aristotle's ethics—without reduction or distortion—into a comprehensive framework of eschatological beatitude that is profoundly indebted to Augustine's surpassing theological vision expressed classically in the last two books of the *City of God*.

well as nonrational causes. In nonrational beings this occurs by way of their God-given natural instincts and appetites. Aquinas takes the whole universe of nonrational nature to relate to God as an instrumental cause relates to a principal cause.[27] But while nonrational beings are moved to an end by being acted upon by the principal cause, only rational beings move to their end by self-determination. They move themselves to their end. And it is the kind of end to which they move themselves that determines the kind of action by which they move themselves toward it in order to attain it (a. 3).[28] For this reason, human actions have an irreducible moral quality. They have the valence of good, specifically intentional good, or the lack, specifically intentional lack, thereof.

The ultimate human end as human must be sought after and attained in an essentially *human* way, that is, in the way characteristic of a rational being. Hence human happiness and especially its perfection, beatitude, can never be a merely sensual reality pertaining to the human strictly as sensate animal. Rather, it must be a moral reality, pertaining to the human as rational animal and therefore as moral agent. Consequently, beatitude does not only entail the created human perfection of eternal life in a resurrection body, but also—indispensably—the perfection of a rightly ordered will, in short, the holiness characteristic of the saints.

Often the end of a particular human action is the achievement of a further end. For example, one might exercise in order to be-

---

27. *ST* I, q. 22, a. 2, ad 4. See chapter 1 for a more detailed consideration of Aquinas's universal teleology.

28. Aquinas takes the whole of a morally relevant action, a "human action," as a quasi-hylomorphic unit of form and matter (*ST* I-II, q. 18, a. 6; *De malo*, q. 2, a. 2, ad 5; *De caritate* 4). For this very reason, a "human action" may fail, that is, become vicious and sinful, because of a deficiency in its form—a lack of the rectitude of the will—or because of a deficiency in its matter—the kind of action chosen. Hence, according to Aquinas, the moral quality of a human action depends on two orders: what an action *is directed to* and what an action *is* (its moral species or kind). For a lucid analysis and presentation of Aquinas's account of these complex matters, see Steven A. Long, *The Teleological Grammar of the Moral Act* (Ave Maria, Fla.: Sapientia Press, 2007), and Joseph Pilsner, *The Specification of Human Actions in St. Thomas Aquinas* (Oxford: Oxford University Press, 2006). For an integration of contemporary bioethics into Aquinas's teleologically constituted moral theology, see Nicanor Pier Giorgio Austriaco, OP, *Biomedicine and Beatitude: An Introduction to Catholic Bioethics* (Washington, D.C.: The Catholic University of America Press, 2011).

come physically fit. Can the hierarchy of such ends be infinite or must there be an ultimate end (*finis ultimus*)? Aquinas argues that an infinite regress of ends makes human action impossible. Not only does each human action have an ultimate end (a. 4), he says, all the human actions of each person have one single ultimate end: "Just as of all [human beings] there is naturally one last end, so the will of an individual [human being] must be fixed on one last end." All penultimate ends are ordered to one, single, overarching ultimate end as means to achieving this end (a. 5).[29] And what obtains for one human being must in virtue of the shared human nature obtain for all: all humans strive for perfection; all intend the ultimate human end (a. 6).

While all human beings intend the ultimate end *formally*, that is, *as* ultimate end, there is a great difference in what humans take the ultimate end to be *materially*. All humans strive for perfection, but what perfection consists in and what good one must obtain to reach it is a matter of interminable controversy—as human history in general and the history of philosophy in particular incontrovertibly demonstrates. The question is answered subjectively in strikingly different ways (a. 7). Objectively, however, there obtains only one answer, according to Aquinas. The whole cosmos is directed to one single ultimate end. God is the objective ultimate end for all things without exception, the *finis ultimus cuius*, the thing itself in which the nature of end is found (a. 8). Yet with regard to the act of achieving it (*finis ultimus quo*), the human ultimate end differs from that of non-rational beings, for humans attain their ultimate end by knowing and loving God, and this *finis ultimus quo*—this active possession by way of the act of knowing and the act of loving—is beatitude, blessedness, that is, perfect participation in divine happiness.

The Universal Principle of Finality Realized in Human Existence

Rational creatures realize this universal finality of the cosmos and all it includes by way of our human agency. This agency is grounded in an intelligibility (our human nature) that is prior to our con-

29. This particular thesis of Aquinas has proven to be highly controversial among contemporary moral philosophers and moral theologians. See chapter 1, pp. 112–22, and especially also the epilogue, pp. 409–25, for a more extensive discussion of this claim.

sciousness and that we are unable to "determine" or even "construct" through arbitrary decisions informed by the quasi-teleology of the imperious will of the modern subject aspiring to sovereignty. Here the clarifying and indeed liberating power of Aquinas's concept of the "will as nature" (*voluntas ut natura*) comes into the picture, the will as ordered to the good and hardwired to desire happiness and therefore as ordered unthematically to God prior to our thinking and willing anything in particular. As such, as hardwired to desire happiness, the human will is actually unable to change arbitrarily the formality of the ultimate end *qua* ultimate end; nor, for that matter, is the will able to change arbitrarily what constitutes objectively the material aspect of the ultimate end, God. In short, humans are unable sovereignly to determine what makes us irreversibly and interminably happy—any more than we can determine our nature.[30]

Contemporary transhumanism is presently attempting to deny this fundamental metaphysical reality. According to this neo-Gnostic version of angelism, the attempted apotheosis of the sovereign self, human nature is an a-teleological, fluid, and hence malleable reality that may be shaped freely along the lines of individual or collective determinations. My insistence throughout this book on the universality of the principle of finality may indeed be understood as an unequivocal indictment of the intellectual climate of late modernity. I will argue in the opening programmatic chapter, "Ordained for Beatitude," that one of the characteristics of the modern era is the widespread rejection of the principle of finality.[31] As it plays out in the anthropological realm, this pervasive dismissal of the principle of finality leads to a crisis in terms of the human being's understanding of himself as a human person. Due to the widespread erroneous dismissal of the finality of human nature, the human self-image as rational animal, as person and nature in one, collapses into the irresolvable antinomy between two contradictory and agonistically compet-

30. See chapter 1 for a further discussion of this important point and for an instructive discussion of its position in the wider framework of classical teleology, see Robert Spaemann and Reinhard Löw, *Natürliche Ziele: Geschichte und Wiederentdeckung des teleologischen Denkens* (Stuttgart: Klett-Cotta, 2005), 11–79.

31. For a nuanced analysis of this complex intellectual process, see Thomas Pfau, *Minding the Modern: Human Agency, Intellectual Traditions, and Responsible Knowledge* (Notre Dame, Ind.: University of Notre Dame Press, 2013), 185–413.

ing self-images, a neo-Gnostic angelism and a naturalistic animalism. The late-modern person vacillates between the self-image of an essentially disembodied sovereign will that submits all exteriority, including the body, to its imperious dictates, and the self-image of a super-primate, a highly advanced animal, gifted or cursed with a developed consciousness that is driven by instincts, passions, and desires beyond its control and understanding into patterns of behavior for which an animal can never be held fully accountable.

Question 2: The Object of Happiness

Question 2 asks which good makes the human happy, not somewhat happy or transiently happy or happy in a certain way, but rather perfectly and everlastingly happy, blessed. Aquinas here is pursuing the question of *what* the perfect good is, what qualifies as the objective ultimate end the attainment of which brings about perfect happiness, beatitude. He shows that God is the complete good, the *bonum consummatum*, the good that has no good beyond itself, and that God consequently is the objective ultimate end the attainment of which makes the human being perfectly happy, blessed. How does Aquinas reach this point?

He picks up at the very beginning an insight from the previous question, namely that all humans agree in their desire to be perfectly and everlastingly happy (q. 1, a. 7). Indeed, their rational appetite, the will, is "hard-wired" to desire happiness in such a way that it cannot not desire happiness. Yet humans quite obviously disagree profoundly over the question of what the good is that would make us perfectly happy. Aquinas first (aa. 1–4) considers the standard exterior goods that people desire: wealth, honor, fame or glory, and power. He adduces four reasons why none of these four exterior goods qualifies as ultimate end of human beings. First, they are all morally indifferent, that is, they can be found among good as well as bad persons. But beatitude, being the highest human good, is incompatible with evil; it cannot be found among wicked persons, yet wealth, honor, fame, and glory can be found among them. Second, none of these goods qualifies as *bonum consummatum*, a good beyond which and next to which one cannot desire another good. The wealthy person might still desire fame and power; the powerful person might still desire wealth and glory. Third, each of these exterior goods can lead to bad consequences, especially wealth, the care and worry over which tends to completely absorb the rich person, as Ecclesiastes poignantly observes: "The surfeit of the rich will not let them sleep.... Riches were kept by their owners to their hurt, and those riches were lost in a bad venture" (Eccl 5:12–14). The same could be said analogously of honor, fame, and power. However, as beatitude is complete fulfillment, no misfortune can emerge from it. Fourth and finally, all external goods depend on exterior causes and are therefore subject to the vicissitudes of luck (*fortuna*). Human life is vulnerable to the loss of any of these goods at any moment. Therefore these exterior goods cannot qualify as candidates for the ultimate human end. Humans are ordered naturally, that is, through interior principles and hence by the immanent dynamic of human nature, to their proper perfection, to perfect happiness. Yet these goods will only—and at best—bring about a fragile, transient, and deeply ambiguous happiness, most likely the surfeit of happiness instead of genuine, even if imperfect, happiness.

The good of the body—first and foremost, good health or more comprehensively, "wellness" with the end of unlimited longevity—also does not qualify as a candidate for the perfect good (q. 5). Aquinas offers two reasons for this. First, as humans cannot be themselves the perfect good, they obviously are destined to an end beyond themselves. Yet, Aquinas states, "when a thing is made for something other than itself, then the ultimate end cannot be constituted by its own continuance in existence." In his second argument, Aquinas seems almost to anticipate as a possible objection the modern appeal to the greatest good of secular humanism, namely interminable human continuance in existence, self-preservation with the end of unlimited longevity, and ideally the overcoming of physical death. Could this not be a way of regarding the human being as perfect good achieved by way of the good of the body? Even given the supposition that the good of the body is the overcoming of physical death, Aquinas would argue that the ultimate human end cannot be something bodily. Why? Because the constitutive principle that makes a human being specifically human is not the body but the rational soul, which Aquinas takes to be the principle or form of the body. He states: "The body is for the soul as matter is for form, and instruments for a principal cause to work through." Furthermore, all the goods of the body are ordained to the goods of the soul as their end. Differently put, humans who simply live with bodily well-being and unlimited longevity as their ultimate end fundamentally misunderstand what it is to be human and will eventually fail to be human in some significant way.

Unsurprisingly, but to the predictable dismay of many of our contemporaries, Aquinas also argues that the pleasure of sense (a. 6) fails as a candidate for the perfect good. Bodily pleasure depends on the contingent condition of the body and hence encounters the same problems Aquinas considered in relationship to the good of the body. Intellectual or spiritual pleasure, however, is another matter because it is achieved only with the attainment of the highest intellectual and spiritual good.

Aquinas expands this insight about the pleasure of the rational soul (a. 7) by drawing upon the distinction between the good, the attainment of which makes a human being perfectly happy (*finis cuius*), from the subjective enjoyment of this good (*finis quo*). Beatitude (*finis ultimus quo*) is indeed a condition of the rational soul, its very perfection and hence a good interior to the soul. But what causes the beatitude of the soul is an objective good exterior to it (*finis ultimus cuius*).

And so Aquinas concludes (a. 8) that humans cannot arrive at perfect happiness, beatitude, by the attainment of any created good. The perfect good (*bonum consummatum*) that satisfies human desire completely transcends creation. Aquinas states:

> The object of the will, that is the human appetite, is the Good without reserve, just as the object of the mind is the True without reserve. Clearly, then, nothing can satisfy [the human] will except such goodness, which is found, not in anything created, but in God alone. Everything created is a derivate good. He alone, who fills with all good things thy desire [Ps 102:5], can satisfy our will, and therefore in him our happiness [*beatitudo*] lies. (*ST* I-II, q. 2, a. 8)

Question 3: The Essence of Happiness

In question 3, Aquinas takes the next step and asks what the subjective human attainment of the objective ultimate end is. Having established in question 2 that the ultimate human end in its objective sense (*finius ultimus cuius*) is God, in question 3 Aquinas first reminds his readers (a. 1) of the crucial distinction between the ultimate human end as something *uncreated*, namely God himself, and the human attainment or enjoyment of the ultimate end, beatitude, as something *created*. The former is the *object* of beatitude, the latter is the *reality* of beatitude. As Aquinas explains, "with respect to its object or cause happiness is uncreated reality, while with respect to its essence it is a creaturely reality."

He next (a. 2) turns to the question of what the subjective attainment of this exterior ultimate end is. In light of the preceding analysis, there is only one answer: perfect subjective happiness, beatitude, consists in the attainment of God. But why is this the case? Simply put, Aquinas understands beatitude as the perfection of human life. The principle of human life—what makes it distinctly human and what makes it surpassingly perfectible—is the rational soul. Hence, beatitude is the perfection of the rational soul and that perfection is the maximal actualization of the rational soul's higher faculties, intellect and will. And because the soul is an active (and not just a passive) principle, the maximal actualization is not an actualization simply by another, but rather a self-actualization. Although it will become apparent that Aquinas thinks that such a self-actualization presupposes an antecedent as well as a concomitant divine help, grace, in order to enable and sustain the rational soul's self-actualization in the *viator* and in a special way in the *comprehensor*.

It is by now clear that Aquinas thinks of happiness, the subjective attainment of the objective ultimate end, as the perfect actualization of being human and hence as an activity. It is "being in act." But could one not also think of this subjective attainment instead as a state of being? In his answer, Aquinas integrates two seemingly incompatible positions that he finds in the philosophical tradition. Aristotle, in his *Nicomachean Ethics*, regards happiness as surpassing activity, as the complete actualization of what it is to be human. The late antique philosopher and theologian Boethius, in his *Consolation of Philosophy* advanced the notion that happiness is a perfect state (*status perfectus*).[32] Aquinas overcomes the apparent contradiction between both views this way: he takes Boethius to be offering a concept of the state of perfection in which the happy person finds himself. He understands Aristotle to be analyzing the very nature of this state as an interior intransitive activity. Beatitude is the subjective perfection of the human being; taken this way it may be described as a state of perfection. Yet because perfection means the full actualization of every being (for whatever can still be further actualized is not yet perfect), beatitude must consist in the ultimate or culminating interior actualization of being human.

In order to clarify what one might call the "psychology of beatitude," Aquinas considers the involvement of the human soul's faculties—the senses, the will, and the intellect—in this surpassing interior activity that is beatitude (aa. 3–5). It is in the context of these considerations that Aquinas introduces the distinction between an imperfect happiness attainable on earth and the perfect happiness that only the *comprehensor* attains in heaven.

While human sensation does not belong essentially to beatitude, Aquinas nevertheless holds that the senses are related to beatitude in both an antecedent and a consequent way (a. 3). Imperfect, earthly happiness is not to be had without the human act of reasoning and understanding, but the act of reasoning and understanding depends in this life on sensory input and so sensation is an antecedent to earthly happiness. In the perfect happiness of the *comprehensor*, after the general resurrection, there will be, Aquinas states, citing

32. *Philosophiae consolationis* 3.2.2–12: "The whole concern of men, which the effort of a multitude of pursuits keeps busy, moves by different roads, yet strives to arrive at one and the same end, that of happiness [*beatitudinis finem*]. Now that is the good which, once a man attains it, leaves no room for further desires. And it is the highest of all goods, containing in itself all that is good, for if there were anything lacking to it, it could not be the highest good, since there would remain something outside it which could be desired. So it is clear that happiness is that state which is perfect since all goods are gathered together in it [*Liquet igitur esse beatitudinem statum bonorum omnium congregatione perfectum*]." Boethius, *Tractates. The Consolation of Philosophy*, trans. H. F. Stewart, E. K. Rand, S. J. Tester (Cambridge, Mass.: Harvard University Press, 1973), 233.

Augustine, "a flowing out from the beatitude of soul into the body and the senses such as to enhance their activities" and so sensation comes to be a consequent of heavenly beatitude.

What about the will? Aquinas takes the will to be that specific appetite that corresponds to the intellect as the sense appetite corresponds to sense. The will is the rational appetite, that is, a fundamentally mental and not sensual faculty (a. 4). To the dismay of voluntarists of all stripes, Aquinas holds that the act of attaining God, the objective ultimate end, beatitude, is primarily an act of the intellect. To be precise, it is an act of the speculative or theoretical (rather than the practical) intellect. The rational appetite, however, is involved in a twofold way in the intellect's act of attaining God. It is involved first antecedently, insofar as humans desire the perfect good and thus begin to seek insight into that which ultimately qualifies as perfect good; and second, as a consequence, because the delight (*delectatio*) that follows upon the intellect's act of attaining God, is an act of the will.

The only higher faculty left as a candidate for the primary and essential actualization of beatitude is the intellect. Aquinas offers three reasons (a. 5) that the essential interior activity of beatitude should be said to occur in the theoretical and not in the practical intellect. First, in the case of the *comprehensor* the most noble object, God, engages the highest human faculty, the theoretical intellect. Second—unlike the judgments of practical reason—the contemplation of the theoretical intellect is sought for its own sake. Finally, it is contemplation that ultimately conforms the human to God and to the angels. And so Aquinas concludes that the ultimate and perfect beatitude in the life to come consists principally in contemplation.

But contemplation of what? Would the forms of the material world qualify as objects of such contemplation? Because Aquinas holds that "forms in the material world do reflect some likeness of higher substances," "by dwelling on them disinterestedly there is a sort of anticipation of true and complete happiness" (a. 6). This would be the contemplation of the metaphysician, the logician, and the mathematician. Yet because the first principles of the theoretical sciences are received by way of the senses—as Aristotle argues in the beginning of the *Metaphysics* and in the closing of the *Posterior Analytics*—these sciences and the contemplation of their objects cannot reach what completely and utterly transcends the senses.

But would the contemplation of separate substances, of angels, qualify as objects of the contemplation that is perfect happiness? Because the object of the mind is truth without reserve (*verum universale*), the object that perfectly actualizes the mind is the first truth (a. 7). But angels, being created, are a derivate reality and a derivative reality is only a derivative truth. God alone is nonderivative, essential truth and only by contemplating God is the human in perfect bliss. Hence the human mind's final perfection consists in the union with God in the perfect act of the intellect and the consequent perfect act of the will (a. 8).[33]

In short, Aquinas understands the beatific vision as involving both of the soul's higher faculties, intellect and will, in their proper relationship. The will can only attain its own proper ultimate end if the intellect—properly prepared by divine assistance (the *lumen gloriae*; *ST* I, q. 12, a. 5)—actively receives the consummate good first as its own proper ultimate end, that is, as the first truth. Contemplating first truth as its proper object, the intellect then proposes it to the will under the aspect of good. The will, perfectly satisfied in its possession, thus attains perfect happiness such that surpassing joy ensues. Importantly, the contemplation of the *comprehensor* is for Aquinas always a *loving* contemplation: the will antecedently desires what contemplation eventually beholds, the consummate good. After the

---

33. In his noteworthy book *Hell and the Mercy of God*, Reimers advances a compelling contemporary argument from the existence of evil for Aquinas's insistence that for perfect happiness the intellect needs to reach the very essence of the first cause: "Confronted with evil, the suffering person asks two questions: (1) what can be done to alleviate this? and (2) how, why did this happen? Even if he cannot make the pain stop, he wants to understand why he is subjected to this evil. Indeed, this questioning, this need for some explanation arises also when the evil is not one that a person experiences personally.... The scandal to philosophy is that the question of evil cannot finally be answered; that there is no account of evil that explains how what we experience or know to be evil can in the final analysis be good. What the book of Job and Aquinas's analysis imply is that the sought-for answer can be found only in the depths of the divine wisdom; that only one who sees the essence of God with his intellect can understand the reason behind evil. Only in this vision of the Divine Essence can the evil truly be overcome" (*Hell and the Mercy of God*, 227).

intellect's attainment of first truth in the beatific vision, the will—its desires now satiated—delights in the consummate good. Delight entails love. As Aquinas explains: "Delight consists in a certain repose of the will ... *the will is at rest though actively loving*" (q. 4, a. 2). The attainment of perfect beatitude in the beatific vision is for Aquinas first and foremost a truth of revelation, a truth to which the Apostles Paul and John attest: "For now we see in a mirror, dimly, but then we will see face to face. Now I know only in part; then I will know fully, even as I have been fully known" (1 Cor 13:12); "And this is eternal life, that they may know you, the only true God, and Jesus Christ whom you have sent" (Jn 17:3). In order to interpret, make intelligible, and defend this truth of faith, Aquinas draws upon the Augustinian theological tradition and supports it by way of the Platonic-Aristotelian philosophical tradition.[34]

Question 3 accentuates and fortifies Aquinas's understanding of happiness as entailing complete self-transcendence (and with it self-forgetfulness) while at the same time, complete self-realization. The complete self-realization occurs in the possession of the uncreated perfect good. At the same time, the possession of the uncreated perfect good entails the most radical self-transcendence. Because the uncreated perfect good in possession is the consummate objective good, the *comprehensor* is completely absorbed by this surpassing good so that while the soul's faculties are perfectly actualized the soul is at rest in the consummate good and hence oblivious of itself. Self-reflexivity belongs to the fallen state; self-forgetfulness to the state of beatitude.

At this point, I must briefly touch upon one of the most intricate theological debates of post-Tridentine Catholic theology reaching right up into the twenty-first century. The issue at stake in this debate lies close to the surface of what Aquinas discusses in question 3. The debate concerns whether humans have a natural desire for the vision of God, and, if so, what this desire is, and how it is elicited. I have entered this debate at length elsewhere and shall therefore not

---

34. The two paradigmatic theological sources in the Augustinian tradition are Augustine, *De civitate dei* XXII.29, and *De genesi ad litteram* XII.26.54–36.69. The two paradigmatic sources in the Platonic-Aristotelian philosophical tradition are Plato, *Republic* VII, 517b–c, and Aristotle, *Nicomachean Ethics* X.7.

enter it again here, although I shall return to it below in the third part of chapter 1.[35] In the following excursus I merely wish to adumbrate what I take to be Aquinas's teaching on this topic insofar as it bears upon the question of the nature and the attainment of beatitude.

Excursus: The Natural Desire for the Vision of God and the Ultimate Human End

As noted above, the proper object of the intellect is being (*ens*) under the aspect of unrestricted truth (*verum universale*). The proper object of the rational appetite, the will, is being under the aspect of the unrestricted good (*bonum universale*). Consequently, humans have a natural desire to know the first truth, the source of all truth, and to attain the consummate good, the realization of all good. And because the first truth and the highest good are one and the same reality, the divine essence, humans have a natural desire for the vision of the divine essence (*desiderium naturale visionis Dei*). Aquinas understands this to be the natural appetite of the intellect according to its *ontological structure*. However, for the created intellect a natural knowledge of the essence of the first cause unmediated by any created effects remains essentially unattainable. Hence, in this life, the first truth can never engage the intellect directly as an "object" that the intellect then might desire to attain. Only by way of the truth of created things, by them engaging the intellect, does the first truth indirectly engage the intellect. Even the most advanced metaphysical contemplation of the first truth remains discursive and ultimately depends on the import of the senses and does therefore not admit a natural intellectual intuition of the divine essence. Yet it is objects that directly engage the senses or the intellect that elicit unconditional specific desires. In this life, the first truth cannot be such an object. The natural desire for the vision of the divine essence remains therefore conditional and oblique. Consequently, the happiness that results from this acquired metaphysical wisdom, though genuine, remains incomplete and transient. Nevertheless, it is the very ontological structure of the created intellect, its finality, that renders intelligible the ultimate significance of divine revelation

---

35. See my *Dust Bound for Heaven*, 129–246, and below, pp. 134–50.

through Christ and this revelation's promise of the beatific vision and the ensuing perfect happiness. God, the first truth, will unite the created intellect, elevated by the created light of glory (*lumen gloriae*), with the quasi-form of his own uncreated essence and thereby grant an immediate participation of the rational creature in the uncreated life of the Trinity. This promise of divine revelation—received by divine faith as a truth revealed by God—now engages the intellect of the wayfarer and elicits an unconditional desire for the vision of God.

In virtue of the ontological structure of the created intellect, the creaturely image of the divine exemplar, its specific natural finality and its gratuitous supernatural call to union with God, there obtains a twofold order of finality, one that pertains to the created natural structure as well as to the supernatural vocation of the created intellect. Importantly, this twofold order of finality, however, does not entail two distinct ultimate ends for the human being, one natural and one supernatural. Rather, there obtains one ultimate end for the human being. This ultimate end is God. In the natural order, God is end as first truth, author of nature, and the common good of the whole universe, the final end of the created intellect (angelic and human). In the supernatural order God is end as the Trinity, the absolutely surpassing reality of participative union of vision and love that characterizes the beatific vision. Grace presupposes and perfects human nature such that the finality of the created intellect is subsumed under and included in the supernatural ultimate end.

Hence, according to Aquinas, in the extant order of providence, the economy of salvation, every human being is called to the same destiny, the vision of the divine essence. From the creation of the first human being on, this *de facto* ultimate human end is a supernatural end because it is not connatural to human nature (*ST* I-II, q. 109, a. 5, co. and ad 3). The desire for this supernatural end is elicited by grace and attained on account of grace. However, this ultimate end is not simply extrinsically imposed on or added to human nature, but rather constitutes the supernatural perfection of the natural striving (*appetitus*) of the intellect for unrestricted truth and of the will for unrestricted good and of the natural, albeit conditional and oblique desire for the vision of God.

Corresponding to the twofold human finality, natural and supernatural, genuine human happiness is also twofold. There is imperfect genuine happiness which is transitory and fragile. Imperfect happiness is proportionate to human nature; it is attained, according to Aristotle's *Nicomachean Ethics*, in the *bios praktikos*, the life of virtue in a well-ordered society, possibly crowned in one's later years by the *bios theoretikos*, the contemplation of the highest truths. Then there is perfect happiness, beatitude, for which all humans are destined. It is inchoately present already in the *viator* on account of sanctifying grace and the theological virtues, faith, hope, and charity infused concomitantly with sanctifying grace. It is perfectly present in the *comprehensor* in the beatific vision, in the beholding of the first truth by the intellect and in the possession of the consummate good by the will. The everlasting, unitive, and therefore perfect beatitude surpasses the capacity of human nature and can be obtained "by the power of God alone, by a kind of participation of the Godhead, about which it is written (2 Pt 1:4) that by Christ we are made partakers of the Divine nature" (*ST* I-II, q. 62, a. 1). God, the first truth, will unite the created intellect—strengthened by a supernaturally infused *habitus*, the light of glory (*lumen gloriae*)—formally with the divine essence such that through this quasi-instrumental medium of the divine essence itself the intellect can see the first truth, possess the consummate good and thus participate directly in the life of the Trinity. Perfect human beatitude is the subjective fruition of the objective ultimate end (*in statu comprehensoris*) through an unmediated participation in the uncreated divine essence, who is the first cause of the rational soul's creation and enlightenment and the rational soul's final end as its universal good. Because the rational soul is the substantial form of the body, it is the whole human being, soul and body, whose final end is to become a partaker of the divine nature, and thus a partaker of the unfathomable bliss of the divine life.[36]

Eternal life is a promise of divine revelation that, according to Aquinas, is fitting to human nature, because in the beatific vision the natural desire for the vision of God is fulfilled, the perfect object of

---

36. See the epilogue, pp. 389–409, for a more extensive discussion of the metaphysical and epistemological entailments of the beatific vision.

the intellect beheld, and the perfect object of the will possessed and thus perfect beatitude achieved. Finite and transient and therefore imperfect happiness corresponds to earthly human existence, an existence faced with the limitations of reason bound to the senses and fraught with original and actual sin. Infinite and therefore perfect happiness, beatitude, corresponds to heavenly human existence, an existence free from actual sin, free from the wounds caused by original sin, free from the limitations of the senses, and free from the corruptibility of the human body.

It is noteworthy that both the happiness of the virtuous person (and also the person immersed in philosophical contemplation) and the happiness of the *viator* are imperfect. Yet the meaning of "imperfect happiness" is different for each because the respective points of reference for each imperfection are diverse. As Aquinas interprets him, Aristotle regards the happiness humans can attain in this life as essentially imperfect because "those [humans] for whom such perfection in this life is possible are *happy as* [humans] [*ut homines*], as if they had not attained felicity absolutely, but merely in human fashion [*modo humano*]."[37] Thus imperfect happiness is still genuine happiness, not a counterfeit of happiness, because they are "happy as human beings" (*ut homines; modo humano*). But what is Aristotle's point of reference for this imperfect happiness? Denis Bradley, in his extraordinary study, *Aquinas on the Twofold Good*, puts the matter succinctly:

Aristotle's sense of the imperfection of human *eudaimonia* is in comparison to God's happiness, not in comparison with any possible human happiness. Aristotle maintains that philosophic contemplation is akin to the contemplation enjoyed by the gods, but he acknowledges that only the gods live a life that is entirely blessed. Human contemplation, although godlike, cannot escape the imperfections of bodily existence; as human it is subject to change and impermanence.[38]

---

37. *Summa contra Gentiles* [hereafter "*SCG*"] III.48.9; the first Arabic number refers to the chapter, the second Arabic number refers to chapter section as explicitly indicated in the English translation of the *SCG*. Alterations are indicated by brackets. Translation from Thomas Aquinas, *Summa contra Gentiles. Book Three: Providence. Part I*, trans. Vernon J. Bourke (Notre Dame, Ind.: University of Notre Dame Press, 1975), 165. See Aristotle, *Nicomachean Ethics* I.10, 1101a18.

38. Bradley, *Aquinas on the Twofold Human Good*, 399.

Taken as the perfection of the kind of existence human nature makes possible, the happiness humans may attain in this life is genuine happiness. Compared to the happiness of the gods, it is essentially imperfect happiness.

Aquinas also understands the happiness Aristotle refers to as essentially imperfect, but for another reason. Unlike Aristotle, Aquinas compares the happiness of the virtuous and contemplative person with the inchoate happiness of the *viator*—whose happiness results from the infused theological virtues of faith, hope, and charity—and the perfect happiness of the *comprehensor* found in the beatific vision. Because the point of reference for the *viator*'s imperfect happiness is the perfect happiness of the *comprehensor* in which the *viator* already participates incipiently, the *viator*'s happiness is only accidentally imperfect.

One might object that to regard the difference between the happiness of the *viator* and that of the *comprehensor* as merely accidental takes too lightly the challenges and difficulties of suffering, loss, and failure that are part of the *viator*'s journey to beatitude. Yet this objection misses the essentially participatory character of the three theological virtues and of the whole supernatural life in God on account of sanctifying grace.[39] Aquinas understands the *viator* in the state of grace in light of Christ's words according to John's Gospel: "Those who love me will keep my word, and my Father will love them, and we will come to them and make our home with them" (Jn 14:23). Sanctifying grace is the created effect of the indwelling of the Trinity in the *viator*. Because the following passage is absolutely central in order to understand the theological constitution of the *viator* according to Aquinas I shall cite it in full:

God is in all things by His essence, power and presence, according to His one common mode, as the cause existing in the effects which participate in His goodness. Above and beyond this common mode, however, there is one special mode belonging to the rational nature wherein God is said to be present as the object known is in the knower, and the beloved in the lover. And since the rational creature by its operation of knowledge and love attains to God Himself, according to this special mode God is said not only

---

39. See chapter 5.

to exist in the rational creature but also *to dwell therein as in His own temple.* So no other effect can be put down as the reason why the divine person is in the rational creature in a new mode, except sanctifying grace.[40]

It is sanctifying grace that makes the difference between the *viator* and the *comprehensor* in a certain way "accidental." In question 4, Aquinas addresses the remaining fundamental difference between the two: the *comprehensor* has "comprehension," that is, definite and irreversible and hence everlasting possession of the ultimate human end; the *viator* does not.

Question 4: The Conditions of Happiness

Aquinas continues the consideration of the subjective ultimate human end (*finis ultimus quo*) in question 4 by asking what else might be necessary for beatitude. What are the conditions of happiness necessary for an embodied and social being? Are pleasure, delight, comprehension, and rectitude or goodness of the will elements of happiness? Are the body—for that matter, a healthy body—external goods, and the companionship of friends necessary for happiness, imperfect and perfect? Aquinas has discussed these matters already in questions 2 and 3. The crucial difference is that he now has established that God is the consummate good that makes human beings perfectly happy and that perfect happiness consists essentially in the beatific vision. The question now is whether certain other goods are necessary for, or have some intrinsic relationship to happiness, imperfect or perfect. As Aquinas enters into the consideration of these matters, he distinguishes four ways in which something may be necessary for something else without, however, being an essential property of it: (1) as a preparation (*antecedenter*), (2) as a perfection (*perficiens*), (3) as an extrinsic help (*coadiuvans extrinsecum*), or (4) as an accompaniment (*concomitanter*).

Pleasure—in the sense of intellectual delight (*delectatio*)—is concomitant with beatitude (a. 1). Delight, Aquinas observes, "is caused by the repose of desire in a good"; it is the immediate resonance of the attainment of a good. And so, he concludes, "delight

---

40. *ST* I, q. 43, a. 3, co.; emphasis added. See chapter 5 for a more detailed consideration of sanctifying grace, especially in relation to charity.

is caused by the very vision of God, and he who sees God has need of no other" (ad 2). This being the case, we might wonder whether—instead of vision—what matters most is actually delight (a. 2). Should we understand delight, joy, bliss, in short, eternal ecstasy to be the real subjective ultimate human end, perfect happiness, instead of the subjective attainment of the objective ultimate end? Are not interminable delight, joy, bliss, ecstasy, what we actually desire? Why should they not constitute the ultimate end? Aquinas takes a position that at first glance might look counterintuitive to most contemporaries who would most likely answer this question positively. Because, as established earlier, perfect subjective happiness means to be fully actualized as a human being, the principal point of full and genuine human beatitude must be the activity (*operatio*) in which the rational appetite, the will, finds its rest and delight—and this is precisely the activity of intellectual vision. And so Aquinas concludes that beatitude "turns on the mind's act of vision, not on the delight." Surpassing delight, self-forgetful ecstasy of joy and bliss issue from the beatific vision, the will's rest in the possession of the consummate good. They accompany the attainment of perfect happiness, but they are not to be confused with subjective beatitude itself.

This being the case, does beatitude then entail comprehension of the consummate good attained? Aquinas clarifies this point by drawing implicitly upon the distinction between the *viator* and the *comprehensor* and by explaining what "comprehensor" does and does not mean (a. 3). The perfect happiness, beatitude, the *comprehensor* enjoys, entails a threefold perfection: (1) complete knowledge of the ultimate end in place of the *viator*'s incomplete knowledge of it by faith; (2) the real presence of the end to the *comprehensor* by way of an interior illumination of the intellect in place of the *viator*'s longing of hope to attain it; and (3) the delight in the possession of the end instead of the *viator*'s initial motion of love toward the thing loved (or even of a real relation of the lover to the thing loved). Hence, "all three must combine in the integral happiness [*beatitudo*], namely vision, the complete knowledge of an end by the mind, comprehension, which implies its presence, and delight or joy, which implies the resting of the lover with the beloved" (a. 3). Importantly, "comprehension" does not mean the result of a discursive knowledge of God by the finite mind, a conceptual grasp so to speak of the divine essence which is impossible for the created mind even in the beatific vision (*ST* I, q. 12, a. 5). "Comprehension," rather, denotes an act of the will. It is "the holding of an object as present and possessed" (ad 1). As Cajetan astutely remarked in his commentary on this passage, "Comprehension is a relation resulting in the will from the vision of the mind. The will is the one term of this relation, the other is the real and immediately known presence of God."[41]

The will plays another crucial role in beatitude. Without the will's rectitude, beatitude cannot be attained (a. 4). Aquinas explains: "The will is rightful when duly bent on its ultimate end." The will's rectitude is required antecedently as a preparation for beatitude, for only someone with a good will can reach the vision of God. It is required concomitantly, as an attendant condition of beatitude. In the vision of God, a vision of pure goodness, the *comprehensor* loves all she loves within the encompassing embrace of God's goodness. The rectitude of the will is a necessary attendant condition of this loving vision.

What about embodiment? Is the body necessary for beatitude? Aquinas answers by way of the familiar distinction between imperfect and perfect happiness (a. 5). Aquinas states: "Happiness has two phases, one incomplete and possible in this life, and the other completed and subsisting in the vision of God. As for the first, the body is clearly needed, for such happiness comes through activity of mind, theoretical and practical." Yet such activity cannot be performed without the imagination which receives input from the senses which are in a bodily organ. But what about the *comprehensor*? Would he not also need the resurrection body for perfect happiness in the beatific vision? Indeed, quite a number of important theologians in the patristic period and in the Middle Ages held that the beatific vision is delayed until the resurrection of the body has

---

41. This passage from the pertinent section of Cajetan's *Commentaria in Summam Theologiae Sancti Thomae Aquinatis* is quoted from Thomas Aquinas, *Summa Theologiae*, vol. 16: *(1a2ae. 1–5), Purpose and Happiness*, ed. Thomas Gilby, OP (New York: McGraw-Hill, 1969), 96, note d.

occurred.[42] Contrary to this theological position, Aquinas holds that it is evident from authority and reason that "the souls of the saints, separated from their bodies, walk by sight in the vision of God's es-

---

42. It was only Pope Benedict XII who, in his 1336 Constitution *Benedictus Deus*, taught the following: "By this constitution which is to remain in force forever, We, with apostolic authority, define the following: according to the general disposition of God, the souls of all the saints who departed from this world before the Passion of our Lord Jesus Christ and also of the holy apostles, martyrs, confessors, virgins, and other faithful who died after receiving the holy baptism of Christ—provided they were not in need of any purification when they died, or will not be in need of any when they die in the future, or else, if they then needed or will need some purification, after they have been purified after death—and again the souls of children who have been reborn by the same baptism of Christ or will be when baptism is conferred on them, if they die before attaining the use of free will: all these souls, immediately [*mox*] after death and, in the case of those in need of purification, after the purification mentioned above, since the Ascension of our Lord and Savior Jesus Christ into heaven, already before they take up their bodies again and before the general judgment, have been, are, and will be with Christ in heaven, in the heavenly kingdom and paradise, joined to the company of the holy angels. Since the Passion and death of the Lord Jesus Christ, these souls have seen and see the divine essence with an intuitive vision and even face to face, without the mediation of any creature by way of object of vision; rather the divine essence immediately manifests itself to them, plainly, clearly and openly, and in this vision they enjoy the divine essence. Moreover, by this vision and enjoyment the souls of those who have already died are truly blessed and have eternal life and rest. Also the souls of those who will die in the future will see the same divine essence and will enjoy it before the general judgment." Heinrich Denzinger, *Compendium of Creeds, Definitions, and Declarations on Matters of Faith and Morals*, ed. Peter Hünermann et al., 43rd ed. (San Francisco, Calif.: Ignatius Press, 2012), no. 1000 (302) [hereafter "Denzinger"]. I quote the magisterial teaching at length because—as far as it goes and as much as it states—it is arguably anticipated with astonishing precision by Aquinas's teaching. See my epilogue below for further discussion of this complex theological issue. For instructive studies of Pope Benedict XII's personal doctrine of the intensive growth in the beatific vision, see Friedrich Wetter, *Die Lehre Benedikts XII. vom intensiven Wachstum der Gottesschau* (Rome: Gregorian University, 1958), and Simon Tugwell, OP, *Human Immortality and the Redemption of Death* (Springfield, Ill.: Templegate, 1990). It is important to realize that, indeed, Benedict XII did not settle authoritatively the question of whether there is an increase in the intensity of the beatific vision and hence of beatitude after the last judgment. Wetter and Tugwell show that the personal opinion of Benedict XII, especially when he was still Cardinal Fournier, was that beatitude is "the condition which is complete with its collection of all goods" (ibid., 147). Hence, as long as some goods are lacking, beatitude is somehow incomplete. From this Fournier concluded that, before the last judgment, "neither men nor angels will be fully blessed. Though they see the essence of God and are blessed ... because they already have the thing that is most important in beatitude, all the same, they do not have all that they legitimately want or could legitimately want" (ibid.). It is important to note that the formal definition of *Benedictus Deus* was restricted to "the essential minimum that needed official clarification" (ibid., 146). See the epilogue for Aquinas's considered position on this important and controversial topic.

sence, which is true happiness." Furthermore, he argues, "since complete happiness is the vision of the divine essence, it does not hinge on the body, and the soul can be happy without it." The question that arises in light of Aquinas's argument is this: does the resurrection body add anything to beatitude? The resurrection body, Aquinas would respond, perfects beatitude, not *intensively*, by contributing to the depth, or intensity of beatitude, but rather *extensively*, contributing to its extension into the resurrection life of the *comprehensor* and thereby expanding beatitude to the embodied mode of existence bringing about comprehensive well-being (*bene esse*). The resurrection body is, so to speak, the "sounding board" for the soul's beatitude. Importantly, even in resurrection life, the human soul remains ordered to inform and enliven a body; for the human being is an essentially embodied being. While the formal principle, the rational soul, continues to subsist after death, this subsistent soul—even in the beatific vision—is not the complete human person. In fact, for Aquinas the hylomorphic constitution of the human being is one of the strongest arguments for the rational intelligibility and defensibility of the revealed truth of the resurrection of the body. The resurrection life in the beatific vision is the life of a complete human being, the life of a hylomorphic body-soul composite.[43]

Because the human is a hylomorphic body-soul composite, human happiness entails not only embodiment but also at least some bodily perfection (a. 6). Imperfect happiness in this life requires health of body, a presupposition for "the activity of virtue," in which such happiness consists according to Aristotle. The perfect happiness of beatitude entails the complete well-being of the body; it is an antecedent as well as a consequent condition for beatitude. It is an antecedent condition because bodily imperfection causing difficulties and a certain burdensomeness would turn the mind away from the beatific vision. Yet the resurrection body does not feel pain, nor does it age, or have bodily desires that might distract from the soul's vision of God. It is a consequent condition because the soul's beatitude flows over into the body which, so to speak, "drinks" from the soul's perfection.

External goods (a. 7) are required for the imperfect happiness at-

---

43. See the epilogue, pp. 425–36, for a more extensive consideration of Aquinas's mature position on this complex question.

tainable in this life. They serve as instruments for the activity of virtue—which is the life of imperfect happiness. External goods, however, are in no way needed for the beatitude of the beatific vision. They rather are completely superfluous for the perfect happiness in which the souls of the blessed find themselves before the resurrection of the body and for the blessed after the resurrection of the body when they are united with a spiritual body free from all imperfections and what we nowadays might call biological needs.

Last but not least, Aquinas considers whether beatitude requires the companionship of friends (a. 8). He again takes recourse to Aristotle and affirms that in this life, one stands in need of the companionship of friends, not in order to use them or take pleasure in them but rather to do them good and take delight in seeing them do good. One may also receive their assistance in one's active life (*bios praktikos*) as well as in one's life of contemplation (*bios theoretikos*). This is also true in the life of the *viator*, the pilgrim, who follows the path (*via*) taught by divine revelation. For the *comprehensor*, however, companionship of friends is not strictly necessary, because such a person "is wholly and completely fulfilled in God." Yet like the resurrection body, the companionship of friends extends beatitude into the resurrection life of the *comprehensor* and thus brings about comprehensive well-being (*bene esse*). "The friendships go along [*concomitanter*], as it were, with perfect happiness" (ad 3). As with the body, there is also here a "flowing over" of the soul's beatitude. Aquinas draws upon Augustine to illustrate his point: "And if [the blessed] can be said to be helped from without, perhaps it is only because they see one another, and rejoice in God at their companionship together." Companionship in heaven is ultimately a doxological friendship; it flows from the delight of the blessed in God and returns to that delight.[44]

Question 5: *The Attainment of Happiness*

In the fifth and final question, Aquinas asks what humans have to do to become happy and what is only God able to do to make them

---

44. See the epilogue for a consideration of the objection that on the supposition of the existence of hell, and *pace* von Balthasar's position of hell being unoccupied (at least by human beings), there must necessarily be sorrow in heaven, a fact that would consequently preclude perfect happiness.

perfectly and everlastingly happy, to grant them a participation in divine happiness. In this question Aquinas continues to focus on the subjective ultimate human end (*finis ultimus quo*), insofar as it consists in the attainment (*adipisci*), the possession (*consequi*), and the enjoyment (*frui*) of the perfect good, God, through the beatific vision.

Aquinas asks first whether in light of their constitution as finite rational beings, humans are actually capable of receiving an infinite uncreated good (a. 1). Consider the central point, articulated in Aquinas's characteristically pithy way: "Happiness means gaining perfect good. Now whoever has the capacity for this good can be brought to bliss. That [the human] has the capacity appears from the fact that his mind [*intellectus*] can apprehend good which is universal and unrestricted and his will can desire it." The intellect has the capacity for unrestricted truth and the will for unrestricted good; intellect and will are therefore capable of receiving the first truth and perfect good, God; they are *capax perfecti boni*. And as the perfect good fulfills all human desire it brings about perfect happiness. Hence, humans have the capacity to attain the perfect happiness of the beatific vision.

Does this then mean—given that beatitude is maximal happiness—that beatitude will be the same for everyone sharing the beatific vision? Aquinas does not think so (a. 2). He adopts Augustine's interpretation of Christ's words related by the Apostle John, "In my Father's house there are many dwelling places" (Jn 14:2), to signify "the various degrees of merit in eternal life" (a. 2, s.c.). What the *viator* may merit on the journey of faith—a journey initiated, sustained, and completed by divine grace—is an increase in charity, the love of friendship with God. The deeper the power of divine love received in this life, that is, the deeper the *viator*'s charity, the greater the *viator*'s capacity for beatitude. While the *objective* ultimate end is the same for all who are on the journey of faith, the *subjective* attainment and fruition of God, the consummate good, varies according to the increase in charity merited in this life by acts of the selfsame grace-given charity. It is the depth of the *viator*'s merited charity that makes the *comprehensor* ever more open and adapted to receive the fruition of beatitude. Between the *comprehensor*'s depth of beatitude and the *viator*'s depth of befriending God in a life of ever intensifying charity, there is a direct correlation of providence, grace, and charity merited by acts of charity.[45] Beatitude thus permits of degrees of intensity that depend on the *comprehensor*'s receptivity which is a function of the depth of his or her charity merited during the life as *viator*.

Aquinas next reiterates the difference between the happiness realized by the *viator* in this life and the happiness of the *comprehensor*, who enjoys the beatific vision (a. 3). But once the *viator* has become a *comprehensor* and has attained beatitude, can it be lost again? Can the *comprehensor* fall away again from the enjoyment of the supreme good, God? Aquinas thinks this to be impossible, for three reasons (a. 4). First, a state of happiness that includes the awareness that one might lose it is not a state of perfect happiness; it resembles the imperfect happiness of this life. Beatitude includes the certitude that it will never forsake us and that we will never fall away from the enjoyment of the perfect good. Second, the realization of beatitude is the vision of God, the supreme good. "Beatific vision" means that the *comprehensor*'s soul is filled with every good, for in the vision the *comprehensor* is united by intellect and will with God, the consummate good. And insofar as "the will is bent towards the ultimate end from necessity, the human cannot but will to be happy and united with the supreme and consummate good." Third, the only reason God would withdraw the beatific vision from the *comprehensor* would be because of some fault due to a lack of the will's rectitude. But the rightness of the will results from the beatific vision; consequently, it is impossible for the *comprehensor* to commit a fault.

Unsurprisingly, Aquinas holds that while we have a native capacity for the beatific vision, we cannot attain the perfect happiness of the vision of God by our own native resources (a. 5). While the created intellect is capable of receiving what is true universally and the will is

---

45. See *ST* I-II, q. 114, a. 8, and for an informative study, Joseph Wawrykow, *God's Grace and Human Action: "Merit" in the Theology of Thomas Aquinas* (Notre Dame, Ind.: University of Notre Dame Press, 1995). For a lucid discussion of Aquinas's theology of merit in the contemporary ecumenical discussion, see Michael Root, "Aquinas, Merit, and Reformation Theology after the *Joint Declaration on the Doctrine of Justification*," *Modern Theology* 20, no. 1 (2004): 5–22.

capable of desiring the universal good, no created intellect can produce from his or her natural resources intellectual and volitional acts proportionate to the uncreated infinite essence of God. Faced with this predicament, must we not acknowledge a tension (if not a paradox) in human nature? If human nature intrinsically cannot achieve by its own powers the perfection, or happiness, of which it is capable and to which it is actually ordained, is human nature then not an absurdity? Aquinas has such an objection in mind when he states:

> Aristotle reasons that a nature which can attain the perfect good, although it needs outside help, is of a higher condition than a nature which can attain without such recourse only a lesser good.... Likewise it is better to be a rational creature who can reach complete happiness, though needing divine help, than a non-rational creature which is not capable of this happiness, but arrives at some partial good under its own natural power. (ad 2)

Because beatitude is a good that surpasses created nature, it cannot be attained by any creaturely action. Rather, humans become perfectly happy—blessed—by the agency of God alone: "Homo beatus fit *solo Deo agente*, si loquamur de beatitudine perfecta" (a. 6; emphasis added).

Yet the attainment of this perfect happiness requires a proper antecedent preparation of the human soul (a. 7). The will must be rightly set on the ultimate end and, assisted by grace, must move toward this end through motions of graced activity called merits. This is the *viator*'s growth in charity, in friendship with God. The beatific vision of God, the objective ultimate human end, is only reached by allowing oneself to be befriended by God and to befriend God through the one who called his followers friends, who stated that those who saw him saw the Father, and who said about himself, "I am the way, the truth, and the life; nobody comes to the Father but through me." All of this is according to the Apostle John (Jn 14:6, 14:9, 15:5).

Admittedly, in his formal analysis of beatitude in *ST* I-II, Aquinas is not quite as explicit about the Christocentric nature of the journey to beatitude as he possibly could or should be. But in *ST* III, Aquinas makes quite clear that Christ is the way. Consider his programmatic prologue:

Being Human 49

Forasmuch as our Saviour the Lord Jesus Christ, in order to "save His people from their sins" (Mt. 1:21), as the angel announced, showed unto us in His own Person the way of truth [*viam veritatis*], whereby we may attain to the bliss [*beatitudinem*] of eternal life by rising again, it is necessary, in order to complete the work of theology, that after considering the last end of human life [*ultimi finis humanae vitae*], and the virtues and vices, there should follow the consideration of the Saviour of all, and of the benefits bestowed by Him on the human race. (*ST* III, prol.)

In light of this Christ-centered and Christ-informed nature of the *viator*'s journey it is not surprising that Aquinas's treatment of happiness ends with the sobering insight that, taken in its general meaning, every human being necessarily desires perfect happiness, beatitude, but that opinions diverge dramatically and, indeed, detrimentally as to *what* beatitude is, *where* beatitude is to be found, and *how* it is to be gained (a. 8). While the will is necessarily directed to the subjective ultimate end of happiness, humans do not know with the same necessity *what* the objective ultimate end is, the attainment of which is the cause of beatitude. Nor do they know *where* and *how* to attain it. In order not to go astray in this most crucial matter, according to Aquinas, humans need divine grace and the gift of faith in divine revelation, whose definitive mediator and subject is Jesus Christ. Christ reveals the identity of divine happiness to be the life of the Trinity, opens the path to reach it, and offers the help necessary to attain it. This is the journey to beatitude. The central characteristics of this journey, its requirements and challenges, are the topic of this book.

FOUR IMPEDIMENTS TO AQUINAS'S TEACHING ON HAPPINESS

After having adumbrated the contours of Aquinas's teaching on happiness and its perfection, beatitude, it is apposite to consider four impediments that make it difficult, if not impossible, for many contemporaries to apprehend, let alone embrace, this teaching. These impediments are often implicit, but also deeply held theological, philosophical, existential, and moral objections.[46] In Aquinas's sprawling

---

46. The following four impediments are objections raised against Aquinas's teaching on happiness mainly from positions external to the Catholic faith and to Catholic

oeuvre, there are numerous instances where he anticipates versions of these four modern objections and offers the conceptual resources, discursive outlines, and anticipatory arguments for contemporary Thomist rebuttals to what seem to many definitive arguments against Aquinas's teaching on beatitude.[47]

The First Impediment: The Protestant Theological Objection

The first impediment, the Protestant objection, comes in two parts. Let us first turn to the more significant part that has its source in the Protestant Reformation, to be precise, in Martin Luther's theology, and arguably arose from Luther's one-sided reading of Augustine's late works on grace. According to Luther's reading of Augustine, after the Fall and the loss of original righteousness, human nature was so corrupted that all human desires—including those for truth and goodness—are now fundamentally misdirected by self-love (*amor sui*), the sinful curvature of humans into themselves (*incurvatio hominis in seipsum*). Under the condition of original sin, the desire for happiness can only be a desire for self-love (*amor sui*), the sinner's self-affirmation over against God. Deeply influenced by this interpretation of Augustine, the young and still Catholic Luther was fundamentally opposed to and launched an attack against the central

---

theology. The most important recent objection raised indirectly against Aquinas's teaching and more directly against a contemporary Thomist interpretation of it comes from the Catholic philosopher Dietrich von Hildebrand who articulates it forcefully in his *Christian Ethics* (New York: David McKay, 1953). In an important essay Michael Waldstein shows definitively that whatever version of Thomism it is that von Hildebrand criticizes does not reflect Aquinas's own teaching and that furthermore Aquinas's doctrine of teleology, the good, and happiness successfully addresses all the concerns that von Hildebrand raises from the perspective of a personalist ethics, especially the contrast between person and nature. I warmly recommend Waldstein's magisterial piece to all those who might share von Hildebrand's concerns: "Dietrich von Hildebrand and St. Thomas Aquinas on Goodness and Happiness," *Nova et Vetera* (English) 1, no. 2 (2003): 403–64.

47. The substance for a rebuttal of the Protestant theological objection may be found in the treatises on sin (qq. 71–89) and grace (qq. 109–14) in *ST* I-II. The elements for a rebuttal of the modern philosophical objection may be found in *SCG* I.13 and II.79–82; in *ST* I, qq. 2–12; and in the early *On Being and Essence* (*De ente et essentia*). The response to the existential objection is contained *in nuce* in Aquinas's treatise on happiness. Miguel Romero has assembled the relevant aspects of Aquinas's thought on the basis of which he advances a compelling argument against the fourth objection.

role medieval theologians had accorded to beatitude. In his 1515/16 lectures at the University of Wittenberg on St. Paul's Letter to the Romans, Luther—while still an Augustinian hermit—takes the culmination of a proper Christian relationship to God to be the renunciation of beatitude (*resignatio in infernum*), should God demand it.[48] Such a demand would imply a deeply voluntarist understanding of God, characteristic of the nominalist *via moderna* in which Luther was trained at the University of Erfurt.[49] According to this view, the divine will can demand something that would not only contradict the self-love of fallen human nature, but also the intrinsic orientation of the created human nature. But this would be a self-contradictory divine act, an act against reason (*contra rationem*), and hence—according to the received consensus of the patristic theological tradition, including Augustine—an act against the divine nature itself.[50] Classical Protestantism—Calvin largely following Luther in this matter—thus inherits at its very heart a genuine dilemma.

Here is one horn of the dilemma: if human nature is so fundamentally damaged by sin that it suffers the loss of its natural inclinations that order it to its natural end (until its divine reconstitution in the resurrection from the dead), human life not elected for divine revelation, faith, and the guidance of the Holy Spirit must be utterly unintelligible, incoherent, unaccountable, and ultimately self-destructive. Yet this is quite obviously not the case. The metaphys-

48. Martin Luther, *Weimarer Ausgabe, Vorlesung über den Römerbrief* (1515/16), (Weimar: Hermann Böhlau und Nachfolger: 1883–2009), 56:388.

49. The best account of the dominant nominalist theologian, Gabriel Biel (whose work Luther studied closely while a student at the University of Erfurt), in the context of a late medieval landscape of variant nominalist trends still remains Heiko Oberman, *The Harvest of Medieval Theology: Gabriel Biel and Late Medieval Nominalism* (Grand Rapids, Mich.: Baker Academic, 2001).

50. For an outstanding recent formulation of the theological problems caused by a radically voluntarist understanding of God, see Pope Benedict XVI's famous Regensburg lecture from September 12, 2006, "Faith, Reason, and the University: Memories and Reflections": "In all honesty, one must observe that in the late Middle Ages we find trends in theology which would sunder this synthesis between the Greek spirit and the Christian spirit. In contrast with the so-called intellectualism of Augustine and Thomas, there arose with Duns Scotus a voluntarism which, in its later developments, led to the claim that we can only know God's *voluntas ordinata*. Beyond this is the realm of God's freedom, in virtue of which he could have done the opposite of everything he has actually done."

ical integrity of human nature with inclinations toward its natural finality remains intact even in the fallen order. Protestant theologians, in order to save appearances, attribute the realization of natural goods and the avoidance of the detrimental consequences of sin to a divine preserving grace that counteracts the devastating effects of original sin. But they must pay a very high price for this theological move; for now the realization of natural goods is effectively itself a work of grace and consequently the natural subject, the very recipient of grace has virtually disappeared. Human nature as such is so evacuated that it becomes *de facto* impossible to distinguish between original sin and human nature. Preserving grace undoes the effects of original sin, but according to Luther, original sin remains an active force in the human being until death and bodily resurrection. It is not surprising that Matthias Flacius Illyricus (1520-77), a Lutheran theologian widely regarded as the most faithful defender of genuine Lutheranism, did not hesitate to make explicit the theological implications of Luther's theological tenets. Consistent with Luther's premises, Flacius Illyricus—in radical opposition to the downplaying of original sin as a mere accident of the human substance, which he regarded as Pelagian sophistry—concluded that with the Fall, original sin has become the substantial form of the human being before God. Later, he put it more sharply: after the Fall, original sin has become identical with the substance of the human being.[51] Unsurprisingly, numerous Lutheran theologians of the day recognized the profoundly errant nature of this theological inference and rightly rejected it. But they failed to track it back to its proximate premises, that is, to central tenets of Luther's theology and to submit these problematic positions to critical theological scrutiny.[52]

51. For two recent accounts of his doctrine of sin, see Heinrich J. Vogel, "The Flacian Controversy on Original Sin," in *No Other Gospel: Essays in Commemoration of the 400th Anniversary of the Formula of Concord 1580-1980*, ed. Arnold J. Koelpin (Milwaukee, Wis.: Northwestern Publishing House, 1980), 1-15; and Ante Bilokapić, "Die Erbsünde in der Lehre des Matthias Flacius Illyricus," in *Matthias Flacius Illyricus—Leben & Werk*, ed. Josip Matešić, Internationales Symposium, Mannheim, 1991 (Munich: Südosteuropa-Gesellschaft, 1993), 43-52. For an instructive retrieval and transposition of the Flacian theological thesis, see the brief chapter, "Thinking Wickedness," in Robert W. Jenson, *On Thinking the Human: Resolutions of Difficult Notions* (Grand Rapids, Mich.: Eerdmans, 2003), 59-73.

52. For a forceful articulation of these tenets, see the treatise Luther regarded to be

Here is the other horn of the dilemma: if human nature is not detrimentally damaged to the point of its destruction by original sin, but is rather seriously wounded and thereby profoundly weakened, the integrity of created human nature remains structurally, and thus in its natural orientation, undamaged by original as well as actual sin. Consequently, like every other created nature, human nature is ordered to a proportionate perfection. Furthermore, like every other created nature, human nature tends to its proportionate perfection by way of a corresponding desire which in the case of human nature is the desire for the attainment of happiness. Yet if this is true, the desire for happiness cannot be simply dismissed as a sinful expression of self-love (*amor sui*).

Classical Protestantism has never been able to overcome this dilemma and has inherited a lingering deep suspicion against everything that resembles even remotely self-love (*amor sui*), the purported trademark of the sinful human incurvature into oneself. Prominent Lutheran theologians in the twentieth century like Karl Holl, Anders Nygren, Hans Joachim Iwand, Philip S. Watson, and Regin Prenter have criticized Aquinas's doctrine of beatitude as a thinly disguised form of eudaimonianism, which is purportedly nothing but the theoretical manifestation of sinful self-love.

Let us now turn to the second, less significant part of the Protestant objection to Aquinas's teaching on beatitude, a characteristically modern, postmetaphysical objection. Numerous modern Protestant theologians harbor the suspicion that Aquinas's teaching on

---

his strongest and best theological work, *On the Bondage of the Will* (*De servo arbitrio*). For a discussion of this matter and for further literature, see chapter 7 in my *Dust Bound for Heaven*, 249–82. A famous week-long theological disputation in thirteen sessions, held in 1560 in the palace at Weimar between Victorinus Strigel and Matthias Flacius Illyricus, brought the central issues to the fore and may be studied in the proceedings published in 1562: *Disputatio de originali peccato et libero arbitrio, inter Matthiam Flacium Illyricum et Victorinum Strigelium, publice Vinariae per integram hebdomadam, praesentibus Illustriss. Saxoniae Principus, Anno 1560. Initio Mensis Augusti*. In the 1577 *Formula of Concord*, Lutheran theologians implicitly rejected the position of Flacius Illyricus (and arguably also of Luther on this matter) and drew again upon the established Scholastic distinction of substance and accident to distinguish between the essence of the human being and original sin: "Satan cannot create a substance; he can only, with God's permission, corrupt accidentally the substance which God has created." *Formula of Concord*, Epitome I.25, in *The Book of Concord*, ed. and trans. Theodore Tappert (Philadephia: Fortress Press, 1959), 469.

the immortality of the rational soul, central to his doctrine of beatitude, expresses a lingering Pelagian impulse—the creature having a quasi-ontological foothold against and a correlative moral claim upon the creator. In order to avoid what they take to be an intrusive tenet of unbiblical Hellenism and in order to remain in step with postmetaphysical modernity, these theologians embrace a "total-death-theory."[53] Death, according to this theory, is understood as annihilation and resurrection as new creation. The looming metaphysical problems of personal identity and continuity between the *viator* and the *comprehensor* that this theory presents are most often waved off with an oblique reference to divine omnipotence and the divine "memory," attributes that supposedly suffice to address the problem. Yet this is an illusion, for the appeal to the divine "memory" is nothing but a misguided attempt to transpose the principle of the continuity of the person's identity from the ontological status of a divinely created, incorruptible subsistent form directly into the divine mind. However, without a robust metaphysical account of divine ideas, the notion of a divine "memory" remains vacuous

---

53. In early Christianity this view was held by the so-called Hypnopsychites and Thnetopsychites, a position refuted effectively by Origen. In the twentieth century, a number of noted German Protestant theologians embraced this view. Among them were Paul Althaus, Karl Barth, Oscar Cullmann, and Werner Elert, not to mention the more radical existentialist positions advanced by Rudolf Bultmann and Herbert Braun in the wake of Martin Heidegger's *Being and Time*. For a representative and characteristically fascinating, albeit erroneous account, see the small but significant volume by the most influential student of Karl Barth in the latter part of the twentieth century: Eberhard Jüngel, *Death: The Riddle and the Mystery*, trans. Iain and Ute Nicol (Philadelphia: Westminster, 1975). Because these views made considerable inroads into Catholic theology, especially in the form of the so-called theory of the resurrection in death (a theological position according to which the individual resurrection occurs at the moment of death), the magisterium of the Catholic church addressed these matters head on in a "Letter on Certain Questions Concerning Eschatology," issued on May 17, 1979, by the Congregation of the Doctrine of the Faith. The document states: "The Church believes (cf. the Creed) in the resurrection of the dead. The Church understands this resurrection as referring to *the whole person*; for the elect it is nothing other than the extension to human beings of the Resurrection of Christ itself. The Church affirms that a spiritual element survives and subsists after death, an element endowed with consciousness and will, so that the 'human self' subsists. To designate this element, the Church uses the word 'soul,' the accepted term in the usage of Scripture and Tradition. Although not unaware that this term has various meanings in the Bible, the Church thinks that there is no valid reason for rejecting it; moreover, she considers that the use of some word as a vehicle is absolutely indispensable in order to support the faith of Christians."

and even with such an account, the suggestion remains profoundly problematic, because even the concept of the divine idea of a singular entity cannot overcome the logical problem of the re-creation of the contingent historical singularity of a supposedly annihilated human person. Any supposed "re-creation" or "new creation" of the annihilated person would be only a copy or a double of the person, but not the selfsame person. Hence, because even divine omnipotence cannot overcome logical contradictions, even on the supposition of a recovery of the metaphysics of divine ideas, the Protestant "total death theory" faces a dilemma: either the principle of personal identity and continuity is to be safeguarded by way of the immortal soul conceived of as incorruptible subsistent form or, absent this metaphysical principle, the new creation of resurrection life will be at best a perfect copy, but not the selfsame person. Modern Protestant theology either must recover a robust metaphysics of the rational soul or swallow the self-defeating prospect of the eschatological double. With the ongoing rejection, root and branch, of classical metaphysics, modern Protestant theology will be in no position to make the "total-death-theory" intelligible and therefore will remain confined to belaboring metaphors.

The purportedly anti-Hellenistic and authentically Semitic "total-death-theory" dies under the weight of its internal metaphysical contradictions. But recall that the Protestant objection has two parts. The other part of the objection, arising from the doctrine of total depravity, has deeper roots that are considerably more difficult to remove. Nevertheless, I intend at least to dislodge this old and deep-seated theological impediment to the appreciation of Aquinas's doctrine of beatitude in chapters 3, 4, and 5. Incidentally, a younger generation of Lutheran theologians has undertaken a noteworthy effort to remove this impediment from the side of Protestant theology—a constructive and hopeful sign for a future deeper reception of Aquinas's doctrine of beatitude in a Protestant context.[54]

---

54. For the discussion in Germany, see Peter Bartmann, *Das Gebot und die Tugend der Liebe: Über den Umgang mit konfliktbezogenen Affekten* (Stuttgart: Kohlhammer, 1998); Rochus Leonhardt, *Glück als Vollendung des Menschseins: Die Beatitudo-Lehre des Thomas von Aquin im Horizont des Eudämonismus-Problems* (Berlin: de Gruyter, 1998); and Stefan Gradl, *Deus beatitudo hominis: Eine evangelische Annäherung an die Glückslehre*

The Second Impediment: The Modern Philosophical Objection

The philosophical objection cuts considerably deeper. It is identical with the very phenomenon of modern atheism and evolutionary naturalism. From Hobbes, Hume, d'Holbach, Feuerbach, Marx, Darwin, Nietzsche, and Freud to the so-called new atheism of Dawkins, Hitchens, Dennett, and Harris, the two central suppositions of Aquinas's doctrine of beatitude are denied: the existence of God, the first cause and final end of the universe, and the endowment of the human being with a subsistent intellectual principle or form, that is, with an immortal rational soul that distinguishes the rational animal fundamentally from all other kinds of animals. The shared presumption of contemporary popularized evolutionary naturalism is that Marx unmasked God as the central ingredient in the opiate of religion generously applied by the ruling classes to the economically exploited and politically oppressed masses, that Freud reduced God to a phenomenon of the subconscious, that Darwin made God as an explanatory principle superfluous, and that Nietzsche finally pronounced God dead.[55]

---

des Thomas von Aquin (Leuven: Peeters, 2004). For the discussion in the United States, next to the sprawling *oeuvre* of Stanley Hauerwas, see among younger scholars especially Rebecca Konyndyk DeYoung, Colleen McCluskey, and Christina Van Dyke, *Aquinas's Ethics: Metaphysical Foundations, Moral Theory, and Theological Context* (Notre Dame, Ind.: University of Notre Dame Press, 2009), and David Decosimo, *Ethics as a Work of Charity: Thomas Aquinas and Pagan Virtue* (Stanford, Calif.: Stanford University Press, 2014). Echoes of the Protestant theological objection can be discerned quite clearly in the otherwise instructive study by Jennifer A. Herdt, *Putting On Virtue: The Legacy of the Splendid Vices* (Chicago: University of Chicago Press, 2008).

55. For those who have a proper grasp of the nature of the Christian faith and of the nature of the empirical sciences and their mathematical modeling, it is obvious that there is no conflict (and that indeed there cannot be a conflict) between "religion and science." The conflict rather lies between the Christian faith and scientism, that is, philosophical naturalism as a normative worldview that demands adherence, aims to impose its views in public institutions, and understands itself as the enlightened supercession of all religions. Admittedly, this conflict was sharpened by the antimetaphysical biblicism of classical Protestant orthodoxy in the early modern period and continued by strong fundamentalist forces in the nineteenth century, especially in England and the United States. Unnuanced biblical literalism, the rejection of the spiritual sense, the neglect of the philosophy of nature and of metaphysics led to a sharp reaction in the uncritical embrace of scientism as a normative point of reference for liberal Protestant theologians.

In light of the selfsame and by now widely popularized evolutionary naturalism, humans increasingly conceive of themselves primarily as the products of subconscious drives, of repressed traumas from childhood and youth, of socioeconomic conditions, of a particular genetic constitution, as a bundle of sense-impressions and emotional states with an irrepressible will-to-power but a fluid and shifting personal identity. In short, humans undergo a disconcerting reification of self and others: humans are just one instance of matter in motion; consciousness, abstractive reasoning, and language are nothing but the odd surpluses that make the human an evolutionarily successful super-primate. Any claim to something purportedly "human" beyond this highly developed matter in motion can only be understood as the effect of an evolutionary strategy of self-projecting anthropomorphisms meant to make existence endurable for the super-primate.

Together with God, the reality of conscience and the stability of personhood disappear. Together with the comprehensive teleology of the universe, the teleology of proper human agency (and with it moral agency) vanishes. The denial of the existence of God and of the spiritual nature and immortality of the rational soul issues in the deepest possible crisis, indeed, the eclipse of what it means to be human and what it means to seek and find happiness. The "death of God" and the concomitant "death of the immortal soul" manifest their destructive effects in a fragmented, alienated, and atomized Western (and increasingly global) sociopolitical, cultural, and spiritual reality.

Any serious attempt adequately to address this most fundamen-

---

One instructive instance is the publication in England of *Essays and Reviews* in 1860, four months after Charles Darwin's *On the Origin of Species* had appeared. It was an endorsement by liberal, broad church theologians from Cambridge and Oxford of the rising scientism, in its naturalist or historicist version, thinly veiled as a theological argument. A dialectic between theological liberalism and fundamentalism set in that falsified the science-religion discussion from both sides. Putting the ideological construct of scientism to the side, there still is an important conversation between the Christian faith and modern science. For a cogent philosophical sorting-out of the issues, see Alvin Plantinga, *Where the Conflict Really Lies: Science, Religion, and Naturalism* (Oxford: Oxford University Press, 2011), and for a lucidly articulated constructive account of how religion and science may rightly and fruitfully inform each other, see Philip A. Rolnick, *Origins: God, Evolution, and the Question of the Cosmos* (Waco, Tex.: Baylor University Press, 2017); Michael Hanby, *No God, No Science? Theology, Cosmology, Biology* (Oxford: Wiley Blackwell, 2013); and from an explicitly Thomist perspective, Gerard M. Verschuuren, *Aquinas and Modern Science: A New Synthesis of Faith and Reason* (Kettering, Ohio: Angelico Press, 2016).

tal and urgent impediment with the care and rigor it deserves would go beyond the scope of the present book. The sustained critical attention that outstanding philosophers and theologians have paid to this impediment in the course of the twentieth and early twenty-first century relieves me of the burden to reproduce their efforts.[56] I shall

56. The classic treatment of modern atheism remains the *magnum opus* by Cornelio Fabro, *God in Exile. Modern Atheism: A Study of the Internal Dynamic of Modern Atheism, from Its Roots in the Cartesian* Cogito *to the Present Day* (New York: Newman Press, 1968). An often criticized but so far not surpassed comprehensive engagement of modern rationalism, empiricism, agnosticism, and naturalism is the remarkable study by Réginald Garrigou-Lagrange, OP, *God, His Existence and His Nature*, 2 vols. (St. Louis, Mo.: Herder, 1934). Indispensable for the retrieval of a nonreductive epistemology remains Jacques Maritain, *The Degrees of Knowledge* (New York: Charles Scribner's Sons, 1959), and for a critical engagement of evolutionary naturalism, Étienne Gilson, *From Aristotle to Darwin and Back Again: A Journey in Final Causality, Species, and Evolution* (San Francisco, Calif.: Ignatius Press, 2009), together with the profound and incisive studies by Charles De Koninck, collected in the first volume of his posthumously published writings. For an incisive recovery of natural theology after and in light of the objections raised by Kant and Heidegger, see Thomas Joseph White, OP, *Wisdom in the Face of Modernity: A Study in Thomistic Natural Theology* (Ave Maria, Fla.: Sapientia Press, 2009). For an astute and accessible rearticulation of five classical proofs of God's existence and for the project of natural theology, see Edward Feser, *Five Proofs of the Existence of God: Aristotle, Plotinus, Augustine, Aquinas, Leibniz* (San Francisco: Ignatius Press, 2017). See also Norman Kretzmann, *The Metaphysics of Theism: Aquinas's Natural Theology in* Summa contra gentiles *I-II*, 2 vols. (Oxford: Clarendon Press, 1997–99); Gaven Kerr, *Aquinas's Way to God: The Proof in* De Ente et Essentia (Oxford: Oxford University Press, 2015); and Denys Turner, *Faith, Reason, and the Existence of God* (Cambridge: Cambridge University Press, 2004). For an accessible account of and defense of the notion of the rational soul, see Ric Machuga, *In Defense of the Soul: What It Means to Be Human* (Grand Rapids, Mich.: Brazos, 2002), and also Keith Ward, *In Defense of the Soul* (London: Oneworld, 1998). On the topic of the human soul and a nonreductive anthropology, see Adrian J. Reimers, *The Soul of the Person: A Contemporary Philosophical Psychology* (Washington, D.C.: The Catholic University of America Press, 2006), and David Braine's *The Human Person: Animal and Spirit* (Notre Dame, Ind.: University of Notre Dame Press, 1992) and *Language and Human Understanding: The Roots of Creativity in Speech and Thought* (Washington, D.C.: The Catholic University of America Press, 2014). For a Thomist engagement of and response to the contemporary naturalist philosophy of mind, see James D. Madden, *Mind, Matter, and Nature: A Thomistic Proposal for the Philosophy of Mind* (Washington, D.C.: The Catholic University of America Press, 2013), and also the above-mentioned book by Verschuuren, *Aquinas and Modern Science*; for two quite different but equally lucid and forceful engagement of the so-called new atheism, see Edward Feser, *The Last Superstition: A Refutation of the New Atheism* (South Bend, Ind.: St. Augustine's Press, 2010), and David Bentley Hart's *Atheist Delusions: The Christian Revolution and Its Fashionable Enemies* (New Haven, Conn.: Yale University Press, 2010) and *The Experience of God: Being, Consciousness, Bliss* (New Haven, Conn.: Yale University Press, 2013).

content myself with first and foremost resituating the philosophical objection metaphysically in chapters 1 and 2. This metaphysical resituating of the philosophical objection will be guided by one of Aquinas's fundamental suppositions: the beliefs a person holds cannot impact the ontological structure of human nature; that is, whatever belief one might hold about happiness, one's will is *de facto* hard-wired for happiness. Given the ontological structure of human nature, there can only be one single objective happiness which perfectly satiates the intellect (ordered to unrestricted truth) and the will (ordered to the unrestricted good)—the first truth and highest good, God. It is for this reason that the human being is "all the way down" *homo religiosus* and it is for the selfsame reason that the secularist assumption that Christianity will give way eventually to atheism is profoundly mistaken. Wherever in the so-called advanced societies of the Western Hemisphere the Christian faith is abandoned, syncretistic cults and occult practices, as well as simple superstition are on the rise. The rapid return of idolatry unmasks secularism as just another, but now increasingly superseded, superstition. The swift replacement of secularism with other and possibly more insidious superstitions diminishes the immediate public force of the philosophical objection. Yet it would be a serious error to assume that such a replacement mitigates the need to address and defeat argumentatively the philosophical objection. I introduced the philosophical objection not only because it arguably remains the central intellectual challenge of our age of unbelief—predicted and prepared by Friedrich Nietzsche, analyzed and addressed in advance by John Henry Newman—but also because it issues into the powerful third impediment, the existential objection.

The Third Impediment: The Existential Objection

Arguably a partial result of the eclipse of what it means to be human, the understanding of and search for happiness has taken a radical experiential turn. The happiness now sought is the emotional state of joy, delight, and especially ecstasy as the apex of an encompassing feeling of well-being that ideally continues, fed by whatever sequence of objects, substances, and events it takes to sustain it.

The a-teleological dynamic of consumption—the trademark of consumer capitalism—collapses action and its purpose to the here and now. Any remaining sense of community and conviviality is no longer based on the common good, let alone on the highest good, God, but rather on sensuality, sentiments, and transient coalitions of proximate interests. Nietzsche announced the return of the Dionysian and what has arrived is the obsession with the body and with orgiastic and analogous experiences of sensual and emotional ecstasy.[57] The fun- and event-centered culture—the most characteristic feature of which is the collection of extraordinary, exhilarating, and possibly transgressive experiences of all sorts—is the direct result of the pervasive search for the feelings of joy, delight, and ecstasy that happiness issues in the here and now.

But what is the objection? It is simply this: given this existentialist understanding of happiness as the result of the instant gratification of some desire and the resulting sensual or emotional elation, a happiness that consists in the attainment of a specific good, even the highest good, is simply meaningless. Such happiness, at least in the life of the *viator*, is the subjective possession of the good itself, the life of virtue and the embrace of the ultimate end in faith, hope, and charity. But it might not issue immediately or at all in tangible sensual joy, delight, and bliss. This has no intellectual, volitional, or emotional traction in a context in which happiness has been definitively disaggregated from meaning and is taken to be nothing but the sensual delight resulting from unencumbered preference satisfaction.

The central issue underlying the existential objection is not simply a false idea or image of happiness that holds people captive to a life of uninhibited preference satisfaction, but rather the corruption of the will. And *pace* Nietzsche, the corrupt will is not a manifesta-

---

57. The spiritual and metaphysical crisis beneath the existential objection is nihilism which in many ways is a direct consequence of the second objection. Nietzsche rightly identified nihilism as the central problem of the modern era and Heidegger wrongly takes metaphysics to be identical or at least complicit with nihilism. For a lucid and profound metaphysical response to the theoretical as well as practical nihilism implicated in the existential objection (with implications for the second objection) inspired and guided by Aquinas's philosophy of being, see Vittorio Possenti, *Nihilism and Metaphysics: The Third Voyage*, trans. Daniel B. Gallagher (Albany: State University of New York Press, 2014).

tion of the impersonal will to power. Rather, as the Italian philosopher Vittorio Possenti puts it strikingly, "while Nietzsche considered the will of the individual to be a fiction, as a part of an erroneous psychology that masks the impersonal will to power, the Thomist, armed with the *Summa*, is able to see that the will to power is an intellectual fiction that disguises the corruption of the will. The genealogical task of unmasking it must be understood from the Thomist viewpoint as the unmasking of pride."[58] The very root of the vice of pride is the absence of the will's rectitude. The key to a response to the existential objection is, therefore, the orientation to the good (the proper formation of conscience), the virtue of religion (enabling acts of true worship of God), and the virtue of charity (enabling acts of unitive love of God or friendship with God). Yet the proper formation of conscience, the virtue of religion, and the virtue of charity presuppose the restitution of the will from corruption to rectitude. In chapters 2 through 6, I begin to address and remove this third impediment.

The Fourth Impediment—An Objection from Disability Studies

In recent decades, Aquinas's teaching on beatitude and especially his position that beatitude is actualized primarily and essentially in the intellect has become extremely controversial. Protestant theological circles that have come under the influence of the recently emerged field of Disability Studies tend to dismiss Aquinas's teaching on beatitude as the paradigmatic case of intellectual elitism and exclusionism, because Aquinas purportedly has no way to account for profound cognitive impairment in his conception of beatitude. These critics regard Aquinas's teaching that beatitude is primarily and essentially actualized in the intellect as a fundamentally misguided instantiation of a morally objectionable intellectualism that he shares with Aristotle (and for that matter with the whole tradition of the perennial philosophy). According to these critics, persons with profound cognitive impairment are not only excluded from the kind of imperfect happiness Aristotle considers in the *Nicomachean Ethics*

---

58. Ibid., 227.

but also, and more importantly, from the beatitude of the *comprehensor* as Aquinas conceives it. One must therefore reject this intellectualism root and branch and conceive of a new theological anthropology that takes its normative cues from the very condition of persons with profound cognitive impairment and then develop on this basis a new understanding of human flourishing that encompasses both the cognitively impaired persons and those who are statistically "normal."[59]

The concerns that drive this critique of Aquinas are indeed of great urgency in contemporary sociopolitical contexts in which disabled persons and especially persons with profound cognitive impairment are increasingly regarded as unproductive and burdensome human surplus, tragically blocked from human flourishing and a life of happiness—a condition that "compassionate" genetic screening and "pre-sorting" is supposed to prevent in the future. Aquinas's critics, however, fail to understand the philosophical presuppositions and theological entailments of Aquinas's position.[60] His hylomorphism accounts for all forms of impairments, including cognitive impairments, as deficiencies of the received matter that in-

---

59. For one of the most forceful contemporary objections to Aquinas's account of the ultimate human end, considered by way of the condition of persons with profound cognitive impairment, see Hans S. Reinders, *Receiving the Gift of Friendship: Profound Disability, Theological Anthropology, and Ethics* (Grand Rapids, Mich.: Eerdmans, 2008), 88–122. I am in deep agreement with the commitments and concerns that inform Reinders's book and give moral force to his overall argument. Reinders's critique of Aquinas is important, however, not because it constitutes a viable objection to him (which it does not), but rather because of the broad acceptance Reinders's critique has found among certain Protestant and Catholic systematic and moral theologians who share a common condition—a commendable commitment to defend the dignity of bodily and cognitively impaired persons in combination with a regrettable lack of familiarity with the philosophical and theological resources Aquinas's thought offers for such a defense.

60. For an astute interpretation and defense of Aquinas's theology in the face of these criticisms, see Miguel J. Romero's "St. Thomas Aquinas on Disability & Profound Cognitive Impairment" (ThD diss., Duke University, 2012); "Aquinas on the *Corporis Infirmitas*: Broken Flesh and the Grammar of Grace," in *Disability in the Christian Tradition: A Reader*, ed. Brian Brock and John Swinton (Grand Rapids, Mich.: Eerdmans, 2012), 101–51; "The Happiness of 'Those Who Lack the Use of Reason,'" *The Thomist* 80, no. 1 (2016): 49–96; "Cognitive Impairment, Moral Virtue, and Our Life in Christ," *Church Life* 4, no. 4 (2014): 79–94; "To Think Theologically about Disability: The Contemporary Challenge and a Proposal," *Culture e Fede (Pontificium Consilium de Cultura)* 24, no. 3 (2016): 203–4; and "The Goodness and Beauty of Our Fragile Flesh: Moral Theologians and Our Engagement with 'Disability,'" *Journal of Moral Theology: Engaging Disability* 6, Special Issue 2 (2017).

hibit the actualization of the rational soul's faculties, but in no way affect the ontological integrity of the rational soul. Humans are by nature vulnerable to bodily defect. The human being was originally created in the state of original righteousness and endowed with sanctifying grace. Natural defects such as impairment, illness, injury, and death are the consequences of the loss of original righteousness due to original sin. But these bodily deficiencies disappear without remainder with natural death and in no way affect the existence of the *comprehensor*. Furthermore, the efficacious nature of the sacraments, especially baptism and the Eucharist, turn all persons who receive these sacraments into *viatores*. The sacrament of baptism removes the stain of original sin and conveys sanctifying grace and with it the seeds of the theological virtues faith, hope, and charity, as well as the gifts of the Holy Spirit, while the Eucharist sustains the state of *viator*. Moreover, persons with profound cognitive impairment cannot commit mortal sins and therefore cannot fall from the state of *viator*. They might be subjectively *viatores in nuce*, yet on account of sacramental efficacy, they are nevertheless *viatores in re*. For this very reason, they will eventually become *comprehensores* and thereby attain the ultimate end to which humans are ordained. Hence, as a matter of fact, Aquinas's philosophical presuppositions and theological entailments seem to secure the full inclusion of persons with profound cognitive impairment into the sacramental *status viatoris* and especially into the resurrection life of the *comprehensor* and hence fully into the life of interminable beatitude. Aquinas's view rests on a fundamental theological axiom that is not often shared by contemporary Protestant and even Catholic theologians. This axiom becomes clear in his treatise on beatitude as well as in his *Literal Exposition on Job*: the totality of a human life cannot be evaluated intelligibly simply in view of the course of our earthly life (its brevity or length and its degrees of flourishing or diminishment). It can only be understood properly as a fully intelligible human life in light of the supernaturally ordained ultimate human end, the *status comprehensoris* and the beatific vision.[61] And precisely because this perspective

---

61. Consider Job 7:1–4, where Job is replying to Eliphaz: "Man's life on earth is combat and his day is like the day of the hireling. Like the slave, he sighs for the shade, or the workingman for the end of his work. So I, too, have passed empty months and I have

sub specie aeternitatis is not available to us in *statu viatoris*, as long as we exercise our judgments in this earthly life, we are inherently unable to evaluate accurately the totality of a human life as fully and intelligibly human. Human persons may die or be killed *in utero*, they may die as young children, as teenagers, as old and full of life as Abraham, they may be persons with profound cognitive or with significant bodily impairment, they may be persons of genius. In none of these cases is their life in its totality intelligible as a human life in the full extension of its reality and flourishing if one supposes earthly life to be indicative of the totality of human life and thus excludes the perspective of eternity, the destiny of the *status comprehensoris* to which God ordains all human beings. Instructed by Aquinas's thought, Dante grasped this truth profoundly and gave it unrivaled poetic expression in his *Divine Comedy*. Increasingly self-consigned to the immanent frame of naturalism, modern

---

counted sleepless nights. If I sleep, I say: When will I arise? And again I will wait for evening, and I will be filled with pains until dark." Consider now the opening lines of Aquinas's *Expositio super Iob ad litteram* 7, lib. 1 (verse 1): "The opinions of men have differed about the condition of this present life. Some held that ultimate happiness was experienced in this life. The words of Eliphaz seem to follow this opinion. The ultimate end of man is in that place where he expects the final retribution for good or evil. So if man is rewarded by God for good deeds and punished for evil deeds in this life, as Eliphaz is eager to prove, it seems necessary to conclude that the ultimate end of man is in this life. But, Job intends to disprove this opinion and he *wants to show that the present life of man does not have the ultimate end in it, but is compared to this end as motion is compared to rest and the journey to the destination.* ... Job intends to strengthen [his arguments] and demonstrates them efficaciously from reason. For clearly, each thing rests when it attains its ultimate end. So once the human will has attained its ultimate end, it must rest in that and must not be moved to desire anything else. Our experience is contrary to this in the present life. For man always desires the future as though he were not happy with the things he has in the present. So clearly the ultimate end is not in this life, but this life is ordered to another end like warfare is ordered to victory and the hired man's day is ordered to his pay. Note however that what we have now is not sufficient in this present life, but desire tends to the future for two reasons. First because of the afflictions of the present life, and so he introduces the example of the slave desiring the shade, saying 'Like the slave,' worn out from the heat, 'he sighs for the shade,' which refreshes him. Second, from the defect of the perfect final good one does not possess here. So he uses the example of the hired man saying, 'or the workman, for the end to his work.' For the perfect good is the end of man. 'So I have passed empty months,' for I considered the past months passed empty for me, because I did not obtain final perfection in them. 'And nights,' i.e. when I should have been resting from my afflictions. 'I have counted sleepless,' i.e. I considered them sleepless because I was delayed in them from the attainment of my end." Emphasis added; trans. Brian Mulladay, OP, available at dhspriory.org/thomas/SSJob.htm#191.

humanity fails to grasp this truth. The more Christians make themselves at home intellectually and existentially in the immanent frame of naturalism, the less will they grasp of the depth and extent of human destiny in everlasting communion with God and the nature of perfect happiness—let alone the reason why the essential actualization of beatitude occurs in the theoretical intellect—of *all* human beings who partake in the resurrection life.[62]

THE ONGOING RELEVANCE OF AQUINAS'S DOCTRINE

Rather than defeating Aquinas's doctrine of happiness, the four objections betray the epochal spiritual, intellectual, and moral crisis in which modern humanity finds itself. There reigns considerable confusion over the questions of what it is to be human, what difference it makes, and what the perfection of being human actually is that generates genuine and lasting happiness. A fresh *ressourcement* in Aquinas's thought is not only salutary but, I argue, mandatory if one wishes to grasp the nature and magnitude of this epochal crisis and also find spiritually, intellectually, and morally sound ways to address and overcome it.[63]

---

62. To the degree to which Catholics consign themselves tacitly and unconsciously to the naturalist and a-teleological immanent frame, they will find it increasingly difficult to affirm the full implications of the assumption of Mary, body and soul, into heaven. See chapter 9 for a deeper consideration of this crucial matter of faith.

63. For one of the most profound and persuasive accounts narrating the way this epochal crisis came to pass and for a precise characterization of its most salient features, see Pfau, *Minding the Modern*. In his *magnum opus* Pfau advances a concise and compelling intellectual narrative of how the notions of "person" and "will" descended into the present disordered framework sanctioned by philosophical naturalism as the only viable one. There are, of course, competing narrative accounts of the passage to modernity; see Lukács, Horkheimer/Adorno, Blumenberg, Dupré, Foucault, MacIntyre, Habermas, Stout, and Taylor. Some are compatible with Pfau's narrative, others incompatible. The incompatible ones are genealogies that tend to stand under the mutually exclusive specters of Hegel, Marx, Nietzsche, and Heidegger. The epistemic, analytic, and hermeneutical usefulness of most of these sweeping intellectual narrations is rather limited because the principles in light of which one judges one account to be preferable or superior to another are held antecedently to and independently from any of these accounts. These principles are, after all, the very presuppositions that inform the account one prefers over others. I happen to prefer Pfau's account and hold it to be compatible with the accounts Dupré and MacIntyre advance, because they all are, albeit in slightly different

While the church is not of this world, it exists in this world and is variously affected by the deep crises and the dominant ideologies that impact a particular era. Theoretically, the four impediments might not affect Catholics, but these nodal points of crisis do in fact profoundly touch Catholics in the present age. The Fathers of the Second Vatican Council already discerned this fact clearly, and in *Gaudium et Spes* advanced a pertinent response that places Christ at its center:

> The Church knows that her message is in harmony with the most secret desires of the human heart when she champions the dignity of the human vocation, restoring hope to those who have already despaired of anything higher than their present lot. Far from diminishing man, her message brings to his development light, life and freedom. Apart from this message nothing will avail to fill up the heart of man: "Thou hast made us for Thyself," O Lord, "and our hearts are restless till they rest in Thee." The truth is that only in the mystery of the incarnate Word does the mystery of man take on light. For Adam, the first man, was a figure of Him Who was to come, namely Christ the Lord. Christ, the final Adam, by the revelation of the mystery of the Father and His love, fully reveals man to man himself and makes his supreme calling clear. It is not surprising, then, that in Him all the aforementioned truths find their root and attain their crown. (nos. 21–22)

One way these impediments tend to affect Catholicism is an increasing readiness to submit tacitly to the postmetaphysical strictures of the naturalist immanent frame by beginning to favor the

---

ways and with differing emphases, informed by principles that belong to philosophy in the perennial sense (*philosophia perennis*): Plato, Aristotle, the Stoa, Neoplatonism, and Aquinas's metaphysical synthesis. The success of Pfau's narrative and its superiority over competing narrations rests not only on his exacting analysis of the central protagonists but especially on the heuristic strength his principles afford for grasping the depth-structure of the epochal crisis we face. For the best recent account of why these principles are not willfully adopted and imposed but rather display their superiority in their discursive success across complex transgenerational lines of cumulative argumentation, see Alasdair MacIntyre's 1988 Gifford Lectures, *Three Rival Versions of Moral Inquiry: Encyclopaedia, Genealogy, and Tradition* (Notre Dame, Ind.: University of Notre Dame Press, 1990). MacIntyre's work may be read best as an extended application of retortion (an argumentative strategy employed already by Plato and Aristotle): if interlocutors representing the alternative accounts wish to engage his argumentation by way of a discursive counterargument, they are able to do so only by drawing upon the very principles they have been denying in their respective alternative accounts. Hence, these interlocutors will have to commit a performative self-contradiction that displays the erroneous character of the position they argue.

"weak thinking" of postmodern philosophy, by prioritizing praxis over doctrine, and eventually by severing the former from the latter. The doctrine of the faith stands increasingly in danger of being regarded as an ideological superstructure that serves as critical reflection upon antecedent praxis in order to improve upon subsequent praxis. For these forms of Catholicism that fail to measure up to the wisdom of the Second Vatican Council, theological thought arises from praxis, returns to praxis, and is constantly justified, energized, but also historicized and hence "fluidified" by praxis. Significantly, in the documents that emerged from the 1985 Synod for the twentieth anniversary of Vatican II, the Synod Fathers had insisted that doctrine cannot be disjoined from praxis, but rather that doctrine must constantly inspire and inform praxis.[64] For only if doctrine indeed constantly inspires and informs praxis does the above teaching of *Gaudium et Spes* stand any chance of traction in late modernity. *Gaudium et Spes* either pronounces a truth about God, Christ, and humanity that obtains and therefore is at once an invitation and a claim on all humanity, or it is merely a specific recommendation for an ecclesial and pastoral praxis in the late 1960s that employed a theological language configured for precisely this practical purpose.[65] In fact, of course, *Gaudium et Spes* is teaching the truth that Christ reveals about the human vocation to beatitude.

---

64. See *The Extraordinary Synod—1985: Message to the People of God* (Boston: St. Paul Editions, 1985). The key text is the Synod Fathers' "Final Report" (37–68). Significantly, the Synod Fathers state: "Special attention must be paid to the four major constitutions of the Council, which contain the interpretative key for the other decrees and declarations. It is not licit to separate the pastoral character from the doctrinal vigor of the documents. In the same way, it is not legitimate to separate the spirit and the letter of the Council. Moreover, the Council must be understood in continuity with the great tradition of the Church, and at the same time we must receive light from the Council's own doctrine for today's Church and the people of our time" (41–42). The Synod Fathers also state: "The false opposition between doctrinal and pastoral responsibilities must be avoided and overcome" (49–50). The increase in relevance of this last statement is directly proportional to the time that has passed since 1985.

65. For a thoughtful interpretation of *Gaudium et Spes* that not only avoids these pitfalls but points into the direction of an ongoing constructive reception of the Pastoral Constitution, see Thomas Joseph White, OP, "Gaudium et Spes," in *The Reception of Vatican II*, ed. Matthew L. Lamb and Matthew Levering (New York: Oxford University Press, 2017), 113–46, as well as his "The 'Pure Nature' of Christology: Human Nature and *Gaudium et Spes* 22," *Nova et Vetera* (English edition) 8, no. 2 (2010): 283–322.

At the present moment, therefore, it seems to me to be of special importance for Catholics to retrieve doctrine, its nature and its object, and especially the doctrine of beatitude in order fully to live up to the gift and promise of the Catholic faith. It is not an exaggeration to say that the church's life depends upon it. Yet the retrieval of doctrine, its nature, and its object, requires the recovery of the fitting intellectual instrument, a science proper to this object—sacred theology. The retrieval of doctrine and the recovery of sacred theology have to go hand in hand.

The Recovery of Sacred Theology

Many works have narrated the effects of modernity on sacred theology and the dissolution of the once unified but internally differentiated academic discipline into a conglomerate of essentially independent disciplines that are only extrinsically bound together by a practical purpose, the education and formation of clergy. For a while history replaced metaphysics as the instrumental science that gave the overall enterprise of theology at least a semblance of coherence. But with the radicalization of historicism and the introduction of psychology and the social sciences into the various academic fields that now make up the theological curriculum, theology has become a thoroughly piecemeal affair. The various disciplines regard themselves as "Wissenschaft," science, by way of the fields, in which they participate—historiography, Semitic and late Hellenistic studies, psychology of religion, sociology of religion, political theory, and moral philosophy. Yet sacred theology whose unifying subject matter is God and God's authoritative and definitive revelation in Jesus Christ—theo-logy, the *Logos* of *Theos* and the unique and elevated science to which the revelation of this *Logos* gives rise—has virtually disappeared and been replaced by a religiously charged anthropology and a pastoral pragmatics that all too often suffers from a shortsighted anti-intellectualism and a misplaced sentimentalism. The following *ressourcement* in Aquinas's theology is motivated by the aspiration of a full recovery of sacred theology as programmatically adumbrated by Pope St. John Paul II in his 1998 encyclical letter *Fides et Ratio*. Because of the centrality of the issue, I shall cite the pertinent passage in full:

With regard to the *intellectus fidei*, a prime consideration must be that divine Truth "proposed to us in the Sacred Scriptures and rightly interpreted by the Church's teaching" enjoys an innate intelligibility, so logically consistent that it stands as an authentic body of knowledge. The *intellectus fidei* expounds this truth, not only in grasping the logical and conceptual structure of the propositions in which the Church's teaching is framed, but also, indeed primarily, in bringing to light the salvific meaning of these propositions for the individual and for humanity. From the sum of these propositions, the believer comes to know the history of salvation, which culminates in the person of Jesus Christ and in his Paschal Mystery. Believers then share in this mystery by their assent of faith.

For its part, *dogmatic theology* must be able to articulate the universal meaning of the mystery of the One and Triune God and of the economy of salvation, both as a narrative and, above all, in the form of argument. It must do so, in other words, through concepts formulated in a critical and universally communicable way. Without philosophy's contribution, it would in fact be impossible to discuss theological issues such as, for example, the use of language to speak about God, the personal relations within the Trinity, God's creative activity in the world, the relationship between God and man, or Christ's identity as true God and true man. This is no less true of the different themes of moral theology, which employ concepts such as the moral law, conscience, freedom, personal responsibility and guilt, which are in part defined by philosophical ethics.

It is necessary therefore that the mind of the believer acquire a natural, consistent and true knowledge of created realities—the world and man himself—which are also the object of divine Revelation. Still more, reason must be able to articulate this knowledge in concept and argument. Speculative dogmatic theology thus presupposes and implies a philosophy of the human being, the world and, more radically, of being, which has objective truth as its foundation. (par. 66)

In the course of the following chapters, especially in chapter 1, I shall develop a cumulative case for the integral unity of sacred theology. The link between beatitude and the natural and supernatural equipment and practical means by which the *viatores* attain beatitude is illustrative of the overarching coherence the unified science of sacred theology affords. Speculative, dogmatic, and moral theology are integral parts of sacred theology.[66] Precisely because of the

---

66. This is also true for biblical and historical theology. Yet to show how they are integral parts of sacred theology would transcend the scope of this book. This task will

central role that metaphysics plays in Aquinas's implementation of sacred theology, his theological thought remains eminently relevant for us today.

Besides being a Thomistic study in eschatology and ethics, the book is an exercise in retrieving Aquinas's salutary understanding of theology as holy teaching (*sacra doctrina*) exemplified by the topic at the very heart of revelation: the universal call of humanity to adoptive sonship through communion with the Son of God, the incarnate Lord, and thereby to eternal life, the everlasting participation in the beatitude of the Trinity. The ongoing relevance of Aquinas's theology becomes obvious if one reconsiders the guidelines for sacred theology stated in *Fides et Ratio*. Again due to its importance, I shall cite the relevant passage in full:

> The interpretation of sources is a vital task for theology; but another still more delicate and demanding task is the *understanding of revealed truth*, or the articulation of the *intellectus fidei*. The *intellectus fidei*, as I have noted, demands the contribution of a philosophy of being which first of all would enable *dogmatic theology* to perform its functions appropriately. The dogmatic pragmatism of the early years of this century, which viewed the truths of faith as nothing more than rules of conduct, has already been refuted and rejected; but the temptation always remains of understanding these truths in purely functional terms. This leads only to an approach which is inadequate, reductive and superficial at the level of speculation. A Christology, for example, which proceeded solely "from below," as is said nowadays, or an ecclesiology developed solely on the model of civil society, would be hard pressed to avoid the danger of such reductionism.
>
> If the *intellectus fidei* wishes to integrate all the wealth of the theological tradition, it must turn to the philosophy of being, which should be able to propose anew the problem of being—and this in harmony with the demands and insights of the entire philosophical tradition, including philosophy of more recent times, without lapsing into sterile repetition of antiquated formulas. Set within the Christian metaphysical tradition, the philosophy of being is a dynamic philosophy which views reality in its ontological, causal and communicative structures. It is strong and enduring because it is based upon the very act of being itself, which allows a full and comprehensive openness to reality as a whole, surpassing every limit in or-

---

have to wait for another work that will have to build upon the crucial work of Yves Congar, OP.

der to reach the One who brings all things to fulfilment. In theology, which draws its principles from Revelation as a new source of knowledge, this perspective is confirmed by the intimate relationship which exists between faith and metaphysical reasoning. (par. 97)

Sacred theology is fundamentally sapiential; its unity is the unity that the reception and ever deeper contemplation of the truth affords. This science has profound practical implications but is irreducible to the postmetaphysical pragmatism that holds reason to be purely instrumental and praxis to have a merely utilitarian end.

The Structure of the Book

Chapter 1 opens up programmatically the whole conceptual and substantive horizon in which Aquinas unfolds the human journey to beatitude. I make a case for restoring the principle of finality or teleology to the very heart of sacred theology. However, in order to advance such a case, I must first signal the centrality of metaphysics as the privileged rational instrument of theology. Returning teleology to the center of theology will have, as I shall argue, several beneficial effects on the work of theology itself. First, it will help in conceiving of the proper distinction and correlation of nature and grace and of the proper understanding of the natural desire for the vision of God. Furthermore, this restitution allows for the recovery of the finality of the created intellect. The intellect's finality is a necessary presupposition for central tenets of Aquinas's doctrine of beatitude: the objective ultimate human end being God and the subjective ultimate human end being primarily a participated perfection of the intellect—the beatific vision.

Chapter 2 extends the metaphysics of finality to the teleological metaphysics of the good. It transitions thus from universal teleology to eternal and natural law, and from there to conscience and the virtue of prudence. In this chapter, I consider the fundamentally *moral nature* of the human journey to beatitude and what this journey presupposes conceptually and in reality: the rectitude of the will, the eternal and the natural law, and especially conscience in relationship to the virtue of prudence. By its conclusion, chapter 2 will have recovered Aquinas's fundamental principle of the teleological metaphysics of the good as it pertains to the *viator*'s journeying to beatitude: to be good is to do the truth.

While chapter 2 focuses on the *natural* presuppositions of the journey to beatitude, chapter 3 thematizes the *soteriological sine qua non* of this sojourn. The *viator* only becomes a *viator* by being first saved from sin, healed, and set on a journey that comprises in one the *viator*'s justification, sanctification, and deification. The satisfaction of Christ on the cross liberates humanity from the estrangement and corruption of sin, thereby restoring humanity to God and reestablishing friendship with God, the life of charity. It is at the cross of Christ where the *viator*'s sojourn begins.

Chapters 4 through 8 follow the sequence in which Thomas Aquinas ordered the virtues that inform the Christian life and thereby the *viator*'s journey in *ST* II-II: first the theological virtues of faith, hope, and charity, followed by the moral virtues of prudence, justice, courage, and temperance. There are, though, three modifications of this overall order: first, prudence is already considered, albeit all too briefly, in chapter 2. Second, because the topic is divine happiness and its attainment, instead of the virtue of justice, there will be a treatment of the corresponding virtue that pertains to God—justice to God, so to speak—which is the virtue of religion. Third and finally, the virtues of courage and temperance are considered under the specifications most relevant to the life of the *viator* on the journey to perfect happiness: martyrdom and chastity.

Chapter 4 treats the theological virtue of faith (with a glance upon hope) and answers the question of how beatitude becomes inchoately present in the *viator*. This chapter makes explicit the fundamental difference between the imperfect happiness of the one who is living, as Aristotle conceived it in the *Nicomachean Ethics*, the life of virtue (*bios praktikos*) and even the life of philosophical contemplation (*bios theoretikos*) on the one hand, and on the other hand the imperfect happiness of the *viator*. The difference rests in the gratuitous gift of divine faith by way of which the "substance of things hoped for," the seed of beatitude is already present in the *viator*'s intellect.

Chapter 5 treats the theological virtue of charity, the acme of the life of sanctifying grace and the divinization it engenders. The chapter focuses on the supernatural actualization and perfection of this journey, on the divinization of the *viator* through a growing friendship with God, induced by sanctifying grace and enacted in a life of charity. It is only after the *viator* has embarked on a life of charity, of friendship with God, that religion, martyrdom, and chastity become possible.

Chapter 6 is dedicated to the recovery of a widely neglected and, indeed, largely forgotten virtue, that is, however, requisite for the rectitude of the will and hence an integral part of the antecedent condition for the attainment of beatitude—the virtue of religion. The virtue of religion actualizes the will's rectitude through acts of honor and reverence due to God. For a baptized and confirmed Christian, acts of the virtue of religion, commanded by charity, contribute essentially to the preparation of the *viator* for attaining the beatitude of the *comprehensor*. Being a *viator* without exercising the virtue of religion is a contradiction in terms. The latter is an entailment of the former and the considered departure from acts of the virtue of religion eventually undermines one's existence as *viator*.

Chapters 7 and 8 address the two paradigmatic temptations the *viator* is faced with on the journey to beatitude. Giving in to these temptations may result in the abandonment of the journey. Resisting each temptation requires the activation of a crucial virtue. Chapter 7 attends to the temptation of the *viator* to abandon or to betray the revealed truth, accepted in faith, either under psychological pressure, threat of physical violence, or simply by the omission of due witness because of fear. It treats as well the virtue that meets this temptation head on, overcomes fear of persecution and death, and keeps the *viator* ordered to the ultimate end: the virtue of courage and its supreme act, martyrdom.

Chapter 8 addresses a widespread daily temptation that the *viator* (particularly as a twenty-first-century user of the internet) is faced with that substitutes the journey for the ultimate end, the beatific vision for another "vision"—pornography, which rouses the lust of the eyes and stimulates the desire for ever fleeting ecstatic moments of venereal pleasure. The emphasis of the chapter, however, does not fall onto the analysis of the problem, but on the recovery of the solution, the recovery of a virtue indispensable for the *viator*'s journey to beatitude—chastity.

Chapter 9, finally, attends to the very exemplar of a Christian *viator*, the Virgin Mary. Not only is her life of religion, courage, and chastity exemplary for all Christian sojourners; even more importantly, she is a beacon of hope for the *viator*: assumed, body and soul, into heaven, Mary embodies in her personal state of beatitude the goal to which all *viatores* are called. Not only has Christ, the head of the church, arisen from the dead and sits in glory at the right hand of the Father, but also his mother—who by Christ's transference from the cross, has become the mother of all his followers—has already been assumed, body and soul, into heaven. And for this reason the whole communion of the saints, the whole body of Christ is already anchored in the glory of God, not only in the head, the risen Christ—which is the absolute *conditio sine qua non* for attaining beatitude—but also already in one, who like the rest of the elect relies completely on the infinite merits of Christ's salvific sacrifice of charity on the cross.

Finally, the epilogue focuses on three central aspects of the state of beatitude: first, the beatific vision as the wayfarer's single ultimate end; second, the resurrection of the body as integral to heavenly beatitude; and third, the inherently communal character of heavenly beatitude. As the beatific vision has only been touched upon briefly in this prologue, it requires a fuller treatment before these three topics can be meaningfully discussed. Hence, the epilogue opens with a treatment of Aquinas's metaphysical and epistemological conception of the beatific vision.

The second part of the epilogue then treats the question whether the beatific vision is the single ultimate human end or whether there are others necessarily correlated to the beatific vision. This question goes to heart of the nature of the beatific vision and the resurrection life. Is subjective beatitude essentially perfective union of the intellect with God and must every other aspect of the resurrection life be understood in light of that or is the beatific vision only one end, admittedly the keystone piece, among a range of goods that altogether constitute the life in "paradise regained"?

The third part of the epilogue addresses the question whether and in which way the *comprehensor*'s beatitude increases after the general resurrection of the body when the *comprehensor*'s soul is reunited with its resurrection body. If the beatitude of the blessed is already perfect as soon as they enter the beatific vision right after their death, what does the body contribute to the *comprehensor*'s beatitude? If it contributes nothing at all, would the resurrection of the body then be superfluous, an empty redundancy? If it does contribute, would this not entail that the *comprehensor*'s beatitude before the general resurrection of the body is less than perfect?

The fourth and final part of the epilogue pertains to a widespread impression that readers gather regarding Aquinas's teaching on eschatology. By concentrating exclusively on Aquinas's treatise on happiness in *ST* I-II, one might get the mistaken impression that the *comprehensores* in heaven are essentially disembodied discrete monads each united individually with God but each also disjoined from all others—God and the individual soul *solus cum solo*. Yet such an impression of a *solus cum solo* beatitude is profoundly misguided, because for Aquinas the *viator*'s journey to beatitude and the *comprehensor*'s life of beatitude is essentially embodied and communal. The *viator* is an embodied human being belonging to the body of Christ, the church; and so is and does the *comprehensor* after the general resurrection of the dead. There is no real difference between the subjective ultimate end of the individual and the collective ultimate human end: in both cases, it is the body of Christ. It is for this very reason Aquinas can startlingly state: the church is the end of everything, *Ecclesia finis omnium*.

APPENDIX: PAUL VI'S "CREDO OF THE PEOPLE OF GOD"

It would be a serious mistake to think one had to "return to the Middle Ages" in order to recuperate Aquinas's theological axiom of the destiny of the *status comprehensoris* to which God ordains all human beings; for this theological axiom is nothing but simply an entailment of the revelation authoritatively communicated by Christ, the apostles, and their successors, the bishops, and received in and held by what Aquinas would call divine faith. (See chapter 4 for a more extensive treatment.) The year 2018 marked the fiftieth anniversary of the closing of the Year of Faith declared by Pope Paul VI in 1967. On the occasion of its closing, Paul VI proclaimed a "Credo of the People of God" that has lost nothing of its relevance as a contemporary reformulation of the Nicene Creed. Consider the following section from the pope's opening reflections:

> In making this profession, we are aware of the disquiet which agitates certain modern quarters with regard to the faith. They do not escape the influence of a world being profoundly changed, in which so many certainties are being disputed or discussed. We see even Catholics allowing themselves to be seized by a kind of passion for change and novelty. The Church, most assuredly, has always the duty to carry on the effort to study more deeply and to present, in a manner ever better adapted to successive generations, the unfathomable mysteries of God, rich for all in fruits of salvation. But at the same time the greatest care must be taken, while fulfilling the indispensable duty of research, to do no injury to the teachings of Christian doctrine. For that would be to give rise, as is unfortunately seen in these days, to disturbance and perplexity in many faithful souls. It is important in this respect to recall that, beyond scientifically verified phenomena, the intellect which God has given us reaches that which is, and not merely the subjective expression of the structures and development of consciousness; and, on the other hand, that the task of interpretation—of hermeneutics—is to try to understand and extricate, while respecting the word expressed, the sense conveyed by a text, and not to recreate, in some fashion, this sense in accordance with arbitrary hypotheses. But above all, we place our unshakable confidence in the Holy Spirit, the soul of the Church, and in theological faith upon which rests the life of the Mystical Body. We know that souls await the word of the Vicar of Christ, and we respond to that expectation with the instructions which we regularly give. But today we are given an opportunity to make a more solemn utterance. (*Solemni Hac Liturgia* [*Credo of the People of God*], pars. 4–6)

The *Profession of Faith* from Pope Paul VI's *Solemni Hac Liturgia*, proclaimed at the end of the Year of Faith, June 30, 1968, articulates authoritatively the material faith that Aquinas's teaching on the journey to beatitude undergirds, explicates, and defends. Furthermore, the "Credo of the People of God" clearly articulates the theological axiom on which Aquinas's teaching on beatitude rests. Therefore, I include the central part of the magisterial document, the Profession of Faith, in this appendix. This Profession is the proximate creedal horizon in which the subsequent chapters undertake a contemporary *ressourcement* in Aquinas's theology of beatitude and the journey thereto.

Profession of Faith

8. We believe in one only God, Father, Son and Holy Spirit, creator of things visible such as this world in which our transient life passes, of things invisible such as the pure spirits which are also called angels,[67] and creator in each man of his spiritual and immortal soul.

9. We believe that this only God is absolutely one in His infinitely holy essence as also in all His perfections, in His omnipotence, His infinite knowledge, His providence, His will and His love. He is He who is, as He revealed to Moses;[68] and He is love, as the Apostle John teaches us:[69] so that these two names, being and love, express ineffably the same divine reality of Him who has wished to make Himself known to us, and who, "dwelling in light inaccessible,"[70] is in Himself above every name, above every thing and above every created intellect. God alone can give us right and full knowledge of this reality by revealing Himself as Father, Son and Holy Spirit, in whose eternal life we are by grace called to share, here below in the obscurity of faith and after death in eternal light. The mutual bonds which eternally constitute the Three Persons, who are each one and the same divine being, are the blessed inmost life of God thrice holy, infinitely beyond all that we can conceive in human measure.[71] We give thanks, however, to the divine goodness that very many believers can testify with us before men to the unity of God, even though they know not the mystery of the most holy Trinity.

---

67. Cf. Denzinger, no. 3002.
68. See Ex 3:14.
69. See 1 Jn 4:8.
70. See 1 Tm 6:16.
71. See Denzinger, no. 804.

The Father

10. We believe then in the Father who eternally begets the Son; in the Son, the Word of God, who is eternally begotten; in the Holy Spirit, the uncreated Person who proceeds from the Father and the Son as their eternal love. Thus in the Three Divine Persons, *coaeternae sibi et coaequales*,[72] the life and beatitude of God perfectly one superabound and are consummated in the supreme excellence and glory proper to uncreated being, and always "there should be venerated unity in the Trinity and Trinity in the unity."[73]

The Son

11. We believe in our Lord Jesus Christ, who is the Son of God. He is the Eternal Word, born of the Father before time began, and one in substance with the Father, *homoousios to Patri*,[74] and through Him all things were made. He was incarnate of the Virgin Mary by the power of the Holy Spirit, and was made man: equal therefore to the Father according to His divinity, and inferior to the Father according to His humanity;[75] and Himself one, not by some impossible confusion of His natures, but by the unity of His person.[76]

12. He dwelt among us, full of grace and truth. He proclaimed and established the Kingdom of God and made us know in Himself the Father. He gave us His new commandment to love one another as He loved us. He taught us the way of the beatitudes of the Gospel: poverty in spirit, meekness, suffering borne with patience, thirst after justice, mercy, purity of heart, will for peace, persecution suffered for justice sake. Under Pontius Pilate He suffered—the Lamb of God bearing on Himself the sins of the world, and He died for us on the cross, saving us by His redeeming blood. He was buried, and, of His own power, rose on the third day, raising us by His resurrection to that sharing in the divine life which is the life of grace. He ascended to heaven, and He will come again, this time in glory, to judge the living and the dead: each according to his merits—those who have responded to the love and piety of God going

---

72. See Denzinger, no. 75.
73. See ibid.
74. See Denzinger, no. 150.
75. See Denzinger, no. 76.
76. See ibid.

to eternal life, those who have refused them to the end going to the fire that is not extinguished. And His Kingdom will have no end.

The Holy Spirit

13. We believe in the Holy Spirit, who is Lord and Giver of life, who is adored and glorified together with the Father and the Son. He spoke to us by the prophets; He was sent by Christ after His resurrection and His ascension to the Father; He illuminates, vivifies, protects and guides the Church; He purifies the Church's members if they do not shun His grace. His action, which penetrates to the inmost of the soul, enables man to respond to the call of Jesus: Be perfect as your Heavenly Father is perfect (Mt. 5:48).

14. We believe that Mary is the Mother, who remained ever a Virgin, of the Incarnate Word, our God and Savior Jesus Christ,[77] and that by reason of this singular election, she was, in consideration of the merits of her Son, redeemed in a more eminent manner,[78] preserved from all stain of original sin[79] and filled with the gift of grace more than all other creatures.[80]

15. Joined by a close and indissoluble bond to the Mysteries of the Incarnation and Redemption,[81] the Blessed Virgin, the Immaculate, was at the end of her earthly life raised body and soul to heavenly glory[82] and likened to her risen Son in anticipation of the future lot of all the just; and we believe that the Blessed Mother of God, the New Eve, Mother of the Church,[83] continues in heaven her maternal role with regard to Christ's members, cooperating with the birth and growth of divine life in the souls of the redeemed.[84]

---

77. See Denzinger, nos. 251–52.
78. See *Lumen Gentium*, no. 53.
79. See Denzinger, no. 2803.
80. See *Lumen Gentium*, no. 53.
81. See *Lumen Gentium*, nos. 53, 58, 61.
82. See Denzinger, no. 3903.
83. See *Lumen Gentium*, nos. 53, 56, 61, 63; cf. Pope Paul VI, "Allocution for the Closing of the Third Session of the Second Vatican Council," *AAS* 56 (1964): 1016, and his *Signum Magnum*, Apostolic Exhortation, May 13, 1967, introduction; available at vatican.va.
84. See *Lumen Gentium*, no. 62; cf. Paul VI, *Signum Magnum*, par. 1.

Original Offense

16. We believe that in Adam all have sinned, which means that the original offense committed by him caused human nature, common to all men, to fall to a state in which it bears the consequences of that offense, and which is not the state in which it was at first in our first parents—established as they were in holiness and justice, and in which man knew neither evil nor death. It is human nature so fallen, stripped of the grace that clothed it, injured in its own natural powers and subjected to the dominion of death, that is transmitted to all men, and it is in this sense that every man is born in sin. We therefore hold, with the Council of Trent, that original sin is transmitted with human nature, "not by imitation, but by propagation" and that it is thus "proper to everyone."[85]

Reborn of the Holy Spirit

17. We believe that our Lord Jesus Christ, by the sacrifice of the cross redeemed us from original sin and all the personal sins committed by each one of us, so that, in accordance with the word of the apostle, "where sin abounded, grace did more abound."[86]

Baptism

18. We believe in one Baptism instituted by our Lord Jesus Christ for the remission of sins. Baptism should be administered even to little children who have not yet been able to be guilty of any personal sin, in order that, though born deprived of supernatural grace, they may be reborn "of water and the Holy Spirit" to the divine life in Christ Jesus.[87]

The Church

19. We believe in one, holy, catholic, and apostolic Church, built by Jesus Christ on that rock which is Peter. She is the Mystical Body of Christ; at the same time a visible society instituted with hierarchical organs, and a spiritual community; the Church on earth, the pilgrim People of God here below, and the Church filled with heavenly blessings; the germ and the first fruits of the

---

85. See Denzinger, no. 1513.
86. See Rom 5:20.
87. See Denzinger, no. 1514.

Kingdom of God, through which the work and the sufferings of Redemption are continued throughout human history, and which looks for its perfect accomplishment beyond time in glory.[88] In the course of time, the Lord Jesus forms His Church by means of the sacraments emanating from His plenitude.[89] By these she makes her members participants in the Mystery of the Death and Resurrection of Christ, in the grace of the Holy Spirit who gives her life and movement.[90] She is therefore holy, though she has sinners in her bosom, because she herself has no other life but that of grace: it is by living by her life that her members are sanctified; it is by removing themselves from her life that they fall into sins and disorders that prevent the radiation of her sanctity. This is why she suffers and does penance for these offenses, of which she has the power to heal her children through the blood of Christ and the gift of the Holy Spirit.

The Word

20. Heiress of the divine promises and daughter of Abraham according to the Spirit, through that Israel whose scriptures she lovingly guards, and whose patriarchs and prophets she venerates; founded upon the apostles and handing on from century to century their ever-living word and their powers as pastors in the successor of Peter and the bishops in communion with him; perpetually assisted by the Holy Spirit, she has the charge of guarding, teaching, explaining and spreading the Truth which God revealed in a then veiled manner by the prophets, and fully by the Lord Jesus. We believe all that is contained in the word of God written or handed down, and that the Church proposes for belief as divinely revealed, whether by a solemn judgment or by the ordinary and universal magisterium.[91] We believe in the infallibility enjoyed by the successor of Peter when he teaches ex cathedra as pastor and teacher of all the faithful,[92] and which is assured also to the episcopal body when it exercises with him the supreme magisterium.[93]

---

88. See *Lumen Gentium*, nos. 5 and 8.
89. See *Lumen Gentium*, nos. 7 and 11.
90. Cf. *Sacrosanctum Concilium*, nos. 5–6; cf. *Lumen Gentium*, nos. 7, 12, 50.
91. See Denzinger, no. 3011.
92. See Denzinger, no. 3074.
93. See *Lumen Gentium*, no. 25.

21. We believe that the Church founded by Jesus Christ and for which He prayed is indefectibly one in faith, worship and the bond of hierarchical communion. In the bosom of this Church, the rich variety of liturgical rites and the legitimate diversity of theological and spiritual heritages and special disciplines, far from injuring her unity, make it more manifest.[94]

One Shepherd

22. Recognizing also the existence, outside the organism of the Church of Christ, of numerous elements of truth and sanctification which belong to her as her own and tend to Catholic unity,[95] and believing in the action of the Holy Spirit who stirs up in the heart of the disciples of Christ love of this unity,[96] we entertain the hope that the Christians who are not yet in the full communion of the one only Church will one day be reunited in one flock with one only shepherd.

23. We believe that the Church is necessary for salvation, because Christ, who is the sole mediator and way of salvation, renders Himself present for us in His body which is the Church.[97] But the divine design of salvation embraces all men; and those who without fault on their part do not know the Gospel of Christ and His Church, but seek God sincerely, and under the influence of grace endeavor to do His will as recognized through the promptings of their conscience, they, in a number known only to God, can obtain salvation.[98]

Sacrifice of Calvary

24. We believe that the Mass, celebrated by the priest representing the person of Christ by virtue of the power received through the Sacrament of Orders, and offered by him in the name of Christ and the members of His Mystical Body, is the sacrifice of Calvary rendered sacramentally present on our altars. We believe that as the bread and wine consecrated by the Lord at the Last Supper were changed into His body and His blood which were to be offered for us on the cross, likewise the bread and wine consecrat-

---

94. Cf. *Lumen Gentium*, no. 23, and *Orientalium Ecclesiarum*, nos. 2, 3, 5, 6.
95. See *Lumen Gentium*, no. 8.
96. See *Lumen Gentium*, no. 15.
97. See *Lumen Gentium*, no. 14.
98. See *Lumen Gentium*, no. 16.

ed by the priest are changed into the body and blood of Christ enthroned gloriously in heaven, and we believe that the mysterious presence of the Lord, under what continues to appear to our senses as before, is a true, real and substantial presence.[99]

Transubstantiation

25. Christ cannot be thus present in this sacrament except by the change into His body of the reality itself of the bread and the change into His blood of the reality itself of the wine, leaving unchanged only the properties of the bread and wine which our senses perceive. This mysterious change is very appropriately called by the Church transubstantiation. Every theological explanation which seeks some understanding of this mystery must, in order to be in accord with Catholic faith, maintain that in the reality itself, independently of our mind, the bread and wine have ceased to exist after the Consecration, so that it is the adorable body and blood of the Lord Jesus that from then on are really before us under the sacramental species of bread and wine,[100] as the Lord willed it, in order to give Himself to us as food and to associate us with the unity of His Mystical Body.[101]

26. The unique and indivisible existence of the Lord glorious in heaven is not multiplied, but is rendered present by the sacrament in the many places on earth where Mass is celebrated. And this existence remains present, after the sacrifice, in the Blessed Sacrament which is, in the tabernacle, the living heart of each of our churches. And it is our very sweet duty to honor and adore in the blessed Host which our eyes see, the Incarnate Word whom they cannot see, and who, without leaving heaven, is made present before us.

Temporal Concern

27. We confess that the Kingdom of God begun here below in the Church of Christ is not of this world whose form is passing, and that its proper growth cannot be confounded with the progress of civilization, of science or of human technology, but that it consists in an ever more profound knowledge of the unfathomable

---

99. See Denzinger, no. 1651.
100. Cf. Denzinger, nos. 1642 and 1651–54, as well as Pope Paul VI, *Mysterium Fidei*, Encyclical Letter, September 3, 1965; available at vatican.va.
101. Cf. *ST* III, q. 73, a. 3.

riches of Christ, an ever stronger hope in eternal blessings, an ever more ardent response to the love of God, and an ever more generous bestowal of grace and holiness among men. But it is this same love which induces the Church to concern herself constantly about the true temporal welfare of men. Without ceasing to recall to her children that they have not here a lasting dwelling, she also urges them to contribute, each according to his vocation and his means, to the welfare of their earthly city, to promote justice, peace and brotherhood among men, to give their aid freely to their brothers, especially to the poorest and most unfortunate. The deep solicitude of the Church, the Spouse of Christ, for the needs of men, for their joys and hopes, their griefs and efforts, is therefore nothing other than her great desire to be present to them, in order to illuminate them with the light of Christ and to gather them all in Him, their only Savior. This solicitude can never mean that the Church conform herself to the things of this world, or that she lessen the ardor of her expectation of her Lord and of the eternal Kingdom.

28. We believe in the life eternal. We believe that the souls of all those who die in the grace of Christ whether they must still be purified in purgatory, or whether from the moment they leave their bodies Jesus takes them to paradise as He did for the Good Thief are the People of God in the eternity beyond death, which will be finally conquered on the day of the Resurrection when these souls will be reunited with their bodies.

Prospect of Resurrection

29. We believe that the multitude of those gathered around Jesus and Mary in paradise forms the Church of Heaven where in eternal beatitude they see God as He is,[102] and where they also, in different degrees, are associated with the holy angels in the divine rule exercised by Christ in glory, interceding for us and helping our weakness by their brotherly care.[103]

30. We believe in the communion of all the faithful of Christ, those who are pilgrims on earth, the dead who are attaining their purification, and the blessed in heaven, all together forming one Church; and we believe that in this communion the merciful love

---

102. Cf. 1 Jn 3:2 and Denzinger, no. 1000.
103. See *Lumen Gentium*, no. 49.

of God and His saints is ever listening to our prayers, as Jesus told us: Ask and you will receive.[104] Thus it is with faith and in hope that we look forward to the resurrection of the dead, and the life of the world to come.

Blessed be God Thrice Holy. Amen.

---

104. Cf. Lk 10:9–10, Jn 16:24.

1

Ordained for Beatitude—
The Finality of the Created Intellect
Sacred Theology, Metaphysics, and the Natural Desire for the Vision of God

> O the depth of the riches and wisdom and knowledge of God!... For from him and through him and to him are all things. To him be glory for ever. Amen.
> —Romans 11:33, 36 (RSV)

> A theology without a metaphysical horizon could not move beyond an analysis of religious experience, nor would it allow the *intellectus fidei* to give a coherent account of the universal and transcendent value of revealed truth.
> —Pope St. John Paul II, *Fides et Ratio*, par. 83

In this opening chapter, I pursue a threefold goal. First, I aspire to restitute the principle of finality, or teleology, to the very heart of theology. For without a comprehensive teleological horizon it is impossible, in the framework of a doctrinally sound and philosophically mature theology, to make sense of human nature, let alone human happiness and its perfection, beatitude. Second, I want to show that such a restitution of teleology to the heart of theology will shed clarifying light onto one of the most intractable debates in modern Catholic theology, the debate over the proper distinction between and correlation of nature and grace as well as the proper understanding of the natural desire for the vision of God. Third, I intend this restitution of the principle of finality to the very center of theology to serve as a case study for the role metaphysics should play as the privileged instrument of sacred theology. I shall use the term "sacred theology" or "holy teaching" (*sacra doctrina*) in order to differentiate the theology that arises from divine revelation from the natural theology of metaphysics. Because I will return to this term shortly, it shall suffice at this point to characterize it thus: rooted in divine revelation, sacred theology has the testimony of the revealing God as its subject matter, principle, and goal. Sacred theology teaches God, is taught by God, and leads to God (*sacra theologia Deum docet, a Deo docetur, et ad Deum ducit*). Only at its own great peril may Catholic theology—so conceived—dare to ignore or even reject the horizon and depth-dimension of intelligibility that metaphysics grants.

In the early twenty-first century, in a pervasive postmetaphysical intellectual climate, this thesis is not altogether uncontroversial, to say the least. One might fittingly characterize it as the elephant in the middle of the living room of contemporary theology. Arguably, the one Doctor of the church largely ignored, dismissed, and even rejected between 1965 and 1998 (the year of the promulgation of Pope St. John Paul II's encyclical letter *Fides et Ratio*) was the one who since the Council of Trent (1545–63) had been, not only by name alone but *de facto* the common doctor (*doctor communis*): Thomas Aquinas.[1] In the years between 1965 and 1998 many if not most Catholic theologians neglected the metaphysics he had developed in continuity with Aristotle and the privileged role it played in his theology as well as in that strand of Catholic theology that regard-

1. The scope of this brief narrative reflects the central topic of the first chapter, the recovery of the role of metaphysics in sacred theology. Yet because the overall focus of the book is the ultimate end, beatitude, the core chapters of this book fall into the parameters, Thomistically conceived, of moral theology whose central concern is the journey to the ultimate end and the overcoming of the impediments that might prevent one from attaining it. In light of this governing theme, the decisive moment of the reemergence of Thomas Aquinas as proposed *doctor communis* occurs already in 1993 with Pope John Paul II's promulgation of the encyclical letter *The Splendor of Truth* (*Veritatis Splendor*). It was with this ongoingly central encyclical letter that a previously misguided instantiation of Catholic moral theology was redirected back on a course commensurate with this book on beatitude and its attainment.

ed him as the *doctor communis* from the Council of Trent onward. Moreover, during these years many if not most Catholic theologians dismissed the disciplined use of metaphysics as a coherent and sustained philosophical discourse in the service of theology and embraced—as latecomers—the by-then, at least in secular circles, old news of a new postmetaphysical era. Under the epochal influence of Martin Heidegger, philosophy became—according to the purportedly irreversible dynamic of an evolving historical fate—postmetaphysical. Catholic theology, bereft of its privileged instrument, turned into a multifarious and only loosely connected hermeneutical enterprise of interpreting biblical texts, historical developments, doctrinal thought-forms, and the never-absent signs of the times in the framework of an all-encompassing historicity of truth.[2]

Since the late 1960s there has been in currency a by-now conventional story meant to provide the fitting etiology of this remarkable phenomenon. It is noteworthy that this story has achieved its quasi-hegemonic status of an unquestioned master narrative simply by the untiring repetition of a plot line that distinguishes itself by the complete absence of demonstrative arguments. As the by-now conventional story goes, in the first decades of the twentieth century, if not already earlier, Scholastic philosophy, not the least in its Thomist version, had become intellectually hollowed out, purportedly exhausted by interminable internecine warfare among various strands of Thomism, irresoluble contradictions, and consequently increasing divisions. Allegedly unable to cope with new intellectual challenges and sociopolitical dynamics it faltered and eventually dissipated. In their respective Gifford Lectures, Alasdair MacIntyre and Ralph McInerny advanced compelling refutations of this widespread master narrative.[3] And even without these refutations it is quite ob-

---

2. For a characteristic expression of this allegedly new epochal situation—the all-too-slow welcome of the Enlightenment in the church and dawning of the comprehensive historicity of truth as the new epochal consciousness of the church—see the programmatic essay by Karl Rahner, "Yesterday's History of Dogma and Theology for Tomorrow," trans. Edward Quinn, in *Theological Investigations* (New York: Crossroad, 1983), 18:3–34, and the incisive rejoinder by Hans Urs von Balthasar, "Human Religion and the Religion of Jesus Christ," in *New Elucidations*, trans. Sr. Mary Theresilde Skerry (San Francisco: Ignatius Press, 1986), 74–87.

3. Alasdair MacIntyre, *Three Rival Versions of Moral Inquiry: Encyclopaedia, Genealogy,*

vious that this conventional story is unable to accommodate the remarkable richness, intellectual diversity, and constructive engagement of the modern intellectual landscape for which, among many others, stand the names of Jacques Maritain, Etienne Gilson, and Louis-Bertrand Geiger; Yves Simon, Ralph McInerny, Charles De Koninck, Benedict Ashley, Lawrence Dewan, and Oliva Blanchette; Erich Przywara, Gustav Siewerth, and Ferdinand Ulrich; Edith Stein and Hedwig Conrad-Martius; Fernand van Steenberghen, Louis de Raeymaeker, Cornelio Fabro, Tomáš Týn, and Vittorio Possenti. Metaphysicians in general, and especially in the Thomist tradition, responded in substantive ways to the restrictions Kant had imposed in his *Critique of Pure Reason* on any future metaphysics, as well as to Heidegger's repeated insinuation concerning the "forgetfulness of Being" that purportedly had characterized metaphysics from Plato to Nietzsche.[4]

This all too long and thorough abstinence from any substantive

---

and Tradition (Notre Dame, Ind.: University of Notre Dame Press, 1990); Ralph McInerny, *Characters in Search of Their Author: The Gifford Lectures Glasgow 1999–2000* (Notre Dame, Ind.: University of Notre Dame Press, 2001), and *Praeambula Fidei: Thomism and the God of the Philosophers* (Washington, D.C.: The Catholic University of America Press, 2006).

4. Heidegger radicalized the critique of metaphysics that Kant had set into motion. According to Heidegger, the concept of being refers intrinsically to finitude. Being is a finite predicate that therefore cannot be applied to God and consequently completely undercuts the analogy of being. The hiatus between God and being is unbridgeable. Overcoming the forgetfulness of being leads, according to Heidegger, only deeper into finitude. A Thomist overcoming of the forgetfulness of being leads, on the contrary, to its origin, its perfect, infinite, actualization, the *ipsum esse subsistens*. For a sustained and nuanced defense of Thomist metaphysics against Kant's epistemological strictures and Heidegger's charge of ontotheology, see White, *Wisdom in the Face of Modernity*; for a spirited attack on Heidegger's charge of the forgetfulness of Being advanced against Christian philosophy, Platonic as well as Aristotelian, see David Bentley Hart, "The Offering of Names: Metaphysics, Nihilism, and Analogy," in his *The Hidden and the Manifest: Essays in Theology and Metaphysics* (Grand Rapids, Mich.: Eerdmans, 2017), 1–44; and for a noteworthy recent rebuttal of Heidegger's charge and for a nuanced engagement of the Thomist position, see Walter Hoeres, *Gradatio entis: Sein als Teilhabe bei Duns Scotus und Franz Suárez* (Heusenstamm: Editiones Scholasticae, 2012). For two astute reversals of Heidegger and reconstructions of metaphysics (the first in the spirit of Platonism, the second by way of a deep recovery of Plato and Aristotle under the guidance of Aquinas's metaphysics of being), see Stanley Rosen, *The Question of Being: A Reversal of Heidegger* (New Haven, Conn.: Yale University Press, 1993), and Oliva Blanchette, *Philosophy of Being: A Reconstructive Essay in Metaphysics* (Washington, D.C.: The Catholic University of America Press, 2003).

employment of metaphysics has worrisome results, to say the least, for Catholic theology. Should, indeed, Catholic theology persist in its indifference to, or positive disavowal of, all metaphysical reflection, it risks a loss greater than it can afford. In arguing for the indispensable role of metaphysics as theology's privileged instrument, one will have to address at least five questions: (1) what theology is, (2) what metaphysics is, (3) which role metaphysics plays in relationship to sacred theology, (4) what might a paradigmatic example of its role as privileged instrument for sacred theology look like, and (5) what difference a substantive employment of metaphysics could make for Catholic theology. Instead of searching for answers to these five questions that would reflect the broadest possible consensus and thereby the smallest common denominator among contemporary Catholic theologians, I hope instead to advance answers that aim at substantive coherence and logical consistency. Furthermore, the paradigmatic example I shall focus on is arguably not only a metaphysical topic of great relevance for theology but also a topic greatly neglected in contemporary philosophy—that to which I have already alluded, the principle of finality.

In the following, I intend to demonstrate that a thorough understanding of the universal principle of finality and especially of the finality characteristic of human nature is crucial for the proper distinction and correlation between nature and grace and the proper understanding of the natural desire for the vision of God. I shall argue that the principle of finality is indispensable for an account of perfect human happiness, that is, beatitude. Furthermore, I will make that case that its renewed consideration will allow Catholic theology to move beyond the impasse of what has been dubbed as "grace-extrinsicism" on the one hand and, "grace-integralism" on the other.

The chapter is comprised of three parts. In the first part, I attend to the first three of the above five questions: what theology is, what metaphysics is, and the role that metaphysics plays in relationship to theology. In the second part, I revisit Aquinas's argument for the universal principle of finality, which in turn furnishes at least an initial answer to the fourth question, namely what a paradigmatic example of metaphysics' role as a privileged instrument for sacred theology might look like. In the final part, I show the difference that the principle of finality makes for rightly distinguishing between and correlating nature and grace as well as for advancing an account of the natural desire for the vision of God that aids in avoiding the respective shortcomings identified in "grace-extrinsicism" and "grace-integralism." This final part serves as an answer to the fifth question, what difference a substantive employment of metaphysics could make for Catholic theology.[5] It will show what difference the principle of finality, especially when applied to the created intellect, makes for overcoming the theological standoff between what has been characterized as "grace-extrinsicism" versus "grace-intrinsicism." The theologically impatient reader might want to turn immediately to the third part where I engage recent and contemporary theologians on the interminable "nature-grace" dispute and read the rest of the chapter in light of the conclusion.

THE PRIVILEGED INSTRUMENTALITY OF METAPHYSICS IN SACRED THEOLOGY

To develop a robust and sufficiently nuanced answer to the question of what sacred theology is and what metaphysics is and what differentiates them requires easily a book-length treatment.[6] In order to maintain a desirable balance between brevity and consistency I will concentrate my efforts in the following on what Thomas Aquinas and his school take Catholic theology and metaphysics to be. This decision is not arbitrary but rather reflective of the century-long recommendation by the Catholic magisterium of Aquinas's way of distinguishing and correlating faith and reason, and theology and

---

5. As the overall argument of the following is not part of metaphysical inquiry proper (although a subset of the argument is) but rather pertains to the nature and task of Catholic theology, it cannot be strictly conclusive. Nevertheless, the argument advances with the aim of making as strong an accumulative case as possible for its two-pronged thesis. The case is made by way of a close consideration of two interrelated and, arguably, central topics of Catholic theology.

6. I have reflected on this matter at greater length in the chapter, "Prelude—Faith and Reason: 'Is There a Cure for Reason's Presumption and Despair?'—Why Thomas Matters Today," in my *Dust Bound for Heaven*, 29–71.

philosophy, most recently in Pope St. John Paul II's 1998 encyclical *Fides et Ratio*. Very much in the spirit of Thomas Aquinas, John Paul II regards the center of Catholic theology to be speculative theology. This most central discipline of Catholic theology, he states, "must articulate the universal meaning of the mystery of the One and Triune God and of the economy of salvation, both as a narrative and, *above all, in the form of argument*." But in order to achieve this task "in concept and argument," "speculative dogmatic theology ... presupposes and implies a philosophy of the human being, the world and, more radically, of being, which has objective truth as its foundation" (par. 66). John Paul II's crucial claim—that the foundation of sacred theology, considered under the aspect of its most central discipline, speculative theology, as well as of the philosophy of being, is objective truth—echoes the most essential theological and philosophical commitment of the *doctor communis* and the school carrying his name.

Precisely because sacred theology and metaphysics are founded in objective truth, Aquinas understands them to be two different instantiations of the most rigorous standard of objective science available: Aristotle's account of scientific knowledge advanced in his *Posterior Analytics*. As is well known, at the center of the *Posterior Analytics* stands the apodictic or demonstrative syllogism. The goal of scientific knowledge is the demonstration—in light of certain indemonstrable first principles—of the attributes and causes of the subject under investigation. Scientific knowledge is achieved when something is shown to belong *per se* to a subject because of what that subject is. Every science is founded on first indemonstrable principles that antecede discursive reason and are reached only by some form of direct, nondiscursive intellectual intuition or insight. Scientific knowledge may be gained both by induction toward these first principles and by deduction from them.[7] Sciences differ formally if they have different sets of first indemonstrable principles.[8]

---

7. As we shall see, while this is normally the case in a natural science, in sacred theology, in contrast, we do not induce the principles so much as gain insight into them when they are revealed to us. The "insight" or induction is given in faith—as revealed principles, which constitute the articles of faith.

8. See Aristotle, *Posterior Analytics* I, 75b37–76a30, and Thomas Aquinas, *Commentary*

Sacred Theology

Sacred theology thus conceived is a science *sui generis*, a science that is fundamentally different from and far superior to a systematic presentation and exposition of the totality of biblical propositions—a procedure characteristic of classical Protestant Scholasticism. It is also far superior to the systematic presentation and exposition of church dogma and doctrine, a procedure characteristic of Catholic traditionalism. Last but not least, sacred theology is far superior to the systematic presentation and exposition of subjective religiosity, individual or collective, in its various literary, symbolic, and ideational expressions—a procedure characteristic of liberal Protestantism as well as Catholic modernism. Aquinas's preferred denomination for this science *sui generis* is *sacra doctrina*, holy teaching or sacred theology. He conceives of sacred theology in analogy with the Aristotelian subordinate sciences and therefore understands holy teaching to be a science that is immediately dependent upon "the knowledge of God and the saints" (*ST* I, q. 1, a. 2, co.).[9]

Admittedly, holy teaching (*sacra doctrina*) is a most unique science, which Aristotle could never have anticipated for at least two reasons. First, an Aristotelian subordinate science proceeds from principles of a higher science. In the frame of reference characteristic of the higher science these principles are still known by natural reason. But this is uniquely not the case with those principles on which sacred theology relies. Unlike all other subordinate sciences, sacred theology proceeds from principles that transcend the whole order of natural reason. Second, from the viewpoint of the compre-

---

on Aristotle's Posterior Analytics, trans. Richard Berquist (South Bend, Ind.: Dumb Ox Books, 2007), 76–84 (Marietti, nos. 143–58). For a contemporary presentation and analysis of Aristotle's theory of scientific knowledge, see Richard McKirahan, *Posterior Analytics, Principles and Proofs: Aristotle's Theory of Demonstrative Science* (Princeton, N.J.: Princeton University Press, 1992), and for an instructive contemporary philosophical engagement, Alasdair MacIntyre, *First Principles, Final Ends, and Contemporary Philosophical Issues* (Milwaukee, Wis.: Marquette University Press, 1990). The best monograph on Aquinas's analogical application of Aristotle's theory of science to theology is still John I. Jenkins, CSC, *Knowledge and Faith in Thomas Aquinas* (Cambridge: Cambridge University Press, 1997).

9. For what is still the best historical study that situates Aquinas's understanding of theology as *sacra doctrina* in his own intellectual milieu, see Marie-Dominique Chenu, OP, *La théologie comme science au XIIIe siècle*, 3rd ed. (Paris: Vrin, 1957).

hensive hierarchy of Aristotelian sciences, sacred theology is utterly superfluous, because, as we will see, metaphysics is in its own way "divine science." In short, the scope of Aristotelian sciences covers all aspects of reality. Yet holy teaching pertains to a reality of which all Aristotelian sciences are necessarily unaware—human salvation. The principles on which holy teaching depends pertain directly to the salvation and hence the eternal destiny of humankind. Therefore, Aquinas argues, in order that the salvation of humankind may come about more suitably and more surely, it is necessary that there be a teaching (*doctrina*) in accord with divine revelation that would surpass human reason and the most comprehensive scientific inquiries it could muster (*ST* I, q. 1, a. 1). This teaching (*doctrina*) in accord with divine revelation is sacred theology.

Sacred theology is an absolute singularity in the universe of Aristotelian sciences; indeed, it would have been completely inconceivable for Aristotle, for it relies directly upon God's own knowledge in which the blessed, by way of the beatific vision, already fully participate and concerns itself with the testimony that the Lord conveys through the incarnate Logos by way of the prophetic and apostolic witness and the inspired authors of the scripture as interpreted by the church's authoritative teaching (*ST* II-II, q. 1). With the exception of the so-called preambles of the faith (*praeambula fidei*),[10] the truths that ground the principles on which sacred theology as a subordinate science relies essentially transcend the capacities of the human intellect in this life.

Two important features of sacred theology follow from this con-

10. The "praeambula ad articulos" (*ST* I, q. 2, a. 2, ad 1) comprise those truths about God and the rational soul that are (1) presupposed by the articles of faith and that (2) can be known by natural reason. See also *ST* II-II, q. 1, a. 5, ad 3. To make explicit the *praeambula fidei*, develop demonstrative arguments for them, and defend them against objections is nothing but the capstone work of metaphysics, as Ralph McInerny convincingly argues in *Praeambula Fidei*, 26–32 and 159–68. For two highly instructive studies that offer a rather comprehensive account of the *praeambula fidei* across Aquinas's sprawling *oeuvre*, see John F. Wippel, "Thomas Aquinas on Philosophy and the Preambles of Faith," in *The Science of Being as Being: Metaphysical Investigations*, ed. Gregory Doolan (Washington, D.C.: The Catholic University of America Press, 2012), 196–220 (at 220, Wippel proposes a list of no less than twelve preambles that can be found in Aquinas's texts), and his "Aquinas on Creation and Preambles of Faith," *The Thomist* 78, no. 1 (2014): 1–36.

ception: first, "God is in very truth the object of this science" (*Deus vere* [*est*] *subiectum huius scientiae*).¹¹ Because sacred theology considers God and all those things that have God as their first cause and final end, the material objects of sacred theology comprise ultimately not only God but also all created reality. Yet in which way does sacred theology then differ from every other science if sacred theology shares all the material objects of all the other sciences? The Thomist tradition came to designate that what specifies a particular science the "formal object which" (*obiectum formale quod*). The "formal object which" denotes the specific aspect under which a distinct science studies all its variant material objects. Sacred theology treats all its material objects "under the aspect of God" (*sub ratione Dei*).

God is the "formal object which" that specifies sacred theology as a distinct science. But how can the practitioners of sacred theology study God, the knowledge of whom exceeds the power of the created intellect? Differently put: what is it that makes the "formal object which" actually knowable to the practitioners of sacred theology? It is the "formal object under which" (*formale obiectum quo*) which comprises the divine communication of revelation and the human reception of divine faith. The objective aspect of the "formal object under which" is God communicating by way of the incarnate Lord, prophets, and apostles such that there is not only a divine manifestation but also cognitive content and hence objective truth. The subjective aspect of the "formal object under which" is the virtue of faith. Faith in its precise theological sense denotes a stable disposition or habit (*habitus*) that is not actively acquired by the believer but rather supernaturally infused by God—hence divine faith. Divine faith is a *theological* virtue, because God as first truth is its sole formal object—

11. *ST* I, q. 1, a. 7: "God is the object [*subiectum*] of this science. The relation between a science and its object is the same as that between a habit or faculty and its object. Now properly speaking, the object of a faculty or habit is the thing under the aspect of which all things are referred to that faculty or habit, as man and stone are referred to the faculty of sight in that they are colored. Hence colored things are the proper objects of sight. But in sacred science, all things are treated of under the aspect of God: either because they are God Himself or because they refer to God as their beginning and end. Hence it follows that God is in very truth the object of this science. This is clear also from the principles of this science, namely, the articles of faith, for faith is about God. The object of the principles and of the whole science must be the same, since the whole science is contained virtually in its principles."

God, the first truth, teaching about himself: "[Divine] faith adheres to all the articles of faith by reason of one mean [*medium*], i.e. on account of the First Truth proposed to us in the Scriptures, according to the teaching of the Church who has the right understanding of them. Hence, whoever abandons this mean [*medium*] [that is, on account of the First Truth], is altogether lacking in [divine] faith" (*ST* II-II, q. 5, a. 3, ad 2). The first truth is the formal object of the divine faith that receives the superior principles of the knowledge of God and the blessed (*scientia Dei et beatorum*) as articles of faith. Hence, "nothing can come under faith, save in so far as it stands under the First Truth, under which nothing false can stand" (*ST* II-II, q. 1, a. 3). Consequently, divine faith enables the faithful (and among them the practitioners of sacred theology) to take the cognitive content of revelation, the articles of faith, as true and absolutely certain first principles from which sacred theology proceeds.[12]

Second, sacred theology, like other sciences, is capable of drawing true conclusions from true principles. Hence, sacred theology is a science that advances demonstrative arguments and therefore makes progress by way of such arguments (*scientia argumentativa*).[13] Now, it is important to realize that sacred theology as a discursive

---

12. For an explanation of God as the principal material object and as the constitutive formal object *quod* and *quo* of divine faith and hence sacred theology, see chapter 4 in this book and for the importance of understanding and defending the inner unity of sacred theology, see my *Dust Bound for Heaven*, 313–46. For a lucid presentation of the notion of sacred theology as a unified science and an astute application of it to the contemporary hyperspecialization of the theological subfields of theology characteristic of the modern academy, see Philip Neri Reese, OP, "Theology, Faith, Universities: From Specialization to Specification in Theology," *New Blackfriars* 92 (2011): 691–704.

13. *ST* I, q. 1, a. 8: "As other sciences do not argue in proof of their principles, but argue from their principles to demonstrate other truths in these sciences: so this doctrine does not argue in proof of its principles, which are the articles of faith, but from them it goes on to prove something else." Of course, Aquinas's conception of sacred theology as a *scientia* subordinate to the *scientia Dei et beatorum* and in particular as *scientia argumentativa* did not go unchallenged in the decades after his death. For an informative introduction to the intense discussion of Aquinas's proposal in the thirteenth and early fourteenth century, see Martin Grabmann, *Die theologische Erkenntnis- und Einleitungslehre des hl. Thomas von Aquin auf Grund seiner Schrift "In Böethium de Trinitate." Im Zusammenhang der Scholastik des 13. und beginnenden 14. Jahrhunderts dargestellt* (Fribourg: Paulusverlag, 1948). For an instructive twentieth-century retrieval, reconstruction, and instantiation of Aquinas's understanding of sacred theology as *scientia argumentativa*, see Paul Wyser, OP, *Theologie als Wisssenschaft: Ein Beitrag zur theologischen Erkenntnislehre* (Salzburg: Pustet, 1938).

science can move its line of argumentation in two directions. The first direction moves away from the first principles to new conclusions, to new insights that are virtually implied in the principles of faith or in proximate conclusions. The second direction moves toward the first principles by way of arguments that elucidate, interpret, and defend these first principles.

In a day and age where all too often the highest exercise of Catholic theology seems to amount to some combination of hermeneutics and pragmatics—a hermeneutical gesture meant to interpret the Gospel in light of the signs of the times and under the stricture of the historicity of truth followed by some effort to extract some tangible yet inherently contingent and utterly transient pastoral application—the very suggestion of sacred theology culminating in speculative theology might appear at best as provocatively heady and, more likely as a decidedly undesirable return to what some time ago was all too quickly ridiculed and facilely dismissed as the science of conclusions (*Konklusionswissenschaft*). Yet it is precisely speculative theology that according to John Paul II "must articulate the universal meaning of the mystery of the One and Triune God and of the economy of salvation, both as a narrative and, *above all, in the form of argument*" (par. 66; emphasis added). Lest Catholic theology abandon the task of articulating the mystery of God *in the form of argument*, the fulcrum of sacred theology must be its very exercise as speculative theology, as an argumentative and discursive science, and not simply as an extrinsically and purely pragmatically connected bundle of exegetical, historical, hermeneutical, and sociocultural studies and inquiries operating under the dogma of historicism—the historicity of truth.[14] To

14. In light of strong antimetaphysical currents in post-Vatican II Catholic theology—currents that exhibit considerable impatience for any form of sustained speculative efforts and that simultaneously insist upon immediate existential authenticity and pragmatic pastoral impact, Lonergan's observation from the 1950s is as pertinent as ever: "Just as the equations of thermodynamics make no one feel warmer or cooler ... so also speculative theology is not immediately relevant to the stimulation of religious feeling. But unless this fact is acknowledged explicitly and systematically, there arises a constant pressure in favor of theological tendencies that mistakenly reinforce the light of faith and intelligence with the warmth of less austere modes of thought." Bernard Lonergan, SJ, "Theology and Understanding," *Gregorianum* 35 (1954): 643. There has obviously been a considerable range in the way Catholic theologians sympathetic to Aquinas's understanding (inside and outside the Thomist school) have taken the analogy between a strictly subordinate science and the uniquely subordinate science of sacred theology. One might think

insist that speculative theology is the culminating exercise of sacred theology does not entail at all the denigration or exclusion from sacred theology of what has been called "positive theology" (to which, rightly conceived, and with the proper qualifications, also belongs biblical exegesis). Positive theology undertakes the analysis of past historical documents in light of the contemporary teaching of the church with the end of ascertaining the church's dogmatic tradition. Crucially, it is not history that provides positive theology with its object, but rather divine faith. Contrary to the positive theologian who discovers and establishes the church's dogmatic tradition, the radical hermeneuticist (who in many instances has replaced the positive as well as the speculative theologian) flatly denies the very possibility to extract or identify the truth in particular historical expressions and theological developments.[15] The radical hermeneuticist not only places himself outside the orbit of the living faith, the virtue of divine faith communally lived in the church, but also unwittingly gives witness to the terminal end of sacred theology as a unified science of God.

Metaphysics

Thomist metaphysics stands, of course, philosophically on its own feet. It does not depend on sacred theology, nor does it in any substan-

---

of the dogmatic works of Matthias Joseph Scheeben, Charles Journet, and Jean-Hervé Nicolas, OP, as exemplary creative instantiations, under modern conditions, of the range in which sacred theology can be conceived of not simply as an interminable hermeneutical enterprise but rather as *scientia argumentativa*. See Matthias Joseph Scheeben, *Gesammelte Schriften*, ed. Josef Höfer et al., 8 vols. (Freiburg: Herder, 1949-67); Charles Journet, *L'Église du verbe incarné: Essai de théologie spéculative*, 5 vols. (Saint-Maurice: Editions Saint-Augustin, 1998-2005); Jean-Hervé Nicolas, OP, *Synthèse dogmatique*, 2 vols. (Paris: Editions Beauchesne, 1985–93). For more recent instantiations, more easily accessible to an English-speaking readership and topically more focused, see among others, Simon Francis Gaine, OP, *Did the Saviour See the Father?: Christ, Salvation, and the Vision of God* (London: Bloomsbury T and T Clark, 2015); Serge-Thomas Bonino, OP, *Angels and Demons: A Catholic Introduction* (Washington, D.C.: The Catholic University of America Press, 2016); and Thomas Joseph White, OP, *The Incarnate Lord: A Thomistic Study in Christology* (Washington, D.C.: The Catholic University of America Press, 2016).

15. Paradigmatic instantiations of the former are Ambroise Gardeil, OP, *Le Donné revélé et la théologie*, 2nd ed. (Paris: Cerf, 1932), and Yves M.-J. Congar, OP, *Tradition and Traditions: A Historical Essay and a Theological Essay*, trans. Michael Naseby and Thomas Rainborough (New York: MacMillan, 1967), and of the latter are Terrence W. Tilley, *Inventing Catholic Tradition* (Maryknoll, N.Y.: Orbis, 2000), and Lieven Boeve, *Interrupting Tradition: An Essay on Christian Faith in a Postmodern Context* (Leuven: Peeters, 2003).

tive way that might weaken its integrity as metaphysics presuppose sacred theology. At the same time fundamental principles of Thomist metaphysics have been recommended warmly and frequently and for good reasons by the Catholic magisterium to Catholic theologians and philosophers. A minimalist and general recommendation can be found in *Fides et Ratio* (pars. 43–44 and 78); a maximalist and rather specific recommendation—misunderstood and in some instances misapplied as a tool of ecclesiastical discipline and therefore understandably, albeit rashly, dismissed by many for reasons extrinsic to the substance proposed—can be found in the twenty-four Thomistic theses.[16] In the following, I simply assume the repeatedly announced "end" or "death" of metaphysics to have been premature—to say the least.[17] The history of philosophy proves to be a most unbiased judge of such precipitate obituaries. As can easily be studied by those who care enough about the truth value of such announcements: Hegel revived comprehensive metaphysical speculation after Kant had submitted it to the strict epistemological delimitation of transcendental critique; Blondel revitalized metaphysical inquiry in the face of the reigning Kantianism at the Sorbonne; Bergson returned to metaphysical inquiry after positivism had declared it definitively and irretrievably dead; Husserl conceived of phenomenology as a renewal of philosophy in the perennial sense (*philosophia perennis*) in the face

16. *Acta Apostolicae Sedis* 6 (1914): 383–86. The twenty-four Thomistic theses are presently most easily available in printed form in Bernard Wuellner, SJ, *Summary of Scholastic Principles* (Chicago: Loyola University Press, 1956), 120–24, and at u.arizona.edu/~aversa/scholastic/24Thomisticpart2.htm. The best commentaries—*sine ira et studio*—still are Édouard Hugon, OP, *Principes de philosophie: Les vingtquatre thèses thomistes* (Paris: P. Tequi, 1922), and Guido Mattiussi, SJ, *Les points fondamentaux de la philosophie thomiste: Commentaire des vingt-quatre thèses approuvées par la S. Congrégation des Etudes*, trans. J. Levillain (Turin: Marietti, 1926). The greatest damage done to these Thomistic theses was not brought about by some philosophical argumentation that resulted in their putative theoretical defeat but rather by a disciplinary misuse of them that resulted in their *de facto* practical defeat and continues to do so for those still chilled by the haunting memories of what they might describe as a Thomist stranglehold on the Curia, the seminaries, and the university faculties in the pre-Conciliar era.

17. For typical recent announcements of the demise of metaphysics—announcements that rely in an all too transparently decisionist attitude on the Heideggerian-Derridean approach to philosophy—see John Caputo and Gianni Vattimo, *After the Death of God*, ed. Jeffrey W. Robbins (New York: Columbia University Press, 2007), and Gianni Vattimo, *Farewell to Truth*, trans. William McCuaig (New York: Columbia University Press, 2007).

of a pervasive historicist skepticism and relativism rampant in the German *Geisteswissenschaften* at the end of the nineteenth century; Stein and Conrad-Martius attempted to integrate Husserl's early realist phenomenology into the Thomist strand of the *philosophia perennis*; Thomist philosophers challenged Heidegger's charges of the forgetfulness of Being and of ontotheology against metaphysics and made significant contributions of their own to the *philosophia perennis* (Maritain, Gilson, Geiger, Fabro, van Steenberghen, de Raeymaeker, Týn, De Koninck, Siewerth, Ulrich, Blanchette, Possenti, et al.); and last but not least, contemporary analytic philosophers have increasingly turned to metaphysical topics (Ross, Lowe, Loux, Mumford, et al.). Of course, not all metaphysics done today stands in the Aristotelian-Thomist tradition, but that, after all, has always been the case.[18]

For the sake of brevity and consistency, I shall limit myself here to the conception of metaphysics that Aquinas articulates in the prologue of his commentary on Aristotle's *Metaphysics*. It shows Aquinas to be not at all interested in "construing" some idiosyncratic metaphysics of his own but, rather, in unfolding a "first philosophy" of which he regards Aristotle's *Metaphysics* to be the most advanced instantiation—and which, quite obviously, Aquinas rereads in intense dialogue with the neo-Platonic tradition represented by Avicenna and Albert, and under the significant influence of Dionysius and Augustine. In short, when Aquinas considers metaphysics he pursues nothing but that tradition of philosophical inquiry and discourse that I have already above called by its traditional designation, philosophy in the perennial sense (*philosophia perennis*).[19] In the order of knowledge that can be acquired naturally, metaphysics is the highest science, transcending and therefore regulating as *sapien-*

---

18. For noteworthy recent instantiations of the Scotist-Suárezian strand of the *philosophia perennis*, see Ludger Honnefelder, *Scientia transcendens: Die formale Bestimmung der Seiendheit und Realität in der Metaphysik des Mittelalters und der Neuzeit (Duns Scotus, Suárez, Wolff, Kant, Peirce) (Paradeigmata)* (Hamburg: Meiner, 1990), and Hoeres, *Gradatio entis*.

19. For an astutely argued account of this understanding of philosophy, see McInerny, *Praeambula Fidei*, 159–306. *Philosophia perennis* is, of course, to a certain degree a contested reality insofar as the precise nature of metaphysics is under dispute between Scotists, Leibnizians, Aristotelian-Thomists, and recent analytic philosophers.

tia rectrix all natural sciences, natural philosophy, and mathematics. Metaphysics holds this elevated position because it is preeminently intellectual, first because it inquires into the highest causes of being, those causes that in the order of knowledge afford the greatest intelligibility; second because it considers the most universal principles, "such as *being*, and those things that naturally accompany being, such as *unity* and *plurality*, *potency* and *act*";[20] and third, because it considers those things that are separate from sensible matter altogether in their being, God and the intellectual substances. Aquinas concludes:

> Therefore in accordance with the three classes of objects mentioned above from which this science derives its perfection, three names arise. It is called *divine science* or *theology* inasmuch as it considers the aforementioned substances. It is called *metaphysics* inasmuch as it considers being and the attributes which naturally accompany being (for things which transcend the physical order are discovered by the process of analysis, as the more common is discovered after the less common). And it is called *first philosophy* inasmuch as it considers the first causes of things.[21]

The formal object of metaphysics is being as such (*ens inquantum ens*) under which aspect metaphysics considers being in general (*ens commune*), the being that belongs to and may be predicated of anything real as well as of the separate substances that are the common and universal causes of being in general. Hence, metaphysics thus conceived is inseparably ontology *and* divine science, philosophy of being *and* natural theology, the latter being the culminating perfection of the former. John Paul II advances this conception of metaphysics in less technical language thus: "Set within the Christian metaphysical tradition, the philosophy of being is a dynamic philosophy which views reality in its ontological, causal and communicative structures. It is strong and enduring because it is based upon the very act of being itself, which allows a full and comprehensive openness to reality as a whole, surpassing every limit in order to reach the One who brings all things to fulfillment" (*Fides et Ratio*, par. 97).

20. Thomas Aquinas, *Commentary on Aristotle's* Metaphysics, trans. John P. Rowan (Notre Dame, Ind.: Dumb Ox Books, 1995), xxix.
21. Ibid., xxxi.

The wisdom that metaphysics affords is the highest wisdom a person can acquire by the natural means of rational scientific inquiry. The superior wisdom that sacred theology affords relies on the gift of revelation and the grace of faith.[22] As grace perfects nature, so does sacred theology "perfect" metaphysics, however neither essentially nor accidentally, but in an existential coordination. While the formal objects of sacred theology and metaphysics remain distinct, the surpassing revelation of the knowledge of God and the blessed (*scientia Dei et beatorum*) harmonizes with the science of metaphysics in its highest conclusions. An active existential cooperation of metaphysical inquiry with the faith issues in an appeal to the natural dimensions of the human person that call for the development and employment of the metaphysical capacities of the human intellect.

Does this also mean that sacred theology presupposes metaphysics in the way grace presupposes nature? In order to clarify the precise relationship between sacred theology and metaphysics a distinction is called for. When considered under the aspect of definite teaching (*doctrina*), that is, in light of the principles on which sacred theology depends as its proper first principles, its sole indispensable foundation is revelation and its reception by way of the infused theological virtue of faith. The direct knowledge of faith, considered in itself, does not depend nor rely upon the antecedent deliveries of metaphysics. Common sense suffices.[23] The situation, however,

---

22. Next to the acquired natural wisdom of metaphysics and the acquired supernatural wisdom of sacred theology, there is the Holy Spirit's infused supernatural gift of wisdom that affords a quasi-experiential knowledge of God. For a lucid treatment of metaphysical wisdom and the two supernatural wisdoms, see the first chapter in Réginald Garrigou-Lagrange, OP, *The Sense of Mystery: Clarity and Obscurity in the Intellectual Life*, trans. Matthew K. Minerd (Steubenville, Ohio: Emmaus Academic, 2017).

23. In his lucidly argued presentation of Aquinas's understanding of holy teaching (*sacra doctrina*) Bruce Marshall advances a convincing argument that according to Aquinas the simple believer, the "old woman" (*vetula*), will always only know the preambles of faith through divine faith. The *vetula* serves as the paradigm for the crucial insight that divine faith considered *simpliciter* does not stand in need of any metaphysical assistance whatsoever. Bruce D. Marshall, "*Quod Scit Una Uetela*: Aquinas on the Nature of Theology," in *The Theology of Thomas Aquinas*, ed. Rik van Nieuwenhove and Joseph Wawrykow (Notre Dame, Ind.: University of Notre Dame Press, 2005), 1–35. It should nevertheless be duly noted that the knowledge of faith in its reliance upon common sense does presuppose implicitly the first conceptions of the intellect. Sacred theology *qua scientia* makes these presuppositions explicit in its account of the knowledge of

changes fundamentally when sacred theology is considered under the aspect of an argumentative or discursive science (*scientia argumentativa*), that is, when it is considered as a unique subordinate science whose first principles are received from a superior science. It is in the context of considering sacred theology under this aspect that Aquinas clarifies the relationship between arguments from authority and arguments from reason:

> This doctrine is especially based upon arguments from authority, inasmuch as its principles are obtained by revelation.... Since ... grace does not destroy nature, but perfects it, natural reason should minister to faith as the natural bent of the will ministers to charity.... Hence sacred doctrine makes use also of the authority of philosophers in those questions in which they were able to know the truth by natural reason. (*ST* I, q. 1, a. 8, ad 2)

It is here, in the exercise of sacred theology as *scientia argumentativa*, that metaphysics comes to play an indispensable role as the privileged instrument of sacred theology. Remember, due to their different formal objects—supernatural divine *revelation* for sacred theology and *being qua being* for metaphysics—they are essentially different but still uniquely related sciences.

Consider this relationship first in regard to sacred theology. The superior *scientia* on which sacred theology depends and which constitutes its principal subject matter lies essentially beyond the reach of metaphysics; for, crucially, the "formal object which" of sacred theology is God including all the central mysteries of the divine life: the Trinity of divine persons, the eternal divine decrees that constitute providence and the whole economy of salvation with the incarnation at the very center. Furthermore, as already mentioned, this supernatural "formal object which" becomes accessible only through a unique and equally supernatural "formal object under which," divine revelation and divine faith. However, all the first principles of metaphysics are included in the knowledge of God and of the blessed (*scientia Dei et beatorum*). Hence, not only can the true principles

---

faith. Formally considered, these conceptions are a central subject matter of metaphysics. For this reason, an unsound metaphysics has the potential to do considerable harm to a theological account of the knowledge of faith, were sacred theology to adopt such an unsound account.

of metaphysics never contradict the first principles of sacred theology—one truth never contradicts another truth—but the former can also shed clarifying light on the superior but surpassingly mysterious principles of revelation. Metaphysics, therefore, can serve as an *instrument* to grant greater clarity (*ad maiorem manifestationem*) to the teaching of sacred theology.

Now consider this relationship in regard to metaphysics. Obviously, sacred theology does not belong to the hierarchy of sciences of which metaphysics is the guiding or governing wisdom (*sapientia rectrix*). Rather, sacred theology, although merely a dependent science, nevertheless transcends this hierarchy. At the same time, even revelation comes by way of being. Revelation presupposes and works with the structures of being and also with the structures of human cognition and understanding. And these—the structures of being, cognition, and understanding—are the proper subject matter of metaphysics. It has been astutely observed "that the conception of a *scientia* of faith, which derives its truth directly from the First Truth itself, is only thinkable in supposition of a metaphysical account of the truth of being."[24] Because revelation comes by way of being, metaphysics becomes the *privileged* instrument of sacred theology.

Consider, finally, this relationship in regard to God, who is the principal material object of sacred theology as well as of metaphysics—albeit in formally completely different ways. Despite this difference, sacred theology and metaphysics share a fundamental and indeed formidable challenge, a challenge that pertains to the way these sciences have access to their central subject matter and if not met puts into question their status as sciences. As it turns out, only when sacred theology avails itself of the help of metaphysical analysis is it able to identify and conceptualize the fundamental challenge and to advance a solution that avoids the shortcomings of classical as well as modern apophatic and rationalist theologies.[25]

---

24. Rudi te Velde, *Aquinas on God: The 'Divine Science' of the* Summa Theologiae (Burlington, Vt.: Ashgate, 2006), 29.

25. For an astute instantiation of the proper use of metaphysics in sacred theology that displays the fruitfulness of applying this instrument with an eye to the contemporary postmetaphysical and profoundly disoriented intellectual climate, especially in late-modern universities, see Thomas Joseph White, OP, "Monotheistic Rationality and Divine Names: Why Aquinas's Analogy Theory Transcends Both Theoretical Agnosti-

Here is the fundamental challenge in a nutshell: neither metaphysics nor sacred theology is able in principle to arrive at the knowledge of God's essence and hence at a knowledge that is precise enough to advance a scientific definition of God. For there is no proper definition achievable in response to the question "What is God?" In the case of sacred theology, the revealed principles, the articles of the faith, depend on higher principles that are absolutely inaccessible to human understanding in this life. In the case of metaphysics, such a definition of God's essence would need to put God into a genus and then name the specific difference that would differentiate God from other species of this genus or posit God as its sole instance. But this is impossible because genus presupposes the distinction of being and essence, and God is the one instance where being and essence are not distinct but one. Hence God transcends every genus; hence no definition of God is possible; hence no proper scientific knowledge of God is achievable.[26]

Because a definition of its central subject matter, God, is unavailable, sacred theology must rely on God's effects, those of grace, that is, revelation (the articles of faith), and those of nature, that is, being in general (*ens commune*), its constitutive principles, and its first cause. At this point it becomes clear why metaphysics plays an indispensable role as privileged instrument of sacred theology. For sacred theology to ignore God's effects of nature not only means to forgo the insights attainable from a metaphysical inquiry that ascends from finite to infinite being but also to commit the claim to transcendence entailed in a divine revelation that is historical and definitive to the enclosure of the immanent frame (Charles Taylor) and hence to unintelligibility. Rudi te Velde puts the matter succinctly:

Without reason's *manuductio* [act of guiding], by which the subject of the revealed doctrine of faith is given an intelligible determination, the Christian *revelatio* cannot be understood to be what it is assumed to be: knowl-

---

cism and Conceptual Anthropomorphism," in *God: Reason and Reality*, ed. Anselm Ramelov, OP (Munich: Philosophia, 2014), 37–79.

26. For a lucid treatment of this complex and challenging problematic, a treatment in dialogue with alternative contemporary proposals, see Turner, *Faith, Reason, and the Existence of God*, esp. chap. 7, "Univocity and Inference: Duns Scotus," 125–48, and chap. 10, "Analogy and Inference," 193–215.

edge which is true of God. Without the *manuductio* of metaphysics, leading to a transcendent reality, the Christian revelation will lapse into the immanence of human history, at least in the sense that its putative reference to transcendence remains unintelligible.[27]

According to Aquinas, a theology that eschews the assistance of metaphysics will most likely fall short in achieving the *intellectus fidei*, the maximum of intelligibility and communicability of the revealed knowledge of God and God's saving work this side of the beatific vision. Sacred theology without metaphysics will also fail in the apologetic task of refuting philosophical objections advanced against the truth of revelation and, last but not least, fail also in the analytic task of identifying the errors that make up theological heterodoxy.

Already in one of his very first works, his commentary on the *De Trinitate* of Boethius, Aquinas formulates what I characterize as metaphysics' role as the privileged instrument of sacred theology. He refers here to "philosophia" in general (which would include also natural philosophy and logic, but which always means first and foremost "first philosophy" as the unifying keystone of "philosophia"). In the third article of the second question he asks whether it is permissible to use philosophical reasoning and authorities in the science of faith, that is, in sacred theology. In the body of the argument, he identifies three ways in which philosophy can be used in sacred theology:

First, in order to demonstrate the preambles of faith, which we must necessarily know in [the act of] faith. Such are the truths about God that are proved by natural reason, for example, that God exists, that he is one, and other truths of this sort about God or creatures proved in philosophy and presupposed by faith. Second, by throwing light on the contents of faith by analogies, as Augustine uses many analogies drawn from philosophical doctrines in order to elucidate the Trinity. Third, in order to refute assertions contrary to the faith, either by showing them to be false or lacking in necessity.[28]

---

27. Te Velde, *Aquinas on God*, 30.
28. *Expostio super librum Boethii de Trinitate* [hereafter "*Expos. de Trin*"], q. 2, a. 3. The translation is taken from Thomas Aquinas, *Faith, Reason, and Theology: Questions I-IV of his Commentary on the* De Trinitate *of Boethius*, trans. Armand Maurer (Toronto: Pontifical Institute of Mediaeval Studies, 1987), 49.

It is quite noteworthy that subsequently he points out that "those ... who use philosophy in sacred doctrine can err in two ways." He then names two abuses that anticipate what in the modern period comes to represent the characteristic self-confidence of a rationalism ready to impose its normative conceptual control over sacred theology:

> In one way by making use of teachings that are contrary to the faith, which consequently do not belong to philosophy but are a corruption and abuse of it. Origen was guilty of this. In another way by including the contents of faith within the bounds of philosophy, as would happen should somebody decide to believe nothing but what could be established by philosophy. On the contrary, philosophy should be brought within the bounds of faith, as the Apostle says in 2 Corinthians 10:5: "We take every thought captive to obey Christ."[29]

Contrary to the glib epistemic self-confidence characteristic of modern rationalism, Aquinas is fully aware of the finitude and fragility of human reason, a finitude due to the natural limitations of creatures and a fragility due to the inherent fallibility of matter in the hylomorphic unity of the rational animal (*animal rationale*) and especially also to the wounds original sin has left in human nature, diminishing the intellect, weakening the will, and inflaming the passions. He therefore regards metaphysical knowledge as *de facto* limited, prone to error, and as inherently perfectible by revelation. But contrary to the epistemic despair characteristic of modern skepticism and fideism, Aquinas regards the human intellect as intrinsically ordered to truth and capable of attaining truth. He therefore regards metaphysics to be a privileged instrument of sacred theology for unfolding argumentatively, explicating, and defending the infinitely higher and more sublime revealed mysteries of the divine faith.

Far from being a hegemonic discourse, sacred theology precisely as an argumentative or discursive science (*scientia argumentativa*) protects the faith from the perennial dangers of its Gnostic mythologization into some arcane knowledge to be enjoyed by those few who are privileged to be so illuminated. Moreover, it further serves to protect the faith from its rationalist or emotivist naturalization

29. Ibid.

into the religiosity that reflects and legitimizes whatever happen to be the dominant sociocultural, political, and economic configurations of the day. By thus shoring up the faith, sacred theology enables and sets free other discourses that flow directly from the faith, first and foremost the ongoing theological and spiritual exegesis and contemplation of scripture in the tradition of typological and figurative reading initiated in the New Testament and developed further by the Church Fathers and, secondly, the profound and evocative writings of the mystics. It is not at all accidental that the Carmelite mystic St. John of the Cross received a solid Thomist philosophical and theological formation as a student and that the confessor of the Carmelite mystic and reformer St. Teresa of Avila was the eminent Dominican Thomist Domingo Bañez. Sacred theology does not inhibit but rather encourages, fosters, and defends authentic mysticism. Moreover, because of its fundamental reliance upon the written word of God together with sacred tradition, sacred theology regards the ongoing interpretation of scripture not only as an absolutely integral practice but also as a necessary precondition for its unique task as an argumentative science (*scientia argumentativa*). In short, while metaphysics is an *instrument of* sacred theology, the interpretation of scripture is *integral to*, indeed, is nothing less than "the very soul" of sacred theology.[30]

---

30. According to the Fathers of the Second Vatican Council, "the 'study of the sacred page' should be the very soul of sacred theology" (*Dei Verbum*, no. 24). One might want to recall two noteworthy recent instances in which two eminent popes display in their own apostolic exercise of *sacra doctrina* the way in which the interpretation of scripture is "the very soul" of sacred theology: in his famous Wednesday audiences stretching from 1979 to 1984, Pope St. John Paul II advanced a profound theological exegesis of the first chapters of Genesis, the Song of Songs, Tobit, the Gospels, and the Letter to the Ephesians into a theologically fully fleshed out and philosophically undergirded theology of the body. See John Paul II, *Man and Woman He Created Them: A Theology of the Body*, trans. Michael Waldstein (Boston: Pauline Books and Media, 2011). One generation later, Pope Benedict XVI undertook a profound retrieval of the concrete face of Jesus by way of a synthetic and theologically sensitive exegesis of the synoptic Gospels. Arguably, this effort can be understood (as Pope Benedict XVI himself did) as a modern correlate to Aquinas's treatment of the life of Christ in the Third Part of the *Summa Theologiae*: Pope Benedict XVI, *Jesus of Nazareth: From the Baptism in the Jordan to the Transfiguration* (New York: Doubleday, 2007), *Jesus of Nazareth: Holy Week: From the Entrance into Jerusalem to the Resurrection* (San Francisco, Calif.: Ignatius Press, 2011), and *Jesus of Nazareth: The Infancy Narratives* (New York: Image Books, 2012).

In the following, I do not wish to map out in any further detail the relationship between sacred theology and metaphysics. Rather, I wish to turn to one of the central principles that metaphysics inquires into—the principle of finality. I wish to argue that a sufficient grasp of the principle of finality is indispensable if sacred theology is to secure the intelligibility of supernatural divine revelation and overcome the typical modern theological mistakes of naturalizing the supernatural on the one hand and, on the other hand, of rendering nature vacuous of any proportionate finality for the sake of the integralist vision of a pure supernaturalism. I will argue that the metaphysical principle of finality as advanced and defended by Thomas Aquinas affords, first, the properly nuanced understanding of the natural desire for the vision of God (and thereby secures the intelligibility of supernatural divine revelation and the gratuity of the beatific vision) and affords, second, the properly nuanced distinction between nature and grace (and secures thereby the intelligibility and distinct surpassing gratuity of salvation and deification in differentiation from the primordial gratuity of creation and original righteousness). The following account of finality begins with an important passage in the *Summa Theologiae*, but subsequently relies almost completely on the argumentation Aquinas advances in the third book of his *Summa contra Gentiles*. In both works, one can observe well how metaphysics plays an indispensable role as privileged instrument in an enterprise that is essentially that of sacred theology.

THE PRINCIPLE OF FINALITY

The exact formulation of the principle of finality is "every agent acts for an end." "Agent" denotes "thing" in the widest sense, for things do not simply exist but have the potency to operate in ways characteristic of them. The universal scope of the principle of finality is widely rejected by modern philosophers who adopt the suppositions of Cartesian mechanism, Spinozist monism, Hobbesian materialism, Lockean empiricism, or Kantian transcendental idealism, let alone contemporary revivals of Humean skepticism and Nietzschean transhumanism. To put the matter differently and more directly:

one way to conceive of modernity is thus—as the intellectual, moral, and political consequences that have ensued from the loss or rejection of the universal principle of finality. In our pervasively anti-teleological age, any attempt at recovering or defending the principle of finality suffers the predictable fate of being first misunderstood, then misconstrued, and eventually dismissed.[31] A comprehensive defense of the principle of finality against the educated among its contemporary detractors is, of course, quite impossible here. However, a first step in this direction might consist in offering an accurate presentation of the principle of finality as initially defended by Aristotle and as subsequently considered in its universal scope by Aquinas.

Aquinas opens the twelfth lecture of his commentary on the second book of Aristotle's *Physics* this way:

[Here] the philosopher ... clarifies certain things which he had assumed, namely, that nature acts for an end and that in some things necessity is not from the causes which are prior in being (which are the matter and the moving cause), but from the posterior causes, which are the form and the end.... He says ... first ... that nature is among the number of causes which act for the sake of something.[32]

Then he steps out of the role of strictly commenting on Aristotle's text and states: "This is important with reference to the problem of providence. For things which do not know the end do not tend toward the end unless they are directed by one who does know, as the arrow is directed by the archer. Hence if nature acts for an end, it is necessary that it be ordered by someone who is intelligent. This is

---

31. For an excellent history of teleological thinking from Plato to the twentieth century and for an astute analysis, engagement, and critique of non- and anti-teleological thinking in contemporary philosophy of science and especially in the philosophy of biology, see Spaemann and Löw, *Natürliche Ziele*; for a still relevant Thomist engagement of modern anti-teleological thinking, see Gilson, *From Aristotle to Darwin and Back Again*; and for a lucid and still highly relevant presentation and defense of the Aristotelian-Thomist metaphysics, see Réginald Garrigou-Lagrange, OP, *Le Réalisme du Principe de Finalité* (Paris: Desclee de Brouwer et Cie, 1932), translated into German as *Der Realismus der Finalität*, trans. Joachim Volkmann (Heusenstamm: Editiones Scholasticae, 2011).

32. Thomas Aquinas, *Commentary on Aristotle's* Physics, trans. Richard J. Blackwell, Richard J. Spath, and W. Edmund Thirkel (Notre Dame, Ind.: Dumb Ox Books, 1999), *In octo libros Physicorum Aristotelis expositio* [hereafter "*In Phys.*"], lib. II, 8, lect. 12 (198b10–33), 125 (Marietti, no. 250).

the work of providence."³³ As Robert Spaemann and Reinhard Löw, in their important work on the history and rediscovery of teleological thinking, rightly observe, Aquinas's statement did not remain without significant consequences.³⁴ While Aristotle understood the finality of human rational agency to be embedded in the finality of nature, he agreed with Plato, who in the tenth book of his *Laws* presented the argument that divine intelligence precedes the finality of nature. Drawing upon Plato and Aristotle, Aquinas argues that the finality of nature must be conceived of as being embedded in an encompassing finality of surpassing intelligence. In subsequent centuries, Aquinas's thesis led to consequences quite contrary to his intention. With the help of the thesis that the causal nature of an end necessarily presupposes a consciousness that anticipates the end, late medieval theologians—to be precise, nominalists like Ockham and Buridan—eliminated teleology from nature. A deeply voluntarist theology came to evacuate the finality of nature.³⁵ The transposition of finality from nature into the divine consciousness and will resulted in understanding the world as devoid of intrinsic finality and instead as a causally determined mechanism of surpassing intricacy that is informed by a finality completely extrinsic to it because superimposed upon it by the inscrutable will of God the world-architect.³⁶

In contrast to this later development, Aquinas understands finality to be intrinsic to natural things. The most fundamental division of being is that between potency and act. Whatever is, is either pure act or a unit composed of two intrinsic principles, potency and act. Hence the deepest root of the metaphysical principle of finality in being is this: passive potency is ordered to the act of reception of form and active potency is the act of the production of form. Therefore, the very constitution of a material substance, a first substance,

33. Ibid.
34. Spaemann and Löw, *Natürliche Ziele*, 68–71.
35. Ibid., 82–88. For an accessible presentation of the Nominalist position and a lucid initial rebuttal, see Edward Feser, *Scholastic Metaphysics: A Contemporary Introduction* (Heusenstamm: Editiones Scholasticae, 2014), 94–100.
36. On the radical transition from classical teleology to modern mechanism, see the instructive study by Simon Oliver, *Philosophy, God, and Motion* (London: Routledge, 2005).

already bespeaks the primacy of final causality. Without act being the finality of potency, both potency and act would become unintelligible. Potency is essentially ordered toward act as is the sense of sight to seeing. This is a fundamental insight Aquinas articulates already in his early *De principiis naturae*:

> The end is the cause of the causality of the efficient cause, because it makes the efficient cause be an efficient cause. And similarly, the end makes the matter be the matter, and the form be the form, since the matter does not acquire a form except on account of the end, and the form does not perfect the matter except on account of the end. Whence it is said that the end is the cause of causes, because it is the cause of the causality in all the causes.[37]

Furthermore, all things composed of essence and existence and all material substances composed also of matter and form subsist in virtue of the substantial form of a specific nature which bequeaths distinct ends to the particular substance. Finality thus accounts for the most fundamental structure of finite being.

As already mentioned, the exact formulation of the principle of finality is "every agent acts for an end" (*omne agens agit propter finem*). The most condensed formulation of the argument for natural finality that Aquinas advances can be found in *ST* I-II (q. 1, a. 2). In the following, I will supplement Aquinas's argumentation there with sections from the third book of the *Summa contra Gentiles* and from his commentary on Aristotle's *Physics*.

Every Agent Acts for an End

Consider the programmatic prologue with which Aquinas sets the stage for *ST* I-II:

> Since, as John of Damascus states, [the human being] is said to be made to God's image, in so far as the image implies *an intelligent being endowed with free-will and self-movement*: now that we have treated of the exemplar, that is, God, and of those things which came forth from the power of God in accordance with His will; it remains for us to treat of His image, that is, [the

---

37. Aquinas, *De principiis naturae*, chap. 4. The citation is from Joseph Bobik, *Aquinas on Matter and Form and the Elements: A Translation and Interpretation of the* De Principiis Naturae *and the* De Mixtione Elementorum *of St. Thomas Aquinas* (Notre Dame, Ind.: University of Notre Dame Press, 1998), 60.

human being], in as much as he too is the principle of his actions, as having free-will and control of his actions. (*ST* I-II, prol.)

The metaphysical relationship between the human being and God is that of image and exemplar. The perfections characteristic of the exemplar are to be found in the image. These perfections are necessarily qualified by the particular finite ontological constitution of the image. As the crowning perfection that the exemplar and the image share is to be the principle of one's own actions, this perfection is to be treated first. Consequently, right after the prologue, Aquinas treats in the first question of human finality in general and the nature of the ultimate end in particular. In the very first article of this first question Aquinas establishes that all human actions must be for the sake of an end. Final causality is constitutive of human action. Actions that are properly called human arise from a deliberate will. And insofar as the object of the will is an end or good, all human actions are for the sake of an end or good. This seems straightforward enough and a time-pressed contemporary reader might be ready to turn to the article that treats the question of whether human actions are what they are by reason of their end. But, as it turns out, this is not the topic of the second article. Rather, in the second article Aquinas raises the question of whether other beings also act for an end or whether acting for an end is proper to human beings. Eager to get to the punchline, a contemporary speed-reader might be prepared to skip over this article and move on. What else in the world should be acting for an end besides human beings? And why would Aquinas even raise such a question?

It is worth recalling at this point that the audience for which Aquinas wrote the *Summa Theologiae* was most likely a particular group of rather advanced beginners, Dominican students sent to the *studia generalia* to undertake advanced studies in sacred theology, in short, to be introduced to sacred theology as an argumentative science (*scientia argumentativa*). They were what we might today call graduate students, already schooled in Aristotelian logic and familiar with the content of scripture.[38] Hence Aquinas does not have to

---

38. See Leonard E. Boyle, *The Setting of the "Summa Theologiae" of Saint Thomas Aquinas* (Toronto: Pontifical Institute of Mediaeval Studies, 1982); Jenkins, *Knowledge and*

tell them explicitly that his demonstration in the first article—that acting for an end is proper to a rational creature—is a so-called *quia* ("that") demonstration (a proof of the fact) that moves from the effect to the cause. Nor does he have to tell them that in the second article he is advancing to the stricter so-called *propter quid* ("why") demonstration (a proof by means of causes) that moves from the cause to the effect. For here he proves that the predicate "acting for an end" (*agere propter finem*) is proper to the rational agent precisely because it is proper to every agent. And being proper to every agent means that acting for an end is common to all agents.[39]

The three objections Aquinas raises against his own line of argumentation at the beginning of the second article might very well reflect the unexamined hermeneutical pre-understanding with which an impatient contemporary reader might approach this article: first, knowledge of the end seems to be a crucial condition for the ability to act for an end. But knowledge of the end presupposes consciousness. Second, to act for an end means ordering one's action to this very end, and such ordering seems to be the work of reason. And third, the end or the good is the proper object of the will, but the will is the rational appetite, and therefore to act for an end must belong properly to the rational being.

These three objections seem to settle the matter and a rushed contemporary reader might as well press on, eager to leave behind what seems like an all too medieval digression. Aquinas, however, deems it important to linger and argue against these seemingly obvious objections that the principle of finality is necessarily universal, that not only the rational agent but indeed every agent acts for an end. Quite obviously, Aquinas uses the term "agent" (*agens*) an-

---

Faith, chap. 3 and 215–19; and M. Michèle Mulchahey, *"First the Bow is Bent in Study": Dominican Education before 1350* (Toronto: Pontifical Institute of Mediaeval Studies, 1998).

39. Aquinas simply assumes that the advanced beginner for whom the *Summa Theologiae* was composed would recall at this point what he had written in *ST* I, q. 2, a. 2: "Demonstrations can be made in two ways: One is through the cause, and is called [*propter quid*], and this is to argue from what is prior absolutely. The other is through the effect, and is called a demonstration [*quia*]; this is to argue from what is prior relatively only to us." For Aristotle and Aquinas on *propter quid* ("why") demonstrations, see Aquinas, *Exposition libri Posteriorum* I, lect. 1–22, 4–103 (Marietti, nos. 7–192), and for *quia* ("that") demonstrations, see lect. 23–25, 104–14 (Marietti, nos. 192–216).

alogically. For in the "sed contra" he marshals for his authority Aristotle who demonstrates in the second book of the *Physics* that not only the intellect but also nature acts for a purpose. So "agent" can refer to a natural agent, like fire or water (nowadays we would speak of a chemical "agent"); to a living but non-sentient agent, a plant; to a sentient and cognizant agent, an animal; and to a rational agent, a human person.

Aquinas's argumentation in his reply is indirect, which indicates that he regards the principle "every agent acts for an end" as a first principle, that is, a principle that cannot be deduced from prior principles but must be demonstrated indirectly by showing that denying the principle leads inevitably to absurd consequences. His argument proceeds in three steps:

(1) If in a number of interlocked causes the first cause is removed, the others are necessarily also removed.

(2) Matter does not receive form unless it is moved to do so by an agent. Hence, some efficient cause accounts for matter receiving form.

(3) An agent does not move except out of an intention for the end.

At this point an attentive contemporary reader might exclaim: "Sleight of hand! Consciousness and intentionality based on reason are smuggled into the argument!" But Aquinas would simply point out that if an agent were not determined to some particular effect, it would not do one thing rather than another. At which point an even more reflective contemporary reader might begin to wonder whether the sleight of hand might not after all occur in the modern understanding of efficient causality where it is tacitly assumed that efficient causality simply entails determination to one end. But it is precisely this function, the determination to one end that Aquinas understands to be the *proprium* of final causality. The final cause is the first of all causes, the cause of causes, precisely because it predetermines the efficient cause to some particular effect. The following *reductio ad absurdum* of the denial of final causality already served above for the rebuttal of the sleight-of-hand charge: "If the agent were not determinate to some particular effect, it would not do one thing rather than another: consequently, in order that it produce a determinate effect, it must, of necessity, be determined to some certain one, which has the nature of an end" (*ST* I-II, q. 1, a. 2).

In his *magnum opus*, *The Way toward Wisdom*, the eminent Dominican Thomist Benedict Ashley summarizes concisely Aquinas's line of argument:

This final causality or teleology as understood by Aristotle and Aquinas, is ... nothing more than precisely this predetermination of a natural efficient cause to produce a specifically determined effect (*provided that this effect is considered in its productive rather than its destructive character*).... As Aristotle said, "Final causality is the cause of causes," since nothing occurs in natural processes except through efficient causes that are predetermined to produce effects that have the regularity of a predictable probability.[40]

Of course, not everything that acts for an end attains its end. Not every terminus is the natural end of a thing. Something might impede the natural motion toward an end. Things do indeed happen by chance. But as Aquinas argues, chance itself presupposes finality:

Among inanimate things the contingency of causes is due to imperfection and deficiency, for by their nature they are determined to one result which they always achieve, unless there be some impediment arising either from a weakness of their power, or on the part of an external agent, or because of the unsuitability of the matter. And for this reason, natural agent causes are not capable of varied results; rather, in most cases, they produce their effect in the same way, failing to do so but rarely. (*SCG* III.73.2)

Chance becomes intelligible as the contingency of causes, a contingency that comes about in three ways: (1) by way of a weakness of the power, that is, a deficiency in relation to the intrinsic finality of the entity; (2) by way of external agency, that is, by way of natural lines of causality converging accidentally and thereby impeding the motion to some natural end; and (3) by way of matter which is the fundamental principle of chance and is as such characterized by an inherent fallibility. This unique feature of matter also presupposes the principle of finality. For the fallibility of matter can only

---

40. Benedict M. Ashley, OP, *The Way toward Wisdom: An Interdisciplinary and Intercultural Introduction to Metaphysics* (Notre Dame, Ind.: University of Notre Dame Press, 2006), 323–24.

be named because matter as potency is ordered toward form as act. Insight into the negative aspect, fallibility, presupposes insight into the positive aspect, finality. In short, we know when something fails to attain its end to begin with because we see that it routinely acts in a certain way. So even failure—precisely inasmuch as we are able to recognize it as failure—is a testament to the universal applicability of the principle of finality. Hence, each of the three ways chance comes about presupposes the principle of finality; hence, without the presupposition of the principle of finality, the concept of chance becomes vacuous.

But not only chance presupposes finality. Something similar is the case with fault (*peccatum*), the absence of something that is due to a certain nature. Fault in natural things presupposes natural finality: "There is no fault to be found, except in the case of things that are for the sake of an end. A fault is never attributed to an agent, if the failure is related to something that is not the agent's end" (*SCG* III.2.7). Absent the natural finality of distinct species, the notion of fault, the absence of what is due to a certain nature, becomes meaningless.

Hence, neither the reality of chance nor the reality of fault can undermine the universal principle of finality. Nor does consciousness of the end as characteristic of the finality of rational agency evacuate natural finality. For noteworthily, Aquinas's demonstration of natural finality does not depend on whether the agent knows and hence consciously intends the end. "Intending an end" does not require consciousness in the natural agent. Rather, the structure of finality—arriving from some determinate principle at some determinate end—is isomorphic in the agency of a rational agent and in the activity of a sentient or natural agent. Aquinas states:

Just as the entire likeness of the result achieved [*tota similitudo effectus*] by actions of an intelligent agent exists in the intellect that preconceives it, so, too, does the likeness of a natural resultant [*similitudo naturalis effectus*] pre-exist in the natural agent; and as a consequence of this, the action is determined to a definite result. For fire gives rise to fire, and an olive to an olive. Therefore, the agent that acts with nature as its principle is just as much directed to a definite end, in its action, as is the agent that acts through the intellect as its principle. (*SCG* III.2.6)

While the structure of finality obtains in all agents, the different constitution of natural substances accounts for the analogical use of the terms "agent" and "end." Rational agents act consciously for the sake of an end (*directive formaliter*); they know the end as end and assign means to achieve the end. Animals know the end only materially (*materialiter tantum*) and are drawn to it by instinct. Plants and other natural agents merely execute the end (*executive tantum*).[41]

Even if the cosmos were indeed eternal and all species eternally stable and fixed—as Aristotle presumed to be the case—there would still remain the question of the preordination of final causality. For while an eternal cosmos and the eternity of stable and fixed species would display the structure of finality, they could not account for its existence. A cosmos that is not eternal and that furthermore suggests a stunning development from the simplest inorganic elements to exceedingly complex forms of organic life only ups the ante. Whence the preordination of finality in the *de facto* extant universe?

Natural finality has an undeniable immediate *a posteriori* evidence and yet it is impossible for natural finality to account for its preordination: this is the starting point for Aquinas's fifth way. Remember, it is the immediate evidence of natural finality that stands at the center of the so-called fifth way: "Natural bodies act for an end, and this is evident from their acting always, or nearly always, in the same way, so as to obtain the best result" (*ST* I, q. 2, a. 3).[42] Like the other four ways, the fifth way is an inductive *quia* demonstration from effect to cause. It *does not* rely on the argument that ascertains the principle that every agent necessarily acts for an end but rather merely on the immediate *a posteriori* evidence of the principle of finality. The fifth way, from the governance of the world (*ex gubernatione rerum*), goes this way:

We see that things which lack intelligence, such as natural bodies, act for an end, and this is evident from their acting always, or nearly always, in

---

41. Réginald Garrigou-Lagrange, OP, *De Beatitudine, de Actibus Humanis et de Habitibus: Commentarius in Summam Theologiam S. Thomae Ia-IIae qq. 1–54* (Turin: R. Berruti, 1951), 38–39.

42. While a defense of the fifth way is not the purpose of the following reflections, a renewed appreciation of the fact that the fifth way is embedded in the epistemically fundamental *a posteriori* evidence of natural finality is a welcome side effect of Aquinas's defense of natural teleology.

the same way, so as to obtain the best result. Hence it is plain that not [by chance], but [by purposeful intention] [*non a casu sed ex intentione*], do they achieve their end. Now whatever lacks intelligence cannot move toward an end, unless it be directed by some being endowed with knowledge and intelligence; as the arrow is shot to its mark by the archer. Therefore some intelligent being exists by whom all natural beings are directed to their end; and this being we call God. (*ST* I, q. 2, a. 3)

The arrow—directed by the archer, released from the bow, and heading toward the aim—serves as Aquinas's prime model for natural finality. Those things that lack reason tend to the end by natural inclination. As they do not know the nature of an end by themselves they cannot ordain anything to an end, but they can be ordained to an end by another. The analogy of the archer and the arrow reappears in *ST* I-II (q. 1, a. 2). Here the analogy prepares and illustrates Aquinas's fundamental thesis about the way God governs the whole of irrational nature: "The entire irrational nature is in comparison to God as an instrument to the principal agent." The arrow, as instrument, relates to the principal agent, the archer, as the entire irrational nature, as instrument, relates to the principal agent, God.

But the analogy of the archer and the arrow entails a deficiency of which Aquinas is fully aware. Already in his discussion of divine governance, he addresses the matter and offers an improved analogy:

The natural necessity inherent in those beings which are determined to a particular thing, is a kind of impression from God, directing them to their end; as the necessity whereby an arrow is moved so as to fly towards a certain point is an impression from the archer, and not from the arrow. But there is a difference, in as much as that which creatures receive from God is their nature, while that which natural things receive from man in addition to their nature is somewhat violent. Wherefore, as the violent necessity in the movement of the arrow shows the action of the archer, so the natural necessity of things shows the government of Divine Providence. (*ST* I, q. 103, a. 1, ad 3)

God as the principal agent of the instrument—the totality of irrational nature—impresses finality by giving things their respective natures so that they act for ends according to their nature in accordance with the overarching will of the divine governor. God governs by way of natural necessity—the instrumentality of proper secondary causes—and not, as the analogy of the archer and the arrow might suggest, by way of violent necessity.

Now recall the third objection noted above, one of the three objections a hurried contemporary reader might have been all too ready to endorse. The end or the good is the proper object of the will; but the will is the rational appetite, and therefore acting for an end must belong properly to a rational being. In his reply to the objection, Aquinas agrees with the fundamental line of the objection, but then applies the analogy of the governor:

> The object of the will is the end and the universal good [*bonum universale*]. Consequently there can be no will in those things that lack reason and intellect, since they cannot apprehend the universal; but they have a natural appetite or a sensitive appetite, determinate to some particular good. Now it is clear that particular causes are moved by a universal cause: thus the governor of a city, who intends the common good, moves, by his command, all the particular departments of the city. Consequently all things that lack reason are, of necessity, moved to their particular ends by some rational will which extends to the universal good, namely by the Divine Will. (*ST* I-II, q. 1, a. 2, ad 3)

Of course, differently from the governor, who acts for an end, the common good (*bonum commune*) of the city, God does not act for an end. Otherwise God would not be the final end of everything, the common good of the whole universe. However, as Aquinas observes in *De veritate*, the divine goodness is, so to speak, the end of God's free acts, yet not in the sense of the divine goodness being the final end of God's acts, as if God were—*horribile dictu*—a self-caused cause (*causa sui*), a plain contradiction in terms of what first cause means, namely uncaused cause—but rather in the sense of *ratio sui*: the divine goodness is the reason or purpose for all of God's free acts *ad extra*.[43] With this important qualification in place one can state that the principle of finality indeed pertains to all of reality.

Let us recapitulate. For Aquinas natural finality is emphatically not simply an entailment of an already presupposed theism. Of course, Jews, Christians, and Muslims are committed to divine prov-

---

43. "Divina bonitas sit eius voluntati ratio volendi omnia, sicut sua essentia est ei ratio cognoscendi omnia" (*De ver.*, q. 23, a. 4). For a helpful commentary on this crucial but complex matter, see Garrigou-Lagrange, *De Beatitudine*, 39.

idence and governance and hence would hold as an axiomatic entailment of the doctrine of creation *ex nihilo* that finality suffuses the whole cosmos. But then again, the will of God might be so absolutely mysterious (as in versions of Christian nominalism and Muslim voluntarism) and the structure of creation so thoroughly devastated by the Fall (as in traditional Lutheranism and Calvinism, and also in Jansenism) that believing in God's providence and governance becomes a matter of blind faith and any natural finality whatsoever comes to be hidden in the abyss of the divine will or buried under the ruinous debris of a devastated cosmos sustained and preserved solely by a completely extrinsic and utterly mysterious divine help. Aquinas will have none of this. He consistently rejects voluntarism in the doctrine of God as well as devastationism in the doctrine of creation. Drawing upon Aristotle, Aquinas argues that to deny natural finality only leads to the very destruction of what "nature" means. As if moved by some premonition of the philosophical confusions and errors that the not-too-distant future would hold, Aquinas, in his commentary on Aristotle's *Physics*, issues a surprisingly prescient warning:

> Aristotle shows ... that ... one who says that nature does not act for the sake of something, destroys nature and the things which are according to nature. For those things are said to be according to nature which are moved continuously by some intrinsic principle until they arrive at some end—not to some contingent end, and not from any principle to any end, but from a determinate principle to a determinate end.[44]

---

44. *In Phys.* II, 8, lect. 14, 199a34–b33 (Marietti, no. 267); translation from Aquinas, *Commentary on Aristotle's* Physics, 133. This insight is of great theological significance, as the arguably greatest Catholic dogmatic theologian of the nineteenth century, Matthias Joseph Scheeben, already made plain in the still important work of his youth, *Nature and Grace*. There he discusses philosophically and dogmatically how the idea of nature includes the idea of its tendency to its own proper good; otherwise, it is not a nature. Scheeben sees this principle worked out in the rejection of Monoenergism and Monotheletism in the seventh century, inasmuch as the latter two become a *de facto* revival of Eutychianism, i.e., by denying Christ his operation, etc., they deny him his nature. If nature is not intrinsically ordered to a proportionate end, it is no longer a nature. Nature is inherently teleological. Its form is determined from the ground up by the end for which it is formed, whence its form is the *quo*, that by which it attains its end. Losing this metaphysical insight casts profound darkness over what is theologically at stake between dyotheletist orthodoxy and monotheletist heterodoxy. See Matthias Joseph Scheeben, *Nature and Grace*, trans. Cyril Vollert, SJ (St. Louis, Mo.: Herder, 1954; reprinted in Eugene, Ore.: Wipf and Stock, 2009), 52–53.

Now it also becomes clear why the often misunderstood principle "nature does nothing in vain" is but a variant of the principle of finality. "In vain" means "for no end," "for no purpose." Doing "nothing in vain" is equivalent to doing "everything for the sake of an end."

If instead of denying the finality of nature, one happens to come to acknowledge it, one has indeed reached a new point of departure for advancing to a deeper understanding of nature, namely nature as art (*ars*) that ineluctably gives witness to a surpassing artist: "Nature is nothing but a certain kind of art, i.e., the divine art, impressed upon things, by which these things are moved to a determinate end. It is as if the shipbuilder were able to give to timbers that by which they would move themselves to take the form of a ship."[45]

Human art is nothing but an imitation of nature, but nature is nothing but the art of a transcendent divine artist. As transcendent first cause the divine artist employs, of course, a whole created order of real secondary causality. Hence, the "divine art, impressed upon things" would be gravely misunderstood were it to be taken along mechanistic lines as a putatively direct divine manipulation or design of unformed "stuff." In such an "intelligent design" scenario, God, the transcendent first cause and final end, would be reduced to the great Demiurge and proper secondary causality to a mere counterfeit.

With the proper understanding of nature as the art of a transcendent divine artist we have reached an appropriate point of transition from Aquinas's demonstration of the principle "every agent acts for an end" to his line of argumentation from this principle to God as final cause of the universe and of each human being.[46] For this purpose, I will turn to the third book of the *Summa contra Gentiles*. Aquinas's argument culminates in the thesis that all things tend to become like God by imitating the divine goodness. The first step in the ascent to this teleological summit is the insight that the end of everything is a good.

---

45. *In Phys.*, 134 (Marietti, no. 268).

46. For a lucid treatment of this complex topic, see Oliva Blanchette, *The Perfection of the Universe according to Aquinas: A Teleological Cosmology* (University Park: Pennsylvania State University Press, 1992).

The End of Everything Is a Good

The principle that every agent acts for an end can be considered in two ways: under the aspect of causality and under the aspect of terminus. So far I have considered finality under the aspect of causality, but now I shall turn briefly to the aspect of terminus. As already mentioned above, not every terminus has the character of a *telos*. Death is not the *telos* of a living being. Rather, the terminus that has the character of a *telos* must be somehow appropriate or fitting (*conveniens*) to the agent, "because the agent would not be inclined to it except by virtue of some agreement (*aliquam convenientiam*) with it" (*SCG* III.3.2). The natural end or *telos* (*debitus finis*) of everything is that "in which the appetitive inclination [*appetitus*] of an agent or mover, and of the thing moved, finds its rest" (*SCG* III.3.3) because this state is perfective of its being. But that which all things desire for their perfection is a good. As Aristotle adroitly states: "The good is that which all desire" (*SCG* III.3.3).[47] The end of each and every created thing is a good, a point of termination for the appetitive inclination, be it the ontological appetite, the sense appetite, or the rational appetite. Aquinas concludes: "If, in fact, nothing tends toward a thing as an end, unless this thing is a good, it is therefore necessary that the good, as good, be the end. Therefore, that which is the highest good is, from the highest point of view, the end of all things" (*SCG* III.17.2). As God is the highest good and God is one, as Aquinas has established by way of cumulative argumentation (in *SCG* I.10–41), it follows that all things are ordered to one end that is God.

All Things Are Ordered to One End That Is God

Recall that the final cause holds the first place among the causes.[48] For it is the final cause to which all other causes owe the fact that they are causes in act, because—as has already been demonstrated—an agent acts only for the sake of an end. Matter is brought to formal act by an efficient cause. Therefore matter actually becomes the matter of the particular thing and a form becomes the form of the selfsame

---

47. Aristotle, *Nicomachean Ethics* I.1, 1094a1.
48. In *SCG* III.17, Aquinas advances seven arguments for this thesis. I will present only the very last argument.

thing through the efficient causality of the agent and consequently through the final cause. But, as Aquinas argues, in the case of interlocked causes, that is, in the case of a so-called *per se* series of causes, the posterior end is the cause of the preceding end being introduced as an end. For a thing is not moved *here and now* by a proximate end unless for the sake of a last end. Consequently: the last end is the first cause of all; to be first cause of all must be appropriate to the first being, that is, to God. Hence, God is the end of all things.

God Is the End of All Things

But how can God be the end of all things? Aquinas distinguishes between two senses of end. There is, first, the end prior in intention and posterior in being. It is the kind of end a rational agent sets up and reaches by his or her own action. There is, second, the end that precedes in the causal order and that also precedes in existence. God is the end of all things in this second sense of end as something preexisting to be attained by everything according to its proper mode. Lest Aquinas be misunderstood at this point, it is imperative to recall that everything that is directed to God as its end is infinitely unequal to the end and therefore attains the end only proportionate to its specific nature.

But *nota bene*: not only is God not the end in the sense of something set up or produced by things. God is also not the end in the sense that something could be added to God by the action of a thing, as if God's own goodness could be increased by being attained by other things. God is the source of enrichment, but is in no way enriched by other things attaining their perfection. For nothing extrinsic to God can be an end to God's goodness; if it were, God's goodness would be imperfect and would not be the end of all things. Moreover, God is not in potency of obtaining something: "Things are not ordered to God as to an end *for which* something may be obtained, but rather so that they may attain Himself from Himself, according to their measure, since He is their end" (*SCG* III.18.5; see also *ST* I, q. 44, a. 4). While the perfect good is in no ways enriched by other things, it is essential for the perfect good to communicate itself "in the sense that an end is said to move" (*ST* I, q. 5, a. 4, ad 2).

The principle that God is the absolute source of enrichment and in no way enriched by other things has famously been challenged especially by process theologians, but also by modern theologians who stood too much under the spell of Hegel's philosophical system of the comprehensive self-differentiation of the Absolute. Abandoning this fundamental principle means unavoidably to submit God to a surpassing finality that encompasses God and the world (Hegel and process theologians) or God and the unity of the created and the uncreated Sophia (Sergius Bulgakov). Using the Trinitarian dogma in the wake of Hegel's and Schelling's theosophic speculations to posit a history in God—in order to justify the overturning of the principle that God is the absolute source of enrichment, the perfection of plenitude and beatitude (*SCG* I.40 and also 100–102)—leads to nothing but the very subjugation of God to the principle of finality, and, more broadly, to the re-mythologization of the Nicene faith.

But how is God the end of all things in the sense of their enrichment by God's goodness or by their attaining divine goodness? Aquinas argues that if all things tend toward God as the ultimate end, so that they may attain God's goodness—according to their measure—it follows that the ultimate end of things is to become like God, to imitate God. Hence, all things tend to become like God by imitating the divine goodness.

All Things Tend to Become like God by Imitating the Divine Goodness

It would obviously be wrong to take "imitation" in a narrow anthropomorphic sense. Instead, Aquinas employs this term in a comprehensive metaphysical sense. Conceived in this way, imitation is the consequence of three truths:

(1) Each thing tends toward a likeness of divine goodness as its end.

(2) Each thing becomes like the divine goodness in respect of all the things that belong to its proper goodness.

(3) If this is the case then the goodness of the thing not only consists in its mere existence (participation in being) but in all the things needed for its perfection.

All things imitate God in their substantial subsistence (*actus primus*), their first perfection, and in their proper operation, their second perfection (*actus secundus*). Hence, imitation is not some finality superadded to the natural finality of things. Rather, imitation designates the ontological status of finite finality itself (*SCG* III.20).

A created being imitates God by perfecting its proper nature via acts through which it attains its end. A higher level of this imitation is to bring other members of one's species into being and thereby to contribute to the continuation and perfection of the species:

> Since a cause, as such, is superior to the thing caused, it is evident that to tend to the divine likeness in the manner of something that causes others is appropriate to higher types of beings.... Again, a thing must be perfect in itself before it can cause another thing.... So, this final perfection comes to a thing in order that it may exist as the cause of others. Therefore, since a created thing tends to the divine likeness in many ways, this one whereby it seeks the divine likeness by being the cause of others takes the ultimate place. (*SCG* III.21.7–8)

Being a cause of others is initiated by the finality toward which the substantial form of created things is ordered by way of its proper inclination: the natural appetite, the sense appetite, or the rational appetite, the will.

In the *locus classicus* of discussing a crucial application of the principle of finality, the natural law, Aquinas refers to these appetites as natural inclinations (*ST* I-II, q. 94, a. 2). All substances have the natural inclination to preserve their own being, according to their nature; all animals have in addition the natural inclination toward sexual reproduction and rearing of the young. As rational animals, human beings have furthermore the natural inclination to good according to the nature of human reason, that is, to know the truth about God and to live in society.

Following the order of natural inclinations, being the cause of others occurs first of all physically through reproduction. It occurs secondly among rational beings through the labor of parents passing on to children language, culture, a life of virtue, and, most importantly, the virtue of justice. It occurs, third, intellectually, in the discursive and dialectical labor characteristic of the pedagogical relationship between teacher and student in regard to the formation of the intellectual virtues, to acquiring knowledge, and gaining understanding and wisdom such that ideally the student himself will become able to elicit insight and foster wisdom in others. Last but not least, being a cause of others occurs in the supernatural order by way of gratuitous grace that contributes to their justification and thereby enables the upbuilding of the ecclesial body of Christ (*ST* I-II, q. 111, a. 1).

Significantly, Aquinas closes his discussion that all things imitate the divine goodness by being causes of others by adducing two weighty theological authorities: the Apostle Paul and the one whom medieval theologians held to be a most brilliant philosopher-convert of St. Paul's preaching in Athens—Dionysius the Areopagite. Aquinas adduces first the theological authority of Dionysius: "Of all things, it is more divine to become a co-worker with God" in order to seal it with the superior apostolic authority of St. Paul who refers to the relationship to the faithful: "We are God's fellow workers, you are God's field, God's building."[49]

In the natural order, the teacher of wisdom who conveys truth and brings about understanding, thereby eliciting a desire for the supreme good, acts in the highest mode of imitating God. In the supernatural order, those who imitate God in the highest degree are the teacher of divine wisdom, the preacher of the Word of God, the interpreter of tongues, and last but not least those who through their example of holy poverty inflame others with the desire to follow the poor Christ.

The Comprehensive Finality of the Universe

In sum, precisely because God is the final end and therefore the first cause of the universe, the principle of finality governs the whole created order in the extant order of divine providence comprising creation, salvation, and divinization. The final end of all God's acts *ad extra* is God, the sovereign goodness. Aquinas observes that God wills "Himself as the end, and other things as ordained to that end; inasmuch as it befits the divine goodness that other things should

---

49. The passage from Dionysius in *SCG* III.21.8 is from *Caelestis hierarchia*, cap. III, no. 2, and the passage from St. Paul is found in 1 Cor 3:9 (RSV).

be partakers therein" (*ST* I, q. 19, a. 2). The divine goodness is the end to which the divine will directs all the eternal decrees that efficaciously unfold the extant order of divine providence, creation, salvation, and divinization, in short, the diverse modes of participation in the divine goodness.

Because the universe is created by God according to God's goodness, it is essentially ordered to God as the final end. Hence, in the created universe every created agent, constituted by a specific nature, acts for an end that is proportionate to and perfective of that nature and is directed to the final end of the universe. In the case of the irrational creature, the specific end is effected by the sense-appetite or the natural appetite. In the case of the rational creature, the determination to one, that is, to the specific end is effected by the rational appetite, the will. After having considered the finality of the whole universe (including rational beings), a crucial task remains, namely to consider in which way God is the final end of each individual human being.

The Natural Finality of the Intellect and the Imitation of God by the Rational Being

When Aquinas applies to rational beings the principle that all things become like God by imitating the divine goodness, he makes a fundamental and far-reaching distinction. It is the distinction between those agents whose second perfection comes about simply by way of their *nature* versus those agents whose second perfection comes about by way of their *intellect*. The distinction is between "natural agents" and "rational agents." It will be crucial for the following to realize that in this important distinction "nature" does not mean the *essence* in respect to its principle of operation but rather *physis* which denotes the teleological axiom "nature is determined *ad unum*." The finality of subrational beings leads not only to one end, but also by one path.[50]

---

50. Needless to say, this axiom applies less and less the higher one moves in the order of living beings, because quite obviously advanced animals do pursue their end of integral species fulfillment by a variety of paths. How would this axiom and therefore the distinction between "nature" as *physis* on the one side and on the other side as the characteristic operation of *essence* come to bear upon human nature itself? Understood as

When Aquinas introduces the distinction between agents whose second perfection comes about exclusively by way of their *physis* and those whose second perfection comes about by way of their intellect he does so in order to introduce an ontologically superior order of finality. It is in natural agents alone that the end is determined by the ontological or natural appetite. They tend to the end by natural inclination alone. Agents endowed with intellect, in comparison, have next to the natural appetite and the sense appetite an appetite superior to both, the rational appetite, which is the will. Precisely because the proper object of the intellect is being (*ens*), and its proper end, the universal truth (*universale verum*), so too the proper object of the rational appetite, the will, is the universal good (*universale bonum*).[51] For, as Aquinas states, "an object of the intellect is only motivating by virtue of the rational meaning of the good [*ratio boni*] which is the object of the will" (*SCG* III.3.7). Agents endowed with intellect determine the end for themselves by considering the ultimate reason for seeking anything at all (*ratio boni*): "Things that know their end are always ordered to the good as an end, for the will, which is *the appetite for a foreknown end*, inclines toward something only if it has the rational character of a good, which is its object" (*SCG* III.16.4; emphasis added).

I can only be drawn to a good that I consider first as a worthwhile end, that is, consider under "the rational character of a good." Only the good that is apprehended (*bonum apprehensum*) actualizes

---

essence, human nature denotes the operative principle of the hylomorphic composite of the rational soul actualizing a living body; the essence denotes the *forma communis* and the *materia communis* of the species *animal rationale*. Understood as *physis*, "nature" denotes in the human being those activities that are determined *ad unum* and therefore fall completely outside of the control of the will, that is, the vegetative functions of the body. Because the rational soul is the substantial form of the body, these vegetative functions are operations of the rational soul; they are its vegetative power that actualizes the life functions of the body. *SCG* IV.11; *De ver.*, q. 4, a. 8; *ST* I, q. 18, aa. 1–2; q. 75, a. 1; q. 78, aa. 1–2.

51. *SCG* III.26.8: "Appetite is not peculiar to intellectual nature; instead, it is present in all things though it is in different things in different ways. And this diversity arises from the fact that things are differently related to knowledge. For things lacking knowledge entirely have natural appetite only. And things endowed with sensory knowledge have, in addition, sense appetite, under which irascible and concupiscible powers are included. But things possessed of intellectual knowledge also have an appetite proportionate to this knowledge, that is, the will. So, the will is not peculiar to intellectual nature by virtue of being an appetite, but only in so far as it depends on intellect."

the "appetite for a foreknown end," thereby eliciting a specific desire, that is, a motion to the end as presented by the intellect. Importantly, Aquinas does not argue that the moral good is directly derivative of the ontological good. Aquinas clarifies this important matter with great precision in *ST* I-II, where he argues that moral judgments are not simply direct inferences from metaphysical principles, even if the knowledge of the metaphysical principles is indispensable for the moral judgments to become effectively evident.[52] Rather, the practical intellect is *intellectus* all the way down; it differs from the speculative intellect only in that the object (*obiectum*) that engages it differs from the object (*obiectum*) that engages the speculative intellect. The object of the speculative intellect is being (*ens*), the object of the practical intellect is being (*ens*) under the apprehension of something as good (*ratio boni*); the end of the speculative intellect is knowledge of the truth; the end of the practical intellect is truth to be done under the aspect of good. Aquinas states: "The practical intellect knows truth, just as the speculative, but it directs the known truth to operation" (*ST* I, q. 79, a. 11, ad 2).[53] In *Reality and the Good*, Josef Pieper stresses that "theoretical reason itself becomes 'in extending,' *per extensionem*, the practical reason ... ; through the extension of knowledge toward willing and acting, the theoretical reason becomes practical." Consequently, "the theoretical and the practical reason are not two distinct powers of the soul. Nor are they two separate and independent operations of one and the same 'basic faculty.'" Rather, "the practical reason ... is nothing but the theoretical reason itself regarded under the aspect of a special function."[54]

This insight matters greatly, for under the influence of powerful modern strands of philosophy—Kantianism in Europe and Prag-

---

52. For a lucid treatment of this important matter, see Ralph McInerny, "Ethics and Metaphysics," in his *Aquinas on Human Action: A Theory of Practice* (Washington, D.C.: The Catholic University of America Press, 2012), 193–206.

53. See also *ST* I, q. 79, a. 11: "It is the speculative intellect which directs what it apprehends, not to operation, but to the consideration of truth; while the practical intellect is that which directs what it apprehends to operation. And this is what the Philosopher says (*De anima* III; 433a14) that *the speculative differs from the practical in its end*. Whence each is named from its end: the one speculative, the other practical—i.e., operative" (emphasis added).

54. Josef Pieper, *Living the Truth: Reality and the Good*, trans. Lothar Krauth, and *The Truth of All Things*, trans. Stella Lange (San Francisco, Calif.: Ignatius Press, 1989), 141–43.

matism in the United States—not a few contemporary moral philosophers and moral theologians, Catholic as well as Protestant, take Aquinas's nuanced differentiation between the speculative aspect and the practical aspect of the one *intellectus* as the occasion to claim him as a central authority for the alleged autonomy of the practical intellect from the speculative intellect. The abiding interest consists in the attempt to make Aquinas's moral thought palpable in a postmetaphysical age by propping it upon a Kantian stem. For Kant indeed unhinges practical reason entirely from theoretical reason and thereby from all knowledge of reality. Pieper rightly stresses that "this is not a harmless unessential speculation for philosophers. In making the practical reason—that is, the power of the soul that determines action—independent of the theoretical reason—that is, the power of the soul that perceives objective being—Kant sees, according to Richard Kroner, nothing less than the conquest of the metaphysics of being, the transfer of the center of gravity from the object to the subject.'"[55] This separation of the practical intellect from the speculative intellect—be it by declaring them to be two distinct faculties or two completely autonomous operations of one faculty—severs in the order of agency the good to be done from the knowledge of the truth and hence detrimentally disassociates the teleology proper to the practical intellect from the ontological principle of finality. Insofar as the good is coextensive with being, and insofar as this pertains in the case of beings endowed with intelligence (*intellectus*) also to the moral good, the ontological principle of finality encompasses also the teleology of human action. For contrary to those modern moral philosophers and theologians who erroneously claim his authority in order to maintain the complete autonomy of practical reason, Aquinas holds that the formality of the final end is given by nature *also* in the moral order (*ST* I-II, qq. 1–5).[56]

After having established that only the apprehended good (*bonum apprehensum*) elicits a motion to the end as presented by the intellect, Aquinas brings the following general metaphysical principle

---

55. Ibid., 142.
56. For reliable guides on this complex terrain, see Stephen L. Brock, *Action and Conduct: Thomas Aquinas and the Theory of Action* (Edinburgh: T and T Clark, 1998), and Long, *The Teleological Grammar of the Moral Act*.

to bear directly on the human intellect: the end of the first agent and mover is the final end of all intermediate agents and movers. Now consider how Aquinas applies this principle to the human intellect:

> Of all parts of [the human being], the intellect is found to be the superior mover, for the intellect moves the appetite, by presenting it with its object; then the intellectual appetite, that is the will, moves the sensory appetites, irascible and concupiscible, and that is why we do not obey concupiscence unless there is a command from the will; and finally the sense appetite, with the advent of consent from the will, now moves the body. Therefore, the end of the intellect is the end of all human actions. "But the end and good of the intellect are the true" [Aristotle, *Nicomachean Ethics* VI.2, 1139a27]; consequently, the first truth is the ultimate end. So, the ultimate end of the whole [human being], and of all his operations and desires, is to know the first truth, which is God. (*SCG* III.25.10)

To know the first truth (*cognoscere primum verum*) is the ultimate end of the human being and all his operations and desires (*omnium operationum et desideriorum eius*).[57] Aquinas makes reference to all desires of the human being only in respect of their ontological structure, converging to one final end, the knowledge of the first truth. One of these desires is the desire to know the cause (*desideriorum cognoscendi causam*).[58] A natural reaction of *admiratio*, wonder, gives rise to the quest of inquiry. This quest is a movement that receives its élan from a natural desire elicited by the encounter with something,[59] and that finds its rest or terminus in the contemplation of the cause of that thing. By the contemplation of its cause, the thing

---

57. The point needs to be pressed that *SCG* III.25.10 and 11 are to be seen in their specific order. *SCG* III.25.10 is the superior end, but can only be reached by way of 25.11, because the human being is not an angel. At this point the specific constitution of the human soul as substantial form of the body and the way human knowledge comes about, needs to be taken fully into account. For such an account, see most recently Ashley, *Way toward Wisdom*, 101–14.

58. *SCG* III.25.11: "Besides, there is naturally present in all [human beings] the desire to know the causes of whatever things are observed" (Naturaliter inest omnibus hominibus desiderium cognoscendi causas eorum quae videntur).

59. Benedict Ashley puts the matter as succinctly as one can in two sentences: "We must begin our knowledge of all being with *ens mobile*, sensible being, as the only 'Being' that we can sense and thus know intellectually. But from that starting point, by observing the order of the sciences we can widen our understanding of beings, even until our notion of 'Being' analogically includes all created being, and through that, as the work of God, we get some idea of God as the First Cause" (*Way toward Wisdom*, 63).

itself is more perfectly understood. The natural desire to know the causes of things arises from the very ontological structure of the intellect itself. Indeed, knowing the causes of things is precisely the operation that perfects the intellect. Aquinas extends this argument to the order of causes:

> For each effect that he knows, [the human being] naturally desires to know the cause. Now, the human intellect knows universal being [*ens universale*]. So, he naturally desires to know its cause, which is God alone .... Now, a person has not attained his ultimate end until natural desire comes to rest. Therefore, for human happiness which is the ultimate end it is not enough to have merely any kind of intelligible knowledge; there must be divine knowledge, as an ultimate end, to terminate the natural desire. So, the ultimate end of [the human being] is the knowledge of God. (*SCG* III.25.12)

Every intellect desires naturally the vision of the divine essence.[60] Aquinas understands this to be the natural *appetitus* of the intellect according to its *ontological structure*. However, for the created intellect a natural knowledge of the essence of the first cause independent from any created effects remains essentially unattainable. The natural desire for the vision of the divine essence remains conditional and oblique, for even the most advanced metaphysical contemplation of the first truth remains discursive and does not permit an intellectual intuition of the divine essence. Consequently the happiness that results from this contemplation, though genuine, remains incomplete and transient.[61] Nevertheless, it is the very ontological structure of the created intellect, its finality, that renders intelligible the ultimate significance of the divine revelation through Christ and its promise of the beatific vision and the ensuing perfect happiness:

---

60. *SCG* III.57: "Omnis intellectus naturaliter desiderat divinae substantiae visionem." In the terms developed at a later time when the alternatives were formulated with greater explicit precision and taking other principles and passages into account, Aquinas arguably taught a *desiderium naturale videndi Deum ut causam primam*, a natural desire to see God as first cause and final end, and not *a desiderium naturale videndi Deum supernaturaliter*, a natural desire to see God according to his proper quiddity, the Trinity of Father, Son, and Holy Spirit.

61. For a lucid treatment and reconstruction of this complex matter and for a proposed solution with which I happen to find myself in complete agreement, see Thomas Joseph White, OP, "Imperfect Happiness and the Final End of Man: Thomas Aquinas and the Paradigm of Nature-Grace Orthodoxy," *The Thomist* 78 (2014): 1–43.

God, the first truth, will unite the created intellect by way of formal causality with the divine essence and thereby grant a created but albeit unmediated participation in the life of the Trinity.

In his metaphysical analysis of the natural desire for the vision of God, Aquinas is concerned with the underlying ontological structure and natural finality in its own relative integrity. "Relative integrity" signifies here that human nature is not *per se* in act. Only particular human beings exist in the concrete order of providence in specific states; they do so, however, in virtue of one shared nature from which all acts characteristic of being human flow. Moreover, the principle of nature accounts for the absolute gratuity of the fact that the concretely extant order of providence coincides with the economy of salvation. For it is precisely the principle of nature that makes it possible to affirm divine gratuity: it is solely in virtue of divine *convenientia* and not due to any exigencies that might arise from human nature itself. Furthermore, only by way of the relative integrity of the principle of nature and especially in light of the entailed principle of finality is it possible to grasp the continuous identity of human nature across various states of the economy of salvation—the original state, the state of corruption, the state of grace, and the final state of blessedness.

THE INDISPENSABILITY OF THE PRINCIPLE OF FINALITY

The accurate distinction and correlation between nature and grace and the correct understanding of the natural desire for the vision of God have proved to be of great importance for sacred theology, to say the least. Since the time the Catholic magisterium in the patristic era had condemned as erroneous the theological positions characteristic of Pelagianism and, in the modern era, those of Baianism and Jansenism, Catholic theologians have developed conceptual distinctions that would avoid the errors that gave rise to Pelagianism and much later to Baianism and Jansenism in the first place.[62] Famously and controversially, in the middle of the twenti-

---

62. Denzinger, nos. 222–30, 370–97, 1901–80, 2301–32. The bibliography of authors who have written on the topic of nature and grace and on the natural desire for the vision

Ordained   135

eth century a new effort was undertaken to resolve the intricacies of these topics in ways that differed considerably from and opposed much of post-Tridentine theology, a new effort that had a strong impact on the Second Vatican Council and on Catholic theology itself in the second half of the twentieth century: the Christian humanism of Henri de Lubac and his school, dubbed by one influential critic as "nouvelle théologie" and by others as "grace-integralism" (in distinction from the nature-grace integrism characteristic of Baius).[63]

---

of God is vast—to say the least. The interested reader may want to consult the extensive bibliographies available in Jacobus M. Ramirez, OP, *De Hominis Beatitudine I* (Opera Omnia, Tomus III), ed. Victorino Rodríguez, OP (Madrid: Instituto de Filosofía "Luis Vives," 1972); Henri de Lubac, *Surnaturel: Études historiques. Nouvelle édition avec la traduction intégrale des citations latines et grecques* (Paris: Desclée de Brouwer, 1991); and Lawrence Feingold, *The Natural Desire to See God According to St. Thomas Aquinas and His Interpreters*, 2nd ed. (Naples, Fla.: Sapientia Press, 2010).

63. De Lubac, *Surnaturel: Études historiques*. See also his *Augustinianism and Modern Theology*, trans. Lancelot Sheppard (New York: Crossroad, 2000); *The Mystery of the Supernatural*, trans. Rosemary Sheed (New York: Crossroad, 1998); *A Brief Catechism on Nature and Grace*, trans. Br. Richard Arnandez, FSC (San Francisco, Calif.: Ignatius Press, 1984); "The Mystery of the Supernatural," in his *Theology and History*, trans. Anne Englund Nash (San Francisco, Calif.: Ignatius Press, 1996), 281–316. For an overview that is as informative as it is sympathetic to Henri de Lubac, see Joseph A. Komonchak, "Theology and Culture at Mid-Century: The Example of Henri de Lubac," *Theological Studies* 51 (1990): 579–602. For a spirited Protestant defense and radicalization of de Lubac's position, see John Milbank, *The Suspended Middle: Henri de Lubac and the Debate Concerning the Supernatural* (Grand Rapids, Mich.: Eerdmans, 2005), and for an equally spirited rejoinder, see my essay "*Desiderium Naturale Visionis Dei—Est autem duplex hominis beatitudo sive felicitas*: Some Observations about Lawrence Feingold's and John Milbank's Recent Interventions in the Debate over the Natural Desire to See God," *Nova et Vetera* (English edition) 5, no. 1 (2007): 81–131. For a nuanced and strong defense of de Lubac's position, see David Braine, "The Debate between Henri de Lubac and His Critics," *Nova et Vetera* (English edition) 6, no. 3 (2008): 543–90. For a critique of Milbank's interpretation of de Lubac and for a spirited defense of the latter, see Edward T. Oakes, SJ, "The Paradox of Nature and Grace: On John Milbank's *The Suspended Middle: Henri de Lubac and the Debate Concerning the Supernatural*," *Nova et Vetera* (English edition) 4, no. 3 (2006): 667–96, and "The *Surnaturel* Controversy: A Survey and a Response," *Nova et Vetera* (English edition) 9, no. 3 (2011): 625–56. See also the respective chapters in the massive collection *Ressourcement: A Movement of Renewal in Twentieth-Century Catholic Thought*, ed. Gabriel Flynn and Paul D. Murray with the assistance of Patricia Kelly (Oxford: Oxford University Press, 2011). For a creative and thought-provoking rearticulation and further development of the topic along the lines traced by Joseph Maréchal, SJ, Maurice Blondel, SJ, Karl Rahner, SJ, Henri de Lubac, SJ, and Hans Urs von Balthasar, see Stephen M. Fields, SJ, *Analogies of Transcendence: An Essay on Nature, Grace, and Modernity* (Washington, D.C.: The Catholic University of America Press, 2016). Fields asserts that all human beings have a supernatural finality due to the universality of prevenient grace. At the same time, Fields seeks an alternative to Rahner's supernatural existential because he takes it—and I think

Early in the twenty-first century, de Lubac's construal and critique of the post-Tridentine theology that developed as a constructive response to Baianism and Jansenism—a response dubbed by de Lubac himself as "grace-extrinsicism"—was subjected to increasing historical, philosophical, and theological scrutiny.[64] After important clarifications regarding matters of textual interpretation and conceptual consistency, in recent years the debate has taken a more constructive turn in search of a new, more nuanced and refined consensus.[65]

What does the metaphysical analysis of the natural desire for the vision of God based on the principle of finality of the created intellect contribute to this debate? I submit that it yields at least three insights that are absolutely central for sacred theology: the first is

---

rightly so—to vacuate the theological significance of nature which Rahner takes to be a mere "remainder concept" of grace. Fields aims at recovering a more robust concept of nature within the obtaining order of grace. While still relying, all too uncritically it seems to me, on Rahner's metaphysics of knowledge for an epistemological framework, he turns to Max Seckler's interpretation and development of Aquinas's account of the natural *instinctus* of faith in order to develop an analogical notion of grace wherein the natural instinct of faith serves as the meeting point between divine and human freedom. By drawing upon Rahner's concept of *Realsymbol* he conceives of nature as grace's sacramental medium because nature and grace are ultimately analogical. Furthermore, Fields asserts an analogy between prevenient grace and sanctifying grace: prevenient grace is the disposition of the formal action of sanctifying grace. Finally, he takes the natural desire for God and prevenient grace, while formally distinct, to be materially the same and as such serving as the material cause of sanctifying grace (see esp. 141–42).

64. McInerny, *Praeambula Fidei*; Feingold, *Natural Desire to See God*; Steven A. Long, *Natura Pura: On the Recovery of Nature in the Doctrine of Grace* (New York: Fordham University Press, 2010); Bernard Mulcahy, OP, *Aquinas's Notion of Pure Nature and the Christian Integralism of Henri de Lubac* (New York: Peter Lang, 2011); and Christopher J. Malloy, "De Lubac on Natural Desire: Difficulties and Antitheses," *Nova et Vetera* (English edition) 9, no. 3 (2011): 567–624.

65. Nicholas J. Healy, "Henri de Lubac on Nature and Grace: A Note on Some Recent Contributions to the Debate," *Communio* 35, no. 4 (2008): 535–64; Guy Mansini, OSB, "The Abiding Theological Significance of Henri de Lubac's *Surnaturel*," *The Thomist* 73, no. 4 (2009): 593–619; Edward T. Oakes, SJ, "Scheeben the Reconciler: Resolving the Nature-Grace Debate," *Nova et Vetera* (English edition) 11, no. 2 (2013): 435–53; Thomas Joseph White, OP, "The 'Pure Nature' of Christology: Human Nature and *Gaudium et Spes* 22," *Nova et Vetera* (English edition) 8, no. 2 (2010): 283–322, "Good Extrinsicism: Matthias Scheeben and the Ideal Paradigm of Nature-Grace Orthodoxy," *Nova et Vetera* (English edition) 11, no. 2 (2013): 537–63, and "Imperfect Happiness and the Final End of Man"; Christopher Smith, "*Surnaturel* Revisited: Henri de Lubac's Theology of the Supernatural in Contemporary Theology" (STD diss., University of Navarra, 2014); Andrew Dean Swafford, *Nature and Grace: A New Approach to Thomistic Ressourcement* (Eugene, Ore.: Pickwick, 2014).

the fundamental significance of the natural desire for the vision of God that is proportionate to the ontological structure and the natural finality of the human intellect. The French Dominican Thomist Marie-Joseph Le Guillou states:

> The very structure of the created [intellect] gives witness to a desired opening in the prolongation of its proper perfection, an opening toward a supernatural surpassing which would be the vision of God Himself, the divine essence. The realization of which, however, being absolutely out of the range of the created [intellect], depends solely on God's good pleasure. Naturally powerless to realize the desire's fulfillment, the created spirit can only wait for the gratuitous gift, which can neither be accessed nor demanded.[66]

Le Guillou aptly summarizes Aquinas's surpassing synthesis that can be found in its most condensed form in chapter 104 of his *Compendium theologiae*: on the one hand, *qua* structure of the created intellect, there obtains a natural desire for ever more perfect knowledge up to and including the knowledge of the essence of the first cause: "The ultimate end of an intellectual creature is the vision of God in His essence" (*Est ... finis ultimus intellectualis creaturae, Deum per essentiam videre*). On the other hand, the intellect is not effectively proportioned to see God and hence lacks the natural disposition for such knowledge. And insofar as the created intellect is by definition unable to present to the will the ultimate good (*bonum ultimum*), which is the essence of the first cause, the will does not actuate a fortified desire, a specific motion to this end as presented by the intellect. Hence the natural desire for the vision of God is but a simple motion, conditional upon some distinct activation—be it a transient and imperfect activation in the form of an elicited philosophical desire to see the essence of God, or be it a permanent and perfect activation through the grace of conversion by way of exterior revelation and proclamation and simultaneously by way of a corresponding interior illumination (*lumen fidei*). The natural desire for the disproportionate finality of the created intellect may be activated transiently and imperfectly by a natural motion, and perfectly and permanently by a supernatural motion.

---

66. Marie-Joseph Le Guillou, OP, "Surnaturel," *Revue des sciences philosophiques et théologiques* 34 (1950): 226–43, at 240 (author's translation).

The second insight this analysis affords is the positive supernatural character of the divine gift. For only God is to himself his proper connatural object. Hence the positive content of the word "supernatural" corresponds to a surpassing order of communion with God, accorded gratuitously. And God is absolutely free to grant such a participation in the surpassing blessedness of the triune life. The fact that God creates intellects capable of such communion in no way obligates God to grant the beatific vision. Of course, nothing at all is owed by God to a creature in a strict sense, but only in a qualified sense insofar as God obligates himself by way of a decree of divine acceptation in matters of merit and reward or by way of divine providence in matters of natural endowments. In short there is no strict debt of nature (*debitum naturae*) that would obligate God absolutely. Aquinas states:

> Debt [*debitum*] may be taken in two ways: first, as arising from merit; and this regards the person whose it is to do meritorious works, according to Rom. 4:4: "Now to him that worketh, the reward is not reckoned according to grace, but according to debt." The second debt regards the condition of nature. Thus we say it is due to a man to have reason, and whatever else belongs to human nature. Yet in neither way is debt taken to mean that God is under an obligation to His creature, but rather that the creature ought to be subject to God, that the Divine ordination may be fulfilled in it, which is that a certain nature should have certain conditions or properties, and that by doing certain works it should attain to something further. And hence natural endowments are not a debt in the first sense but in the second. But supernatural gifts are due in neither sense. (*ST* I-II, q. 111, a. 1, ad 2)

Because supernatural gifts are due in neither sense so also does the aptitude to receive supernatural gifts, that is, supernatural perfectibility, constitute a *debitum* in neither sense. The ontological structure and natural finality of the created intellect would neither be rendered absurd nor essentially frustrated were the supernatural end withheld in principle. For *qua* nature, the ontological structure of the created intellect has a proportionate natural finality—on a trajectory analogous to the supernatural finality—that yields a genuine, albeit transitory and therefore always imperfect happiness.

The third insight this analysis yields is the necessity to maintain the integrity of the respective created natures in the extant order of providence, that is, in the encompassing economy of salvation. Only if there obtains a finality proportionate to the created intellect can the two central features of attaining the ultimate end in its surpassing perfection be made intelligible and thus safeguarded: the surpassing gratuity (that presupposes the gratuity of creation but is not entailed by it) and the transcendent fulfillment of the proportionate finality of human nature in a genuinely supernatural perfection. Without the proportionate finality of human nature toward which humans are able to move based on the faculties proper to human nature, there would exist no passive potency for sanctifying grace to presuppose and to perfect. In order for the human being—*qua* human—to be elevated to the supernatural ultimate end, and in this supernatural actuation not to be transmuted into some other specific nature, the gratuitous transcendence of the ultimate end requires the relative, but proper integrity of a specific nature—the created intellect, the subsistent form of a living body. And this necessarily entails first that there obtains a finality proportionate to the created intellect, a finality essentially conducive to such an elevation. This entails secondly a natural desire for the vision of God that remains conditional and oblique. In sum, by way of its ontological structure and natural finality, the human intellect simply opens up to the divine gratuity, to the good pleasure of God.

In the extant order of providence with the original supernatural destination of humanity to eternal communion with God, the natural final end in its proper integrity pertains only to the hypothetical state of pure nature. Yet positing in light of revelation a single concrete ultimate end that is essentially supernatural makes it necessary to distinguish between two orders of finality. For the genuinely surpassing gratuity of attaining the ultimate end and perfect happiness can only be maintained without unsavory paradoxes or, worse, some putative divine exigency, if there obtains a finality that is proportionate to the natural faculties of the created intellect. Importantly, however, in virtue of the ontological structure of the created intellect and its specific finality, the two orders of finality *do not* entail two distinct ultimate ends for the human being, one natural and one supernatural. Rather, there obtains only one ultimate end for the human being. This ultimate end is God: as first truth, author of nature, and the common good of the whole universe, the final end of the created intellect (angelic and human), and as the Trinity, the absolutely surpassing reality of participative union of vision and love that characterizes the beatific vision. The intellect's proper object is being (*ens*) and its proper end truth (*verum*); and contemplation is the act of the intellect in which truth is enjoyed for its own sake. Because all truth presupposes tacitly the first truth, the end of the intellect is not just contemplation of truth, but of truth itself, God. In the extant order of providence, the economy of salvation, this finality is always already subsumed within the supernatural ultimate end, the beatific vision. The proper perfection of the intellect is contemplation, be it as natural contemplation or as infused contemplation. Dispelling the legitimate concern that contemplation might be nothing but a rarified activity of some privileged intellectual elite, Benedict Ashley rightly stresses that "'contemplation' simply means an awareness of God in all aspects of our world and our lives, even when that awareness remains rudimentary and nameless. The mystic attains this awareness intensely, but it is not beyond the simplest and earthiest human being even without the special elevation of grace to be aware that this is God's world and we are God's."[67]

Grace presupposes human nature and also perfects it such that the finality of the created intellect is subsumed to and included in the supernatural final end. Hence, the natural final end is neither extrinsic to the supernatural ultimate end nor intrinsic to it. Rather, their relationship is analogical. There obtains an analogy of proper proportionality between the supernatural ultimate end and the natural finality of the created *intellectus*. While the general obediential potency as well as the natural potency extend to all created natures, the specific obediential potency does not. A tree has the natural potency to grow and to decay, and it also has the obediential potency in relationship to divine omnipotence to be uprooted and instantaneously replanted on another continent. The same is true for a stone,

---

[67]. Benedict M. Ashley, OP, "Integral Human Fulfillment according to Germain Grisez," in *The Ashley Reader: Redeeming Reason* (Naples, Fla.: Sapientia Press, 2006), 225–69, at 269. For a beautiful rendition of this complex subject matter, see Pieper, *Happiness and Contemplation*.

a horse, or a human. But a tree cannot be elevated into the beatific vision by divine omnipotence without in the course of it being transformed into a created intellect and thereby ceasing to be a tree. Not all created natures have the aptitude to receive the same motion from God. The specific obediential potency of created intellects denotes the very aptitude to receive supernatural motions like sanctifying grace, theological virtues, and the light of glory. Only for created intellects, angels and humans, is the beatific vision the surpassing gratuitous perfection of their natures. In short, it is in virtue of the specific ontological structure and finality of the created intellect that human nature and its proportionate finality are characterized by a specific obediential potency to supernatural perfection through grace. It is precisely the finality of human nature—determined ultimately by the specific finality of the created intellect—that radically distinguishes the gratuitous actualization of the specific potency of the intellect to the first truth, its elevation by sanctifying grace, from the general obediential potency and its actualization by general divine omnipotence. The specific obediential potency thus corresponds to humans being created in the image of God and therefore being naturally *capax Dei*.

In sum, the principle of finality is not only indispensable for a correct understanding of nature and consequently of human nature and hence of the created intellect. Rather, the principle of finality is also indispensable for a correct understanding of grace perfecting human nature by elevating it in the prolongation of the proper perfection of the created intellect's specific finality. The insights that the metaphysical analysis of the principle of finality affords might shed some light onto the reasons why one of the most protracted conflicts of modern Catholic theology did not admit of a ready and simple solution. Most, albeit not all, parties in the confrontation between the more recent grace-integralism and the older grace-extrinsicism that developed in the aftermath of the condemnations of Baianism and Jansenism had neglected or repudiated parts of the resources necessary in order to arrive at a constructive resolution of the conflict. I would like to suggest that both parties in their respective opposing extremes failed to maintain the ordered unity of the finality of nature together with the ontological structure and proper finality of the created intellect—arguably a unique achievement of Aquinas's synthesis.

Grace-integralism characteristically tends to overemphasize the intrinsic *appetitus* of the created intellect at the cost of the ontological condition of the created intellect in the hylomorphic unity with the body as one integrated material substance. It tends to fall short on fully accounting for the finality proportionate to human nature as a hylomorphic unity of soul and body. Bereft of the natural finality characteristic of the hylomorphic unity, human nature tends to become, as was rightly said, nothing but a "vacuole" for grace.[68]

Grace-extrinsicism characteristically tends to overemphasize the distinct integrity of the finality proportionate to human nature to the point that two completely distinct orders of finality were posited with two completely distinct ultimate ends for the human being. In its more extreme form, that is, in its Suarezian instantiation as it became normative in the tradition of Jesuit Scholastic formation up to and including the schooling that Henri de Lubac underwent, the fallen state of human nature was posited to be virtually identical with a state of "pure nature" that was assumed to obtain had humanity been created originally without the gift of grace. Here "pure nature" becomes more than a purely hypothetical state that never obtained in the extant order of providence but merely served as a conceptual proviso to safeguard the absolute gratuity of sanctifying grace already in the state of original righteousness in relationship to human nature *qua* created.[69] In short, whenever "pure nature" turns from naming a strictly hypothetical state that never *de facto* obtained in the extant order of providence into naming a presumably undamaged post-Fall state, a state simply bereft of the supernatural and preternatural *auxilia* characteristic of the state of original righteousness, the critique advanced by Henri de Lubac hits its target. Besides displaying a somewhat disconcerting theological insensitivity about

---

68. This problem is probably most transparent in Henri de Lubac's *A Brief Catechesis on Nature and Grace*, trans. Richard Arnandez, FSC (San Francisco, Calif.: Ignatius Press, 1984). For an extensive analysis and astute critique of nature as a mere "vacuole" for grace, see Long, *Natura Pura*, 52–109.

69. See Francisco Suarez, SJ, *Opera Omnia* (Paris: Vivès, 1857), Tome VII (*De statibus humanae naturae*), Prolegomenum IV, cap. VIII-IX.

the dangers that come along with a use of "natura pura"—betraying possibly too great an indebtedness to the overconfidence in human nature characteristic of Renaissance humanism—this problematic form of grace-extrinsicism at the same time displays a surprising lack of appreciation for the unique ontological structure and finality of the created intellect as Aquinas's metaphysical analysis had laid bare: *intellectus* carries in its own structure the orientation to realize itself, to achieve full flourishing, in a transcendent end, the contemplation of the first truth.

An extreme and characteristically modern form of *grace-extrinsicism* can be observed in the work of the influential moral philosopher Germain Grisez, who conceives of the human being as a rational animal without *intellectus*.[70] In his desire to expunge completely the alleged "other-worldliness" of classical Catholic moral theology, Grisez forcefully rejects a teleologically ordered and intrinsically intelligible hierarchy of goods and ends as well as *intellectus*, the corresponding receptor of the intelligibility of this order in the human being. However, only *intellectus* can account for an overarching finality of human nature, a hierarchy of ends at the top of which stands the contemplation of truth, of the first truth. Yet without *intellectus*, there cannot obtain any proportionality whatsoever between the finality of human nature and its supernatural fulfillment. The rational animal thus conceived is not *capax Dei*. Yet a creature that is not *capax Dei* is also not *capax beatitudinis*. For, as stated in the prologue, beatitude is "the perfect good of an intellectual nature" (*ST* I, q. 26, a. 1). Denying such a hierarchy of goods and ends, a hierarchy that may be perceived and understood in virtue of the *intellectus* has far-reaching consequences. Together with the other new natural law theorists, Grisez postulates instead of such a hierarchy a number of goods that are equally basic. On this supposition, the act of prioritizing one good over another cannot be the result of a judgment that is arrived at in virtue of the intellect's insight into the ontological hierarchy of goods. Absent such a hierarchy as well as *intellectus* and given a num-

---

70. See his *The Way of the Lord Jesus Christ: Christian Moral Principles* (Chicago: Franciscan Herald Press, 1983), esp. 809–10, and his "A Critique of Russell Hittinger's Book, *A Critique of the New Natural Law Theory*," *The New Scholasticism* 62, no. 4 (1988): 438–65, esp. 459–60.

ber of equally basic goods, the prioritization will depend completely on the agent's appetitive faculty, the will and the passions. The moral quality of the will and the passions depends, however, on the way they are molded, habituated into virtues or vices, by way of secondary volitions. Yet these secondary volitions are not open anymore to be guided by the *intellectus* that takes its cues from the ontological hierarchy of ends. Rather, the ultimate source from which these secondary volitions arise is the agent's sheer willfulness. What sits *de facto* at the very heart of Grisez's account is modernity's greatest good—subjective sovereignty. So much in all brevity on this widely influential yet deeply problematic version of grace-extrincism.[71]

While modern Catholic theology can largely be narrated by way of this paradigmatic controversy at the center of which stands the speculative challenge of integrating in a metaphysically sound way the *universal* principle of finality and the *specific* finality of the created intellect, other strands of modern theology display a similar problematic. The almost unanimous modern philosophical rejection of a comprehensive natural finality and especially of the finality of the created intellect seems to encourage two characteristic tendencies in modern theology: an encompassing theological supernaturalism and an encompassing ontotheological naturalism (or quasi-supernaturalism).

The first tendency is to absorb the finality proportionate to human nature into a comprehensive theologically-funded finality, into the teleology of a single divine gratuity—one seamless stream of continuity from the first act of creation *ex nihilo* to the final perfection of the new creation. This seamless continuity of a single gratuity obliterates the crucial difference—metaphysical as well as theological—between the ontological participation of finite being (*ens per participationem*) in the act of being (*actus essendi*) in virtue of a gratuitous and radically free diffusion of divine goodness *ad extra* (*dare esse*) by way of God's transcendent final, efficient, and exemplary causality, on the one hand, and, on the other hand, the unmediated unitive participation in the divine life and beatitude of the blessed that the triune God grants in virtue of adoptive sonship by way of transcendent formal

---

71. For a more extensive critical engagement of Grisez's account, see the epilogue, pp. 409–25, below.

causality (*quo*) of the divine essence itself.[72] A paradigmatic instantiation of such an encompassing theological supernaturalism is Sergius Bulgakov's sophiology, the systematically most consistent and speculatively brilliant account—possibly since Origen—of an *a priori* universal salvation which according to its internal systematic logic is all-embracing and includes eventually also Satan.[73]

The second characteristic tendency is to absorb the finality proportionate to human nature via sublation into the all-encompassing dynamic of the all-embracing self-differentiation of the Absolute Spirit, of which creation, history, and religious self-consciousness are nothing but integral necessary moments. Due to the lack of any genuine gratuity, this teleology, driven by the inner dialectic of the self-differentiation of the Absolute (construed as subjectivity), is nothing but surpassingly—natural. The most ambitious modern instantiation of such an encompassing ontotheological naturalism is, of course, Hegel's theosophy of the Absolute Spirit, arguably the most penetrating and sophisticated secularization of Christianity to date.

Some theologians, while unable to affirm the finality proportionate to human nature, at the same time wish to resist both of the above characteristic consequences. In their honorable desire not to be impaled on either one of these two horns—supernaturalism or naturalism—they seek to exercise some damage control by appealing to some versions of what one might best characterize as a fundamental postmetaphysical exemption from the dilemma they face. This postmetaphysical exemption takes three forms.

(1) One dominant group claims the combined Kierkegaardian, Barthian, and Wittgensteinian exemption from all forms of "natural theology" and "metaphysics" and thereby, unavoidably, pursues nothing but a barely camouflaged version of the supernaturalist alternative: "nature" is taken to be vacuous, epistemically or ontologically, or both. Yet even in the postmetaphysical lexicon of grace, the word "nature" still serves a useful function, namely as a semantic in-

---

72. For the metaphysics of the beatific vision, see the epilogue, pp. 389–409.
73. Sergius Bulgakov, *The Bride of the Lamb*, trans. Boris Jakim (Grand Rapids, Mich.: Eerdmans, 2002), and "On the Question of the Apocatastasis of the Fallen Spirits (In Connection with the Doctrine of S. Gregory of Nyssa)," in *Apocatastasis and Transfiguration*, trans. Boris Jakim (New Haven, Conn.: Variable Press, 1995), 7–30.

dicator intrinsic to the grammar of gratuity: every gratuity requires a point of reference, a nongratuity in distinction from which gratuity receives its distinct meaning. In reference to the gratuity of salvation, the word "nature" serves this auxiliary grammatical function. While putatively indispensable for the grammar of grace, it lacks any genuine substantial reference. "Nature" has been reduced to a mere semantic token signifying the "other" that gratuity always *qua* gratuity entails, the "other" that is always already constituted by gratuity, ontologically as well as salvifically.[74]

Two of the most significant representatives of this first dominant group of postmetaphysical theologians are related to the "post-liberal" Yale School, a group of Protestant theologians who have taught and still teach at Yale University and who variously reflect certain Barthian theological concerns and commitments and certain Wittgensteinian philosophical concerns and commitments that fund a consistent postmetaphysical mode of theological discourse. The work of these two theologians document instructively the consequences of jettisoning the finality proportionate to human nature and the ontological structure and distinct finality of the created intellect. In her important work *Christ the Key*, Kathryn Tanner explicitly adopts the nature-grace paradigm and advances an idiosyncratic Protestant version of *grace-integralism*.[75] Because of the allegedly complete malleability of human nature under the always already extant reality of transcendent uncreated grace, human nature without grace remains radically unintelligible, a contingent conglomerate of traits that receive unification and direction, and come to flourish, only in virtue of the grace of the incarnation. At the same time, this grace remains completely transcendent, because there obtains no correlation whatsoever between a completely malleable human nature and a grace

---

74. For a characteristic instantiation of a hamartiologically driven epistemological exemption along Kierkegaardian-Barthian lines, see Alan J. Torrance, "*Auditum Fidei*: Where and How Does God Speak? Faith, Reason, and the Question of Criteria," in *Reason and the Reasons of Faith*, 27–52, and *Persons in Communion: An Essay on Trinitarian Description and Human Participation, with special reference to Volume One of Karl Barth's Church Dogmatics* (Edinburgh: T and T Clark, 1996). For a spirited instantiation of an epistemically driven ordinary language exemption taken along Barthian-Wittgensteinian lines, see Stanley Hauerwas, *With the Grain of the Universe: The Church's Witness and Natural Theology* (Grand Rapids, Mich.: Brazos, 2001).

75. Tanner, *Christ the Key* (Cambridge: Cambridge University Press, 2010).

that is always completely *ad extra*: in virtue of the incarnation, every human being is objectively attached to Christ and thereby *de facto* redeemed. It is for this reason that the ontology of the coordination of the human and divine nature of Christ becomes the key for understanding God's salvific attachment to humanity and the always already objectively graced state of human nature. Tanner's insistence on the complete malleability (and hence a-teleology) of human nature and simultaneously on the always already graced (and hence extrinsically and gratuitously teleologized) human nature—in virtue of an ontologized incarnation-centered understanding of salvation—seems at first glance more like a qualified version of grace-extrinsicism. But despite all her affirmations of the contrary, her metaphysically vacuous concept of human nature makes grace-integralism unavoidable. For considered without the grace of the incarnation human nature is nothing but a vacuous placeholder for the grace of the incarnation. Certainly, grace is utterly gratuitous and completely *ad extra* (echoing ironically the strongest notion of a general *potentia oboedientialis*), but—paradoxically—only the grace of the incarnation enables human nature to be what it is supposed to be and to flourish the way it is supposed to flourish. Due to this ontologization of grace and of redemption, Tanner's decidedly Protestant version of grace-integralism, however, takes a calamitous quasi-naturalistic turn. While human nature is graced, and, in virtue of the incarnation now attached, or better, coordinated to God as Spirit, the human nevertheless remains only all too human. An incarnationally ontologized salvation turns out to be nothing but the unilateral divine realization—*ex solo opere divino operato*—of the humanity of the human. Without *intellectus*, a union of intellect and will between God and human becomes inconceivable and so do divinization and the beatific vision become equally inconceivable.

In contrast to Tanner, David Kelsey, in his lengthy *magnum opus*, *Eccentric Existence: A Theological Anthropology*,[76] advances a pronounced version of *grace-extrinsicism*. My few comments cannot do even minimal justice to the scope, complexity, and depth of Kelsey's work. Nevertheless, I shall assay a few pertinent observations. According to Kelsey, as far as I can see, human nature, biologically de-

---

76. Kelsey, *Eccentric Existence* (Louisville, Ky.: Westminster John Knox, 2009).

fined via human DNA, is not structurally ordered to a transcendent final end. Only by being addressed by God's Word does the human being, a living body, become a person, that is, a personal body, and enter in his or her concrete unsubstitutable existence into a story with the God who calls—eccentric existence. Bereft of the ontological structure of the created intellect and its distinct finality, the human being—in virtue of what one must assume is due to the general obediential potency in which every creature stands to God's omnipotence—enters into a relationship with God, but one that has to remain essentially extrinsic, purely *ad extra*, because the human being can never be more than just, even if ever so intimately, coordinated to God. Consequently, Kelsey conceives of eschatological consummation as the intimacy of Trinitarian circumambience: eccentric human existence remains forever eccentrically coordinated to the divine circumambience. While the constituent theocentrism of Kelsey's theological anthropology is to be commended, it is nevertheless the case that without *intellectus* a union of intellect and will between God and human becomes inconceivable and so do divinization and the beatific vision become equally inconceivable. Without the metaphysics of the separate subsistence of *intellectus* and its specific finality, divine circumambience (be it interior or exterior or both), remains the ontological limit of consummation, an eternal "coordination" of greatest proximity, but absolutely no unitive participation, that is, no communion in the full and substantive sense.

(2) Another group of late-modern theologians claims the exemption of contemporary scientism, namely the pseudo-philosophical strictures that modern natural science purportedly imposes on all nonscientific discourse. These theologians pursue a barely camouflaged version of the naturalist alternative: while they might affirm a regional emergent finality of the human animal, the materialist or at least reductively naturalist strictures that contemporary natural science allegedly imposes lead them to reject the ontological structure and the specific finality of the created intellect together with any genuinely supernatural end of humanity. The final state is conceived of at best as a technologically perfected and maximally extended, that is, unending state of natural human flourishing in a world that is characterized by the absence of corruption and evil, in short, the

Ordained   149

utopia of a paradise regained, an eternal vacation resort of sorts that remains untroubled by something as outlandish to the contemporary materialist mindset as the unitive participation in the life of the triune God. The naturalist, liberal Protestant version of this eschatology relies on the utopia of a technological perfectibility of human nature, while the preternaturalist Evangelical Protestant version relies on an act of divine cosmological intervention.[77] In either case, the state of everlasting perfection envisioned remains captivated by the strictures of a merely naturalistic perfection of creation.

(3) A third group simply declares defeat to be victory by giving up Christian theology and the Christian faith altogether. The denial of a finality proportionate to human nature becomes part and parcel of an outright rejection of all finality. Spinoza's *Deus sive natura* arrives—via Nietzsche's embrace of the eternal return of all things—at the Deleuzian celebration of a multiple and fissured self encompassed by the "fold," the absolutely immanent vortex of the play of power—an interpretation of reality that converges in a most remarkable way with the anti-teleological materialism characteristic of much of contemporary natural science: despite all appearances to the contrary an inescapable arbitrariness reigns unceasingly. It is unsurprising that in these circles an increasingly popular spiritual option is a Westernized adaptation of Buddhism.[78] Such a "Buddhism lite" is the less costly consequence to be drawn from the absolute

---

77. The conceptual framework for a naturalist, liberal Protestant version of eschatology was established in Immanuel Kant's influential 1794 essay, "The End of All Things," in *Religion within the Boundaries of Mere Reason and Other Writings*, ed. and trans. Allen Wood and George Di Giovanni (Cambridge: Cambridge University Press, 1998), 193–205, and nuanced in the long "science and religion" symbiosis that culminates in the development of a "religious naturalism," exemplified well in the works, among others, of Philip J. Hefner: see *The Human Factor: Evolution, Culture, and Religion* (Minneapolis, Minn.: Augsburg Fortress, 2000) and *Technology and Human Becoming* (Minneapolis, Minn.: Augsburg Fortress, 2003). A characteristic example of the preternaturalist Evangelical Protestant version of such an eschatology would be an influential work of the leading New Testament scholar N. T. Wright, *Surprised by Hope: Rethinking Heaven, the Resurrection, and the Mission of the Church* (New York: HarperOne, 2008).

78. For an account suffused with the acid of irony, see Testsuo-Marcel Kato (pseudonym), *Traité de Bouddhisme Zen à l'usage du bourgeois d'Occident* (Paris: Éditions du Parc, 1998). (This is the first work of the French writer and philosopher Fabrice Hadjadj.) For a straightforward adaptation of Buddhism to a normative framework of scientific naturalism, see Owen Flanagan, *The Bodhisattva's Brain: Buddhism Naturalized* (Cambridge, Mass.: MIT Press, 2011).

rejection of the metaphysical principle of finality, the more costly one being, of course, the ecstatic nihilism whose bittersweet cup its prophet and priest, Friedrich Nietzsche, drank to the last draught.

CONCLUSION

By this point it should be transparent that the way Aquinas conceives of sacred theology is far from arbitrary, idiosyncratic, or antiquated. Rather, sacred theology thus conceived is nothing but a consistent application of the fundamental axiom that grace does not abolish but presupposes and perfects nature (*gratia non tollit naturam sed perficit eam*). And, as was shown, the denial of the finality of nature "destroys nature and the things which are according to nature."[79] Applied with consistency, such a denial eventually undercuts any substantive theological notion of creation. Nature abhors a vacuum: as soon as metaphysics loses its status as the privileged instrument of sacred theology, other instruments—that is, postmetaphysical and antimetaphysical strands of contemporary philosophy—fill the vacuum, as the history of post-Vatican II Catholic theology makes all too plain.

Hence, quite obviously, the denial of the finality of nature and the consequent metaphysical evacuation of nature itself have profound consequences for the way sacred theology is conceived and done. Bereft of the fundamental axiom that grace does not abolish but rather presupposes and perfects nature, Catholic theology begins to vacillate between the poles of a purely pragmatic accommodationism to whatever form of postmetaphysical philosophy happens to be momentarily fashionable and an equally postmetaphysical escapist, fideist, or traditionalist supernaturalism. Moreover, bereft of its once privileged instrument, the metaphysics in the tradition of the *philosophia perennis*, sacred theology will lose access to the intelligibility of the universal principle of finality this metaphysics affords. Yet this principle is absolutely indispensable in order to offer an account of the finality of the created intellect, a necessary presupposition for understanding why the ultimate human end is God and why beatitude is primarily a perfection of the intellect.

79. *In Phys.* II.8, lect. 14, 199a34–b33, 133 (Marietti no. 267).

2

Equipped for Beatitude—
To Be Good Is to Do the Truth

Eternal Law, Natural Law, Prudence, and Conscience

> It is the most perfect state of any thing that it not only is good in itself but also causes goodness in others.
> —Thomas Aquinas, *On There Being Only One Intellect*[1]

The journey to beatitude, analogous to any other journey, requires the wayfarer to actualize all the faculties necessary to proceed on the sojourn and to reach the destination. It has become patent already in the prologue as well as in the previous chapter that the human faculties most central for the journey to beatitude are the intellect and the will. Furthermore, it also has become clear already that wayfarers proceed by way of genuine human actions, that is, morally qualified actions, good and evil. The ultimate human end can only be achieved by way of moral agency based on the fundamental principle, *to be good is to do the truth.*

This chapter extends the metaphysics of finality to the metaphys-

---

1. *De unitate intellectus contra Averroistas*: "Est enim perfectissimum uniuscuiusque rei ut non solum sit in se bonum, sed ut bonitatem in aliis causet." In Ralph McInerny, *Aquinas Against the Averroists: On There Being Only One Intellect* (West Lafayette, Ind.: Purdue University Press, 1993), 136 (Latin) and 137 (English).

ics of the good, which is the metaphysics of morals. It moves from the previous consideration of a universal teleology to the eternal law and the natural law, and from there to conscience and the virtue of prudence. These fundamental elements of a metaphysics of the good are indispensable for eventually understanding one central prerequisite of the *viator* on the journey to beatitude: a rightly ordered will. I will discuss the rectitude of the will explicitly only in chapter 6 in conjunction with the virtue of religion. Yet without the central elements of the metaphysics of morals in place, the concept of a rightly ordered will remains a freewheeling and ultimately empty notion. In order to demonstrate their current relevance, I shall not unfold these central elements abstractly but rather in the context of their contemporary contestation. Recall the philosophical and the existential objections to Aquinas's doctrine of beatitude that I adumbrated in the prologue. In a combination characteristic of late modernity, they form one single impediment with a philosophical aspect, the anthropocentric turn, and an existential aspect, the rise of subjective sovereignty. This specifically late-modern configuration becomes especially relevant when one considers the reality of conscience. When conceived as a function of subjective sovereignty, conscience is necessarily mistaken for its counterfeit—with detrimental consequences for the will's rectitude and hence the *viator*'s journey to beatitude.

In the first part of this chapter, I shall therefore put onto the canvas with the broadest strokes the anthropocentric turn to the subject and the emergence of subjective sovereignty as the dominant self-image. In the second part, I will propose as a cure for this detrimental anthropocentrism the return to the metaphysics of being and its three fundamental premises regarding the transcendentals being, truth, and the good. In the third part, I will turn to the eternal and the natural law and show that based on the ontological constitution of finite being, each being is first and foremost directed to its own perfection, to the full actualization of its nature, and that by the selfsame actualization of its nature, every being is directed to the twofold good of the universe, the order among the parts and the ordering of the whole universe to God. In the fourth part, I will consider the natural participation of the eternal law by the human being—the primordial conscience (*synderesis*)—and in the fifth part its characteristic activity, *con-scientia*. In the sixth part, I will draw out the crucial difference between conscience and the virtue of prudence. In the seventh part, I will address the complex phenomenon of the erroneous conscience and will in the subsequent part draw out the subtle but crucial differences between it and the distinctly modern phenomenon of the counterfeit of conscience. In the conclusion, finally, I will return to the principle that *to be good is to do the truth*. From the previous discussion, it will have become patent that this is the fundamental principle of the metaphysics of the good as it pertains to the *viator*'s journey to beatitude. For the good is that which is in accord with reality—a reality whose measure is the first truth who is the sovereign good. It will also have become clear that the whole moral motivation of rational beings depends upon the voice of primordial conscience, the natural habitual awareness of the precepts of the natural law. The typically modern crisis of moral motivation—Why should I pursue the good? Why should I be moral in the first place?—turns out to be a direct consequence of the anthropocentric turn and the subsequent flight from the encompassing teleology, of which the primordial conscience is an integral part.

THE ANTHROPOCENTRIC TURN AND SUBJECTIVE SOVEREIGNTY

In the early decades of the twenty-first century, an observant spectator might perceive the striking ambiguity that haunts the self-image of late-modern humanity in the Western Hemisphere. The rapidly accelerating progress of the scientific penetration of the natural world and the ensuing technological domination of the whole planet seem to have advanced humanity into a quasi-divine position, a collective Demiurge. Sovereignty, once upon a time an exclusive attribute of divinity, seems now to fall to humanity collectively, and in rather far-reaching specific ways to each individual human subject.

In the affluent parts of the Western Hemisphere, subjective sovereignty is exercised by way of the unfettered rule of one's will over ideally everything exterior to one's will, from myriads of consumer goods to varyingly branded identities, and last but not least, ideological and religious affiliations. The precious and tenaciously defended privilege of subjective sovereignty is, of course, choice. The scope of choice is seen as directly proportional to the degree of subjective sovereignty—an increase in the former indicates an increase in the latter.

However, the interpretation of reality that the natural sciences communicate to the public presents a jarringly different picture—a picture that calls into question the very possibility of subjective sovereignty. The human mind is understood as an epiphenomenon of the brain's neurological processes; human choices are predicted with statistical precision and unmasked as ultimately driven by nothing other than the interests of the "selfish gene." According to the naturalist savants of the most advanced life sciences, humans are nothing but highly sophisticated primates that will eventually be transparent without remainder to the scientific gaze and therefore open to comprehensive governance by way of the most advanced psychological and technological means of manipulation.

Thus the modern subject, the product of the anthropocentric turn, vacillates between two competing self-images. On the one side, we find the gnostic angelism of the putatively disembodied sovereign self that may submit to its will an absolutely malleable and fluid exteriority. And on the other side we find the materialist animalism of a super-primate that is the accidental product of the intricate interplay between random genetic mutation and specific ecological niche preferment. The extremes touch each other insofar as transhumanism—an outgrowth of the fantasies of the sovereign self—and posthumanism—the reductive understanding of the human being as super-primate—coincide in their *de facto* erasure of the embodied rational being.

As always, so also in our contemporary context, deeply shaped by the utopian pretenses of transhumanism and posthumanism, sovereignty has two aspects, the sovereign agent and the objects upon which sovereignty is exercised. The interminable struggle in late-modern technologically advanced, economically consumer-capitalist, and politically putatively liberal societies of the Western Hemisphere is to avoid at all costs being subjected to—and thereby objectified by—the sovereignty of others and simultaneously to maximize one's possibilities of exercising subjective sovereignty.

In our robustly secular and deeply skeptical Western societies, subjective sovereignty is the one transcendence the modern subject remains certain of, because it is self-produced. This particular form of transcendence is a decidedly immanent transcendence; its outer horizon is death. For death defies all strategies of maintaining or increasing subjective sovereignty, albeit with one significant exception: namely the unique strategy of folding death into the last act of one's own subjective sovereignty by sovereignly determining the terminus of oneself and the subsequent annihilation of one's body. Sovereign self-destruction unmasks the dead-end into which the anthropocentric turn ultimately leads: the self-image of subjective sovereignty can be consistently maintained to the very end only if it is sealed by an act of sovereign self-destruction. It is this ironic consequence that betrays the profound pretention and falsehood of this self-image.[2]

THE METAPHYSICS OF BEING:
BEING, TRUTH, AND THE GOOD

What might be the cure for this pervasive but profoundly false self-image?[3] I would submit, in all due modesty, that the only lasting cure will be nothing short of undoing the anthropocentric turn itself. Quite obviously, the world cannot be saved in the course of one academic sabbatical, let alone the anthropocentric turn undone in a single book chapter. But a first modest step in this direction might consist in this: to consider the most fundamental and radical alternative to anthropocentrism, an alternative, noteworthily, that is not simply

---

2. One of the most profound probings into the subjective sovereignty's "heart of darkness" is Fyodor Dostoyevsky's masterwork *Demons*, epitomized in the character Kirillov.

3. The following section is deeply indebted to Josef Pieper's interpretation of Aquinas in his *Reality and the Good*, which in the English translation forms the second part of the book *Living the Truth* (San Francisco, Calif.: Ignatius Press, 1989).

the contradictory to subjective sovereignty, that is, some imagined competitive sovereignty of an "Other" in capital letters, as most moderns would misunderstand divine sovereignty, an imagined competitive super-sovereignty out to annihilate or at least curtail subjective sovereignty. Unsurprisingly, in order to protect subjective sovereignty, such a competitive super-sovereignty must be placated, bribed, or simply declared nonexistent. Such a cure, of course, would not get at all to the root of the problem but only intensify the anthropocentric turn. Rather, getting to the root of the problem would mean to undertake the labor of recovering the primordial reality of the transcendent good and its noncompetitive sovereignty. This recovery would afford once again direct access to an objective moral reality in the light of which we can begin to understand the deeply problematic nature of the anthropocentric turn. This program of recovery forms an important part of the Thomist engagement of modernity.

At the heart of this program stands the comprehensive retrieval of the metaphysics of being which in its full depth is necessarily a metaphysics of creation. It rests on the fundamental Thomistic principle "to create is to give existence" (*creare est dare esse*). This principle marks the crucial ontotheological difference between the transcendent creative source of all existence, the subsistent act of existing itself (*ipsum esse subsistens*), the very giving of being, the "dare esse" (*ipsum esse creatum*),[4] and the participated act of being (*actus essendi*) the term of which is the "datum," the gift of the contingent existence of discrete beings (*ens per participationem*). Nothing less than such a recovery will reach deep enough in order to eradicate the bitter roots from which the anthropocentric turn arises.

This Thomist metaphysics of being entails three fundamental premises, premises I cannot develop, let alone defend, but only

---

4. What each being (*ens per participationem*) participates by way of its act of being (*actus essendi*) is not the divine essence immediately (*ens per essentiam*), but the gift of being (*ipsum esse creatum*) that is the first creature, so to speak (because it does not subsist independently from the *actus essendi* of the *ens per participationem*), and the closest created similitude of the uncreated divine essence. See *In librum beati Dionysii de divinis nominibus expositio* [hereafter "*In de Div. Nom.*"], c. 5, l. 2 (Marietti, no. 660): "Ipsum esse creatum est quaedam participatio Dei et similitudo ipsius." See also *Scriptum super libros Sententiarum magistri Petri Lombardi episcopi Parisiensis* [hereafter "*Sent.*"] I, q. 8, a. 1, q.c. 1, ad 2; q. 8, a. 12; *De ver.*, q. 21, a. 2, ad 2; q. 22, a. 2, ad 2; *SCG* III.66.

name and in the following suppose as true, because I intend to focus on one (albeit crucial) consequence of these premises—the primordial conscience. It is the reality of the primordial conscience that allows us best to confront the problem of subjective sovereignty and in principle already to overcome it. But first the three fundamental premises entailed in the metaphysics of creation:

First, the ontological premise: God is the measure of all things (*Deus omnium entium est mensura*). Through God's creative knowledge all real things are what they are. Differently put, all created things have their pre-form, their model, in the intellect of God; the divine knowledge is their exterior formal cause. Aquinas puts it thus:

> Natural things from which our intellect gets its scientific knowledge measure our intellect. Yet these things are themselves measured by the divine intellect, in which are all created things—just as all works of art find their origin in the intellect of the artist. The divine intellect, therefore, measures and is not measured; a natural thing both measures and is measured; but our intellect is measured, and measures only artifacts, not natural things.[5]

In the last sentence Aquinas refers to the realm of *technē* or *ars*, the vast realm of human creative ingenuity. But the intellect's ability to give the measure depends on the antecedent reception of the measure by the intellect. Aquinas states: "The intellect receives its measure from objects; that is, human knowledge is true not of itself, but it is true because and insofar as it conforms to reality" (*ST* I-II, q. 93, a. 1, ad 3). Thus *the second premise, the epistemological premise*, follows directly from the ontological premise: *pace* Kantian critical idealism and Husserlian transcendental phenomenology, human cognition attains the truth of real things. In the order of being, the measure that the extant thing receives by way of the original gift of being is its essence, its substantial form. In the order of knowledge, the measure that the intellect receives from the extant thing by way of the senses is the intentional form. The measure that constitutes the thing, its substantial form, and the measure that the object communicates to the intellect, its intentional form, are identical in essence but subsist in different modes of being, *esse reale* and *esse intentionale*.

From the epistemological premise follows the *third premise which*

---

5. *De ver.*, q. 1, a. 2, resp. (*Truth*, 1:11).

pertains to the order of action. Here is one of Aquinas's many formulations of this principle: "The will does not have the character of a first rule; it is rather a rule which has a rule, for it is directed by reason and the intellect."[6] The intellect's relation to reality antecedes the will's relation to it. As the rational appetite, the will depends on the prior deliveries of the intellect. The intellect's proper object is being and the intellect's proper end is truth. Affirming the primacy of the intellect over the will, Aquinas states that "the good, as truth, is related more primarily to knowledge than it is related, as good, to the will."[7] The human good is therefore not what the will sovereignly determines it to be. Rather, the human good is that which is first and foremost in accord with reality. But what is "reality"?

"Reality" is one of those concepts that belong to the very bedrock of Aquinas's metaphysics. For Aquinas "reality" means primarily two things expressed by the two Latin words *realis* and *actualis*; the one is derived from the Latin *res*, thing, the other from *actus*, action. *Res* signifies everything that is presented to our sense perception or our intellectual cognition; it signifies what has being independently of our thinking. *Actualitas*, on the other hand, signifies the opposite to whatever is merely potential. Reality in the sense of *actualitas* means realized potentiality. And thus to be good means not only to be directed toward realization, but rather also to be "realized" and hence fully in accord with reality. Aquinas states: "Every being is perfect insofar as it is realized, and imperfection lies in this that its potentiality is not realized" (*ST* I-II, q. 3, a. 2). Absolute *actualitas*, the absolute transcendence of the infinite subsistent act of existing itself (*ipsum esse subsistens*; *ST* I, q. 8, a. 2) is, of course, the sovereign good, God.[8]

THE ETERNAL AND THE NATURAL LAW

In virtue of the ontological constitution of all finite being (*ens per participationem*) by way of the act of being (*actus essendi*), each being is first and foremost directed to the full actualization of its own

---

6. *De ver.*, q. 23, a. 6 (*Truth*, 3:119).
7. *ST* I-II, q. 19, a. 3, ad 1; see also *De ver.*, q. 21, a. 3.
8. Pieper, *Living the Truth*, 111.

being according to its nature. Simultaneously, by the selfsame actualization of its own being, every creature is directed to the twofold good of the universe: the order among the parts and the ordering of the whole universe to God.[9] Aquinas holds it to be an entailment of the sovereign good, God, that God in all eternity by an act of the divine will intends the end of a perfect universe as the true manifestation of his sovereign goodness. No single being, however, is able perfectly to manifest this surpassing goodness. Therefore, God created an abundance of diverse beings with a plethora of different perfections. Thereby the universe as a whole more perfectly manifests and participates in God's goodness. However, beings are more like God when they act and cause being. For this very reason, Aquinas argues, God created all things in a state of potency to their particular type of action. When each being performs its particular type of action, it contributes to the perfection of the universe. And because God creates and guides creatures to their proper perfection in light of the same end (the perfection of the whole), each being acts in accord with its particular mode of participating the act of being (*actus essendi*) which is its primary perfection, the substantial form. Through these acts, which are its secondary perfections, each being reaches its specific end. These secondary perfections are the way each being participates in the eternal law, the *ratio* by way of which God governs the universe.[10] God's *ratio*, the eternal law, has imprinted upon all beings natural inclinations to their proper natural ends. Precisely by following their natural inclinations all beings pursue their own perfection and contribute to the perfection of the whole universe.

Now, rational beings participate in this *ratio* in a unique way, a way proper to their intellect. In analogy to the eternal law, Aquinas calls this natural cognitive participation of rational beings in eternal law "natural law" (*ST* I-II, q. 91, a. 2).[11] In virtue of the nat-

---

9. See esp. *SCG* I.29 and III.23–32. On this topic, now available in English, see the important essay by Charles De Koninck, "The Primacy of the Common Good against the Personalists," in *The Writings of Charles De Koninck*, ed. and trans. Ralph McInerny (Notre Dame, Ind.: University of Notre Dame Press, 2009), 2:63–108.

10. For a lucid discussion of this complex topic, see John Rziha, *Perfecting Human Actions: St. Thomas Aquinas on Human Participation in Eternal Law* (Washington, D.C.: The Catholic University of America Press, 2009).

11. Aquinas understands the natural law fundamentally as the rational creature's

ural law, rational creatures are "partakers of a share of providence, by being both provident for [themselves] and for others" (*ST* I-II, q. 92, a. 2). This participation occurs by way of the natural inclination of practical reason to the proper act and end of the rational being: "On the part of practical reason, [the human being] has a natural participation of the eternal law, according to certain general principles" (*ST* I-II, q. 91, a. 3, ad 1). Aquinas calls this natural participation of the eternal law by the human being *synderesis*, which in a nutshell denotes the primordial conscience. What is *synderesis*? Aquinas distinguishes two aspects of the human intellect, speculative reason and practical reason. The end of each is truth: for speculative reason truth in the theoretical order; for practical reason truth in the order of agency. Theoretical and practical reason are only able to pursue and achieve their end, truth, in virtue of certain fundamental principles that reside in the intellect as innate habits or dispositions. The innate habit of speculative reason contains the first principles of abstract reason, the innate habit of practical reason contains the first principles of action. The principle of noncontradiction is based upon the concept of being, which is the proper object of the speculative reason; the first principle and the first precept of *synderesis* is based upon the concept of the good which is the proper object of practical reason.

SYNDERESIS AS PRIMORDIAL CONSCIENCE

Synderesis, the primordial conscience, is a natural, innate stable disposition or habit (*habitus*) of the human mind. In virtue of this unique *habitus* human beings are enabled and indeed ordered "to have a primary and infallible judgment about the good as the end and the meaning of human action."[12] This destination toward such a primary and infallible judgment is possible because this innate natural *habitus* contains the first principle and the first precept of practi-

---

participation in the eternal law, which "is nothing else than the type of Divine Wisdom, as directing all actions and movements" (*ST* I-II, q. 93, a. 1). For an instructive treatment of this crucial aspect of Aquinas's sapiential moral theology, see Rziha, *Perfecting Human Actions*, 199–230.

12. Pieper, *Living the Truth*, 153.

cal reason. Its first principle is "good is that which all things seek after," and its first precept is "good is to be done and pursued, and evil is to be avoided" (*ST* I-II, q. 94, a. 4).[13] It is important to realize that the first precept "does not primarily signify an obligation to do the good. Rather, it expresses the attraction of the good.... It is this urgency of the truth within the good, within the very attraction of the good, that is at the heart of the intimate awareness of duty and obligation."[14] The first precept expresses the inherent attraction of the good as understood good. The natural *habitus* of first principle and first precept enable the rational creature not only to move to some perceived good but to realize the character of good (*ratio finis*). Because good is the perfection that all beings desire (*ST* I, q. 5, a. 1) and to which all beings move as their final end (*ST* I, q. 5, a. 4), the primordial conscience (*synderesis*) enables the human *qua rational* being to realize the teleology of the good by participating, by way of the natural law, in the eternal law. Genuine human freedom arises precisely from the rational being's proper *rational* participation in the eternal law and is perfected when the rational being acts fully in accord with the eternal law.[15]

Incidentally, on the supposition of the fundamental teleological ordering of the universe, the so-called naturalistic fallacy—the illicit naturalistic or metaphysical transition from "is" to "ought," from the order of being to the moral order, a putative fallacy invented by David Hume and named by G. E. Moore—is a mute concern.[16] For, be-

---

13. Aquinas explains: "*Good* is the first thing that falls under the apprehension of the practical reason, which is directed to action: since every agent acts for an end under the aspect of good. Consequently, the first principle in practical reason is founded on the notion of good, i.e. that *good is that which all things seek after*. Hence this is the first precept of law, that *good is to be done and pursued, and evil is to be avoided*" (*ST* I-II, q. 94, a. 2).

14. Servais Pinckaers, OP, *Morality: The Catholic View*, trans. Michael Sherwin, OP (South Bend, Ind.: St. Augustine's Press, 2001), 100.

15. Rziha, *Perfecting Human Actions*, 265: "For Thomas, freedom does not come from a blind movement of the will or sense appetites but comes from the will and sense appetites being determined by human reason to intend and choose acts in accord with the ultimate end of humanity.... Hence, freedom is bound up in rationality, which derives its light and intellectual forms from the eternal law.... Authentic human freedom is first and foremost caused by the eternal law and only caused by the human through the soul's participation in the eternal law."

16. One can, of course, argue that *synderesis* does not exist. But the burden of the proof rests with the one who advances such an argument. For the overwhelming empirical

longing without remainder to the extant teleologically ordered universe, human beings—as all other created beings—are teleologically constituted by way of their natural inclinations (*ST* I-II, q. 94, a. 2). As a tendency to its proper end or good, the "ought" is embedded in the "is" of every being and especially in those beings that realize their perfection through the exercise of practical reason. The primordial conscience, *synderesis* is not only a formal but a teleological principle interior to practical reason itself.

There is one further implication given with the interior teleological constitution of practical reason. Because the primordial conscience (*synderesis*) is a habitual light, it prevents the dictates of conscience from ever becoming heteronomous. For the dictates of conscience are nothing but the concretization, by way of judgment, of those principles and precepts that are constitutive of the teleological ordering of practical reason itself. For this very reason, an objective teleological ethics grounded in the primordial conscience and in the natural inclinations remains untouched by the false binary of heteronomy and autonomy, the direct result of the anthropocentric turn that haunts most modern moral philosophy.[17] Turning away from the primordial conscience and with it from the teleological order of reality and embracing instead the negative freedom of sovereign self-determination, the anthropocentric turn and the consequent sovereign subjectivity give rise to a pervasive counterfeit of conscience, the presumptuous "authenticity" of self-will. This counterfeit is condemned to a neverending vigilance against the constant threat of a hostile "takeover" by other sovereign self-wills, be they human "others" or a supposed divine "Other" misconceived in the false self-image of subjective sovereignty.

---

evidence in human history speaks for the existence of *synderesis*. For a modern discussion of the problem raised by Hume expressly in his anonymously published 1739/40 *Treatise of Human Nature Being an Attempt to Introduce the Experimental Method of Reasoning into Moral Subjects* (III.I.1), and coined as "naturalistic fallacy" by G. E. Moore in his 1903 *Principia Ethica* (chap. 2), see *The Is-Ought Question*, ed. William Donald Hudson (London: Macmillan, 1969). For a substantive treatment of this problematic and an in-depth analysis of Aquinas's philosophical justification for the transition from "is" to "ought," see Piotr Lichacz, "Did St. Thomas Aquinas Justify the Transition from 'Is' to 'Ought'?" (STD diss., University of Fribourg, 2008).

17. See J. B. Schneewind, *The Invention of Autonomy: A History of Modern Moral Philosophy* (Cambridge: Cambridge University Press, 1998).

THE PRIMORDIAL CONSCIENCE
AND ITS ACT, *CON-SCIENTIA*

We must now turn to the *act* of the primordial conscience. Aquinas calls this act *con-scientia*, "knowing together." Recall that Aquinas defines the primordial conscience (*synderesis*) as "a natural *habitus* of first principles of action, which are the universal principles of the natural law."[18] *Synderesis* names practical reason as "perfected by a completely determined *habitus*."[19] The natural determination of practical reason consists in "a primordial perception of the good proper to [the human being]."[20] The intellect in its theoretical and in its practical aspect intuits self-evident principles antecedent to rational deliberation, but consequent to learning the terms of these principles through basic sense experience. Aquinas explains this matter succinctly in the context of discussing the question whether any *habitus* is natural, that is, innate:

> The understanding of first principles is called a natural habit. For it is owing to the very nature of the intellectual soul that [a human being], having once grasped what is a whole and what is a part, would at once perceive that every whole is larger than its part: and in like manner with regard to other such principles. Yet what is a whole, and what is a part—this he cannot know except through the intelligible species which he has received from phantasms: and for this reason, the Philosopher at the end of the *Posterior Analytics* shows that knowledge of principles comes to us from the senses. (*ST* I-II, q. 51, a. 1)

How does this understanding of conscience spell out on the operational level?[21] "Knowing together" (*con-scientia*) signifies the actualization of the natural *habitus* of the first principles of moral truth

---

18. *De ver.*, q. 16, a. 1 (*Truth*, 2:304). See also his *Sent.* II, d. 24, q. 2, a. 3, and *ST* I, q. 79, a. 12.

19. *De ver.*, q. 16, a. 2, ad 5 (*Truth*, 2:310).

20. Servais Pinckaers, OP, *The Sources of Christian Ethics*, trans. Sr. Mary Thomas Noble, OP (Washington, D.C.: The Catholic University of America Press, 1995), 384.

21. The Greek term for this actualization is συνείδησις and its Latin literal translation is *con-scientia*. By the time the Apostle Paul wrote his letters, both terms were common in popular everyday usage of Greek and Latin. Paul uses συνείδησις frequently: see Rom 2:15; 1 Cor 8:7, 10, 12; 10:28–29; 2 Cor 1:12–13; 1 Tm 1:19; Ti 1:15.

in two respects (*ST* I, q. 79, a. 13).[22] There occurs, first, a concrete judgment of practical reason to be followed, secondly, by a command of reason that applies this knowledge to action (*ST* I-II, q. 19, a. 5). The judgment of "knowing together" (*con-scientia*) normally occurs prospectively, that is, antecedent to the execution of a specific exterior act. But it also may occur retrospectively, consequent to the execution or the omission of some specific exterior act.

CONSCIENCE AND THE VIRTUE OF PRUDENCE

In order to gain a deeper understanding of the objective nature of primordial conscience and its actualization in *con-scientia* we must appreciate how *con-scientia* relates to the principal cardinal virtue, prudence, which Aquinas defines as "right practical reason." "Prudence imprints the inward seal of goodness upon all free activity of [the human being]."[23] Hence: "What is prudent and what is good are substantially one and the same; they differ only in their place in the logical succession of realization. For what is good must first have been prudent."[24] What difference does the virtue of prudence make if indeed, as Aquinas claims, "*synderesis* moves prudence [i.e., the knowledge of truth in the practical order], just as the understanding of principles moves science [i.e., the knowledge of truth in the theoretical order]" (*ST* II-II, q. 47, a. 6, ad 3)?

To be sure, the virtue of prudence does make a crucial difference. For this particular virtue concretizes the third premise, the premise that pertains to the order of action. Recall Aquinas's formulation of this premise: "The will does not have the character of a first rule; it is rather a rule which has a rule, for it is directed by reason and the intellect."[25] Consistent with this rule, Aquinas conceives of prudence as having a cognitive as well as a commanding quality (*ST* II-II, q. 48, a. 1). Willing and acting depend upon prudence in precisely

---

22. See also *De ver.*, q. 17, a. 1, and *Sent.* II, d. 24, q. 2, a. 4.
23. Pieper, *The Four Cardinal Virtues: Prudence, Justice, Fortitude, Temperance* (Notre Dame, Ind.: University of Notre Dame Press, 1966), 7–8.
24. Ibid.
25. *De ver.*, q. 23, a. 6 (*Truth*, 3:119).

this: the concrete moral action of the will receives its measure from the command (*iudicium*) of prudence (*ST* I-II, q. 64, a. 3). Aquinas puts this matter quite explicitly in article 13 of his treatise *On the Virtues in General*: "Reason ... relates to the things that it puts into effect as being *their* standard and measure.... By contrast, it relates to the things about which it reflects, as something that is measured and regulated relates to *its* standard and measure. For the good of our intelligence is what is true, and our intelligence attains that precisely by corresponding to the thing that it understands."[26] Importantly, in this function of giving the measure to the concrete moral action to the will by way of command, prudence as the perfective excellence of practical reason is precisely an extension of speculative reason. Unlike the divine intellect, the human intellect must receive the measure before it can give the measure. Josef Pieper puts the matter as clearly as one could wish:

> Knowledge of being is "lengthened" and transformed into decision and command. The imperative is founded upon an indicative; the latter makes the former possible. Essentially prior to the decision and command is the purely perceptive statement. The "image" of the real precedes and underlies the "plan" of all realization. Decision and command, in which the practical reason is realized, signify, then, a knowledge which turns toward the will. But knowledge is an essential identity of the mind with the objective reality. The relation of these two facts reveals the measure and the manner in which the practical reason proper, which on its part determines the free act, is essentially bound up with the objective reality which is perceived in our knowledge of being.[27]

Aquinas's account of practical reason comes thus to stand in the sharpest possible contrast to all modern accounts of practical reason, accounts that in the wake of the anthropocentric turn move the human into a quasi-divine position: "practical" reason becomes now essentially creative, indeed, constructive, that is, in short, sovereign.

With the utterly realist nature of the virtue of prudence firmly established, the question nevertheless remains: how is the act

---

26. *De virtutibus in communi* [hereafter "*De virt.*"], q. un., a. 13. Translation from Thomas Aquinas, *Disputed Questions on the Virtues*, ed. E. M. Atkins and Thomas Williams, trans. E. M. Atkins (Cambridge: Cambridge University Press, 2005), 98.
27. Pieper, *Living the Truth*, 144.

of "knowing together" (*con-scientia*) to be understood in relationship to prudence? Among the three acts of the virtue of prudence—to take counsel (*consiliari*), to judge (*iudicare*), and to command (*praecipere*)—*con-scientia* comprises the second act when this judgment is right and certain, that is, when it is indeed properly formed by the virtue of prudence (*ST* II-II, q. 47, a. 8). *Con-scientia*, in and of itself, however, is not efficacious in choosing and doing the good. Consider the morally weak person. Following Aristotle, Aquinas calls such a person incontinent. The incontinent person "knows what he ought to do, his conscience is all right, but his knowledge of the good is not complemented by an effective appetitive disposition to good as good. That is why in the crunch, in choosing ... he goes wrong."[28] While judgments of *con-scientia* are absolutely indispensable for moral goodness, simple *con-scientia* lacks the power of execution.[29] What remains indispensable for efficaciously choosing and doing the good, are the two other acts of the virtue of prudence, counsel and command, in concert with the remaining cardinal virtues of justice, fortitude, and temperance.[30] At its very best, that is,

28. Ralph McInerny, "Prudence and Conscience," *The Thomist* 38 (1974): 291–305, at 303.

29. Command (*imperium*) is an act of the reason moved by the will (*ST* I-II, q. 17, a. 1). When *imperium* is an act integral to the virtue of prudence (instead of being the result of precipitation or thoughtlessness), Aquinas calls it *praecipium*, command as informed by right judgment. Indeed, he regards the act of command (*praecipere*) as the principal act of prudence. Practical reason is directed to action. Therefore, after counsel or deliberation and judgment, the third act of prudence is "to command [*praecipere*] which act consists in applying to action the things counselled and judged. And since this act approaches nearer to the end of practical reason, it follows that it is the chief act of the practical reason, and consequently of prudence" (*ST* II-II, q. 47, a. 8).

30. In *ST* II-II, q. 53, a. 3, Aquinas lays out the contours of the ideal act of taking counsel which comprises five steps: "*Memory* [*memoria*] of the past, *intelligence* [*intelligentia*] of the present, *shrewdness* [*solertia*] in considering the future outcome, *reasoning* [*ratiocinatio*] which compares one thing with another, *docility* [*docilitas*] in accepting the opinions of others. He that takes counsel descends by these steps in due order." That these five steps are not solitary events in the agent's soul but, on the contrary, reflect primarily distinct aspects of the dynamic of social interaction of deliberation becomes clear when one considers Aquinas's important statement in *ST* I-II, q. 14, a. 3, resp.: "Counsel properly implies a conference held between several; the very word [*consilium*] denotes this, for it means a sitting together [*considium*], from the fact that many sit together in order to confer with one another." I am indebted to Raymond F. Hain IV for having learned to think about counsel as a primarily social activity. See the section "Is Consilium a Social Activity?" in his instructive dissertation, "Practical Virtues: Instrumental

when it is right and certain, the antecedent judgment of *con-scientia* is an integral component of the virtue of prudence.

Once the *habitus* of prudence has been diminished or completely lost due to contrary acts of imprudence (*ST* II-II, q. 53) and the act of counsel prevented by precipitation (a. 3) or by thoughtlessness (a. 4), the flight from the *synderistic* indicator of moral truth paves the way for one to indulge in the counterfeit of conscience, the presumptuous "authenticity" of self-will. Regarding its own decisions as intrinsically infallible expressions of a sovereign self-determination, the counterfeit forgoes counsel. The decisions the counterfeit posits create the semblance of a true and therefore good conscience precisely because the counterfeit's decisions are held as infallible. By feigning authenticity, the sovereign self-determination produces a counterfeit that blocks access to the *synderistic* root of right judgment.

The Erroneous Conscience

But how does this phenomenon of the counterfeit of conscience, which produces a simulacrum of the true and therefore good conscience, relate to the phenomenon of the erroneous conscience? Could the counterfeit of conscience not be understood as an instantiation of the erroneous conscience? That this is not the case will become plain when we understand the characteristics of an erroneous conscience.

The judgment of *con-scientia*, the application of the universal principles of *synderesis* to a particular case, is fallible. When properly informed by prudence, that is, when conformed to right intention according to the principles and precepts of *synderesis* and when subjectively certain, the judgment of *con-scientia* is practically true and right. But the agent might suffer from ignorance and might therefore be objectively burdened by an erroneous conscience. Hence, the characteristic deficiency of an erroneous conscience is ignorance. Such ignorance can be voluntary or involuntary, vincible or invincible (*ST* I-II, q. 76).

Practical Reason and the Virtues" (PhD diss., University of Notre Dame, 2009), 177–82, and more recently his important essay "Consilium and the Foundations of Ethics," *The Thomist* 79, no. 1 (2015): 43–74.

The dictate of conscience binds and must be obeyed; therefore, a dictate issuing from an objectively erroneous conscience must nevertheless be subjectively obeyed. Aquinas rightly insists upon this point. But does such an insistence not open the door to the authenticity of self-will, the counterfeit of conscience? Consider how Aquinas distinguishes between the objective and the subjective perspective:

> Conscience is said to bind in so far as one sins if he does not follow his conscience, but not in the sense that he acts correctly if he does follow it.... Conscience is not said to bind in the sense that what one does according to such a conscience will be good, but in the sense that in not following it he will sin.... A correct conscience and a false conscience bind in different ways. The correct conscience binds absolutely and for an intrinsic reason; the false binds in a qualified way and for an extrinsic reason.[31]

The erroneous conscience does indeed bind, not because it is correct, but because the judgment of *con-scientia* is all a person can go by—at the moment. Nevertheless, the erroneous conscience can be identified eventually as such because it depends upon the logical priority of the correct conscience, which applies the principles of *synderesis* rightly. From the agent's perspective the way to find out whether one has acted from an erroneous conscience or not occurs in light of instruction, counsel, or self-examination by way of a consequent judgment of *con-scientia*, either in the form of a moral self-critique that elicits regret and remorse in the case of a formerly erroneous conscience or in the form of a simple retrospective affirmation that one's true and therefore good conscience has indeed also been right. Precisely because of the innate *habitus* of *synderesis*, the principle and therefore the concrete possibility of self-correction always obtains. For this reason it is the case that while the erroneous conscience indeed binds, it does not automatically excuse. Aquinas explains:

> If ... reason or conscience should err voluntarily, either directly or because of negligence, being in error about something one is held to know, then such error does not prevent the will which is in accord with erring reason or conscience from being evil.... Similarly, supposing error of reason or

---

31. *De ver.*, q. 17, a. 4, resp. (*Truth*, 2:331–32); see also *ST* I-II, q. 19, a. 5. Aquinas holds the correct conscience to bind absolutely and for an intrinsic reason because a judgment of *con-scientia* that is practically true is necessarily also right.

conscience which proceeds from a non-excusing ignorance, evil in the will necessarily follows. However, such a [person is not perplexed], because he can correct his error, since his ignorance is both vincible and voluntary. (*ST* I-II, q. 19, a. 6 and ad 3)

Culpable erroneous conscience is caused either by negligence (see *ST* II-II, q. 54; lack of due solicitude), which makes it indirectly voluntary, or by willful ignorance (see *ST* I-II, q. 76), which makes it directly voluntary. In his *Commentary on the Sentences*, the young Aquinas offers a pithy summary of this complex matter: to follow one's erring conscience means to be unable to avoid sinning (*peccatum non evaditur*), but to act against one's conscience means to directly incur sin (*peccatum incurritur*).[32] To turn intentionally against the judgment of conscience is always culpable because it means that one cuts oneself off from the very possibility of following moral truth. To follow one's erring conscience means to do what seems subjectively right but what is objectively wrong. With this insight, we have reached the point where we can name the difference between the erroneous conscience and the counterfeit of conscience.

The Erroneous Conscience and the Counterfeit of Conscience

First, from the objective perspective afforded by the Thomist metaphysics of the good and its entailed moral science, the reality of an erroneous conscience presupposes an objective moral order and reliable knowledge of it. For a consistent moral subjectivism and the concomitant rule of self-will, on the contrary, an erroneous conscience is an utterly meaningless notion. By positing its own dictates of self-will, the subjectivist counterfeit of conscience is, by definition, infallible. Because it is the law of its own dictates, there is nothing in light of which the counterfeit of conscience can possibly err.[33] In the wake of the anthropocentric turn, "sincerity," "authenticity," and "being at peace with oneself" become the new criteria of a radically subjectivist conception of moral judgment in service of the

---

32. *Sent.* II, d. 39, q. 3, a. 3. Cf. also his later *Quaestiones quodlibetales* [hereafter "*Quod.*"] III, q. 12, a. 2, ad 2.

33. Johann Gottlieb Fichte's subjective idealism offers probably the most consistent but also most problematic account of the inherently infallible conscience.

sovereign self. These new criteria are intended to mute the voice of the primordial conscience and thereby to unhinge the "rule of ethical truth."[34]

Second, from the agent's perspective, the very possibility of an erroneous conscience entails an antecedent and a consequent personal duty. The antecedent duty is to avoid ignorance and imprudence. Formulated positively, the antecedent duty is always to seek counsel, to have one's conscience formed by those one regards as wiser and better informed than oneself, and first and foremost, to avail oneself of the instruction by and guidance of those whose specific vocation is to instruct conscience by teaching the secondary precepts of the natural law. The consequent duty is to avoid negligence and indifference by way of a regular examination of conscience, a sincere review of past judgments, and repentance of acts done due to an erroneous conscience.

Third, in light of Aquinas's doctrine of conscience, the counterfeit of conscience is objectively a result of willful ignorance or at least of negligence and thoughtlessness. In the worst case, the counterfeit is an intentional, self-conscious flight from conscience: by positing decisions of the self-will, a person acts in direct opposition to the judgments of a correct conscience.

Does this mean that the counterfeit of conscience is able to extinguish *synderesis*? Aquinas addresses this question explicitly. He denies that *synderesis* can be extinguished in its root, through a loss of the innate *habitus*, "for this light belongs to the nature of the soul, since by reason of this the soul is intellectual."[35] But regarding the actualization of the *habitus*, *synderesis* can indeed be deflected toward the contrary of *synderesis* whenever "the force of concupiscence, or of another passion, so absorbs reason that in choice the universal judgment of *synderesis* is not applied to the particular act."[36] It is here that Aquinas points to what we might call the dark secret of the counterfeit of conscience. What looks to the person fleeing primordial con-

---

34. John Henry Cardinal Newman, *Certain Difficulties Felt by Anglicans in Catholic Teaching* (London: Longmans, Green, and Co, 1888; reprinted in Westminster, Md.: Christian Classics, 1969), 2:175–378, at 246.
35. *De ver.*, q. 16, a. 3, resp. (*Truth*, 2:312).
36. Ibid.

science like the sovereignly posited decisions of self-determination is indeed the product of a profound self-deception. The flight from primordial conscience actually makes the moral agent subject to the power of the sensual passions and the variegated desires of the will to which they give rise. However, because the primordial conscience cannot be destroyed, but only fled from or suppressed, the counterfeit of conscience must be willfully maintained, directly or—more frequently—indirectly. For all the decisions the counterfeit sovereignly posits remain exposed to the "habitual light" that the first principle and the first precept of *synderesis* shed on the agent's reason. The counterfeit is therefore inherently unable to gain the peace that is characteristic of a conscience that is both subjectively true and therefore good and objectively correct.[37]

CONCLUSION: TO BE GOOD IS TO DO THE TRUTH

Where have we arrived? At Aquinas's sobering suggestion that to be good is to do the truth. This is the fundamental principle of the metaphysics of the good as it pertains to the *viator*'s journey to beatitude. For the good is that which is in accord with reality—a reality whose measure is the first truth who is the sovereign good. Every human being *qua* rational being has received a natural innate *habitus* that reflects the measure that the rational being received in its rational nature: while the sphere of theoretical thinking is governed by the fundamental principle of noncontradiction, the sphere of practical thinking is governed by *synderesis*, the first principle of the natural law. In Aquinas's words: "The original direction of all our actions toward the end is necessarily brought about by the natural law" (*ST* I-II, q. 91, a. 2, ad 2). The whole moral motivation of rational beings depends upon the voice of primordial conscience, the natural habitual awareness of the precepts of the natural law. From a Thomist perspective the typically modern crisis of moral motivation—Why should I pursue the good? Why should I be moral in the first

37. But even for a conscience, truly so called, such a peace remains a fragile reality unless it is one of the fruits of the Spirit (*ST* I-II, q. 70) arising from the gifts of wisdom and counsel (*ST* II-II, qq. 45 and 52).

place?—is a direct consequence of the anthropocentric turn and the subsequent flight from the encompassing teleology, of which the primordial conscience is an integral part. This flight produces the counterfeit of conscience, the authenticity of self-will that interminably vacillates between three versions of self-justification: moral nihilism ("There is neither good nor evil," "Good and evil are strictly subjective success terms"), moral skepticism ("Human beings are inherently incapable of discerning reliably moral good and evil"), and moral sovereignty ("I am the creator and arbiter of my own moral code").

These accretions of the anthropocentric turn commit those who come under their spell to constant performative self-contradictions in everyday life because persons who hold these views nevertheless continue to act toward ends that are first perceived as goods. And it is precisely this that makes these actions intelligible in the first place. Intelligible actions however are, as G. E. M. Anscombe and Alasdair MacIntyre have shown, the basic units of human moral agency.[38] And these units have an irreducibly teleological structure, a structure that as Aquinas has argued necessitates a single final end. Hence, modern agents, beholden by the false self-image of subjective sovereignty, *de facto* display the first principle of practical reason, follow the first precept of the natural law, and for the most part also acknowledge an at least tacit knowledge of some of the secondary precepts of the natural law. As Alasdair MacIntyre has pointedly stated in his still eminently relevant study from 1990, *Three Rival Versions of Moral Enquiry*, "the Thomist...discerns in the continuous reappropriation of [the deracinated and fragmented moral rules of European modernity], and in the recurring resistance to discarding them, evidence of the work of *synderesis*, of that fundamental initial grasp of the primary precepts of the natural law, to which cultural degeneration can partially or temporarily blind us but which can never be obliterated."[39] In the following conclusion, MacIntyre makes the implicit organizing principle of my reflections explicit:

---

38. G. E. M. Anscombe, *Intention*, 2nd ed. (Ithaca, N.Y.: Cornell University Press, 1963); Alasdair MacIntyre, "The Intelligibility of Action," 63–80.
39. MacIntyre, *Three Rival Versions of Moral Enquiry*, 194.

So the Thomist claims to be able to render intelligible the history of both modern morality and modern moral philosophy in a way which is not available to those who themselves inhabit the conceptual frameworks peculiar to modernity. They cannot hope to understand themselves in the only terms which they and their institutions allow themselves for understanding. And their own theories, the theories of those imprisoned within modernity, can thus provide only ideological rationalizations, the rationalizations of modern deontology, modern consequentialism, and modern contractarianism.[40]

Modern deontology, consequentialism, and contractarianism are moral theories that emerge in the wake of the anthropocentric turn. As the history of modernity has demonstrated, these moral theories turned out to be utterly unfit to contain the power of subjective sovereignty that the anthropocentric turn unleashed.

Aquinas's metaphysics of the good with its special emphasis on *synderesis*, natural law, and the virtue of prudence advances a compelling account of why this is the case and thereby offers a powerful analytic device that allows us accurately to gauge the profoundly problematic implications of the anthropocentric turn for moral theory and especially for the moral life. Aquinas's realist metaphysics opens up the ontological and epistemological horizon in which the philosophical errancy of the anthropocentric turn comes into full light.

What Aquinas's metaphysics of being and the good cannot do, and of course was never meant to do, is to turn us back efficaciously from the perennial existential crisis, a crisis that the anthropocentric turn has only intensified. Even when we do not flee the voice of primordial conscience but are attentive to it, there remains a pressing question: how can one be good and therefore do the truth without first encountering the truth in such a direct and personal way that we find ourselves not only claimed by the truth but fall in love with its surpassing goodness such that we become effectively good?

Aquinas, of course, holds the faith characteristic of an orthodox Christian, which is the faith of the church, namely, that the sovereign good has become incarnate. Yet with this claim Aquinas beck-

---

40. Ibid.

ons us to ascend from metaphysics to mystagogy, from the philosophy of the sovereign good to the elevated science of sacred theology he called "holy teaching" (*sacra doctrina*). This holy teaching rests on one breathtakingly simple and breathtakingly outlandish axiom: the first truth and the sovereign good are at hand in the utter humility and vulnerability of the human nature that the incarnate Logos assumed from among a people God created for that purpose. Here is the ultimate stumbling block for the sovereign self, with its pride and despair. Here too, however, is the concrete hope that we might enter a new life in which death has been definitively overcome precisely by the incarnate sovereign good. In this new life the pursuit of subjective sovereignty can be relinquished because the cage of immanent transcendence has been opened from the outside by the sovereign good. In the personal encounter with the one who, according to the Apostle John, says "I am the truth" (Jn 14:6), the one who gives his life for his enemies and calls us to become his friends, it becomes obvious: primordial conscience tells us, "To be good is to do the truth." This is the fundamental principle that subsists as habitual light in the practical reason and enjoins the first precept of the natural law. But in order to *become* good in the first place—that is, good unconditionally and absolutely (*simpliciter*), not merely conditionally and in a certain respect (*secundum quid*)—so that we can effectively do the truth, we must be united by way of the infused theological virtues of faith, hope, and charity with the One who is the truth *simpliciter*, because only he can state the truth that he is: "I am the truth" (Jn 14:6) and "Before Abraham was, I AM" (Jn 8:58). For according to John the incarnate sovereign good also says, "Apart from me you can do nothing" (Jn 15:5; RSV).

3

Liberated for Beatitude— Saved from Sin

Christ's Passion on the Cross, the Surpassing Act of Charity

> In the justification of the ungodly, justice is seen, when God remits sins on account of love, though He Himself has mercifully infused that love. So we read of Magdalen: *Many sins are forgiven her, because she has loved much* (Lk 7:47).
> —Thomas Aquinas, *ST* I, q. 21, a. 4, ad 1

What actually makes a human being a wayfarer to the ultimate end, beatitude? How does one become a *viator*? The purpose of this chapter is to show that becoming a wayfarer to beatitude is not simply a matter of making up one's mind and doing it. Rather, before humans may embark on the sojourn to beatitude they must be made fit for it by becoming configured to the ultimate end—they must be constituted as wayfarers. For without being configured to the ultimate end and thus constituted as wayfarers, we can neither approach nor attain the ultimate end, beatitude. To put it into theological terms, the topic of this chapter is the soteriological constitution of the *viator* as *viator*. God makes humans into wayfarers in the first place by saving them from sin and thus freeing them for the journey to beatitude, a journey that comprises in one the wayfarer's justification, sanctification, and deification. Aquinas shows that it is at the foot of the cross of Christ where humans are constituted as wayfarers and where the wayfarer's sojourn begins. Christ's passion on the cross, the surpassing act of charity, liberates humanity from the estrangement and corruption of sin, restores humanity to God, and reestablishes the primordial order of charity, the friendship with God. Configured to the ultimate end, thus constituted as wayfarers, humans are fit to embark on the sojourn to beatitude.

As I did in the first two chapters, also in this chapter I shall unfold the topic under discussion in the context of a pertinent contemporary issue. In this chapter the issue will be the ecumenical challenge of reappropriating Aquinas's soteriology in which a central biblical motif—almsgiving as the first and foremost means of repaying the debt of sin—has fallen into almost complete oblivion. However, there has been a noteworthy initiative in biblical exegesis to reclaim and put into center stage this very biblical motif.[1] This important initiative offers a key to access the very heart of Aquinas's soteriology in a fresh and contemporaneously relevant way. At the heart of this soteriology sits the order of charity which is essential for the theological constitution of the *viator* and the nature of the journey to beatitude. As it turns out, both the wayfarer and the sojourn itself belong to the order of charity and can only be understood in light of it.

Gary Anderson's book *Sin: A History* is as salutary and salient for Protestants who find the very notion that almsgiving might be a means to repay the debt of one's sins theologically objectionable because they regard it as unbiblical as it is for Catholics who have forgotten the theological meaning of almsgiving and with it its biblical roots. Did not, after all, the Reformation unmask almsgiving as a means to repay the debt of one's sins as the most pernicious, sinful attempt at "self-redemption" (*Selbsterlösung*) and was not the

---

1. Gary A. Anderson, *Sin: A History* (New Haven, Conn.: Yale University Press, 2009). For two discussions and engagements of the book, as informative as instructive, see Paul J. Griffiths's review, "In the Red," *Commonweal* 137, no. 2 (January 29, 2010): 25–26, and Bruce D. Marshall's review essay, "Treasures in Heaven," *First Things* 199 (January 2010): 23–26. For an excellent exegetical study on the Gospel of Matthew that extends Anderson's argument into the New Testament, see Nathan Eubank, *Wages of Cross-Bearing and Debt of Sin: The Economy of Heaven in Matthew's Gospel* (Berlin: Walter de Gruyter, 2013).

important Lutheran reformer Johannes Bugenhagen (1485–1558), a close friend of and co-operator with Martin Luther, acclaimed as a social reformer precisely for the invention and broad implementation of the "common chest" that was meant in one fell stroke to get rid simultaneously of beggars and of almsgiving?[2] To put it in different and more conciliatory terms, Anderson's book is of significant ecumenical relevance, and that for at least two reasons: first, the book—in light of its argument for an undeniable grammar of sin as debt and of almsgiving as the first and foremost means of repaying this debt—invites Protestants to reconsider whether one of their most cherished polemics against the Catholic faith might indeed be biblically unfounded. And second—in light of some rather peculiar developments, to say the least, in Catholic life and piety since the 1960s—Anderson's book invites contemporary Catholics to rediscover the biblical warrants for more than a few traditional Catholic practices of piety and their concomitant beliefs. In order to contribute directly to the latter—the Catholic rediscovery—and indirectly to the former—the Protestant reconsideration—I take *Sin: A History* as the welcome occasion for a *ressourcement* in Thomas Aquinas's theology of sin and redemption, a theology equally relevant, I would like to submit, for contemporary Catholics and Protestants.[3] That sin

---

2. The Bugenhagen scholar Kurt K. Hendel puts the matter as succinctly as one can wish: "The poor chest, envisioned as the community's chief means of caring for its poor, was a centralized, carefully administered, accountable system. Its focus was carefully defined. For the sake of efficiency and control, Bugenhagen expected all resources designated for the care of the poor to be deposited in and disbursed from the poor chest. *Begging was strictly opposed, and private almsgiving was discouraged.* The Reformer also suggested that the poor be identified and evaluated, and that only the worthy poor receive regular support." "The Care of the Poor: An Evangelical Perspective," *Currents in Theology and Mission* 15 (1988): 532 (emphasis added). "Although love for neighbor and the service of God were obviously not new concepts, they were now promoted as the sole impetus for the care of the poor since the good works piety of the medieval church was rejected by the evangelical reformers. Bugenhagen also recognized that the decentralized, voluntary almsgiving of the Middle Ages had to be reformed both for theological and practical reasons. He maintained, therefore, that caring for the poor was not a matter of free choice but a responsibility of the individual Christian and of the Christian community, and he proposed the organized, centralized, and regulated system of the poor chest as a corrective for the decentralized practice of begging and almsgiving. Indeed, begging was repeatedly forbidden in the church orders." "Johannes Bugenhagen: A Retrospect on His 500th Birthday," *Currents in Theology and Mission* 12 (1985): 285.

3. For a comprehensive study of this topic, see Romanus Cessario, OP, *The Godly*

is first and foremost a debt in need of being repaid is, indeed, central to Aquinas's way of understanding the incarnation and the passion of Christ. And realizing this is tantamount to realizing that Aquinas is a profoundly biblical theologian who synthesized a tradition of patristic and medieval exegesis and theology, and that his synthesis to a surprising degree anticipates and confirms Anderson's important exegetical rediscovery.

In the following, I would like to prepare the ground for bringing Aquinas's theology of sin and redemption into a constructive dialogue with Anderson's book. However, in this brief chapter, I shall be able to act merely as a tour guide who will take the reader on one particular path through Aquinas's mature *magnum opus*, his *Summa Theologiae*, a path rarely taken in recent years; it is to be hoped that now, emboldened by Anderson's exegetical argument, other readers will take the path more frequently.

This tour will comprise three stations. It will commence in *ST* I-II with Aquinas's discussion of the debt of punishment consequent upon sin. From there I will turn to his interpretation of Christ's priesthood and passion in *ST* III. Finally, at the third station, I will attend to the all-important but often misunderstood human participation in Christ's satisfactory sacrifice. Here I will turn briefly to baptism, the Eucharist, and alms deeds. It will become clear that the debt of punishment on account of sin is not simply cancelled through Christ's expiation for the sins of the whole world. Rather, the debt of punishment becomes, in and through Christ's expiatory sacrifice in charity, the occasion for the sinner to be restored to the order of charity, a restoration in which the sinner's participation is indispensable, indeed, crucial. To put the matter in simple conceptual terms: the debt of punishment—an indispensable entailment of divine justice—is transformed by the order of divine charity into an instrument that restores sinners to the

---

Image: Christ and Salvation in Catholic Thought from Anselm to Aquinas (Petersham: St. Bede's Publications, 1990), and more recently "Sonship, Sacrifice, and Satisfaction: The Divine Friendship in Aquinas and the Renewal of Christian Anthropology," in his *Theology and Sanctity*, ed. Cajetan Cuddy, OP (Ave Maria, Fla.: Sapientia Press of Ave Maria, 2014), 69–98. For a most recent, thoroughly researched and adroitly argued treatment, see Daria Spezzano's excellent article, "'Be Imitators of God' (Eph 5:1): Aquinas on Charity and Satisfaction," *Nova et Vetera* (English edition) 15, no. 2 (2017): 615–51.

very order of charity itself and thus configures them to the ultimate end, thereby constituting them as wayfarers.

THE STAIN OF SIN AND THE DEBT OF PUNISHMENT: VIOLATING THE ORDER OF CHARITY

Allow me first to recall briefly Aquinas's fundamentally Augustinian concept of evil and sin. Evil is a partial privation of good and, more specifically, the absence of a specific good that is due. Sin is either the absence of a due act, interior or exterior, in reference to God or an act contrary to what is due to God. Consequent upon original sin, all powers of the human soul are left destitute of their proper order whereby they are naturally directed to virtue. Aquinas has in mind this destitution of the proper order of intellect, will, and the sense appetites when he considers the four wounds of human nature consequent upon sin: ignorance, malice, weakness, and concupiscence.[4] Moreover, and more important for our concerns, sin causes a stain on the soul (*macula peccati*) and furthermore incurs a liability of punishment (*reatus poenae*), which is to be understood as a debt of punishment (*debitum poenae*).

Hence, besides contributing its part to the four wounds of hu-

---

4. *ST* I-II, q. 85, a. 3: "As a result of original justice, the reason had perfect hold over the lower parts of the soul, while reason itself was perfected by God, and was subject to Him. Now this same original justice was forfeited through the sin of our first parent, as already stated [q. 81, a. 2]; so that all the powers of the soul are left, as it were, destitute of their proper order, whereby they are naturally directed to virtue; which destitution is called a wounding of nature. Again, there are four of the soul's powers that can be the subject of virtue, as stated above [q. 61, a. 2], viz. the reason, where prudence resides, the will, where justice is, the irascible, the subject of fortitude, and the concupiscible, the subject of temperance. Therefore in so far as the reason is deprived of its order to the true, there is the wound of ignorance; in so far as the will is deprived of its order to the good, there is the wound of malice; in so far as the irascible is deprived of its order to the arduous, there is the wound of weakness; and in so far as the concupiscible is deprived of its order to the delectable, moderated by reason, there is the wound of concupiscence. Accordingly these are the four wounds inflicted on the whole of human nature as a result of our first parent's sin. But since the inclination to the good of virtue is diminished in each individual on account of actual sin, as was explained above [aa. 1–2], these four wounds are also the result of other sins, in so far as, through sin, the reason is obscured, especially in practical matters, the will hardened to evil, good actions become more difficult and concupiscence more impetuous."

man nature, every sinful act leaves two things, a stain on the sinner's soul and the sinner's guilt. What does Aquinas mean by "stain on the sinner's soul" and why should it matter? He explains that the human soul has a twofold splendor (*nitor*): one from the natural light of reason whereby human beings are directed to their actions; the other from the illumination of the divine light, that is, the wisdom and grace whereby humans are perfected in order to do good and fitting actions. "Now, when the soul cleaves to things by love, there is a kind of contact in the soul" (*ST* I-II, q. 86, a. 1). Consequently, when human beings sin, they cleave to certain things contrary to the light of reason and contrary to the divine law. The loss of the splendor of the human soul is occasioned by such contact, which "is metaphorically called a stain on the soul." Aquinas holds that "the stain of sin remains in the soul even when the act of sin is past" (*ST* I-II, q. 86, a. 2). For the stain "denotes a blemish in the brightness of the soul, on account of its withdrawing from the light of reason or of the divine law."[5]

The second thing each actual sin leaves after the act is the sinner's liability for punishment (*reatus poenae*; *De malo*, q. 2, a. 2, ad 14). Significantly, Aquinas interprets this liability for punishment as a debt of punishment (*debitum poenae*).[6] The sinner stands in the position of debtor in relationship to divine justice. What is actually due to the sinner is punishment. Consequently, the Fathers of the English Dominican Province, in their translation of the *Summa Theologiae*, render the liability for punishment (*reatus poenae*) itself as "debt of punishment," a felicitous decision I will make my own in the following. Sin, being either the absence of a due act in reference to God or an act contrary to what is due to God, disturbs the universal order of divine governance. And because God delights in the order of divine justice, punishment is due as the payment that balances out the equality of justice.

It is admittedly rather strange for and even offensive to modern

---

5. This stain of sin remains as long as the human being remains out of this light, that is, until the human being repents and returns to the light of reason and the divine law.

6. *Sent.* IV, d. 21, q. 1, a. 3, q.c. 2: "Ad secundam quaestionem dicendum, quod quicumque est debitor alicujus, per hoc a debito absolvitur quod debitum solvit; et quia reatus nihil est aliud quam debitum poenae; per hoc quod aliquis poenam sustinet quam debebat, a reatu absolvitur."

sensibilities that, according to Aquinas, God is both merciful *and* just, that justice is as much a divine perfection as is mercy, and that in the absolute simplicity of the divine essence, mercy and justice are one.⁷ Hence, even when love and mercy rule, the requirements of divine justice must be met lest God act against justice. Unsurprisingly, when in *ST* I-II, q. 86, a. 6, Aquinas addresses the question whether the debt of punishment remains after sin, he insists in the *sed contra* (with reference to 2 Kgs 12:13–14, the prophet Nathan communicating God's message to David regarding his crimes of adultery and murder) that "a man is punished by God even after his sin is forgiven: and so the debt of punishment remains, when the sin has been removed" (*ST* I-II, q. 87, a. 6, s.c.). In unfolding his own answer to the question, Aquinas considers two aspects of the sin: the guilty act and the subsequent stain on the soul.

By the guilty act, the sinner has transgressed the order of divine justice, and thus only an act of penal compensation (*recompensatio poenae*) will restore him to the equality of justice. According to the order of divine justice, the one who has too much indulged his own will and has consequently transgressed God's commandments suffers, either willingly or unwillingly, something contrary to what he would wish. "This restoration of the equality of justice by penal compensation is also to be observed in injuries done to one's fellow [humans]. Consequently it is evident that when the sinful or injurious act has ceased there still remains the debt of punishment" (*ST* I-II, q. 87, a. 6). And what removes this debt of punishment is satisfaction.

The order of divine justice could, of course, have been accommodated differently by God. If God had somehow willed to liberate human beings from sin without satisfaction, God could have done so, of course, without acting against justice. In *ST* III, where Aquinas

---

7. Cf. *ST* I, q. 3, and *ST* I, q. 21, esp. a. 4: "Whether in Every Work of God There Are Mercy and Justice?" In the response to the first objection, Aquinas anticipates in a nutshell the way he conceives divine mercy and justice to be one in God, but to be ordered in God's works by way of love such that justice is always grounded in mercy: "In the justification of the ungodly, justice is seen, when God remits sins on account of love, though He Himself has mercifully infused that love." For a more detailed interpretation of the relationship of divine mercy and divine justice in the divine economy, see my essay "Human Sexuality in a Fallen World: An Economy of Mercy and Grace," *Nova et Vetera* (English edition) 15, no. 2 (2017): 433–64.

considers Christ's passion, he advances an important argument why it is most suitable for the healing of the human soul that God does not simply forgive without satisfaction. He states:

> A judge, while preserving justice, cannot pardon fault without penalty, if he must visit fault committed against another.... But God has no one higher than Himself, for God is the sovereign and common good of the whole universe. Consequently, if [God] forgive sin, which has the formality of fault in that it is committed against Himself, [God] wrongs no one: just as anyone else, overlooking a personal trespass, without satisfaction, acts mercifully and not unjustly. (*ST* III, q. 46, a. 2, ad 3)

Aquinas grants that it is not absolutely necessary for God that satisfaction be made for human sins, but he insists that satisfaction is indeed most suitable for the healing of the human soul. What he has in mind here has, of course, all to do with Christ who "by His Passion made satisfaction for the sin of the human race" (*ST* III, q. 46, a. 1, ad 3, echoing 1 Jn 2:2). But we do not understand Christ's act of satisfaction fully if we do not appreciate first in what way the removal of the debt of punishment by way of satisfaction is indeed most suitable for the healing of the human soul. In order to understand this point in greater fullness, we need to return to the stain of sin on the human soul and ask, how is the stain of sin removed? It is evident, Aquinas holds, "that the stain of sin cannot be removed from the soul, without the soul being united to God" (*ST* I-II, q. 87, a. 6). For, after all, it was through being separated from God that the soul suffered the loss of its splendor.

Now, how does Aquinas think this removal of the stain and this union of the soul with God is to come about? First and foremost, the will is the faculty of the human soul by way of which the human is united to God—in this life, I should add. And therefore the stain of sin can be removed only if the will accepts the order of divine justice. That means for Aquinas one of two things: either the human being on his *own accord* takes upon himself the punishment of past sins, or the human being bears patiently the punishment that God inflicts.[8]

---

8. In both ways, Aquinas says, "punishment avails for satisfaction ... and although satisfactory punishment, absolutely speaking is against the will, nevertheless in this particular case and for this particular purpose, it is voluntary."

Aquinas explores this satisfactory punishment with great interest. Because a satisfactory punishment is in some way voluntary, it is transferable under one specific condition. He states: "Since those who differ as to the debt of punishment, *may be one in will by the union of love*, it happens that one who has not sinned, bears willingly the punishment for another: thus even in human affairs we see [people] take the debts of another upon themselves" (emphasis added). And so "one may bear another's punishment, in so far as they are, in some way, one" (*ST* I-II, q. 87, a. 8). It is not surprising then that already in his treatment of the debt of punishment in the context of the wider discussion of human sin, Aquinas announces the key theme that later in *ST* III unites the sacraments with Christ's passion: "*Christ bore a satisfactory punishment*, not for His, but for our sins" (*ST* I-II, q. 87, a. 7, ad 3; emphasis added).

We need one more piece in place to understand fully why Aquinas regards satisfaction to be most suitable for the healing of the human soul. And this piece pertains to the central role of charity. What belonged to the splendor of the human soul originally was charity. For in the state of original righteousness, because of the gift of sanctifying grace, humans adhered to God by charity.[9] Original sin destroyed this adherence by charity to humanity's final end, union with God. So what is at stake in satisfactory punishment is twofold: (1) satisfaction restores the order of charity by way of a satisfaction accepted voluntarily in charity for the person wronged and for the wrongdoer; (2) substitutionary satisfaction presupposes a union of charity between the wrongdoer and the person who makes satisfaction.[10] Remember, Aquinas holds that "when a soul cleaves to things

---

9. *ST* I-II, q. 87, a. 3: "Now in every order there is a principle whereby one takes part in that order. Consequently if a sin destroys the principle of the order whereby [the human being's] will is subject to God, the disorder will be such as to be considered in itself, irreparable, although it is possible to repair it by the power of God. Now the principle of this order is the last end, to which [the human being] adheres by charity."

10. Eleonore Stump put this crucial point—easily missed or misunderstood in Aquinas's theology—in a felicitously succinct way: "Because, on Aquinas's view, the point of making satisfaction is to return the wrongdoer's will to conformity with the will of the person wronged, rather than to inflict retributive punishment on the wrongdoer or to placate the person wronged, it is possible for the satisfaction to be made by a substitute, provided that the wrongdoer allies himself with the substitute in willing to undo as far as possible the damage he has done. So Aquinas thinks that one person can make satisfaction for another

by love, there is a kind of contact in the soul" (*ST* I-II, q. 86, a. 1). If the wrongdoer loves the person who makes satisfaction for him, there is a kind of contact in the soul of the wrongdoer with this person. *And if this person is a divine person, there is a kind of contact in the soul of the wrongdoer with God.*[11] Christ's satisfaction for human sin in charity both to God the Father and to the wrongdoer allows for, invites, and, by way of sanctifying grace, brings about a restoration of charity through which the human adheres again to his or her final end, union with God. And adhering to God through charity inchoately attaches the soul to God such that the soul's splendor is restored. This leads us to our second station, Christ as priest and Christ as victim, Christ who bore in his passion a satisfactory punishment for our sins, a punishment borne voluntarily, and more importantly, as a supreme act of charity, which restores all humanity to the supreme divine order of charity.

CHRIST'S PRIESTHOOD AND PASSION ON THE CROSS

At the outset of his consideration of Christ's priesthood, Aquinas enumerates three reasons why human beings are required to offer sacrifice—"sacrifice" meaning, most broadly, everything that is offered to God in order to raise the human spirit to God: "First, for the remission of sin, by which [the human] is turned away from God.... Secondly, that [the human] may be preserved in a state of grace, by ever adhering to God, wherein his peace and salvation consist.... Thirdly, that the [human] spirit ... be perfectly united to God: which will be most perfectly realized in glory" (*ST* III, q. 22, a. 2). Now, precisely these effects were conferred on us by the humanity of Christ: first, the blotting out of our sins (Rom 4:25), second, the reception of the grace of salvation (Heb 5:9), and third, acquiring the perfection of glory (Heb 10:19). And therefore Aquinas concludes, "Christ Himself, as [human], was not only priest, but also a perfect victim, being

---

only to the extent to which they are united, or that one person can atone for another insofar as they are one in charity." *Aquinas* (New York: Routledge, 2003), 435.

11. *ST* I-II, q. 86, a. 1, ad 2: "The act of the will consists in a movement towards things themselves, so that love attaches the soul to the thing loved."

at the same time victim for sin, victim for a peace-offering, and a holocaust" (*ST* III, q. 22, a. 2). And so Christ's priesthood expiates human sin, and this in two respects. For two things are required for the perfect cleansing from sins. They correspond to the two things sin comprises—namely, the stain of sin (*macula peccati*) and the debt of punishment (*reatus poenae*; *ST* III, q. 22, a. 3).

The debt of punishment is entirely removed by the satisfaction that Christ offers for all humanity to God the Father. The stain of sin is blotted out by sanctifying grace, the principle of the divine life in the human being which the sinner receives through baptism[12] and which after its loss through mortal sin can subsequently be restored through the sacrament of penance (*ST* III, q. 89, a. 1). For by grace the sinner's heart is turned to God. Now, remember Aquinas's principle: "When the soul cleaves to things by love, there is a kind of contact in the soul" (*ST* I-II, q. 86, a. 1). As charity is a divinely infused virtue, the originating principle of which is sanctifying grace, by charity the soul cleaves again to God—with whom there is therefore a kind of contact in the soul, which is the soul's splendor. Aquinas teaches that the priesthood of Christ produces both these effects.[13]

Three points are crucial: first, Christ's satisfaction comports fully with divine mercy and divine justice:

That man should be delivered by Christ's Passion was in keeping with both His mercy and His justice. With His justice, because by His Passion Christ made satisfaction for the sin of the human race; and so man was set free by Christ's justice: and with His mercy, for since man of himself could not satisfy for the sin of all human nature ... God gave him His Son to satisfy for him.... *And this came of more copious mercy than if He had forgiven sins without satisfaction.* Hence it is said (Eph 2:4): "God, who is rich in mercy, for His exceeding charity wherewith He loved us, even when we

---

12. *ST* III, q. 69, a. 4. Aquinas expresses the effect of baptism most beautifully in his brief response to the question "Whether the Effect of Baptism Is to Open the Gates of the Heavenly Kingdom?" (*ST* III, q. 69, a. 7): "To open the gates of the heavenly kingdom is to remove the obstacle that prevents one from entering therein. Now this obstacle is guilt and the debt of punishment. But it has been shown above ... that all guilt and also all debt of punishment are taken away by Baptism. It follows, therefore, that the effect of Baptism is to open the gates of the heavenly kingdom."

13. *ST* III, q. 22, a. 3: "For by its virtue grace is given to us, by which our hearts are turned to God.... Moreover, He satisfied for us fully, inasmuch as 'He hath borne our infirmities and carried our sorrows' (Is 53:4)."

were dead in sins, hath quickened us together in Christ." (*ST* III, q. 46, a. 1, ad 3; emphasis added)

Second, Christ's satisfaction allows for a human participation, if the human being is united with Christ in charity:

> Christ's Passion is applied to us even through faith, that we may share in its fruits, according to Rom 3:25: "Whom God hath proposed to be a propitiation, through faith in His blood." But the faith through which we are cleansed from sin is not *lifeless faith*, which can exist even with sin, but *faith living* through charity; that thus Christ's Passion may be applied to us, not only as to our minds, but also as to our hearts. And even in this way sins are forgiven through the power of the Passion of Christ. (*ST* III, q. 49, a. 1, ad 5; emphasis added)

Third, Christ's sacrifice on the cross restores humanity to the order of charity: "Christ's Passion was the *offering* of a *sacrifice*, inasmuch as He endured death of His own free-will out of *charity*" (*ST* III, q. 47, a. 4, ad 2; emphasis added). Satisfaction pertains to the debt of punishment, which refers to justice. Sacrifice, by way of which satisfaction is made, pertains to the restoration of the inchoate union between soul and God, which refers to charity. A sacrifice in perfect charity can make satisfaction precisely because in satisfaction the affection and devotion of the offerer is what is measured. And Christ's human affection and devotion, because of their hypostatic union with the divine nature, were absolutely perfect. It is here that Aquinas's understanding of Christ's human nature as the *instrument* of his divinity comes into full play. He had inherited this theologoumenon from patristic theology.[14] Christ's sacrifice was most efficacious for blotting out sins, because Christ's human nature operated by virtue of the divine.[15]

---

14. For an extensive discussion of this crucial aspect of Aquinas's Christology, see Theophil Tschipke, OP, *Die Menschheit Christi als Heilsorgan der Gottheit unter besonderer Berücksichtigung der Lehre des heiligen Thomas von Aquin* (Freiburg: Herder, 1940). See also the recent French translation: *L'humanité du Christ comme instrument de salut de la divinité*, trans. Philibert Secretan (Fribourg: Academic Press, 2003).

15. *ST* III, q. 22, a. 3, ad 1. In order to support this understanding, Aquinas appeals to a famous passage from Augustine's *De Trinitate* (4.14), a passage frequently cited by medieval theologians: "Four things are to be observed in every sacrifice—to whom it is offered, by whom it is offered, what is offered, for whom it is offered; the same one true Mediator reconciling us to God by the sacrifice of peace, was one with Him to Whom it was offered, united in Himself those for whom He offered it, at the same time offered it Himself, and was Himself that which He offered."

How do we remain continuously united with this sacrifice out of charity through which Christ made a perfect satisfaction for the sins of all humanity? When considering Christ the priest and Christ the victim, Aquinas anticipates the answer to this question by pointing to the Eucharistic sacrifice: "The Sacrifice which is offered every day in the Church is not distinct from that which Christ Himself offered, but is a commemoration thereof" (*ST* III, q. 22, a. 3, ad 2). He cites from Augustine's *De civitate Dei* (X.20): "Christ Himself both is the priest who offers it and the victim: the sacred token of which He wished to be the daily Sacrifice of the Church." Thus we reach our third and final station.

BEING RESTORED TO CHARITY BY PARTICIPATING IN THE SACRIFICE OUT OF CHARITY

Thomas Aquinas is very clear that there is only one explicitly revealed way to secure the effects of Christ's passion.[16] We must be configured to Christ, and this occurs sacramentally in baptism. He appeals to Romans 6:4: "For we are buried together with Him by baptism into death." It is for this reason that at baptism, no punishment of satisfaction is imposed upon the candidates, because they are fully delivered by Christ's satisfaction. It is an altogether different matter, however, after baptism. Aquinas states: "But because, as it is written (1 Pt 3:18), 'Christ died but once for our sins,' therefore [one] cannot a second time be likened unto Christ's death by the sacrament of Baptism. Hence it is necessary that those who sin after

---

16. It would go beyond the scope of this chapter to discuss Aquinas's profound and still eminently pertinent theory of conceiving of the sacraments as instrumental causes. The theory of sacramental causality that he advances in the *Summa Theologiae* is intimately connected with his account of the instrumentality of Christ's sacred humanity that is operative in the sacraments. As an instrument joined to the instrumentality of the sacraments, Christ's sacred humanity moves the graced person united to him towards perfection and finally to the surpassing participation in divine happiness, beatitude. The instrumentality of the sacraments contributes efficaciously to this end by renewing and deepening the graced person in the divine friendship of charity. For an instructive and penetrating account of the instrumental causality of the sacraments in Aquinas and the Thomist tradition, see Reginald M. Lynch, OP, *The Cleansing of the Heart: The Sacraments as Instrumental Causes in the Thomist Tradition* (Washington, D.C.: The Catholic University of America Press, 2017).

Baptism be likened unto Christ suffering [*configurentur Christo patienti*] by some form of punishment or suffering which they endure in their own person" (*ST* III, q. 49, a. 3, ad 2). The undergoing of penance and, if necessary, purgatory are the requisite punishments of satisfaction for post-baptismal sins. The superior end of penance and purgatory, however, is not simply satisfaction but rather purification, the removal of those obstacles—the wounds of sin—that hinder the attainment of the ultimate end, our everlasting participation in divine happiness.

Aquinas regards baptism as an objective incorporation into the passion and death of Christ and consequently the communication of Christ's passion to every baptized person "so that he is healed just as if he himself had suffered and died" (*ST* III, q. 69, a. 2). And because Christ's passion is a sufficient satisfaction for all the sins of all human beings, the baptized person is consequently "freed from the debt of all punishment due to him for his sins, just as if he himself had offered sufficient satisfaction for all his sins" (*ST* III, q. 69, a. 2). Hence baptism is the sacrament that accounts for the first consequence of sin, the debt of punishment.

But now we must turn to what is even more important, and what, according to Aquinas, is the true end of Christ's passion. Remember that Aquinas insists that the stain of sin on the soul can be removed only by the soul's reattachment to God in charity. For, after all, it was through being separated from God that the soul suffered the loss of its splendor. Aquinas thinks this reattachment of the soul comes about by way of the will. For the will is the faculty of the human soul by way of which the human adheres to God: "when the soul cleaves to things by love, there is a kind of contact in the soul" (*ST* I-II, q. 86, a. 1). And charity is exercised by the faculty of the will. So when the soul cleaves to God by charity, there is a contact in the soul, the soul is reattached to God in charity—and that is nothing but the incipient union of the soul with God in charity.[17]

---

17. This incipient union of the soul with God in charity is the beginning of the mystical life to which every baptized Christian is called. See on this topic, indispensable for Christian existence in the twenty-first century, the important work by John G. Arintero, OP, *The Mystical Evolution in the Development and Vitality of the Church*, 2 vols., trans. Jordan Aumann, OP (St. Louis, Mo.: Herder, 1949).

And here the Eucharist comes fully into play. Aquinas understands the Eucharist in immediate correlation to and distinction from baptism:

> Baptism is the sacrament of Christ's death and Passion, according as [one] is born anew in Christ in virtue of His Passion; but the Eucharist is the sacrament of Christ's Passion according as [one] is made perfect in union with Christ Who suffered. Hence, as Baptism is called the sacrament of Faith, which is the foundation of the spiritual life, so the Eucharist is termed the sacrament of Charity, which is "the bond of perfection" (Col 3:14). (*ST* III, q. 73, a. 3, ad 3)

The key word here is *charity*, which, according to Colossians 3:14, is the bond of perfection. Unlike baptism, which "is directly ordained for the remission of punishment and guilt" (*ST* III, q. 79, a. 5, ad 1), the Eucharist is given for those baptized into Christ's death to be nourished and perfected through Christ. What does Aquinas have in mind here?

As is well known, Aquinas consistently considers the Eucharist in two respects, as sacrament under the aspect of communion and as sacrifice under the aspect of offering. Considered as a sacrament, the Eucharist has a strengthening and perfecting power. According to the intensity of the bond of charity between Christ and us as we devoutly receive Christ's sacred body and blood, we grow in charity, and consequently we participate with ever-growing devotion in the Eucharistic sacrifice by uniting in charity our own spiritual self-offering with Christ's sacrifice to the Father.

Considered as a sacrifice under the aspect of offering, the Eucharist has a satisfactory power pertaining to post-baptismal sins. If one were to consider only the quantity of what is being offered—the sacred body and blood of Christ of the one sacrifice on Calvary—this offering suffices to satisfy for all punishment. Yet crucially, Aquinas reminds us that in satisfaction, the affection and the devotion—in short, the effects of charity—of the offerer or the one for whom it is offered are weighed, and not the quantity of the offering. Hence, he states, "although this offering suffices of its own quantity to satisfy for all punishment, yet it becomes satisfactory for them for whom it is offered, or even for the offerers, according to the measure of their devotion, and not for the whole punishment" (*ST* III, q. 79, a. 5). The measure of affection and devotion is the measure of the union of charity between the offerer or the one for whom it is offered and Christ. For it is by this charity that he is united with Christ's sacrifice. Hence the unity in distinction of sacrifice and sacrament integrates the demand of justice into an ever-intensifying circle of charity.

This is the sacramental pillar of the restored arc of the order of charity. I shall now turn to the other pillar of the restored arc of the order of charity, the human participation by way of mercy, which is an effect of charity. Alms deeds stand out most crucially here because they integrate the demands of justice and satisfaction into the encompassing circle of the sacrifice in charity. For ultimately both pillars denote offerings out of charity, that is, sacrifices "offered to God in order to raise the human spirit to God in charity."

Some, however, might want to ask whether alms should be understood at all as acts of charity rather than exclusively as acts of justice; Daniel 4:24 (according to the Vulgate) states: "*Peccata tua elemosynis redime*" (Redeem your sins with alms). And satisfaction is an act of justice. Now, Aquinas responds to this objection, as usual, with a distinction. Almsgiving is reckoned among the works of satisfaction and hence as an act of justice insofar as the pity for the one in distress is directed to the satisfaction for one's own sin. But insofar as almsgiving is directed to please God, it has the character of a sacrifice. And an act of mercy united with Christ in charity, that is, done for God's sake, has the character of a sacrifice (*ST* II-II, q. 32, a. 1, ad 2 and 3). So how does Aquinas understand alms? He defines almsgiving as "a deed whereby something is given to the needy, out of compassion and for God's sake" (*ST* II-II, q. 32, a. 1). An alms deed is motivated by mercy and, as mercy is an effect of charity, alms deeds are acts of charity through the medium of mercy. Aquinas is adamant about this aspect of alms deeds. Whereas almsgiving can be materially without charity, to give alms "formally," that is, genuinely for God's sake with delight and readiness, is possible only with charity (ad 1).

Aquinas usefully draws upon a traditional distinction of alms deeds and regards them as suitably reflecting the various needs of our neighbor. Seven bodily alms deeds correspond to the needs of the body: feeding the hungry, giving drink to the thirsty, clothing the naked, harboring the harborless, visiting the sick, ransoming the captive, and giving burial to the dead. Seven spiritual alms deeds correspond to the needs of the soul: prayer, instruction, counseling, comforting, reproving, pardoning the injury, and bearing one another's burdens (*ST* II-II, q. 32, a. 2).

What makes the discussion of alms in Aquinas's theology so instructive is that, in his way of thinking, alms deeds follow the logic of sacrifice and satisfaction that already characterized the sacramental pillar of the restored arc of charity: the demands of justice—satisfaction—are integrated in the overarching horizon of the sacrifice in charity. The human response of satisfaction to the demands of justice, paying the debt of punishment, is elevated to a human participation in the sacrifice in charity.

CONCLUSION

To conclude, I would like to return to the beginning. The one single bond that in Aquinas's theological synthesis holds together the debt of punishment consequent upon sin, substitutionary satisfaction, Christ's sacrifice on the cross, and our participation in that sacrifice through baptism, Eucharist, and alms deeds is the one bond of perfection, which is charity. In his commentary on St. Paul's Letter to the Colossians, Aquinas comments on the bond that stood against us on account of our debt of guilt. Colossians 2:13–14 states: "And you, who were dead in trespasses and the uncircumcision of your flesh, God made alive together with [Christ], having forgiven us all our trespasses, having canceled the bond which stood against us with its legal demands; this he set aside, nailing it to the cross" (RSV). Consider Aquinas's terse but poignant commentary on this passage:

> But how has God forgiven us? I answer that a person incurs two things by sinning, that is, a debt of guilt, and slavery to the devil. And so he explains how sins are forgiven: first, our being freed from slavery to the devil, and second, he mentions the removing of the debt of guilt.
>
> He says, *having canceled the bond that stood against us*; this bond or written decree [*chirographum decreti*] ... is a warranty usually employed in contracts. And whoever violates God's bond is subject to a debt of punishment.... Now

the memory of this violation is called a bond. And it is Christ who has forgiven all by having canceled the bond, that is, the memory of the transgression, *which stood against us*.... The term *bond* is used because its violation is not forgiven in such a way as to bring it about that there was never any sin. Rather, such sin is not remembered by God as something to be punished...

How did Christ cancel this bond? On the cross, for *this he set aside, nailing it to the cross*. It was the custom for a bond to be torn up once a person had fulfilled all his obligations. Now man was in sin and Christ paid for this by his suffering.... And therefore, at the moment of Christ's death this bond was canceled and destroyed. And so he says, *this he set aside, nailing it to the cross*, by which he took away our sin by making satisfaction to God.[18]

Augustine famously stated: "God created us without us, but he did not save us without us."[19] And, according to Aquinas, the very point of the active human participation in God's saving activity is the restoration of the human soul to divine charity, in virtue of which the soul cleaves to God, such that there is a kind of contact in the soul with God, an inchoate union between the soul and God. The very access to this inchoate union with God in charity is our participation in Christ's satisfactory sacrifice in charity. The debt of punishment is not simply cancelled in Christ. Rather it becomes the very occasion for the sinner's restoration to the order of charity and the sinner's soul to the splendor that comes from cleaving to God in charity. Active participation (*participatio actuosa*) in Christ's sacrifice in charity is the way God chose most fittingly for sinners to become *viatores* and for *viatores* to become *comprehensores*. We can see now how Aquinas adopts the biblical mercantile grammar of debt and payment and employs it as an instrument of charity, to the end of restoring the sinner to the order of charity and of thereby configuring the wayfarer to the ultimate end, the beatitude of the beatific vision that consists in the union of charity with God. "For," as the Apostle John teaches, "God is love" (1 Jn 4:8; RSV).

18. *Super Epistolam ad Colossenses* II, lect. 3. Translation from Thomas Aquinas, *Commentary on Colossians*, ed. Daniel A. Keating, trans. Fabian Larcher, OP (Naples, Fla.: Sapientia Press, 2006), 61 (Marietti, nos. 112–15).

19. St. Augustine, *Sermo* 169, 11.13, in *Patrologia Latina*, ed. J.-P. Migne (Paris, 1841–55) [hereafter "*PL*"], 38:923.

4

The Beginning of Beatitude—
The Substance of Things Hoped For
The Virtue of Faith

"The object of faith is that whereby [the human being] is made one of the Blessed."
—Thomas Aquinas, *Summa Theologiae*[1]

In this chapter I address the question how, according to Aquinas, after the wayfarer has been configured to the ultimate end and thereby constituted as *viator*, beatitude comes to be inchoately present in the wayfarer. In the course of these considerations, one all-important difference comes clearly into focus: the difference between the imperfect happiness of someone who is living, as Aristotle conceived it in the *Nicomachean Ethics*, the life of virtue (*bios praktikos*) and even the life of philosophical contemplation (*bios theoretikos*) and, by contrast, the imperfect beatitude of the *viator*. This vital difference between the imperfect happiness of the former and the imperfect beatitude of the latter is caused by the gratuitous gift of faith by way of which the seed of beatitude, the "substance of things hoped for," comes to be present in the wayfarer's intellect.

To have identified and illuminated this inchoate presence of beatitude in the wayfarer is arguably the single most important achieve-

---

1. *ST* II-II, q. 2, a. 5: "Fidei objectum per se est id per quod homo beatus efficitur."

ment of Aquinas's teaching on faith. Yet since the Protestant Reformation faith has become a disputed theological topic and since the Enlightenment it has become a philosophically contested phenomenon. Aquinas's teaching on faith, lest it be detrimentally misunderstood, must be accessed by way of what might at first glance look like a detour. Because belief and belief-formation are a central preoccupation in contemporary philosophical theories of knowledge, I must clarify briefly the difference between a philosophical inquiry into belief and belief formation and a theological inquiry into the nature of divine faith.

After this initial methodological clarification, I will first adumbrate the intellectual dynamic that had the greatest impact on modern theology and its special preoccupation with the nature of faith—the modern turn to the subject. Modern theologies of faith are—with a few noteworthy exceptions—characteristically anthropocentric, while Aquinas's theology of faith is profoundly theocentric. A proper appreciation of this difference is crucial for gaining access to the depths of Aquinas's account of divine faith. In the second part, I will turn to Aquinas's treatment of the theological virtue of faith where I will focus on faith as a dynamic movement of the wayfarer's intellect into God. In the subsequent third part, I will illustrate the ongoing pertinence of Aquinas's theology of faith by showing how one of the arguably greatest dogmatic theologians of the last couple centuries—Matthias Joseph Scheeben—creatively drew upon Aquinas in advancing one of the most profound and comprehensive theologies of faith in the modern period. In an important but all too brief fourth part, I will consider the way in which divine faith is received, held, and communicated by way of the indispensable but contemporaneously much maligned instrumentality of propositions, the articles of faith. Their increasing erosion by turning them into nothing but "activating symbols" is part of the ongoing tendency of anthropocentrizing divine faith, of submitting it to the hermeneutical hegemony of the sovereign subject. In the conclusion, finally, I shall return to the problem of the anthropocentric turn to the subject, for this problematic is of dramatic importance for every theology of faith. Because divine faith is irreducibly theocentric,

The Beginning

in order to be configured to the ultimate end, beatitude, and thereby be constituted as a wayfarer, one must exit the maze of self-centered subjectivity in order to receive the inchoate beginning of beatitude in the gift of faith and thus be enabled to embark on the journey to its surpassing plenitude.

Before I begin, however, I must make an initial methodological clarification. What is faith? This question may initiate, on the one hand, a *philosophical* inquiry into the nature and characteristics of belief and into the corresponding act of assent. The branch of philosophical inquiry to which such an investigation belongs is contemporaneously called "epistemology."[2] Yet the same question, "What is faith?," may, on the other hand, initiate an inquiry that is genuinely *theological* in nature. Such an inquiry is *formally* different from a philosophical inquiry into the nature of belief and assent.[3] Because the aspect under which something is studied constitutes the unity of the inquiry, the formality that constitutes the unity of theological inquiry (in distinction from philosophical inquiry) is the specific intelligibility afforded by faith in divine revelation. The formal description "what is intelligible in the light of divine revelation" is constitutive of sacred theology or holy teaching (*sacra doctrina*).[4] The

---

2. John Henry Newman's 1870 classic *An Essay in Aid of a Grammar of Assent* (Notre Dame, Ind.: University of Notre Dame Press, 1979) represents a conceptually rigorous effort at clarifying philosophically matters of belief and assent, an intellectual achievement that anticipated key insights of recent analytic philosophy. For a lucid interpretation and defense of Thomistic epistemology in conversation with contemporary analytic philosophy, see Paul A. MacDonald, *Knowledge and the Transcendent: An Inquiry into the Mind's Relationship with God* (Washington, D.C.: The Catholic University of America Press, 2009).

3. "Formally" is the condensed adverbial indication of the *ratio formalis obiecti*, the precise aspect under which something is the object of a specific scientific inquiry.

4. In *ST* I, q. 1, a. 3, Thomas Aquinas puts the matter in the following way: "Sacred doctrine is one science [*una scientia*]. The unity of a faculty or habit is to be gauged by its object, not indeed, in its material aspect [*materialiter*], but as regards the precise formality [*secundum rationem formalem obiecti*] under which it is an object.... Because Sacred Scripture considers things precisely under the formality of being divinely revealed, whatever has been divinely revealed possesses the one precise formality [*in una ratione formali obiecti*] of the object of this science." Aquinas specifies further in *ST* I, q. 1, a. 7: "In sacred science [*sacra doctrina*] all things are treated under the aspect of God; either because they are God Himself; or because they refer to God as their beginning and end.... This is clear also from the principles of this science, namely the articles of faith, for faith is about God. The object of the principles and of the whole science must

following considerations are going to rely explicitly on the inchoate but definite intelligibility that divine revelation bestows on those who receive it in faith. In his *Tractates on the Gospel of John* (29.6), Augustine famously stated: "Believe so that you may understand" (*Crede, ut intelligas*). In short, these considerations stand in the long Augustinian-Thomist tradition of "faith seeking understanding" (*fides quaerens intellectum*), which in its scientific form is the work of sacred theology.

CONTEMPORARY THEOLOGY IN LIGHT OF THE MODERN TURN TO THE SUBJECT

The following exercise in sacred theology takes place in an intellectual context quite different from the one in which Aquinas undertook his theological inquiry into the nature of faith. What separates the contemporary intellectual context from Aquinas's might still be characterized best by the familiar formula of "the modern turn to the subject." This turn to the subject came to a first full flowering in the new anthropocentrism of Renaissance humanism. From then on theological inquiry into the nature of faith became increasingly (though not without ongoing significant resistance from the Dominican Thomist tradition) dazzled by the phenomenon of self-reflexive subjectivity. And consequently, it became acutely preoccupied with a new question: how can the subjective consciousness achieve absolute certitude (*certitudo super omnia*) of a truth that is genuinely supernatural? Under theocentric conditions, Aquinas's inquiry into the nature of faith began and ended with God and was thus essentially grounded in the divine truth on which the certitude of faith was understood to depend *objectively*. Differently put: according to Aquinas, the certitude of faith is first and foremost a function of its cause, divine truth.[5] Furthermore, under theocentric conditions it is

---

be the same, since the whole science is contained virtually in its principles." For a philosophically astute analysis of Aquinas's reception of the Aristotelian concept of "scientia" (first and foremost from the *Posterior Analytics*) and for its analogical application to *sacra doctrina* as a *scientia* subaltern to the *scientia Dei et beatorum*, see Jenkins, *Knowledge and Faith in Thomas Aquinas*.

5. Only secondarily is the certitude of faith also dependent on its possessor. See ST II-II, q. 4, a. 8.

obvious that faith—divine faith as a gift of grace—is the beginning of beatitude. As will be seen later in this chapter, Aquinas argues that through faith the intellect becomes in a certain inchoate way informed by God as the first truth, while the will, through charity, is in a certain inchoate way already united with God as the ultimate end. The gift of divine faith thus contains, according to Aquinas, the very substance of beatitude.

Under anthropocentric conditions, however, matters changed dramatically. With Renaissance humanism, the self-consciousness of the human subject moved into the center, not only as the investigating subject, but now primarily also as the investigated object—and the absolute certitude of faith is now sought first and foremost in the primary object of investigation, the human subject.[6] In consequence, many of the post-Tridentine Catholic theologians became preoccupied with the absolute certitude of subjective consciousness: "How can the believer become certain of the supernatural or divine nature of the motive of his or her assent to divine revelation?" And so in the context of their increasingly complex and comprehensive theological treatises "De fide," numerous post-Tridentine Catholic theologians came to dedicate a special section to the discussion of this particular question, a section that came to be entitled "De analysi fidei."[7] Around 1585, Gregory of Valentia, SJ, was the first to introduce the term "analysis fidei." From the early seventeenth century on, the rational psychology of the act of faith, the "analysis fidei," became commonplace, especially in Jesuit Baroque Scholasticism. Most notably and most famously, Francisco Suárez, SJ, in his treatise

---

6. Drawing upon Wilhelm Dilthey's characterization of Renaissance humanism, Karl Eschweiler states felicitously: "All [theoretical and practical] judging was rooted and ended in the self-consciousness of the *homo-homo*." *Die zwei Wege der neueren Theologie: Georg Hermes—Matth. Jos. Scheeben. Eine kritische Untersuchung des Problems der theologischen Erkenntnis* (Augsburg: Filser, 1926), 33 (author's translation). For a thoughtful treatment and astute analysis of the ways Eschweiler's theology eventually became fraught with severe problems of a primarily political nature, see Thomas Marschler, *Karl Eschweiler (1886–1936): Theologische Erkenntnislehre und nationalsozialistische Ideologie* (Würzburg: Pustet, 2011). Eschweiler's book *Die zwei Wege der neueren Theologie* has, however, lost nothing of its heuristic fecundity and analytic relevance for understanding Catholic theology and especially the theology of faith in the course of and after the modern turn to the subject.

7. Eschweiler, *Die zwei Wege der neueren Theologie*, 35.

De fide,[8] and Cardinal Juan de Lugo, SJ, in his treatise *De virtute fidei divinae*,[9] set off and framed a complex and highly involved discussion of the "analysis fidei" that deeply influenced all subsequent treatises "De fide." Even for the opponents of this form of "new theology of faith," Suarez and Lugo became the standard points of reference and of critique.[10] Concordant with the modern turn to the subject, in most of the subsequent treatments of the "analysis fidei" the rational psychology of the *act* of faith took the center stage of the philosophical and theological energy invested into the theological treatise "De fide." Eventually, this treatise dealt almost exclusively with a critical inquiry informed by rational psychology into the ultimate foundation of certitude (*certitudo super omnia*) of the self-reflexive subject, that is, of subjectivity *per se*. Under the influence of the Enlightenment, the anthropocentric emphasis only intensified, to the point of reducing faith to an exclusively natural rational act of belief (rationalism) or to an essentially a-rational taste or feeling for supernatural truth (fideistic traditionalism)—though not without notable exceptions.[11] Importantly, after the modern anthropocentric turn, it

---

8. Francisco Suárez, SJ, *De triplici virtute theologica: fide, spe, et charitate*, vol. 12 in his *Opera Omnia* (Paris, 1856–78).

9. Juan de Lugo, SJ, *De virtute fidei divinae* (Lyon, 1646).

10. For an accessible summary with encyclopedic fecundity and characteristic even-handedness, see Avery Dulles, SJ, *The Assurance of Things Hoped For: A Theology of Christian Faith* (New York: Oxford University Press, 1994), esp. 54–58 and 105–7. And for a comprehensive analysis of the various accounts of the "analysis fidei" from the seventeenth to the nineteenth century, see Aloys Schmid, *Untersuchungen über den letzten Gewißheitsgrund des Offenbarungsglaubens* (Munich: Ernst Stahl, 1879).

11. The Dominican Thomist tradition consistently resisted these developments. Other exceptions reflecting a different intellectual pedigree would be Johann Adam Möhler's *Symbolism: Exposition of the Doctrinal Differences Between Catholics and Protestants as Evidenced by Their Symbolical Writings* (New York: Crossroad, 1997 [1832]), Johann Evangelist von Kuhn's *Einleitung in die katholische Dogmatik* (1859), and John Henry Newman's Catholic *oeuvre*. Dulles perceives a notable resemblance between Adam Möhler's pre-Vatican I theology of faith and Matthias Joseph Scheeben's post-Vatican I theology of faith. Both abandon anthropocentrism. Dulles states: "In its essentials Scheeben's approach to faith resembles Möhler's final position. Both of them were opposed to systems that base faith on inner experience or rational self-assertion, thus making it, in effect, a conquest of the human spirit. Instead they called for a radical shift whereby anthropocentrism is abandoned. Faith, they affirmed, is a reverent submission to a word that comes from above, a personal word of address from a gracious God. Only those who are willing to become like little children, trusting in the word of another, can enter into the household of faith" (Dulles, *The Assurance of Things Hoped For*, 91).

has become dramatically unclear whether, and if so how, faith leads to and indeed is the very beginning of beatitude.

Eventually the First Vatican Council, in the dogmatic constitution on the Catholic Faith, *Dei Filius*, exposed and condemned the errors of what arguably are two distinct though mutually exclusive offshoots of modern anthropocentrism—a naturalist rationalism and a supernaturalist fideistic traditionalism.[12] Both diminish divine faith: the former to a "rational faith," a rational examination—propelled by real doubt—and eventual justification of the truths of faith before the bar of reason (a pure interior natural rationalism of the self-reflexive subject),[13] and the latter to a fideistic and a-rational, purely tradition-mediated "givenness" of the faith that would habituate and form the person linguistically and affectively for the eventual reception of an interior supernatural and supra-rational self-manifestation of God (a pure interior supernaturalism of the subject).[14]

After the Fathers of the First Vatican Council had reasserted the proper doctrinal framework for a Catholic theology of faith, the later nineteenth century and the twentieth up to the Second Vatican Council witnessed a lively debate over the "analysis fidei" among the likes of Joseph Kleutgen, SJ, Matthias Joseph Scheeben, Pierre Rousselot, SJ, Hans Urs von Balthasar, and the Dominican Thomist school.[15] The debate of these years might best be characterized by the tension caused, on the one hand, by the attempt to mediate what were seen to be legitimate modern anthropocentric concerns with the older theocentric patristic and medieval tradition and, on the other hand, by the attempt to overcome what was understood to be an anthropocentric distortion by a theocentric rectification.

---

12. Regarding the former, see Denzinger, nos. 3010 and 3014, and for the respective canons, see nos. 3035–36. Regarding the latter, see no. 3009, and for the respective canon, see no. 3033.

13. For the prototype of this trend, see the works of Georg Hermes (1775–1831).

14. For the prototype of this trend, see the works of Louis Eugène Bautain (1796–1867).

15. Dulles, *Assurance of Things Hoped For*, chaps. 4 and 5. For an exhaustive study of the complex debates over the inner constitution of the act of faith in nineteenth- and early twentieth-century Catholic theology, see Roger Aubert, *Le problème de l'acte de foi: Données traditionelles et résultats des controverses récentes* (Louvain: E. Warny, 1958).

What has become ever stronger though, it seems, in the second half of the twentieth century, that is, after the Second Vatican Council, is a considerably deepened turn to the subject endowed with libertarian and self-transcending freedom. In not a few quarters of contemporary Catholic theology, the act of faith has become the fulcrum of the unfathomable freedom of self-transcending subjectivity, the act of all acts—in which we achieve ultimate self-realization—even if such self-realization be conceived dialectically as the very self-abandonment to an Other.[16] The subject who believes asks what the nature of the act is that he undertakes when he believes; what kind of epistemic status the beliefs of the believing subject have; what the nature of the certitude is that pertains to those beliefs; how the subject acquires these beliefs by way of the intellectual and volitional operations of the mind; how the beliefs the subject holds might have developed historically and might still be developing; how they are psychologically, socially, and culturally informed or even conditioned; and how those beliefs might inform the subject existentially and pragmatically.

And so, much of contemporary Catholic theology of faith in Europe and in North America seems errant in the maze of self-reflexive subjectivity, Catholic theology now being predominantly absorbed with various aspects of the subject: its unavoidable construction of religious meaning, its autonomous rationality, its existential authenticity, its prelinguistic primordial religious experience, its unfathomable libertarian freedom, its primordially and inescapably graced nature, and (last but not least) its sociohistorical, cultural, and economic location.[17]

---

16. This self-reflexive subjectivity plays itself out quite differently in English-speaking Catholic theology. See Tilley, *Inventing Catholic Tradition* and *Faith: What It Is and What It Isn't* (Maryknoll: Orbis, 2010). For German-speaking Catholic theology, see, e.g., Markus Tomberg, *Glaubensgewißheit als Freiheitsgeschehen: Eine Relecture des Traktats 'De analysi fidei'* (Regensburg: Pustet, 2002).

17. The most constructive modern phenomenology and psychology of belief delivering the best recognition and integration of the subject into the theology of faith is arguably to be found in the Catholic *oeuvre* of John Henry Newman, especially in the works leading up to and including his 1870 *Essay in Aid of a Grammar of Assent*. For a recent comprehensive study of Newman's achievement in the context of the problematic of the *analysis fidei*, see Wilhelm Tolksdorf, *Analysis fidei: John Henry Newmans Beitrag zur Entdeckung des Subjektes beim Glaubensakt im theologiegeschichtlichen Kontext* (Frankfurt: Peter Lang, 2000).

One lesson learned in retrospect is that once Renaissance humanism had entered and once Molinism had penetrated ever deeper into the maze of self-reflexive subjectivity, it seemed close to impossible for contemporary Catholic theology of faith to find the exit. All paths seemed to turn inexorably to the center of the maze—the modern subject. In light of this situation, it does not seem to be surprising that in recent times the magisterium of the Catholic church has set up unequivocal theological signposts in order to guide Catholic theologians in their consideration of the question "What is faith?" into the direction of the exit from the maze of modern subjectivity. In his 2007 encyclical letter *Spe Salvi*, in the very important seventh paragraph, Pope Emeritus Benedict XVI gives a crucial magisterial answer to the question "What is faith?" and thereby, arguably, offers Ariadne's thread to an errant contemporary Catholic theology of faith.[18] I understand *Spe Salvi*'s teaching in the central seventh paragraph to be nothing less than a salutary magisterial invitation encouraging a fresh start for reconceiving the theological inquiry "De fide" in the early twenty-first century. To this end, *Spe Salvi* offers pertinent impulses that aim at overcoming the modern turn to the subject and theology's subsequent entrapment in the maze of self-reflexive subjectivity. At the very least, the encyclical letter clearly invites theologians to rethink critically the disproportionately privileged position that the rational psychology of the "act of faith"—the "analysis fidei"—has traditionally played in many if not most modern Catholic treatises "De fide."

The pertinent part of the seventh paragraph of *Spe Salvi* states:

In the eleventh chapter of the *Letter to the Hebrews* (v. 1) we find a kind of definition of faith which closely links this virtue with hope.... "Faith is the *hypostasis* of things hoped for; the proof of things not seen." For the Fathers and for the theologians of the Middle Ages, it was clear that the Greek word *hypostasis* was to be rendered in Latin with the term *substantia*. The Latin translation of the text produced at the time of the early Church therefore reads: *Est autem fides sperandarum substantia rerum, argumentum non ap-*

---

18. What Pope Benedict XVI articulated in his encyclical letter *Spe Salvi* with special reference to Thomas Aquinas finds a broader treatment in Pope Francis's 2013 encyclical letter *Lumen Fidei*, esp. in pars. 23–36. See my article "Enlightenment: Reflections on Pope Francis' Encyclical Letter *Lumen Fidei*," *Nova et Vetera* (English edition) 12, no. 1 (2014): 1–10.

parentium—faith is the "substance" of things hoped for; the proof of things not seen. (par. 7)

Significantly, at this point in the encyclical letter, Pope Benedict turns to no other theological authority but Thomas Aquinas in order to elucidate the nature of faith:

> Saint Thomas Aquinas, using the terminology of the philosophical tradition to which he belonged, explains it as follows: faith is a *habitus*, that is, a stable disposition of the spirit, through which eternal life takes root in us and reason is led to consent to what it does not see. The concept of "substance" is therefore modified in the sense that through faith, in a tentative way, or as we might say "in embryo"—and thus according to the "substance"—there are already present in us the things that are hoped for: the whole, true life. And precisely because the thing itself is already present, *this presence of what is to come also creates certainty* [emphasis added]; this "thing" which must come is not yet visible in the external world (it does not "appear"), but because of the fact that, as an initial and dynamic reality, we carry it within us, a certain perception of it has even now come into existence.... Faith draws the future into the present, so that it is no longer simply a "not yet." The fact that this future exists changes the present; the present is touched by the future reality, and thus the things of the future spill over into those of the present and those of the present into those of the future. (par. 7)

This passage is informed by a tacit yet striking theocentrism, which should not be too surprising; for in this very part *Spe Salvi* passes on an important teaching from the First Vatican Council's Dogmatic Constitution on the Catholic Faith, *Dei Filius*, a constitution that is meant to check and correct the anthropocentric distortions of the understanding of divine faith, distortions that emerged in Catholic theology subsequent to and in response to the Enlightenment. Consider the opening lines of the constitution's third chapter, entitled "De fide," which amount to nothing less than a formal definition of the essence of divine faith:

> Since human beings are totally dependent on God as their creator and lord, and created reason is completely subject to uncreated truth [*veritas increata*], we are obliged to yield to God the revealer full submission of intellect and will by faith. This faith, which is the beginning of human salvation, the Catholic Church professes to be a supernatural virtue, by means of which, with the grace of God inspiring and assisting us, we believe to be true what

he has revealed, not because we perceive its intrinsic truth by the natural light of reason, but because of the authority of God himself, who makes the revelation and can neither deceive nor be deceived.[19]

The passage concludes with a citation of Hebrews 11:1. In continuity with the formal definition given by the Fathers of the First Vatican Council, Pope Benedict XVI understands Hebrews 11:1 to offer a kind of definition of faith. I will follow suit in the following theological reflection on the nature of divine faith. For it seems to me that it is this kind of definition of faith—as interpreted in *Dei Filius* and *Spe Salvi*—that enables us to break free from the anthropocentrism that is the root cause of the disproportionate attention given to the psychology of the act of faith.

Given the reading of Hebrews 11:1 advanced by *Dei Filius* and especially *Spe Salvi*, three features should hold the place of primacy in a theological analysis of the nature of that faith which the tradition rightly calls "divine faith." First, *habitus*: "Faith is a *habitus*, that is, a stable disposition of the spirit, through which eternal life takes root in us and reason is led to consent to what it does not see." Second, *substance*: "Through faith, in a tentative way, or as we might say 'in embryo'—and thus according to the 'substance'—there are already present in us the things that are hoped for." "Faith draws the future into the present, so that it is no longer simply a 'not yet.'" "Substance" denotes here a tangible beginning of an eventual fulfillment; it indicates that faith is in a concrete way eschatologically inchoative. Third, the uncreated truth (*veritas increata*) who can neither deceive nor be deceived, which—as we will see—is the all-important formal object or motive cause of the act of assent.

In light of what should hold primacy in a theological inquiry into the nature of divine faith, *Dei Filius* and *Spe Salvi* urge contemporary Catholic theologians to turn their attention to the reality that precedes and that elicits the act of faith, to the reality that makes the act of faith the kind of act it is and brings about the infused operative quality that makes possible and facilitates the act of faith. In order to get an initial handle on this change of perspective and direction, we

---

19. *Decrees of the Ecumenical Councils*, vol. 2: *Trent–Vatican II*, ed. Norman P. Tanner, SJ (Washington, D.C.: Georgetown University Press, 1990), 807.

must go upstream and listen again to the very source to which *Spe Salvi* points us, the theology of the common doctor, Thomas Aquinas. However, lest my *ressourcement* in Aquinas's theology might appear as a merely antiquarian and therefore inconsequential enterprise, I will demonstrate his contemporaneity by drawing upon a theological interlocutor who—at least to my German sense of theologically qualified time and chronology—belongs to the immediate theological past: the great nineteenth-century dogmatic theologian Matthias Joseph Scheeben (1835–88). And because I think that, as a matter of fact, we are still (at least in matters of theology) in the very long nineteenth century wrestling with fundamentally the same theological issues (only now in a relatively decayed post-intellectual form), Scheeben arguably is still a theological contemporary. Scheeben was profoundly concerned about the detrimental theological consequences of the modern turn to the subject and was profoundly committed to the full recovery of a theocentric supernatural theology of faith and beatitude.

THOMAS AQUINAS

If, indeed, according to *Spe Salvi*, faith is the beginning of eternal life, then the direct object of faith—that which precedes and determines faith—should be that whereby the human being attains eternal life. Hence, the object of faith cannot simply be true things about God, but must be God himself. In Aquinas's crisp language: "The object of faith is that whereby [the human being] is made one of the Blessed" (*ST* II-II, q. 2, a. 5).[20] "The act of the believer does not terminate in a proposition, but in a thing" (*res* here in the sense of reality which can be a thing or a person).[21] In order to appreciate the act of faith and the specific infused principle of activity or *habitus* that makes acts of faith possible, one must first and foremost inquire into the relation of the act to its proper object. It is the object that specifies the act, which in turn specifies the respective principle of activity or *habitus*. Consequently, at the beginning of *ST* II-II, Aquinas

---

20. *ST* II-II, q. 2, a. 5: "Fidei objectum per se est id per quod homo beatus efficitur."
21. *ST* II-II, q. 1, a. 2, ad 2: "Actus autem credentis non terminatur ad enuntiabilia, sed ad rem."

opens his treatise on the first of the three theological virtues (i.e., faith) with a consideration of the object of faith, moves then to the act of faith, and finally considers the habit and virtue of faith. In one of his very first essays, Marie-Dominique Chenu, OP, the influential Dominican theologian and Thomist scholar, rightly regards the object of faith to be the very key to Aquinas's treatise on faith.[22] By extension, we should add—and this is, incidentally, a side thesis of this chapter—that the object of faith, as understood by Aquinas, is the key to grasping the theological significance of the three essential features of faith identified by *Dei Filius* and *Spe Salvi*: first and foremost, the *veritas increata*, secondly, the eschatologically inchoative substance, and finally, the supernatural *habitus*. Heeding this magisterial signal, a theological consideration of the question "What is faith?" should turn first to faith's object.

The Object of Faith

In light of the contemporary ordinary English meaning of the noun "object," the "object of faith" (*obiectum fidei*) is an admittedly less than felicitous technical term. It has its remote origin in Aristotle's epistemological considerations and later became a staple term in Western medieval philosophy and theology. Contemporary connotations of "object" collide head-on with what "object" (*obiectum*) actually denotes in Aquinas's use. But once rightly understood, it is the very "object of faith" that provides the key to understanding what kind of act faith is, and what kind of *habitus* makes possible this kind of act.

Let me state up front the proper denomination of "object" as Aquinas uses it in the treatise on faith in the *Summa Theologiae*: "The term [*obiectum*] 'object' stands for the reality, thing or person, that engages an act."[23] What needs to be highlighted is the verb "engage." The medieval thinkers deployed "object" (*obiectum*) in connection with apprehensive and appetitive powers that convey "whence the

---

22. Marie-Dominique Chenu, OP, "Pro supernaturalitate fidei illustrando," *Xenia Thomistica* 3 (1925): 307.

23. T. C. O'Brien, OP, "Appendix 1: Objects and Virtues," in St. Thomas Aquinas, *Summa theologiae*, vol. 31: *Faith (2a2ae 1–7)*, trans. T. C. O'Brien (Cambridge: Cambridge University Press, 2006), 178.

act of apprehension or appetition originates."[24] Lawrence Dewan puts the complex matter succinctly:

> In the case of apprehension, "obiectum" expresses movement from the thing toward the soul. In the case of appetition, it expresses movement from the soul toward the thing. This suggests that in using the word "obiectum" concerning an apprehensive power, one is expected to imagine something moving from the thing apprehended to the one who apprehends: perhaps the best illustration would be sound traveling from the gong or bell to the ear. Color, for example, would be imagined as behaving somewhat similarly. The "obiectum" would be what is hurled at and strikes the observer. To call something an "obiectum" would be something like calling it "striking," "a striking thing." On the other hand, in the case of motive or appetitive powers, the "obiectum" is "that which we go for," the target of our pursuit, that at which we hurl ourselves.[25]

The powers of apprehension and appetition are passive potencies; they are receptive of their objects before their specific activities are actualized. The "object" has a causal function upon the act of apprehension; it is from the "object" (let us say, color) that the act of apprehension (seeing) receives its specific determination that distinguishes it from other kinds of acts of apprehension (hearing or smelling). As the "object" determines the act, Aquinas takes it as operating after the manner of a formal principle. For this reason the "object" is denominated as "formal objective" or "formal object." In his early commentary on Lombard's *Sentences* he offers a helpful summary of the precise meaning of "formal object":

> Because everything acts to the degree that it is actual and so through its form, and because for the passive powers the object is the actuating element, therefore that aspect of the object to which a passive power is proportioned is that which is formal in the object. And in reference to it powers and habits are differentiated, because they derive their species from this formal aspect of the object [i.e., formal objective].[26]

I will return to the topic of "formal object" later in this chapter.

---

24. Lawrence Dewan, OP, "'Objectum': Notes on the Invention of a Word," in his *Wisdom, Law, and Virtue: Essays in Thomistic Ethics* (New York: Fordham University Press, 2007), 414.

25. Ibid.

26. *Sent.* III, q. 24, a. 1, q.c. 1; trans. T. C. O'Brien, "Appendix 1: Objects and Virtues," 181.

If you gain a distinct sense that by considering the full meaning of "object" you are leaving behind the epistemic presuppositions entailed in the Cartesian rupture between *res cogitans* and *res extensa* as well as those entailed in the Kantian rupture between the transcendental ego and the "thing in itself" (*das Ding an sich*)—you are right. You are, as a matter of fact, being directed to the exit of the maze of modern subjectivity with its interminable succession of aporetic epistemologies. According to the realist epistemology of the *philosophia perennis*, there obtains a primordial causal, that is, specifying, engagement of the apperceptive faculties by the "object," which precedes and indeed enables the secondary epistemological reflection of this dynamic.[27] Moreover, this engagement of the act by the object presupposes an order between human beings and their world. We see the color of the apple, we hear the sound of the bell, we feel the wetness of the rain. "Object" denotes realities, persons, and things in view of our distinct engagement by them and interaction with them.[28] By virtue of our apprehensive powers we are receptive to persons and things, and by virtue of our appetitive powers we interact with persons and things. They become "objects" (*obiecta*), not by any change in themselves, but by being known and desired in a term that might best be characterized as "intentional union." As T. C. O'Brien aptly puts it: "With respect to knowledge, it is the actuality of being itself that 'allows' knowledge and to which the knowledge is a reaction. In the case of appetition, it is the goodness, therefore the actual being, of the object that prompts and evokes the corresponding love, desire, hope."[29]

It is at this very point that we come to appreciate fully Aquinas's teaching that faith, hope, and charity are theological virtues—they facilitate acts of faith, hope, and charity, which have God as their

---

27. Besides the recent book by MacDonald, *Knowledge and the Transcendent*, see the two classics of Thomist epistemology: Maritain, *The Degrees of Knowledge*, and Étienne Gilson, *Thomist Realism and the Critique of Knowledge*, trans. Mark A. Wauck (San Francisco, Calif.: Ignatius Press, 1986).

28. See chap. 5, "Perception and Abstraction," in James Ross's important book *Thought and World: The Hidden Necessities* (Notre Dame, Ind.: University of Notre Dame Press, 2008) for a lucid and astute defense of what amounts to an essentially Aristotelian-Thomist epistemology (absent Scholastic technicalities) in conversation with and critical engagement of contemporary analytic philosophy of mind.

29. O'Brien, "Appendix 1: Objects and Virtues," 182.

respective "object." This means that God unites himself to the human in such a way that the human can know, hope in, and love God, for—remember—"object" denotes here the term of an intentional union of cognition and appetition. God becoming "object" does not change God, but it reduces cognitive and appetitive powers to certain kinds of acts—in short, it specifies them. These acts in turn specify the operative *habitus* that empower the intellect and will to perform acts that entirely surpass their natural orientation. Consider Aquinas's terse statement: "Now we derive from God ... knowledge of truth. ... Accordingly, faith makes us adhere to God, as the source whence we derive the knowledge of truth, since we believe that what God tells us is true" (*ST* II-II, q. 17, a. 6). However, God is not just the material object of faith insofar as we believe truths about God and in relationship to God. Rather, by clinging to God himself as the very motive of our assent to the content of faith, we reach God in his very being. And so Aquinas stresses: "When we believe God [by faith], we [reach God himself] by believing [*credendo Deum attingimus*]; for which reason it was stated ... that God is the object of faith, not only because we believe in a God [*credimus Deum*] but because we believe God [*credimus Deo*]" (*ST* II-II, q. 81, a. 5).[30] Believing God by faith, cleaving to God by hope, and loving God by charity denote three kinds of acts facilitated by the three theological *habitus* that have God as their object.

We have reached the point where we must turn to the object of faith. Because faith is essentially an act of the intellect—*cum assensu cogitare*—the "object" receives a title appropriate to the intellect's orientation: "first truth" (*prima veritas*), a concept we encountered in *Dei Filius* under the slight variation of "uncreated truth" (*veritas increata*).

First Truth

Truth does not reside in things but in the intellect. But what is the case for the human intellect must supereminently be the case for the divine intellect. Truth resides first and foremost in the divine in-

---

30. I have modified the English translation of the Dominican Fathers. They translated *attingere* with "reaching out to," which does not do full justice to Aquinas's intention. Rather, *attingere* must be translated with "to arrive at," "to reach."

tellect, first truth (*prima veritas*), or with Vatican I, uncreated truth (*veritas increata*). Jesus can truthfully say "I *am* the truth" because he is the Son of God, the Word incarnate, begotten truth. As Aquinas puts it in *De veritate*: "[If] truth is taken properly in whatever pertains to God, it is predicated essentially; yet it is appropriated to the person of the Son."[31] To predicate truth essentially of God means that truth is identical with the divine essence:

> His being [*esse suum*] is not only conformed to His intellect, but it is the very act of His intellect; and His act of understanding is the measure and cause of every other being and of every other intellect; and He Himself is His own existence and act of understanding [*et ipse est suum esse et intelligere*]. Whence it follows not only that truth is in Him but that He is truth itself, and the sovereign and first truth [*ipse sit summa et prima veritas*]. (*ST* I, q. 16, a. 5)

All created things, in virtue of their participation in the act of being, can be said to be true insofar as they conform to their divine exemplar. And sure enough, for human beings, as endowed with intellect, this means that we can participate in God and God's knowledge by inquiring into created truth.

But what happens when the sovereign and first truth (*summa et prima veritas*) becomes object of a cognitive act? Specified directly by the first truth, the act must be a participation in an entirely more perfect supernatural manner of divine knowledge. "Believing God, we reach God himself" (*ST* II-II, q. 81, a. 5). It is thus that the first truth (not truth from God or about God or in relation to God, but the prototype and exemplar of all truth) as object of faith specifies the act of faith, which in turn specifies the *habitus* of divine faith.[32]

But now we must remember that faith is not vision: "Faith is the 'substance' of things hoped for; the proof of things not seen" (Heb 11:1). The first truth in its proper species is the unmediated ob-

---

31. *De ver.*, q. 1, a. 7 (*Truth*, 1:36).
32. For an astute and penetrating interpretation of this crucial aspect of Aquinas's theology of faith, see Juan Alfaro, SJ, "Supernaturalitas fidei iuxta S. Thomam," *Gregorianum* 44 (1963): 501–42 and 731–87. In his opening thesis statement, Alfaro lucidly captures the very core of Aquinas's doctrine of divine faith: "Divine faith is directed to the vision of God as its beginning: this is the fundamental perspective of St. Thomas as he elaborates the theology of faith. The supernaturality of faith becomes intelligible in light of the supernaturality of the vision of God to which faith tends" (501; author's translation).

ject of the beatific vision of the blessed, the *comprehensores*, in heaven. Only insofar as *it does not appear* is the first truth the object of faith.[33] But how then does the "obiectum" engage the intellect and thus specify the act of faith? Aquinas gives us a clue right at the beginning of his treatise on faith: "The object of every cognitive habit [*habitus*] includes two things: first, that which is known materially, and is the material object [*materiale obiectum*], so to speak, and, secondly, that whereby it is known, which is the formal aspect of the object [*formalis ratio obiecti*]" (*ST* II-II, q. 1, a. 1). We are returning now to the crucial distinction between the material object of faith (*credere Deum*), believing in God, and the formal aspect of the object of faith (*credere Deo*), believing God himself.

The Formal and the Material Objects of Faith

By distinguishing between the formal and the material objects and by also taking object as the end toward which the will is directed, Aquinas identifies a threefold relationship between the act of faith and its divine object. In order to express this threefold relationship, he adopts the popular Augustinian formula, widely used in the tradition (*ST* II-II, q. 2, a. 2). I introduced it partially already above: *credere Deo*, to believe God—faith is the reverent submission to God as revealer, the acceptance of God as *prima veritas*. This is faith's formal object. *Credere Deum*, to believe in God—faith is assent to what God has revealed, first and foremost about himself. This is faith's material object. Both believing God (*credere Deo*) and believing in God (*credere Deum*) indicate the intellect's relationship to God. Finally, tending toward God (*credere in Deum*). Faith is a dynamic movement into God. This aspect signifies the intellect's act informed by an affective union with its end, charity. This threefold relationship between the act of faith and its object does not designate three distinct acts but rather the three aspects constitutive of every consummate act of faith. Hence, while being essentially an intellectual act,

---

33. *De ver.*, q. 14, a. 8, ad 3: "First Truth, insofar as it appears in its proper form, is the object of the vision of heaven. But, in so far as it does not appear, it is the object of faith. So, although the object of both acts is the same thing in reality, it differs in intelligible aspect. The object thus formally different makes the species of the act different" (*Truth*, 2:245).

trust and affectivity are integral to—as Aquinas would put it—"living" or "formed" faith.[34] When God engages the human intellect and thus becomes its object, God engages the intellect first and foremost *formally*, as first truth, who reveals himself in the person of the Word—scripture and tradition constituting "one single deposit of the Word of God," as *Dei Verbum* teaches (no. 10).[35]

For most theological uses, the distinction between the formal and the material objects of the act of faith suffices, the formal object being, as *Dei Filius* states, "the authority of God revealing." However, if we want to attain a deeper appreciation, on the one hand, of "the authority of the First Truth who is revealing," or differently put, the "truthfulness of God in speaking"[36] and, on the other hand, of what aspect of the formal object specifically accounts for faith being a supernatural, infused *habitus*—the beginning of eternal life in the believer—then we are well advised to avail ourselves of the time-honored distinction between the mediating "formal object under which" (*quo*) and the terminative "formal object which" (*quod*).[37]

The mediating "formal object under which" (*obiectum formale quo*) is the authority of the first truth in revealing, the truthfulness of God in speaking; it is the medium by reason of which the term is at-

---

34. *ST* II-II, q. 4, a. 3: "The act of faith is directed to the object of the will, i.e., the good, as to its end: and this good which is the end of faith, viz., the Divine Good, is the proper object of charity. Therefore charity is called the form of faith in so far as the act of faith is perfected and formed by charity." In his commentary on this passage, O'Brien states, as tersely as rightly: "Only in one who loves God does faith reach its fully intended meaning as the beginning of eternal life." Thomas Aquinas, *Summa theologiae*, vol. 31 (2a2ae 1–7); *Faith*, 125. For a brilliant and exacting study of the precise correlation between the theological virtues of faith and charity in Aquinas's theology, see Michael S. Sherwin, OP, *By Knowledge and by Love: Charity and Knowledge in the Moral Theology of St. Thomas Aquinas* (Washington, D.C.: The Catholic University of America Press, 2005).

35. We do not have to go very far into the theological past in order to find a clear expression of the "obiectum fidei" under the title of "First Truth." In 1910, Pope Pius X states in "Sacrorum antistitum": "Faith is not a blind inclination of religion welling up from the depth of the subconscious under the impulse of the heart and the inclination of a morally conditioned will but is the genuine assent of the intellect to a truth that is received from outside by hearing [*ex auditu*]. In this assent, given on the authority of the all-truthful God, we hold to be true what has been said, attested to, and revealed by the personal God, our Creator and Lord " (Denzinger, no. 3542).

36. Dulles, *Assurance of Things Hoped For*, 188.

37. For an explanation of these terms, see the sections "Sacred Theology" and "Metaphysics" in chapter 1, pp. 93–109.

tained, the personal God who is supreme and first truth.[38] The term attained is the "formal object which" (*obiectum formale quod*), by reason of which the material object is attained. Moreover, the terminative "formal object which" (*quod*), by way of the act of faith, specifies the supernatural disposition of faith. Romanus Cessario puts the terminative aspect of the formal object succinctly: "As a theological virtue, the virtue of faith unites the believer—through the mediation of Christ's human nature and historical ministry—to the persons of the Blessed Trinity."[39] It is this intentional union with the Trinity that requires the stable disposition of faith to be nothing less than a grace-infused (instead of acquired) and hence strictly supernatural *habitus* that ushers in the beginning of beatitude.

MATTHIAS JOSEPH SCHEEBEN

In order to demonstrate that the distinction between the "formal object under which" (*quo*) and the formal object "which" (*quod*) is of ongoing theological relevance, I turn to Matthias Joseph Scheeben, arguably one of the most profound and most productive Catholic theologians of the last two centuries. In his theology of faith, he conveys—in ways still pertinent for contemporary Catholic theology—the theological substance behind the important conceptual distinction between the "formal object under which" (*quo*) and the "formal object which" (*quod*).

One of Scheeben's unquestioned achievements as the leading German dogmatic theologian of the nineteenth century was the retrieval of the essential supernatural character of the Christian faith in the aftermath of the grievous distortions inflicted upon the understanding of divine faith, especially by rationalism, but also by fideistic traditionalism. Scheeben developed his mature theology of faith in the first volume of his monumental *Handbook of Catholic Dogmat-*

---

38. Ibid.: "In adhering to God as revealer the believer accepts God as the one whose word is supremely deserving of assent, trust, and obedience. The authority of God who speaks is inseparable from the authority of God's word, but the word as a created reality cannot be the formal object, or motive, of faith."

39. Romanus Cessario, OP, *Christian Faith and the Theological Life* (Washington, D.C.: The Catholic University of America Press, 1996), 61.

ics,⁴⁰ which began to appear in 1873, only three years after the abrupt termination of the First Vatican Council. I shall rely here, however, on a later and slightly more comprehensive version of his theology of faith, a fifty-seven-column monographic entry in the fifth volume of *Wetzer and Welte's Lexicon of the Church*.⁴¹ In this late version of Scheeben's theology of faith, which appeared in the year of his death in 1888, he had the opportunity to expand and nuance his earlier account, and more importantly, the opportunity to react to his critics, first and foremost his erstwhile Roman teacher, Joseph Kleutgen, SJ.⁴² The single most important dogmatic point of reference for both versions of his theology of faith is, of course, the 1870 Dogmatic Constitution on the Catholic Faith, *Dei Filius* from the First Vatican Council. All sections of his treatment presuppose this dogmatic constitution, and large portions of it consist of an interpretation and further unfolding of the Council's teaching on faith.

The Mediating Formal Object of Faith "Under Which"
Let us first turn to the mediating "formal object under which." Scheeben illuminates the theological substance of this indispensable

40. The edition I have been consulting is vol. 3 of Scheeben, *Gesammelte Schriften*.
41. Matthias Joseph Scheeben, "Glaube," in *Wetzer und Welte's Kirchenlexikon, oder Encyclopädie der katholischen Theologie und ihrer humanen Hilfswissenschaften* (1888), 5:616–74. We get an initial idea of the richness and complexity of Scheeben's theology of faith from the simple fact that it takes him eleven sections—each comprising several subsections—to cover the topic in all of its aspects and ramifications. He treats of, first, the name and notion of faith as such in German, Latin, Greek, and Hebrew; second, the concept and nature of theological faith; third, the motive causes of faith, its formal object, and its character as objective divine faith; fourth, the material object of faith and its character as a transcendent faith; fifth, the motive causes of faith's credibility and its character as reasonable faith; sixth, the church's presentation of God's Word, the authority of church doctrine and its character as Catholic faith; seventh, the grace of faith as its supernatural cause and faith's character as supernatural; eighth, human cooperation and faith's character as an act of human freedom; ninth, the resolution or reduction of faith to all its constitutive principles; tenth, the properties of faith that constitute or complete its specific perfection; and, finally, eleventh, the necessity of faith (that is, faith as a necessary means of salvation; and faith as a matter of obligation due to a precept). In the handbook chapter as well as in the later lexicon monograph, we encounter a fully integral, nonreductive account of the nature, structure, and plenitude of the Christian faith.
42. Unsurprisingly, the conflict pertained to the *analysis fidei*, which Kleutgen once called the "crux theologorum." For an all too brief characterization of the point of conflict, see note 48 below, and for a helpfully concise discussion see Dulles, *Assurance of Things Hoped For*, 90.

aspect of the formal object by drawing upon the analogy of the social phenomenon of natural authority in contexts in which assent is demanded and willingly given. He calls this phenomenon "authority faith" (*Autoritätsglaube*). Authority faith is "a firm holding as true, or a decided judgment of the mind, that does not rest on its own insight or direct acquaintance ... with the object of that judgment, but on the insight or knowledge made over to us by another intelligent being."[43] In his recent important monograph on Scheeben, *Romance and System*, Aidan Nichols felicitously renders Scheeben's core concept this way: "To 'believe' in the appropriate sense of the word is to enjoy a conviction whose 'ground and norm' lie elsewhere, in the entertaining of truth by another."[44] "Authority faith" arises essentially from the respect and esteem of the person who gives witness and who teaches, from the dignity of the person and his or her spiritual and intellectual perfections.[45] "Authority faith" is more perfect and more pronounced in accordance with how completely the one who witnesses and teaches due to his superiority over the hearer can duly claim or even command faith from the hearer. The ultimate witness and perfect teacher not only offers his judgments as the foundation for the hearer's convictions but also prescribes his judgments as the norm for the hearer's convictions. This authority is, of course, far from an extrinsic and presumptuous imposition upon the believer. After all, the authority of the "auctor" that stands behind every "auctoritas" and who requests assent to the truth of the Gospel is none other than the selfsame "auctor" of the very act of faith itself, insofar as it is this "auctor" who makes the act of faith possible in the first place, and as its engendering principle must be cooperating in it.[46] The "auctor" of faith is God, externally as well as internally. "Authority faith" is thus nothing else than one side of the selfsame coin of which faith's essential supernaturalism is the other side. Differently put, faith's mediating "formal object under which" (*quo*) and its ter-

---

43. *Handbuch*, 1:287; translation from Aidan Nichols, OP, *Romance and System: The Theological Synthesis of Matthias Joseph Scheeben* (Denver, Colo.: Augustine Institute Press, 2010), 22.

44. Nichols, *Romance and System*, 22.

45. Scheeben, "Glaube," 620.

46. Ibid., 621.

minative "formal object which" (*quod*) are one and the same object, in the words of *Dei Filius*, the *veritas increata*, the truth who is "auctor" of all.

The "auctor" of all, by exercising his authority by way of the temporal missions of the incarnate Lord and the Holy Spirit, offers himself as the reliable ground for the certitude of the requested assent. Because it is God who proposes himself in such a way, it is most fitting and proper to respond with "authority faith." Scheeben regards the relationship between parents and children as the principal paradigm for the way "authority faith" arises naturally in human relations. The parents who speak authoritatively and thereby demand the child's assent, vouch in virtue of their moral truthfulness that they require faith only for what they themselves understand to be true, and to the degree that, because of the proper functioning of their intellect, they can exclude the danger of error. Consequently, the content of their speech can be held true by the child based on their integrity and authority as well as if it came directly from the child's own insight. The trust, respect, and obedience of the child to its parents are integral components of the child's genuine freedom, its proper flourishing toward adulthood. The child's relationship to the parents serves as the prime natural analogue of the relationship between God, the "Father of Spirits" (*pater spiritum*; Heb 12:9) and all created spirits: divine faith is grounded in a relationship in which the authority and credibility of the one who speaks are exhaustively and exclusively entailed in the divine nature of the speaker.[47] "Authority faith" is essentially an assent to truths because of the authority of the one who speaks. The assent of the intellect is commanded by the will in virtue of the respect and trust that the person speaking elicits and the credentials the person has. The assent proper to "authority faith" does not arise from a theoretical inference or a practical judgment, though such inferences and judgments may indeed precede faith proper in some way to prepare the assent integral to the act of "authority faith." The assent integral to the act of divine faith, however, entails its own intellectual motive, because the divine credentials must, of course, be perceived and understood by the in-

---

47. Ibid., 622.

tellect in the very assent of divine faith.[48] This means that, in the case of genuine theological faith, God presents himself as "auctor" to the person externally by word and sign as well as internally as God who speaks—the intellect being illumined by the light of faith. Theological faith thus is divine faith in the sense that the authority to which the believer submits and the credibility to which the believer assents are essentially contained in the divinity by whom the believer is addressed. In sum, the mediating "formal object under which" (*quo*) denotes the motive cause of the assent of faith.

The Terminative "Formal Object Which"

Let us now turn to the terminative formal object "which" (*quod*) that accounts for the intentional union between the human intellect and the persons of the Trinity. According to Scheeben, it is this aspect of the formal object of faith that, by way of the act of faith, determines the transcendent *formal* causality of the theological faith, its character as a supernaturally infused *habitus*. In virtue of the assent of faith, there comes about such an intimate and perfect union and assimilation of the believer's knowledge with God's knowledge that the supernatural formal causality issues in nothing short of an inchoate participation in God's own life and knowledge and, consequently, in some tangible anticipation of the supernatural knowledge of God in the beatific vision.[49] Scheeben goes so far as to use the term "transplantation" (*Überpflanzung*) in order to describe how, in this most intimate intentional union, the power and dignity of the divine knowledge comes to be implanted in the believer's

---

48. In his 1873 *Handbuch* Scheeben had criticized Lugo's and Kleutgen's construal of the intellectual motive of faith as overly rationalistic, as a mechanically logical operation by way of which the believer demonstrates to him- or herself the truth of the content of faith (312). Kleutgen responded by charging Scheeben with excessive voluntarism; he regarded Scheeben's construal as it was advanced in the *Handbuch* (replacing God's *veracitas* as the decisive intellectual motive of faith with God's *auctoritas*) as theoretically unsustainable. In his later monographic lexicon entry, Scheeben responded to Kleutgen's criticism (633) and admitted that the acknowledgment of God's infallible knowledge and truthfulness are integral to the intellectual motive of faith. This acknowledgment, however, he insists is not produced by an implicit syllogism but rather is concomitant with the acts of reverence and attachment, trust, and faithfulness produced by the will as God introduces Himself externally and internally as "auctor."

49. Scheeben, "Glaube," 654.

faith.⁵⁰ Scheeben regards this "transplantation" of the power and dignity proper to the divine knowledge to be the truly divine certitude appropriate to the dignity of the Word of God communicating itself not only externally but also internally to the believer. This certitude is decidedly theocentric: it rests in an intentional union that anticipates the beatific vision. In other words, certitude is caused by the inchoate intentional union the final end of which is the formal union (by way of the *lumen gloriae*) of the intellect with God in the beatific vision. The intentional union means that the human intellect is elevated beyond itself by God to the very height of the divine principle and receives a certitude that corresponds to the dignity of this principle. The one who has divine faith in virtue of grace adheres to the first truth itself as it is in itself, such that the *prima veritas* can unfold itself in the intellect of the believer with the will and judgment of the human submitted to the first truth.⁵¹

So far, we have seen Scheeben's way of substantiating what is at stake in the notion of faith's terminative "formal object which" (*quod*): a theological account that grants a profound theological intelligibility to the church's teaching that divine faith is a grace-infused and hence strictly supernatural *habitus* of the intellect that ushers in the beginning of beatitude. Let us finally turn to the material object of faith, the first truth revealed.

THE MATERIAL OBJECT OF FAITH

Here I will have to be all too brief, because a proper consideration of this important topic would go far beyond the scope of this chapter. Simply put, the material object includes God as the thing (*res*) reached by the act of faith and everything else that God reveals, not only as factually true but also what God promises and commands. Because divine faith, however, is not vision, it must be received, held, and communicated according to the mode of the receiv-

---

50. Ibid., 625.
51. In Newman's terminology, the one who has divine faith suspends the principle of private judgment in matters of faith, while the one who lacks divine faith submits matters of divine faith to the principle of private judgment. Scheeben cites Aquinas, *ST* II-II, q. 5, a. 3, ad 1.

er, that is, according to the mode of the human being in the state of pilgrimage (*in statu viatoris*) and not in the state of beatitude (*in statu visionis*).⁵² What is utterly simple in the mind of subsistent truth can be assented to by the believer only in a composite manner. Therefore God chooses an instrumentality conducive to human understanding and to the nature of giving assent—truth-bearing statements that can be sufficiently grasped in order to enable a simple assent. These propositions of faith can in no way be instruments extrinsic to the divine communication of the truth. Rather, as instruments of God's own truthfulness, they participate in the one formality or meaning that constitutes divine faith.⁵³ God as first truth in being (*prima veritas in essendo*) and God as first truth in speaking (*prima veritas in dicendo*) cannot be divorced from each other. Nor can the first truth in speaking be divorced from the proper instruments, the propositions of faith. Consequently, it is erroneous to reduce these propositions of faith to the status of "activating symbols" or "effective channels" of an essentially ineffable mystery.⁵⁴ Such a move also jettisons the first truth as faith's formal object. Rather, assent is given to the articles of faith because they are revealed by God, the first truth (*prima veritas*), who does not deceive and cannot be deceived. The propositions of faith are absolutely integral to the material object of the faith, the very thing (*res*) that is reached by the act of faith.⁵⁵

CONCLUSION

At this point we are able to appreciate the full weight of Aquinas's pithy statement from *De veritate*: "Faith, which through assent unites [the human being] to divine knowledge, has God as its prin-

---

52. On Aquinas's use of the Scholastic axiom "What is received is received according to the mode of the receiver" (*quidquid recipitur ad modum recipientis recipitur*), see the instructive study by John F. Wippel, "Thomas Aquinas and the Axiom 'What is received is received according to the mode of the receiver,'" in *Metaphysical Themes in Thomas Aquinas II* (Washington, D.C.: The Catholic University of America Press, 2007), 113–22.

53. Cessario, *Christian Faith and the Theological Life*, 57.

54. Dulles, *Assurance of Things Hoped For*, 194.

55. Recall that *res* is a transcendental and signifies all that can become the term of a knowing act. Yet the medium of a knowing act of discursive reasoning characteristic of human earthly existence are propositions.

cipal object, and anything else as a consequent addition."[56] Scheeben transposed Aquinas's teaching into the image of "transplantation" (*Überpflanzung*). The object of faith is for both theologians the key to understanding divine faith as the personal, intentional union between God and the believer. The object of faith is not an abstract reality but the Trinity, both first truth and perfect beatitude. As unitive and as eschatologically inchoative, divine faith is utterly theocentric. Divine faith is elicited by and is directed toward its object, the first truth, who is not some abstract truth, but subsistent truth, the Trinity.

Now we are in a better position to appreciate the full theological implications of the teaching of *Spe Salvi* on the nature of divine faith: the object of faith is the key to understanding the theocentric, unitive, and eschatologically inchoative character of divine faith. The *essentially* supernatural object of faith is the key to understanding the infused *habitus* of divine faith itself as supernatural, first, *in mode* (*quoad modum*), because the *habitus* is supernaturally caused and directed to a supernatural end. Secondly and surpassingly, on account of the intentional union between knower and known, between believer and the divine truth believed, the infused *habitus* of divine faith must also be *substantially* supernatural (*quoad substantiam*). Divine faith is a tangible down payment, a substantive foreshadowing—in *Spe Salvi*'s felicitous words: "'in embryo'—and thus according to the substance" (par. 7)—of the beatific vision in glory.

What about the maze of self-reflexive subjectivity the modern turn to the subject has gotten us into? How do we get out? Where is Ariadne's thread? By now, the guide to the exit I propose should be quite obvious. Ariadne's thread is indeed nothing but the object of faith under the title of "first truth." By following this thread consistently, Catholic theology will eventually find its way out of the maze of modern self-reflexive subjectivity. The subject as agent of the act of faith is neither faith's cause nor the arbiter of its content. Hence, by being barred from playing a constitutive role, the subject is healed and elevated to play the proper participatory role of a creature ordered and, in virtue of living faith (*viz.*, divine faith formed

---

56. *De ver.*, q. 14, a. 8 (*Truth*, 2:245).

and thus perfected by charity), drawn into the beatitude of the Trinity. The subject's free act of assent is facilitated by a disposition that cannot be acquired but is elicited and informed by the divine personal truth. As Scheeben aptly put it: "As little as human beings can justify themselves, as little can they make themselves have divine faith."[57] The subject is far from being erased, reified, or diminished; the subject is rather rectified (should I say "eccentrified"?) and elevated in the course of being engaged by faith's object. Consequently, risking the danger of painting with an all too broad brush, I hazard the claim that in the contemporary transition from the modern turn to the subject toward the postmodern despair about and flight from modern subjectivity, genuine divine faith and its proper theological understanding must unavoidably issue in an inversion of anthropocentrism, that is, in the restitution of proper theocentrism. It would be, however, a grave error to assume that anthropocentrism and theocentrism would relate to each other like two sides of the same coin, such that an inversion would be simply like turning a coin upside down.

The precise relationship between anthropocentrism and theocentrism is probably the point of my greatest agreement and at the same time sharpest disagreement with Karl Rahner's way of negotiating anthropocentricity and theocentricity in theology. They are indeed not opposites (here is the agreement); but, crucially, they also are not one and the same thing (here is the sharp disagreement). In his essay, "Theology and Anthropology," Rahner argues that natural as well as revealed theology are fundamentally both transcendental anthropology.[58] That is, to say something about God is to say something automatically about the human being and vice versa and, furthermore, these two kinds of statements are connected with one another not only in respect of their object but also in respect of the process of knowing itself. Rahner's approach depends completely on the supposition that Kant's transcendental idealism (as read through the lens of Heidegger's interpretation of Kant) constitutes an epoch-

---

57. Scheeben, "Glaube," 656.

58. Karl Rahner, "Theology and Anthropology," trans. Graham Harrison, in his *Theological Investigations* (New York: Herder and Herder, 1972), 9:28–45.

al moment in the history of philosophy behind which theology cannot return. While Rahner in the above essay—rightly—holds that the anthropocentric turn must be purged from its aspirations to self-sovereignty, his endorsement of Kant's and Heidegger's analyses commits him to the position that such a necessity can under no circumstances entail a *carte blanche* return to Aquinas's metaphysics and epistemology. If Kant's analysis in the *Critique of Pure Reason* indeed obtains, Rahner is justified in claiming that it is essential to begin every dogmatic discussion with our structures of knowing, that is, the *a priori* possibility of knowing this fact of dogma. But it is far from clear that Kant's epistemological analysis in his *Critique of Pure Reason* and Heidegger's phenomenological account of *Dasein* in his *Being and Time* do indeed obtain and it is at the same time quite clear that Rahner's Kant- and Heidegger-inspired reinterpretation of Aquinas in *Spirit in the World*, while undoubtedly brilliant, is profoundly problematic.[59]

In short, it would be a grave error to assume that anthropocentrism and theocentrism would relate to each other like two sides of the same coin, such that an inversion would be simply like turning a coin upside down. Entertaining such an erroneous assumption would mean becoming imprisoned by a false image of this particular inversion. Rather, such an inversion would be more like a true "reformatio"; for anthropocentrism, in principle, must reduce God

---

59. See Karl Rahner, *Spirit in the World*, trans. William Dych (New York: Herder and Herder, 1969). At this point, it is impossible to enter into the kind of thoughtfully critical engagement that Rahner's thought deserves as well as requires. I shall at least name the most problematic tenets of his account: being as interiority, knowing as self-knowledge, the knowledge of first principles, the anticipation of being and the knowledge of God, and, finally, the nature of the *species intelligibilis* and sensible knowledge, in short, all the entailments of the *conversio ad phantasmata*, especially the historicity of truth. Indispensable starting points for such a critical engagement remain Bernhard Lakebrink, *Klassische Metaphysik: Eine Auseinandersetzung mit der existentialen Anthropozentrik* (Freiburg: Rombach, 1967); Cornelio Fabro, *La svolta antropologica di Karl Rahner*, in his *Opere Complete* 25 (Segni: Editrice del Verbo Incarnato, 2011); and, more accessible for an English-speaking readership, White, *Wisdom in the Face of Modernity*. For an account of the circumstances and the substantive philosophical reasons that led Rahner's *Doktorvater* Martin Honecker to reject as doctoral dissertation in philosophy what was later published as *Spirit in the World*, see the substantive study by Vincent Berning, *Martin Honecker (1888–1941): Auf dem Wege von der Logik zu Metaphysik—Die Grundzüge seines kritisch-realistischen Denkens* (Weilheim: Gustav-Siewert-Akademie, 2003).

to a function of human fulfillment and happiness; and, because of the unavailability of a theodicy that is fully satisfying on a rational level, the fate of much of modern religious anthropocentrism is its eventual decline into atheistic humanism.[60] Theocentrism, by contrast, due to the surpassing nature of the gratuitous ultimate end of the human being, *viz.*, eternal communion with God, allows for the perfect beatitude of the human being in concert with and as part of the perfection of the whole cosmos.[61] Consequently, neither in the inchoate perfection *in via* nor in the final perfection of the beatific vision is God ever a function of a human fulfillment and happiness that would be an end in itself to which God might offer eternal assistance—as an anthropocentric eschatology will have to assume, of course, erroneously. Rather, human fulfillment and happiness in the beatific vision are the gratuitous specific human realization of the whole cosmos participating in its final end, God, so that the life of the Trinity "may be all in all" (1 Cor 15:28), as a theocentric eschatology rightly holds. By way of the simultaneously infused theological virtues of faith, hope, and charity, the Christian achieves in this life an intentional union with the triune God and—far from being destroyed—is inchoately but unfathomably perfected.

For a precise characterization of the inchoate as well as unfathomable nature of this perfection *in statu viatoris*, I will leave the last word to the *doctor communis*. It was after all Scheeben's theological genius to maximize Aquinas's profound insight in his own teaching: "As [a person] in his intellective power participates in the Divine knowledge through the virtue of faith, and in his power of will participates in the Divine love through the virtue of charity, so also in the nature of the

---

60. Eschweiler (*Die zwei Wege der neueren Theologie*, 265n8) rightly observes that a certain form of modern mysticism that displays theocentric rhetoric is nothing but the acme of religious anthropocentrism ("God in *us*," "Jesus in *us*"). The 1,200-page study on the emergence and intellectual history of modern atheism by Cornelio Fabro, *God in Exile*, has lost nothing of its pertinence for coming to understand the insidious consequences that are entailed in the modern turn to the subject for our capability to behold the formal object of divine faith, the first truth.

61. Far from announcing the anthropocentric turn (as some twentieth-century interpreters of Aquinas erroneously claimed), the Christocentrism of the *Summa Theologiae*—Christ the incarnate "Deus pro nobis" as its keystone—is genuinely theocentric in that the *ordo salutis* is ordered essentially to the participation in the blessedness of the triune God.

soul does he participate in the Divine Nature, after the manner of a likeness, through a certain regeneration or re-creation" (*ST* I-II, q. 110, a. 4). In his discussion of the missions of the divine persons Aquinas famously states:

> There is one special mode belonging to the rational creature wherein God is said to be present as the object known is in the knower, and the beloved in the lover. And since the rational creature by its operation of knowledge and love attains to God Himself, according to this special mode God is said not only to exist in the rational creature, but also to dwell therein as in his own temple. (*ST* I, q. 43, a. 3)

This is nothing but the objective reality that "'in embryo'—and thus according to the substance" subsists in living faith, the presence of "things that are hoped for: the whole, true life" (*Spe Salvi*, par. 7), which is the very beginning of beatitude, our participation in divine happiness. It is this presence of "things that are hoped for" in the *viator* that draws the *viator* forward on the journey to the perfect, interminable actualization of the whole, true life, to beatitude.

5

The Road to Beatitude— Divinization and Friendship with God
The Virtue of Charity

> Charity is not a virtue of human beings qua human beings, but insofar as, by sharing in grace, they become gods and the children of God, in keeping with 1 John 3:1, "You see what charity the Father has bestowed on us, so that we are called, and have become, the children of God."
>
> —Thomas Aquinas, *On Charity*[1]

In the previous chapter, I focused on the very beginning of the journey to beatitude, on the substance of things hoped for as received, beheld, and affirmed in the theological virtue of faith. In this chapter, I shall consider the supernatural actualization and perfection of this journey, the justification, sanctification, and finally divinization of the *viator* through a growing friendship with God, induced by grace and enacted in a life of charity. As I did already in earlier chapters, I will unfold this supernatural dynamic in the context of its contemporary contestation.

In the first part, I will expand upon and deepen the analysis of the modern turn to the subject by highlighting its most character-

---

1. *De caritate*, q. un., a. 2, ad 15. Translation from Thomas Aquinas, *On Charity*, in *Disputed Questions on the Virtues*, 121.

istic two-sided feature, the immanent frame with its unique counterfeit transcendence on the one side, and, on the other side, the loss of the absolute transcendence of God and with it the supernatural. In order to prepare the genuinely supernatural character of divine grace, I will introduce, in the second part, some key elements of Aquinas's metaphysics of participation. The ontological reality of finite beings participating the closest similitude of the divine nature (*ipsum esse creatum*) through their own act of being (*actus essendi*) is an indispensable condition for understanding Aquinas's conception that in the elect rational creatures, this participation finds its perfection in virtue of grace and charity in acts that surpass the natural proportion of this participated nature, inchoately in the life of the *viator* and perfectly in the beatific vision of the *comprehensor*. In the third part, I shall adumbrate the main features of Aquinas's profound theology of grace focusing first on actual grace and the beginning of faith and subsequently on sanctifying grace. In this part, which is the very heart of the chapter, I will discuss Aquinas's thesis that sanctifying grace is a certain formal participation of the divine nature the wayfarer already enjoys, a participation that is the source of the supernatural life of charity. In the subsequent fourth part, I shall finally turn to the theological virtue of charity. Charity, according to Aquinas, is the wayfarer's incipient connaturality with divine things, the greatest intimacy possible with God in this life of pilgrimage to the ultimate end. As friendship with God, charity is an incipient partaking in the very life of the triune God, an inchoate sharing (*communicatio*) of the divine beatitude. The effect of charity on the wayfarer is an increasing conformation to the God who is love (1 Jn 4:8). In the conclusion, I shall finally return to the chapter's beginning, late-modern anthropocentrism, and suggest that we may learn from Aquinas's metaphysics of participation and theology of divinization that the only genuine realization of subjectivity comes about in the self-forgetful self-realization of the wayfarer's ever deepening sharing of the divine beatitude in the life of charity.

MODERNITY'S ANTHROPOCENTRIC TURN

As already stated at the beginning of chapter 2, the late-modern subject vacillates uneasily between two competing self-images, between, on the one side, what might be called the *gnostic angelism* of subjective sovereignty that may submit to its will an absolutely malleable and fluid exteriority and, on the other side, the *materialist animalism* of a super-primate determined by its genetic makeup and its particular ecological niche. The utopian existentialist self-image of the sovereign subject and the dystopian competing naturalist self-image of the super-primate constantly destabilize each other precisely because they are nothing but the two contradictory effects brought about by the modern anthropocentric turn.[2] This turn, prepared in the Italian Renaissance, ushered in by Cartesian rationalism and Humean empiricism, and solidified by Kant's critical idealism, raised the specter of the irreconcilable bifurcation between a gnostic angelism and a materialist animalism. Both self-images of the age are false and hence ultimately uninhabitable by human beings. The flight from the unbearably reductive self-image characteristic of the materialist animalism of the super-primate ends up in the equally erroneous self-image of the gnostic angelism of the sovereign self. As the latter self-image, though attractive, is impossible to sustain consistently over an extended period of time, the resulting frustration leads to the predictable resignation to the self-image of the super-primate which again turns out to be unbearable. Hence the ceaseless vacillation. Yet, noteworthily, both poles of this vacillation share the anthropocentric condition of immanentism and its specific subject-produced transcendence.

The utopian angelist version of immanent transcendence arises from the endless surplus of desires for finite goods that is fueled by

2. In his *Critique of Pure Reason*, Kant advances a profound analysis of this distinctly modern problematic and—tacitly presupposing the ontological and epistemological entailments of the anthropocentric turn—elevates the problematic to the dignity of one of the four antinomies of pure reason, the antinomy between causality according the laws of nature and spontaneity, in short the antinomy between determination and freedom. See Immanuel Kant, *Critique of Pure Reason*, ed. and trans. Paul Guyer and Allen W. Wood (Cambridge: Cambridge University Press, 1997), 459–550 (A444/B472–A452/B480).

the subject's will to sovereignty. As the fulfillment of each of these desires is transitory, each fulfillment is transcended by a renewed desire for a finite good and its, at best, transitory fulfillment. The interminable vacillation between desire, transitory fulfillment, and the return of desire issues into the immanent transcendence of the bad infinity of an endless extension of finite goods. The dystopian animalist version of immanent transcendence is characterized by the replacement of finite desires with instinctual drives. Freed from the illusions of conscience and responsible agency, the super-primate's activity arises from the conflagration of variegated constellations of drives and instincts. The immanent transcendence of materialist animalism arises from the complete dependency of human existence upon a complex and contingent matrix of biochemical processes. If commitments, convictions, customs, and preferences are indeed mere epiphenomena of such a matrix of neurological and biochemical processes that issue into distinct drives, urges, and instincts, what is the case today might not be the case tomorrow. "Identity" denotes nothing but a transitory state, an event, and the event horizon of continuous contingent change constitutes the unique transcendence of this dystopian self-image.

Needless to say, the strictly immanent transcendence to which both self-images of the late-modern age give rise force the spiritual soul into the proverbial Procrustean bed that cuts it off from the true transcendence whose encounter and contemplation grants the only lasting happiness to the human person.[3] Precisely in this regard Thomas Aquinas turns out to be of continuing relevance for contemporary philosophy and theology "after the anthropocentric turn." This relevance consists in his uncompromising commitment to the participated wisdom characteristic of a consistent philosophical and theological theocentrism. The participated wisdom he pursues and displays is most accentuated in his consistent theological supernaturalism that is rooted in divine revelation and supported by a meta-

---

3. The Thomist thinker who had a deep grasp of the late-modern problematic of immanent transcendence and advanced a powerful Thomist response to it was the German philosopher Josef Pieper. See especially his *Leisure: The Basis of Culture* and *Happiness and Contemplation*, both translated by Gerald Malsbary (South Bend, Ind.: St. Augustine's Press, 1998).

physics of being that opens up from finite being to the absolute and objective transcendence of uncreated being itself, that is, the universal cause of all being. Arguably, Aquinas offers the philosophical and theological resources necessary for a thorough undoing of the anthropocentric turn and for recovering a genuine theocentrism in the natural as well as the supernatural order. At the very center of this recovery stands the metaphysical and theological notion of participation.

Cornelio Fabro and others have shown convincingly that the concept of participation plays a central role in Aquinas's metaphysics.[4] Unfolded along the lines of the ontological participation of effects in their causes, the notion of participation affords a rich and nuanced philosophy of being. When consistently developed along the lines of the participation of finite being in uncreated being, such an inquiry into the principles of being issues into a metaphysics of creation. The metaphysics of creation rests on the fundamental principle "to create is to give being" (*creare est dare esse*), or to render it more precisely, to create is to grant being (*ipsum esse creatum*), which each creature participates by its act of being (*actus essendi*) and in virtue of which the creature is, so to speak, a possessor of being (*habens esse*). The act of being (*actus essendi*) through which each creature participates the closest created similitude to the divine nature itself, the gift of being, the *dare esse* (*ipsum esse creatum*),[5] marks

---

4. Cornelio Fabro, *La nozione metafisica di partecipazione secondo San Tommaso d'Aquino, Opere Complete* 3 (Segni: Editrice del Verbo Incarnato, 2005 [1939]); Fabro, "The Intensive Hermeneutics of Thomistic Philosophy: The Notion of Participation," *Review of Metaphysics* 27, no. 3 (1974): 449–91; L.-B. Geiger, *La participation dans la philosophie de s. Thomas d'Aquin* (Paris: Vrin, 1942); Rudi te Velde, *Participation and Substantiality in Thomas Aquinas* (Leiden: Brill, 1995); John F. Wippel, *The Metaphysical Thought of Thomas Aquinas: From Finite Being to Uncreated Being* (Washington, D.C.: The Catholic University of America Press, 2000), 94–131. For the surpassing theological importance of the concept of participation for Aquinas's doctrine of grace, see Marcello Sánchez Sorondo, *La gracia como participación de la naturaleza divina según Santo Tomás de Aquino* (Salamanca: Universidad Pontificia, 1979).

5. Recall what was already stated in chapter 2: each being (*ens per participationem*) participates by way of its act of being (*actus essendi*) not directly and immediately the divine essence itself (*ipsum esse subsistens*; *ens per essentiam*) but rather the gift of being (*ipsum esse creatum*) that is, the first created reality and the closest created similitude of the uncreated divine essence. See *In de Div. Nom.*, c. 5, lect. 2 (Marietti, no. 660): "Ipsum esse creatum est quaedam participatio Dei et similitudo ipsius." See also *Sent.* I, q. 8, a. 1, q.c. 1, ad 2; a. 12; *De ver.*, q. 21, a. 2, ad 2; q. 22, a. 2, ad 2; *SCG* III.66.

the crucial ontotheological difference between the transcendent source of all being, the absolutely transcendent infinite subsistent act of existing itself *(ipsum esse subsistens; ens per essentiam)*, the giving of being *(ipsum esse creatum)*, and each participating, that is, finite being *(ens per participationem)*.

The ontological reality of the natural participation of all finite beings through their act of being *(actus essendi)* in the gift of being *(ipsum esse creatum)*—a participation by way of efficient causality—allows Aquinas to consider analogically the surpassing supernatural participation of the rational creature immediately in the divine nature *(ipsum esse subsistens)*—a participation by way of formal causality. This supernatural participation rests on sanctifying grace as its quasi-ontological foundation and is realized in the acts of the supernatural infused disposition or habit *(habitus)* of charity, the most eminent of the three theological virtues, issuing in an inchoate union with God.

PARTICIPATION AS PERFECTIVE— NATURAL AND SUPERNATURAL

According to the ontological participation and teleological dynamism of all finite beings, each being is first and foremost directed to its own perfection, to the full actualization of its specific nature. Simultaneously, by way of the selfsame actualization of its specific nature, every creature is directed to the twofold good of the universe: the order among the parts and the ordering of the whole universe to God.[6] Nothing short of the universe's perfection is the fitting manifestation of God's wisdom and goodness. Toward that end, Aquinas argues, God created an abundance of diverse beings with a plethora of different perfections in order that the universe as a whole may more perfectly manifest and participate in God's goodness. Consider Aquinas's argument from the *Summa contra Gentiles*:

---

6. See esp. Thomas Aquinas, *SCG* I.29 and III.23–32. On this topic, now available in English, see the important essay by Charles De Koninck, "The Primacy of the Common Good," 2:63–108, and especially the excellent study by Blanchette, *The Perfection of the Universe according to Aquinas*.

Since every created substance must fall short of the perfection of divine goodness, in order that the likeness of divine goodness might be more perfectly communicated to things, it was necessary for there to be a diversity of things, so that what could not be perfectly represented by one thing might be, in more perfect fashion, represented by a variety of things in different ways. For instance, when a [human person] sees that his mental conception cannot be expressed adequately by one spoken word, he multiplies his words in various ways, to express his mental conception through a variety of means. And the eminence of divine perfection may be observed in this fact, that perfect goodness which is present in God in a unified and simple manner cannot be in creatures except in a diversified manner and through a plurality of things. Now, things are differentiated by their possession of different forms from which they receive their species. And thus, the reason for the diversity of forms in things is derived from this end. (*SCG* III.97.2)

Creatures participate God's goodness not only by participating their act of being (*actus essendi*), but to a much greater degree by imitating God through their characteristic operations, thereby causing—proportionate to their specific natures—distinct states of being. For this very reason, Aquinas argues, God created all things in a state of potency to their specific type of operation that is the full realization of their specific nature. By realizing their specific nature through these operations, all creatures contribute to the perfection of the universe. All creatures achieve their secondary perfection by operating in proportion to the particular mode of their participation in the act of being which is their primary perfection, their substantial form. These secondary perfections are the way each being participates in the eternal law, the *ratio* by way of which God governs the universe.[7] God's *ratio*, the eternal law, has imprinted upon all beings natural inclinations to their specific natural ends. By following their natural inclinations all beings pursue their own perfection and contribute to the perfection of the whole universe. It should be emphasized that the rational creature's participation in the eternal law is, of course, a much greater participation because it occurs according to freedom and intelligence.

Yet God's wisdom ordains that the perfection of the universe transcends the finality proportionate to finite created natures, that

---

7. For a lucid discussion of this complex topic, see Rziha, *Perfecting Human Actions*.

it transcends the perfection that arises from the participation of finite being in the act of being. The only possible participation that transcends the participation of a creature in the created similitude (*ipsum esse creatum*) of the divine nature (*ens per participationem*) by way of its act of being (*actus essendi*) must be an utterly unique and surpassingly mysterious immediate participation in the divine nature itself *by way of the divine nature itself*, in short, nothing but a kind of immediate formal participation in in the transcendent uncreated being (*ens per essentiam*), by way of the infinite subsistent act of existing itself (*ipsum esse subsistens*).[8] For this surpassing end God has created rational creatures (angels and humans) as dynamic images of the divine triune exemplar (*ST* I, q. 93, aa. 1 and 3). Their perfect realization as images consists in their immediate formal union with the divine exemplar. As the deposit of the faith—conveyed by scripture, transmitted by tradition, and affirmed by dogma—teaches, God is a trinity of subsistent relations, persons in the fullest ontological sense (*ST* I, q. 29, a. 4). Hence, participation of the created image in the divine exemplar occurs by way of a conformation to the image of the Trinity.[9] This conformation, flowing from the divine nature, is realized by way of the operations characteristic of the specific faculties rational creatures are endowed with, intellect and will. Aquinas explains:

> God is in all things by His essence, power, and presence, according to His one common mode, as the cause existing in the effects which participate in His goodness. Above and beyond this common mode, however, there is one special mode belonging to the rational nature wherein God is said to be present as the object known is in the knower, and the beloved in the lover. And since the rational creature by its operation of knowledge and love attains to God Himself, according to this special mode God is said not only to exist in the rational creature, but also to dwell therein as in His own temple. (*ST* I, q. 43, a. 3)

The will is formed by the theological virtue of charity, while the intellect is formed by the theological virtue of faith and then (more

---

8. For the metaphysics of the beatific vision, see the epilogue, pp. 389–409.
9. See D. Juvenal Merriell, *To the Image of the Trinity: A Study in the Development of Aquinas's Teaching* (Toronto: Pontifical Institute of Mediaeval Studies, 1990).

perfectly even) as faith formed by charity, by the Holy Spirit's gift of wisdom. Through charity and wisdom, the elect human beings are made participators "of the divine Word and of the Love proceeding, so as freely to know God truly and to love God rightly" (*ST* I, q. 38, a. 1). Elected by God to this surpassing final end, the blessed *qua* creatures participate the divine nature not only through their own act of being but rather participate the divine nature in virtue of a formal deifying union with the divine nature that finds its perfection in acts of vision, attainment, and beatitude that surpass the natural proportion of this participated nature. Aquinas points to the divine ordination of humanity's supernatural ultimate end in the very first article of the *ST*: "[The human being] is directed to God, as to an end that surpasses the grasp of his reason." Then Aquinas quotes the Vulgate rendition of a crucial passage he returns to whenever he discusses the supernatural final end to which humanity is ordained, namely, Isaiah 64:4, a passage that the Apostle Paul quotes in 1 Corinthians 2:9: "The eye has not seen, O God, besides Thee, what things Thou hast prepared for them that wait for Thee" (*ST* I, q. 1, a. 1). In order to carry out this *ordinatio* of his wisdom, God "who moves all things to their due ends" (*ST* II-II, q. 23, a. 2) and thereby orders all things sweetly, adds supernatural forms to the natural powers of the rational beings. The first of these supernatural forms, sanctifying grace, poured into the very essence of the soul, is the ontological principle and root of all the other supernatural forms or *habitus*, the theological virtues, the infused moral virtues, and the gifts of the Holy Spirit.[10] Thus, their intellects being informed by the theological virtue of faith and their wills by the theological virtue of charity, the *viatores* become, through faith and charity, inchoately participators "of the Divine Word and of the Love proceeding, so as freely to know God truly and to love God rightly" (*ST* I, q. 38, a. 1).

Among these supernatural infused *habitus* charity is of surpassing eminence, first because charity is a certain participation of the Holy Spirit such that all the gifts of the Holy Spirit are rooted in charity. Secondly and even more importantly, charity is of surpassing emi-

---

10. *ST* I, q. 43, a. 3, ad 1: "Sanctifying grace disposes the soul to possess the divine person."

nence because already in this life of the *viator*, charity affords an inchoate union with God. It is for this very reason Aquinas maintains that God is present in the souls of the just not only as the transcendent first efficient cause by his essence, power, and presence, but also as an object of the love of charity and of the connatural knowledge concomitant with charity and, hence, as a guest and friend. The formal cause of the indwelling of the Trinity is this quasi-experiential knowledge rooted in sanctifying grace and afforded by the love of charity.[11] Because union, which is due to charity, presupposes conversion, which is due to actual grace, and the elevation of human nature, which is due to sanctifying grace, I shall treat first of grace and then of charity.

GRACE

Gratia in Aquinas's use is an analogical notion with many nuances. In its widest sense, *gratia* denotes a freely given quality that renders the recipient pleasing. In a more restricted sense, *gratia* denotes the assistance (*auxilium*) of the first mover, whether due to nature or above nature, that is, natural (every motion proportionate to the nature of a being), preternatural (extraordinary strengthening, extension, or protection of natural capacities), or supernatural (e.g., miracles in the strictest sense). Finally, in its most proper sense—the sense exclusively used in the following—*gratia* denotes a strictly supernatural gift of God to the rational creature for the purpose of salvation, divinization, and eventual union of the rational creature with God—sanctifying grace (*gratia gratum faciens*). This supernatural gift is either actual or habitual. As actual, sanctifying grace is a quality that is supernatural and transient; as habitual, it is a quality that is supernatural and permanent (albeit forfeitable), an "entita-

---

11. The infused *habitus* of sanctifying grace and the quasi-experiential knowledge of charity are conjoined formal causes of the indwelling of the Trinity. See Barthélemy Froget, OP, *The Indwelling of the Holy Spirit in the Souls of the Just According to the Teaching of St. Thomas Aquinas*, trans. Sydney A. Raemers (Westminster, Md.: Newman Press, 1952), and for a more comprehensive and conceptually more penetrating study that compares and conrasts Aquinas's account with those of St. Albert the Great, St. Bonaventure, and other interlocutors, see Francis L. B. Cunningham, OP, *The Indwelling of the Trinity: A Historico-Doctrinal Study of the Theory of St. Thomas Aquinas* (Dubuque, Iowa: Priory Press, 1955).

tive *habitus*" inhering in the very essence of the recipient's spiritual soul. When considering the effect of sanctifying grace, Aquinas distinguishes between operating and cooperating grace; both are different effects of the same grace, the effect of operating grace being that God moves while the human being is moved, and the effect of cooperating grace being that God moves the human being and the human being moves himself (again by virtue of God's movement). Thus sanctifying grace can be considered in four respects: (1) as operating actual grace, (2) as cooperating actual grace, (3) as operating habitual grace, and (4) as cooperating habitual grace.

First, I shall focus on actual grace, and especially on operating actual grace, for two reasons: first, in human persons who have reached the age of reason—hence in every adult convert to the faith—actual grace is an indispensable preparation for the reception of sanctifying grace. Second, because the intellectual appetite, the will, stands at the center of the inchoate act of union in the life of the *viator*, it is crucial to understand how God moves the will toward this union. Fundamentally, Aquinas conceives of the movement of the will to God as a conversion to God.[12] This conversion is threefold: the first conversion occurs in the *initium fidei*, the beginning of faith, which is the disposition necessary to receive the *habitus* of sanctifying grace. Based on the received *habitus* of sanctifying grace, the second conversion occurs—the continuous turning to God by acts of charity, acts that merit beatitude. This continuous turning to God through growth in charity creates the disposition necessary for the third conversion. This final conversion turns the *viator* into a *comprehensor* who has full possession of God in the beatific vision, a possession that issues into the perfect love of God and the perfect beatitude of the *comprehensor*.

---

12. Aquinas ranks the threefold conversion according to the order of perfection and not according to the chronological order, as I will do in the following discussion: "The first is by the perfect love of God; this belongs to the creature enjoying the possession of God; and for such conversion, consummate grace is required. The next turning to God is that which merits beatitude; and for this there is required habitual grace, which is the principle of merit. The third conversion is that whereby a [human being] disposes himself so that he may have grace; for this no habitual grace is required; but the operation of God, Who draws the soul towards Himself, according to Lament. 5.21: *Convert us, O Lord, to Thee, and we shall be converted*" (*ST* I, q. 62, a. 2, ad 3).

ACTUAL GRACE AND THE BEGINNING
OF FAITH (*INITIUM FIDEI*)

The beginning of faith, the *initium fidei*, denotes the special divine motion—operating actual grace—by which God efficaciously orders the human will to God as its final end and simultaneously signifies the absolutely crucial and indispensable, but albeit ultimately limited place of justification in the order of salvation and divinization. This "turning of the will," its rectification or effective justification, issues in the will's desire for God as the overarching specific good.[13] Because the will is the efficient cause of all human acts and because it moves all the other powers of the soul to their acts, the will is the first principle of sin (*ST* I-II, q. 74, a. 1). And consequently, of all the powers of the soul, the will has been most fundamentally infected by original sin (*ST* I-II, q. 83, a. 3; *De malo*, q. 4, a. 2). For that reason, it is necessary first and foremost that the will be justified, that is, that the rectitude of the will be restored effectively from evil to good. In the *initium fidei* therefore actual grace is first of all operating actual grace.[14] Aquinas states: "An external cause alters free choice, as when God by grace changes the will of a human being from evil to good, as Prv. 21:1 says: 'The heart of the king is in God's hands, and God will turn it whithersoever he willed.'"[15] This changing of the will from evil does not violate or contradict the will's proper operation. For "the will advanced to its first movement in virtue of the instigation [*instinctus*] of some exterior mover [*exterior movens*]"

---

13. Aquinas distinguishes the special motion of operating actual grace very clearly from the will's universal motion to the *bonum universale*: "God moves man's will, as the Universal Mover, to the universal object of the will, which is good. And without this universal motion, man cannot will anything. But man determines himself by his reason to will this or that, which is true or apparent good. Nevertheless, sometimes God moves some specially [*specialiter*] to the willing of something determinate, which is good; as in the case of those whom He moves by grace" (*ST* I-II, q. 9, a. 6, ad 3).

14. "God acts directly on the radical orientation of the will." Bernard Lonergan, SJ, *Collected Works of Bernard Lonergan*, vol. 1: *Grace and Freedom: Operative Grace in the Thought of St. Thomas Aquinas*, ed. Frederick E. Crowe and Robert M. Doran (Toronto: University of Toronto Press, 2000), 128. Lonergan's insight does not contradict the fact that every free act of the will is informed by the intellect (*ST* I-II, q. 77, a. 2).

15. *De malo*, q. 16, a. 5; Thomas Aquinas, *The De Malo of Thomas Aquinas*, ed. Brian Davies, trans. Richard Regan (Oxford: Oxford University Press, 2001), 877.

(*ST* I-II, q. 9, a. 4), who is God himself (a. 6). Thanks to the divine *instinctus*, the appetitive inclination of the will tends now to God himself as the overarching specific good.[16]

Aquinas uses the notion of an external cause to refer to God's alteration of free choice and thus treats of operating actual grace as an instantiation of external transcendent causality. "External" is here distinguished from "internal," where the latter is the proximate cause in the order of secondary causality. God as external cause is in no way extrinsic to the creature's nature or existence but external only to the creature's proximate secondary causality. Lonergan puts the matter succinctly: "God as external principle moves the will to the end, and in special cases he moves it by grace to a special end. Conspicuous among the latter is conversion, which is expressed entirely in terms of willing the end."[17] It is precisely the metaphysics of participation, of the act of being (*actus essendi*) in its ontological differentiation from and correlation to the finite being itself (*ens per participationem*) on the one hand, and on the other hand, the ontological differentiation between the gift of being, the *dare esse* (*ipsum esse creatum*) and the subsistent act of existing itself (*ipsum esse subsistens; ens per essentiam*) that prevents this "externality" from being understood in the modern sense of a "first cause," issued by a "highest" or "perfect" being—that is, infinitely superior to all other causes and beings but still on an ontic continuum and hence in a competitive relationship of non-transcendent causality with them because a "first" cause, thus conceived, does not transcend the ontic level of secondary causality. God's external causality remains transcendent causality all the way down and hence is not competitive with the internal proximate causality of the will—whose first universal mover, of course, is the selfsame transcendent universal cause, God.[18]

---

16. At this point, I can only stress the pivotal role that the term *instinctus* plays in the development of Aquinas's thoroughly anti-Semipelagian theology of grace. For a full account, see Max Seckler, *Instinkt und Glaubenswille nach Thomas von Aquin* (Mainz: Grünewald, 1961), and more recently and accessibly, Michael S. Sherwin, *By Knowledge and By Love: Charity and Knowledge in the Moral Theology of St. Thomas Aquinas* (Washington, D.C.: The Catholic University of America Press, 2005), 139–44.

17. Lonergan, *Grace and Freedom*, 125.

18. Lonergan, in his interpretation of Aquinas's theology of operating grace, overcomes this nocuous modern misunderstanding thanks to the "theorem of divine tran-

Under the category of God as external transcendent cause, operating grace is identical with the very act of the will willing God as supernatural end. The distinction between *operating* and *cooperating* actual grace denotes the different effects of God's actual grace in the *initium fidei*. When Aquinas responds to the question whether human beings can prepare themselves for grace without the external aid of grace, he states the following: "To prepare oneself for grace is, as it were, to be turned to God."[19] To prepare oneself for the gift

---

scendence," which he sees at work in Aquinas: "The Thomist higher synthesis was to place God above and beyond the created orders of necessity and contingence: because God is universal cause, his providence must be certain; but because he is a transcendent cause, there can be no incompatibility between terrestrial contingence and the causal certitude of providence" (Lonergan, *Grace and Freedom*, 81–82). It would be a mistake, however, to create a competitive relationship between what Lonergan describes as a theorem and Aquinas's metaphysics of being. Lonergan characterizes a theorem as "something known by understanding the data already apprehended and not something known by adding a new datum to the apprehension, something like the principle of work and not something like another lever, something like the discovery of gravitation and not something like the discovery of America" (147). The theorem is consequent upon the cosmic emanation scheme operative in Aquinas's metaphysics so that the former presupposes the latter: "For an instrument is a lower cause moved by a higher so as to produce an effect within the category proportionate to the higher; but in the cosmic hierarchy all causes are moved except the highest, and every effect is at least in the category of being; therefore, all causes except the highest are instruments" (Lonergan, *Grace and Freedom*, 83).

19. "Hoc autem est praeparare se ad gratiam, quasi ad Deum converti" (*ST* I-II, q. 109, a. 6). Here is the important passage in full: "Now in order that man prepare himself to receive this gift, it is not necessary to presuppose any further habitual gift in the soul, otherwise we should go on to infinity. But we must presuppose a gratuitous gift of God, Who moves the soul inwardly or inspires the good wish. For in these two ways do we need the Divine assistance as stated above (aa. 2, 3). Now that we need the help of God to move us, is manifest. For since every agent acts for an end, every cause must direct its effect to its end, and hence since the order of ends is according to the order of agents or movers, man must be directed to the last end by the motion of the first mover, and to the proximate end by the motion of any of the subordinate movers; . . . And thus since God is the first Mover simply, it is by His motion that everything seeks Him under the common notion of good, whereby everything seeks to be likened to God in its own way. Hence Dionysius says (*Div. Nom.* iv) that *God turns all to Himself*. But He directs righteous men to Himself as to a special end [*ad specialem finem*], which they seek, and to which they wish to cling, according to Ps. lxxii. 28, *it is good for Me to adhere to my God*. And that they are *turned* to God can only spring from God's having *turned* them. Now to prepare oneself for grace is, as it were, to be turned to God; just as, whoever has his eyes turned away from the light of the sun, prepares himself to receive the sun's light, by turning his eyes towards the sun. Hence it is clear that man cannot prepare himself to receive the light of grace except by the gratuitous help of God moving him inwardly" (Et ideo quod homo convertatur ad Deum, hoc non potest esse nisi Deo ipsum

of habitual grace *is* to be turned to God. As transcendent first cause, God moves interiorly as a cause genuinely external to the order of secondary causality. In other words, one's own act of preparation is caused by God without that act's losing its integrity as the will's proper operation, being drawn toward its end—but now being the special end of adhering to God. There is no ontological difference between operating and cooperating grace; rather, they are the two distinct effects of God's selfsame actual grace.[20] These two distinct effects pertain each to one specific aspect of the voluntary action. For, as Aquinas states, "in a voluntary action, there is a twofold action, viz., the interior action of the will, and the external action: and each of these actions has its object. The end is properly the object of the interior act of the will: while the object of the external action, is that on which the action is brought to bear" (*ST* I-II, q. 18, a. 6).

The interior action is concerned solely with the end itself; the external action pertains to the means that lead to the end, means that can entail proper proximate ends of their own, which are respectively objects of interior actions of the will. The first effect of actual grace pertains to the interior action of the will. Regarding this action, the will is moved and God is the sole mover.[21] The operating actual grace of conversion *is* the very action of the will willing God as the overarching special good to be desired, that is, as willing God as the supernatural end.[22] The second effect of actual grace per-

---

convertente. Hoc autem est praeparare se ad gratiam, quasi ad Deum converti: sicut ille qui habet oculum aversum a lumine solis, per hoc se praeparat ad recipiendum lumen solis, quod oculos suos convertit versus solem. Unde patet quod homo non potest se praeparare ad lumen gratiae suscipiendum, nisi per auxilium gratuitum Dei interius moventis) (*ST* I-II, q. 109, a. 6).

20. *ST* I-II, q. 111, a. 2, ad 4: "Operating and co-operating grace are the same grace; but are distinguished by their different effects."

21. *ST* I-II, q. 111, a. 2: "Now there is a double act in us. First, there is the interior act of the will, and with regard to this act the will is a thing moved, and God is the mover [*istum actum, voluntas se habet ut mota, Deus autem ut movens*]; and especially when the will, which hitherto willed evil, begins to will good. And hence, inasmuch as God moves the human mind to this act, we speak of operating grace."

22. Lonergan explains: "The *voluntas mota et non movens* is the reception of divine action in the creature antecedent to any operation on the creature's part. So far from being a free act, it lies entirely outside the creature's power. But though not a free act in itself, it is the first principle of free acts, even internal free acts such as faith, fear, hope, sorrow, and repentance" (*Grace and Freedom*, 424). Accordingly, the internal act of faith,

tains to the exterior action. Aquinas states: "Since [the exterior act] is commanded by the will, ... the operation of this act is attributed to the will. And because God assists us in this act, both by strengthening our will interiorly so as to attain to the act, and by granting outwardly the capability of operating, it is with respect to this that we speak of cooperating grace" (*ST* I-II, q. 111, a. 2).

Consequently, as Aquinas emphasizes, "God does not justify us without ourselves, because whilst we are being justified we consent to God's justification [*justitiae*] by a movement of our free-will. Nevertheless this movement is not the cause of grace, but the effect; hence the whole operation pertains to grace."[23] Already acts of prayer asking for God's help are the effect of cooperating actual grace—but only *secundum quid*, only in a broader, analogical sense.

Allow me to explain: while this kind of cooperating actual grace is a virtually unavoidable entailment of Aquinas's doctrine of actual grace in the process of conversion before and leading up to the beginning of faith (*initium fidei*), the qualification *secundum quid* seems nevertheless to be apposite. The reason for this is as follows: the distinction between actual operating and cooperating grace makes it possible to explain the difference between prejustificatory motions of grace in which God moves us and we are moved, on the one hand, and on the other hand, our actions in which we act moved by God— but not as yet justified. However, the prejustificatory actual grace we cooperate with in view of justification is not cooperating grace in the strict sense, as cooperating grace *simpliciter* is reserved to habitual grace that alone allows for our stable habitual cooperation with God. This notion of cooperating grace in its strict sense seems to be implied in Aquinas's preface at the beginning of *ST* I-II, q. 113: "We have now to consider the effect of grace: (1) the justification of the ungodly, which is the effect of operating grace; and (2) merit, which is

---

arising from the new principle, is a free act, an act of *liberum arbitrium*: "Now the act of believing is an act of the intellect assenting to the Divine truth at the command of the will moved by the grace of God, so that it is subject to the free-will [*liberum arbitrium*] in relation to God; and consequently the act of faith can be meritorious" (*ST* II-II, q. 2, a. 9).

23. *ST* I-II, q. 111, a. 2, ad 2: "Deus non sine nobis nos iustificat, quia per motum liberi arbitrii, dum iustificamur, Dei iustitiae consentimus. Ille tamen motus non est causa gratiae, sed effectus. Unde tota operatio pertinet ad gratiam."

the effect of cooperating grace." Hence, prejustificatory actual grace with which we cooperate must be qualified as *secundum quid*, as being a quasi-cooperative actual grace, a grace that disposes us toward justification but remains prejustificatory.

To summarize: the difference between *voluntas mota et non movens* and *voluntas mota et movens* is the difference between willing the end and willing the means leading to this end.[24] The gift of grace comes first as a transitory assistance (*auxilium*), as actual grace, with two distinct effects: operating grace, moving the human being interiorly, and cooperating grace *secundum quid*, the human being moving himself to act, as moved by cooperating grace. Importantly, the assistance (*auxilium*) of actual operating grace remains absolutely indispensable from the beginning of faith (*initium fidei*) right up until the grace of final perseverance, which is according to Aquinas—following Augustine's position advanced in his treatise *On the Gift of Perseverance* (*De dono perseverantiae*)—nothing but a motion of operating actual grace. Furthermore, as the infused *habitus* of sanctifying grace cannot reduce itself to act, the actual divine assistance (*auxilium*) of a first motion is also required for such acts of sanctifying grace.

The central function of actual grace in the first conversion, the

---

24. *Voluntas mota et movens* simply renders the actualization of acquired freedom in the efficacious choice of means, as the will's proximate causality is now directed to its special end, God himself. In his commentary on St. Paul's Epistle to the Romans Aquinas applies this actualization of the acquired freedom to the reality of the spiritual person, that is, the person who is moved by the higher prompting (*superiori instinctu*) of the Holy Spirit: "Homo spiritualis non quasi ex motu propriae voluntatis principaliter, sed ex instinctu Spiritus Sancti inclinatur ad aliquid agendum.... Non tamen per hoc excluditur quin viri spirituales, per voluntatem et liberum arbitrium operentur, quia ipsum motum voluntatis et liberi arbitrii Spiritus Sanctus in eis causat, secundum illud Phil. II: *Deus est qui operatur in nobis velle et perficere*" (*Super Epistolam ad Romanos* [hereafter "*In Rom.*"] 8.3; *S. Thomae Aquinitatis Doctoris Angelici in Omnes S. Pauli Apostoli Epistolas Commentarii*, 1:111). Thus, cooperating grace is nothing but the grace of conversion, the willing of the supernatural end, but now as moving the will to will the means leading to this end. Lonergan rightly stresses that "in both cases the same theory of instrumentality and of freedom is in evidence: the will has its strip of autonomy, yet beyond this there is the ground from which free acts spring; and that ground God holds and moves as a fencer moves his whole rapier by grasping only the hilt. When the will is *mota et non movens, solus autem Deus movens, dicitur gratia operans*. On the other hand, when the will is *et mota et movens, dicitur gratia cooperans*.... In actual grace divine operation effects the will of the end to become cooperation when this will of the end leads to an efficacious choice of means" (Lonergan, *Grace and Freedom*, 147).

initium fidei, is the creation of the disposition that allows the reception of sanctifying grace. For as all appropriate matter must be rightly prepared in order to become disposed for the reception of a specific form, so analogously the human will must be rightly disposed in order to receive the *habitus* of sanctifying grace. With the first conversion completed and the will justified such that it desires God as the surpassing specific good, the human being at the age of reason is properly disposed to receive the *habitus* of sanctifying grace.

SANCTIFYING GRACE

Aquinas introduces the ontologically surpassing reality of sanctifying grace from the perspective of the mystery of God's creative love outwardly (*ad extra*) which is the source of all participation, whether natural or supernatural. God's general love (*dilectio communis*) grants to all beings—by way of their participation in the act of being—their natural existence (*esse naturale*).[25] Yet by his special love (*dilectio specialis*), God draws the elect rational creature beyond the condition of its nature (*supra conditionem naturae*) to a participation in the divine good (*participatio divini boni*). "It is by this love that God simply wishes the eternal good, which is Himself, for the creature" (*ST* I-II, q. 110, a. 1). Then Aquinas concludes: "Accordingly, when [someone] is said to have the grace of God, there is signified something [supernatural] bestowed on [that person] by God [*significatur quiddam supernaturale in homine a Deo proveniens*]" (*ST* I-II, q. 110, a. 1). "To have the grace of God" points to an infused *habitus*, something that comes forth directly from God beyond the act of being (*actus essendi*)—but nevertheless always by way of it—a

25. In the following section I am indebted to two important recent studies on the topic of deification in the teaching of Thomas Aquinas: Bernard Blankenhorn, OP, *The Mystery of Union with God: Dionysian Mysticism in Albert the Great and Thomas Aquinas* (Washington, D.C.: The Catholic University of America Press, 2015), and Daria Spezzano, *The Glory of God's Grace: Deification according to St. Thomas Aquinas* (Ave Maria, Fla.: Sapientia Press, 2015). See also the magisterial and by now classic account offered by Sánchez Sorondo, *La gracia*, and also his "La grazia come partecipazione della natura divina: implicazioni antropologiche dei misteri della fede Cristiana," in *Doctor Communis: Credere, amare, e vivere la verità, The Proceedings of the XIII Plenary Session of the Pontifical Academy of Saint Thomas Aquinas in the Year of Faith, 21–23 June 2013* (Vatican City: Libreria Editrice Vaticana, 2014), 83–93.

unique supernatural participation in the divine goodness.[26] However, lest the soul be mistaken for a divine substance, this *habitus* must be thought of as inhering in the soul like an accidental quality, which exists by way of the substantial form in which it inheres. Hence, while not divine, the soul "becomes godlike in its condition."[27] Consider Aquinas's nuanced argument:

> Because grace is above human nature, it cannot be a substance or a substantial form, but is an accidental form of the soul. Now what is substantially in God, becomes accidental in the soul participating the Divine goodness, as is clear in the case of knowledge. And thus because the soul participates in the Divine goodness imperfectly, the participation of the Divine goodness, which is grace, has its being in the soul in a less perfect way than the soul subsists in itself. Nevertheless, inasmuch as it is the expression or participation of the Divine goodness, it is nobler than the nature of the soul, though not in its mode of being. (*ST* I-II, q. 110, a. 2, ad 2)

The *habitus* of sanctifying grace is essentially nothing but a certain participation of the divine nature. While not a substance, but an accidental form, an infused quality, this unique participation—in Matthias Joseph Scheeben's apt rendition—"shares with substance the function of being a single common substratum of the various supernatural faculties and acts."[28] For this reason Aquinas rejects an all too easy solution advanced by Peter Lombard, namely the identification of this infused quality with the theological virtues of faith, hope, and charity. Aquinas takes the theological virtues as starting points

---

26. Matthias Joseph Scheeben is one of the most congenial nineteenth-century interpreters of Aquinas's theology of sanctification and deification. Already in his first major work, *Nature and Grace* (1861), he demonstrated a deep understanding of Aquinas's doctrine of sanctifying grace: "The supernatural principle is not really a new substance, but inheres in a substance, is linked with the essential, basic faculties belonging to this substance, and makes them capable of a higher domain of activity. It is present in the natural substance and faculties as a form determining them to a new existence, power, and activity. Therefore it is called a [*habitus*], whereby the soul exists in a definite way, especially with regard to a certain end and to acts of life." *Nature and Grace*, 152–53.

27. Scheeben, *Nature and Grace*, 154.

28. Ibid.: "The supernatural principle of life, or supernature, does not have quite the same relation to its acts as the nature of things has to its acts, as though it were a substance; it is not a substance. Yet if we consider it minutely, we can say with St. Thomas that it shares with substance the function of being a single, common substratum of the various supernatural faculties and acts. It is not one of these faculties or all of them taken together; it is their common substructure."

for his own argument: the difference between sanctifying grace and the theological virtues is the real and not merely conceptual distinction between the supernatural principle and cause and the supernatural effect (*ST* I-II, q. 110, a. 3). His argument unfolds in three steps. First, virtue is a disposition of what is perfect and perfect is what is disposed according to its nature. Second, the infused virtues dispose the human being in a surpassing manner to a surpassingly supernatural end, deification, union with God. Third and consequently, these virtues must dispose the human being in relation to some higher nature, a nature in which the human being must somehow participate, in short, to a participation of the divine nature (*Hoc autem est in ordine ad naturam divinam participatam*). Aquinas tops off this conclusion with 2 Peter 1:4, a crucial biblical text that he usually cites when he points to the divine *ordinatio* of the human being's supernatural end: to become partakers of the divine nature (*divinae consortes naturae*). The infused virtues are derived from and ordered to this "light of grace which is a participation of the Divine Nature [*ipsum lumen gratiae, quod est participatio divinae naturae*]." It is because of the reception (*acceptatio*) of this divine nature that human beings are regarded as regenerated or reborn as sons of God. And precisely because sanctifying grace, the supernatural principle, shares the characteristic of a substance, it serves as the "principle and root" (ad 3) of all the infused virtues, first and foremost of the theological virtues: faith, hope, and charity.[29]

29. The metaphysical underpinnings of Aquinas's doctrine of sanctifying grace not only have decidedly anti-Pelagian but also and equally clear—although obviously *avant la lettre*—anti-Lubacian implications. If infused grace was simply the theological virtues, then grace would graft onto natural inclinations in the human being already sufficiently disposed so as to be inclined toward the supernatural object of faith, hope, and charity. But because human nature is absolutely disproportionate to the supernatural final end to which it is ordained in the extant order of providence, the natural inclinations are not sufficiently disposed to this supernatural final end. Consequently, a surpassing infused "organism," a quasi-nature or substratum of grace is needed to elevate the natural inclinations toward God. Only by way of such an infused quasi-nature, the *habitus* of sanctifying grace, can the theological virtues, the infused moral virtues, and the gifts of the Holy Spirit be coordinated within an "organic" spiritually structured and informed life of sanctification and divinization. Evidence yet again that—*pace* Henri de Lubac—there is no natural tendency toward the supernatural, *formally* considered, in Aquinas's mature theology. For a more extensive discussion of this matter, see chaps. 5–6 of my *Dust Bound for Heaven*, and, more recently, White, "Imperfect Happiness and the Final End of Man."

To summarize: while the second conversion is initiated by way of operating actual grace in the *initium fidei*, it is completed by way of the infusion of sanctifying grace. This grace is a supernatural albeit created *habitus*, an infused form and hence an accidental quality informing the soul with divine light and thereby elevating the very essence of the soul. By way of sanctifying grace the rational creature participates inchoately in the divine nature itself. In the order of sanctification or deification, sanctifying grace is the primary perfection, the quasi-ontological principle that elevates human nature in such a way that now the inclinations of the spiritual soul are well disposed to be inclined to the supernatural object of the theological virtues—God. The secondary perfection comes about by way of the infused *habitus* of faith, hope, and charity and their specific actions. The theological virtues do not merely order the human person rightly to God through a submission of will and intellect—as does the infused virtue of religion. Rather, the actions specific to the theological virtues "arrive at" or "touch" (*attingant*) God (*ST* II-II, q. 23, a. 3; q. 81, a. 5) and therefore unite the human person to God. In order to understand this extraordinary claim and how Aquinas arrives at it we need to turn now to the theological virtue of charity, whose beginning characterizes the second conversion and whose perfection belongs to the third.

CHARITY

We recall that the third conversion comes about by the perfect love of God which occurs irreversibly and everlastingly when the rational creature enjoys the possession of God in the beatific vision. Remember also that in order to acquire the right disposition for the reception of a specific form, appropriate matter needs to be specifically prepared. Analogously, for this third and final conversion to come about, a specific preparation of the human being endowed with sanctifying grace is called for. What disposition does the third conversion require and does the second conversion bring about?

Aquinas develops his answer along the lines of the overarching axiomatic principle that grace presupposes and perfects nature. Every creature realizes its secondary perfection by way of actions that contribute to the realization of the final end of its specific nature. The rational creature whose nature has been elevated by sanctifying grace realizes the secondary perfection by way of actions that contribute to the realization of the supernatural final end of its elevated nature. Realizing this supernatural secondary perfection of the human nature elevated by sanctifying grace prepares the proper disposition for the final perfect conversion, the reception of the grace of glory. But because the human being is created *toward* the image of the Trinity, that is, as a dynamic image ordered to be conformed to its divine exemplar, the actions that move human nature to its perfection must be operations of those very faculties through which the human image is conformed to the triune exemplar—intellect and will. And because sanctifying grace is the created effect of the indwelling Trinity, the conformation of the intellect and the will to the triune exemplar must be appropriated to the temporal missions of the Son and the Spirit.

The Holy Spirit is the subsistent relation of love (*vinculum caritatis*) between the Father and the Son. Therefore, "taken personally, love is the proper name of the Holy Spirit" (*ST* I, q. 37, a. 1). The temporal missions of the Son and of the Holy Spirit terminate in the respective conformation of the intellect and the will—the infused *habitus* of divine faith conforms the intellect to the Son, the Word, who is truth itself, and the infused *habitus* of charity conforms the will to the Holy Spirit, who is love itself. Charity is nothing less than a participation in the love of the Father and Son, who love each other principally and all creatures by the Holy Spirit (*ST* I, q. 37, a. 2). As sanctifying grace, the originating principle of the theological virtues, is a participation in the divine nature, so is charity a participation in the Holy Spirit (*ST* II-II, q. 23, a. 3, ad 3).

For the actions of the theological virtue of charity to be voluntary and hence meritorious, they must proceed from an intrinsic principle: "Given that the will is moved by the Holy Spirit to the act of love, it is necessary that the will also should be the efficient cause of that act" (*ST* II-II, q. 23, a. 2). Charity requires a supernatural but intrinsic form added to the natural power of the will, by means of which the Holy Spirit moves it. In opposition to Peter Lombard's position, Aquinas insists that charity is "formal" in us; that is, as a proper, intrinsic, and therefore created *habitus*, which is genuinely the principle of the actions specific to the theological virtue of charity.[30]

As an infused *habitus*, charity enables the will to supernatural actions, first by directing the will to the divine good as its supernatural end, second, by commanding actions of the other virtues to this supernatural end, and third, by providing the foundation of the gifts of the Holy Spirit, gifts that dispose one to be moved by the Holy Spirit. Fourth and finally, charity enables the will when acting with cooperating grace to produce Spirit-filled works proportionate to eternal life and to thereby merit beatitude by virtue of the power of the Holy Spirit moving the person to eternal life. Far from being any problematic holdover from early fifth-century Semipelagianism (as it was called only much later in the wake of the Protestant Reformation),

---

30. *ST* II-II, q. 23, a. 2, ad 3: "Charity works formally. Now the efficacy of a form depends on the power of the agent, who instills the form.... But because it produces an infinite effect, since, by justifying the soul, it unites it to God, this proves the infinity of the Divine power, which is the author of charity." Not infrequently Orthodox theologians have voiced the following concern about Aquinas's doctrine of "created charity," that is, of charity as an infused *habitus*: it purportedly constitutes a buffer or even amounts to an opposition between the human person infused with charity and the immediate presence of the Holy Spirit. But this is not the case at all. Rather, the notion of *infused* charity avoids a theology of the activity of the Holy Spirit as merely extrinsic and nontransformative and so is very close indeed to the deepest Orthodox theological commitments. After all, Aquinas's doctrine of infused charity is all about divinization. Furthermore, *teleologically*, this created form disposes us to immediate contact with the Holy Spirit living in us and, moreover, allows us, so to speak, to touch God's face, to love God as he is in himself, and so to be in contact with the uncreated life of God. In terms of *efficient* causation, this created form is the result of the Holy Spirit inhabiting us. Finally and most crucially, the notion of *created* charity affords the insight that, *formally*, charity in us is something created that does not affect immediately the essence of God. What difference does this make? Consider the following: someone in the state of grace commits a mortal sin and thereby forfeits the *habitus* of charity and the friendship with God. The notion of created charity allows us to understand why this mortal sin is not simultaneously the sin against the Holy Spirit. If charity were the immediate uncreated effect of the indwelling Holy Spirit, it would be hard if not impossible to explain why a grave sin against charity would not be identical with the sin against the Holy Spirit, that is, identical with the implicit but nevertheless direct negation of the Holy Spirit himself. The notion of infused charity as created form avoids this problematic consequence. In sum, infused charity is not a buffer or opposition between us and the immediate presence of the Holy Spirit, but is rather the created effect of that immediate presence and a created condition for an ultimate and immediate communion in love with God in himself.

for Aquinas merit is the fitting product of the principle of human cooperation with actual and habitual grace. When considered under the aspect of the Holy Spirit's agency—charity is after all a participation in the Holy Spirit—the merit of actions specific to charity is condign, that is, a strict merit, because the Holy Spirit as the divine agent alone can merit in the proper sense. When considered under the aspect of the proximate secondary causality of human cooperating agency, the merit of actions specific to charity is only congruous and acknowledged by God's merciful *ordinatio* as meritorious.[31] Actions specific to the theological virtue of charity merit an increase in the infusion of charity, that is, a greater conformity to the Holy Spirit, so that eventually—if not forfeited by an act of mortal sin—charity deifies the will and brings about already in the life of the *viator* an inchoate union with the triune God.

Aquinas conceives of this charity-produced union as the most perfect and profound interpersonal relationship with the triune God: through the sacramental character of baptism the created dynamic image participates in Christ's death and resurrection, becomes thereby part of the mystical body whose head is Christ and from whom all graces flow *qua* headship, and receives interiorly sanctifying grace and with it the *habitus* of charity. Thus the created dynamic image becomes increasingly conformed to the divine triune exemplar and thereby rightly disposed for the reception of the grace of glory, the perfect participation in the divine nature which is nothing but the life and beatitude of the divine persons.

The very essence of the future perfection, as well as its preparation for it by way of charity, is the participation of the divine triune beatitude. Charity is the sharing (*communicatio*) of the divine beatitude already into the very life of the *viator*. Aquinas elucidates this *communicatio* of the divine beatitude, this inchoate union of the *viator* with God in two ways: first by way of mapping the friendship between Christ and his disciples onto the Aristotelian concept of perfect friendship, and secondly, by exploiting the structural analogy between the natural passion of love (*amor, dilectio*) and the super-

---

31. *ST* I-II, q. 114, aa. 1 and 2. For a noteworthy study of the development of Aquinas's doctrine of merit, see Wawrykow, *God's Grace and Human Action*.

natural love of charity (*caritas*)—for both transform the lover into the beloved object.

Let us first turn to friendship. Aquinas uses Aristotle's concept of perfect friendship from *Nicomachean Ethics* VIII as the framework that allows him to unfold the full theological implications of the dominical words from John 15:5, "No longer do I call you servants ... but I have called you friends."[32] Aquinas sees the theological implications as twofold: first, by virtue of the temporal missions of the Son and the Spirit, perfect friendship between God and a human person is possible precisely on the terms of Aristotle's account of perfect friendship. Second, Aristotle's structural account of perfect friendship affords a deeper understanding of the unitive dynamic of charity.[33]

Aquinas achieves both purposes by focusing upon two central features of Aristotle's account of perfect friendship, the *amor amicitiae* and the *communicatio* of the *bonum honestum* (*ST* II-II, q. 23, a. 1). Friendships of pleasure and use are characterized by *amor concupiscentiae*, the *ratio* of which is to wish the good of the beloved object for oneself, for reasons of pleasure or use. Perfect friendship, on the contrary, is characterized by *amor amicitiae*, the *ratio* of which is benevolence: to love someone as to wish good to them. To qualify as perfect friendship this love must be mutual; and most importantly, this mutual well-wishing must be founded on some *communicatio*, the sharing of some genuine good. Because of the radical disproportion in natures, Aristotle holds that there can be no true *communicatio* between a god and a human being.[34] Yet Aquinas rightly points out that by way of their indwelling and the ensuing elevation of human nature the temporal missions of the Son and the Spirit overcome this impediment and thus make possible a genuine *communicatio* between the triune God and the rational creature. The substance of this *communicatio* is nothing but God's own beatitude.

---

32. Aristotle, *Nicomachean Ethics*, trans. H. Rackhamm, Loeb Classical Library 73 (New York: G. P. Putnam's Sons, 1926), 1156b8–1157a.

33. For a comprehensive and lucid treatment of friendship as the paradigm by way of which Aquinas explicates the logic of redemption, see Holger Dörnemann, *Freundschaft als Paradigma der Erlösung* (Würzburg: Echter, 1997).

34. Aristotle, *Nicomachean Ethics*, 1158b35–1159a13.

Aquinas states: "Since there is a communication between [the human being] and God, inasmuch as [God] communicates his [beatitude] to us, some kind of friendship must needs be based on this same communication.... Charity is a friendship of [the human being] for God, founded upon the [*communicatio*] of everlasting [beatitude]" (*ST* II-II, q. 23, a. 1; q. 24, a. 2).

Aquinas takes the *communicatio* of eternal beatitude as an explanatory principle for every aspect of his treatment of charity: (1) charity is one virtue with the divine goodness as its end; (2) charity is gratuitously infused; (3) charity is proper to rational creatures with a capacity for eternal life; and (4) all things should be loved with respect to God as the first principle of beatitude. All these aspects are intimately connected with charity's foundation on God's *communicatio* of a share in his own beatitude as final end.

In order to account for the union of charity Aquinas exploits the structural analogy between the natural passion of love (*amor, dilectio*) and the supernatural love of charity (*caritas*) (*ST* I-II, qq. 26–28). Here are his three operative principles: first, love (*amor*) is a *passio*; second, all love transforms the lover; third, with God as the beloved object, charity is the highest kind of love. As to the first principle: while *passio* applies first and properly to the concupiscible appetite, it can also, by extension, apply to the intellectual appetite, the will, in which the love of charity is a principle of movement. The fundamental principle applies to all kinds of love, including charity: "The appetible object gives the appetite ... a certain adaptation to itself, which consists in [a pleasing affinity] [*complacentia*] with that object, and from this follows movement towards the appetible object" (*ST* I-II, q. 26, a. 2). As to the second principle: love brings about union by virtue of the principle of affinity (*complacentia*): "The lover stands in relation to that which he loves, as though it were himself or part of himself" (*ST* I-II, q. 26, a. 2, ad 2). The effect of love is therefore a mutual indwelling (*ST* I-II, q. 28, a. 2). Consequently, in application of the third principle, "the love of charity is of that which is already possessed, since the beloved is, in a manner, in the lover, and, again, the lover is drawn by desire to union with the beloved" (*ST* I-II, q. 66, a. 6).

But which form exactly does the loving affinity characteristic of all love take in the love of true friendship (*amor amicitia*)? According to Aquinas, in the love of true friendship, the principle of affinity takes the following form: willing the good to the other as to oneself, one apprehends the friend as another self, *alter ipse* (*ST* I-II, q. 28, a. 1), which entails a mutual indwelling of sorts: "every love makes the beloved to be in the lover, and vice versa" (a. 2). But there is one all-important difference between natural loves and supernatural charity: in the case of natural loves, likeness (*similitudo*) *causes* love. Yet in the case of the theological virtue of charity, likeness *is the effect* of love, the consequence of a gift from God of a similitude between the created dynamic image and the divine exemplar. Hence the indwelling of the Holy Spirit (together with the Father and the Son) is the cause of the union of charity. Because of the sharing (*communicatio*) of beatitude and the increasing conformation of the will to the Holy Spirit, charity affords nothing less than "connaturality for Divine things" (*ST* II-II, q. 45, a. 2). By, so to speak, spiritually "touching" the very face of God—and the operations of infused charity do nothing less than that—the human person gains a knowledge of God by connaturality that is as immediate and intimate as it is ineffable.

To summarize: a creature participates the closest similitude of the divine nature, the gift of being, *dare esse* (*ipsum esse creatum*) through its own act of being (*actus essendi*), but in elect rational creatures, this participation finds its perfection in acts that surpass the natural proportion of this participated nature. In the latter, by virtue of grace and charity, their participation in the gift of being by way of their act of being is surpassingly perfected by a quasi-ontological formal participation in the divine nature itself (*ipsum esse subsistens; ens per essentiam*) that already in the *viator* makes possible the act of inchoate union with God. Charity unites the *viator* formally with the divine nature itself, whose essence is love, a love that subsists personally as the Holy Spirit.

CONCLUSION

The point has been reached where it is apposite to return to the beginning, to the irreconcilable contradiction interior to the anthropocentric turn. One of the overarching reasons for the anthropocentric turn was the attempt at achieving the full realization of human subjectivity and, indeed, sovereignty. Yet instead, we are faced with two dominant but false self-images of the anthropocentric age, a gnostic angelism and a materialistic animalism, whose interminable *agōn* destroys what the anthropocentric turn had set out to achieve. The familiar opening lines of Dante's *Divine Comedy* capture the situation well: *Nel mezzo del cammin di nostra vita mi ritrovai per una selva oscura, che la diritta via era smarita.*[35] Midway upon the journey of our life, having wandered from the straight and true and thus finding ourselves lost in the dark and hard wood of late-modern anthropocentrism, we may learn from Aquinas's metaphysics of participation and theology of divinization this: the genuine realization of subjectivity comes about only in what is best called a self-forgetful self-realization. This self-forgetful self-realization is nothing but the twofold participation of the human being in the origin and end of all things: first *qua* rational creature through intellect and will in the first truth and sovereign good and, secondly, *qua* created image through the conformation to the divine exemplar in an everlasting union of vision and love with God. The first participation is the creaturely condition of the possibility for the latter participation, and the latter is the surpassing fulfillment of the former. In more technical Thomist terms: participation in God according to our rational nature is the ground and obediential potency for supernatural participation.

The key to this self-forgetful self-realization is simultaneously the key to overcoming the destructive contradiction interior to the anthropocentric turn. The key is to become even in this life as *viator* in the Christ-centered friendship with the triune God, through grace and charity, changed into an *alter ipse* of the divine friend. *Alter ipse*

35. In his noted translation, Charles S. Singleton renders this opening stanza thus: "Midway in the journey of our life I found myself in a dark wood, for the straight way was lost." Dante Alighieri, *Inferno 1: Italian Text and Translation*, trans. Charles S. Singleton (Princeton, N.J.: Princeton University Press, 1970), 2–3.

amicus, a friend is another self. This is also true for the *viator* in relationship with God. Being befriended by God through charity and growing in this friendship transforms the *viator* into the image whose divine exemplar is Christ. When the created image conforms to the divine exemplar, then and only then is the self perfectly realized, as *alter ipse* of the triune God, that is, as *comprehensor*.

Becoming a *comprehensor* is the only authentic human *self-realization*. And this self-realization can be achieved only in union with God because this union, the beatific vision, is the fullest realization of what is constitutive of a self—the unitive acts of intellect and will that through the grace of glory and the perfection of charity are now formally united with the first truth and the sovereign good. This realization of the self is *self-forgetful* because the surpassing object of these unitive acts is not the self, *ipse*, but the *alter ipse*, the self's uncreated, transcendent origin. "Self-forgetful self-realization" is a contemporary way of identifying the eschatological *comprehensor*, the divinized soul in its perfection (as principle and substantial form of a resurrection body) participating in such a way in the divine nature—subsistent being itself and love itself—that the created dynamic image finally becomes completely conformed to its divine exemplar such that as the divine exemplar is identically subsistent being and love so the created image now divinized is completely "being-love." Thus the Apostle John names what obtains inchoately in the *viator* and perfectly in the *comprehensor*: "God is love, and he who abides in love abides in God, and God abides in him" (1 Jn 4:16; RSV). The objective beatitude of the *comprehensor* is the *alter ipse*, the Blessed Trinity, and the subjective beatitude of the *comprehensor* is the beatific vision. Divinization through friendship with God, the self-forgetful self-realization as the triune God's *alter ipse*, is the true end and resolution of the anthropocentric turn.

6

The Preparation for Beatitude— Justice toward God
The Virtue of Religion

> May religion bind us to the one Almighty God.
> —Augustine, *Of True Religion*[1]

> Religion ... denotes properly a relation to God. For it is He to Whom we ought to be bound as to our unfailing principle; to Whom also our choice should be resolutely directed as to our last end; and Whom we lose when we neglect Him by sin, and should recover by believing in Him and confessing our faith.
> —Thomas Aquinas, *ST* II-II, q. 81, a. 1

> Religion approaches nearer to God than the other moral virtues, in so far as its actions are directly and immediately ordered to the honor of God. Hence religion excels among the moral virtues.
> —Thomas Aquinas, *ST* II-II, q. 81, a. 6

This chapter is about justice; to be precise, justice to God. Justice is an expression of the will's rectitude and, as we will see, the will's rec-

---

[1]. "Religet nos religio uni omnipotenti Deo." Augustine, *De vera religione* 55 (*PL* 34:172), cited by Thomas Aquinas in *ST* II-II, q. 81, a. 1.

titude is an antecedent condition for the wayfarer's attainment of beatitude. But justice to God creates a special problem. Aquinas defines the cardinal virtue of justice as "rendering to everybody his [or her] due by a constant and perpetual will" (*ST* II-II, q. 58, a. 1). But because justice is "the virtue of actions among equals" (*ST* I-II, q. 61, a. 3, ad 2), constitutively asymmetrical relationships—children to parents, citizens to their homeland, and, first and foremost, rational creatures to their creator—cannot fall directly under the virtue of justice. For the constitutive inequality characteristic of these relationships makes it impossible to render what is properly due. Consequently, acts of moral excellence that pertain to these essentially asymmetrical relationships must belong to virtues different from justice in the strict sense. Yet insofar as some due is rendered, they must nevertheless still be related to justice.

This chapter is therefore dedicated to the recovery of a virtue akin to justice, a virtue that has suffered widespread neglect and oblivion—the virtue of religion. This virtue is requisite for the rectitude of the will and thus forms an integral part of the antecedent condition for the attainment of beatitude. The virtue of religion actualizes the will's rectitude through acts of honor and reverence due to God. For a baptized and confirmed Christian, acts of the virtue of religion, commanded by charity, contribute essentially to the preparation of the *viator* for attaining the beatitude of the *comprehensor*. Being a *viator* without exercising the virtue of religion is a contradiction in terms. The latter is an entailment of the former and the considered departure from acts of the virtue of religion eventually undermines one's existence as *viator* and gravely endangers one's attainment of beatitude.

As in earlier chapters, I also will demonstrate the ongoing pertinence of the virtue of religion in the contemporary context of its secular contestation, marginalization, and outright rejection. In the first part, I will sketch the widespread phenomenon of "doing without religion" in the contemporary immanent frame of secularism and in contrast with it articulate Aquinas's account of the virtue of religion. In the second part, I will clarify how the use of "religion" in the virtue of religion relates to and differs from the five currently dominant uses of "religion." After that clarification, in the third part, the point has been reached to unfold Aquinas's account of the virtue of religion. Based on this account, I will attend in the fourth part to the crucial connection between the rectitude of the will and the attainment of perfect and everlasting beatitude and show subsequently, in the fifth part, that the rectitude of the will is absolutely central to the virtue of religion. In the sixth part, I shall finally review the five currently dominant uses of "religion" in light of the fully recovered virtue of religion. In the conclusion, I will drive home the absolute indispensability of the virtue of religion for the wayfarer's attainment of perfect and everlasting beatitude.

THE CONTEMPORARY IMMANENT FRAME OF SECULARISM—DOING WITHOUT RELIGION

Pope Francis, then-cardinal Jorge Mario Bergoglio, in his notes addressed to his fellow cardinals during the congregations of cardinals preceding the 2013 conclave, named what he regards to be the most pressing margins of human existence to which the Catholic church is called to evangelize: the margins of the mystery of sin, of pain, of injustice, of ignorance—and of doing without religion. Arguably, doing without religion is an increasingly widespread mode of living in the secular societies of the Western Hemisphere.[2] For very good reasons, Pope Francis identifies this pervasive mode of living as one of the margins of human existence, for it is neither neutral nor benign. Rather, doing without religion constitutes a significant impediment to attaining the surpassing final end to which humanity is ordained in the extant order of providence—to perfect and everlasting happiness in union with God. The *Catechism of the*

[2]. For the standard Western narrative of how it came to pass that large segments of European and North American societies are doing without religion, see Charles Taylor's *magnum opus*, *A Secular Age* (Cambridge, Mass.: Belknap Press, 2007). See Matthew Rose, "Tayloring Christianity: Charles Taylor is a Theologian of the Secular Status Quo," *First Things* (December 2014), available at firstthings.com/article/2014/12/tayloring-christianity, for an astute critique of Taylor's ambitious project. Taylor arguably promotes a problematically resigned Christian spirituality that stands in grave danger of accommodating itself all too willingly to the new secular establishment of doing without religion.

Catholic Church renders this surpassing final end in its programmatic opening statement thus: "God, infinitely perfect and blessed in himself, in a plan of sheer goodness freely created man to make him share in his own blessed life."[3]

Thomas Aquinas advances an account of the virtue of religion that is theologically profound, philosophically robust, and especially relevant for a context in which doing without religion has become a widespread phenomenon. He takes the virtue of religion to be indispensable for attaining the surpassing final end to which divine providence has ordained humanity—genuine and everlasting beatitude in communion with God. To put Aquinas's central insight in a nutshell: the gratuitous ultimate end of perfect and everlasting participation in the divine life—the beatific vision—is unattainable without the *viator* practicing the virtue of religion. This vital virtue signifies the stable disposition, formed by charity, to submit one's will to God in the interior act of devotion, to direct one's intellect completely to God in the interior act of prayer, and to render one's due honor and reverence to God in exterior acts of adoration, sacrifice, oblation, tithes, and vows. The necessary relationship that, according to Aquinas, obtains between the attainment of the surpassing ultimate end and the exercise of the virtue of religion may usefully be cast into this syllogism:

(1) If humanity is ordained to the gratuitous supernatural final end of union with God, then the virtue of religion is indispensable for the attainment of this end.

(2) Humanity is ordained to the gratuitous supernatural final end of union with God.

(3) Consequently, the virtue of religion is indispensable for attaining this end. Doing without religion constitutes a grave imped-

3. The passage continues the following way: "For this reason, at every time and in every place, God draws close to man. He calls man to seek him, to know him, to love him with all his strength. He calls together all men, scattered and divided by sin, into the unity of his family, the Church. To accomplish this, when the fullness of time had come, God sent his Son as Redeemer and Savior. In his Son and through him, he invites men to become, in the Holy Spirit, his adopted children and thus heirs of his blessed life." *Catechism of the Catholic Church. Second Edition Revised in Accordance with the Official Latin Text Promulgated by Pope John Paul II* (Vatican City: Libreria Editrice Vaticana, 1997) [hereafter "*CCC*"], §1.

iment in regard to attaining the ultimate end and places one, therefore, on a margin of human existence.

The major premise encapsulates the crucial claim. In the following, I shall advance a brief systematic rereading of Aquinas's warrant for this premise.

But why should doing without religion constitute one of the margins of human existence in the first place? For the educated elites of the Western Hemisphere, doing without religion is the welcome effect of an ineluctable progress from ignorance and bigotry to enlightenment and tolerance. For them, doing without religion does not constitute at all one of the margins of human existence but, quite on the contrary, the precondition for the ultimate flourishing of the sovereign self. Therefore, in order to answer the question above in a theologically sound way, two tasks must be accomplished: first, the recovery of the virtue of religion that has suffered unjust neglect from philosophers and theologians during the latter part of the twentieth century and the first decades of the twenty-first century; and second, the recovery of the reason why the virtue of religion is indispensable for attaining the surpassing ultimate end—perfect and everlasting happiness in union with God. Because accomplishing the first task presupposes the accomplishment of the second, I shall attend to them in reverse order. Yet first of all, two preliminary questions must be answered: one, how does the use of "religion" in the virtue of religion relate to and differ from the currently dominant uses of "religion"? And two, what essentially is the virtue of religion?

THE VIRTUE OF RELIGION VERSUS "RELIGION" IN CONTEMPORARY PARLANCE

There are at least five currently dominant uses of the term "religion" from which the virtue of religion must be clearly distinguished.[4]

---

4. These five contemporary uses of the term "religion" are far from comprehensive. Rather, they are of paradigmatic significance for the reconsideration of the virtue of religion in the current intellectual, political, social, and cultural climate of the Western Hemisphere. Incidentally, already in 1912, the American naturalist psychologist of religion James Henry Leuba, who was committed to the program of an explanatory reductionism

Political Liberalism's Use of "Religion"

The first is the quite recent but now widespread secularist—or in the European context, "laicist"—use of "religion," a use that has risen to the position of virtually unchallenged hegemony in the secular media of Europe and North America. This use is so utterly influential because it is part of the conceptual matrix of a normative secularism that frames—primarily by way of the media—the public discussion in virtually all Western societies. The positive contrastive terms to this negative use of "religion" are "secular reason" and its present instantiation, "secular discourse." "Religion" stands for sets of beliefs that are presumably more or less arbitrary in nature, beliefs impossible to warrant and adjudicate rationally. Because of its inherently irrational nature—so secularist reasoning goes—"religion" must establish its claims by way of more or less subtle forms of violence, ranging from psychological manipulation to open terror, torture, and religious war.[5] In order to secure peace in the public square, a pure "secular" reason and discourse must dominate the public sphere, while "religion" in all shapes and forms is to be relegated to the private, or at best, social sphere. While in virtually all Western societies there exists, of course, a constitutional right to religious freedom, the political and judicial powers of current Western liberal democracies interpret this religious freedom not as a constitutional human right antecedent to normative political categories of "public" versus "private," but merely as a political right within them. Normatively framed in such a way, the right to religious freedom turns into a right of free exercise that pertains first and foremost to the private sphere and, under increasingly restrictive conditions, also to the social sphere. According to this by now quasi-hegemonic secularist interpretation of the freedom of religion, the public sphere belongs exclusively to "secular" reason and discourse. Religious be-

---

of religion to physiological phenomena, collected no fewer than forty-eight different definitions of "religion." See his *A Psychological Study of Religion: Its Origin, Function, and Future* (New York: Macmillan, 1912), 339–61.

5. For a robust critique and deconstruction of this founding myth of modern political liberalism, see William T. Cavanaugh, *The Myth of Religious Violence: Secular Ideology and the Roots of Modern Conflict* (New York: Oxford University Press, 2009).

lief and practice are constitutionally protected as long as they remain within the parameters of the private and social spheres.

The "founding theory" of this construal of "public" and "private" was advanced by John Rawls in his *magnum opus*, *A Theory of Justice*, and fine-tuned in his later *Political Liberalism*.[6] Jürgen Habermas, in his somewhat more nuanced and sophisticated approach to religion by way of his speech act theory, seeks to assign to "religion" a role in the deliberative political process of lawmaking characteristic of liberal procedural democracies.[7] "Religion," in Habermas's theory of communicative action, becomes identical with the speech acts of believers. He differentiates strictly between the unregulated and the regulated public discourse. In the unregulated public discourse, religious reasoning is permitted, while in the regulated deliberative public discourse that involves lawmaking, religious reasoning is strictly prohibited. Hence, Habermas distinguishes in the "public" between a wider social public and a more specific and restrictive political public. While Rawls requires all citizens committed to "religion" to translate their arguments into a language that is accessible to all citizens, Habermas expects a similar translation process only in regard to the restricted deliberative public discourse that pertains directly to lawmaking. Rawls and Habermas share the underlying assumption that there exists a "rational discourse" whose normative commitments are, in essence, different from the rational commitments that a "religious" interlocutor would hold. Hence, a person who, in the restricted deliberative public discourse of lawmaking, draws conceptually and semantically, let's say, on Mill's *Utilitarianism*, Kant's *Critique of Practical Reason*, or Hegel's *Philosophy of Right*, differs cat-

---

6. John Rawls, *A Theory of Justice*, rev. ed. (Cambridge, Mass.: Harvard University Press, 1999), and *Political Liberalism*, expanded ed. (New York: Columbia University Press, 2005).

7. On this, see especially his *A Theory of Communicative Action*, 2 vols. (Boston: Beacon Press, 1985); *Religion and Rationality: Essays on Reason, God, and Modernity* (Cambridge, Mass.: MIT Press, 2002); *Between Naturalism and Religion: Philosophical Essays* (Cambridge: Polity Press, 2008); *Nachmetaphysisches Denken 2* (Frankfurt: Suhrkamp, 2012); and together with Joseph Ratzinger, *The Dialectics of Secularization: On Reason and Religion* (San Francisco, Calif.: Ignatius Press, 2006). For Habermas on Rawls, see Habermas's important essay, "Reconciliation through the Public Use of Reason: Remarks on John Rawls' Political Liberalism," *Journal of Philosophy* 92, no. 3 (1995): 109–31.

egorically from a person who draws conceptually and semantically on Augustine's *City of God*, Aquinas's *Summa Theologiae*, or for that matter, the social encyclicals of Pope Leo XIII. Holding such tacitly operative convictions as Rawls and Habermas do is, of course, nothing but a sophisticated way of being beholden by a rather unreflective (should one say quasi-"religious") attitude about unexamined Enlightenment presuppositions. And, incidentally, Charles Taylor, in his probing engagements of Habermas's political thought, has pressed the question quite convincingly of whether nonreligious philosophical systems do not share central characteristics of their "religious" counterparts.[8] If Taylor is right—and I think he is—the distinction between a pure "secular reason" and merely "religious views" is a self-serving fiction of political liberalism.[9] This secularist use of "religion," integral to the strategic global outreach of free-market consumer capitalism, constitutes the most preeminent and also most subtle instance of what Pope Francis has astutely identified as the "colonization of the mind."

American Protestantism's Use of "Religion"

There exists a second, quite different but equally problematic dominant use of "religion." Whereas the first use is programmatically "secular," the second use is uniquely Christian, alive among various strands of Protestantism, first and foremost in North America, and there especially among Baptists, Pentecostals, Evangelicals, and new post-denominational and post-institutional Christian movements. This particular type of stridently anti-ecclesial and anticlerical strands of American Protestantism is in many ways a continuation of seventeenth-century radicalism—for example, the Diggers, Levelers, Ranters, and Fifth Monarchy Men—a radicalism that

---

8. For an instructive and accessible exchange regarding these issues between Habermas and Taylor and a condensed version of Taylor's critique of Habermas, see "Dialogue: Jürgen Habermas and Charles Taylor," in *The Power of Religion in the Public Sphere: Judith Butler, Jürgen Habermas, Charles Taylor, Cornel West*, ed. Eduardo Mendieta and Jonathan VanAntwerpen (New York: Columbia University Press, 2011), 60–69.

9. For a striking analysis and critique of how the artificial restrictions of Rawlsian secularist rationalism have emptied public discourse of intellectual and moral substance and authenticity, see Steven D. Smith, *The Disenchantment of Secular Discourse* (Cambridge, Mass.: Harvard University Press, 2010).

has periodically resurfaced, as for instance in William Blake's sharply antinomian view of religion.[10]

Like the first use, the second one also has a distinctly negative connotation. Here "religion" means "organized religion," a linguistic marker that identifies negatively institutional management, dissemination, and control of Christian beliefs and behavior. "Religion" in this sense is critiqued and dismissed as an inauthentic and estranged institutional temptation to works-righteousness. It is contrasted with the positive ideal of a non-institutional, "free," and therefore purportedly authentic faith in Jesus. Often, especially among the younger generation, "religion" is taken to be the polar opposite of "relationship," these two terms being set up as an antinomy. The exercise of what is seen as "traditional, institutional religion" is not an expression of a "relationship" with Jesus Christ, but is its *de facto* denial. This use has its roots in the constitutive individualism and the operative anti-Catholicism that are at the heart of what is characteristically American about American Protestantism.[11]

The Consumer-Capitalist Use of "Religion"

A third dominant use of "religion" differs from the first two in that it lacks their principally negative connotations. This use refers to comprehensive worldviews or "spiritualities" that pertain to ultimate matters and that answer what one might usefully call "Life Questions" such as: "What should I live for, and why?"; "What should I believe, and why should I believe it?"; "What kind of person should I be?"; and "What is meaningful in life, and what should I do in order to lead a fulfilling life?"[12] Hinduism, Buddhism, Judaism, Islam,

---

10. On seventeenth-century radicalism, see the excellent work by Christopher Hill, *The World Turned Upside Down: Radical Ideas during the English Revolution* (New York: Viking Press, 1972), and on William Blake, see E. P. Thompson, *Witness against the Beast: William Blake and the Moral Law* (New York: New Press, 1993), and G. E. Bentley Jr., *The Stranger from Paradise: A Biography of William Blake* (New Haven, Conn.: Yale University Press, 2001).

11. This dominant use is best captured not by this or that book—their name is legion—but by the extremely popular YouTube video by Jefferson Bethke, "Why I Hate Religion, But Love Jesus," available at youtube.com/watch?v=1IAhDGYlpqY.

12. I borrow these questions from Brad S. Gregory, who, in the introduction to *The Unintended Reformation: How a Religious Revolution Secularized Society* (Cambridge, Mass.: Belknap Press, 2012), advances an astute discussion of these life questions.

Christianity, and innumerable other religions constitute distinct species of the overarching genus of a spiritual worldview option. In Western capitalist consumer societies governed by an alternatively dogmatic or axiomatic relativism—that is, by the unfettered rule of the free market—"religions" constitute spiritual commodities in the ambit of a comprehensive wellness lifestyle liberalism to be sampled, acquired, returned, or discarded by their demanding consumers.[13]

The Religionswissenschaft Use of "Religion"

A fourth dominant use of "religion" is found primarily among cultural anthropologists, as well as sociologists and philosophers of religion. According to this use, "religion" denotes a unique constant in the evolution of the *homo sapiens*, the origin and ultimate point of reference of which is a prelinguistic and prereflective awareness of the primordially "numinous" or "sacred." "Religion" expresses a fundamental and ultimately ineffable experience of "being-in-the-world," of utter dependency, contingency, and finitude toward death, but also of unity with the cosmos, with ancestors, with the totality of life, and last but not least, with the numinous or sacred. The *interior* perspective of each religion is not reflective of a distinct transcendent truth about God or the world. Rather, it is a distinct reception and expression of what remains essentially ineffable but is universally shared by all religions. The *exterior* scientific methodologies of *Religionswissenschaft* facilitate a genealogical account of "religions" as the emerging cultural-historical expressions of a primordial anthropological constant in the evolution of *homo sapiens*. Under the gaze of the exterior scientific perspective, "religions" become the object of historical, linguistic, cultural-anthropological study in the "departments of religion" found in contemporary secular colleges and universities.[14] The theoretical commitments hidden in such a notion of

---

13. For a lucid critique of this use of "religion," see Graham Ward, "The Commodification of Religion or the Consummation of Capitalism," *The Hedgehog Review* 5, no. 2 (2003): 50–65.

14. For the most substantive and comprehensive account that deploys this use of "religion," see Robert Bellah's commanding *magnum opus*, *Religion in Human Evolution: From the Paleolithic to the Axial Age* (Cambridge, Mass.: Belknap Press, 2011). For an astute identification of the tacit but normative theological framework characteristic of liberal Protestantism that arguably informs Bellah's account in this extraordinary work,

"religion" have their roots either in the reductive naturalist accounts of "religion" advanced in the "natural history of religion" during the Enlightenment period[15] or in the romantic anti-Enlightenment experiential-expressivist concept of "religion." Also, given that liberal Protestantism (represented especially by Schleiermacher) and Catholic Modernism favored an understanding of "religion" as arising from a faculty completely different from the intellectual and volitional faculties, such an emphasis on religion as a feeling or awareness that is essentially preconceptual and prelinguistic would only underscore religion as something essentially ineffable.[16] Unsurprising, therefore, is the probably most central tenet of "religion" according to liberal Protestantism and Catholic Modernism: the doctrine that religious experience arises fundamentally from the transcendental constitution of human subjectivity itself, a subjectivity that emerges slowly but inexorably in the long history of human evolution and that extends itself into the intersubjectivity of linguistically configured complexes of symbol and ritual. Consequently, religious narratives and doctrines purportedly constitute secondary and inherently insufficient linguistic and conceptual expressions of these

---

see Thomas Joseph White, OP, "Sociology as Theology: Robert Bellah's Book Renews the Liberal Protestant Project," *First Things* (June 2013), available at firstthings.com/article/2013/06/sociology-as-theology, and for a devastating Augustinian critique of Bellah's grand narrative, see Paul J. Griffiths, "Impossible Pluralism: Choosing Between Universal Academic History and Christian Faith," *First Things* (June 2013), available at firstthings.com/article/2013/06/impossible-pluralism.

15. See paradigmatically David Hume's *Dialogues Concerning Natural Religion* and *The Natural History of Religion*, best accessible in David Hume, *Dialogues and Natural History of Religion*, ed. J. C. A. Gaskin (Oxford: Oxford University Press, 1993).

16. The early nineteenth-century *locus classicus* of this use of "religion," paradigmatic for liberal Protestantism, is the programmatic work of the young Friedrich Schleiermacher, *On Religion: Speeches to Its Cultured Despisers*, trans. John Oman (Louisville, Ky.: Westminster John Knox Press, 1994), especially the second speech, "The Nature of Religion." For a similarly programmatic work on the Catholic side, paradigmatic for what came soon after to be called Catholic Modernism, see Alfred Loisy (writing as A. Firmin), "La définition de la religion," *Revue du clergé français* 18 (1899): 193–209, "L'idée de la révélation," *Revue du clergé français* 21 (1900): 250–71, and *Autour d'un petit livre* (Paris: Alphonse Picard et fils, Éditeurs, 1903). For a lucid and penetrating contemporaneous critique of the use of "religion" Loisy advances, see Eugène Portalié, "'Dogma and History': Part 3 of 'Autour des fondements de la foi,' 1904," in *Defending the Faith: An Anti-Modernist Anthology*, ed. and trans. William M. Marshner (Washington, D.C.: The Catholic University of America Press, 2017), 121–85.

primordial religious experiences of the sacred, or in Rudolf Otto's famous term, the *mysterium tremendum et fascinosum*.[17]

The Use of "Religion" in Protestant Dialectical Theology

A fifth conventional use of "religion" has become prevalent in one influential strand of twentieth-century Protestant theology. Karl Barth and his disciples deploy the liberal Protestant notion of "religion" as a contrast term that puts into relief the principal concept of Barth's theology—"revelation." In the Barthian theological scheme, "religion" represents a fundamental and irrepressible human dynamic arising again and again from the postlapsarian universal condition of original sin—"natural theology" purportedly constituting its purest expression. Barth takes "religion" to be a basic phenomenon of humanity under the condition of original sin—"religion" as the again and again recurring attempt of humanity to placate, manipulate, and eventually control the living, radically free, and transcendent God. This phenomenon can only be checked again and again by the recurring event of the divine self-communication in Christ through the Holy Spirit as witnessed to by scripture. Whenever Christianity itself becomes "religion" in this problematic sense, according to Barth, it calls again and again for the deconstructing and purifying event of the God's Word to break in anew, accompanied by the critical work of dialectical theology. *Ecclesia semper reformanda*: the church must be constantly reformed by the Word, because "religion" again and again raises its ugly Pelagian head in it, a recurring dynamic that requires constant vigilance and when necessary, unhesitating purgation.

In his theological critique of "religion," Barth fuses Calvin's radicalization of Augustine's critique of pagan religion in the first ten books of the *City of God* with the famous projection theory of Ludwig Feuerbach's *The Essence of Christianity*, so that his hyper-

---

17. Among the paradigmatic twentieth-century works that encapsulate this use of "religion" are Rudolf Otto's *Das Heilige. Über das Irrationale in der Idee des Göttlichen und sein Verhältnis zum Rationalen* (Breslau: Trewendt, 1917), translated as *The Idea of the Holy: An Inquiry into the Non-Rational Factor in the Idea of the Divine and Its Relation to the Rational*, trans. John W. Harvey (London: Oxford University Press, 1950); and Mircea Eliade's *The Sacred and the Profane: The Nature of Religion* (New York: Harcourt, Brace and Co., 1959).

Augustinian use of "religion" signifies the ever recurring attempt of a humanity, fundamentally alienated from God, to project their hopes, wishes, and desires onto a fabricated product, the religious idol. The agent of this theological critique of "religion" is, unsurprisingly, a dialectical theology exclusively funded by God's self-revelation in Christ.[18]

Significantly, the notion of "religion" (*religio*) as used in the virtue of religion cannot be subsumed under any of these five dominant contemporary uses of "religion." Rather, as we will see later, the virtue of religion puts fundamentally into question the central assumptions on which each of the five dominant uses of "religion" rests. Having accomplished the first preliminary task, we must turn to the second and examine what the virtue of religion signifies and what its proper definition is.

THE VIRTUE OF RELIGION ACCORDING TO THOMAS AQUINAS

Thomas Aquinas is the first theologian to compose a comprehensive and complete treatise on the virtue of religion in which he develops an original and unitary conception of what he regards as the most eminent of the moral virtues.[19] Drawing upon Cicero, Isidore of Seville, and especially Augustine, he conceives of *religio* as a specific moral excellence that comprises a set of operations characteristic of the human being as a rational creature. It denotes both

---

18. For the by-now classical expression of this notion of "religion," see Karl Barth, *Kirchliche Dogmatik* I/2, §17, "Gottes Offenbarung als Aufhebung der Religion" (Zürich: Theologischer Verlag Zürich, 1940), 304–97. This part of Barth's *Church Dogmatics* is now available in an affordable English edition: Karl Barth, *On Religion: The Revelation of God as the Sublimation of Religion*, trans. Garrett Green (New York: T and T Clark, 2006).

19. *ST* II-II, qq. 80–100. In his introduction to *La virtù di religione*, the Italian Dominican Thomist Tito Centi, OP, characterizes "St. Thomas as the primary origin of the treatise *De religione*. It is to be traced back to him, because it has been his achievement for the first time to put together and, so to speak, invent the argument [for the virtue of religion].... Undoubtedly, already before St. Thomas much had been said about devotion, adoration, prayer, sacrifice, vows, and oaths, but what had remained unclear was the link that made all these actions exercises of one single virtue that is specifically different from the theological virtues and the other moral virtues." Tommaso d'Aquino, *La Somma Teologica*, vol. 18 (Siena: Salani, 1967), 8 (author's translation).

interior and exterior operations (interior acts of devotion and prayer and exterior acts of adoration, sacrifice, oblation, tithes, vows, etc.) by way of which the human being renders what is due to the source of all being and life, to "the first principle of the creation and government of things" (*ST* II-II, q. 81, a. 3). Because these acts denote a human excellence in relationship to a common object (the *habitus*—a stable disposition hard to lose) that enables and facilitates these specific acts, *religio* constitutes a distinct virtue.[20] It "denotes properly a relation to God."[21] By the proper and immediate acts that the *habitus* of *religio* elicits (such as adoration and sacrifice), the human being is directed to God alone (*ST* II-II, q. 81, a. 1, ad 1). As already observed at the beginning of the chapter, this virtue is akin to the cardinal virtue of justice, which Aquinas defines as "rendering to everybody his [or her] due by a constant and perpetual will" (*ST* II-II, q. 58, a. 1). But because justice is "the virtue of actions among equals" (*ST* I-II, q. 61, a. 3, ad 2), constitutively asymmetrical relationships—children to parents, citizens to their homeland, and, first and foremost, rational creatures to their creator—cannot belong directly to the virtue of justice. For the constitutive inequality characteristic of these relationships makes it impossible to render what is properly due. Consequently, acts of moral excellence that pertain to these essentially asymmetrical relationships must belong to virtues different from justice in the strict sense, but insofar as some due is rendered, they must nevertheless still be related to justice. Hence, *religio* cannot be a subjective part of justice—that is, one of the species into which a cardinal virtue may be divided. Rather, it must be a potential part of justice. And so, as "a virtue which resembles a cardinal virtue without manifesting its complete specific nature," the virtue of religion occupies a position similar to "piety" (*pietas*; *ST* II-II, q. 101) and "observance" (*observantia*; *ST* II-II, q. 102).[22] These two virtues facil-

---

20. *ST* II-II, q. 81, a. 3: "Habits [*habitus*] are differentiated according to a different aspect of the object. Now it belongs to religion to show reverence to one god under one aspect, namely as the first principle of the creation and government of things."

21. *ST* II-II, q. 81, a. 1: "Religio proprie importat ordinem ad Deum."

22. Kevin D. O'Rourke, OP, in St. Thomas Aquinas, *Summa theologiae*, vol. 39: (2a2ae. 80–91), *Religion and Worship* (New York / London: Blackfriars and McGraw-Hill Book Company / Eyre and Spottiswoode, 1964), xxiii.

itate those acts of rightly acknowledging what is due and what cannot be rendered according to the order of justice in the constitutively unequal relationships all human beings have to their parents and to their homelands. *A fortiori*, no rational creature is able to render what is justly due to God. The virtue of religion is the operative *habitus* that enables human beings to exercise the greatest approximation to justice possible in the most asymmetrical relationship of all, the rational creature to "the first principle of the creation and government of things."[23]

Consider the real (and not merely stipulative) definition of the virtue of religion that the noted Hungarian Dominican Thomist, Alexander M. Horvath, formulates based on Aquinas's account: *religio* is (1) a moral virtue, whose (2) acts (3) through an ordination of reason refer (4) to God as the first principle in order (5) to testify our reverence and submission and to participate in God's gifts. The *formal* cause of the acts of the virtue of religion is the ordination of reason to God. Reason's ordination to God occurs in regard to interior religious acts (submission of the will, mental prayer, etc.) by way of a purely transcendental relation to God and in regard to all exterior acts by way of a predicamental relation to God. The *efficient* cause of this ordination is its very *ratio*, the judgment and command of reason that are the very origin of the relation to God, be it transcenden-

---

23. *ST* II-II, q. 81, a. 3. The first principle (*primum principium*) signifies the transcendent universal source and cause of all that exists. As every cause contains the perfections characteristic of its proper effect to a higher degree than the effect, all genuine extant perfections are in a surpassing way characteristics of the first principle. These perfections include among others intellect, will, life, personhood, and with them love, justice, mercy, providence, and blessedness. Given this understanding—implicitly as a vague awareness to which conscience gives rise or explicitly as the knowledge natural theology affords—it is a dictate of natural reason that the first principle is to be honored by way of acts of adoration and sacrifice. However, as the metaphysical knowledge of the first principle's perfections remains notional and limited and its implicit awareness weak and insecure, the former tends to a reductive, depersonalized rationalization (Plato's religion and Hindu mysticism) and the latter to a multi-personal mythologization (the pantheon of pagan deities). Only by way of a personal self-introduction to Abraham and Moses and culminating in the incarnate Logos, Jesus Christ, does the first principle's identity, "He Who Is," as triune Lord become accessible—to faith, an act of assent to a testimony that surpasses and simultaneously affirms what natural reason is implicitly aware of or may come to know explicitly as the existence of the first principle of the creation and government of things.

tal or predicamental. The *material* cause signifies everything that is taken up or chosen as an offering in order to signify the honor that is due to God. These things may include acts of the will, the intellect, or the other virtues and all things that, through their ordination, may be ordered to God directly or indirectly. The *final* cause, the cause of all causes, is the person's intention to testify reverence and submission to God and to participate in God's gifts.

From the formal and material cause of the acts of the virtue of religion issues the formal object of *religio*—*cultus*. *Cultus* signifies what is offered to God and that through which God is honored and revered; that is, all the acts that the *habitus* of *religio* elicits and commands. *Cultus* broadly understood signifies (1) the act of *religio* (oblation), (2) the matter or object in and through which oblation is exercised, and (3) the end (*finis*) of oblation, which is reverence of God and participation in God's gifts.[24]

The virtue of religion presupposes some rudimentary universal knowledge of God's existence and providence and is rooted in the third inclination of the natural law. The principles of the natural law govern and guide the acquired virtue of religion.[25] It is this mostly tacit and implicit knowledge of God and its rootedness in the natural law that account for the integrity of the *formal* cause of the acquired virtue of religion, the ordination of reason and of its *ratio*, the judgment and command of reason to exercise acts of religion. The *material* cause—everything taken up or chosen as offering in order to signify the honor that is due to God—may be more or less deficient due to the state of wounded nature (*status naturae corruptae*) in which humanity finds itself after the Fall (*ST* I-II, q. 109, a. 2). Importantly, the *de facto* deficiency of its material cause does not compromise the *formal* integrity of religion as a moral virtue. It is precisely this constitutive formal integrity that affords the definition of the virtue in the first place. Aquinas states:

---

24. Alexander M. Horvath, OP, *Annotationes ad II-II Quaest. 81–91 De Virtute Religionis* (Pro Manuscripto) Pontificum Institutum Internationale "Angelicum" (Rome: Tipografia Agostiniana, 1929), 3–8.

25. *ST* I-II, q. 94, a. 2: "Thirdly, there is in [the human being] an inclination to good, according to the nature of his reason, which nature is proper to him; thus [the human being] has a natural inclination to know the truth about God and to live in society."

A virtue is that which makes its possessor good, and his act good likewise, wherefore we must needs say that every good act belongs to a virtue. Now it is evident that to render anyone his due has the aspect of good, since by rendering a person his due, one becomes suitably proportioned to him, through being ordered to him in a becoming manner. But order comes under the aspect of good.... Since then it belongs to religion to pay due honor to someone, namely to God, it is evident that religion is a virtue. (*ST* II-II, q. 81, a. 2)

The *formality* of the object of all the operative *habitus*—including *religio*—and the formal integrity of their respective acts account for the teleological perfectibility of human nature (regarding the good of moral excellence). As grace does not destroy but rather presupposes and perfects nature, it is divine grace that, in the extant order of providence, accounts for the surpassing perfection of the virtue and the agent, a perfection that comes about by way of the healing and elevation of human nature by sanctifying grace and the infusion of the theological virtues, especially charity.

The acquired virtue of religion differs from its infused analogue in that, in the case of the latter, the material cause is definitively perfected by way of divine and human instruction. According to Aquinas, the New Law of the Gospel and human law (that is, Christ's mandates and the additional determinations of the church) establish what specific things are to be done in reverence of God (*ST* II-II, q. 81, a. 2, ad 3). Furthermore, and more importantly, the acts of the infused virtue of religion are commanded by the three theological virtues, faith, hope, and charity, and formed by the virtue of charity, which already unites the person in some fashion with God "by a union of the spirit" (*ST* II-II, q. 82, a. 2, ad 1). Furthermore, in order to make the human soul amenable to the motions of the Holy Spirit, the human being receives, together with the theological virtue of charity also the gifts of the Holy Spirit, infused *habitus* of their own. The Apostle Paul states, in Romans 8:15: "You have received the spirit of adoption of sons, whereby we cry, Abba, Father." Precisely because it is the Holy Spirit who moves to this effect, to have such filial affection toward God, Aquinas argues, there must be a corresponding gift of the Holy Spirit, a stable disposition that facilitates and elicits such acts: "Since it belongs properly to piety to pay duty and worship to one's father, it follows that piety, whereby, at the Holy Spirit's instigation, we pay worship and duty to God as our Father, is a gift of the Holy Spirit" (*ST* II-II, q. 121, a. 1).

The gift of piety perfects the infused virtue of religion. While the latter elicits acts of worship to God the creator, the former elicits worship to God the Father. Last but not least, the person receives the infused virtue of religion and the gift of piety by way of the infusion of sanctifying grace. Yet sanctifying grace itself is received in turn in virtue of an instrumental cause that imprints a seal or character on the soul that efficaciously capacitates the graced person to the worship of the triune God. This very seal or character that the rational soul receives is the effect of the sacraments, first and foremost of baptism.[26] Because of the seal of baptism and the gift of piety, the *cultus* of *religio* is now worship of the Father through the Son in the Holy Spirit.

Unsurprisingly, but nevertheless significantly, Aquinas regards the virtue of religion to be "the chief among the moral virtues" (*ST* II-II, q. 81, a. 6, s.c.). The virtue of religion acquires its surpassing preeminence among the moral virtues from its relationship to the objective final end to which the agent is ordered—God. The closer something is to this end, the greater is its goodness. Because the virtue of religion, whose acts are directly ordered to the honor of God, approaches nearer to God than any other moral virtue, this virtue holds a position of preeminence among all the moral virtues.[27]

This brief account and definition of the virtue of religion shall suffice. We are now in a position to turn to a pair of interconnected tasks. The first task is to show that and why according to Aquinas the virtue of religion is indispensable for the attainment of one's

---

26. *ST* III, q. 63, a.1: "As is clear from what has been already stated [*ST* III, q. 62, a. 5] the sacraments of the New Law are ordained for a twofold purpose; namely, for a remedy against sins; and for the perfecting of the soul in things pertaining to the Divine worship according to the rite of the Christian life." For an instructive account of Aquinas's understanding of the sacraments as instrumental causes, see Lynch, *The Cleansing of the Heart*.

27. *ST* II-II, q. 81, a. 6: "Whatever is directed to an end takes its goodness from being ordered to that end; so that the nearer it is to the end the better it is. Now moral virtues ... are about matters that are ordered to God as their end. And religion approaches nearer to God than the other moral virtues, in so far as its actions are directly and immediately ordered to the honor of God. Hence religion excels among the moral virtues."

subjective final end—beatitude. The second task that remains is to make simply explicit what is entailed in having accomplished the first, namely that in the Thomist framework the virtue of religion is absolutely central for genuine human flourishing.

THE ATTAINMENT OF PERFECT AND EVERLASTING BEATITUDE AND THE RECTITUDE OF THE WILL

As discussed in detail in my prologue, according to Aquinas, the happiness of the human being is twofold (*duplex*): first, the genuine but transitory, and therefore imperfect, happiness corresponds to the finality proportionate to human nature: the human being has the natural potency to obtain this beatitude, and so *can* obtain it; second, the everlasting, unitive, and therefore perfect, beatitude surpasses the capacity of human nature and can be obtained "by the power of God alone, by a kind of participation of the Godhead, about which it is written (2 Pt 1:4) that by Christ we are made partakers of the Divine nature" (*ST* I-II, q. 62, a. 1). The perfect beatitude of the human being is the subjective fruition of the objective ultimate end by way of an unmediated direct union of the intellect and the will with God, who is the first cause of the rational soul's creation and enlightenment and who also is the rational soul's final end as the soul's universal good.[28] And insofar as the rational soul is the

28. *ST* I-II, q. 3, a. 8: "Final and perfect happiness can consist in nothing else than the vision of the Divine Essence. To make this clear, two points must be observed: first, that [human beings are] not perfectly happy, so long as something remains for [them] to desire and seek; secondly, that the perfection of any power is determined by the nature of its object. Now the object of the intellect is *what a thing is*, i.e., the essence of a thing, according to *De Anima* iii. 6. Wherefore the intellect attains perfection, in so far as it knows the essence of a thing. If therefore an intellect know the essence of some effect, whereby it is not possible to know the essence of the cause, i.e., to know of the cause *what it is*, that intellect cannot be said to reach that cause simply, although it may be able to gather from the effect the knowledge that the cause is. Consequently, when [the human being] knows an effect, and knows that it has a cause, there naturally remains in [the human being] the desire to know about that cause, *what it is*. And this desire is one of wonder, and causes inquiry, as is stated in the beginning of the *Metaphysics* I, ch. 2.... If therefore the human intellect, knowing the essence of some created effect, knows no more of God than *that He is*, the perfection of that intellect does not yet reach simply the First Cause, but there remains in it the natural desire to seek the cause. Wherefore it is not yet perfectly happy.

substantial form of the body, it is the whole human being, soul and body, whose final end in the extant order of divine providence—gratuitously decreed from all eternity as merited by Christ—is to become a partaker of the divine nature, and thus a partaker of the unfathomable bliss of the divine life.[29]

Significantly, there obtains an essential requirement for the attainment of this everlasting perfect beatitude. In order to illustrate this requirement, Aquinas adduces a central principle of the philosophy of nature and puts it to analogical use in his theological argument of fittingness (*convenientia*): "Matter cannot receive a form, unless it be duly disposed thereto" (*ST* I-II, q. 4, a. 4). Material cannot be shaped unless it is duly prepared. Wood must be cut and dried in order to receive the form of fire; iron must be heated in order to receive the form of a plow. Similarly, nothing achieves its end unless it is well adapted to the end. And therefore no one can attain perfect beatitude without a right good will.[30]

The rectitude of the will is, of course, necessarily a *concomitant* condition of attaining perfect happiness. For "happiness or bliss by which [the human being] is made most perfectly conformed to

---

Consequently, for perfect happiness the intellect needs to reach the very Essence of the First Cause. And thus it will have its perfection through union with God as with that object, in which alone [human] happiness consists."

29. *ST* I, q, 26, a. 3. As one noted interpreter of Aquinas's thought rightly emphasizes, "[Human beings] cannot know that they are capable of attaining the vision of God except through faith based on divine teaching. That God actually does ordain [human beings] to Himself is a revealed truth known only by faith. Only the believer can hope and pray for this divine gift." Bradley, *Aquinas on the Twofold Human Good*, 524. See also *Comp. theol.* II, c. 7. Aquinas states explicitly: "The ultimate happiness [of the human being] consists in a supernatural vision of God: to which vision [the human being] cannot attain unless he be taught by God.... Hence, in order that a [human being] arrive at the perfect vision of heavenly happiness, he [or she] must first of all believe God, as a disciple believes the master who is teaching him" (*ST* II-II, q. 2, a. 3).

30. *ST* I-II, q. 4, a. 4: "Final Happiness consists in the vision of the Divine Essence, Which is the very essence of goodness. So that the will of him who sees the Essence of God, of necessity, loves, whatever he loves, in subordination to God; just as the will of him who sees not God's Essence, of necessity, loves whatever he loves, under that common notion of good which he knows. And this [to love everything our will loves in explicit subordination to God, or to love everything our will loves in implicit subordination to God, namely by loving God within the common notion of goodness [*sub communi ratione boni*] is precisely what makes the will right. Wherefore *it is evident that Happiness cannot be without a right will*" (emphasis added).

God, and which is the end of human life, consists in an operation" (*ST* I-II, q. 55, a. 2, ad 3), and this operation that realizes the perfect conformity to God entails necessarily the *concomitant* rectitude of the will.

But the rectitude of the will, the will properly set on the ultimate end, is also a condition *antecedent* to attaining perfect beatitude. Why so? Could God not conceivably have created a rational creature that, in the original state, is endowed with a will rightly ordered to the ultimate end and that, in the next instance after its creation, would be elevated by God to the attainment of the ultimate end and to perfect and everlasting beatitude in the beatific vision? Because any answer to this question refers necessarily to the mystery of the divine wisdom and will, Aquinas advances an argument of *convenientia*, of what seems to be most fitting for divine wisdom. It is worth quoting at length:

> The order of Divine wisdom demands that it should not be thus; for as is stated in *De Caelo* ii. 12, *of those things that have a natural capacity for the perfect good,* one *has it without movement,* some *by one movement,* some *by several.* Now to possess the perfect good without movement, belongs to that which has it naturally; and to have Happiness naturally belongs to God alone. Therefore it belongs to God alone not to be moved towards Happiness by any previous operation. Now since Happiness surpasses every created nature, no pure creature can [fittingly] gain Happiness, without the movement or operation, whereby it tends thereto. But the angel, who is above [the human being] in the natural order, obtained it, according to the order of Divine wisdom, by one movement of a meritorious work.... whereas [the human being] obtains it by many movements of works which are called merits. Wherefore also according to the Philosopher (*Ethic.* i. 9), happiness is the reward of works of virtue. (*ST* I-II, q. 5, a. 7; emphasis added)

The reception of the gratuitous gift of perfect and eternal beatitude requires antecedent movement or operation by the embodied rational creature. And such movement—initiated by grace, ordered by the restored rectitude of the will to God, and united inchoatively with God by way of the theological virtue of charity—merits the attainment of everlasting perfect beatitude. "Merit" denotes the essential cooperation of rational creatures with divine grace in attaining the ultimate end and their perfect beatitude.[31] Aquinas takes Augustine's universally accepted axiom, "God created us without us: but he did not will to save us without us," to be the guiding theological principle that accounts for the proper preparation of the rational creature for eternal union with God.[32] The proper preparations of the created image, the human being, to receive an essentially disproportionate, surpassing realization of its perfection—conformity to and union with the exemplar—are acts chosen and executed by a right good will. But the goodness of the will depends on the intention of the end. The last end of the human will is the sovereign good, God. Hence, for the will to be good, the will has to be properly set on the ultimate end, God, the sovereign good. The sovereign good—God's own infinite goodness—relates to the divine will as its proper object. In other words: God, always and in all, wills his own goodness, and God wills things apart from himself by willing his own goodness, the sovereign good (*ST* I, q. 19, a. 2, ad 2). Hence, God wills also our will to be ordered to the sovereign good. And so for the rectitude of the human will to obtain, the human will must be properly conformed to the divine will.[33] Consequently, the rectitude of the human will, the intellectual appetite, depends on the intellect being instructed by the natural and the divine law (*ST* I-II, q. 19, a. 4) and on the will being thus ordered by right reason and the acquired moral virtues to a due end (*ST* I-II, q. 55, a. 4, ad 4), and by sanctifying grace, the theological virtues, the infused moral virtues, and the gifts of the Holy Spirit to the gratuitous ultimate end.

---

31. *ST* I-II, q. 111, a. 2, esp. ad 2; q. 114, a. 2. For an excellent analysis and interpretation of the theological concept of "merit" in Thomas Aquinas, see Wawrykow, *God's Grace and Human Action*. And for an astute ecumenical defense of this concept, see Root, "Aquinas, Merit, and Reformation Theology."

32. Augustine, *Sermo* 169.11.13 (*PL* 38:923).

33. *ST* I-II, q. 19, a. 9: "As stated above [a. 7], the goodness of the will depends on the intention of the end. Now the last end of the human will is the Sovereign Good, namely, God, as stated above [q. 1, a. 8; q. 3, a. 1]. Therefore the goodness of the human will requires it to be ordained to the Sovereign Good, that is, to God. Now this Good is primarily and essentially compared to the Divine will, as its proper object. Again, that which is first in any genus is the measure and rule of all that belongs to that genus. Moreover, everything attains to rectitude and goodness, in so far as it is in accord with its proper measure. Therefore, in order that [the human being's] will be good it needs to be conformed to the Divine will."

THE RECTITUDE OF THE WILL AND
THE VIRTUE OF RELIGION

The rectitude of the will finds its proper realization in virtues that are about *operations*. The paradigm is the virtue of justice, which applies the will to its proper act (*ST* I-II, q. 59, a. 5), thereby realizing its rectitude *in actu*.[34] "Wherefore," Aquinas concludes, "all such virtues as are about operations, bear, in some way, the character of justice" (*ST* I-II, q. 60, a. 3). The virtue of religion resembles the virtue of justice, for it is also about operations, but it is not an integral part of justice. Rather, it is annexed to it because its operations fall short of justice due to the impossibility to render what exactly is due in the relationship of the rational creature to the creator.[35]

Precisely because the virtue of religion belongs to a family of related virtues whose head is the virtue of justice—which applies the will to its proper act and thereby actualizes the will's rectitude—it would be a grave error to mistake the virtue of religion for some supererogatory moral excellence that is up to one's personal discretion.[36] Aquinas emphasizes that "it belongs to the dictate of natural reason that [the human being] should do something through reverence for God. But that [the human being] should do this or that determinate thing does not belong to the dictate of natural reason, but is established by Divine or human law" (*ST* II-II, q. 81, a. 2, ad 3).

Natural reason dictates the very *ratio* of the virtue of religion,

---

34. *ST* II-II, q. 58, a. 1: "Justice is a *habitus* [a stable disposition of the will] whereby a [human being] renders to each one what is his due *by a constant and perpetual will*" (emphasis added).

35. *ST* II-II, q. 80, a. 1: "Whatever [the human being] renders to God is due, yet it cannot be equal, as though [the human being] rendered to God as much as he [or she] owes Him, according to Psalm 115:12: *What shall I render to the Lord for all the things that He hath rendered to me?*" While the strict equality of commutative justice is out of the question, there must be some semblance of equality, as Aquinas, after all, understands the virtue of religion as a part of justice: "Religion is ... a moral virtue, since it is a part of justice, and observes a mean, not in the passions, but in actions directed to God by establishing a kind of equality in them. And when I say *equality*, I do not mean absolute equality, because it is not possible to pay God as much as we owe Him, but equality in consideration of [the human being's] ability and God's acceptance" (*ST* II-II, q. 81, a. 5, ad 3).

36. For the most comprehensive recent study of the virtue of religion in the thought of Thomas Aquinas, see Robert Jared Staudt, "Religion as a Virtue: Thomas Aquinas on Worship through Justice, Law, and Charity" (PhD diss., Ave Maria University, 2008).

namely that reverence to God is due and this due is so necessary "that *without it moral rectitude cannot be ensured*" (*ST* II-II, q. 80, a. 1; emphasis added). Without the acts of the virtue of religion, moral rectitude cannot be ensured. And if moral rectitude is deficient, the integrity and unity of the cardinal virtues is compromised, if not lost. This sequence of entailments leads to two problematic alternatives pertaining to those who do not have charity—that is, those whom Aquinas would have called practitioners of pagan virtue.

The first alternative is what is conventionally considered as straightforwardly Aristotelian: as moral rectitude requires the practice of the virtue of religion and because Aquinas assumes that pagans were able to practice the acquired moral virtues, or as he also calls them, the social or political virtues (*ST* I-II, q. 61, a. 5), pagans were able to practice the virtue of religion. What complicates, or even undercuts, this alternative is that according to Aquinas, it is impossible for human beings in the state of wounded nature to fulfill the natural duty to love God above all things (*ST* I-II, q. 119, a. 3). Yet, falling short of this natural love of God above all things "in the appetite of his rational will" (ibid.), the human being in this state seems incapable of acquiring the specific *habitus* of *religio*, the *cultus* of God as "the first principle of the creation and government of things" (*ST* II-II, q. 81, a. 3).

This complication at the heart of the first alternative compels consideration of the second alternative, which is conventionally considered as the Augustinian one. As moral rectitude requires the practice of the virtue of religion, and because the acquired moral virtue of religion is only a counterfeit, moral rectitude cannot be assured. Yet, without moral rectitude, the unity, and with it the integrity, of the cardinal virtues is destroyed. Hence, all moral virtues except the infused moral virtues are mere counterfeits. Only the virtue of religion that is infused and formed by charity is a genuine virtue because, through healing grace, the natural love of God above all things can again be exercised. But Aquinas expressly denies this consequence (*ST* I-II, q. 61, a. 1, a. 5).

Each alternative leads to unsavory consequences that, as a matter of fact, contradict aspects of Aquinas's complex doctrine of virtue. Certain aspects of both the straightforwardly Augustinian and the straightforwardly Aristotelian approach find support, but others do not. It would be all too precipitous to conclude at this point that Aquinas's attempt to integrate Aristotle's virtue ethics and Augustine's theology of sin and grace into one coherent system ultimately failed. Neither of the all too conventional alternatives matches the daring and depth of Aquinas's actual synthesis. Rather, as David Decosimo puts it rather felicitously in his recent *Ethics as a Work of Charity*, "Aquinas strives to be Aristotelian by being Augustinian and vice versa."[37] In order to appreciate how Aquinas does this, it is apposite to recall the various distinctions he makes between the perfection and imperfection of virtue in different respects and between different sets of virtues.[38]

37. Decosimo, *Ethics as a Work of Charity*, 9. Decosimo's book is an important intervention on the complex and controverted matter of Aquinas's teaching on the acquired and the infused moral virtues. His conceptually astute and textually meticulous analysis and interpretation demonstrates that what are conventionally considered as the straightforwardly Aristotelian and Augustinian alternatives are ultimately unhelpful interpretive strategies because they fall, in their respective ways, short of the daring and depth of Aquinas's synthesis.

38. The following core distinctions rest on the "co-existence theory," the supposition that the Christian can have both acquired and infused moral virtues, not only in general, but simultaneously and specifically. For a helpful analytic map of this complex discussion among Thomist virtue ethicists, see Angela McKay Knobel, "Two Theories of Christian Virtue." *American Catholic Philosophical Quarterly* 84, no. 3 (2010): 600–618. On this highly complex and hotly disputed question, even in view of considerable counterarguments, I still hold the "co-existence theory" to be (1) Aquinas's own implicitly held theory and (2) despite its complexity the theory that saves all the appearances best. For arguments supporting this theory in recent times, see Anthony J. Falanga, CM, *Charity the Form of the Virtues According to Saint Thomas* (Washington, D.C.: The Catholic University of America Press, 1948); Robert Florent Coerver, *The Quality of Facility in the Moral Virtues* (Washington, D.C.: The Catholic University of America Press, 1946); Daniel Westberg, *Right Practical Reason: Aristotle, Action, and Prudence in Aquinas* (Oxford: Clarendon Press, 1994); Bradley, *Aquinas on the Twofold Human Good*; and Thomas M. Osborne Jr., "Perfect and Imperfect Virtues in Aquinas," *The Thomist* 71, no. 1 (2007): 39–64. Support for this theory can also be found in Pieper, *The Four Cardinal Virtues*; Michael Sherwin, OP, "Infused Virtues and the Effects of Acquired Vice: A Test Case for the Thomistic Theory of Infused Cardinal Virtues," *The Thomist* 73, no. 1 (2009): 29–52; Markus Christoph, SJM, "Justice as an Infused Virtue in the *Secunda Secundae* and Its Implications for Our Understanding of the Moral Life" (PhD diss., University of Fribourg, 2010), esp. chap. 3; and Decosimo, *Ethics as a Work of Charity*. The one point about which I find myself in disagreement with Decosimo is his thesis that every single good meritorious act of a person in the state of grace is *simultaneously* an act of the natural virtue and of the corresponding supernatural virtue.

The first distinction between perfection and imperfection pertains to the supernatural final end and regards the crucial difference between acquired and infused moral virtues. While the theological virtues are always infused, moral virtues can be acquired or infused. Infused moral virtues are perfect and simply true, for they conduce to the supernatural final end. Because acquired moral virtues do not, they are imperfect in this respect (*ST* I-II, q. 65, a. 2).

The second distinction between perfection and imperfection pertains to what is conducive to the principal good, the ultimate final end. Here Aquinas introduces two distinctions. The first distinction pertains to what conduces directly to the principal good, the ultimate final end, versus what leads away from it. Virtues that conduce to the principal good, the ultimate final end, are perfect and simply true. They are the infused moral virtues we encountered already above. What leads human beings away from the ultimate final end can only be an apparent good, and what conduces to it is consequently a counterfeit virtue. The second distinction pertains to acquired moral virtues and differentiates between those that are directed to the virtuous good, the good *simpliciter*, or the good in itself (*bonum honestum*), and those that are directed to a merely useful or pleasurable good (*bonum utile*; *bonum delectabile*).[39] In the latter we encounter again the counterfeit virtues.[40] But the former, those directed to the virtuous good (*bonum honestum*), are true but imperfect virtues. Because they are true, they can be perfected when referred to charity. Consider the following: civic fortitude is directed to the welfare of the state (*conservatio civitatis*), which is a *bonum honestum*. Consequently, civic fortitude is a true, albeit imperfect virtue—imperfect, unless it is referred by charity to the principal good and ultimate final end, whereby it becomes a perfect and simply true virtue.[41]

---

39. *ST* I-II, q. 39, a. 2: "Every virtuous good results from these two things, the rectitude of the reason and the will."

40. *ST* II-II, q. 23, a. 7: "If this particular good is not a true, but an apparent good, it is not a true virtue that is ordered to such a good, but a counterfeit virtue." Then Aquinas cites at length Augustine, who uses the example of the miser whose prudence, justice, temperance, and courage are counterfeit virtues because his particular good is not a true but an apparent good.

41. *ST* II-II, q. 23, a. 7: "If, on the other hand, this particular good be a true good, for

The third distinction between perfection and imperfection pertains to the very constitution of moral virtues *qua habitus*. According to Aquinas, moral virtues are virtues *simpliciter* because they make the persons who possess them good and render their activity good too—good in respect to the connatural final end proportionate to human nature, not good in the sense of acceptable to God as meritorious of an increase in charity.[42] Moral virtues in the full sense of the term (virtues *simpliciter*) are to be differentiated from nonmoral or "natural virtues." The latter are virtues in only a qualified sense (virtues *secundum quid*) because they indicate a vague natural inclination either to true goods common to all human beings or to the specific form such an inclination takes in an individual soul/body composite.[43] This mere disposition to act (*virtus inchoata*) is fundamentally different from and imperfect in relation to the acquired *habitus* that is stable and difficult to lose (*difficile mobile*). Compared with this natural virtue (*virtus inchoata*), an acquired moral *habitus* is perfect, true, and simple. For the difficulty to lose it (*difficile mobile*) belongs to the *ratio* of virtue; it is proper to virtue *per se*.

In light of these central distinctions, we are now in a position to consider again the acquired virtue of religion and the solution Aquinas advances, a solution that the two conventional alternatives do not consider. Aquinas immediately grants the fundamental Augustinian point, but in an Aristotelian way: among the acquired moral virtues, the virtue of religion indeed has a unique deficiency. For, in regard to this unique acquired virtue, it matters significantly that human beings in the state of wounded nature are unable to exercise the natural love of God above all things. Hence, far from being a mere semblance or counterfeit of virtue, the acquired virtue of religion is

---

instance the welfare of the state, or the like, it will be a true virtue, imperfect, however, unless it be referred to the final and perfect good. Accordingly, no strictly true virtue is possible without charity."

42. ST I-II, q. 56, a. 3: "Since virtue is that *which makes its possessor good, and his work good likewise*, these latter habits are called virtues simply [*simpliciter*]; because they make the work to be actually good, and the subject good simply."

43. ST I-II, q. 58, a. 4, ad 3: "The natural inclination to a good of virtue is a kind of beginning of virtue, but is not perfect virtue. For the stronger this inclination is, the more perilous may it prove to be, unless it be accompanied by right reason, which rectifies the choice of fitting means towards the due end."

nevertheless a uniquely imperfect virtue. Like all the other acquired virtues, it is imperfect in respect to the supernatural ultimate end.

But unlike all the other acquired moral virtues, the virtue of religion is also imperfect in respect to the proper realization of the *cultus* of God as the first principle of the creation and government of things. Recall, *cultus* results from the formal and the material cause of the acts of *religio*. Here Aquinas is Aristotelian, but in an Augustinian way: the formal cause, reason's ordination to God, and the efficient cause, the *ratio* of this ordination, accounts for the constitutive integrity, the proximate perfection characteristic of an acquired operative *habitus*. But its material cause—everything taken up or chosen as offering in order to signify the honor that is due to God—remains *de facto* deficient. For the proper perfection of the material cause presupposes the capacity to exercise the natural love of God above all things *qua* final end. Only if human beings were able, in the state of wounded nature, to exercise this natural love of God above all things would the virtue's proper *ratio*, the judgment and command of reason, be matched consistently and stably by an equivalent volition of God as ultimate good. Hence, despite its formal integrity *qua* specifying object and despite its proper *ratio*, the *cultus* of the acquired virtue of religion remains *de facto* deficient. However, due to its *formal* integrity, the acquired virtue of religion is able to ensure moral rectitude and, consequently, also the unity of the acquired moral virtues. While not at all a counterfeit of virtue, the acquired virtue of religion, due to its material imperfection, nevertheless produces necessarily a deficient *cultus*. The material imperfection that causes the deficient *cultus* is overcome only through the restoration of the capacity of the natural love of God above all things. Yet this restoration comes about only by healing grace and the infusion of faith, hope, and charity (*ST* I-II, q. 109, a. 3).

And there is more: the person who receives, together with faith, hope, charity, and all the other infused moral virtues, also the infused virtue of religion receives in addition an imprinted seal or character on the soul that efficaciously capacitates him or her to the worship of the triune God. This very seal or character that the soul receives is the effect of the sacraments, first and foremost, of baptism: "The sacraments of the New Law [which derive their power especially from Christ's passion; *ST* III, q. 62, a. 5] are ordained for a twofold purpose, namely for a remedy against sins, and for the perfecting of the soul in things pertaining to the Divine worship according to the rite of the Christian life" (*ST* III, q. 63, a. 1). The New Law and its correlative human law (that is, Christ's commands and the additional determinations of the church) establish what determinate things are to be done in reverence of God.[44] Thanks to the gift of piety, the range of what is to be done for the sake of reverence to God, now worshiped as Father, is remarkably expansive: "By the gift of piety [a human being] pays worship and duty not only to God, but also to all [human beings] on account of their relationship to God. Hence it belongs to piety to honor the saints, and not to contradict the Scriptures whether one understands them or not.... Consequently [piety] also assists those who are in a state of unhappiness" (*ST* II-II, q. 121, a. 1, ad 3). The gift of piety and the theological virtue of charity display a similar structure. In each, the unique relationship with God—in the case of piety worship of God as Father and in the case of charity friendship with God—includes those to whom God's fatherhood and friendship extends.[45]

The theological virtues have God as their direct object; faith and hope are directly engaged by God as their immediate object, and the theological virtue of charity already realizes a certain union with God, the perfect ultimate end. Higher virtues, like faith, hope, and charity, can command the acts of lower virtues.[46] The acts of the infused perfect virtue of religion—commanded by faith, hope, and charity (*ST* II-II, q. 81, a. 5, ad 1)—are not in reference directly to God (like believing God, hoping in God, loving God with God's own shared love of charity), but rather are about things referred to the ultimate end; they are acts issued by faith, hope, and charity and are

---

44. *ST* II-II, q. 81, a. 2, ad 3: "It belongs to the dictate of natural reason that [the human being] should do something through reverence for God. But that he should do this or that determinate thing does not belong to the dictate of natural reason, but is established by Divine and human law."

45. See *ST* II-II, q. 23, a. 1, ad 2 and ad 3.

46. *ST* II-II, q. 81, a. 5, ad 1: "The theological virtues faith, hope, and charity have an act in reference to God as their proper object, wherefore, by their command, they cause the act of religion, which performs certain deeds directed to God."

done out of due reverence for God.[47] There obtains a unique relationship between the theological virtue of charity and the infused moral virtue of religion. By way of charity, the Christian adheres to God "by a union of the spirit" (*ST* II-II, q. 82, a. 2, ad 1). For this reason, charity is the form of all the infused moral virtues, first and foremost the virtue of religion. But the relationship between charity and the infused virtue of religion goes even deeper: "It belongs immediately to charity that [the human being] should give himself to God, adhering to him by a union of the spirit; but it belongs immediately to religion, and, through the medium of religion, to charity which is the principle of religion, that [the human being] should give himself to God for certain works of Divine worship [*divini cultus*]" (*ST* II-II, q. 82, a. 2, ad 1). The person who adheres to God by a union of the spirit receives a supernatural principle or cause that issues immediately in the infused *habitus* of religion and orders that person immediately to acts of divine worship, *cultus divini*. In short, it is impossible for a person who adheres to God by a union of the spirit not to practice the virtue of religion. These works of divine worship arise from two principal interior operations facilitated by the infused *habitus* of religion.

Devotion is the first and is a special act of the will "to devote [oneself] to God so as to subject [oneself] wholly to God (*ST* II-II, q. 82, a. 1)."[48] Devotion applies the will to its proper act, namely, to refer all the other moral virtues to the service of God, who is the ultimate end. Devotion, the principal operation of the virtue of religion (that is, of actualizing the will's rectitude regarding what is due to God) ensures that the service of God constitutes the end or purpose of all

---

47. *ST* II-II, q. 81, a. 5. But how do the theological virtue of charity and the infused moral virtue of religion relate exactly? By way of charity, the Christian adheres to God by a union of the spirit (*ST* II-II, q. 82, a. 2, ad 1). And for this reason, charity informs all the infused moral virtues, also the virtue of religion; but here the relationship goes deeper. For "it belongs immediately to charity that [the human being] should give himself to God.... but it belongs immediately to religion (and through the medium of religion, to charity ...) that [the human being] should give himself to God for certain works of Divine worship" (*ST* II-II, q. 82, a. 2, ad 1).

48. *ST* II-II, q. 82, a. 1, ad 1: "Since devotion is an act of the will whereby [a human being] offers himself for the service of God Who is the last end, it follows that devotion prescribes the mode of human acts, whether they be acts of the will itself about things directed to the end, or acts of the other powers that are moved by the will."

the other acts of religion and, indeed, of all the other moral virtues.[49] The second principal operation of the virtue of religion is *prayer*, the surrendering of one's mind to God by presenting the mind to God and asking becoming things of God (*ST* II-II, q. 83, a. 1; a. 3, ad 3). Devotion and prayer are the interior constitutive acts of the infused virtue of religion, and among the two, devotion holds the position of primacy.[50] Exterior acts of adoration, sacrifice, oblation, vows, tithes, and others become proper acts of the infused virtue of religion only by way of their mediation through the interior acts of devotion and prayer. The infused virtue of religion is analogous to the theological virtue of charity in that, similar to the way charity unites all the other infused virtues with the last end (by being their form) and commands acts of all the other virtues, the infused virtue of religion unites all the other infused moral virtues by submitting their acts to the interior worship of God.

"RELIGION" REVISITED IN LIGHT OF THE VIRTUE OF RELIGION

After having completed the two interconnected tasks—showing that and why according to Aquinas the virtue of religion is indispensable for the attainment of one's subjective final end, beatitude, and making explicit the necessary entailment, namely that in the Thomist framework the virtue of religion is absolutely central for genuine human flourishing—we return now to the dominant contemporary uses of "religion." Each of these contemporary uses has its own complex reasons. As suggested in the above opening discussion of these uses, some of these reasons are to be found in the profound

---

49. *ST* II-II, q. 82, a. 1, ad 1: "The mover determines the manner or mode of action of the object it moves. The will moves the other powers of the soul to their actions, and because it is concerned with the end, the will also moves itself to the means which lead to the end. Hence, since devotion is an act of the will by which a man promptly offers himself to the service of God who is the last end, devotion determines the mode of human acts, whether they are actions of the will concerning the means to the end, or acts of the other powers moved by the will" (O'Rourke's translation).

50. As O'Rourke rightly stresses in his commentary: "As the first and principal act of religion, inward devotion must be in every religious act, otherwise it will not be a true act of religion at all, though it may have the external appearance" (*ST* II-II, qq. 80–91, 39:257).

problems connected with the self-understanding and self-constitution of modernity in general and of the modern subject in particular, especially in light of the modern anthropocentric turn. Other reasons are related to the complex phenomenon of the commodification of all lifeforms in a global capitalist system with a totalizing technological penetration and domination of human life. Others again are rooted in the complex development of diverse movements of religious reform and revolution in Europe and North America in the sixteenth and seventeenth centuries. Others may be found in the recent development of the academic discipline of "religious studies" (*Religionswissenschaft*) and others again in theological criticisms of this discipline and its methodologically imposed theological blinders. To ask what difference the virtue of religion would make to each one of these variegated uses and in the course of such a treatment to do justice to the interior complexity of each of them transcends the scope of this chapter. All I intend to do at this point is to indicate and adumbrate some of the directions of further constructive as well as critical thought about these diverse uses of "religion" that become possible when these uses are examined from the perspective of the virtue of religion. With the brevity and incompleteness of the following sketch, I hope to invite and indeed provoke a deeper and more searching theological investigation of how the recovery of the virtue of religion might complicate, transform, or even undo most of these contemporary uses of "religion."

Political Liberalism's Use of "Religion"

Recall that the specific moral excellence of the virtue of justice is to render "to everybody his [or her] due by a constant and perpetual will" (*ST* II-II, q. 58, a. 1). Hence, it is according to the very nature of the virtue of justice to transcend and to encompass both the public and the private spheres. All the operative virtues that are annexed to justice share this essential feature. The virtue of religion, rightly understood and practiced—which is the essential feature of virtue *simpliciter*—resists submission to the superimposition of a political disciplinary distinction that compromises the essence of the virtue itself. And what holds for the acquired virtue of religion holds even more so for the infused virtue of religion. While rooted in the person's soul in the interior acts of devotion and prayer, true *cultus* arises from there to take an ineluctably public, communal, and also a quasi-political form. Being directed to the highest good, the *summum bonum*, reverence of and honor to the first principle of the creation and government of things, the first truth and sovereign good—in short, the triune Lord—this virtue is only practiced authentically according to its nature when it is practiced in the political public such that the political public itself is rightly ordered to the first principle of the creation and government of things.

Now, to say the least, this is obviously not how contemporary democracies constitute themselves in the spirit of sovereign secularism. Banishing the practice of the virtue of religion from the political public is a constitutive element of their self-understanding. Of course, to force the virtue of religion into the purely private sphere is to force it to turn into its own counterfeit.[51] During his apostolic journey to the U.S. in September 2015, Pope Francis made the following pointed statement that pertains to the essentially public nature of the virtue of religion: "Religious freedom certainly means the right to worship God, individually and in community, as our consciences dictate. But *religious liberty, by its nature, transcends places of worship and the private sphere of individuals and families*. Because religion itself, the religious dimension, is not a subculture; it is part of the culture of every people and every nation."[52]

Not only does the virtue of religion suffer from the profoundly alienating imposition of its privatization, but also does the body politic suffer eventually. One of the foremost German legal philosophers of the second half of the twentieth century, Ernst-Wolfgang Böckenförde, argued famously—and persistently—that a truly just, and therefore free, democratic society lives from moral sources that

---

51. For an astute contemporary theological analysis of this pernicious dynamic, see Douglas Farrow, *Desiring a Better Country: Forays in Political Theology* (Montreal: McGill-Queens University Press, 2015).

52. Emphasis added. Pope Francis made this symbolically charged statement in his speech at a meeting for religious liberty with the Hispanic community and other immigrants at the Independence Mall in Philadelphia, September 26, 2015, available at vatican.va/content/francesco/en/speeches/2015/september/documents/papa-francesco_20150926_usa-liberta-religiosa.html.

transcend its scope, sources that secular liberalism *per se* cannot provide and replenish on its own terms, but on which a truly free and just society at the same time vitally depends.[53] These sources are fundamentally connected with and accessed by way of the public practice of the virtue of religion. And this practice of *religio*, according to Böckenförde, will be ideally and preferably Christian because it is nothing but the Christian understanding of the human being that is presupposed in the tenets and the program of genuine liberalism: the human being as created in the image of God and, therefore, endowed with an indelible dignity and an intrinsic orientation toward transcendence, an orientation expressed first and foremost in humanity's universal desire for knowledge and happiness and consequently in the public practice of the virtue of religion that gives honor and reverence to the first principle of the creation and government of things, the triune creator and Lord who is the fount of every good. By privatizing the virtue of religion, late-modern secularist democracies cut themselves off from the transpolitical moral and spiritual roots that fund the public ethos of their own citizens.[54] This development leads to the transformation of the citizen into the essentially private consumer of goods, the sovereign self in the order of consumption, for whom the public "secular discourse" is nothing else but the interminable negotiation of the competing interests of consumers, customers, and clients.

American Protestantism's Use of "Religion"

The virtue of religion undermines the modern American Evangelical and post-denominational dichotomization between inauthentic "organized religion" and authentic free individual faith and spirituality. For the proper practice of the infused virtue of religion does, as we have seen, entail an ordered relationship between, on the one hand, the deep interior submission of the will and mind to

---

53. Ernst-Wolfgang Böckenförde, *State, Society and Liberty: Studies in Political Theory and Constitutional Law*, trans. J. A. Underwood (New York: Berg, 1991).

54. The contraction of religion to private belief is already powerfully at play in post-Restoration England, e.g., in John Locke's *Four Letters on Toleration* (London: Ward, Lock, and Tyler, 1876). For a brief but astute discussion, see Pfau, *Minding the Modern*, 308–11.

God—a profound personal "spirituality," the end and purpose of which is nothing but holiness, the inclusion of everything into the ordered relationship with God (*ordo ad Deum*)—and, on the other hand, personal and communal practices that can only be facilitated and sustained by way of what some rather infelicitously choose to call "organized religion." Hence, the practice of the virtue of religion entails *necessarily* the full existential involvement of the person and, simultaneously, their communal, public, and institutional embodiments. The virtue of political justice and the politically organized body politic are correlative realities; analogously, the virtue of religion and the organized ecclesial body politic, the visible one, holy, catholic, and apostolic church, are correlative realities. Abolish the latter, and you will eventually lose the former. Yet together they form the Catholic religion, about which Pope Paul VI, in his address during the last general meeting of the Second Vatican Council on December 7, 1965, offers a characterization that completely transcends the familiar dichotomy between "organized religion" and authentic, free faith and spirituality:

> The Catholic religion ... in a certain sense ... is the life of mankind. It is so by the extremely precise and sublime interpretation that our religion gives of humanity (surely man by himself is a mystery to himself) and gives this interpretation in virtue of its knowledge of God: a knowledge of God is a prerequisite for a knowledge of man as he really is, in all his fullness; for proof of this let it suffice for now to recall the ardent expression of St. Catherine of Siena, "In your nature, Eternal God, I shall know my own." The Catholic religion is man's life because it determines life's nature and destiny; it gives life its real meaning, it establishes the supreme law of life and infuses it with that mysterious activity which we may say divinizes it.[55]

The Consumer-Capitalist Use of "Religion"

Because all moral excellence presupposes a discerning moral agency, the virtue of religion, when properly practiced, profoundly puts into question the dynamic of commodification characteristic of

---

55. Pope Paul VI, "Address during the Last General Meeting of the Second Vatican Council," December 7, 1965. For a lucid and profound introduction to the Catholic religion precisely along the lines of Pope Paul VI's characterization, see Thomas Joseph White, OP, *The Light of Christ: An Introduction to Catholicism* (Washington, D.C.: The Catholic University of America Press, 2017).

late-modern consumer capitalism and its concomitant lifestyle liberalism. The will's ordination to the supreme good, realized in the acts of the virtue of religion as commanded by the theological virtue of charity, constitutes an objective real relation of the human being to God. This real relation averts the subtle dynamic of religious estrangement that is the very heart of late capitalism's universal commodification that turns religion into just another consumable item enriching the lifestyle options of the putatively sovereign self.

The Religionswissenschaft Use of "Religion"

As has become sufficiently clear by now, the virtue of justice and all its practices are about *operations*, that is, about interior or exterior acts in relationship not to oneself (as the virtues of courage and temperance are), but rather in relationship to specific others. These operations are specified by their object that communicates itself to individual agents as they are embedded in their specific cultural-linguistic matrix of religious practices. The very constitution of the virtue of religion by its specific object thus problematizes the experiential-expressivist interpretation of "religion." The reason is the following: the *interior* formal constitution of the virtue of religion as moral excellence for a practitioner of religion and the *exterior* explanatory perspective of experiential-expressivism are mutually exclusive. Adopting the exterior explanatory perspective of experiential-expressivism means to understand the operations of the virtue of religion as rituals, customs, and disciplines that symbolically express some preconceptual and prelinguistic awareness of the numinous or sacred. According to this explanatory framework, there cannot exist a justice-like virtue of religion, for such a virtue would entail the purported existence and furthermore knowledge of some personal Other to whom honor and reverence are due. Practicing the virtue of religion, on the other hand, presupposes formally the existence and at least inchoate knowledge of such an Other, and that necessarily makes experiential-expressivism for such a practitioner a misguided, reductively nonreferential strategy of explanation. Hence, if experiential-expressivism—being a reductive explanatory strategy—were to be applied consistently to the virtue of religion, the latter would instan-

Preparation   289

taneously lose its intelligibility as a moral excellence. For justice, or a virtue close to justice, to be intelligible (let alone operative), it must formally presuppose the objective reality that specifies its acts.

The Use of "Religion" in Protestant Dialectical Theology

As has become sufficiently clear in the course of this chapter, the Barthian theological critique of "religion" does not apply to the virtue of religion in the way Thomas Aquinas conceives it primarily—namely in its proper Christian instantiation as an infused moral virtue. Recall, Barth takes religion to be a human phenomenon indicative of original sin. It is the ever recurring human attempt to manipulate, placate, and eventually control the living, free, and transcendent God. Yet according to Aquinas, human nature when healed and elevated by sanctifying grace is free from such a purportedly ever recurring sinful dynamic. The infused virtue of religion is a gift of grace that presupposes not only divine and justifying faith, but also the efficacious sacramental mediation of grace through the church's sacraments, especially baptism and the Eucharist. In short, there cannot exist any infused moral virtue of religion without the grace that flows from the head, the incarnate, crucified, and risen Lord, through the sacraments to the members of Christ's body, the church. The infused virtue of religion depends upon the capital grace that flows from Christ, the head of the body, the church, into the members of the body. The very Christological, sacramental, and ecclesiological rootedness of the infused virtue of religion and Barth's theological critique of "religion" are mutually exclusive. Barth's use of "religion" requires a permanent critique of religion in all shapes and forms that is funded by a sustained hermeneutics of suspicion in regard to Christianity and its manifold religious practices. Aquinas's understanding of religion as a virtue akin to the virtue of justice, on the contrary, allows for an encompassing positive hermeneutics of religion.

A Modern Theological Use of "Religion" Congruent with the Virtue of Religion

As has become clear in the course of these considerations, the virtue of religion can be defended against the Barthian critique of "religion" in its instantiation as an infused moral virtue, a virtue that is a direct consequence of sanctifying grace and the indwelling Holy Spirit. Yet it is also possible, on a more fundamental level, to defend the virtue of religion as a necessary constant of created human nature, a constant that, after the Fall, is enacted in weakened and variously compromised ways. Hence, the acquired virtue of religion is not simply a surd; rather, precisely in its imperfection, the virtue of religion remains a distinct moral excellence that reflects aspects of truth about the human condition *vis-à-vis* the creator.

One eminent Catholic thinker of the modern period who captures this insight well is John Henry Newman. Awareness of God, of the self, and of human need characterizes, according to his view, "natural religion." According to his semantics, natural religion stands in opposition, on the one hand, to civilized or artificial religion (the religion of liberalism) and, on the other hand, to revealed religion that culminates in Jesus Christ. Because of the Fall, natural religion in actual practice focuses on the dark side of the human predicament. Natural religion depicts the human being first and foremost in need of expiation in order to be reconciled to God. Hence, Newman takes atonement to be central to natural religion. Consequently, practices of sacrifice and prayer—fueled by a hope of deliverance from suffering and confidence in divine providence—are the most common traits of natural religion.[56] Newman's use of "religion" in his notion of natural religion amounts to possibly the best modern appreciation of what, on the one hand, is true and valid as a moral virtue in the acquired virtue of natural religion encountered in countless instantiations outside of the orbit of the special revelation that culminates in Christ and what, on the other hand, is the surpassing perfection of the virtue of religion—a *habitus* infused by sanctifying grace and formed by charity, the inchoative union with God. On the supposition of Newman's understanding of natural religion and of revealed religion—an understanding that, incidentally, is fully congruent with Aquinas's understanding of the acquired and the infused

---

56. John Henry Newman, "The Influence of Natural and Revealed Religion Respectively," in *Fifteen Sermons Preached before the University of Oxford between A.D. 1826 and 1843* (Notre Dame, Ind.: University of Notre Dame Press, 1997), 16–36, and his *An Essay in Aid of a Grammar of Assent*, 95–107 and 303–17.

virtues of religion—doing without religion is both *contra naturam* and *contra gratiam*, and consequently amounts to a uniquely modern margin of human existence, a margin made possible by the advent of the surpassing perfection of *religio* as instantiated in the human life and oblation on the cross of the incarnate Lord. Doing without religion becomes a possibility only after natural religion has been perfected by revealed religion. By spurning revealed religion, one necessarily also forgoes natural religion and is consequently left with doing without religion. Doing without religion constitutes the most elusive, and simultaneously the deepest, form of injustice the human being is capable of—injustice against God, the first principle of the creation and government of things, the triune creator and Lord.

Practicing this injustice of doing without religion is, of course, far from the often-announced end of religion. On the contrary, doing without religion introduces the ultimate counterfeit of *religio*, the last religion, ushered in silently but devastatingly in modern philosophy with the anthropocentric turn and the adoption of the principle of immanence.[57] The "last religion" is the counterfeit religion of the sovereign self, the erection of the quasi-divine self-will and its unquenchable desires for all imaginable semblances of true happiness. John Henry Newman characterized its central feature as infidelity. With remarkable prescience he states in his 1873 sermon "The Infidelity of the Future":

The special peril of the time before us is the spread of that plague of infidelity, that the Apostles and our Lord Himself have predicted as the worst calamity of the last times of the Church. And at least a shadow, a typical image of the last times is coming over the world. I do not mean to presume to say that this is the last time, but that it has had the evil prerogative of being like that more terrible season, when it is said that the elect themselves will be in danger of falling away.... Accordingly, you will find, certainly in the future, nay more, *even now, even now*, that the writers and thinkers of the day do not even believe there is a God. They do not believe either the *object*—a God personal, a Providence and a moral Governor; and secondly, what they *do*

---

57. See Fabro's unjustly neglected, but still utterly relevant, *God in Exile*. For the third edition of the Italian original and the first edition of Fabro's complete works, see Cornelio Fabro, *Introduzione all' ateismo moderno*, Opere Complete 21 (Segni: Editrice del Verbo Incarnato, 2013).

believe, viz., that there is some first cause or other, they do not believe with faith, absolutely, but as a probability.... Christianity has never yet had experience of a world simply irreligious.[58]

In 1883, only ten years after Newman delivered his all too clairvoyant homily, Friedrich Nietzsche published the first two parts of his *Thus Spoke Zarathustra: A Book for All and None*. Zarathustra personifies the spirit of infidelity and utters, as clearly as one could wish, the *credo* of this counterfeit *cultus* of the sovereign self: "But to reveal my entire heart to you, my friends: *if* there were gods, how could I stand not to be a god! *Therefore* there are no gods."[59]

It would be rash to dismiss the *credo* Nietzsche states through the mouth of Zarathustra as an all too radical departure from the genuine humanist secularism espoused by modern liberalism; for Nietzsche understood all too well that the worship (*cultus*) of the "last religion" is the worship of humanity (*cultus humanitatis*) instead of the worship of God (*cultus Dei*). And the worship of humanity arguably sits, of course, at the very heart of modern liberalism. Pope Paul VI, in his address during the last general meeting of the Second Vatican Council on December 7, 1965, expresses this point with all desirable clarity: "The Church of the council has been concerned ... with man—man as he really is today: living man, man all wrapped up in himself, man who makes himself not only the center of his every interest but dares to claim that he is the principle and explanation of all reality."[60]

---

58. "The Infidelity of the Future. Opening of St. Bernard's Seminary, 2nd October 1873," in *Faith and Prejudice and Other Unpublished Sermons of Cardinal Newman*, ed. The Birmingham Oratory (New York: Sheed and Ward, 1956), 117 and 124–25.

59. Zarathustra continues thus: "Even in knowing I feel only my will's lust to beget and to become; and if there is innocence in my knowledge, then this happens because the will to beget is in it. Away from God and gods this will lured me; what would there be to create, after all, if there were gods? But I am always driven anew to human beings by my ardent will to create; thus the hammer is driven toward the stone.... I want to perfect it, for a shadow came to me – the stillest and lightest of all things once came to me! The overman's beauty came to me as a shadow. Oh, my brothers! Of what concern to me anymore – are gods! – Thus spoke Zarathustra." Friedrich Nietzsche, *Thus Spoke Zarathustra*, ed. Adrian Del Caro and Robert B. Pippin, trans. Adrian Del Caro (Cambridge: Cambridge University Press, 2006), 65–67.

60. Pope Paul VI, "Address during the Last General Meeting of the Second Vatican Council," December 7, 1965, available at vatican.va.

While the *cultus* of the "last religion," the worship of humanity, culminating in the celebration and adoration of the self, sovereign beyond good and evil, is still approaching its apogee, Aquinas's account of the essential relationship between the attainment of beatitude and the practice of the virtue of religion makes plain that the *cultus* of the "last religion" compromises the rectitude of the will detrimentally and thereby thwarts the attainment of the ultimate end. Unsurprisingly, the modern counterfeit *cultus* directed to a counterfeit transcendence does not adduce to happiness, but rather to a world bereft of true transcendence and delivered over to the immanent frame's iron cage, the ideal breeding ground of spiritual sloth (*acedia*) and metaphysical boredom and hence the source of an extensive collective unhappiness in constant need of simultaneous anesthetization and titillation by entertainment, sex, or drugs and other "wellness" tactics—a very far cry from the noonday ecstasy of Nietzsche's *Übermensch*.[61]

CONCLUSION

It is nothing but the virtue of religion that actualizes the will's rectitude through acts of honor and reverence due to God. Minimally, doing without religion is a failure to do justice to the most fundamental and most essential relationship, that of the rational creature to the creator. Precisely because "it belongs to the dictate of natural reason that [the human being] should do something through reverence to God" (*ST* II-II, q. 81, a. 2, ad 3), doing without religion is a mode of existence contrary to the dictate of natural reason. And because the dictate of natural reason is always according to nature, doing without religion is against human nature (*contra naturam humanam*) and constitutes a unique margin of human existence.

For a baptized and confirmed Christian, acts of the virtue of religion commanded by charity are meritorious and thus contribute essentially to preparing the *viator*, the wayfarer, for attaining the ultimate end and perfect beatitude as *comprehensor*, as partaker in the

---

61. For a deeper consideration of *acedia* as the root cause of typically modern boredom, see chapter 8, pp. 350–58.

beatific vision. But for a baptized and confirmed Christian, due to neglect or indifference, not to practice the acts of the infused virtue of religion as established by divine and human law is a serious sin of omission, and to commit intentional acts of irreligion and irreverence is a grave sin of commission (*ST* II-II, q. 97, preamble; q. 122, a. 3). As the acts of religion are commanded by God—they fall under the precepts of justice and are expressed as revealed divine law in the second commandment of the Decalogue, where they make explicit a dictate of natural reason (*ST* II-II, q. 122, a. 3)—intentional acts of irreverence and irreligion cause persons who know the precept to lose friendship with God and do damage to the rectitude of their will and, consequently, err from the path to everlasting perfect beatitude. For a baptized and confirmed Christian, doing without religion is something contrary to God's grace (*contra gratiam Dei*) that in view of the supernatural ultimate end of eternal unitive beatitude constitutes a perilous placement at the periphery of human existence.[62]

"*Nel mezzo del cammin di loro vita si ritrovarono per una selva oscura, che la diritta via era smaritta.*"[63] Midway upon the journey of their lives, having wandered from the straight and true, and thus finding themselves lost in a dark and hard wood of indifference, irreverence, and irreligion, all of these persons—whether Christian or not—still desire happiness. They seek the universal good to which their will is directed by necessity, but with the rectitude of the will compromised, or even corrupted, they will not find what they crave even in fame, wealth, pleasure, power, a long life, and the accumulation of

---

62. Displaying indifference or even open contempt to the Lord's Day by neglecting the public worship of God, prayer, recollection, and resting in God and replacing it with the *cultus* of the "last religion" and its characteristic rituals, with wellness, sports, entertainment, and, of course, shopping, is the most widespread and widely accepted form of irreverence and irreligion practiced by baptized Christians in the West—supposing, of course, they do not belong to the working class of the new service industry that has to cater around the clock to the demands of the counterfeit *cultus*. To advance the objection that this phenomenon is merely the result of the around-the-clock work and consumption schedule of Western consumer societies run amok is to confuse the effect with the cause. Western modern capitalism is, to a large degree, the result of the replacement of the good life (to which the virtue of religion is central) with the "goods life" (to which the counterfeit virtues of acquisitiveness and self-indulgence are central). See Gregory, *Unintended Reformation*, especially chaps. 4–5.

63. "Midway in the journey of our life I found myself in a dark wood, for the straight way was lost" (Alighieri, *Inferno*, trans. Singleton, 2–3).

things. Because all of these are, at best, only aspects of the universal good, the persons possessing them still desire the universal good *in toto*. Short of attaining it, they will ultimately fail in their quest of finding perfect and everlasting beatitude.

Recall the syllogism from the introduction and its major premise: if humanity is ordained to the gratuitous supernatural final end of union with God, then the virtue of religion is indispensable for the attainment of this end. The systematic rereading of Aquinas has yielded a coherent, and arguably compelling, warrant for this premise. It has also afforded a Thomistic recapitulation of Pope Francis's identification of a religionless wasteland. In the practical order, where the mandate and challenge of a new evangelization is paramount, Pope Francis exemplifies in his own papal ministry a crucial insight of Aquinas's treatment of humanity's surpassing ultimate end: the subjective attainment of beatitude, fruition, is necessarily accompanied by joy. And insofar as the theological virtue of charity brings about an inchoative participation in the life of God, in the final attainment of everlasting beatitude, the Christian life, even in the midst of profound suffering, is one of deep joy, a joy that arises from the inchoative union with God in charity (*ST* II-II, q. 28, a. 1). That is why the deep joy of the saints attracts almost irresistibly. Hence, persons lost in the dark and hard wood of indifference, irreverence, and irreligion are best encountered with the joy that is one of the fruits of the Holy Spirit.[64] Encountering such joy might serve as the first impulse of desiring the happiness that blossoms in the existential center of faith—the life of charity, the inchoative friendship with God, the very beginning of eternal beatitude—and that moves us from the margin where both religion is eschewed and ignorance abounds. Becoming a *viator* presupposes receiving at least some knowledge through reason and through faith of the journey's destination—God.

Becoming a *viator*, a wayfarer—the universal ordination of all human beings in the extant order of divine providence—has one char-

---

64. Following the Vulgate, Catholic tradition as synthesized and interpreted by Aquinas lists twelve fruits of the Holy Spirit: charity, joy, peace, patience, kindness, goodness, generosity, gentleness, faithfulness, modesty, self-control, and chastity (see *ST* I-II, q. 70, a. 3, as well as *CCC* §1832).

acteristic, indeed one indispensable feature: the ready submission of the will and intellect to God. From these two interior acts, devotion and prayer, flow all other interior and exterior acts of the virtue of religion. Thus joyfully and devoutly, the *viator* says, "I incline my heart to perform thy statutes, forever, to the end" (Ps 119:112; RSV).

7

Perseverance on the Journey to Beatitude—Reclaiming Martyrdom
The Virtue of Courage

> The cause of all martyrdom is the truth of faith.
> —Thomas Aquinas, *ST* II-II, q. 124, a. 5

> *It is not the suffering but the cause that makes the martyr*, as Augustine says.... One suffers for Christ by suffering not only for the faith of Christ but for any just deed done for the love of Christ: *blessed are those who are persecuted for justice's sake* (Matt 5:10).
> —Thomas Aquinas, *Commentary on the Letter of Saint Paul to the Romans*[1]

> As long as the Gospel is preached in this world—and that means to the end of time—the Church will also have martyrs.... Certainly, there may be times in which martyrs are fewer and times in which they are more; but to say that at certain times there are no martyrs at all would be to deny the Church's existence at that time.
> —Erik Peterson, "Witness to the Truth"[2]

---

1. *In Rom.* VIII, lect. 7. Translation from Thomas Aquinas, *Commentary on the Letter of Saint Paul to the Romans*, ed. J. Mortensen and E. Alarcón, trans. F. R. Larcher, OP, Latin/English Edition of the Works of St. Thomas Aquinas 37 (Lander, Wyo.: The Aquinas Institute for the Study of Sacred Doctrine, 2012), 241.

2. Erik Peterson, "Witness to the Truth," in *Theological Tractates*, ed. and trans. Michael J. Hollerich (Stanford, Calif.: Stanford University Press, 2011), 156–57.

In this chapter I shall address one characteristic temptation that the *viator* is faced with on the journey to beatitude—to abandon or to betray the revealed truth, accepted in divine faith, either under psychological pressure, threat of physical violence, or simply by the omission of due witness because of fear. More importantly, however, I shall consider the virtue that meets this temptation, overcomes fear of persecution and death, and keeps the *viator* ordered to the ultimate end: the virtue of courage and its supreme act, martyrdom.

According to the Gospel of John, Christ, the incarnate Logos, through whom all things were made (Jn 1:3) spoke thus of himself: "I am the way, and the truth, and the life; no one comes to the Father but by me" (Jn 14:6; RSV). His coming was announced by his precursor, John the Baptist, whose mission was to testify: "He came for testimony [ματυρία], to bear witness [ματυρειν] to the light, that all might believe [πιστευειν] through him" (Jn 1:7; RSV).

Testifying (ματυρειν) to Christ, who is the truth, is the principal activity of all whom Christ calls to be his friends (Jn 15:15) and who carry out the love of this friendship—charity—by doing what he commands (Jn 14:15, 23). As the Spirit of truth will bear witness to Christ, so will the disciples bear witness, filled with the Spirit of truth (Jn 15:26). Even in the earliest apostolic tradition, the Greek verb ματυρειν takes on the connotation, not only of testifying, but also of being a witness to the point of shedding one's own blood (*usque ad sanguinem*), in short, to the point of being martyred. After Pentecost, for the apostles and eventually for the whole "Church of God, the pillar and bulwark of the truth" (1 Tm 3:15; RSV), "fighting the good fight of the faith" (1 Tm 6:12; RSV) came to mean first and foremost to testify to Christ, who is the truth. For most, if not all of the apostles, and for innumerable faithful after them, such testifying led and continues to lead to a deeper imitation of Christ who, in Aquinas's words, "offered the example for all, to die for the truth."[3]

---

3. *Sent.* IV, d. 7, q. 3, a. 2, q.c. 1, arg. 2: "Christ gave to all the example of dying for the truth." See also the following statements from various other works: "there are some who, although they do not fear death, abhor an abject death. And even to the contempt of such a death did our Lord inspire men by the example of His death." SCG IV.55.20, found in Thomas Aquinas, *Summa contra Gentiles, Book Four: Salvation*, trans. Charles O'Neil (Notre Dame, Ind.: University of Notre Dame Press, 1975), 243. "In order that Christ's death might not only be the price of the redemption but also an example of

Christ's exemplary death was preceded by the martyrdom of St. John the Baptist and was soon to be followed by the martyrdoms of St. Stephen and St. James.[4] Since then martyrdom has been regarded by the Catholic church as a unique perfection of charity in the imitation of Christ, testifying to the truth to the point of shedding one's own blood (*usque ad sanguinem*).

On December 3, 2012, the Catholic layman Devasahayam Pillai was beatified in Nagercoil, in the southern state of Tamil Nadu, India.[5] Belonging to an upper-caste family, Bl. Pillai had encountered the Christian faith while a soldier. In 1745, at the age of thirty-three, he was baptized and received the name Devasahayam, a Tamil rendering of the biblical name Lazar, "God has helped." In 1752, after enduring imprisonment and brutal torture for three long years, Bl. Pillai was executed for refusing to renounce the Catholic faith. The Catholic church recognized Devasahayam Pillai as having undergone death voluntarily at the hands of those who acted in hatred of the faith (*in odium fidei*).

On May 25, 2013, Fr. Giuseppe Puglisi was beatified in Palermo, Sicily.[6] In 1993, on his fifty-sixth birthday, he had been assassinated by Mafia killers. The Catholic church acknowledged Bl. Giuseppe Puglisi to have died a martyr. But he did not die because his murderers hated the Catholic faith and thus persecuted the faithful, and especially prelates and priests.[7] Rather, he was murdered because of

---

virtue, namely in order that men should not fear to die for the truth." *Quod.* II, q. 1, a. 2; found in Thomas Aquinas, *Quodlibetal Questions 1 and 2*, trans. Sandra Edwards (Toronto: Pontifical Institute of Mediaeval Studies, 1983), 76. "But the good shepherd goes before them by example.... And Christ does go before them: for he was the first to die for the teaching of the truth ... and he went before all into everlasting life." *Lectura super Ioannem* 10, 4, lect. 1 (Marietti, no. 1374); found in Thomas Aquinas, *Commentary on the Gospel of John, Part II*, trans. James A. Weisheipl and Fabian R. Larcher (Petersham: St. Bede's Publications, 1980), 116–17.

4. See St. John Paul II, *Veritatis Splendor*, Encyclical Letter, August 6, 1993, par. 91, available at vatican.va.

5. See Anto Akkara, "Newly Beatified Indian Lay Martyr Praised for Refusing to Reject Faith," *Catholic News Service*, December 4, 2012, available at catholicnew.com/data/stories/cns/1205075.htm.

6. John L. Allen, Jr., "Don Pino: The Most Important Beatification of the Early 21st Century," *National Catholic Reporter*, May 10, 2013, available at ncronline.org/blogs/all things-catholic/don-pino-most-important-beatification-early–21st-century.

7. This kind of martyrdom *pro fide* would have been typical during the persecutions

his unequivocal witness as a parish priest to truth and justice. In his local context in Palermo, this meant not only avoiding any lie and secrecy about the activities of the Mafia but also actively giving witness to truth and justice in order to protect persons, especially teenagers and young adults, from the Mafia's pernicious influence. The Catholic church recognized Fr. Puglisi as having died at the hands of those who acted in hatred of virtue and truth (*in odium virtutis et veritatis*).

How does the criterion of martyrdom for the sake of virtue and truth (*pro virtute et veritate*) relate to what in recent centuries has been the traditional criterion of martyrdom for the faith (*pro fide*)? Does the criterion of martyrdom because of the hatred of virtue and truth replace, expand, or develop the traditional criterion of martyrdom because of the hatred of the faith? To put the question in paradigmatic biblical terms: how does the martyrdom of John the Baptist, who, as the Roman Missal puts it, "died a Martyr for truth and justice"[8]—because he denounced Herod's living in open contempt of the divine law (Mk 6:18)—relate to the martyrdoms of Stephen the Deacon and James the Apostle, who were killed because they publicly testified to Christ (Acts 6:8–7:60; 12:1–2)?

In this chapter, I wish to display the contemporary relevance of Thomas Aquinas's teaching on martyrdom. His careful construal of the act of martyrdom gives rise to a nuanced notion of martyrdom, a notion that affords a theologically sound integration of the criterion of undergoing death voluntarily at the hands of those who act in hatred of virtue and truth (*in odium virtutis et veritatis*) into the paradigmatic criterion of undergoing death voluntarily at the hands of those who act in hatred of the faith (*in odium fidei*).[9]

---

in the first Christian centuries under the pagan *Pax Romana* or—to pick just two among many modern instances—in Portugal after the socialist revolution in 1910 or during the Spanish Civil War. It may be noted that on October 13, 2013, on the ninety-sixth anniversary of the miracle of the sun at Fatima, Pope Francis not only solemnly consecrated the whole world to the Immaculate Heart of the Blessed Virgin and Mother of God but also beatified five hundred persons who were martyred in hatred of the faith (*in odium fidei*) during the Spanish Civil War.

8. Collect of the Mass on the Memorial of the Passion of St. John the Baptist, Martyr, August 29, Daily Roman Missal, ed. James Socias, 7th ed. (Woodridge, Ill.: Midwest Theological Forum, 2012), 1918.

9. For the most recent comprehensive study of Aquinas's account of martyrdom

I will argue that the magisterial tradition has affirmed Aquinas's argument while circumscribing it and making it more precise and, furthermore, that recent magisterial teaching has affirmed this integral notion of martyrdom. In the conclusion, guided by Aquinas's analysis, I will offer some tentative reflections on testifying to the truth to the point of shedding one's own blood (*usque ad sanguinem*) in contemporary Western secular societies, where in the twentieth and twenty-first centuries being killed *in odium virtutis et veritatis* has become a more frequent occurrence—a situation noticeably different from that of Africa and Asia, where martyrdom *in odium fidei* is dramatically increasing in frequency.[10]

THOMAS AQUINAS ON MARTYRDOM

The Cardinal Virtues

Aquinas defines martyrdom as the principal act of the virtue of fortitude (*fortitudo*). In order fully to appreciate everything this definition entails, it will be useful to attend to the virtue of fortitude, one

---

in relation to his Christology and his virtue ethics, see Patrick M. Clark, *Perfection in Death: The Christological Dimension of Courage in Aquinas* (Washington, D.C.: The Catholic University of America Press, 2015), and for a profound theological meditation on martyrdom, see Servais Pinckaers, OP, *The Spirituality of Martyrdom: To the Limits of Love*, trans. Patrick M. Clark (Washington, D.C.: The Catholic University of America Press, 2016).

10. The following reflections presuppose the central distinction between inquiring theologically into the nature of martyrdom on the one hand and, on the other hand, establishing canonically the indispensable criteria for demonstrating a case of authentic martyrdom. The latter was undertaken exhaustively by Pope Benedict XIV (then Cardinal Prosper Lambertini) in the third volume of *De servorum Dei beatificatione et beatorum canonizatione* (Rome, 1748). Cardinal Lambertini wrote this massive work in 1734–38 after having overseen as Promoter of Faith all canonization processes from 1708 to 1727 under Popes Clement XI, Innocent XIII, and Benedict XIII. In 2006, Benedict XVI said of him: "My Predecessor Benedict XIV, rightly considered 'the master of the Causes of Saints' deserves a grateful mention" ("Letter of His Holiness Benedict XVI to the Participants of the Plenary Session of the Congregation for the Causes of Saints," April 24, 2006, available at vatican.va). The former, as I will demonstrate, was pursued in an exemplary way by Aquinas in his *Summa Theologiae*. While the two inquiries belong together like two sides of a coin, I will only pursue the question of the inner theological constitution of testifying to the truth to the point of shedding one's own blood (*usque ad sanguinem*), and thus pursue the question of what is proper to the theological notion of martyrdom, but will not discuss the canonical criteria for its demonstration—with one important exception that is of relevance for Aquinas's line of theological argumentation.

of the four cardinal virtues. A "cardinal" or principal virtue is one on which other virtues depend or "hang" just as a door depends or hangs on a hinge (*cardo*).[11] The cardinal virtues have a special claim to that which is characteristic of all the virtues, and that is first and foremost to act steadfastly (*firmiter operari*).[12] Among the four cardinal virtues there is a distinct hierarchy. Cognizance of this hierarchy is indispensable for a proper understanding of fortitude's principal act in relationship to the other cardinal virtues and in relationship to the theological virtues of faith, hope, and charity. The hierarchy of virtues arises from two principles: first, the better a virtue is, the higher it is (*ST* II-II, q. 123, a. 12); second, good in human acts depends on these acts being regulated by the due rule (*debita regula*). From this latter principle follows another, namely, that human virtue which is a principle of good acts must consist in attaining the due rule of human acts. There are two such rules, one governing the other. The first is God and the second is reason regulated by God (*ST* II-II, q. 23, aa. 3 and 6). The infused theological virtues, whose object is God, and the infused moral virtues, which are ordered to God, directly attain the first rule, God, while the acquired intellectual and the moral virtues only attain the second rule, human rea-

---

11. Aquinas offers a detailed explanation in his *De virt.*, q. un., a. 12, ad 24 (see also *De virtutibus cardinalibus*, q. un., a. 1): "A virtue is called 'cardinal,' i.e. fundamental, because other virtues depend upon it as a door does on a hinge [*cardo*]. And since a door is an entrance to a house, the *theological* virtues do not possess the character of cardinal virtues, since they are concerned with the ultimate end, and there is no way to move from the ultimate end and enter anything else. It suits the theological virtues that the other virtues rest on them as a solid base.... Similarly, the *intellectual* virtues are not called 'cardinal,' because some of them complete us for the *contemplative* life, for example, wisdom, knowledge, and intelligence. That life, though, is an end, and therefore does not have the character of a door. (The *active* life, by contrast, for which the *moral* virtues complete us, is like a door to the contemplative life.) *Skill* does not have virtues that are dependent upon it, and therefore cannot be called 'cardinal.' However, *practical wisdom*, which gives guidance in the active life, is counted among the cardinal virtues." Aquinas, *Disputed Questions on the Virtues*, 92.

12. "Fortitude above all lays claim to praise for steadfastness. Because he that stands firm is so much the more praised, as he is more strongly impelled to fall or recede. Now, man is impelled to recede from that which is in accordance with reason, both by the pleasing good and the displeasing evil. But bodily pain impels him more strongly than pleasure.... And among the pains of the mind and dangers those are mostly feared which lead to death, and it is against them that the brave man stands firm. Therefore fortitude is a cardinal virtue" (*ST* II-II, q. 123, a. 11).

son. Among the theological virtues, that virtue ranks highest which most attains God—charity. Among the cardinal virtues, that virtue ranks highest which most attains human reason. As the *habitus* that perfects reason is prudence, it is the first and highest in the order of cardinal virtues.[13] The virtue of justice realizes this good of reason among human beings, for it is the nature of justice "to establish the order of reason in all human affairs." Fortitude and temperance safeguard this good by moderating the acts of the sense appetite, the passions, lest human beings be drawn away from the good of reason by the fear of bodily pain and death or by the attraction of sensual pleasure. Because the fear of danger and death has the greatest power to withdraw a person from the good of reason, fortitude ranks above temperance, which moderates or withholds the appetite from sensual pleasure. And so Aquinas concludes: "To be a thing essentially ranks before effecting it, and the latter ranks before safeguarding it by removing obstacles thereto. Wherefore among the cardinal virtues, prudence ranks first, justice second, fortitude third, temperance fourth, and after these the other virtues" (*ST* II-II, q. 123, a. 12).

The Cardinal Virtue of Fortitude

Unlike patience (*ST* II-II, q. 136) and perseverance (*ST* II-II, q. 137), which are potential parts annexed to fortitude as secondary to the principal virtue, "fortitude ... is about the greatest dangers wherein one must proceed with caution" (*ST* II-II, q. 140, a. 2, ad 3). Hence, the cardinal virtue of fortitude is about the danger of death (*ST* II-II, q. 23, a. 4), and the principal act of fortitude is endurance, that is, the strength to continue to pursue the good of reason as specified by prudence even under the threat of death, an endurance that moderates fear and curbs daring (a. 3). The danger of death is faced primarily in combat, but also in other situations:

> A brave man behaves well in face of danger of any other kind of death; especially since man may be in danger of any kind of death on account of virtue: thus may a man not fail to attend on a sick friend through fear of deadly infection, or not refuse to undertake a journey with some godly object in

---

13. On the absolute centrality of prudence for the moral life, see the instructive discussion in Romanus Cessario, OP, *The Moral Virtues and Theological Ethics*, 2nd ed. (Notre Dame, Ind.: University of Notre Dame Press, 2009), 72–93.

view [*ad aliquod pium negotium prosequendum*] through fear of shipwreck or robbers. (*ST* II-II, q. 123, a. 5)

The supreme test of spiritual endurance finally is visited upon the martyr: "Martyrs face the fight that is waged against their own person, and this for the sake of the sovereign good [*summum bonum*] which is God; wherefore their fortitude is praised above all. Nor is it outside the genus of fortitude that regards warlike actions, for which reason they are said to have been *valiant in battle* [*fortes facti in bello*] [Heb 11:34]" (*ST* II-II, q. 123, a. 5, ad 1).[14]

Fortitude may subsist in the subject as an acquired *habitus*, but also as an analogous *habitus*, infused together with the theological virtue of charity (*ST* I-II, q. 65, a. 3).[15] While the acquired cardinal virtue of fortitude is directed to the common good, the infused virtue of fortitude is directed to the supernatural final end, the enjoyment of God, an end that inchoately engages the faithful already by way of the theological virtues of faith, hope, and charity.[16] The ac-

---

14. In this essential order of the cardinal virtues, fortitude comes to stand in the position close to the lowest, least important one. In the concrete interplay of the cardinal virtues, however—that is, in the order of operation—there obtains an all-important feedback loop. For the habits of moral virtue correct the sense appetites, and because of these habits we desire right ends that, when aided by prudence, allow us to make good judgments. In other words, the proper operation of prudence presupposes proper habituation in justice, courage, and temperance (*ST* II-II, q. 47, a. 13, ad 2; *ST* I-II, q. 58, a. 5). Consequently, what comes last in the essential order of the cardinal virtues comes first in their order of operation. Inordinate fear weakens and obstructs the virtue of justice and, most detrimentally, the proper operation of prudence. Without the virtue of fortitude there simply is neither true and perfect prudence nor true and perfect justice. Impaired prudence issues in a tangibly hampered moral life and consequently in diminished human flourishing.

15. Under the gift of fortitude, Aquinas observes: "Charity is the root of all the virtues and gifts" (*ST* II-II, q. 139, a. 2, ad 2). On the complex and highly controversial question of how acquired and infused moral virtues cooperate according to Aquinas, see the recent extensive and penetrating study by Christoph, "Justice as an Infused Virtue." Regarding the consequences, an act of infused virtue implies for acquired virtue as a *habitus*, he states: "Every act of an infused virtue contains per se the perfection of its natural counterpart, and therefore the supernatural act itself works for the development of a positive disposition for good deeds according to the rule of reason. This can be the case although the act in itself is of a higher order (sc. supernatural)" (213).

16. See also *De virt.*, q. un., a. 10. Lee Yearly offers a helpful summary of the three parts that, according to Aquinas, a virtue can have: "First are the qualities, the component parts, that help shape a single virtue's action; for example, memory and foresight in prudence. Second are those distinctive virtues, allied virtues, that share the essential

quired virtue of fortitude is essentially civic fortitude (*fortitudo civilis*) which strengthens a person's mind in matters of human justice, while the gratuitously infused virtue of fortitude (*fortitudo gratuita*) strengthens a person's soul in the good of divine justice (*iustitia Dei*).[17]

Civic fortitude is a type of the acquired *habitus* of fortitude. Under the condition of human nature wounded by sin (*in statu naturae corruptae*), the acquired cardinal virtues cannot reach the ideal of perfect virtue (*ST* I-II, q. 109, a. 2). However, because civic fortitude is directed to the welfare of the state (*conservatio civitatis*), it is a true, albeit imperfect virtue—imperfect, that is, unless it is referred by charity to the final end and perfect good, the enjoyment of God (*ST* II-II, q. 23, a. 7), whereby it becomes a true virtue *simpliciter*.[18] (The necessary precondition for reaching this final end is of course to be justified by God through faith in Jesus Christ by way of sanctifying grace.) This matter will be of considerable significance later. For, as we will see, in the case of the martyr who "gave his life in witness to truth and justice,"[19] acts of civic fortitude—guided by right reason and directed to the welfare of the *res publica*—are referred by charity to God such that they fall under the rule of the measure of the divine law in regard to the supernatural final end.[20] Consequently, such acts of civic

---

characteristic of the primary virtue but fail to express it fully, even if they may express other qualities of the primary virtue more fully than it does; for example, the wit to judge when exceptions to rules are needed (*gnome*). Third are those separable and substantially different activities of virtue, the types of a virtue, that appear when the virtue operates in distinct spheres of life; for example, military and political prudence." Lee H. Yearly, *Mencius and Aquinas: Theories of Virtue and Conceptions of Courage* (Albany: State University of New York Press, 1990), 184.

17. "Just as civic fortitude [*fortitudo civilis*] strengthens a man's mind in human justice [*iustitia humana*], for the safeguarding of which he braves the danger of death, so gratuitous fortitude [*fortitudo gratuita*] strengthens man's soul in the good of *Divine justice* [*iustitia Dei*], which is through faith in Christ Jesus, according to Rom 3:22" (*ST* II-II, q. 124, a. 2, ad 1).

18. *ST* II-II, q. 23, a. 6: "Charity attains God Himself that it may rest in Him, but not that something may accrue to us from Him." See also a. 7: "Accordingly it is evident that simply true virtue [*virtus vera simpliciter*] is that which is directed to man's principal good; thus also the Philosopher says (*Phys.* VII, text 17) that *virtue is the disposition of a perfect thing to that which is best*: and in this way no true virtue is possible without charity."

19. *Veritatis Splendor*, par. 91.

20. In the fully matured theology of his later years, Thomas Aquinas is adamant

fortitude referred by charity to God do become formally congruent with acts of infused fortitude that are always intrinsically informed by charity.[21] Referred by charity to God, such acts of fortitude are guided by right reason that is illumined by divine faith. As we will see shortly, divine faith illuminating the intellect is the final cause that enables charity to command such acts of fortitude and thereby refer them to God. For both the acquired and the infused virtue of fortitude, the principal act is endurance. In the case of the infused virtue of fortitude, when this principal act is brought to its term in the voluntary endurance of death *pro fidei veritate*, it constitutes martyrdom in its perfect form (*ST* II-II, q. 124, a. 4).

In the next section, I will show that, according to Aquinas, when an act that may be originally one of civic fortitude is referred by charity to God (the ultimate end) as a witness to the divine law, a witness endured even in the face of the danger of death and indeed endured while being put to death, such an act does become formally congruent with the act of martyrdom characteristic of the infused virtue of fortitude. Markus Christoph formulates lucidly the principle that accounts for this dynamic: "The graced agent is directed to supernatural union with God by charity and the infused virtues, and this new orientation becomes the first principle of all of his acts. Consequently, if such a person fulfills any virtuous deed that is determined superficially by natural standards, it will finally be directed to that supernatural end, i.e. it will be always a supernatural act since every moral act is measured in respect to the final end."[22]

---

about the fact that for the person who has the theological virtue of charity there do not exist any acts of natural acquired virtue (of true, but not perfect virtue) that if not referred to God by charity might remain somehow neutral, that is, might qualify as acts that are neither meritorious nor blameworthy. According to Aquinas, this is emphatically not the case, as he states in *De malo*, q. 2, a. 5, ad 7: "Not every act, even considered individually, is meritorious or demeritorious, although every act is good or evil. And I say this on behalf of those without charity, of those who cannot merit. But for those with charity, every act is meritorious or demeritorious." Thomas Aquinas, *On Evil*, ed. Brian Davies, trans. Richard Regan (Oxford: Oxford University Press, 2003), 113.

21. Conversely, as Christoph rightly points out, "the formal object of acquired virtue is inclusively present in infused virtue, granted that the object of the natural virtue is elevated to conform to the divine rule" ("Justice as an Infused Virtue in the *Secunda Secundae*," 211).

22. Ibid., 213.

The Principal Act of Fortitude—Martyrdom

It is imperative not to pass too quickly over the fundamental point Aquinas makes: martyrdom is the principal act of fortitude. What does this mean? Fortitude and temperance safeguard and support the human being in the good of reason. What right reason has specified, these two virtues *safeguard* from attacks, lures, or oppositions of the antecedent acts of the sense appetites and *support* with proper consequent acts of the sense appetites. The moral virtues fortitude and temperance thus align the passions to the order of right reason and thereby help secure the attainment of the moral good. Passions that are principally to be cultivated are passions consequent upon the judgment of reason, while passions that are principally to be curbed—or transformed into consequent passions—are passions antecedent to the judgment of reason. Passions consequent to the judgment of reason can come about and increase the goodness of an action in two ways, as Aquinas observes:

> First, by way of redundance: because ... when the higher part of the soul is intensely moved to anything, the lower part also follows that movement; and thus the passion that results in consequence, in the sensitive appetite, is a sign of the intensity of the will, and so indicates greater moral goodness.— Secondly, by way of choice; when ... [a person], by the judgment of his reason, chooses to be affected by a passion in order to work more promptly with the co-operation of the sensitive appetite. And thus a passion of the soul increases the goodness of an action. (*ST* I-II, q. 24, a. 3, ad 1)

The good of reason has an object—truth—and an effect—justice (*ST* II-II, q. 124, a. 1). The principle "action follows being" (*operari sequitur esse*) determines the relationship between the object and the effect of reason, for "it belongs to justice to establish the order of reason in all human affairs" (*ST* II-II, q. 123, a. 12).[23] To establish the order of reason in all human affairs is first and foremost to

---

23. *ST* I-II, q. 31, a. 5: "The intellect penetrates to the essence [of a thing]; for the object of the intellect is *what a thing is*" (Intellectus penetrat usque ad rei essentiam; obiectum enim intellectus est "quod quid est"). *De ver.*, q. 23, a. 6: "The will does not have the character of the first rule; it is rather a rule which has a rule, for it is directed by reason and the intellect. This is true not only in us but also in God, although in us the will is really distinct from the intellect" (*Truth*, 3:119).

acknowledge the true order of ends and subsequently to desire that order of ends rightly. The first pertains to prudence, the second pertains to justice.[24] The cardinal virtue of justice includes as one of its potential parts the virtue of truthfulness (*veracitas*) (*ST* II-II, q. 109). Truthfulness pertains to the moral debt of justice "insofar as, out of equity, one [person] owes another a manifestation of the truth" (*ST* II-II, q. 109, a. 3). Under the condition of human nature wounded by sin (*in statu naturae corruptae*), the virtues of truthfulness and justice are resisted by the mendacious and the unjust. Aquinas states an all-too-familiar fact: "On account of justice which he pursues, and also on account of other good deeds, [a person] encounters mortal adversaries" (*ST* II-II, q. 123, a. 11, ad 3).

Endurance is the principal act of the virtue of fortitude and martyrdom, endurance under the assault of persecution until death, and is the perfection of the principal act of the infused virtue of fortitude, which—being always already informed by charity and sustained by infused patience and perseverance—is intrinsically referred to love of God and neighbor. "Martyrdom consists essentially in standing firmly to truth and justice against the assaults of persecution" (*ST* II-II, q. 124, a. 1).

Aquinas argues that martyrdom is specifically an act of the virtue of fortitude.[25] In this context he makes explicit that the truth in which the martyr stands firm is the truth of faith, which is nothing but the first truth (*prima veritas*), faith's object.[26] The martyr does

---

24. *ST* I-II, q. 19, a. 3, ad 1: "The good considered as such, i.e., as appetible, pertains to the will before pertaining to the reason. But considered as true it pertains to the reason, before, under the aspect of goodness, pertaining to the will: because the will cannot desire a good that is not previously apprehended by reason."

25. *ST* II-II, q. 124, a. 2: "It belongs to fortitude to strengthen [a person] in the good of virtue, especially against dangers, and chiefly against dangers of death, and most of all against those that occur in battle. Now it is evident that in martyrdom [a person] is firmly strengthened in the good of virtue, since he cleaves to faith and justice notwithstanding the threatening danger of death, the imminence of which is moreover due to a kind of particular contest with his persecutors.... Wherefore it is evident that martyrdom is an act of fortitude; for which reason the Church reads in the office of Martyrs: They 'became valiant in battle' [Heb 11:34]." Proper of the Saints, January 20, Saints Fabian and Sebastian, Martyrs, *The Saint Dominic Missal*, Latin-English (New York: Saint Dominic Missal, 1959), 784.

26. *De ver.*, q. 14, a. 8, ad 3: "First truth, in so far as it appears in its proper form, is the object of the vision of heaven. But, in so far as it does not appear, it is the object of

not abandon faith and justice despite the imminent dangers of death (*fidem et iustitiam not deserit propter imminentia pericula mortis*), an imminence due to a unique contest with his persecutors (*quae etiam in quodam certamine particulari a persecutoribus immanent*). What is at stake in this contest for the persecuted faithful is the unshatterable unity of the interior act of faith and the exterior act of confession. In the exterior act of confession, the truth of the faith becomes an act of the virtue of truthfulness (*veracitas*). Aquinas does not hold that the exterior verbal confession of the faith is a constant requirement for every one of the faithful in virtually all possible circumstances—on the contrary. However, when the faith itself is attacked by unbelievers or when the honor of God and the good of the neighbor are at stake, the interior act of faith may not be separated from the exterior act of confession. In such situations, the simplicity of truthfulness (*veracitas*) requires the identity of the latter and the former: "Simplicity is so called from its opposition to duplicity, whereby, to wit, a [person] shows one thing outwardly while having another in his heart: so that simplicity pertains to this virtue. And it rectifies the intention, not indeed directly (since this belongs to every virtue), but by excluding duplicity, whereby a [person] pretends one thing and intends another" (*ST* II-II, q. 109, a. 2, ad 4).

Aquinas offers three specifications of the kinds of instances when the exterior verbal confession of the faith is due. First, "the end of faith, even as of the other virtues, must be referred to the end of charity, which is the love of God and our neighbor. Consequently when God's honor and our neighbor's good demand, [a person] should not be contented with being united by faith to God's truth, but ought to confess his faith outwardly" (*ST* II-II, q. 3, a. 2, ad 1). Second, "in cases of necessity where faith is in danger, everyone is bound to proclaim his faith to others, either to give good example and encouragement to the rest of the faithful, or to check the attacks of unbelievers" (ad 2). Third, "if there is hope of profit to the faith or if there be urgency, a [person] should disregard the disturbance of unbelievers, and confess his faith in public" (ad 3). Illuminated by

---

faith. So, although the object of both acts is the same thing in reality, it differs in intelligible aspect. The object thus formally different makes the species of the act different" (*Truth*, 2:245).

faith, informed by charity, and guided by a well-formed conscience, right reason enables the faithful to recognize the situations when these specifications obtain and when, consequently, the interior act of faith must be perfected by the exterior act of confession.

Common to each of these three specifications is the centrality of charity. The end of faith and of the other virtues must be referred to the end of charity, the enjoyment of God in friendship with God that includes the love of neighbor for the sake of God's love for the neighbor. What is referred to the end of charity can only be referred to that end by charity itself. That is, it may be an act elicited by acquired moral virtue or by the analogous gratuitously infused moral virtue; in both cases, charity commands the act of the moral virtue.[27] When such an act is referred to God by charity, the act becomes informed by charity so that a formal congruence now obtains between this act and an act elicited by the analogous gratuitously infused moral virtue that is intrinsically informed by charity.[28] Hence, the chief motive cause of martyrdom is charity:

> Charity inclines one to the act of martyrdom, as its first and chief motive cause, being the virtue commanding it, whereas fortitude inclines thereto as being its proper motive cause, being the virtue that elicits it. Hence martyrdom is an act of charity as commanding, and of fortitude as eliciting. For this reason also it manifests both virtues. It is due to charity that it is meritorious, like any other act of virtue: and for this reason it avails not without charity. (*ST* II-II, q. 124, a. 2, ad 2)

On the basis of Christ's words in John 15:13, that "greater love has no man than this, that a man lay down his life for his friends" (RSV),

---

27. *ST* II-II, q. 23, a. 8: "In morals the form of an act is taken chiefly from the end. The reason of this is that the principle of moral acts is the will, whose object and form, so to speak, are the end. Now the form of an act always follows from a form of the agent. Consequently, in morals, that which gives an act its order to the end, must needs give the act its form. Now it is evident ... that it is charity which directs the acts of all other virtues to the last end, and which, consequently, also gives the form to all other acts of virtue: and it is precisely in this sense that charity is called the form of the virtues, for these are called virtues in relation to 'informed' acts." See also ad 3: "Charity is said to be the end of other virtues, because it directs all other virtues to its own end. And since a mother is one who conceives within herself and by another, charity is called the mother of the other virtues, because, by commanding them, it conceives the acts of the other virtues, by the desire of the last end."

28. See *De virt.*, q. un., a. 10.

Aquinas regards martyrdom as the strongest proof of the perfection of charity.[29] He confirms this point in the following article. The perfect notion of martyrdom is *usque ad sanguinem*, the act of endurance that entails giving up voluntarily what is most difficult for human beings to part with because it is the recipient of all present good—the body. Consequently, the perfect notion of martyrdom requires that a human being suffer death for Christ's sake. Aquinas states:

> A martyr is so called as being a witness to the Christian faith, which teaches us to despise things visible for the sake of things invisible, as stated in Heb. 11. Accordingly, it belongs to martyrdom that a [person] bear witness to the faith in showing by deed that he despises all things present, in order to obtain invisible goods to come. Now so long as a [person] retains the life of the body he does not show by deed that he despises all things relating to the body. For [humans] are wont to despise both their kindred and all they possess, and even to suffer bodily pain, rather than lose life. Hence Satan testified against Job (Jb 2:4): *Skin for skin, and all that a man hath he will give for his soul* (Douay,—*life*) i.e. for the life of his body. Therefore the perfect notion of martyrdom requires that a [person] suffer death for Christ's sake. (*ST* II-II, q. 124, a. 4)

Whence does the motion of grace come for such a perfect act of martyrdom? As in the case of Bl. Devasahayam Pillai, a martyrdom to the point of shedding one's own blood (*usque ad sanguinem*) might occur in the greatest isolation from other faithful and from the consolation the sacraments afford. What sustains martyrdom in any circumstance, but especially in the situation of extreme isolation, is the Holy Spirit's gift of fortitude. Aquinas regards the gifts of the Holy Spirit as the Spirit's motions of the human mind: "In the gifts of the Holy Spirit, the position of the human mind is of one moved rather than a mover."[30] Beyond the theological virtues of faith, hope,

---

29. *ST* II-II, q. 124, a. 3: "Of all virtuous acts, martyrdom is the greatest proof of the perfection of charity: since a [person's] love for a thing is proved to be so much the greater, according as that which he despises for its sake is more dear to him, or that which he chooses to suffer for its sake is more odious. But it is evident that of all those goods of the present life a [human being] loves life itself most, and on the other hand he hates death more than anything, especially when it is accompanied by the pains of bodily torment.... And from this point of view it is clear that martyrdom is the most perfect of human acts in respect to its genus, as being the sign of the greatest charity, according to John 15:13: *Greater love than this no man hath, that a man lay down his life for his friends*."

30. *ST* II-II, q. 52, a. 2, ad 1; see also *ST* I-II, q. 68, aa. 1–2. For an astute discussion of

and charity, the gifts of the Holy Spirit form the crowning capstone of the primacy of grace in the life of every Christian, but especially in the martyr's existence *in extremis*:

> [A person's] mind is moved by the Holy Spirit, in order that he may attain the end of each work begun, and avoid whatever perils may threaten. This surpasses human nature: for sometimes it is not in [a person's] power to attain the end of his work, or to avoid evils or dangers, since these may happen to overwhelm him in death. But the Holy Spirit works this in [a person], by bringing him to everlasting life, which is the end of all good deeds, and the release from all perils. A certain confidence of this is infused into the mind by the Holy Spirit Who expels any fear of the contrary. It is in this sense that fortitude is reckoned a gift of the Holy Spirit. (*ST* II-II, q. 139, a. 1)

Martyrdom for the Sake of Virtue and Truth

In *ST* II-II, Aquinas establishes that martyrdom is a virtuous act (q. 124, a. 1), that it is an act of fortitude (a. 2), that it is an act of the greatest perfection (a. 3), and that death is essential to the perfect notion of martyrdom (a. 4). In the fifth article, finally, he addresses directly the question that most concerns the argument of this chapter: is faith alone (*sola fides*) the cause of the act of martyrdom? While earlier arguments have prepared the direction he takes on this matter, the *sed contra* he advances does not permit any lingering doubt. He takes a passage from Christ's Sermon on the Mount to refer to martyrdom, an interpretation that is backed by the "ordinary gloss" (*glossa ordinaria*), a collection of biblical glosses, from the leading Church Fathers and early medieval theologians, copied into the margins of the Vulgate.[31]

In his response, Aquinas first recapitulates what he established in the previous articles: "Martyrs are so called as being witnesses, because by suffering in body unto death they bear witness to the

---

the gifts of the Holy Spirit, see Steven A. Long, "The Gifts of the Holy Spirit and Their Indispensability for the Christian Moral Life: Grace as *Motus*," *Nova et Vetera* (English edition) 11, no. 2 (2013): 357–73.

31. *ST* II-II, q. 124, a. 5, s.c.: "*On the contrary*, It is written (Matt. 5:10): *Blessed are they that suffer persecution for justice's sake*, which pertains to martyrdom, according to a gloss, as well as Jerome's commentary on this passage. Now not only faith but also the other virtues pertain to justice. Therefore other virtues can be the cause of martyrdom."

truth; not indeed to any truth, but to the truth which is in accordance with godliness, and was made known to us by Christ: wherefore Christ's martyrs are His witnesses. Now this truth is the truth of faith. Wherefore the cause of martyrdom is the truth of faith" (a. 5). The *final* cause of every act of authentic martyrdom is the truth of faith. But insofar as the truth of faith includes the truth of the divine law that yields the measure for all the moral virtues, the act of martyrdom also seems to be *formally* constituted by the truth of divine faith. (It is worth remembering that, in matters of human agency, the form of the act is largely constituted by its end, the final cause.) Moreover, martyrdom seems to include *materially* the way of life in word and deed that gives rise to the hatred of virtue and truth in those who find themselves challenged or even convicted by this way of life. Aquinas continues his answer in a way that fully affirms this initial assumption:

But the truth of faith includes not only inward belief, but also outward profession, which is expressed not only by words, whereby one confesses the faith, but also by deeds, whereby a person shows that he has faith, according to James 2:18, *I will show thee, by works, my faith*. Hence, it is written of certain people (Ti. 1:16): *They profess that they know God but in their works they deny Him*. Thus all virtuous deeds, inasmuch as they are referred to God, are professions of the faith whereby we come to know that God requires these works of us, and rewards us for them: and in this way they can be the cause of martyrdom. For this reason the Church celebrates the martyrdom of Blessed John the Baptist, who suffered death, not for refusing to deny the faith, but for reproving adultery. (*ST* II-II, q. 124, a. 5)

John the Baptist becomes the paradigm for martyrdom for the sake of virtue and truth. The principles of this martyrdom are several. All virtuous acts, inasmuch as they are referred to God, are professions of the faith. Faith is formally constituted by the certain revealed knowledge that virtuous acts (pursuing good and avoiding sin) are required by God and are integral to friendship with God. This makes faith the final cause of martyrdom.[32] Faith in its proper constitution, however, is always already informed by charity: For

---

32. *ST* II-II, q. 124, a. 2, ad 1: "Martyrdom is related to faith as the end in which one is strengthened, but to fortitude as the eliciting *habitus*."

"the act of faith is directed to the object of the will, i.e., the good, as to its end; and this good which is the end of faith, viz., the Divine Good, is the proper object of charity. Therefore, charity is called the form of faith in so far as the act of faith is perfected and formed by charity" (*ST* II-II, q. 4, a. 3).

Aquinas understands charity as perfecting and thus forming faith insofar as it quickens (*informari*) the act of faith (*ST* II-II, q. 4, a. 3, ad 1). Faith, as a perfecting *habitus* of the intellect, makes present to the will the last end (*ST* II-II, q. 4, a. 7), and charity, as the perfecting *habitus* of the will, desires the last end. Hence, as quickening or informing the acts of all the other virtues, "charity ... directs the act of all other virtues to the last end and ... consequently ... gives the form to all other acts of virtue" (*ST* II-II, q. 23, a. 8). Therefore, faith and charity both command the acts of all the other virtues—faith as final cause and charity as efficient cause. By making the surpassing good of the ultimate end present to the will, faith as final cause enables the efficient cause, charity. Faith thereby commands the act of martyrdom in the order of finality. For the sake of love of God and neighbor, charity, in turn, commands the act of martyrdom, now in the order of efficacy: "Inward faith, with the aid of charity [*fides interior mediante dilectione*], causes all outward acts of virtue, by means of the other virtues, commanding, but not eliciting them" (*ST* II-II, q. 3, a. 1, ad 3).

The theological virtues of faith and charity command the acts of the infused moral virtues, acts that are mediated by the specific *habitus* to which these acts belong and that are specified by their object. Yet while commanded by the higher virtues, these *habitus* immediately elicit their proper acts.[33] The *habitus* of fortitude principally elicits the act of endurance, while the *habitus* of patience elicits its

33. Consider Aquinas's description of the relationship of the infused moral virtues to charity: "The difference between eliciting and commanding an act is that the *habitus* or active potency elicits that act which it produces in respect to an unmediated object, but it commands an act that is produced by way of an inferior mediating *habitus* or active potency in regard to an object of that latter active potency" (Hoc enim interest inter elicere actum et imperare, quod habitus vel potentia elicit illum actum, quem producit circa obiectum nullo mediante, sed imperat actum, qui producitur mediante potentia vel habitu inferiori circa obiectum illius potentiae). *Sent.* III, d. 27, q. 2, a. 4, q.c. 3; author's translation.

continuation and the *habitus* of perseverance its completion. When commanded by an ever-greater charity and thereby referred to God with ever-greater intensity, the *habitus* of fortitude elicits its perfect act, which is endurance to the very shedding of one's blood (*usque ad sanguinem*), the act of perfect martyrdom.[34]

In his response to the three objections of *ST* II-II, q. 124, a. 5, Aquinas defends, applies, and even extends this principle. All three objections forward in different ways a well-known position: allegedly, faith alone (*sola fides*), that is, the public verbal confession of the Christian faith is the sole cause of martyrdom; the decisive motive cause in the persecutors must be exclusively hatred of the faith (*odium fidei*).

On the basis of 1 Peter 4:15–16, the first objection argues that one is said to be a Christian because one holds the Christian faith. And "therefore only faith in Christ gives the glory of martyrdom to those who suffer." Aquinas grants the principle that faith in Christ is constitutive of martyrdom, but differentiates between the public verbal confession of the faith and the public witness that is entailed in living a virtuous Christian life:

A Christian is one who is Christ's. Now a person is said to be Christ's, not only through having faith in Christ, but also because he is actuated to virtuous deeds by the Spirit of Christ, according to Rom. 8:9, *If any man have not the Spirit of Christ, he is none of His*; and again because in imitation of Christ he is dead to sins, according to Gal. 5:24, *They that are Christ's have crucified their flesh with the vices and concupiscences*. Hence to suffer as a Christian is not only to suffer in confession of the faith, which is done by words, but also to suffer for doing any good work, or for avoiding any sin, for Christ's sake, because this all comes under the head of witnessing to the faith. (*ST* II-II, q. 124, a. 5, ad 1)

Hence not only were St. John of Cologne, OP, and St. Fidelis of Sigmaringen, OFM Cap., both martyrs, having been killed because

---

34. According to Aquinas's doctrine of faith, the existence of faith under the dispensation of the Old Law allows us to understand the paradigmatic potential martyr of the Old Testament, Susanna (Dn 13), and the martyrs of 2 Mc 7 as precursors to John the Baptist. "As to those under the Old Testament who through faith were acceptable to God, in this respect they belonged to the New Testament: for they were not justified except through faith in Christ, Who is the Author of the New Testament" (*ST* I-II, q. 107, a. 1, ad 3).

of their witness to the Catholic faith; so too was St. Maria Goretti, who was killed in defending her chastity. The doing of any good work and the avoidance of sin are commanded and thus informed by charity and, by way of charity, they are referred to God. These virtuous acts are as such a testifying of the faith, because divine faith yields the knowledge of God's truth that guides infused prudence in determining how best to refer all specific human acts to God.

At this point the second objection comes into play. If a martyr is a kind of witness and witness is borne to truth alone, could one then not be called a martyr for upholding the truths of geometry? This is obviously absurd. Hence only the divine truth, which is held by faith alone, is the cause of martyrdom. In his reply, Aquinas first points to the crucial connection between martyrdom and truths that pertain to the worship of the Godhead (*pertinent ad cultum divinitatis*) and hence are called truths according to godliness (*secundum pietatem*). He appeals somewhat obliquely to the virtue of religion, a virtue annexed to the virtue of justice. The first and principal act of the virtue of religion is the interior act of devotion, the submission of one's will to God and hence to the divine law. All the other acts of the virtue of religion, and indeed, all the other moral virtues have their end and purpose in the act of devotion (*ST* II-II, q. 82). As a potential part of justice, and as being due to God *qua* creator, the act of devotion, commanded by charity, realizes the rectitude of the will in relationship to God. The act of devotion commits the will to the service of God according to God's will as expressed in the divine law. All truth according to godliness (*secundum pietatem*) falls under the divine law. Aquinas then goes on to state: "Since every lie is a sin, as stated above (q. 110, aa. 3, 4), avoidance of a lie, to whatever truth it may be contrary, may be the cause of martyrdom in as much as a lie is a sin against the Divine Law" (*ST* II-II, q. 124, a. 5, ad 2).

Hence the defense of any truth, be it theoretical or factual, can become the cause of martyrdom, given that the observance of the divine law belongs essentially to the worship of God (*cultus divinitatis*), to which pertains the virtue of religion, whose principal act is the act of devotion. The devout person does not lie because the divine law prohibits lying (which in its core is nothing but duplicity) and prescribes acts of the virtue of truthfulness (*veracitas*). Hence, the defense of any truth can become the cause of martyrdom when its denial is understood as unfaithfulness to the divine law and consequently as a betrayal of what pertains essentially to the first and principal act of the worship of God (*cultus divinitatis*), interior devotion.

The third objection focuses on the common good by arguing that those virtuous acts that are directed to the common good are preferable to and more important than those that are not. According to *Nicomachean Ethics* I.2 the good of the body politic (*res publica*) is better (*potior*) than the good of the private person, and thus it seems that those who die in defense of the *res publica* should be regarded as martyrs. But this contradicts the established practice of the church which does not celebrate those as martyrs who die defending their *res publica* in a just war. Hence faith alone must be the cause of martyrdom.

In his response Aquinas maintains the superiority of the common good over the private good, but integrates this hierarchy of the human good in the natural order into an encompassing and perfecting hierarchy of the divine good (where the common good is indistinguishable from the private good) in the supernatural order. The good of one's *res publica* is special (*praecipuum*) among human goods. Yet the divine good is better (*potius*) than the human good. And the divine good (being that which the theological virtues already somewhat attain and being that to which all moral virtues are directed by the virtue of religion) is the cause of martyrdom. But then he adds: "Since human good may become Divine, for instance when it is referred to God, it follows that any human good in so far as it is referred to God, may be the cause of martyrdom" (*ST* II-II, q. 124, a. 5, ad 3).

Among human goods the most eminent is the common good of the *res publica*. Hence, the defense of the *res publica* is a good more eminent than any merely private human good. But the divine good is an infinitely higher common good.[35] Can acts of virtue pertaining

---

35. I agree with Charles De Koninck's interpretation of the common good according to Thomas Aquinas as advanced in his *Primacy of the Common Good against the Personalists* and as concisely summarized by Yves Simon in his review "On the Common Good": "The subordination of the temporal common good to the supernatural good should not

to the proximate common good be referred to the ultimate common good? In other words, can a death suffered in defense of the *res publica* and referred to God by charity qualify as martyrdom? Aquinas's answer seems to imply a positive response. And, indeed, in an earlier parallel discussion he did advance such a positive response:

> The uncreated good surpasses all created good. Hence any created end, whether it be in common or a private good, cannot confer so great a goodness on an act as can the uncreated end, when, to wit, an act is done for God's sake. Hence, when a person dies for the common good without referring it to Christ, he will not merit the aureole; but if he refer it to Christ he will merit the aureole and he will be a martyr; for instance if he defend his country from an attack of an enemy who designs to corrupt the faith of Christ, and suffer death in that defense.[36]

---

be mistaken for the subordination of a good that is common to a good that is private; the higher good to which all temporal good is subordinated is itself a common good (19). 'The supernatural good of the individual person is essentially subordinated to the supernatural common good, in such a way that it is impossible to distinguish between the supernatural virtue of a man and the supernatural virtue of the same man considered as part of the heavenly city.'" *Writings of Charles De Koninck*, 2:168. De Koninck's *Primacy of the Common Good* can be found in the same volume (63–108).

36. *Sent.* IV, d. 49, q. 5, a. 3, q.c. 2, ad 11 (*ST Suppl.*, q. 96, a. 6, ad 11). What kind of scenario might Aquinas have had in mind? Quite likely he was thinking about his own brother Rinaldo. First a partisan of Emperor Frederick II, Rinaldo joined the papal party after Pope Innocent IV deposed the emperor in 1245. In 1246, Frederick II put Rinaldo to death on charges of conspiracy. Frederick II had been persecuting the church in Italy in a systematic manner and was widely regarded, not as the protector of the faith the emperor was supposed to be, but rather as a notorious *corruptor fidei*. Hence his deposition and consequent delegitimization by Innocent IV. Rinaldo's death consequent upon opposing Frederick II falls under the criterion of, in Aquinas's words from the *Scriptum*, defending one's "country from an attack of an enemy who designs to corrupt the faith of Christ, and suffer death in that defense." According to early sources, Aquinas's deceased sister Marotta appeared to him in a dream and related to him that Rinaldo enjoyed a martyr's aureole in heaven. The earliest account of this story is related in Gérard de Frachet's *Vitae Fratrum Ordinis Praedicatorum* which was completed in 1260, while Aquinas's *Scriptum super libros Sententiarum* was in the process of completion around 1256. Jean-Pierre Torrell, OP, relates this story and marshals the sources in his magisterial biography, *Saint Thomas Aquinas*, vol. 1: *The Person and His Work*, trans. Robert Royal (Washington, D.C.: The Catholic University of America Press, 1996), 3. For the date of the completion of Aquinas's *Scriptum*, see ibid., 332, and for the date of the completion of the *Vitae Fratrum*, see William A. Hinnebusch, OP, *The History of the Dominican Order*, vol. 2: *Intellectual and Cultural Life to 1500* (New York: Alba House, 1973), 281–82. But Aquinas might also have thought more broadly about a wider category of cases under which his own brother and many other Christian soldiers might fall. He might have been thinking, for instance, of the battle of Legnica/Liegnitz in Silesia on April 9, 1241, where most of an army of

This is the position of the young Thomas Aquinas in the process of completing his extensive commentary on Peter Lombard's *Sentences*. By the time he composed the *Disputed Questions on Truth* (*Quaestiones disputatae de veritate*), his position had developed. This more nuanced view he continued to hold until relatively late in his life, when he worked on the *Disputed Questions on Evil* (*Quaestiones disputatae de malo*). Consider the later position crisply stated in *De veritate*: "In one who has charity there can be no act of virtue not formed by charity. For, either the act will be directed to the proper end, and this can be only through charity in one who has charity, or the act is not directed to the proper end, and so is not an act of virtue."[37]

On the supposition that the Christian soldier, "who defends his country from an attack of an enemy who designs to corrupt the faith of Christ" (*ST Suppl.*, q. 96, a. 6, ad 11), has charity, he must refer this act, elicited by acquired fortitude, to the supernatural end. Without such a referral, the soldier's act would indeed be a blameworthy act. Given such a referral, however, the act does become formally congruent with an act elicited by the infused virtue of fortitude, which is essentially informed by charity and all the acts of which are directly commanded by charity. The act of referral is absolutely essential for such formal congruence to obtain. But whether indeed the dying Christian soldier made such an act of referral can only be known by God. Because the *ecclesia militans* on her pilgrimage on earth does not have any ordinary access to this particular divine knowledge, she lacks the necessary warrant for a declaration of martyrdom "before the church." What might be the case "before God" can at best only be surmised hypothetically.

Catholic knights and infantry, led by the Polish Duke Henry II, known as the Henry the Pious, lost their lives in defense of their *res publica Christiana* against an invading Mongolian army. And to move away from Aquinas's proximate historical context, a more recent instance along the lines of his argument would arguably be the death of Polish Catholic soldiers who fell on the field of battle defending their *res publica* in 1939 against the brutal and unjustified attack launched by Nazi Germany, an attack that, as it became obvious only all too soon, aimed at the destruction of the Polish culture, the Polish intelligentsia, and the eventual suppression of the Catholic church.

37. *De ver.*, q. 14, a. 5, ad 13 (*Truth*, 2:236). See also *De malo*, q. 2, a. 5, ad 7.

The Martyriological Criterion of the Imitation of Christ

Yet there is another issue of much greater weight that prevents the acknowledgment of soldier martyrs "before the church" in principle. Not only does the church on earth (*ecclesia militans*) lack any knowledge about the crucial act of referral at the moment of the soldier's death, a referral that would impart the absolutely indispensable "form" of the act of martyrdom. But also and more importantly, the question of the proper "matter" of this species of acts must be raised. Is defense of one's *res publica Christiana* from an attack of an enemy who intends to corrupt or suppress the Christian faith a proper "matter" for martyrdom "before the church"? As is well known, the Italian city states and northern European nation-states that began to emerge soon after Aquinas's death all too eagerly adopted the rhetoric of martyrdom for soldiers fallen in defense of the *patria*—"It is sweet and proper to die for the fatherland" (*dulce et decorum est pro patria mori*).[38] Every soldier who dies for the sake of the *patria* is a "martyr" of that very *patria*. In light of such flagrant abuse of the Christian notion of martyrdom by newly emerging political constellations inside of Christendom, the church began to lay down explicit norms about the proper "matter" of the act of martyrdom. The natural good of voluntary death in battle for the justified defense of the *res publica* (*Christiana*), referred by charity to God, the supernatural final end, does not qualify as proper "matter" for martyrdom "before the church." In his *On the Beatification of the Servants of God and the Canonization of the Blessed* (*De servorum Dei beatificatione et beatorum canonizatione*) III.18, Prosper Cardinal Lambertini, later Pope Benedict XIV, offers an extensive discussion of the above text by Aquinas and of its commentaries and affirms that a necessary condition for the perfect notion of martyrdom to the point of shedding one's own blood (*usque ad sanguinem*) is the per-

---

38. For the rhetorical-political transferal of martyrdom from dying for the heavenly *patria* to dying for the political *patria* in the context of the emerging late-medieval national kingdoms, such as France, and city states, such as those in Italy, see Ernst H. Kantorowicz, *The King's Two Bodies: A Study in Medieval Political Theology* (Princeton, N.J.: Princeton University Press, 1957), 232–72: "The Christian martyr... who had offered himself up for the invisible polity and had died for his divine Lord *pro fide*, was to remain—actually until the twentieth century—the genuine model of civic self-sacrifice" (234–35).

fect imitation of Christ, that is specifically, the nonresistance against the attackers, persecutors, and eventually executioners of death.[39] Hence, the "matter" of the kind of act that leads to the death of the Christian soldier dying in defense of the *res publica* (*Christiana*), referred by charity to God, is a "matter" that is *per se* licit, that is, it has the potency of becoming, by way of referral, a meritorious act. Nevertheless, the "matter" lacks a crucial perfection characteristic of the perfection of martyrdom: the perfect imitation of Christ. Due to this imperfection, this kind of act does not qualify as proper "matter" for martyrdom "before the church."

The magisterial criterion of nonresistance does not affect the heart of Aquinas's argument. Rather, the criterion provides careful magisterial precision and circumscription in a way that integrates Aquinas's position into the older patristic tradition: nonresistance constitutes an essential characteristic of the proper "matter" of the act of martyrdom "before the church" because this characteristic resembles most closely the imitation of Christ.[40] Furthermore, the church on earth (*ecclesia militans*) can obtain reliable testimony about whether the criterion of nonresistance has been fulfilled or not.

With this circumscription in place, it is possible for the magisterium to affirm the basic thrust of Aquinas's argument in such a way that it indeed accounts for the martyrdom of Fr. Puglisi at the hands of the Mafia.[41] First, Fr. Puglisi witnessed as a Catholic priest to the

39. Third edition (Rome, 1748), 225. For this information and for a concise summary of Cardinal Lambertini's discussion, I rely on the commentary in Thomas von Aquin, *Summa Theologica: Deutsch-lateinische Ausgabe* (*Die Deutsche Thomas-Ausgabe*), vol. 36: *Die letzten Dinge* (Heidelberg / Graz: F. H. Kehrle / Styria, 1961), 409–10, and especially on the commentary in vol. 21: *Tapferkeit, Masshaltung* (1. Teil) (Heidelberg / Graz: F. H. Kehrle / Styria, 1961), 485–89.

40. At this point I leave unaddressed the question of whether a death in defense of the *res publica*, referred by charity to God, could legitimately be understood as a case of martyrdom "before God"—not unlike the voluntary death *in odium fidei* (for one of the truths of the Catholic faith) or *in odium virtutis et veritatis* undergone by a material, but not formal heretic.

41. This fundamental affirmation can be found expressly in a specific formulation in Prosper Cardinal Lambertini (later Pope Benedict XIV), *De servorum Dei beatificatione et beatorum canonizatione*, and is cited affirmingly by Benedict XVI: "The concept 'martyrdom' as applied to the Saints and Blessed martyrs should be understood, in conformity with Benedict XIV's teaching, as '*voluntaria mortis perpessio sive tolerantia propter Fidem Christi, vel alium virtutis actum in Deum relatum*' (*De Servorum Dei beatificatione et Beatorum canonizatione*, Prato 1839–1841, Book III, chap. 11, 1). This is the constant teaching of

divine truth as received by divine faith. His testifying to the truth entailed his witness in word and action to virtue and justice and to their rule, the divine law. Second, Fr. Puglisi was deeply committed to the common good of the *res publica* he served in as priest and as citizen, a commitment that as priest he constantly referred by charity to God. Third, Fr. Puglisi underwent death voluntarily without resisting his assassins.

Fr. Puglisi's case discloses the perennially true core of Aquinas's argument: any act of witness to virtue and justice is a defense of the *res publica*, and if this defense is referred by charity to God, the person who is killed without offering resistance for the sake of the witness to virtue and justice can indeed be acknowledged as martyr "before the church." Conversely, Aquinas's thesis, rightly understood, discloses what is unique about the kind of martyrdom represented by Fr. Puglisi's prophetic witness and death: it is a martyrdom whose proximate cause was the zeal for the common good of the *res publica* referred by charity to the divine good, the common good of the *Civitas Dei*, the heavenly city. For nothing (with the exception of a criminal and corrupt regime) undercuts the common good of a *res publica* more than widespread organized and secretive crime that involves corruption, fraud, exertion, blackmailing, money laundering, and murder. When motivated by love of God and neighbor, and undertaken with the goal of redirecting the human good of the *res publica* to the divine good of the *Civitas Dei* such that the defense of the common good of the *res publica* becomes formally congruent with directing persons to the common good of the heavenly city— which is the end of faith—exposing, condemning, and fighting organized crime can be a proximate cause of martyrdom. The case for such a martyrdom is made by Aquinas's argument, as affirmed and magisterially specified by the norm of nonresistance. Bl. Giuseppe Puglisi's martyrdom for the sake of virtue and truth (*pro virtute et veritate*) not only follows a paradigm set by St. Thomas More and

---

the Church" ("Letter of His Holiness Benedict XVI to the Participants of the Plenary Session of the Congregation for the Causes of Saints," April 24, 2006). The decisive passage is *vel alium virtutis actum in Deum relatum*. This "other act of virtue related to God" is quite obviously an instance of the set that Aquinas understands basically as professions of faith: "All virtuous deeds, inasmuch as they are referred to God, are professions of the faith" (*ST* II-II, q. 124, a. 5).

St. John Fisher, but rather opens up this paradigm definitively in ways that will make it possible to consider along similar lines the death of many priests, sisters, and lay persons who were killed in various parts of the world because they testified to the truth by witnessing to virtue and justice, and of Catholic priests and laypersons who were executed or tortured to death under the Nazi regime.[42]

According to Aquinas's analysis, martyrdom is always a divine gift of grace, and what is meritorious about it is the depth of the act of charity, of friendship with God, that follows through on the gift of grace and commands the act of martyrdom. The heroism of martyrdom is in the end always a heroism of friendship with God, remaining faithful to the will of God as revealed in the divine law and thereby testifying to the truth. While martyrdom's final cause is faith, its primary motive cause is charity, an efficacy perfected by the exterior motion of divine inspiration, the gift of fortitude. Yet the proximate cause for the act of martyrdom is "all that comes under the head of witnessing to the faith," which includes the doing of any good work and the avoidance of any sin (*ST* II-II, q. 124, a. 5, ad 1).[43]

---

42. According to the church's understanding, St. Teresa Benedicta a Cruce (1891–1942) died a martyr, as did St. Maximilian Mary Kolbe (1894–1941) and Bl. Franz Jägerstätter (1907–43). Arguably, the same might be true of Fr. Franz Reinisch (1903–42) and Fr. Bernhard Lichtenberg (1875–1943). Thomas Schubeck, SJ, makes an analogous case for the Salvadoran martyrs in his important article "Salvadoran Martyrs: A Love that Does Justice," *Horizons* 28 (2001): 7–29. Regarding Archbishop Oscar Romero (1917–80) who had been declared a "servant of God" in 1990 by John Paul II, Benedict XVI, in his Angelus address from March 25, 2007, made the following statement: "The 'yes' of Jesus and Mary is renewed in the 'yes' of the saints, especially the martyrs who are killed because of the Gospel. I stress this because yesterday, on March 24, the anniversary of the assassination of Archbishop Oscar Romero, Archbishop of San Salvador, we celebrated the Day of Prayer and Fasting for Missionary Martyrs: bishops, priests, religious and lay people killed in fulfilling its mission of evangelization and human promotion." Pope Francis's decree from February 3, 2015, to ratify the death of Archbishop Oscar Romero as a martyrdom in hatred of the faith (*in odium fidei*), stands in clear continuity with Benedict XVI's earlier assessment: Archbishop Romero was not only assassinated for the sake of virtue and truth (*pro virtute et veritate*), but, indeed, in *odium fidei*. He was, after all, assassinated in a highly significant fashion—at the altar while saying Mass. This symbolic execution in and of itself suggests first and foremost *odium fidei*. He was beatified in San Salvador on May 23, 2015, in the presence of a quarter-million people. For an extraordinarily instructive account of Archbishop Romero's martyrdom in the context of his life and witness in El Salvador, see Matthew Whelan, "The Land of the Savior: Oscar Romero and the Reform of Agriculture" (PhD diss., Duke University, 2016).

43. There is a perfect consonance between Aquinas's teaching and that of Benedict XVI on the synthesis of grace and freedom in the martyr's ultimate act of charity:

Consequently, according to Aquinas, martyrdom for the sake of virtue and truth (*pro virtute et veritate*) does not replace, expand, or develop martyrdom for the sake of the faith (*pro fide*); rather, the former is integral to the latter: "The cause of all martyrdom is the truth of faith" (*ST* II-II, q. 124, a. 5).

THE CONTEMPORARY RELEVANCE OF AQUINAS'S INTEGRAL DOCTRINE OF MARTYRDOM

Recall the important teaching on martyrdom that Pope St. John Paul II advances in the third part of *Veritatis Splendor*: "Martyrdom, the exaltation of the inviolable holiness of God's law" (pars. 90–94). In this encyclical letter he conceives of martyrdom as a witness of fidelity to the holy law of God, a witness that is understood to confirm "the existence of negative moral norms regarding specific kinds of behavior, norms which are valid without exception" (par. 90). The stories of Susanna, John the Baptist, Stephen the Deacon, James the Apostle, and the countless martyrs of Revelation 13:7–10 are explicitly mentioned. The spectrum clearly covers both martyrdom for the sake of the faith (*pro fide*) and martyrdom for the sake of virtue and truth (*pro virtute et veritate*), understood by *Veritatis Splendor* "as an affirmation of the inviolability of the moral order, [that] bears splendid witness to the holiness of God's law and to the inviolability of the personal dignity of man, created in God's image and likeness" (par. 92). According to *Veritatis Splendor*, martyrdom for the sake of the faith (*pro fide*) and martyrdom for the sake of virtue and truth (*pro virtute*

"Once again, where does the strength to face martyrdom come from? From deep and intimate union with Christ, because martyrdom and the vocation to martyrdom are not the result of human effort but the response to a project and call of God, they are a gift of his grace that enables a person, out of love, to give his life for Christ and for the Church, hence for the world.... Yet it is important to stress that God's grace does not suppress or suffocate the freedom of those who face martyrdom; on the contrary, it enriches and exalts them: the Martyr is an exceedingly free person, free as regards power, as regards the world; a free person who in a single, definitive act gives God his whole life, and in a supreme act of faith, hope, and charity, abandons himself into the hands of his Creator and Redeemer; he gives up his life in order to be associated totally with the Sacrifice of Christ on the Cross. In a word, martyrdom is a great act of love in response to God's immense love" (Benedict XVI, General Audience, Papal Summer Residence, Castel Gandolfo, August 11, 2010).

et veritate) form one integral and seamless unity. Bl. Giuseppe Puglisi falls under it, as does Bl. Devasahayam Pillai. However, in light of *Veritatis Splendor*, Fr. Puglisi's martyrdom seems to be more characteristic of "today's growing secularism, wherein many, indeed too many, people think and live 'as if God did not exist'" (par. 88). The encyclical addresses directly the question of what it means to testify to the truth in a secular world of deeply disturbing moral waywardness:

Martyrdom is an *outstanding sign of the holiness of the Church*. Fidelity to God's holy law, witnessed to by death, is a solemn proclamation and missionary commitment to the point of shedding one's own blood [*usque ad sanguinem*], so that the splendor of moral truth may be undimmed in the behavior and thinking of individuals and society. This witness makes an extraordinarily valuable contribution to warding off, in civil society and within the ecclesial communities themselves, a headlong plunge into the most dangerous crisis which can afflict man: the *confusion between good and evil*, which makes it impossible to build up and to preserve the moral order of individuals and communities. By their eloquent and attractive example of a life completely transfigured by the splendor of moral truth, the martyrs and, in general, all the Church's Saints, light up every period of history by reawakening its moral sense. By witnessing fully to the good, they are a living reproof to those who transgress the law (cf. *Wis* 2:12).[44]

In an important letter from the year 2006, Pope Benedict XVI continued to emphasize the different shape martyrdom takes in profoundly changed cultural contexts:

The martyrs of the past and those of our time gave and give life [*effusio sanguinis*] freely and consciously in a supreme act of love, witnessing to their faithfulness to Christ, to the Gospel and to the Church. If the motive that impels them to martyrdom remains unchanged, since Christ is their source

---

44. Par. 93. Martyrdom is nothing but the extraordinary perfection of the ordinary testifying to the truth to which all Christians are called: "Although martyrdom represents the high point of the witness to moral truth, and one to which relatively few people are called, there is nonetheless a consistent witness which all Christians must daily be ready to make, even at the cost of suffering and grave sacrifice. Indeed, faced with the many difficulties which fidelity to the moral order can demand, even in the most ordinary circumstances, the Christian is called, with the grace of God invoked in prayer, to a sometimes heroic commitment. In this he or she is sustained by the virtue of fortitude, whereby—as Gregory the Great teaches—one can actually 'love the difficulties of this world for the sake of eternal rewards' [*Moralia in Job*, VII, 21, 24; *PL* 75:778: 'huius mundi aspera pro aeternis praemiis amare']" (*Veritatis Splendor*, par. 93).

and their model, then what has changed are the cultural contexts of martyrdom and the strategies *"ex parte persecutoris"* [on the part of the persecutor] that more and more seldom explicitly show their aversion to the Christian faith or to a form of conduct connected with the Christian virtues, but simulate different reasons, for example, of a political or social nature.[45]

In Western secular societies, the hatred of the faith on the part of the persecutors of the faith is increasingly camouflaged behind political and social ideals and norms propagating human progress, liberation, and authenticity along the lines of a collectivized radical individualism of the sovereign self—ideals and norms that are increasingly enforced by way of legal regulations that contradict the Gospel and human dignity. Depending on what the particular focus of this witness is, it might become the occasion for strong opposition, social ostracization, discrimination, and even persecution. It was not hyperbole or alarmism, but rather sober Christian realism faced with an increasingly militant secularism that moved the late Francis Cardinal George, then archbishop of Chicago, to make the famous remark to a group of priests that he might very well die peacefully in his bed, but that his successor might quite likely die in prison and his successor would "die a martyr in the public square."[46] While not all Christians are called to the perfect act of martyrdom, all Christians are called to testify to the truth and hence to acts of in-

---

45. "Letter of Pope Benedict XVI to the Participants of the Plenary Session of the Congregation for the Causes of Saints," April 24, 2006.

46. Francis Cardinal George, OMI, "The Wrong Side of History," The Cardinal's Column, *Catholic New World: Newspaper for the Archdiocese of Chicago* (October 21–November 3, 2012), 1. With his startling remark Cardinal George entertained a historical possibility that was unthinkable for much of American Christianity until quite recently, a perspective which European Christians, especially in light of the cataclysmic events of the twentieth century, had to entertain much earlier. In 1951, the Thomist philosopher Josef Pieper offered his own startling remark: "To put it plainly, one speaks of Christianity as a power of sabotage, of resistance. In Christian terminology, one speaks of Christianity as the Church of the martyrs. The tyrant and the martyr are two figures of the political order that depend on each other. And when one thinks further, the tradition of Western reflection on history regards the Antichrist as sovereign universal ruler in the final term of history; one can escape his power neither by way of exterior nor by way of interior emigration. The only possibility, as it appears, to comport oneself in relation to Antichrist is indeed identical with triumphing over him—it is resistance, the extreme form of which is the witness of the martyr." Josef Pieper, "Sur l'espérance des martyrs," in *Espoir humain et espérance chrétienne: Semaine des intellectuels catholiques, 24 au 31 mai 1951, Centre catholique des intellectuels français* (Paris: P. Horay, 1951), 80 (author's translation).

choate martyrdom. On August 11, 2010, on the occasion of the memorial of John the Baptist's martyrdom, Pope Benedict XVI stated:

> Dear brothers and sisters, celebrating the martyrdom of St. John the Baptist reminds us too, Christians of this time, that with love for Christ, for his words and for the Truth, we cannot stoop to compromises. The Truth is the Truth; there are no compromises. Christian life demands, so to speak, the "martyrdom" of daily fidelity to the Gospel, the courage, that is, to let Christ grow within us and let him be the One who guides our thoughts and our actions.[47]

Contemporary Western secular culture is characterized by two correlated features: on the one hand, on the surface an increasing religious and ideological pluralism and beneath the surface the strong operative belief in the "sovereign self," and, on the other hand, an increasingly aggressive statist laicism that introduces legal instruments of a *de facto* naturalist normativity that insinuates that matters of transcendent truth are arbitrary and hence irrelevant to human flourishing. In such a sociopolitical setting, testifying to the truth by way of prophetic acts of witnessing to virtue and justice becomes increasingly relevant as a persuasive witness that precedes and prepares the way for a discursive argumentation for the truth of the Gospel. For an increasing number of people, at least in the West, such Christian witness becomes the first encounter with the Gospel. In such a setting, the martyr for the sake of virtue and truth (*pro virtute et veritate*) is nothing but a missionary prototype *in extremis* of testifying to the truth. When such a witness to virtue and truth will eventually be challenged and interrogated by the powers that be, he or she might find inspiration in the encyclical letter *Lumen Fidei*, where Pope Francis refers to the martyr Hierax who was asked by the Roman prefect Rusticus, "Where are your parents?" He responded: "Our true father is Christ, and our mother is faith in him" (par. 5). Aquinas offers a continuously pertinent theological account for the fact that the witness to virtue and truth is perfectly integral to the witness of Christ: "The cause of all martyrdom is the truth of faith" (*ST* II-II, q. 124, a. 5). And the truth of faith is the

---

47. Pope Benedict XVI, General Audience, Papal Summer Residence, Castel Gandolfo, August 11, 2010.

unfailing guide of the *viator* on the journey to beatitude, indeed, the very substance of things hoped for that faith beholds is the inchoate presence of beatitude in the wayfarer. At one point on this sojourn, a *viator* might come to the realization that the only way to remain faithful to the journey's goal is to become a martyr and enter there and then into heavenly beatitude.

8

Protecting the Journey to Beatitude— Achieving Selfless Self-Control
The Virtue of Chastity

> All that is in the world, the lust of the flesh and the lust of the eyes and the pride of life, is not of the Father but is of the world. And the world passes away, and the lust of it; but he who does the will of God abides for ever.
>
> —1 John 2:16–17 (RSV)

> Has virtue ... lost its good name? Has the virtue of chastity in particular ceased to be respectable? Or is chastity no longer recognized as a virtue? It is not just a question of reputation. The use of a noun, and lip service to it, are not decisive. What matters is whether virtue is made welcome in the human soul, the human will. If not it ceases to have any real existence. Mere respect for the words "virtue" and "chastity" has no great significance.
>
> —Karol Wojtyla, *Love and Responsibility*, 143

In this chapter I will tackle a widespread daily temptation that the *viator* (especially as a twenty-first-century user of the internet and mobile electronic devices) is faced with: substituting the journey to the ultimate end, perfect happiness, the journey to the beatific vision, with another "vision"—pornography—that rouses the lust of the eyes and stimulates the desire for fleeting ecstatic moments of sexual pleasure. In line with Aquinas's constant emphasis that truth grounds good, this chapter depicts how lust entails the devaluation of the true good and excessive valuation of pleasure. The emphasis of the chapter, however, does not fall onto the analysis of the problem, but onto the recovery of a largely forgotten, but ultimately vital solution, the recovery of a virtue indispensable for the *viator*'s journey to beatitude—chastity.

Today in America and in Europe, we live in a culture of excess. Food is plentiful in both grocery stores and restaurants; material goods line the shelves of our emporia; videos, movies, and games abound on multiple digital devices; and even information flows over us so that we can scarcely recall today what we watched, listened to, or read yesterday. Along with this remarkable abundance comes an equally remarkable wastefulness. Together, abundance and wastefulness make up the excess that marks contemporary Western culture. Excess is both a sign of a disordered appetite and an invitation for the vices of gluttony and lust that encumber proper human flourishing and endanger the dignity of ourselves as well as the persons with whom we interact.

One particular and pressing instance of such excess has been the rapidly widening availability and consumption of pornography, especially since the introduction of the internet and mobile electronic devices. While exact statistics may be hard to come by, it is indubitable that internet porn is both plentiful and easily accessible to both adults and children who log onto their computers or peruse their smartphones.[1] The staggeringly widespread perusal of pornography

---

1. Websites commenting on the issue of internet pornography frequently offer statistics, but given the difficulties in determining the nature and extent of the use of the internet for pornographic purposes, such statistics must be acknowledged—as they often are on the websites themselves—with some caution. It gives one pause, however, and an urgent occasion to take in the magnitude of the problem, when one considers what one of the internet porn industry's largest providers reports about its "business." In January 2016, PornHub claimed its site streamed seventy-five gigabytes of data per second in 2015—enough to fill 175 million sixteen-gigabyte iPhones—a total of 87.8 billion views, up 10 billion from 2014 and another 15 billion over 2013 (statistics available at pornhub.com/insights). An estimated 87 percent of college-age men—and around 30 percent of women—double-click for sex either weekly or every day. See enough.org/stats_porn_industry.

by adults, youth, and even children is not only profoundly harmful but also indicative of considerable moral errancy, an errancy that is a grave impediment for the journey to beatitude. For pornography, as the *Catechism of the Catholic Church* points out, is an evil because it "offends against chastity because it perverts the conjugal act, the intimate giving of the spouses to each other. It does grave injury to the dignity of its participants (actors, vendors, the public), since each one becomes an object of base pleasure and illicit profit for others. It immerses all who are involved in the illusion of a fantasy world" (CCC §2354).[2] What is important here is that the moral evil of pornography threatens and eventually corrupts two fundamental moral goods: the dignity of the human person and the intimately conjoined virtue of chastity.[3]

2. See also the resources offered at the end of the most pertinent 2007 pastoral letter from Bishop Robert W. Finn of the Diocese of Kansas, "Blessed Are the Pure of Heart: A Pastoral Letter on the Dignity of the Human Person and the Dangers of Pornography," available at issuu.com/knightsofcolumbus/docs/323. Consider the following public echo of the church's teaching expressed on November 18, 2004, by Dr. Mary Anne Layden, co-director of the Sexual Trauma and Psychopathology Program at the University of Pennsylvania, at a U.S. Senate subcommittee on pornography: "Pornography, by its very nature, is an equal opportunity toxin. It damages the viewers, the performers, and the spouses and the children of the viewers and the performers. It is toxic mis-education about sex and relationships. It is more toxic the more you consume, the 'harder' the variety you consume and the younger and more vulnerable the consumer" (available at ccv.org/wp-content/uploads/2010/04/Judith_Reisman_Senate_Testimony-2004.11.18.pdf).

3. Because the virtue of chastity resides in the agent, and because my principal concern in this chapter is the virtue of chastity and its diminishment, loss, and recovery, my analysis of the effects of the consumption of internet pornography will be focused on the individual consumer. This concentration, however, is not at all meant to belittle the detrimental effects of pornography on others, especially on spouses (usually wives) and on the performers. Not only the above-cited *CCC*, but also empirical studies unmask the lie that no one else is harmed by consuming pornography. Two studies are especially relevant if one wants to reflect on the danger of pornography consumption for Christian marriage: first, on the relationship between pornography consumption and attitudes supporting violence against women, see Gert Martin Hald et al., "Pornography and Attitudes Supporting Violence against Women: Revisiting the Relationship in Nonexperimental Studies," *Aggressive Behavior* 36 (2010): 14–20; second, on the association between pornography consumption with weakened commitments to one's intimate partner, see Nathaniel M. Lambert et al., "A Love That Doesn't Last: Pornography Consumption and Weakened Commitment to One's Romantic Partner," *Journal of Social and Clinical Psychology* 31 (2012): 410–38. A third study is relevant for considering the alarming rate of mental health issues and correlated trauma among female adult performers: Corita R. Grudzen et al., "Comparison of the Mental Health of Female Adult Film Performers and Other Young Women in California," *Psychiatric Services* 62 (2011): 639–45. Referring to the last study, Warren Kinghorn (to whom I am

While it still seems obvious to many that pornography injures human dignity, it has become less obvious, or even unintelligible to many, that pornography offends against chastity. John Grabowski, in his insightful book *Sex and Virtue*, points out that

> one of the most maligned and misunderstood virtues in contemporary culture is chastity. The word often evokes connotations of inhibition, prudery, dysfunction, and perhaps even neurosis. This is especially true in a culture that sees sexual expression and pleasure as integral to personal health, happiness, and fulfillment. If one has to be sexually active to realize oneself, then continence or celibacy can seem perverse and any form of sexual restraint suspect. If sexual expression is not necessary [sic] limited to monogamous covenantal relationships for it to be seen as good, then even the notion of fidelity can come to be seen as arbitrary and oppressive.[4]

Quite contrary to the contemporary maligning and misunderstanding of chastity, it is nothing but the virtue of chastity that addresses the particular form of disordered excess that pertains to human sexuality. For this very reason, chastity is integral to genuine human flourishing. Against the common modern prejudice and, indeed, resentment against chastity, I will advance an argument for the rehabilitation of the virtue of chastity in conversation with Thomas Aquinas, whose moral theology remains a crucial point of reference for the Catholic church's consistent magisterial insistence throughout the previous and the present centuries on the irreducibly rational and moral nature of human procreative acts. One of the most pertinent lessons to be learned from Aquinas—and here he is the surpassing synthesizer of the theological wisdom of the most eminent Church Fathers and monastic authors—is that while the vice of lust has a carnal object, the root cause of this vice has a spiritual nature. Lust is one

---

indebted for pointing me to these and the other empirical studies cited) astutely observes: "When ... one views a pornographic product, one is very likely to be looking at the exposed body of one who has been raped, sexually degraded or otherwise devalued; to treat her as 'just an image' is a direct offense against charity, in that [one] refuses to see the other as one who is loved by God. Viewing such images, even if it results only in an additional 'click' for an Internet site, perpetuates these cycles of degradation" (personal communication with the author, May 31, 2012). Considered in light of Aquinas's moral theology, viewing pornography products is indeed an offense against justice as well as charity. However, spelling this claim out in detail lies beyond the scope of this chapter.

4. John S. Grabowski, *Sex and Virtue: An Introduction to Sexual Ethics* (Washington, D.C.: The Catholic University of America Press, 2003), 71.

of the maladies of the soul preventing the achievement of happiness, and especially its perfection, beatitude. Thus, uprooting the vice of lust means attending to the spiritual nature of its root cause. In order to make this solution intelligible I will need to take three prior steps, and hence the chapter will comprise four parts.

In the first part, I will use Aquinas's moral psychology to clarify the nature of chastity and its indispensability for the moral integrity of the human person in sexual as well as in other moral matters. Understanding the anthropological framework underlying Aquinas's account of chastity is necessary for a proper understanding of the negative spiritual roots from which the present problem arises. In the second part, I will have recourse to his analysis of vice in order to specify the vice of lust and the way he conceives the possible loss of chastity. In the third part, I will identify the spiritual root cause that gives rise to one preeminent foe of chastity in our days—the frequent, secretive, and in some cases, compulsive consumption of internet pornography. The spiritual root of this vine is old: spiritual apathy, *acedia*, as well as its modern offshoots, boredom and *ressentiment*. The malaise is identified in 1 John—the lust of the flesh, the lust of the eyes, and the pride of life—where the author notes how it is always in search of an ever-transient rush to fill the void (1 Jn 2:16). Lust, enkindled and fueled by the consumption of pornography, turns into a potent spiritual foe and serious threat to the chastity of the single person, to conjugal chastity, and eventually to the well-being of marriages. In the fourth and concluding part, I will propose a spiritual practice that rests on Aquinas's thoroughly Augustinian insistence that chastity is restored, preserved, and perfected from above. This theological axiom must inform all Christian practices that intend to tackle any form of intemperance at its spiritual root.

THE ULTIMATE END OF THE HUMAN BEING AND THE VIRTUE OF CHASTITY

Because the extant order of providence is supernatural, humanity is ordered to one ultimate end. And because grace presupposes and perfects human nature such that the finality of the created intellect is subsumed under and included in the supernatural ultimate end, there obtains a twofold finality, natural and supernatural. Correspondingly, there obtains an imperfect natural and an infinitely surpassing, perfect supernatural happiness.[5] From the first moment of human creation, humanity (essentially endowed with a finality proportionate to human nature) was *de facto* ordained for and called to partake in the life and love of the Trinity, and hence to live and love forever. The originally granted divine life of charity was subsequently lost with the Fall, and only regained in virtue of Christ's redemptive passion and death on the cross (*ST* III, q. 48, aa. 1–6).[6] Due to the supernatural character of the extant providential order, human beings flourish genuinely and lastingly only when they pursue those natural goods that contribute to natural happiness in light of their supernatural vocation (*ST* II-II, q. 152, a. 2). Only when the finality proportionate to human nature is further ordered to and elevated by the supernatural end can the human being flourish permanently and perfectly. Hence, when Aquinas refers to the "order of reason" to which the virtues conform, he understands it to be in accordance with the truth of real things as encountered and engaged by human beings in the scope of the extant supernaturally informed order of providence. The order of reason is a theonomic order of a *de facto* supernatural orientation that variously participates in the eternal law, that is, divine reason, and includes both nature and grace.[7]

---

5. See esp. *Expos. de Trin.*, q. 6, a. 4, ad 3. See also *ST* I-II, q. 3, aa. 3, 5, 6; q. 4, aa. 5, 7, 8. For the most recent comprehensive account of this profoundly complex topic, see Ramirez, *De Hominis*, and more accessibly and recently the explicatory notes by Servais Pinckaers, OP, in S. Thomas d'Aquin, *Somme Théologique: La Béatitude*, Éditions de La Revue des jeunes (Paris: Cerf, 2001).

6. On the complex and controversial question of nature and grace in the interpretation of Thomas Aquinas, see most recently the nuanced and comprehensive account of Jean-Pierre Torrell, OP, "Nature and Grace in Thomas Aquinas," in *Surnaturel: A Controversy at the Heart of Twentieth-Century Thomistic Thought*, ed. Serge-Thomas Bonino, OP, trans. Robert Williams (Ave Maria, Fla.: Sapientia Press, 2009), 155–88. CCC in its first section states clearly and beautifully: "God, infinitely perfect and blessed in himself, in a plan of sheer goodness freely created man to make him share in his own blessed life. For this reason, at every time and in every place, God draws close to man. He calls man to seek him, to know him, to love him with all his strength. He calls together all men, scattered and divided by sin, into the unity of his family, the Church. To accomplish this, when the fullness of time had come, God sent his Son as Redeemer and Savior. In his Son and through him, he invites men to become, in the Holy Spirit, his adopted children and thus heirs of his blessed life" (§1).

7. *ST* I-II, q. 19, a. 4: "It is from the eternal law, which is the Divine Reason, that

In complete concord with the antecedent Christian tradition, Aquinas regards chastity as indispensable for moral integrity in sexual matters and hence for human flourishing. Two elementary truths account for the indispensability of chastity. The first one is the Christian, anti-Manichean, and anti-spiritualist axiom that the sexual powers found in the human being are a genuine good.[8] Aquinas states: "Just as the preservation of the bodily nature of one individual is a true good, so, too, is the preservation of the nature of the human species a very great good. And just as the use of food is directed to the preservation of life in the individual, so is the use of [procreative sexual] acts directed to the preservation of the whole human race" (*ST* II-II, q. 153, a. 2). *Concupiscentia* in its elementary form is nothing but the natural inclination of every creature with a sensitive nature to seek the good proper to its nature (*ST* I-II, q. 30, a 1). Procreative sexual union and the concomitant sexual pleasure fall among the delectable goods that concupiscence seeks. And this natural inclination itself, Aquinas argues, reason apprehends as being good.[9]

---

human reason is the rule of the human will, from which the human will derives its goodness. Hence it is written (Ps. 4:6, 7): *Many say: Who showeth us good things? The light of Thy countenance, O Lord, is signed upon us*: as though to say: 'The light of our reason is able to show us good things, and guide our will, in so far as it is the light of (*i.e.*, derived from) Thy countenance.' It is therefore evident that the goodness of the human will depends on the eternal law much more than on human reason: and when human reason fails we must have recourse to the Eternal Reason." Importantly, the order of reason encompasses and transcends human discursive rationality. Moreover, due to the surpassingly sublime character of divine reason and the divine mysteries, the one order of reason entails a twofold order of knowledge, each order different from the other in epistemic principle and object. See Romanus Cessario, OP, "*Duplex Ordo Cognitionis*," in *Reason and the Reasons of Faith*, ed. Paul J. Griffiths and Reinhard Hütter (New York: T and T Clark International, 2005), 327–38. According to the twofold order of knowledge the eternal law becomes somewhat known by way of reason (natural law) and in an essentially surpassing, but complementary mode by way of revelation received by faith: "Although the eternal law is unknown to us according as it is in the Divine Mind: nevertheless, it becomes known to us somewhat [*aliqualiter*], either by natural reason which is derived therefrom as its proper image; or by some sort of additional revelation [*vel per aliqualem revelationem superadditam*]" (*ST* I-II, q. 19, a. 4, ad 3). For a lucid and penetrating analysis and discussion of this topic, see Rziha, *Perfecting Human Actions*.

8. Attending to the different emphases in the tradition on the goodness of the body, of sexuality, the reproductive act, and even marriage would go far beyond the scope of this chapter. It should, however, not be passed over unmentioned that Aquinas takes a considerably more positive stand on the goodness of sexuality and the inherent dignity of the procreative act than do many of his theological predecessors.

9. *ST* I-II, q. 94, a. 2: "All those things to which [the human being] has a natural

The second elementary truth is the axiom that the most necessary acts for the preservation of the individual human being as well as the human species—eating, drinking, and procreating—are irreducibly acts of the human being *qua* human being and hence *human acts* (*actiones humanae*) (*ST* I-II, q. 1, a. 1). Neither in their eating and drinking nor in the exercise of their procreative powers are human beings mere animals who are led by instinct.[10] Despite being animals biologically, humans essentially transcend animality in virtue of being living beings with a rational nature (*animal rationale*). Hence, Aquinas argues that the more necessary a thing is for the preservation of the individual and the human species, and the more intense the pleasure that accompanies the respective acts, the more important it is "to observe the order of reason" (*ST* II-II, q. 153, a. 3). In order not to misunderstand intemperance and lust right from the start, one must not mistake them to be vices because of the amount of sensual pleasure their practitioners feel. Rather, intemperance and lust are vices because the sensual pleasure is indulged in inordinately.

Because the human being is inescapably *animal rationale*, attempting to abdicate from the theonomic order of reason is not concomitant with embracing some allegedly innocent state of nature but is rather concomitant with quite simply—sinning. Human beings cannot abdicate from being human, that is, from following the order of reason and applying right reason to action.[11] Because acts of human

---

inclination are naturally apprehended by reason as being good, and consequently as objects of pursuit."

10. Aquinas has worked out this truth in an analysis as subtle as it is extensive in his treatise on the passions in *ST* I-II, qq. 22–48, a treatise that is presently enjoying a renewed interest. See chap. 3 in my *Dust Bound For Heaven* for an overview of the recent, fast-growing literature on the passions and for the argument that only when the irreducible spiritual dimension of human affectivity is fully recovered along Aquinas's lines will theological anthropology become invulnerable to the equally pernicious tendencies of early modernity to reduce the human to the mind and of late modernity to reduce the human to the body. For detailed and instructive recent treatments of the passions in Aquinas, see Robert Miner, *Thomas Aquinas on the Passions: A Study of Summa Theologiae 1a2ae 22–48* (Cambridge: Cambridge University Press, 2009), and Nicholas E. Lombardo, OP, *The Logic of Desire: Aquinas on Emotion* (Washington, D.C.: The Catholic University of America Press, 2010).

11. *ST* II-II, q. 47, a. 2, s.c., referring to Aristotle, *Nicomachean Ethics* VI.5: "Prudence is right reason applied to action." Right reason apprehends the end according to the order of reason and the eternal law (*ST* I-II, q. 21, a. 1).

sexuality are not animal operations led by instinct but rather irreducibly human acts, there is a distinct virtue—a dispositional excellence informed by right reason—that pertains to human sexuality. As Josef Pieper states: "Chastity as a virtue ... is constituted in its essence by this and nothing else, namely, that it realizes the order of reason in the province of sexuality."[12]

The theonomic order of reason entails, first, that one not obstruct or pervert the procreative purpose that is immanent to the sexual power, but rather fulfill it in marriage with its threefold good of *fides* (spousal faithfulness and friendship), *proles* (children), and *sacramentum* (instrumentality of salvation).[13] The order of reason implies, second, that the moral integrity of the human person is to remain intact in all respects and under all circumstances, and third, that love of neighbor and justice (giving what is due to the other person) be practiced among all persons (especially spouses, parents, and children, unborn as well as born).[14] What is at stake in the virtue of chastity that upholds the order of reason in sexual matters, as Pieper aptly puts it,

---

12. Pieper, *The Four Cardinal Virtues*, 155. While I have taken the quotations from this edition, I would like to refer the reader to the original 1939 edition of Pieper's treatise. In the original version—"standing on its own feet" so to speak—the ongoing relevance of the virtue of "selfless self-discipline and proper measure" becomes most forcefully tangible: Josef Pieper, *Zucht und Mass: Über die vierte Kardinaltugend* (Leipzig: Hegner, 1939).

13. For Aquinas, it is a sign of the corruption of natural reason when it is not anymore understood broadly in any given social whole that "human nature rebels against an indeterminate union of the sexes and demands that a man should be united to a determinate woman and should abide with her a long time or even for a whole lifetime" (*ST* II-II, q. 154, a. 2). While the commitment until death of one of the spouses is a precept of the natural law, the absolute and principled indissolubility of *matrimonium* pertains to the sacramental character of Christian marriage. While the former, the natural law precept, is in principle accessible to natural reason, the latter is not. Both, the former and the latter, are indisputably obvious only to human reason enlightened by the doctrine of the Gospel as taught by the church.

14. The staggering number of abortions procured annually in the Western Hemisphere (and increasingly globally) by teenagers and young adults outside of matrimony bespeaks in an all-too-sad way Aquinas's argument against fornication: "Simple fornication [heterosexual intercourse outside of marriage] is contrary to the love of our neighbor, because it is opposed to the good of the child to be born ... since it is an act of generation accomplished in a manner disadvantageous to the future child" (*ST* II-II, q. 154, a. 2, ad 4). Hence, even children not yet conceived are morally part of the community of human beings, insofar as these "preborn" children become by way of the natural teleology of the procreative act inchoate objects of the love of neighbor and of the justice due to others.

is the purpose of sex as it was intended originally in the first creation, and ennobled by Christ in the New Creation ... the existential structure of the moral person, as established in nature and in grace; ... [and the] order among men as guaranteed not merely by natural justice, but also by the higher justice of *caritas*, that is, supernatural love of God and man. Chastity realizes in the province of sex the order which corresponds to the truth of the world and of man both as experienced and as revealed, and which accords with the twofold form of this truth—not that of unveiled evidence alone, but that of veiled evidence also—that is, of mystery.[15]

In short, the virtue of chastity enables us to regulate from within the desire for sexual pleasure, and to direct it to our ultimate end.

Far from being prudishness—a fearful contempt of sexuality as a "necessary evil," unavoidable but ultimately subhuman—chastity preserves the very dignity of what is a genuine good. As such, the virtue of chastity belongs to a more comprehensive moral excellence, the virtue of temperance (*temperantia*).[16] Temperance—or better "selfless self-discipline and proper measure" as Pieper renders this virtue—is the virtue that preserves the inner order of the human being concerning the most elementary forces of human self-preservation, the nutritive and sexual sense appetites: "The discipline of temperance defends [the human being] against all selfish perversion of the inner order, through which alone the moral person exists and lives effectively."[17] This makes temperance one of the four cardinal virtues, and chastity an indispensable subclass, or species, of it.

In the overall structure of the moral integrity of the human person, the intellectual virtue of prudence (or practical wisdom) holds primacy among the four cardinal virtues, followed by justice, courage, and temperance. The cardinal virtues are dispositional excellences that enable the realization of the human good according to the order of reason—prudence by identifying and commanding the appropriate specific act, justice by attending to the good of others and hence giving them their due, courage by overcoming fear pertaining to whatever

---

15. Pieper, *Four Cardinal Virtues*, 158.
16. For a recent concise and clear introduction to Aquinas's understanding of chastity, see Grabowski, *Sex and Virtue*, 78–84. For a slightly more extensive treatment, see Albert Plé, OP, *Chastity and the Affective Life*, trans. Marie-Claude Thompson (New York: Herder and Herder, 1966), 115–49.
17. Pieper, *Four Cardinal Virtues*, 150.

threatens our bodily integrity and existence, and temperance by protecting the inner order from the ever-present power of our internal sense appetites.[18] In this essential order of the cardinal virtues, temperance comes to stand in the lowest, least important position. When we consider the concrete interplay of the cardinal virtues, however, that is, in the order of operation, we find an all-important feedback loop. For the habits of moral virtue correct the sense appetites, and because of these habits, we desire right ends that, when aided by prudence, allow us to make good judgments. In other words, the proper operation of prudence presupposes proper habituation in justice, courage, and temperance (*ST* II-II, q. 47, a. 13, ad 2; q. 58, a. 5). Consequently, what comes last in the essential order of the cardinal virtues comes first in their order of operation. Inordinate desire for sensual pleasure weakens and obstructs the virtues of courage and justice and, most detrimentally, the proper operation of prudence. Aquinas tersely observes: "As the philosopher states ... *pleasure above all corrupts the estimate of prudence* [*existimatio prudentiae*], and chiefly sexual pleasure which absorbs the mind and draws it to sensible delight" (*ST* II-II, q. 53, a. 6). Selfless self-discipline and proper measure maintain the inner order of

---

18. Aquinas offers a summary of the essential order among the cardinal virtues in a brief passage in the context of his discussion of fortitude in *ST* II-II, q. 123. In a. 12 he states: "Now reason's good is man's good; according to Dionysius (*Div. Nom.* iv) prudence, since it is a perfection of reason, has the good essentially: while justice effects this good, since it belongs to justice to establish the order of reason in all human affairs: whereas the other virtues safeguard this good, inasmuch as they moderate the passions, lest they lead man away from reason's good. As to the order of the latter, fortitude holds the first place, because fear of dangers of death has the greatest power to make man recede from the good of reason: and after fortitude comes temperance, since also pleasures of touch excel all others in hindering the good of reason. Now to be a thing essentially ranks before effecting it, and the latter ranks before safeguarding it by removing obstacles thereto. Wherefore among the cardinal virtues, prudence ranks first, justice second, fortitude third, temperance fourth, and after these the other virtues." An even briefer summary can be found in the discussion of temperance in *ST* II-II: "As the philosopher declares (*Ethic.* i. 2) *the good of the many is more godlike than the good of the individual*, wherefore the more a virtue regards the good of the many, the better it is. Now justice and fortitude regard the good of the many more than temperance does, since justice regards the relations between one man and another, while fortitude regards dangers of battle which are endured for the common weal: whereas temperance moderates only the desires and pleasures which affect man himself. Hence it is evident that justice and fortitude are more excellent virtues than temperance: while prudence and the theological virtues are more excellent still" (*ST* II-II, q. 141, a. 8).

the person against the encroachments of this powerful desire, thus ensuring that prudence arrives at a right estimate. Without the virtue of temperance there simply is no "true and perfect prudence."[19] Impaired prudence issues in a tangibly hampered moral life and consequently in diminished human flourishing.[20]

It is only at this point that we can properly appreciate all the entailments of the feedback loop between the moral virtues and prudence. The virtue of chastity is indispensable not only for the realization of the virtue of prudence in sexual matters, but also for the undisturbed proper operation of prudence in general. In other words, where the virtue of chastity is feeble and frail, the virtue of prudence will be encumbered and possibly corrupted. But more importantly, where the virtue of chastity is completely wanting—displaced by the vice of intemperance—charity, the love of friendship with God, might very well also be rejected outright. For there are not only venial, but also mortal sins against chastity.

This feedback loop between temperance and the other cardinal virtues becomes a matter of importance for postlapsarian human existence: after the loss of original righteousness and the withdrawal of the original gift of sanctifying grace, human beings live in an existential predicament in which the acts of the sense appetites, the passions, can revolt at any moment because the rational appetite, the will, has been connatively weakened. Imagine a rider upon a horse that suddenly bolts—either away from a real or imagined danger or toward an enticing pleasure. If the rider does not have firm control of the reins, how will he or she ever reach his or her destination? In sexual matters, without the support of the virtue of chastity, the virtues of prudence and justice cannot properly develop, because they will constantly be left unsettled by the desire for inordinate sexual pleasure—especially if this desire has been habituated into the

---

19. See the pertinent discussion of whether prudence can be in the sinner in *ST* II-II, q. 47, a. 13.

20. It is important to distinguish those persons whose acquired virtue of prudence has been severely impaired and even corrupted by the vice of lust from those whose acquired prudence is simply imperfect. While the deliberations and estimates of the former, especially in the case of the corruption of prudence, turn out to be false, the deliberations and estimates of the latter are limited in scope.

vice of lust, a particularly damaging subclass of the vice of intemperance.

As already stated, intemperance and lust are vices, because the agent indulges in inordinate sensual pleasures. Therefore the virtue of temperance is not first and foremost about regulating the amount of pleasure to be had ("moderation")—although temperance is *also* about this—but is principally about the pursuit of those pleasures (*delectationes*) that are in accord with the order of reason and related to the ultimate end. In short, pleasure is by no means absent from the exercise of the virtue of temperance. Commenting on Aristotle, Aquinas observes that there are pleasures "characteristic of the temperate man precisely as he enjoys his own activity; and these he does not avoid but rather seeks."[21] As secondary ends are related to the final end, rightly ordered sensual pleasures are concomitant with virtuous activity that is ordered to the final end. Hence, according to Aquinas, the enjoyment of rightly ordered pleasure is integral to the moral life.

THE VICE OF LUST AND THE LOSS OF CHASTITY

Aquinas clarifies the central criterion of inordinate pleasure when he considers lust (*luxuria*) in its broader sense: "Lust is any kind of surfeit" (*luxuria est quaelibet superfluitas*; ST II-II, q. 153, a. 1, ad 1). Lust (*luxuria*) in the wider sense is indexed to anything being in excess. Lust signifies the person "debauched with pleasures" (*luxuriosus quasi solutus in voluptates*), as Aquinas tersely quotes from Isidore's *Etymologia*. But Aquinas thinks it right to reserve the term *luxuria* in its specific and precise sense for the kind of sensual pleasure that is most intense—in short, for sexual pleasure. The primary reason for this stricter conception of lust is that temperance and intemperance concern those natural desires (*concupiscentiae naturales*) that are directed to the preservation of human nature: the desires for food and sex (*concupiscentiae ciborum et venereorum*; ST II-II, q. 142,

---

21. *In decem libros Ethicorum Aristotelis ad Nicomachum expositio* VII, lect. 12 (Marietti, no. 1497). Translation from Aquinas, *Commentary on Aristotle's* Nicomachean Ethics, trans. C. I. Litzinger, OP (Notre Dame, Ind.: Dumb Ox Books, 1993), 464.

a. 2, ad 2). "Hence," Aquinas states, "temperance is properly about pleasures of food and drink and sexual pleasures. Now, these pleasures result from the sense of touch. Wherefore it follows that temperance is about pleasures of touch" (*ST* II-II, q. 141, a. 4). Touch, the somesthetic sense, is the basis of all the other senses (*ST* I, q. 75, a. 5; *De ver.*, q. 22, a. 5) and hence holds primacy in respect to all natural desires of the human as a sensual being. Sensual desires and the sensual pleasures human beings seek are so strong because they are so basic to sustaining human nature through nutrition and procreation. Indulging intentionally and regularly in the pleasures of the palate inordinately—intemperance in matters of food—and consequently having acquired the respective *habitus* to do so, constitutes the vice of gluttony. Indulging intentionally and regularly in inordinate sexual pleasures—intemperance in matters of sex—and consequently having acquired the *habitus* to do so, constitutes the vice of lust.[22] Aquinas reckons the effects of gluttony on a person's mind quite differently from the effects of lust: "[Sexual] pleasures ... more than anything else work the greatest havoc in [one's] mind."[23] While he does not elaborate on this matter in detail, one can surmise that this effect of sexual pleasures is due to their surpassing intensity and to their complex connection with other desires that find their proper realization in conjugal union, desires for intimacy and comfort. The desire for inordinate sexual pleasure, when heeded and habituated as the vice of lust, can—due to the vehemence of the passions to which the vice of lust gives rise—frequently acquire a powerful and even absorbing reality. For this reason, Aquinas tersely states, "intemperance is the chief corruptive of prudence [*intemperantia maxime corrumpit prudentiam*]; wherefore the vices opposed to prudence arise

---

22. Aquinas treats the important topic of the increase and diminishment of *habitus* in *ST* I-II, qq. 52–53. For a concise treatment of this crucial subject, see Vernon J. Bourke, "The Role of *Habitus* in the Thomistic Metaphysics of Potency and Act," in *Essays in Thomism*, ed. Robert E. Brennan, OP (New York: Sheed and Ward, 1942), 101–10 and 370–73; for a more comprehensive philosophical analysis of *habitus*, see George P. Klubertanz, SJ, *Habits and Virtues* (New York: Appleton-Century-Crofts, 1965); and for the indispensability of *habitus* in the context of a fully developed theological virtue ethics, see Cessario, *The Moral Virtues and Theological Ethics*, 34–44.

23. *ST* II-II, q. 153, a. 1, ad 1: "Luxuria principaliter quidem est in voluptatibus venereis, quae maxime et praecipue animum hominis resolvunt."

chiefly from lust, which is the principal species of intemperance" (*ST* II-II, q. 153, a. 5, ad 1).

Aquinas's analysis of the vice of lust comprises two further components that are of consequence for our deliberations. First, according to a venerable tradition of patristic and monastic spiritual theology that Aquinas receives and affirms, lust is not only a species of intemperance, but also a capital or principal vice. A capital vice, he argues, is "one that has a very desirable end, so that through desire for that end, [one] proceeds to commit many sins.... The end of lust is [sexual] pleasure, which is very great. Wherefore this pleasure is very desirable as regards the sensitive appetite, both on account of the intensity of the pleasure, and because such like concupiscence is connatural to [the human being]" (*ST* II-II, q. 153, a. 4).

Second, Aquinas distinguishes between inordinate and disordered forms of lust. While the inordinate forms of lust include all forms of an inordinate enjoyment of the pleasure entailed in the sexual act that violate relations with others and hence constitute also grave sins against justice, the disordered forms of lust betray the natural teleological order of the procreative act and thus constitute "vices against nature" (*vitia contra naturam*; *ST* II-II, q. 154, a. 12), and sins against God the creator of that natural, teleological order.[24] Confirming Aquinas's important distinction, the *Catechism* states: "Sexual pleasure is morally disordered when sought for itself, isolated from its procreative and unitive purposes" (*CCC* §2351). According to Aquinas's distinction and in light of the church's teaching, the consumption of pornography, undertaken for the end of obtaining sexual pleasure—for oneself and by oneself—from depicted sexual objects and simulated sexual acts, arises from inordinate lust that terminates in disordered forms of lust.[25]

---

24. *ST* II-II, q. 154, a. 12, ad 1: "Just as the ordering of right reason proceeds from man, so the order of nature is from God Himself; wherefore in sins contrary to nature, whereby the very order of nature is violated, an injury is done to God the Author of nature."

25. While Aquinas understands disordered forms of lust to be much graver offenses than inordinate forms of lust, in the order of justice, adultery, and rape would be considered much graver offenses than masturbation and the consumption of pornography, all of which are disordered forms of lust. Yet when considered in the order of justice, pornography figures as a grave offense against the dignity of all participants (actors, vendors, viewers, and the public). Finally, in order to maintain a properly balanced view of the

There are four entailments of Aquinas's analysis of the capital vice of lust and the loss of chastity that deserve closer consideration. Only by attending to these four entailments do we come to grasp the nature and the extent of the damage that the loss of chastity inflicts upon attaining our final end and the happiness to which humanity is ordained.

First, it is worth taking into account that to make a deliberate act of inner consent of *delectatio* in images, scenes, or movies that give rise to sexual lust may in some cases damage and in other cases destroy the virtue of charity, that is, the friendship with God (*ST* II-II, q. 23, a. 1), and with it the infused virtue of chastity.[26] While the question of what constitutes such a deliberate act is, of course, complex and beyond the scope of this chapter, it is apposite to consider at least the central distinction to which any answer will need to conform. It is the distinction between a delectation that is the immediate result of acts of the sense-appetite that occur without the command of reason (*ST* I-II, q. 17, a. 7; q. 154, a. 5) and a deliberate act of consent, commanded by reason.[27] It is the deliberate act of consent commanded by reason that is incompatible with the presence

---

whole matter, it is imperative to keep in mind that, according to Aquinas, sexual sins are not the worst; rather, the worst sins are "those which are directly against God, and sins that are injurious to the life of one already born, such as murder" (*ST* II-II, q. 154, a. 3).

26. In *ST* I-II, q. 74, a. 8, Aquinas states the principle that allows us to demarcate the damage from the destruction of the virtue of charity and with it the infused virtue of chastity: "That a man in thinking of fornication takes pleasure in the act thought of, is due to his desire being inclined to this act. Wherefore the fact that a man consents to such a delectation, amounts to nothing less than a consent to the inclination of his appetite to fornication: for no man takes pleasure except in that which is in conformity with his appetite. Now it is a mortal sin, if a man deliberately chooses that his appetite be conformed to what is in itself a mortal sin. Wherefore such a consent to delectation in a mortal sin, is itself a mortal sin." See also *ST* I-II, q. 88, a. 5, ad 2; *ST* II-II, q. 154, a. 4; *Sent.* II, d. 24, q. 3, a. 4; *De ver.*, q. 15, a. 4; and *Quod.* XII, q. 22, a. 1 (237; Marietti, no. 258). In these passages Aquinas is touching only briefly on the very important but complex issue of what he calls *consensus in delectationem* and what later moral theologians termed *delectatio morosa*, one of the interior sins of lust. The topic deserves a more extensive and nuanced treatment than I can offer in this place. For an informative discussion, see Marie-Michel Labourdette, OP, *Cours de Théologie Morale*, vol. 15: *La vie sexuelle: La chasteté* (unpublished manuscript, Toulouse), 170–75.

27. *ST* II-II, q. 35, a. 3: "The consummation of sin is in the consent of reason.... Wherefore if the sin be a mere beginning of sin in the sensuality alone, without attaining to the consent of reason, it is a venial sin on account of the imperfection of the act."

of charity in the agent and is, therefore, a mortal sin. But there are other, more subtle and elusive forms of volitional consent that are venial sins, sins that do not immediately destroy the friendship with God. Developing Aquinas's distinction further, Karol Wojtyła (Pope St. John Paul II), in the above-cited *Love and Responsibility*, helpfully delineates the very fine, but crucially important line between sensual desire and volitional consent:

> Neither sensuality nor even concupiscence is a sin in itself, since only that which derives from the will can be a sin—only an act of a conscious and voluntary nature (*voluntarium*).... Further, a sensual reaction, or the "stirring of" carnal desire which results from it, and which occurs irrespectively and independently of the will, cannot in themselves be sins.... The source of this desire is the power of concupiscence (*appetitus concupiscibilis* as St. Thomas calls it), and so not the will. Concupiscence of the senses tends to become active "wanting," which is an act of the will. The dividing line between the two is however clear. Concupiscence does not immediately aim at causing the will fully and actively to want the object of sensual desire: passive acquiescence suffices.
>
> Here we stand on the threshold of sin, and we see that concupiscence, which seeks continually to induce the will to cross it, is rightly called the "germ of sin." As soon as the will consents it begins actively to want what is spontaneously "happening" in the senses and the sensual appetites. From then onwards, this is not something merely "happening" to a man, but something which he himself begins actively doing—at first only internally, for the will is in the first place the source of interior acts, of interior "deeds." These deeds have a moral value, are good or evil, and if they are evil we call them sins.[28]

Wojtyła's analysis can easily be applied to the common scenario of someone who, while perusing the internet, is inadvertently confronted with sexually suggestive or even pornographic imagery that elicits an instantaneous sensual reaction. Following Aquinas, Wojtyła distinguishes between the passive acquiescence to this sensual reaction and the active desire, and between the active desire and the deliberate interior act of consent in delectation commanded by reason (which according to Aquinas does entail taking counsel and

---

28. Karol Wojtyła (Pope John Paul II), *Love and Responsibility*, trans. H. T. Willetts (New York: Farrar, Straus and Giroux, 1981), 161–62.

making a judgment).[29] It is only the latter *consensus in delectationem* that Aquinas understands to be a mortal sin.[30]

Second, Aquinas offers a morally salient and still pertinent phenomenology of the incontinent person as distinguished from the intemperate person. The temperate person, the person who has the *habitus* of selfless self-discipline and proper measure, finds it easy to abide by the order of reason in matters of food, drink, and sex. In the temperate person the desire for sensual and spiritual pleasures is directed to and integrated in the proper pursuit of the final end. In the intemperate person, the desire for sensual pleasures is inordinate; sensual pleasure becomes an inordinately pursued end; for some it might even become the final end. The pursuit of what is good for its own sake, the *bonum honestum* according to the order of reason, is abandoned, and consequently the intemperate person is unable to act well with consistency.

Between the temperate and the intemperate stand those who struggle with vehement desires (*ST* II-II, q. 143, a. 1). Those who, while struggling with these strong desires, abide by the order of reason, are continent; they exercise self-control by choosing to perform distinct temperate acts. Those who, while struggling with these strong desires, fall short of the order of reason and fail to exercise acts of temperance, are incontinent. The root of incontinence is a failure of the will. Aquinas helpfully identifies two forms of such a failure of the will, both of which are of immediate relevance to the consumption of pornography: the refusal to think about our acts, which is the sin of impetuosity (*praevolatio*), and the failure to follow through on our own best judgment, which is the sin of weakness (*debilitas*) (*ST* II-II, q. 156, a. 1).

---

29. The virtue of prudence "is right reason applied to action," which entails three interior acts: (1) to take counsel (to inquire), (2) to judge what has been discovered by way of inquiry, and (3) to command, that is, to apply to action what has been counseled and judged (*ST* II-II, q. 47, a. 8). Being directed to a false end, a deliberate act of consent in such a delectation is an instance of false prudence (*ST* II-II, q. 47, a. 13). It is, indeed, a failure of prudence in the proper sense.

30. On the important issue of the intensification and the remission of *habitus*, see Aquinas's detailed treatment in *ST* I-II, qq. 52–53. On the complex but relevant topic of the effect of infused virtues on acquired vices, see the instructive essay by Sherwin, "Infused Virtue and the Effects of Acquired Vice."

Due to the failure of the will, the incontinent person lacks the power of resistance to sexual pleasures. He or she gives in to a sudden attack of the sexual appetite, but afterwards deeply regrets having been overpowered by sexual passion. The intemperate person, on the contrary, is committed to the vice of lust without moral qualms (*ST* II-II, q. 156, a. 3). In this person, consequently, Aquinas observes, only false prudence is operative: "Whoever disposes well of such things as are fitting for an evil end, has false prudence, insofar as that which he takes for an end, is good, not in truth but in appearance.... This is the prudence of which the Apostle says (*Rom.* 8:6): *The prudence* (Douay, *wisdom*) *of the flesh is death*, because ... it places its ultimate end in the pleasures of the flesh" (*ST* II-II, q. 47, a. 13).[31]

For the incontinent as well as the intemperate person, indulging in the custom of watching the simulacra presented by internet pornography may sooner or later issue in a habituated, intensifying "necessity," a compulsion to watch these simulacra again and again.[32] For whatever is experienced as lustful in watching them only lasts a short while and, moreover, subsides over time despite the same stimulus; hence, having the recurring experience of what makes the vice attractive in the first place will require a higher frequency as well as a greater potency. This compulsion works itself out differently in the incontinent and the intemperate.

Third, Aquinas—with the help of Augustine—offers a first step toward a deeper understanding of the reasons why the consumption of internet pornography can easily become compulsive and thus lead to the slow destruction of moral self-possession: "Concupiscence,

---

31. See also more extensively *ST* II-II, q. 55, aa. 1 and 2.
32. According to Dr. David Kupfer, chairman of the DSM-V task force with the American Psychiatric Association, in 2008 "sex addiction [was] not listed as a disorder in the current edition of the *Diagnostic and Statistical Manual of Mental Disorders* (DSM), the bible of psychiatric disorders, but it [was] being considered by a work group on non-substance-related addictions for inclusion in the next edition [in 2013]." Allen Salkin, "No Sympathy for the Sex Addict," *The New York Times*, September 7, 2008, available at topics.nytimes.com/topics/reference/timestopics/subjects/s/sexual_addiction/index.htm. For a nuanced empirical study that works toward a conceptual clarification of problematic internet pornography use, see Chad T. Wetterneck et al., "The Role of Sexual Compulsiveness, Impulsivity, and Experiential Avoidance in Internet Pornography Use," *The Psychological Record* 62 (2012): 3–18.

if indulged, gathers strength: wherefore Augustine says (*Conf.* 8.5): *Lust served became a custom, and custom not resisted became necessity*" (*ST* II-II, q. 142, a. 2).[33] Concupiscence indulged and habituated gathers such strength that it takes on the nature of a certain kind of necessity that compels the judgment of free choice (*liberum arbitrium*) in such a way that the attribute "free" (*liberum*) becomes increasingly vacuous. This resembles and—for an increasing number of clinicians—actually constitutes addiction.[34] Indeed, what seems most characteristic and paradoxical of compulsive behaviors, such as the regular consumption of pornography, is that there is little delectation found in the simulacra viewed, only an ongoing craving. Evidence suggests that in advanced cases of compulsive perusal, no consummatory pleasure is gained, and the appetitive pleasure, which arises from imaging something desirable, is in need of ever stronger visual stimulation in order to be experienced at all. Eventually, appetitive pleasure likewise ceases to be experienced but continues to be craved.[35]

There obtains, fourth and finally, a subterranean connection between longstanding, illicit sexual pleasures and the corruption of natural reason. Aquinas assumes that longstanding and culturally accepted but *per se* illicit sexual practices arising from the vice of lust contribute to the corruption of natural reason (*ST* II-II, q. 154, a. 2, ad 1) such that not much if anything besides the first principle of the natural law remains naturally accessible to such a culturally corrupted reason. In such a context it requires grace and the moral catechesis

---

33. In Maria Boulding's translation, Augustine's analysis in *Confessions* 8.5 takes on a new, pertinent ring: "The truth is that disordered lust springs from a perverted will; when lust is pandered to, a habit is formed; when habit is not checked, it hardens into compulsion. These were like interlinking rings forming what I have described as a chain, and my harsh servitude used it to keep me under duress." St. Augustine, *The Confessions*, trans. Maria Boulding, OSB, in *The Works of St. Augustine: A Translation for the 21st Century* I/1 (Hyde Park, N.Y.: New City Press, 1997), 192.

34. For a study by a Christian philosopher that is as innovative as it is thoughtful on how the category of "habit" allows us to overcome the simplistic alternatives of "disease" versus "choice" in the understanding of addiction, see Kent Dunnington, *Addiction and Virtue: Beyond the Models of Disease and Choice* (Downers Grove, Ill.: Intervarsity Press, 2011).

35. A number of articles on internet pornography, compulsive behaviors, and addiction can be found in the journal *Sexual Addiction and Compulsivity*.

of the church to restore reason to its full created capacities of natural moral reasoning.[36]

If Aquinas is right about these connections, then we should expect just the sort of cultural symptoms documented, for example, by sociologist Jill Manning, who perceives a correlation between the repeated consumption of "cyberporn" and an increased appetite for more graphic types of pornography, a growing number of people struggling with compulsive and addictive sexual behavior, increased marital distress, and risk of separation and divorce.[37] Manning also cites statistics from the American Academy of Matrimonial Lawyers, who in 2002 reported that, for example, 56 percent of divorce cases involved one party having "an obsessive interest in pornographic websites."[38]

---

36. In contemporary late-modern Western culture, the broadly accepted contraceptive mentality, that is, the principled separation of sexual activity from procreation and the redirecting of sexual activity to the primary if not exclusive purpose of sexual pleasure (possibly but not necessarily in combination with the expression of personal affection and intimacy), and the widely shared moral indifference to the unborn human being, arguably indicate a considerable corruption of natural reason. The fact that it is virtually impossible to communicate rationally to those engrossed in the contraceptive mentality that the current transvaluation of morals betrays the gift of life, abandons the order of reason, and is largely borne from the vice of lust might be an indication of how far the corruption of natural reason has already progressed. Hence the familiar and pervasive charge that the Catholic church's teaching on the procreative and unitive ends of the conjugal act is hopelessly out of touch with the dominant spirit of the time might very well be correct, but for precisely this reason it also betrays the profound corruption of natural reason from which the plaintiff, the dominant spirit of the time, suffers. For this reason the very methodology of empirical studies on self-perceived effects of the consumption of pornography is vulnerable to the self-deceptive assessments of those answering the questionnaires and consequently offer little else than a mirror of a collective and hence largely imperceptible indulgence in the vice of intemperance. For an empirical study whose methodology is vulnerable to such critical questioning, see Gert Martin Hald and Neil M. Malamuth, "Self-perceived Effects of Pornography Consumption," *Archives of Sexual Behaviour* 37 (2008): 614–25.

37. See Jill C. Manning's testimony for the Hearing on "The Impact of Internet Pornography on Marriage and the Family," Subcommittee on the Constitution, Civil Rights and Property, Committee on Judiciary, United States Senate, Washington D.C., August 2005, available at s3.amazonaws.com/thf_media/2010/pdf/ManningTST.pdf.

38. See J. Dedmon, "Is the Internet Bad for Your Marriage? Online Affairs, Pornographic Sites Playing Greater Role in Divorces," 2002 press release from American Academy of Matrimonial Lawyers, cited in Jill Manning's testimony above.

THE SPIRITUAL ROOT OF THE PROBLEM: *ACEDIA* AND HER DAUGHTERS

The church on earth (*ecclesia militans*) is continuously faced with the varying consequences of the connative woundedness of the human will and is aware of the truth expressed in 1 John: "All that is in the world, the lust of the flesh, and the lust of the eyes and the pride of life, is not of the Father, but of the world" (1 Jn 2:16; RSV). This inspired exhortation has profoundly influenced subsequent theological reflection on sin and vice from Evagrius of Pontus and John Cassian to Augustine, from Pope Gregory the Great to Thomas Aquinas. A contemporary rehabilitation of the virtue of chastity cannot afford to ignore the classical Christian analysis of the negative spiritual root that gives rise to acts and to vices contrary to and eventually destructive of chastity. Synthesizing and systematizing the spiritual wisdom of the Church Fathers, Aquinas's moral psychology enables the retrieval of a robust appreciation of both the nature of chastity and the nature of its spiritual foes.

To understand and appreciate the nature and the indispensability of the virtue of chastity in sexual matters is not necessarily to understand the notoriously elusive negative spiritual root that gives rise to the lust of the eyes and the lust of the flesh, the typical symptoms of the capital vice of lust, which in turn has further offspring. Identifying this root is a separate task, especially if one holds that in a particular society, such as our own, the lust of the eyes and the flesh are both encouraged and easily facilitated.[39] However, a theological analysis, informed by the moral theology of Thomas Aquinas, of the prevalence of pornography and its addictive nature will not need to get entangled in intricacies of assessing and evaluating contemporary data, but will rather inquire into the spiritual and moral deficiencies that account for this moral problem.

---

39. Consider the *cri de coeur* by the president of Morality in Media: "Pornography is now more popular than baseball. In fact, it has become America's pastime, and we are awash in it. Porn is on our computers, our smart phones, and our cable or satellite TV. It's common in our hotels and even in many retail stores and gas stations. For many men—and increasingly, women—it is part of their daily lives." Patrick A. Trueman, "The Pornography Pandemic," *Columbia* (November 2011): 24.

In order to identify the spiritual root of said problem we must turn to a largely forgotten vice, another of the capital vices: *acedia*, sloth, better rendered as "spiritual apathy"—a profound sorrow about the spiritual good.[40] In this section, I will first, by way of entry into unfamiliar territory, propose two modern offsprings of spiritual apathy (*acedia*)—boredom, or *ennui*, and *ressentiment*. Next, I will treat the vice of *acedia* itself, and finally I will turn to one of this vice's perennial offsprings, what the tradition of patristic and monastic spiritual theology identified as the sixth "daughter" of *acedia*, the "wandering of the mind" (*pervagatio mentis*), with the other five daughters of *acedia* being malice, spite, faint-heartedness, despair, and sluggishness in regard to the commandments.

Acedia, which is concomitant with the loss of hope and charity and with a profound weakening if not loss of faith, is an insidious vice, and today we tend to know it by one of its most common effects: *ennui* or boredom.[41] The vice of spiritual apathy is the aversion

---

40. Richard Regan in his translation of Thomas Aquinas's *De malo, On Evil* (Oxford: Oxford University Press, 2003), 361. Basil Cole rightly observes that "the most neglected capital vice in the literature of spiritual theology in our times is *acedia*." Basil Cole, OP, *The Hidden Enemies of the Priesthood: The Contributions of St. Thomas Aquinas* (Staten Island, N.Y.: Society of St. Paul, 2007), 215. In order to address this lacuna, a noticeable effort has been undertaken recently to recover a fuller awareness of this particularly damaging vice. See Rebecca Konyndyk DeYoung's "Resistance to the Demands of Love: Aquinas on the Vice of *Acedia*," *The Thomist* 68, no. 2 (2004): 173–204, *Glittering Vices: A New Look at the Seven Deadly Sins and Their Remedies* (Grand Rapids, Mich.: Brazos, 2009), 79–98, "Aquinas on the Vice of Sloth: Three Interpretive Issues," *The Thomist* 75, no. 1 (2011): 43–64, and with Colleen McCluskey, and Van Dyke, *Aquinas's Ethics*, 175–81. For an extension of DeYoung's analysis and argument, see Matthew Levering's instructive chapter "Sloth and the Joy of the Resurrection" in his *The Betrayal of Charity: The Sins that Sabotage Divine Love* (Waco, Tex.: Baylor University Press, 2011), 41–62. The indispensable classic study remains Siegfried Wenzel, *The Sin of Sloth: Acedia in Medieval Thought and Literature* (Chapel Hill: University of North Carolina Press, 1967).

41. *Acedia* is arguably the root cause of the typically modern boredom (*Langeweile*) of which Martin Heidegger has offered an intriguing phenomenological analysis. Due to the inescapably supernatural character of the extant providential order, *acedia* itself becomes the theological key to Heidegger's phenomenological analysis of boredom. He gains his insights into boredom from a philosophically intentional though theologically unacknowledged stance ("bracketed" by Heidegger's phenomenological method) within the existential horizon of *acedia*. The scope of his analysis coincides with the existential horizon of *Dasein zum Tode* which is nothing but a shrewd philosophical elevation of *acedia* to the constitutive characteristic of *Dasein*, being-in-the-world ("Die Verfallenheit Daseins an die Welt"). See Martin Heidegger, *Die Grundbegriffe der Metaphysik: Welt—Endlichkeit—Einsamkeit, Freiburger Vorlesung 1929/30*, ed. Friedrich-Wilhelm von

and the inward resistance to the interior divine good, charity, through which the Holy Spirit effects inchoately the realization of a person's supernatural orientation to eternal communication in the life and love of the Trinity. As this realization is not instantaneous but progressive, the life effected by sanctifying grace (shaped by the theological and the infused moral virtues) always involves the struggle with old sinful patterns. The perfective elevation into the divine good is, consequently, an arduous process that entails a conscious struggling against and dying to old weaknesses and vices. In short, the process is open to contrariety that issues in aversion and resistance: "This divine good is a source of sadness for human beings because of the contrariety of the spirit to the flesh, since 'the flesh lusts against the spirit,' as the Apostle says in Gal. 5:17. And so when desire of the flesh [*affectus carnis*] is dominant in human beings, they have distaste for spiritual good as contrary to their good" (*De malo*, q. 11, a. 2).[42]

The reference to Galatians 5:17 indicates that the desire of the flesh, the *affectus carnis*, signifies the lingering effects of sin that form obstacles to the arduous realization of a life transformed and patterned by divine charity. Aquinas is intensely aware that the Pauline *sarx* signifies not only an obstacle but an opposition to the divine good. This opposition usually arises from the sense appetites and issues in attacks of the passions. As long as the rational appetite, the will, clings in charity and hope to Christ, the person is able to withstand the opposition arising from the sense appetites.[43] However, failing to rely on charity and hope, a person might acquiesce in the movement of the sense-appetite by giving the consent of reason: "The movement of sloth is sometimes in the sensuality alone, by rea-

---

Herrmann (Frankfurt a.M.: Vittorio Klostermann, 1983), 117–249; translated into English as *The Fundamental Concepts of Metaphysics: World, Finitude, Solitude*, trans. William McNeill and Nicholas Walker (Bloomington: Indiana University Press, 1995), 78–167. For a robust and relevant analysis of *acedia* as the source of the pervasive boredom modern people face, see the penetrating study by the Christian philosopher R. J. Snell, *Acedia and Its Discontents: Metaphysical Boredom in an Empire of Desire* (Kettering, Ohio: Angelico Press, 2015).

42. Regan (trans.), 669–70.

43. For a discussion of the complex matter that is as nuanced as it is clear, see Cessario, *Moral Virtues and Theological Ethics*, 117–23. He helpfully points out that "this kind of union ... can coexist—think of Christ alone with the apostles in the storm (Mk 4:35–41)—with even the most violent movements of the sense appetites" (121).

son of the opposition of the flesh to the spirit, and then it is a venial sin; whereas sometimes it reaches to the reason, which consents in the dislike, horror and detestation of the Divine good, on account of the flesh utterly prevailing over the spirit. In this case, it is evident that sloth is a mortal sin" (*ST* II-II, q. 35, a. 3).

Acedia creates a void to be filled not with what one has come to detest, the divine good, but with transient rushes of pleasure—primarily sexual pleasure—to ward off the *ennui* of life bereft of its *telos*, the divine good.[44] But the simulacra that promise such rushes of pleasure betray. They only increase the craving, breed compulsion, and intensify spiritual apathy. Unchecked, such detestation of the divine good issues in a sadness that cannot remain without consequences, for "no human being can long remain pleasureless and sad."[45] Aquinas perspicaciously observes in *De malo*: "Due to the sadness conceived regarding spiritual goods, their minds then wander over the illicit things in which the carnal spirit takes pleasure. And in avoiding such sadness, we note the progression wherein human beings indeed first avoid spiritual goods and then attack them."[46] The flight from sadness, which begins with avoiding and resisting spiritual goods and ends with attacking them, represents with uncanny accuracy the anti-Christian *ressentiment* typical of secular, post-Christian societies. The collective ideological, cultural, social, and political aversion to the di-

---

44. For a contemporary fictional account of addiction to pornography—initially fostered, in large part, by boredom—see Russell Banks, *Lost Memory of Skin* (New York: HarperCollins, 2011). The protagonist—"the Kid"—notes that "maybe what the psychologists and the shrink in prison were trying to get the addicts to overcome was boredom instead of desires and cravings, and in reality the main cause for addiction is being bored" (346). Dunnington's pertinent philosophical analysis of the malaise of late-modern culture echoes Banks's perceptive fictional account. Bereft of the *telos* that the divine good affords, many modern persons suffer from a deep sense of arbitrariness that haunts their decisions. Consequently, "addictions provide compelling motivation toward specific ends in a way that is otherwise inaccessible to the modern person who can find no final criterion to justify activity in a definite direction.... If there is a uniquely modern disease, it is the disease of modern boredom, for which addiction is one of the rare proven antidotes" (Dunnington, *Addiction and Virtue*, 116). For an analysis, consonant with Dunnington's, that proposes the keeping of the Sabbath as a spiritual and cultural antidote to boredom, see the insightful essay by Nicholas E. Lombardo, OP, "Boredom and Modern Culture," *Logos* 22, no. 2 (2017): 36–59.

45. *De malo*, q. 11, a. 4, citing *Nicomachean Ethics* VIII.5, 1157b15–16 (trans. Regan, 677).

46. Ibid. (679).

vine good (previously received and embraced) might very well issue in a collective spiritual state of *acedia*.

Hence boredom is only one shoot that springs from the collective *acedia* pervading this secular age. Another one of its shoots is *ressentiment*. Max Scheler, in his influential phenomenology of feeling states, has offered an astute analysis of this distinctly modern spiritual attitude. *Ressentiment* arises from the weakness of the will and issues in contempt of those moral values one despairs of achieving oneself. And this *ressentiment*, according to Scheler, not only characterizes the modern secular individual but also the most influential strand of modern secular moral theory: it motivates the whole modern subjective theory of moral values, an approach to ethics currently best known as emotivism.[47] If moral values amount to nothing but subjective phenomena of the human mind without independent meaning and existence (a position held by a variety of naturalist, positivist, and pragmatist philosophers) one, of course, never can be found lacking in light of an objective standard of moral values.[48] In a chapter entitled "Chastity and Resentment" in his *Love and Responsibility*, Wojtyła advances Scheler's analysis by instructively relating it to and differentiating it from Aquinas's analysis of *acedia*:

Resentment possesses ... the distinctive characteristics of the cardinal sin called sloth. St. Thomas defines sloth (*acedia*) as "a sadness arising from the

---

47. For two of the most incisive and classical criticisms of emotivism in the English-speaking context, see C. S. Lewis, *The Abolition of Man* (San Francisco, Calif.: HarperOne, 2001); and Alasdair MacIntyre, *After Virtue*, 3rd ed. (Notre Dame, Ind.: University of Notre Dame Press, 2007).

48. "The *ressentiment*-laden man, who in his insufficiency is oppressed, tormented, and frightened by the negative judgment of his existence which flows from an objective hierarchy of values—and who is secretly aware of the arbitrary and distorted character of his own valuations—'transvalues' the idea of value itself by *denying* the existence of such an objective hierarchy.... The man of *ressentiment* ... wreaks vengeance on the idea whose test he cannot stand by pulling it down to the level of his factual condition. Thus his awareness of sin and nothingness explodes the beautiful structure of the world of values, debasing the idea for the sake of an illusory cure. 'All values, after all, are "only" relative and "subjective"—they vary with the individual, with desire, race, people, etc.'" Max Scheler, *Ressentiment*, ed. Lewis A. Coser, trans. William W. Holdheim (New York: Cronwell-Collier, 1961), 145–46. The original work is *Über Ressentiment und moralisches Werturteil* (Leipzig: Wilhelm Engelmann, 1912), 77–78. There is hardly any other place in modern secular society more thoroughly penetrated by *ressentiment* than the late-modern secular research university. There is also hardly any other place where the virtue of chastity is met with such unqualified contempt of *ressentiment*.

fact that the good is difficult." This sadness, far from denying the good, indirectly helps to keep respect for it alive in the soul. Resentment, however, does not stop at this: it not only distorts the features of the good but devalues that which rightly deserves respect, so that man need not struggle to raise himself to the level of the true good, but can "light-heartedly" recognize as good only what suits him, what is convenient and comfortable for him. Resentment is a feature of the subjective mentality: pleasure takes the place of superior values.[49]

In other words, while its root condition is spiritual apathy, the typically modern condition of *ressentiment* carries the inner logic of *acedia* further—to contempt of what is truly good and to cleaving to what is individually agreeable. Therefore, a proper appreciation of the dynamics characteristic of this *ressentiment* goes a long way toward helping us understand a large part of the motivation behind the widespread maligning of chastity in contemporary culture: the true and objective good inherent in the virtue of chastity indicates an objective moral standard that amounts to a salient critique of the prevalent moral relativism and subjectivism in matters of human sexuality. I shall now turn from the consideration of *acedia* itself to a very important subspecies of one of her so-called six classical daughters—curiosity—as a specific instantiation of the wandering of the mind after unlawful things.

If one consults the spiritual wisdom of the Church Fathers, one quickly learns that the capital vice of *acedia* rarely comes alone, but issues in other vices that persons affected by *ressentiment* are especially prone to develop. Free from the modern penchant for originality, Aquinas turns to the theological authority of Pope St. Gregory the Great, who in his *Moralia in Job* famously assigns to the vice of spiritual apathy the six daughters of malice, spite, faint-heartedness, despair, and sluggishness in regard to the commandments, and the wandering of the mind after unlawful things.[50] This *pervagatio mentis*,

---

49. Wojtyła, *Love and Responsibility*, 143–44.
50. The pertinent section from Pope Gregory's *Moralia in Job* can be found in vol. 3.2 (31.87–88; 489–91) of the only complete English translation of this important work: S. Gregory the Great, *Morals on the Book of Job*, trans. James Bliss, in *A Library of Fathers of the Holy Catholic Church*, trans. Members of the Church of England, vols. 18, 21, 23, 31 (Oxford / London: John Henry Parker / F. and J. Rivington, 1844–50): "From melancholy there arise malice, rancor, cowardice, despair, slothfulness in fulfilling the commands, and

this wandering of the mind after unlawful things, takes initial shape in one of its subspecies, a vice hardly anymore recognized as such—curiosity (*curiositas*). Curiosity is the first allegedly innocent step that can soon lead to habitual pornographic voyeurism and addiction. In his brief but incisive treatment of the vice of curiosity, Aquinas lets Augustine deliver the authoritative principle: "Concupiscence of the eyes makes [one] curious" (*ST* II-II, q. 167, a. 2, s.c.).[51] The scriptural authority adduced is the already quoted 1 John 2:16. In his response, Aquinas regards the inordinate and undisciplined consideration of sensible things as sinful, first, "when the sensible knowledge is not directed to something useful, but turns [one] away from some useful consideration," and second, "when the knowledge

---

a wandering of the mind after unlawful objects" (490). It is not without interest for our topic that in Gregory's grammar *tristitia*, translated as "melancholy," holds the place of *acedia* and that despair (*desperatio*) is one of its consequences. For the Latin original, see *Sancti Gregorii Magni Moralia in Job*, ed. Marc Adriaen, lib. 23–35, *CCSL* 143B (Turnhout: Brepols, 1985), 1610.28–30: "De tristitia, malitia, rancor, pusillanimitas, desperatio, torpor circa praecepta, uagatio mentis erga illicita nascitur." For an instructive study that makes the convincing case that Gregory's *Moralia in Job* constitutes a theologically still relevant Christological and ecclesiological commentary on the book of Job in the form of a spiritual exegesis inspired by Augustine's *De doctrina christiana*, see Katherina Greschat, *Die Moralia in Job Gregor des Großen: Ein christologisch-ekklesiologischer Kommentar* (Tübingen: Mohr Siebeck, 2005).

51. In *De Vera Religione*, completed on the eve of his priestly ordination (390), Augustine engages in a lengthy discussion of curiosity (38.69–54.106) in the context of the threefold concupiscence of carnal desire, pride, and curiosity, a triad largely inspired by 1 Jn 2:16 (38.70): "Here those three vices are signified, because by the lust of the flesh the lovers of the lowest kind of pleasure are signified, by the lust of the eyes the curious and the inquisitive, by worldly ambition the proud." *True Religion* [*De vera religione*], trans. Edmund Hill, OP, in *The Works of St. Augustine: A Translation for the 21st Century* I/8, 77. In his late homilies on 1 Jn, Augustine emphasizes the wide scope of curiosity. In light of the items named one might surmise that, had Augustine known about internet pornography, its consumption might very well have made this list: "He calls all curiosity the desire of the eyes. How extensive is curiosity? It is in spectacles, in theatres, in the devil's sacraments, in magic, in evil deeds." *Homilies on the First Epistle of John* [*Tractatus in Epistolam Joannis ad Parthos*], trans. Boniface Ramsey, *The Works of St. Augustine: A Translation for the 21st Century* III/14, 49. For an illuminating study on curiosity in Augustine's thought, see Joseph Torchia, OP, *Restless Mind: Curiositas & the Scope of Inquiry in St. Augustine's Psychology* (Milwaukee, Wis.: Marquette University Press, 2013), and for a profound meditation on intellectual appetite *ad mentem S. Augustini*, see Paul J. Griffiths, *Intellectual Appetite: A Theological Grammar* (Washington, D.C.: The Catholic University of America Press, 2009), chaps. 11–12, which deal with curiosity and unfold in highly instructive ways pertinent aspects of Augustine's thought from the latter part of *De Vera Religione*.

of sensible things is directed to something harmful, as looking on a woman [or a man] is directed to lust" (*ST* II-II, q. 167, a. 2). In his response to an objection it almost seems as if Aquinas had a prophetic knowledge of the future rise of internet pornography: "Sight-seeing [*inspectio spectaculorum*] becomes sinful, when it renders [one] prone to the vices of lust and cruelty on account of things [one] sees represented. Hence Chrysostom says that such sights make [people] adulterers and shameless" (*ST* II-II, q. 167, a. 2, ad 2).[52]

In his *Confessions*, Augustine offers a strikingly powerful analysis of this pernicious dynamic, a dynamic that comes to new life in Maria Boulding's gripping translation. In a psychologically intriguing passage in *Confessions* VI, Augustine narrates an event in the life of his close friend Alypius—an event that caused Alypius being "assailed by an entirely unexpected craving for gladiatorial entertainments."[53] Dragged by some fellow students to the stadium to watch gladiatorial fights, Alypius determines to keep his eyes shut and his mind detached from the occurrences around him:

When they arrived and settled themselves in what seats they could find, the whole place was heaving with thoroughly brutal pleasure. He kept the gateway of his eyes closed, forbidding his mind to go out that way to such evils. If only he could have stopped his ears, too! At a certain tense moment in the fight a huge roar from the entire crowd beat upon him. He was overwhelmed by curiosity, and on the excuse that he would be prepared to condemn and rise above whatever was happening even if he saw it, he opened his eyes, and suffered a more grievous wound in his soul than the gladiator he wished to see had received in his body.... As he saw the blood he gulped the brutality along with it; he did not turn away but fixed his gaze there and drank in the frenzy, not aware of what he was doing, reveling in the wicked contest and intoxicated on sanguinary pleasure.... What more need be said? He watched, he shouted, he grew hot with excitement, he carried away with him a madness that lured him back again not only in the company of those by whom he had initially been dragged along but even before them, dragged along others.[54]

---

52. John Chrysostom, *In Matth.*, hom. 6, in *Patrologia Graeca*, ed. J.-P. Migne (Paris, 1857–66) [hereafter "*PG*"], 57:72.
53. Augustine, *Confessions* 6.8 (trans. Boulding, 146).
54. Ibid. (146–47). Contrary to certain versions of contemporary pop psychology, indulging in "sightseeing," in the *inspectio spectaculorum*, does not serve as an innocuous

The causal connection between curiosity, the visual reception of scenes of intense violence that elicit an overpowering reaction of the passions—sanguinary pleasure—in the soul, the passive acquiescence in the evil perceived and the resulting powerful craving for more scenes that would elicit sanguinary pleasure—all of this matches with remarkable accuracy the personal narratives of compulsive consumption of pornography.[55]

It is a perennial truth that the lust of the eyes and the lust of the flesh feed each other. The concupiscence of the eyes inflames the concupiscence of the flesh—and vice versa—and unchecked concupiscence lived out is nothing but the sin of intemperance, the willful abandoning of the virtue of temperance, that is, of selfless self-discipline and proper measure (see *ST* II-II, q. 142, a. 2).

A SPIRITUAL REMEDY PROPOSED

On the threshold of the concluding section, it might be of help to recapitulate the main steps of the argument. In the first section, I demonstrated the indispensability of chastity for genuine human flourishing in light of our final end and chastity's significance in relation to the proper operation of prudence. In the second section, I adumbrated the vice of lust and described the ways chastity can break down over time and lust become a habit. In the third section, I probed the spiritual root cause of the problem, the capital vice of *acedia* and its various offshoots. In this fourth and final section, I shall consider the moral and spiritual resources available to uproot the interrelated capital sins of *acedia* and lust and sever their various spiritual offshoots, and thereby address the forces that issue in the consumption of pornography. I will end by proposing one particular

---

(or at least less damaging) outlet for urges that might otherwise be lived out. (It has been suggested by some such pop psychologists that freely making available child porn on the internet would reduce child sex crimes.) Augustine's keen psychological insight into the unexpected craving that befell Alypius should serve as a sobering warning.

55. See the website of Morality in Media (National Center on Sexual Exploitation), available at moralityinmedia.org, for such accounts, and also a particularly instructive account in Norman Doidge, MD, *The Brain That Changes Itself: Stories of Personal Triumph from the Frontiers of Brain Science* (New York: Vintage, 2007), 109–12.

spiritual remedy that focuses on the root cause of *acedia* and attends positively to the virtue of chastity.

Before considering such pertinent moral and spiritual resources, it is apposite to recall the Thomistic framework established in the first section. The proper starting point afforded by Aquinas's moral theology is *concupiscentia*, the natural inclination to procreative sexual union and the concomitant delectable good of sexual pleasure. Pornography consumption is vicious not because *concupiscentia* is evil, but because a delectable good, that is, sexual intimacy and procreative union, is pursued in a gravely inordinate way, a way that not only offends against justice, charity, and chastity, but that is also ultimately life-denying. Indulging in *acedia*, boredom, and *ressentiment*, the consumer of pornography still seeks inordinately some good, a gravely misplaced good, but a good nonetheless. It is in virtue of the enduring integrity of the fundamental structure of the natural inclination toward the good befitting human nature (the intelligible good and the delectable good) that the proposed moral and spiritual resources enable the human being to turn from the misplaced goods sought inordinately to the final end of the human being that encompasses the imperfect happiness of genuine, but finite, human flourishing as well as the perfect happiness of life with and in God. The gravity of the concern gives justifiable urge to the quest for a proximate and sustainable solution, and—irrespective of the time needed—each solution must be in accord with the dignity of the human person and hence with the order of reason. Recall that the order of reason comprises nature as well as grace. Hence, there are different kinds of resources available. The first kind pertains to the natural capacity to address challenging, difficult, and potentially threatening situations by way of the acquired moral virtue of courage or fortitude; the second kind pertains to sanctifying grace and the infused moral virtues.

The cardinal virtue of courage has its root in the basic human capacity of resilience; courage persists in the good of reason and orders the irascible power to acts that strive to achieve a difficult good (*bonum arduum*) that accords with the dignity of the human person. We need to keep in mind that it is axiomatic for Aquinas that the kind of virtuous life that accords with human dignity and with the ordination to eternal communion with the Trinity involves in principle the striving after a difficult good. To put the matter differently, the human capacity of resilience and the corresponding virtue of courage are indispensable *in via* to the pursuit and achievement of the final end to which humanity is ordained.[56] In *De veritate*, Aquinas offers what might arguably be considered a prime example of mobilizing the hidden resources of resilience:

> No habit corrupts all the powers of the soul. Consequently, when one power is corrupted by a habit, [one] is led by any rectitude that remains in the other powers to ponder and to take action against that habit. If, for example, someone has his concupiscible power corrupted by the habit of lust, he is urged by the irascible power to attempt something hard, and its exercise will take away the softness of lust.[57]

What Aquinas has in mind is that a grave obstacle in the way of pursuing the *bonum arduum*—having been corrupted by the habit of lust, for example—elicits from the virtue of courage acts of resilience that will contribute to the diminishment of the habit of lust such that prudence, whose estimates had become erroneous by being absorbed by sensual pleasure, can increasingly coordinate the acts of resilience into coherent strategies. Such strategies of resilience are characteristic of the incontinent person, who still has sufficient rectitude "in the other powers to ponder and to take action against that habit."

Aquinas's recommendation exemplifies the realism of his moral psychology and, more importantly, offers a discipline available in principle to everyone. However, some cases, where the consump-

---

56. In his important study *Resilience and the Virtue of Fortitude: Aquinas in Dialogue with the Psychosocial Sciences* (Washington, D.C.: The Catholic University of America Press, 2006), Craig Steven Titus offers a helpful definition of resilience that comprises the physiological, psychosocial, and spiritual dimensions of the human person: "First, resilience is the ability to cope in adverse conditions; it endures, minimizes, or overcomes hardships. Second, it consists in resisting destructive pressures on the human person's physiological, psychosocial, and spiritual life; that is, it maintains capacities in the face of challenges, threats, and loss. Third, resilience creatively constructs and adapts after adversity; it implies recovering with maturity, confidence, and wisdom to lead a meaningful and productive life" (29). One central aspect in what Titus calls a "composite definition" is that resilience encompasses the full range of the order of reason, nature, and grace.

57. *De ver.*, q. 24, a. 10 (*Truth*, 3:179).

tion of pornography has become deeply compulsive, call for measures that reach deeper than the courageous application of rigorous self-discipline and the equally courageous concentration of all of one's powers on an arduous good to be achieved. The *habitus* might already be too deeply rooted and might have already developed too severe a compulsiveness for a remaining rectitude in other powers "to ponder and to take action against that habit." Hence, the strategy of resilience—guided by prudence and courage—might entail the restoration of the corrupted power by way of counseling or therapy.[58] Such an effort becomes itself the pursuit of a proximate difficult good the end of which is the removal of the obstacle that encumbers and possibly even undercuts the pursuit of the moral life and the friendship with God.

But in the case of the Christian, resilience also has an important spiritual dimension, and this is the awareness that the rectitude of a corrupted power is restored from above. One central characteristic of resilience and its moral correlative, the virtue of courage, is the capacity to take initiative (*aggredi*). In *Resilience and the Virtue of Fortitude*, Craig Steven Titus not only demonstrates convincingly the intimate link between resilience and courage, but also, and more importantly, points out how deeply involved the passion of hope and, in the case of the Christian, especially the theological virtue of hope are in the exercise of resilience as guided by prudence and courage.[59] The theological virtue of hope, first and foremost, is a potent spiritual medicine against *acedia*, and against the despair to which spiritual apathy can lead.

By thematizing the infused virtue of hope I have already anticipated the second kind of resource, the one on which the Christian should rely first and foremost—sanctifying grace and the infused moral virtues. The theological virtue of hope relies on the help that

---

58. Here is the proper instance to emphasize the role of an accountability partner or of an accountability community. The importance of personal friendship must be emphasized at this point and the centrality of recovering a vision of the good that surpasses the alleged good that is sought in the compulsive perusal of internet pornography. For a compelling account of drawing upon the therapeutic model of the twelve-step movement and at the same time transcending it into a vision of transformative friendships, see Dunnington, *Addiction and Virtue*.

59. Titus, *Resilience and the Virtue of Fortitude*, 146.

comes from divine omnipotence, resting on the insight of faith that nothing is impossible for God, especially God's mercy.

I have established above that in the extant providential order, due to the wounds of original sin, chastity is restored, preserved, and perfected from above, that is, by way of healing and sanctifying grace. This restoration, preservation, and perfection of chastity is greatly aided by what Aquinas calls the "general virtue" of chastity, or "spiritual chastity":

> The spiritual union of the mind with certain things conduces to a pleasure which is the matter of a spiritual chastity metaphorically speaking, as well as of a spiritual fornication likewise metaphorically so called. For if the human mind delight in the spiritual union with that to which it behooves it to be united, namely God, and refrains from delighting in union with other things against the requirements of the order established by God, this may be called a spiritual chastity.... Taking chastity in this sense, it is a general virtue, because every virtue withdraws the human mind from delighting in a union with unlawful things. Nevertheless, the essence of this chastity consists principally in charity and the other theological virtues, whereby the human mind is united to God. (*ST* II-II, q. 151, a. 2)

Spiritual chastity arises directly from the theological virtues of faith, hope, and charity, which unite the human mind to God. As a general virtue, spiritual chastity qualifies the other virtues such that in their exercise the spiritual union of the mind with God and with everything that is consonant with the will of God and the order established by God is preserved.[60] The proper exercise of the other virtues in union with each other entails that "every virtue withdraws the human mind from delighting in a union with unlawful things." Put differently, the general virtue of chastity is an immediate entailment of the friendship with God that is realized by the union of mutual charity between God and the Christian. Spiritual chastity preserves this friendship from the slightest betrayal of the beloved

---

60. Spiritual chastity fosters the spiritual union with the one whom Aquinas calls "our wisest and greatest friend" and makes one cleave to his counsels: "The counsels of a wise friend are of great use, according to Prv. 27:9: *Ointment and perfumes rejoice the heart: and the good counsels of a friend rejoice the soul*. But Christ is our wisest and greatest friend. Therefore His counsels are supremely useful and becoming" (*ST* I-II, q. 108, a. 4, s.c.).

friend by thought, intention, or action. Consequently, it is spiritual chastity that protects the Christian from the profound spiritual betrayal at the very depth of the human soul, the detestation of the divine good and consequently of the very friendship with God.

But if spiritual chastity is to be fortified after being weakened, it needs potent medicine—and that medicine can be found in an active and persistent discipline of prayer. The restoration and protection of chastity, however, call especially for *communal* intercessory prayers. For such communal practices of prayer acknowledge explicitly the fact that the restoration and protection of chastity depend on the providence and grace of God. Moreover, in virtue of the fact that prayers of petition are means through which divine predestination is fulfilled with certainty (*certitudinaliter*),[61] these communal practices of prayer rely explicitly on the prayers of the mother of God, the saints, and the faithful.

In conclusion, I shall propose one such communal practice and discipline.[62] I regard it as one of the utmost important spiritual initiatives that addresses the problem of pornography head on (not at its contemporary shiny electronic surface but at its hidden spiritual root): the Angelic Warfare Confraternity promoted by the Order of Preachers. This confraternity "seeks to foster the connection between chastity and the other acquired and infused virtues, especially charity; which enables one to love and reverence [one's] own body as well as the bodies of others."[63] The members of the Angelic Warfare Confraternity engage in a disciplined practice of daily prayer and support each other in prayer while they draw upon the

---

61. *ST* I, q. 23, a. 8; *ST* II-II, q. 83, a. 2. See also *ST* II-II, q. 83, a. 11, ad 2: "The saints impetrate whatever God wishes to take place through their prayers: and they pray for that which they deem will be granted through their prayers according to God's will."

62. I understand this practice of prayer to be a spiritual discipline that is categorically different from and not a substitute for the kind of counseling or therapy advisable for persons who experience what clinicians might be increasingly inclined to diagnose as a form of gravely compulsive behavior, indeed, as an addiction. Because the root of the problem is a spiritual one, the healing from the addictive behavior will, however, ultimately be overcome only when the negative spiritual root (*acedia* and her daughters) is eradicated. It is the latter that the practice of prayer addresses.

63. Fr. Brian T. Mullady, OP, *The Angelic Warfare Confraternity*, 4th ed. (New Hope, Ky.: The St. Martin de Porres Lay Dominicans, 2006), 25. More information about the Angelic Warfare Confraternity can be found at angelicwarfare.org.

intercessions of the Virgin Mary and on Aquinas, the confraternity's patron saint. Far from being a convenient but inconsequential outlet of pious and prudish impulses, the Confraternity's practice of prayer reflects a pertinent theological truth about the efficaciousness of prayer. As Aquinas states: "Since prayers offered for others proceed from charity ... the greater the charity of the saints in heaven, the more they pray for wayfarers, since the latter can be helped by prayers: and the more closely they are united with God, the more are their prayers efficacious" (*ST* II-II, q. 83, a. 11). In order to protect and liberate ourselves from the lust of the flesh, the lust of the eyes, and the pride of life, we might pray:

> Dear Jesus, I know that every perfect gift and especially that of chastity depends on the power of your Providence. Without you, a mere creature can do nothing. Therefore, I beg you to defend by your grace the chastity and purity of my body and soul. And if I have ever imagined or felt anything that could stain my chastity and purity, blot it out, Supreme Lord of my powers, that I may advance with a pure heart in your love and service, offering myself on the most pure altar of your divinity all the days of my life. Amen.[64]

In *Love and Responsibility*, Wojtyła stresses that for virtue to be "rehabilitated" it must be "made welcome in the human soul, the human will. If not it ceases to have any real existence."[65] If we are to benefit from a spiritual union of the mind with God and with everything that is consonant with the will of God and the order established by God, then spiritual chastity is needed. And in order to sustain spiritual chastity, an intentional discipline of prayer is essential. For "by praying [one] surrenders [one's] mind to God, since [one] subjects it to Him with reverence and, so to speak, presents it to Him" (*ST* II-II, q. 83, a. 3, ad 3). Subjecting one's mind with rev-

---

64. Ibid., 32. These prayers are propitious not only for Christians who pray for themselves and for each other, but also as intercessory prayers for a pornographic culture and especially for those who are not motivated to pray or who may not be Christians. The prayers of the Angelic Warfare Confraternity include the following fifteen general petitions: "1. For our social and cultural climate; 2. For our relationships; 3. For modesty in dress and movements; 4. For our five senses; 5. For our sensuality; 6. For our imagination; 7. For our memory; 8. For our power of estimation; 9. For our affectivity; 10. For our intellect; 11. For our will; 12. For our conscience; 13. For our hearts; 14. For self-surrender; 15. For love."

65. Wojtyła, *Love and Responsibility*, 143.

erence to God and a life of spiritual chastity will remain most fragile without the concomitant contrition for one's sins, for having offended God and having harmed one's neighbor, and without availing oneself of the healing power of the sacraments, regular sacramental confession and reconciliation and equally regular Mass attendance and holy communion.

The chapter has now come full circle. In the first part, I argued that in light of the ultimate end of the human being the virtue of chastity turns out to be indispensable for genuine human flourishing. Moreover, I showed that Aquinas makes a compelling case that for its proper operation the virtue of prudence relies significantly upon the virtue of temperance and, in particular, the virtue of chastity. In the second part, I undertook a form of moral *ressourcement* by recovering Aquinas's analysis of the vice of lust and by showing how Aquinas's moral psychology assists in understanding how the breakdown of chastity and the habituation in lust ensue. In light of this analysis, I argued in the third part that the spiritual root cause of the pervasive contemporary consumption of pornography is the capital vice of *acedia* and its various offshoots. In the fourth and final part, I identified the moral and spiritual resources that in light of Aquinas's moral theology hold the best promise to uproot *acedia* and lust and to restore, protect, and perfect the virtue of chastity. The latter matters greatly, for the virtue of chastity is a principal protector of human dignity. In the order of action, conjugal chastity realizes one's own human dignity and acknowledges the dignity of one's spouse. More comprehensively, and pertaining to all persons, it is the chaste person whose gaze can genuinely behold and affirm the dignity of the other.[66] Last but not least, it is the chaste person who is free from the lure of the enticing, the titillating, the demeaning, and the base

---

66. For the most congenial and influential recent vindication and development of Aquinas's teaching on the moral integrity of the person and the indispensability of the virtue of chastity by way of a biblical theological commentary, see Pope St. John Paul II, *Man and Woman He Created Them*, esp. 225–78. Especially pertinent is chap. 2 (225–378), which is an interpretation of Mt 5:27–28. This chapter concludes with the important section "The Ethos of the Body in Art and Media" (364–67). For a magisterial introduction and interpretation of Pope St. John Paul II's theology of the body, see Michael Maria Waldstein, *Glory of the Logos in the Flesh: Saint John Paul's Theology of the Body* (Ave Maria, Fla.: Sapientia Press, 2019).

and who is, hence, free to utilize the internet and the smartphone as what they are—nothing but subordinate means in the service of ends determined by the virtue of prudence in accord with the order of reason rightly oriented to the ultimate end, beatitude. In a culture of excess the chaste person is the truly free person—free from the inordinate valuation of pleasure, especially sexual pleasure, and free to advance as *viator* on the journey to beatitude.

9

The Exemplar of Beatitude— Hope for the Wayfarer
The Blessed Virgin Mary's Bodily Assumption into Heaven

> Arise, O Lord, and go to thy resting place, / thou and the ark of thy might.
> —Psalm 132:8 (RSV)

> Our Lady's Assumption, the final history of the body of the woman who gave birth to God, is ... not so much an exception to the rule, but much more a fulfilling in advance of what is promised to the whole Mystical Body of Christ.
> —Hugo Rahner, SJ, *Our Lady and the Church*[1]

This concluding chapter considers the very exemplar of the wayfarer: the Virgin Mary. Not only is her life of religion, courage, and chastity exemplary for all wayfarers; even more importantly, she is a beacon of hope for the *viator*: assumed, body and soul, into heaven, the Virgin Mary embodies in her personal state of beatitude the ultimate end to which all *viatores* are called. Not only has Christ, the head of the church, arisen from the dead and sits in glory at the

---

1. Hugo Rahner, SJ, *Our Lady and the Church*, trans. Sebastian Bullough, OP (Bethesda, Md.: Zaccheus Press, 2004 [1961]), 123–24.

right hand of the Father, but also the one who is his mother, and by transference of Christ under the cross, the mother of all his followers, has already been assumed, body and soul, into heaven. And for this reason the whole communion of the saints, the whole body of Christ is already anchored in the glory of God, not only in the head, the risen Christ—which is the indispensable condition, the *conditio sine qua non*—but also already in one, who like the rest of the elect relies completely on the infinite merits of Christ's salvific sacrifice of charity on the cross.

In the first part of this chapter, I shall entertain a "what if" thought experiment in which the supposition of divine faith sets the stage for the subsequent theological inquiry. In the second part, I will unfold Aquinas's unjustly ignored meditation on the Angelic Salutation and in the third part I will draw out the theological implications most pertinent for the wayfarer. Because of her glorious assumption, body and soul, into heaven, Mary has become the eschatological icon of the church. She reveals to the church, the mystical body of Christ, the church's own final end. As the human exemplar of fully attained heavenly beatitude of soul and body she becomes for the wayfarer a principal reason for hope in also attaining the selfsame ultimate end.

AN OPENING THOUGHT EXPERIMENT

As the book is approaching its end, in the sense of its *terminus* as well as its *telos*, I would like to invite the esteemed reader to enter into a "what if" thought experiment with me. What if we were to bracket for the duration of reading this last chapter a notion of "faith" we might have encountered in recent Catholic theology, a notion of a "faith" that allegedly all people hold at least implicitly in virtue of our purportedly universally graced existence, a nonthematic faith in transcendence, meaning, and goodness, a faith that in light of the state of the world is always paired with doubt, a faith that can at best be solidified into a strong opinion, maybe even into a conviction, but that remains always tentative and always open to revision in light of possible new and conflicting evidences or simply more compelling alternatives. What if we were to bracket this all too widespread notion of faith, the faith of the seeker, the faith based on the measure of our own private judgment? What if instead we had a dream? What if we were to dream that faith in all of its aspects was a gift given directly from God to each one of us personally? What if we were to dream that faith was based on a testimony that ultimately comes from God and that we believe to come from God and therefore are able to hold with absolute certainty because we believe God? What if this faith were to contain distinct truths communicated by God by way of entrusted messengers whom we believe because we believe them to be God's messengers entrusted by God with the testimony that conveys distinct truths about God? What if this faith were part and parcel of our friendship with God, a friendship enabled, initiated, and ensured by God, such that the knowledge conveyed by faith were always inherently part of the personal friendship initiated by God and indeed inherently part of an inchoate union with God? What if faith were "the substance of things hoped for; the proof of things not seen" (Heb 11:1), so that "through faith, in a tentative way, or as we might say 'in embryo'—and thus according to the 'substance'—there [were] already present in us the things that are hoped for: the whole, true life"?[2] What if—lest this faith become wayward and ossified—God had appointed guardians of the faith that would allow it to grow and to remain faithful to the truth conveyed by God? And what if the faith itself were certain about these guardians of the faith and certain that God would guide these guardians through the Holy Spirit? Would it not be most appropriate to call such a faith, a faith that has its origin and end in God, a faith that is a gift from God and anchored in God's truthfulness—*divine* faith?[3]

Because the dreaming goes so well, let us go on for a moment and ask, what if a contemporary theologian had put this matter into a compelling contemporary theological idiom. For example, in the following way:

---

2. Pope Benedict XVI, *Spe Salvi*, Encyclical Letter, November 30, 2017, par. 7, available at vatican.va.
3. For a more detailed discussion of divine faith, see chapter 4, pp. 193–223.

The sole objectivity of the faith is the subjectivity of the Church. For the objectivity of the faith is guaranteed by the Spirit of God, who judges everything, but is judged by nobody. This Spirit, however, is present in the Church as her subjectivity and nowhere else present [as such]. One cannot want to apply the final measure oneself. The final measure, insofar as it is tangible at all, is the Church from that moment on that the Spirit of Truth has united Himself with her, and with me, the individual only insofar as I stand in the Church and insofar as I have handed over my faith into hers.... Because [the Church] in freedom overpowered by the Spirit, is always the obedient servant of the truth—in this way alone, but in this way also unconditionally, is [the Church] the one who rules over our faith.... Faith is faith that hears the Church and believes in the Church.[4]

Let us continue our dream. What if this theologian were Karl Rahner and what if he had written these words in the opening pages of a book on the assumption of Mary, a book that he never published during his life? And what if he were to recommend the following attitude for approaching theologically the mystery of the assumption? Consider again the Karl Rahner from 1951:

What is the right beginning for our endeavor to understand what the Church proclaims about the Holy Virgin and her eternal destiny? The humble reverence [*Ehrfurcht*] in face of the mystery of God, a reverence in which the human being does not make himself the measure of truth, and the unconditional faith in relationship to the Church and her teaching and in the Church as the necessary medium of our own understanding of the faith, a faith that is the measure for everything else and that can be measured only by itself and no other criteria.[5]

What if we were to assume this framework of divine faith? Equipped with the reverence Rahner recommends, we would encounter the following as a teaching of the faith that makes divine faith explicit in one specific regard: "We pronounce, declare, and define it to be a divinely revealed dogma: that the Immaculate Moth-

---

4. Karl Rahner, *Maria, Mutter des Herrn: Mariologische Studien* (Freiburg: Herder, 2004), 13–14 (author's translation). The quotation is taken from Karl Rahner's 1951 monograph *Assumptio Beatae Mariae Virginis*, which was published for the first time only in the posthumous edition of his complete works. For detailed information about the reasons for this delayed publication, see Regina Pacis Meyer's instructive introduction to the volume (xi–lv).

5. Ibid., 18 (author's translation).

er of God, the ever Virgin Mary, having completed the course of her earthly life, was assumed body and soul into heavenly glory." Thus states the dogma of the Assumption of the Blessed Virgin Mary as it was defined and promulgated by Pope Pius XII on November 1, 1950, in the Apostolic Constitution *Munificentissimus Deus*.[6] The dogma of the Assumption of the Blessed Virgin into heaven, body and soul, expresses a truth integral to the divine faith we have come presently to assume. The truth made explicit and specified (we could also say "defined") in the dogma belongs to the essence of divine faith; it is an article of this faith as much as the articles specified in the Apostolic Creed and the Nicene Creed, that is, among others, that God is triune, that Jesus Christ is the Son of God incarnate, that he was raised from the dead on the third day and ascended into heaven. All of these truths and numerous others are divinely revealed and therefore integral to divine faith.[7]

In the following theological meditation, in which I am going to consider the very capstone of human participation in divine happiness already fully realized, I am going to be true to the thought experiment and presuppose the truth of the dogma as integral to the

---

6. "Pronunciamus, declaramus et definimus divinitus revelatum dogma esse: Immaculatam Deiparam semper Virginem Mariam, expleto terrestris vitae cursu, fuisse corpore et anima ad caelestem gloriam assumptam" (Denzinger, no. 3903). For the best recent theological interpretation and defense of the dogma of the assumption, see Matthew Levering, *Mary's Bodily Assumption* (Notre Dame, Ind.: University of Notre Dame Press, 2014).

7. Unsurprisingly, therefore, *Munificentissimus Deus* clearly states: "Hence, if anyone, which God forbid, should dare willfully to deny or call into doubt that which We have defined, let him know that he has fallen away completely from the divine and Catholic faith" (Quamobrem, si quis, quod Deus advertat, id vel negare, vel in dubium vocare voluntarie ausus fuerit, quod a Nobis definitum est, noverit se a divina ac catholica fide prorsus defecisse) (Denzinger, no. 3904). For further clarification, see "Doctrinal Commentary on the Concluding Formula of the *Professio Fidei*," issued by the Congregation for the Doctrine of the Faith on June 29, 1998. In par. 11, the commentary states: "To the truths of the first paragraph belong the articles of the faith of the Creed, the various Christological dogmas and Marian dogmas; the doctrine of the institution of the sacraments by Christ and their efficacy with regard to grace; the doctrine of the real and substantial presence of Christ in the Eucharist and the sacrificial nature of the eucharistic celebration; the foundation of the Church by the will of Christ; the doctrine on the primacy and infallibility of the Roman Pontiff; the doctrine on the existence of original sin; the doctrine on the immortality of the spiritual soul and on the immediate recompense after death; the absence of error in the inspired sacred texts; the doctrine on the grave immorality of direct and voluntary killing of an innocent human being."

divine faith we presently assume "as if." Given divine faith, I will explore the truth itself that the dogma conveys. I will first consider the antecedent revealed truths that give rise to the church's faith in the assumption of the Virgin Mary into heaven. These antecedent revealed truths afford divine faith an indispensable understanding of the surpassing theological fittingness of her assumption. Of course, God's omnipotence makes it possible for God to assume any human being into heaven, body and soul—presupposing in this counterfactual, of course, that the instantaneous sanctification of this person by operative grace would be a necessary entailment of such an act of divine omnipotence. Fittingness, *convenientia*, however, assumes that God orders all the works of salvation wisely and that divine faith is enabled by God to trace the wisdom of such ordering and to praise the beauty of such wisdom. By way of interpreting a brief meditation by Thomas Aquinas I will suggest how the assumption of the Virgin Mary is rooted theologically in her plenitude of grace and in her divine motherhood.

Given the assumption of Mary into heaven, I will then consider, albeit only briefly, the most salient ecclesiological and eschatological consequences of this revealed truth of divine faith. As the dogmatic theologian Louis Bouyer states in his important book *The Seat of Wisdom*, "her Assumption is the pledge of the glory Christ will give to his Spouse, as he has already given it to his Mother."[8]

GRATIA PLENA—DEIPARA—ASSUMPTA

Let us consider Thomas Aquinas's theological meditation on the angel's salutation *Ave, gratia plena*, a piece Aquinas composed in the year 1269. The work falls into the early part of Aquinas's second Parisian regency, the period during which he commenced and completed the enormous Second Part of the *Summa Theologiae*.[9] In

---

8. Louis Bouyer, *The Seat of Wisdom: An Essay on the Place of the Virgin Mary in Christian Theology*, trans. A. V. Littledale (New York: Pantheon, 1962), 202.

9. Thomas Aquinas, *In salutationem angelicam vulgo "Ave Maria" expositio* (1269), in *Opuscula Theologica* (Rome: Marietti, 1954), 2:239–41; translated into English as *The Angelic Salutation*, trans. Joseph B. Collins (New York: Wagner, 1939). Concerning the exact date on which Aquinas delivered this sermon, see the instructive commentary and notes provided by Jean-Pierre Torrell, OP, in Saint Thomas d'Aquin, *Somme Theologique*.

this brief but nevertheless rich theological meditation on the angel's salutation, Aquinas demonstrates well how the church's faith moves from the Virgin Mary's plenitude of grace to her divine motherhood and from her divine motherhood to her assumption into heaven. His brief treatise is rooted in a thoroughly *theological* reading of scripture and thus helps us see that the church's faith in the assumption of the Virgin Mary arises from the witness of scripture. For Aquinas's theological meditation allows us to understand the assumption immediately in relationship to the plenitude of grace residing in Mary and in relationship to her divine motherhood, two truths shining forth from the first chapter of the Gospel of Luke. To put it differently: given the immaculate conception of the Virgin Mary, a truth solemnly defined on December 8, 1854, by Pope Pius IX in the papal bull *Ineffabilis Deus*, her assumption does indeed follow as a fitting consequence in the economy of salvation. However, we would seriously misunderstand the church's faith in the assumption of Mary into heaven if in hindsight we were to reduce this truth of divine faith to a mere necessary entailment of the dogma of the Immaculate Conception. Rather, it is important for a full appreciation of the meaning of the assumption to realize and remember that the truth of the Virgin Mary's assumption into heaven is a direct consequence of the witness of the Gospel of Luke itself, namely, a witness of the plenitude of grace that resides in her and a witness of her divine motherhood.

As is well known, Aquinas did not teach the immaculate conception of the Virgin Mary in her mother's womb. Rather, at a time when a variety of theological positions were still explored and de-

---

Le Verbe Incarné en ses mystères (3a, qq. 27–34). Tome 1, L'entrée du Christ en ce monde (Paris: Cerf, 2003), 363, and *Recherches thomasiennes: Études revues et augmentées* (Paris: Vrin, 2000), 285n4. Torrell provides a French translation in *Le Verbe Incarné*, 363–70. For other important findings by Torrell, see the appendix "S. Thomas et la vierge Marie," 340–53, esp. 368n1, and the "notes explicatives," esp. 264–68. For recent treatments of Aquinas's Mariology, see T. A. Mullaney, OP, "Mary Immaculate in the Writings of St. Thomas," *The Thomist* 17 (1954): 433–68; Daniel Ols, OP, "La Bienheureuse Vierge Marie selon saint Thomas," in *Littera Sensus Sententia: Studi in onore del Prof. Clemente J. Vansteenkiste, O.P.*, ed. Abelardo Lobato, OP (Milan: Massimo, 1991), 435–53; and Aidan Nichols, OP, "The Mariology of St. Thomas," in *Aquinas on Doctrine: A Critical Introduction*, ed. Thomas G. Weinandy, Daniel A. Keating, and John P. Yocum (London: T and T Clark, 2004), 241–60.

fended, he taught the perfect sanctification of Mary in her mother's womb immediately after the ensoulment (which Aquinas assumed—based on the best scientific theory of his day—did not occur right at conception). Ironically, from the hindsight of the development of doctrine, it is this particular trait of Aquinas's Mariology that lends special significance to his brief treatise. For it allows us to attend to the direct theological relationship between the plenitude of grace present in Mary and her divine maternity, on the one side, and her assumption into heaven, body and soul, on the other side. In short, his meditation allows us—in hindsight, after the promulgation of the dogma of the Immaculate Conception in 1854—to realize that, indeed, her immaculate conception is for the sake of her divine maternity, while her assumption is a culmination of both of these prior graces.[10]

How does Aquinas proceed in his brief meditation? First, he points out something contemporary readers of scripture would most likely fail to notice, namely, that wherever in scripture angels encounter human beings it is never the angel who greets and expresses reverence to the human being—with the sole exception of the annunciation. Aquinas gives three reasons why it is improper, under normal circumstances, for angels to express reverence to humans, but why it is quite proper and decent for human beings to do so in regard to angels.

First, angels surpass human beings in ontological dignity. For angels have a spiritual and incorruptible nature while humans have a corruptible one. Second, angels are of the utmost familiarity with God and, in addition, are God's assistants in the order of providence as well as in the economy of salvation, while human beings, due to sin, are in and of themselves unrelated to and far removed from God. Third, and most importantly, angels enjoy the surpassing splendor of

10. For a detailed elaboration of the preeminence of the divine maternity and of the predestination of the Virgin Mary to divine maternity as the final cause of her immaculate conception (Christ's salvific death on the cross being the meritorious cause) and as the root cause, the principle, that comes to full realization first in her association with Christ's suffering and death and then also her eternal association with Christ in his perfect victory, see the unjustly forgotten Mariology by Reginald Garrigou-Lagrange, OP, *The Mother of the Saviour and Our Interior Life*, trans. Bernard J. Kelly, CSSP (Dublin: Golden Eagle, 1949).

divine grace; they participate in the divine light itself to the highest degree. It is for this reason, Aquinas surmises, that an angel always appears with light. Human beings, however, even if they participate in the light of grace, do so only to a small degree and in a somewhat obscure manner. Now, according to the Gospel of Luke, the angel indeed explicitly greets the Virgin Mary and pays her reverence. And this is the case, Aquinas argues, because Mary exceeds the angel in at least three regards.

First, she exceeds the angel in the degree of grace, for the plenitude of grace indicates a maximum of perfection that scripture attests nowhere about any angel.[11] Aquinas regards this truth to be established simply on the basis of the witness that the literal sense of scripture affords. According to Aquinas, the plenitude of grace is of surpassing significance and constitutes the fundamental principle of Mariology. The plenitude of grace pertains, first, to the soul of Mary such that she is enabled perfectly to do good and avoid sin, and, second, to her body, in that the overflow (*redundantia*) of grace from her soul to her body enables her to give birth to the Son of God.[12] Finally, the plenitude of grace pertains, third, to the restitution (*refusio*) of grace in all human beings. Aquinas emphasizes in this important third aspect of her plenitude of grace that the Virgin Mary is the only other person apart from Christ (considered in his humanity) to receive grace for every other human being.[13]

---

11. By way of a handy summary, we can turn for one brief moment to the *Summa Theologiae*, where in the third part Aquinas considers the mother of God in the proper theological context of Christology. Here is his argument why she indeed received in the womb the plenitude of grace: "In every genus, the nearer a thing is to the principle, the greater the part which it has in the effect of that principle, whence Dionysius says (*Coel. Hier.* iv) that angels, being nearer to God, have a greater share than [human beings], in the effects of the Divine goodness. Now Christ is the principle of grace, authoritatively as to His Godhead, instrumentally as to His humanity: whence (Jn 1:17) it is written: *Grace and truth came by Jesus Christ*. But the Blessed Virgin Mary was nearest to Christ in His humanity: because He received His human nature from her. Therefore it was due to her to receive a greater fulness of grace than others" (*ST* III, q. 27, a. 5).

12. Aquinas, "In salutationem angelicam vulgo 'Ave Maria' expositio" (Marietti, nos. 1115–17).

13. Ibid. (no. 1118). The Blessed Virgin did not receive this grace simply as a passive instrument of the Holy Spirit, but precisely as a human person, endowed with a principle of agency and of cooperation with God's grace. Being full of grace allows her to perform an act of perfect freedom, the freedom of realizing the surpassing good God enables her

Second, Mary exceeds the angel in divine familiarity. The angel expresses this in the sentence, "The Lord is with you." And this, Aquinas points out, is the case in three utterly unique ways: first of all, Father and Son together have a familiarity with her in a way different from any other creature, angel or human: "The child to be born of you will be called holy, the Son of God" (Lk 1:35b; RSV). Moreover, due to being in her womb, God the Son has a familiarity with Mary, indeed as a son, while he has familiarity with the angel only as Lord but not as Son. In short, while God is the angel's Lord, God is also the Virgin Mary's Son.[14] This single circumstance makes her indeed the single most important creature of the whole universe. And finally, the Holy Spirit has familiarity with her because he overshadows her and hence dwells in her as in the Temple. Consequently, according to Aquinas, God has greater familiarity with the Virgin

---

by grace to realize: "Behold, I am the handmaid of the Lord; let it be to me according to your word" (Lk 1:38). And therefore the Virgin Mary *merited* the grace for every other human being. Lest the charge of an undue exaltation of the Virgin Mary be put at the feet of Thomas Aquinas (and the whole preconciliar Mariology, for that matter), let me emphasize that Mary merited *de congruo proprie* (congruously) what Jesus merited *de condigno* (in strict justice). Aquinas explains how such meriting *de congruo* is based on friendship with God: "One may merit the first grace for another congruously: because [a person] in grace fulfills God's will, and it is congruous and in harmony with friendship that God should fulfill [that person's] desire for the salvation of another, although sometimes there may be an impediment on the part of him whose salvation the just [person] desires" (*ST* I-II, q. 114, a. 6). In reference to this passage, Garrigou-Lagrange offers a pertinent and indeed famous example: "In this way, a good christian [sic] mother, for example, can by her good works, her love of God and of her neighbour, merit the conversion of her son *de congruo proprie*. St. Monica obtained the conversion of St. Augustine by that kind of merit as well as by her prayers: 'The son of many tears,' said St. Ambrose, 'could not be lost'" (*Mother of The Saviour*, 180–81). Because the Mother of God, due to her plenitude of grace, has the highest degree possible for a human being of friendship with God, she merits *de congruo proprie* in virtue of the rights of friendship (*in iure amicabili*), the grace for every human being. See Pope St. Pius X, *Ad Diem Illum Laetissimum*, Encyclical Letter, February 2, 1904, for a magisterial confirmation of the Blessed Virgin as mediatrix of grace: "We are ... very far from attributing to the Mother of God a productive power of grace—a power that belongs to God alone. Yet, since Mary carries it over all in holiness and union with Christ and has been associated by Christ in the work of redemption, she merits for us *de congruo* [in a congruous manner], in the language of the theologians, what Christ merits for us *de condigno* [in a condign manner], and she is the supreme minister of the distribution of graces" (Denzinger, no. 3371).

14. Indeed, as Aquinas emphasizes in the *Summa Theologiae*, the Virgin Mary is the mother of the person of the Son—the person of the Son being the incarnate Logos (*ST* III, q. 35, a. 4, co.; ad 2 and 3).

Mary than with any angel, because Father, Son, and Holy Spirit, the whole Trinity, is with her. And so the angel rightly expresses reverence to Mary, for she is the mother of the Lord, *mater Domini*, hence *Domina*, and therefore worthy of surpassing reverence.

But Mary not only exceeds the angel in plenitude of grace and in familiarity with God. Rather, and this is the third aspect, Aquinas emphasizes that she exceeds the angel also in regard to purity. After having received the plenitude of grace, the Virgin Mary is free from any form of sin (original, mortal, and venial) and in that of similar purity as the angel, but different from the angel, she is also—in virtue of her divine maternity—the source of purity in others. Hence her purity surpasses that of the most pure and holy creature, the angel.

At this juncture we need to halt for a moment and recapitulate in order to appreciate the full import of Aquinas's brief account so far. The triune God, Father, Son, and Holy Spirit, abides with the Virgin Mary in an utterly singular way and hence has familiarity with her to a degree that exceeds God's familiarity with any other creature. To put it differently, according to the witness of scripture, as divine faith receives it under the guidance of the church's teaching and as Aquinas understands it through the medium of divine faith, Mary holds that very place of singularity in the universe that according to the erroneous assumptions of the adoptionist Christological heresy Jesus holds. Jesus was not a human person adopted by God and elevated to the highest level of adoptive divinity possible for a creature—as was held by ancient adoptionism long ago and was held in recent times and still is held in present times by strands of liberal Protestantism and Catholic Modernism. Rather, the Virgin Mary was the distinct human person chosen by God for divine maternity and because of it was eventually assumed, body and soul, into the glory of heaven. The principle *gratia plena* constitutes her whole existence from beginning to end. Mary is the most fully divinized human person from the moment of her coming into existence, as the particular human being she is, to her glorification in heaven. While Aquinas has no particular reason to state the matter in the context of his interpretation of the Angelic Salutation, in an ecumenical post-Reformation setting it is important, however, to mention explicitly that the Catholic church recognizes the privilege of the Virgin Mary's preservation from original sin and her existence *gratia plena* in light of the merits of Christ, just as analogically she is associated in prayer in the mystery of the cross, only because of the merits of her Son and in dependence upon them.

Now we are prepared to turn to the section of Aquinas's meditation where the assumption is mentioned—indeed very briefly, but completely as a matter of fact, not at all as something that is up for debate or in need of an elaborate theological defense or justification. Due to the fullness of grace residing in her, the Virgin Mary was free from any stain of sin. For this very reason she was also preserved from the curse of sin. Aquinas only briefly gestures to the curses of Genesis 3:16–19. Interestingly, he does not distinguish between the curses applying to the man and those applying to the woman. For Aquinas states that in every regard the curse of sin was not going to affect her. There is first Genesis 3:16a: "I will greatly multiply your pain in childbearing; in pain you shall bring forth children" (RSV). Contrary to this curse, Aquinas in accord with the received tradition states that Mary conceives the Son of God without loss of her virginity (*sine corruptione*), bears him in consolation (*in solatione*), and gives birth to him in joy (*in gaudio*). She is, second, preserved from having to eat bread in the sweat of her face (Gn 3:19) because, according to St. Paul in 1 Corinthians 7, virgins are released from the solicitude of this world and are free for God alone. And finally and most importantly, Mary is preserved from the common destiny of humanity to have to return to the dust. "And from this," Aquinas states, "the Blessed Virgin was preserved, because of her bodily assumption into heaven. For we believe that after her death she was raised up again and borne to heaven."[15] He concludes by citing Psalm 132 (131):8: "Arise, O Lord, and go to thy resting place, thou and the ark of thy might" (RSV). Because Christ's humanity, in virtue of divine election and predestination, is the all-sufficient

---

15. Thomas Aquinas, *In salutationem angelicam vulgo 'Ave Maria' expositio* (Marietti, no. 1123): "Et ab hac immunis fuit Beata Virgo, quia cum corpore assumpta est in caelum. Credimus enim quod post mortem resuscitata fuerit, et portata in caelum. Psal. CXXXI, 8: 'Surge, Domine, in requiem tuam; tu, et arca sanctificationis tuae.'" For the theologically delicate question of whether the Virgin Mary underwent death, see note 17 below.

and hence all-powerful instrument of human salvation and because Christ receives his humanity from Mary, she can indeed rightly be considered the ark of God's might. And if indeed she is the latter she must be preserved from all stains of sin, original, mortal, and venial. For otherwise she could not be the ark in which the Spirit of God dwells. At this point it should at least be mentioned that the dogma of the Immaculate Conception does provide greater clarity, as it allows for a more penetrating theological understanding of the fact that, like every other human being after the Fall, the Virgin Mary incurred the *debt* of original sin.[16] However, unlike every other human being after the Fall, she was preserved from incurring the *stain* of original sin from the first instance of her existence. To put the matter differently: the grace is not "Adamic," it is not a grace "stretching forth" so to speak from the state of original righteousness to the Virgin Mary. Rather, her grace is "Christic." Unlike every other human being after the Fall, she is free from sin in virtue of her immaculate conception, but like every other human being after the Fall and like the human nature of Christ, she is subject to imperfections and has the capacity to suffer and die. She is full of grace (*plena gratia*) and sinless, but in complete conformity with the suffering and death of Christ by whom her grace is merited. Precisely because her grace is Christ-conforming, it leads her into an exemplary union with the paschal mystery.

What does it mean to be preserved from the consequences of original sin? Original humanity before the Fall was not preserved naturally from death. Rather, like other composite creatures due to a composite nature, the human being is in principle vulnerable to decomposition and corruption. Hence the preservation of original humanity from natural death was a fortification that original humanity received as part of the gifts of original righteousness and sanctifying grace. Due to preservation, growth, and perseverance in sanctifying

---

16. Arguably, this is what Aquinas intends to maintain in *ST* III, q. 27, a. 5, ad 2, where he holds that if some human being after the Fall had not contracted original sin, "this would be derogatory to the dignity of Christ, by reason of His being the universal Saviour of all." It is here that Aquinas does not make the distinction between the debt of original sin that indeed pertains to all human beings (and that distinguishes Christ also from Mary and makes him also her savior) from incurring the stain (from which Mary was preserved in virtue the merits of Jesus Christ the savior of the human race).

grace, at the eventual point of natural death there would have occurred a transference, body and soul, into heaven. If the plenitude of grace that the Virgin Mary received, exceeded that of the angel and if her familiarity with God also exceeded the one the angel has with God, she must in both exceed original humanity or at least not lack anything in regard to anything that original humanity had received in the state of original righteousness. That means first and foremost that the consequences of the Fall, the withdrawal of original sanctifying grace and the destruction of the state of original righteousness do not apply to her. Hence what was taken from original humanity and has been superabundantly restored and surpassed by Christ's salvific death and resurrection is already realized in and for Mary.[17]

17. A proper treatment of the Virgin Mary's conformity to the cross, a treatment necessary, it seems to me, to approach rightly the theologically delicate question of whether the mother of God underwent death would go far beyond the scope of this chapter. As is well known, an older Eastern tradition holds that she died, while a more recent Western tradition holds that she underwent a kind of exaltation to God without death in an ecstatic spiritual love. As a brief substitute for a proper treatment, I shall adduce two theological authorities, the former having been the teacher and doctoral advisor of the latter. First I shall turn again to Garrigou-Lagrange's *Mother of the Saviour*, a superb preconciliar Mariology that incidentally is fully compatible with the Mariology of the Second Vatican Council and that, according to my understanding, advances an interpretation of the death of Mary that succeeds in synthesizing the central concerns of the Eastern and the Western traditions: "Man was not made immortal at the beginning otherwise than by a special privilege. The Incarnate Word willed to take passible flesh. Mary's flesh was passible too. Thus the deaths of Jesus and Mary were consequences of the inherent weakness of human nature left to itself and unsustained by any preternatural gift. Jesus, however, mastered death by accepting it for our salvation. Mary united herself to Him in His death, making for us the sacrifice of His life in the most generous martyrdom of heart the world has ever known after that of Our Saviour. And when, later on, the hour of her own death arrived, the sacrifice of her life had been already made. It remained but to renew it in that most perfect form which tradition speaks of as death of love, a death, that is to say, in which the soul dies not simply in grace or in God's love, but of a calm and supremely strong love which draws the soul, now ripe for heaven, away from the body to be united to God in immediate and eternal vision. Mary's last moments are described by St. John Damascene in the words 'She died an extremely peaceful death'" (*Mother of the Saviour*, 135–36). The second theological authority I shall adduce is Pope St. John Paul II, who addressed the question in his general audience of June 25, 1997: "It is true that in revelation death is present as a punishment for sin. However, the fact that the Church proclaims Mary free from original sin by a unique divine privilege does not lead to the conclusion that she also received physical immortality. The Mother is not superior to the Son who underwent death, giving it a new meaning and changing it into a means of salvation. Involved in Christ's redemptive work and associated in his saving sacrifice, Mary was able to share in his suffering and death for the sake of humanity's redemption. What Severus of Antioch says about Christ also applies to her: 'Without a preliminary death, how could the resurrection have

MARIA ASSUMPTA: REALIZED ANTICIPATION OF THE CHURCH'S END

On the basis of what has been said so far it might seem as if the assumption would separate Mary most radically from us: the Virgin highly exalted, body and soul in the glory of God and perfectly conformed to Christ, her Son. What does the Virgin Mary have to do with us and what, in turn, we with her? Do not the unique privileges of the mother of God separate her categorically from us?[18] Continuing our thought experiment that divine faith indeed obtains, at least three theological conclusions are to be drawn.

First, in the Virgin Mary, assumed body and soul into heaven, the economy of salvation is present as completed, as having already reached its *telos* in one human person. This is first and foremost the case—as elaborated in the first part—because of Mary's singular relation to Christ as mother of God. This unique relation is integral to the incarnation of the Word of God and reaches its perfection in the everlasting presence, body and soul, of the mother with her Son in the eternal glory of God. One of the great Catholic theologians of the twentieth century, a convert from Lutheranism, put the matter succinctly in *The Seat of Wisdom*, published about ten years after the promulgation of the dogma of the Assumption, but still before the Second Vatican Council. The passage merits being quoted in full:

Each one of these souls, these living members of Christ and his Spouse who make but one flesh in one and the same Spirit, will remain distinct, all the more so in that each brings its own indispensable element to the harmony of universal charity. But, if there is one distinguished forever from all the rest by a role, a quality, a gift of grace of incomparable excellence,

---

taken place?' ... To share in Christ's resurrection, Mary had first to share in his death.... Whatever from the physical point of view was the organic, biological cause of the end of her bodily life, it can be said that for Mary the passage from this life to the next was the full development of grace in glory, so that no death can ever be so fittingly described as a 'dormition' as hers." Pope John Paul II, *Theotokos—Woman, Mother, Disciple: A Catechesis on Mary, Mother of God* (Boston: Pauline Books and Media, 2000), 201–2.

18. For a lucid and profound theological treatment that completely defuses this concern that is often put on the threshold of what some regard as a troubling "high Mariology" reflective of a purported "fulfillment theology," see Thomas Joseph White, OP, "The Virgin Mary and the Church: The Marian Exemplarity of Ecclesial Faith," *Nova et Vetera* (English edition) 11, no. 2 (2013): 375–405.

it is Mary herself. For Mary will forever remain the person through whom the Word was born in the world, and the one through whom his Spouse was born for him, by means of his death. Mary will ever express within Christ's Spouse, the Church, what, in her, transcends even the quality of Spouse, namely, divine Motherhood. This incomparable dignity, which, in and for the Church, belongs personally to Mary alone, will be invested with so great splendour because it shows forth the greatest condescension of grace, the most amazing token of the divine love for the creature, namely, the *kenosis* of the eternal Son who made his creature child of God.

In this way, Mary is the realization in a single person, at the centre and, we might say, the culmination of history, of all that is most noble and perfect to be realised by the whole world at the end of history. All the graces given to each person, just as, before her, they led up to the grace which was hers, so, from now on, flow from her. In her grace as Mother of God, she is full of grace in an absolute sense. She prefigures, and, as it were, pre-contains all the graces the Church will ever receive; and the supreme grace, uniquely transcendent, of mother of grace itself in its divine source, belongs to the Church and testifies, within it, to its quality of Spouse, only because it belongs for ever to Mary, the first and surpassing realisation of the Church whose collective personality is realised only in individual persons.[19]

The Virgin Mary lives already now the fulfillment of human life in the beatific vision, united in love with God for which human beings were originally created and toward which they were ordered by original righteousness and elevated by sanctifying grace. The final end of humanity and the ensuing perfect happiness are realized in the Virgin Mary—the complete embodied human perfection united by intellect and will with God. The present life of the mother of God in heaven is infinitely more real than ours, a life of surpassing completion and perfection, a life without the imperfections of sin, natural evil, the fallibility and corruptibility of material substances, of contingency, and of death, but in virtue of the participation in the divine life, a life of infinite compassion and mercy—all of this fully human in personal, embodied identity.

Second, *Maria Assumpta* is the anticipated Eschaton in history. Together with Christ the head of the church, she as one fully belonging to the church already now constitutes the transhistorical perfec-

---

19. Bouyer, *Seat of Wisdom*, 200–201. The English translation appeared first in England in 1960.

tion of the church. This is at least what the Fathers of the Second Vatican Council teach. Consider *Lumen Gentium*, no. 63:

> The blessed Virgin, through the gift and office of the divine motherhood which unites her with the Son the redeemer, and by reason of her singular graces and gifts, is also intimately united to the church: the mother of God is the type of the church, as already St. Ambrose used to teach, that is to say, in the order of faith, charity and perfect union with Christ. For in the mystery of the church, which is also rightly called mother and virgin, the blessed virgin Mary has taken precedence, providing in a pre-eminent and singular manner the exemplar both as virgin and as mother.[20]

Consider, furthermore, the date of the dogma's promulgation: instead of August 15, the ancient feast day of the assumption, it was promulgated on November 1, the feast day of all saints. I take the theological significance of this to be the following: while in virtue of her divine motherhood being the first and foremost of the communion of saints, the Virgin Mary does as such belong inherently to the communion of saints. For she is, after all, a human person, a creature, all the way down. Hence her assumption, body and soul, into heaven pertains profoundly to the whole communion of saints. Again, Bouyer puts the matter in succinct theological terms:

> Just as in Mary was first effected that perfect union with Christ on the Cross that the whole Church is to realise in the course of its history, so the perfect union with Christ in glory was also accomplished in Mary, as soon as her earthly history was ended, as it will be accomplished for the whole Church at the end of all history.... Christ's Ascension does not mean that he has left us to our present condition, since he has gone only to prepare a place for us, that where he is we also may be; no more does Mary's Assumption mean her separation from us. As her Son is represented in the epistle to the Hebrews as *semper vivens ad interpellandum pro nobis* (7:23), so she remains, as the constant belief of the Church assures us, at his side, the interceder *par excellence*. Already, her blessedness is perfect, present, as she is, with God who has placed in her his delight. But, more than ever, the contemplative prayer which raises her above the angels, in the bliss of an eternal Eucharist, carries an irresistible intercession, on her part, that sinners, all of us countless children of hers, may come to be united to her in her Son.[21]

---

20. *Decrees* (ed. Tanner), 2:896.
21. Bouyer, *Seat of Wisdom*, 201–3.

Not only has Christ, the head of the church, arisen from the dead and sits in glory at the right hand of the Father, but also the one who is his mother, and by transference of Christ under the cross, the mother of all his followers, has already been assumed, body and soul, into heaven. And for this reason the whole communion of the saints, the whole body of Christ is already anchored in the glory of God, not only in the head, the risen Christ—which is the absolute *conditio sine qua non*—but also already in one, who like the rest of the elect relies completely on the infinite merits of Christ's salvific sacrifice of charity on the cross.

Third, if the Virgin Mary was assumed into heaven, body and soul, heaven must be part of creation and must have the extension of at least two human bodies. The resurrection body is a glorified, incorruptible body, but it is still a body and hence has spatial extension, circumscription, and position. Some Lutheran theologians in the Reformation period taught the ubiquity of Christ's body. According to their ontological interpretation of the communication of properties (*communicatio idiomatum*) of the incarnate Lord, Christ's body is taken to be omnipresent as Christ's divine nature is omnipresent *qua* divine substance. Rejecting, in addition, the traditional belief in the assumption of the mother of God into heaven, body and soul, and assuming simultaneously the "sleep of the soul" allowed them to forego the affirmation of a created heaven. It also meant that there was no ecclesial beginning (*inchoatio*) of an already obtaining eschatological reality.

The Virgin Mary's assumption, body and soul, entails on the contrary the reality of created heaven, of an eschatological presence and not just a promised future that might obtain for God in the eternal *nunc* of the divine midday but not yet for the church on earth (*ecclesia militans*). Rather, created heaven is a reality already in the world in which the *ecclesia militans* struggles on. Hence the complete remaking of the cosmos, the new heavens and the new earth, has begun with Christ's resurrection and ascension into heaven but has continued into the life of the church in and through the assumption of the Virgin. The church exists on earth, in purgatory, and already in heaven, the created heaven—and in the case of Mary, body and soul, in the eschatological perfection of glory. The time of the church is always already fulfilled eschatological time, fulfilled in head and body, fulfilled in Christ and in his mother. Fulfillment does not mean completion and perfection, but a concrete beginning (*inchoatio*), the commencement of the completion and of the perfection. The church on earth still struggles; there will be failures, betrayals, persecutions in the *ecclesia militans* as there have been, but the church in heaven (*ecclesia triumphans*) already is in place in eschatological perfection and completion in her most eminent member who constantly intercedes for all the other members of the body of Christ on earth and in purgatory.

I have begun this chapter with a memorable theological statement by Karl Rahner. I shall end it with an equally memorable theological statement from his older brother, Hugo Rahner. It is to be found in his small but important book *Our Lady and the Church*:

> Our Lady's Assumption, the final history of the body of the woman who gave birth to God is ... not so much an exception to the rule, but much more a fulfilling in advance of what is promised to the whole Mystical Body of Christ. And, moreover, it is not only promised, but in a sense already realized.... When the Church celebrates the Assumption, she is celebrating her own final glory.[22]

CONCLUSION

What Christ has accomplished for the sake of all humanity, he has already fulfilled comprehensively for his mother, who under the cross has become our mother and through her assumption, body and soul, into heaven has become the eschatological icon of the church where she reveals to the church, the mystical body of Christ, the church's own final end. In Mary, in whom all of faithful Israel is gathered, and who in virtue of her divine maternity is the first of Christ's body, the church already is anchored in heaven, and heaven is reaching into the *ecclesia militans*. The stunningly beautiful Baroque churches of my home area in Franconia, Germany, embody this vision in the vertical continuity between the *ecclesia militans* at worship in the nave and, as depicted on the walls as various apostles, martyrs, saints, and bishops, and as depicted on the ceiling paint-

---

22. H. Rahner, *Our Lady and the Church*, 123–28.

ings, the *ecclesia triumphans*, being simultaneously with the *ecclesia militans* at worship, eternally glorifying the Trinity. The *ecclesia militans* opens up vertically right into heaven and when the faithful look up to the ceiling they see heaven open and closest to the risen Christ they see the mother of God in heavenly glory. In virtue of the divine faith they hold, the faithful understand perfectly well that the open heaven depicted on the ceiling is not one of a future to come but of a present that here and now impacts the *ecclesia militans* down below. And so it would be most natural for the faithful to join St. Gabriel and St. Elisabeth in greeting Mary and simultaneously asking her for her prayer: "Hail Mary, full of grace, blessed are you among women, and blessed is the fruit of your womb, Jesus. Holy Mary, Mother of God, pray for us sinners, now and in the hour of our death."

With this prayer we have reached the end of this "what if" thought experiment. It is time to wake up from our dreaming and face again our cold, gray, and drab world in which we might (always haunted by doubt) dare the wager of faith based on a nonthematic existential prompting. Or at least this is what the secular simulacrum of faith, the comprehensive rule of private judgment in matters of revealed religion, would want us to believe. But what if we have no good reason to entertain the preceding reflections as a "what if" thought experiment of a hypothetically supposed divine faith? What if divine faith is the only faith worth having? What if sacred theology is inherently bound to and fed, illumined, and guided by divine faith? What if this theology is the only theology worth doing? For after all, as *Spe Salvi* emphasizes, "'in embryo' there are already present in us the things that are hoped for: the whole, true life."[23] And having received the very substance of the whole, true life in divine faith, must it not be similar to what the Psalmist expresses: "When the Lord restored the fortunes of Zion, we were like those who dream" (Ps 126:1; RSV)? Such dreaming is nothing but the *viator*'s incipient participation in the beatitude of the *comprehensor* of whom there exists one fully embodied realization already now—the Virgin Mary after her glorious assumption into heaven, body and soul.

23. Benedict XVI, *Spe Salvi*, par. 7.

Epilogue
God—Man's Beatitude

The book has arrived at its end. Its main purpose has been to engage the reader in a substantive *ressourcement* in Thomas Aquinas's teaching on the ultimate human end—beatitude—on the journey to that end, and on its central way stations. This *ressourcement* took the form of an argument developed from three main theses. (1) Theology needs a robust teleological orientation to succeed, and the loss of theology's proper theocentricity has impoverished contemporary theology. (2) The neglect of metaphysics and especially the metaphysics of final causality has also impoverished contemporary theology. (3) Thomas Aquinas and the school that issued from his philosophical and theological teaching offer a fecund model for integrating the primordial human vocation to the vision of God as the ultimate end with a robust metaphysics in a theocentric vision that is, theologically, unsurpassed in scope and depth and, spiritually, of unexhausted plenitude.

There are, of course, many topics that had to remain untouched or could only be acknowledged in passing. This book does not pretend to be a comprehensive treatise—which one would rightly expect to address all the questions pertaining to eschatology. The central purpose of this book, rather, has been to recapitulate, from a Thomist perspective and in critical dialogue with the late-modern philosophical and theological context, the primordial human vocation to the beatific vision. As Thomas Joseph White has exquisitely expressed:

God—Man's Beatitude

We are called to know God in the eschaton, in ecstatic joy, by which the intellect is taken out of preoccupation with itself and into the unique contemplation of the Trinity. St. Thomas insists that in charity we love God for God's own sake, *only for the goodness of God's own self*, through a love and admiration of God that place him above every other good, even our own good of eternal happiness.[1]

One abiding intention throughout the book has been the recovery, in the wake of the modern anthropocentric turn, of the proper theocentricity of Christian faith, life, and theology. Yet such theocentricity as Aquinas pursues it consistently and comprehensively in all of his philosophical and theological thought does not go unchallenged and is not always rightly understood in a late-modern context in which the anthropocentric turn has been relentlessly intensified and all too deeply internalized.[2] Under the pressure of distinct modern objections, some of Aquinas's interpreters and commentators have caused a variety of distinctly modern objections, concerns, and misunderstandings through certain simplifications, reductions, and imbalances in their presentation of Aquinas's considered philosophical and theological positions. In this epilogue I shall respond to a serious objection, defuse a widespread concern, and address a fateful misunderstanding.

The serious objection that I shall address was raised by the eminent Catholic moral theologian Germain Grisez. His objection against Aquinas's teaching on the ultimate end is two-pronged. The first prong consists in a critique of Aquinas's philosophical thesis that there obtains formally at any one given time only a single final end for human action. The second prong consists in the rejection of Aquinas's related theological thesis that the ultimate end of the hu-

---

1. White, *The Incarnate Lord*, 69.
2. This anthropocentric turn has been extended in programmatic revisionist ways to the thought of Thomas Aquinas himself in an intellectually brilliant albeit profoundly problematic attempt to align Aquinas with the modern turn to the subject. For an instructive exemplar, see Johannes Baptist Metz's "bringing up-to-date" of Karl Rahner's early works *Spirit in the World* and especially *Hearer of the Word* while working on his own programmatic *Christliche Anthropozentrik: Über die Denkform des Thomas von Aquin* (Munich: Kösel, 1962). One of the most penetrating critiques of the philosophical premises funding this revisionist interpretation of Aquinas is still Cornelio Fabro's *La svolta antropologica di Karl Rahner* (Segni: Editrice del Verbo Incarnato, 2011).

man being is God alone and that the beatific vision satisfies all human desires. The widespread concern that I shall defuse pertains to what is seen as Aquinas's failure to integrate the resurrection body in his account of beatitude, an account uniquely construed around the beatific vision. The fateful misunderstanding that I finally shall address claims that Aquinas promotes a *solus cum solo* beatitude, that is, an anti-communal and anti-social beatitude, a scenario in which the heavenly realm is replete with monads all individually absorbed in God and at the same time absolutely isolated from and indifferent to each other. Such a scenario is purportedly entailed in Aquinas's statement that "if there were but one soul enjoying God, it would be happy, though having no neighbor to love" (*ST* I-II, q. 4, a. 8).

In order to establish the proper metaphysical and theological horizon in which the objection, concern, and misunderstanding can be effectively addressed and overcome, it is necessary to turn once more to Aquinas's account of the beatific vision. After considering (1) Aquinas's account of the vision of God, I shall attend to (2) Aquinas's thesis that God is the single ultimate human end, after which I shall reflect on (3) the resurrection of the body in relationship to heavenly beatitude and conclude with (4) the communal character of heavenly beatitude.

THE BEATIFIC VISION

In his consideration of divine beatitude in the First Part of the *Summa Theologiae* Thomas Aquinas states: "The beatitude of an intellectual nature consists in an act of the intellect. In this we may consider two things—namely the *object of the act*, which is the thing understood; and the *act itself*, which is to understand [*intelligere*]" (ST I, q. 26, a. 3; emphasis added). The study of the object of beatitude—*objective uncreated beatitude*—is commensurate with the theology of God. I discussed the beatitude proper to God in the prologue; I shall return therefore to objective beatitude here in the epilogue only briefly in order to attend to one crucial feature of the beatific vision about which the Latin theology of the West and the Greek theology of the East differ significantly. We shall focus principally on the subject of beatitude—*subjective created beatitude*—for it will only be in light of

Aquinas's account of the *comprehensor*'s beatitude in the vision of God that his central thesis that the beatific vision is the one ultimate human end can best be understood and defended.[3]

Objective or Uncreated Beatitude

The ultimate end toward which divine faith is directed and which divine faith inchoately anticipates in the substance of things hoped for (see chapter 4), is nothing but the total, unrestricted, and immediate union of the *comprehensor*'s intellect and will with God, the complete unitive participation in God's transcendent perfection of beatitude, the life of the Trinity. In heaven, the qualitatively new human existence of the *comprehensor* has as its object God, that is, in William Hoye's apt formulation, "the same supreme *esse per essentiam* who is invincibly unknowable, who is totally present in all being, who contains all beings in himself, who is, in short, the actuality of all acts and, therefore, the perfection of all perfections."[4] The total object of the beatific vision is nothing other than the divine essence in its uncompromising, absolute transcendence.

The absolute transcendence of the infinite subsistent act of existing itself (*ipsum esse subsistens*) entails the radical negation of an alternative and indeed incompatible notion of transcendence that emerged in the post-Christian ambience of nineteenth-century European high culture, and acquired widespread acceptance among the artistic and cultural elite of that period. This alternative notion of transcendence found an original and intriguing articulation in the poems of Friedrich Hölderlin and especially of Rainer Maria Rilke's *Duino Elegies*.[5] Both poets invoke transcendence as the other, invisible side of immanence—for Hölderlin it is to be found in the cosmic

---

3. For a discussion of the meaning of "object" (*obiectum*) and "subject" (*subiectum*) in Aquinas's thought—which is just the opposite of the conventional modern meaning it takes after the anthropocentric turn to the subject, see above the first part of chapter 4.

4. William J. Hoye, *Actualitas Omnium Actuum: Man's Beatific Vision of God as Apprehended by Thomas Aquinas* (Meisenheim: Anton Hain, 1975), 146. In the following discussion, I am gratefully indebted to Hoye's excellent and unjustly forgotten study on metaphysics and epistemology of the beatific vision according to Aquinas.

5. See Friedrich Hölderlin, *Selected Poems and Fragments*, trans. Michael Hamburger, ed. Jeremy Adler (London: Penguin, 1998), and Rainer Maria Rilke, *Duino Elegies & The Sonnets of Orpheus: A Dual-Language Edition*, trans. Stephen Mitchell (New York: Vintage, 2009).

order and for Rilke in an ineffable interiority. This transcendence is understood to convey its own unique numinosity and therefore requires a corresponding innerworldly religiosity. According to this alternative vision, fueled by Romanticism's protest against the materialist immanent frame of much of the Enlightenment, transcendence and immanence together constitute the totality of the world in its comprehensive worldliness and only together convey the full depth of a purely world-based experience of existence. The experience of existence invoked in Hölderlin's and Rilke's art relates to the visible (*Diesseits*) and the invisible (*Jenseits*) of one eternal reality—the world.[6]

Considered in light of divine revelation and the metaphysics of creation, Hölderlin and Rilke's understanding of transcendence is a counterfeit. It is nothing but a more hidden aspect of the immanence of the world understood to form the absolute horizon of existence.[7] The transcendence that divine revelation discloses, to which scripture gives ample witness, that Christian theology maintains from the very beginning, and that Aquinas presupposes in his doctrine of the beatific vision, differs radically from the post-Christian counterfeit one finds in the works of Hölderlin and in Rilke's late poems. Eternal life is not simply the natural correlate to the indestructability of the rational soul; eternity is not merely one's everlasting natural subsistence in the world once one's earthly life is over. Rather, eternity is the uncreated absolute transcendence that is essentially the mode of existence characteristic of God in his absolute, unapproachable transcendence of holiness and glory. Only in virtue of God's infinite condescension

---

6. Heidegger, in his later work, elevates Hölderlin's and Rilke's vision (albeit in different ways) to lasting ontological significance: only in the poet's language does the epiphany of *Seyn* occur. Yet Heidegger's ontologizing reading of Hölderlin and Rilke takes again away what it first gives. By configuring the transcendence of *Seyn* as one of a primordial temporality, transcendence comes to mean the essential finitude of being transcending into—nothing. See William J. Richardson, SJ, *Heidegger: Through Phenomenology to Thought* (The Hague: Martinus Nijhoff, 1963), on transcendence, finitude, and temporality esp. 272–79; on Rilke, 391–400; on Hölderlin, 423–33, 440–72.

7. The arguably most profound theological interpretation and critique of Hölderlin and Rilke (the latter being treated in conjunction with Heidegger) can be found in Hans Urs von Balthasar's *Apokalypse der deutschen Seele: Studien zu einer Lehre von letzten Haltungen*, 3 vols., 3rd ed. (Freiburg: Johannes Verlag Einsiedeln, 1998); on Hölderlin, 1:293–345; on Heidegger and Rilke, 3:193–315.

and unfathomable mercy and love, and by way of the surpassing gratuity of sanctifying grace does eternity also come to mean the gratuitous participation of the blessed in the absolute transcendence of the divine eternity. The eternal life of the beatific vision is solely a matter of divine electing love. The ontological constitution of the human being only predisposes and enables the human being for beatitude. The absolute transcendence of God, the eternity in the strict sense that divine revelation discloses and the metaphysics of creation articulates is radically reserved for God. It is a surpassing holiness and glory unapproachable by any created power, even the very greatest. This transcendence denotes the absolute sovereignty of God the creator, who—according to Aquinas—cannot be subsumed univocally together with the creature under any genus and therefore concept, even that of being.[8]

Only when we begin to appreciate this absolute divine transcendence do we also begin to appreciate what a participation in the divine life might presuppose and entail. Only then can we appreciate the surpassing dignity of the intellect—the disposing and enabling principle—and sanctifying grace—the enabling power: the intellect disposes to and sanctifying grace brings about a new creation that not only participates in but also enters into the absolute divine transcendence by way of a most intimate union with God's triune life and beatitude.

The Exact Object of the Beatific Vision— God's Essence or Theophanies?

That the vision of God is a graced participation in the absolute transcendence of God's own beatitude was a conviction shared early in patristic theology. But there was debate among the patristic theologians over what the exact object of the vision was. The poles of the debate were marked by two central passages from the New Testament and their corollaries:

"No one has ever seen God" (Jn 1:18). From this passage it was concluded that no creature can view the essence of God.

---

8. For a defense of Aquinas's analogy of being, see chap. 10 in my *Dust Bound for Heaven* and White, "Monotheistic Rationality and Divine Names."

"Beloved, we are God's children now; what we will be has not yet been revealed. What we do know is this: when he is revealed, we will be like him, for we will see him as he is" (1 Jn 3:2). From this passage it was concluded that in heaven the blessed will see God as he is himself.

The Greek Fathers tended to take the first as the normative principle and read the second in light of the first. John Chrysostom, Dionysius the Areopagite, and John Damascene would be major theological representatives of the apophatic tradition. They assumed that heavenly theophanies—proportionate to human epistemic capacities—would emanate from the divine essence so as to manifest the invisible divinity to the beatified creature.[9] The Latin theology of the West took its lead from Augustine (and Gregory the Great) who interpreted the first passage as referring to the visual sense and thus pertaining to earthly human existence, a vision that would eventually be superseded in the case of the blessed by the beatific vision as described in the second passage. Taking the second as the proper account of the supernatural reality of the beatific vision, Augustine developed the view that in the beatific vision the divine essence is beheld directly, that is, without any interposed medium.[10]

In the first part of the thirteenth century, a lively debate ensued among theologians at the University of Paris over the two positions developed in the patristic period. In 1241, the bishop of Paris, William of Auvergne (who before becoming a bishop had been a master

---

9. For an instructive introduction to this theological tradition with its apogee in the fourteenth-century Byzantine theologian Gregory Palamas, see Vladimir Lossky, *The Vision of God*, trans. Asheleigh Moorhouse (Yonkers, N.Y.: St. Vladimir's Seminary Press, 1983). For the important discussion of how Palamas's mature account of the vision of God compares to, contrasts with, and possibly accords compatibility with Aquinas's account of the beatific vision, see the instructive studies by A. N. Williams, *The Ground of Union: Deification in Aquinas and Palamas* (Oxford: Oxford University Press, 1999), and Édouard Divry, OP, *La transfiguration selon l'orient et l'occident: Grégoire Palamas—Thomas d'Aquin: vers un dénouement oecuménique* (Paris: Téqui, 2009). For an extraordinary study that approaches Aquinas and Palamas by way of a common source, Maximus the Confessor, see Antione Lévy, OP, *Le créé et l'incréé: Maxime le confesseur et Thomas d'Aquin: aux sources de la querelle palamienne* (Paris: Vrin, 2006).

10. See especially Augustine's *Epistula CXLVII* (*Liber ad Paulinam de videndo Dei*), in *CSEL* 44: *S. Aureli Augustini Operum Sectio II: S. Augustini Epistulae* (Leipzig: Freytag, 1904), 274–331.

of theology at the University of Paris), convened a council of theological masters and subsequently condemned the proposition: "The divine essence *in se* is seen neither by human nor by angel." Theologians were to adhere to the contrary position, namely that the blessed and the angels will see the divine essence *in se*.[11] The magisterial specification did not, however, result in a complete and unqualified dismissal of the theological concerns expressed in the position of the Greek Fathers. Rather, Bishop William's magisterial judgment first and foremost accorded the beatific vision a prominent place among the mysteries of the faith to be explored further by theologians. Furthermore, his judgment indicated the direction in which theologians were expected to move in order to achieve a better theological integration of the two respective truths. A first important breakthrough in this matter occurred in the thought of Albert the Great, Aquinas's teacher, who began to synthesize the Dionysian and Augustinian theologies of the beatific vision by interpreting the Dionysian theophanies as the *lumen gloriae*.

Taking the 1241 magisterial decision as his doctrinal point of departure, Aquinas continued his teacher Albert's work of theological integration. Aquinas's considered position is that humans may know the divine essence, but not in this life and even in the beatific vision, not comprehensively. While the epistemological limitations of this life will be overcome in the beatific vision, the ontological difference between the finite creatureliness of the blessed and the uncreated infinity of the divine essence remains forever. Thus, in Aquinas's view, the Latin position, made to a certain degree normative in 1241, pertains to the eschatological overcoming of the epistemological limitations characteristic of this life, while the Greek *agnosia* pertains to the ineradicable permanence of the ontological difference between creator and creature.[12]

---

11. For more detailed accounts of the debate and for the full documentation of the 1241 magisterial judgment by Bishop William of Auvergne, see the outstanding studies by Hyacinthe-François Dondaine, OP, "L'objet et le 'medium' de la vision béatifique chez les théologiens du XIIIe siècle," *Recherches de théologie ancienne et médiévale* 19 (1952): 60–130, and Wicki, *Die Lehre*.

12. Aquinas's synthesis was, of course, not the last word for the theologians of the thirteenth and fourteenth century in their ongoing effort to elucidate the mystery of the beatific vision. It would go far beyond the scope of this epilogue to adumbrate the

In the First Part of the *Summa Theologiae*, after an initial treatment of how God is in himself (*secundum seipsum*) in questions 3–11, Aquinas turns in question 12 to the consideration of how God is actually known by us, that is, how God is in human knowledge (*qualiter sit in cognitionem nostrum*). Aquinas's synthesis of the Latin and the Greek positions receives a pronounced articulation in this text; his characteristic synthesis comes about in three moves. First, he states the fundamental epistemological problem that leads some theologians to hold the position that no created finite intellect whatsoever can see the uncreated infinite essence of God:

> Since everything is knowable according as it is actual, God, Who is pure act without any admixture of potentiality, is in Himself supremely knowable. But what is supremely knowable in itself, may not be knowable to a particular intellect, on account of the excess of the intelligible object above the intellect; as, for example, the sun, which is supremely visible, cannot be seen by the bat by reason of its excess of light. Therefore some who considered this, held that no created intellect can see the essence of God. (*ST* I, q. 12, a. 1)

In a second move, he establishes the Augustinian reasons for the magisterially established position of 1241 in contradistinction to the Greek position. *Agnosia* is not tenable, Aquinas argues,

> for as the ultimate beatitude of [the human being] consists in the use of his highest function, which is the operation of his intellect; if we suppose that the created intellect could never see God, it would either never attain to beatitude, or its beatitude would consist in something else beside God; which is opposed to faith. For the ultimate perfection of the rational creature is to be found in that which is the principle of its being; since a thing is perfect so far as it attains to its principle.... Hence it must be absolutely granted that the blessed see the essence of God. (*ST* I, q. 12, a. 1)

In a third move, Aquinas finally receives and integrates the legiti-

---

positions of Henry of Ghent, Godfrey of Fontaines, Duns Scotus, Durandus of Saint-Pourçain, and Peter Auriol, among others, or even to consider the objections they raised against Aquinas's account. The Thomist who addressed these variegated proposals and their objections according to Aquinas's philosophical principles and theologicial views was John Capreolus, OP, whose defense of Aquinas's teaching on the vision of God is made available in the noteworthy study by Karl Forster, *Die Verteidigung der Lehre des heiligen Thomas von der Gottesschau durch Johannes Capreolus* (Munich: Karl Zink Verlag, 1955).

mate concern of the Greek position. In the first and third objections of article 1, he gives voice to the Greek position by adducing two central authorities of the apophatic tradition and the most important biblical passage backing it—Dionysius, Chrysostom, and John 1:18:

It seems that no created intellect can see the essence of God. For Chrysostom (Hom. xiv. in Joan.) commenting on John 1:18, "No man hath seen God at any time," says: "Not prophets only, but neither angels nor archangels have seen God. For how can a creature see what is increatable?" Dionysius also says (Div. Nom. i), speaking of God: "Neither is there sense, nor image, nor opinion, nor reason, nor knowledge of Him." (*ST* I, q. 12, a. 1, obj. 1)

After laying out the basic objection, based on scripture and a strand of the theological tradition, Aquinas articulates the crucial philosophical objection that Dionysian apophaticism would raise against the Augustinian position:

Further, the created intellect knows only existing things. For what falls first under the apprehension of the intellect is being [*ens*]. Now God is not something existing; but He is rather super-existence [*Sed Deus non est existens, sed supra existentia*] as Dionysius says (Div. Nom. iv). Therefore God is not intelligible; but above all intellect [*Ergo non est intelligibilis; sed est supra omnem intellectum*]. (*ST* I, q. 12, a. 1, obj. 3)

Significantly, in his response to these two objections, Aquinas does not refute the position of the Greek theologians but rather resituates it by arguing that the Greek Fathers negated only the kind of vision that God alone could have of himself:

Both of these authorities speak of the vision of comprehension. Hence Dionysius premises immediately before the words cited, "He is universally to all incomprehensible," etc. Chrysostom likewise after the words quoted says: "He says this of the most certain vision of the Father, which is such a perfect consideration and comprehension as the Father has of the Son." (*ST* I, q. 12, a. 1, ad 1)

His response to what is in many ways the key argument of Dionysius for radical apophaticism is greatly instructive:

God is not said to be not existing as if He did not exist at all, but because He exists above all that exists; inasmuch as He is His own existence [*inquantum est suum esse*]. Hence it does not follow that He cannot be known at all, but that He exceeds every kind of knowledge; which means that He is not comprehended [*Unde ex hoc non sequitur quod nullo modo possit cognosci, sed quod omnem cognitionem excedat, quod est ipsum non comprehendi*]. (*ST* I, q. 12, a. 1, ad 3)

The eschatological vision of God is an immediate vision, but it is not a vision of comprehension (*visio comprehensionis*) in the strict sense. I shall attend below to the reasons Aquinas offers for an immediate intellectual vision of the divine essence and against a comprehensive knowledge of the divine essence as only God comprehends God: in one, infinite act of existence that is identical with the infinite act of exhaustive and perfect understanding—comprehension—of the divine essence.

Created Beatitude: The Subjective Participating Beatitude of the Blessed

Having clarified this fundamental point in article 2 of question 12, Aquinas addresses how the intellectual vision of the divine essence comes about in the blessed. Does the vision of God's essence require some created likeness, in short, theophanies? His answer turns on Aristotle's epistemological principle that sensing and knowing involve a formal union of the power or faculty with its object through taking on its form. The substantial form that makes a thing what it is, is also the form that makes the intellect understand the object.[13] In the thing

---

13. Aristotle, *De anima* III.8, 431b29. Consider Aquinas's interpretation of Aristotle's argument: "Obviously the soul is not simply identical with the things it knows; for not stone itself, but its formal likeness exists in the soul. And this enables us to see how intellect in act is what it understands; the form of the object is the form of the mind in act. Thus the soul resembles the hand. The hand is the most perfect of organs, for it takes the place in man of all the organs given to other animals for purposes of defence or attack or covering. Man can provide all these needs for himself with his hands. And in the same way the soul in man takes the place of all the forms of being, so that through his soul a man is, in a way, all being or everything; his soul being able to assimilate all the forms of being—the intellect, intelligible forms; and the senses, sensible forms." Thomas Aquinas, *Commentary on Aristotle's De Anima*, trans. Kenelm Foster, OP, and Sylvester Humphries, OP (New Haven, Conn.: Yale University Press, 1951), §§789–90. Two excellent introductions to Aquinas's metaphysics of knowledge are John Peifer, *The Mystery of Knowledge* (Albany, N.Y.: Magi Books, 1964), and Yves R. Simon, *An Introduction to Metaphysics of Knowledge*, trans. Vukan Kuic and Richard J. Thompson (New York: Fordham University Press, 1990). The classical reappropriation of Aquinas's metaphysics of knowledge under modern scientific conditions, still unsurpassed in its speculative scope

the form has a natural existence (*esse naturale*) and in the intellect an intentional existence (*esse intentionale*). Aquinas calls the form in its intentional existence "species."[14]

While it would go far beyond the scope of this epilogue to enter into the details of Aquinas's metaphysics of knowledge, it is absolutely essential for a proper understanding of the way intellection in general (and the vision of God in particular) comes about to appreciate that it is not the *species* of the object that is present in knowledge, but that the object is present in knowledge *through* or *by way of* the *species*. In short, the *species intelligibilis* is not a "what" (*quod*), but rather a "through which" (*quo*). Unlike in modern epistemologies (first and foremost John Locke's), in Aquinas's metaphysics of knowledge there is no representation that separates the concept from the object it expresses.[15]

---

and integrative ingenuity, is Jacques Maritain's *The Degrees of Knowledge* (*Distinguish to Unite*), trans. Gerald B. Phelan (New York: Scribner's Sons, 1959). Indispensable for a renewed contemporary appreciation of Aquinas's theory of perception is a full recovery of the role of the *vis cogitiva* in relationship to the active intellect in the process of abstraction. For such a recovery see Anthony J. Lisska's *Aquinas's Theory of Perception: An Analytic Reconstruction* (Oxford: Oxford University Press, 2016). The classic account remains George P. Klubertanz, SJ, *The Discursive Power: Sources and Doctrine of the Vis Cogitiva According to St. Thomas Aquinas* (St. Louis, Mo.: Modern Schoolman, 1952).

14. For an lucid interpretation and reappropriation of the crucial distinction between natural and intentional being in Aquinas's metaphysics of knowledge, see Stephen L. Brock, "Intentional Being, Natural Being, and the First-person Perspective in Thomas Aquinas," *The Thomist* 77, no. 1 (2013): 103–33.

15. Étienne Gilson articulates well the difficulty modern interpreters of Aquinas's metaphysics of knowledge face: "Practically speaking, it is almost impossible to speak of [the species] except as if the species were an image, an equivalent or substitute for the object; and St. Thomas himself so speaks. But it is important to understand that the species of an object is not one being and the object another. It is the very object under the mode of species; that is, it is still the object considered in action and in the efficacy it exerts over a subject. Under this one condition only can we say that *it is not the species of the object that is present in thought, but the object through its species*. And as it is the form of the object which is its active and determining principle, so it is the form of the object which the intellect which knows it, through its species, becomes. *The whole objectivity of human knowledge depends in the last analysis upon the fact that it is not a superadded intermediary, or a distinct substitute which is introduced into our thought in place of the thing. It is, rather, the sensible species of the thing itself which, rendered intelligible by the agent intellect, becomes the form of our possible intellect.*" Étienne Gilson, *The Christian Philosophy of St. Thomas Aquinas*, trans. L. K. Shook, CSB (Notre Dame, Ind.: University of Notre Dame Press, 1994), 227–28 (emphasis added). For an in-depth analysis of Aquinas's metaphysics of knowledge with a special focus on the particular functions of the *species impressa* and the

God—Man's Beatitude 399

Aquinas takes the *species* to be a purely transparent formal medium "through which" (*quo*) the intellect attains its object. Without such a formal medium *quo* the intellect cannot attain its object. Hence, the vision of God requires such a formal medium *quo*. Yet quite obviously, in the vision of God, no created and hence finite formal medium *quo* suffices to effect the formal cognitive union between the created finite intellect of the *comprehensor* and the uncreated infinite divine essence. Hence, the divine essence itself must serve as this formal medium *quo*. Aquinas concludes that in the beatific vision, the uncreated infinite essence of God is the object (*quod*) as well as the formal medium *quo* of the *comprehensor*'s vision. Consider Aquinas's argument from his *Compendium*:

> The divine essence ... has this exclusive characteristic, that our intellect can be united to it without the medium of any likeness. The reason is that the divine essence itself is its own existence or esse [*quia et ipsa divina essentia est eius esse*], which is true of no other form. Knowledge always requires the presence of some form in the intellect; and so, if any form that exists by itself, for example, the substance of an angel, cannot inform an intellect, and yet is to be known by the intellect of another, such knowledge has to be brought about by some likeness of the thing informing the intellect. But this is not necessary in the case of the divine essence, which is its own existence. Accordingly *the soul that is beatified by the vision of God is made one with Him in understanding. The knower and the known must somehow be one.*[16]

---

species expressa in the beatific vision, see Alexander von Zychlinski, "Die species impressa und expressa beim beseligenden Schauakt nach der Lehre des hl. Thomas von Aquin. Eine thomistische Studie" (ThD diss., University of Breslau, 1918).

16. *Comp. theol.* II, c. 9 (emphasis added). How the finite knower and the infinite known can be conceived of as somehow being one Aquinas addresses most extensively in *De Veritate*: "It is not necessary ... for the divine essence to become the form of the intellect but only to become related to the intellect after the manner of a form [*se habeat ad ipsum ut forma*]. Consequently, just as one actual being results from matter and a form which is a part of the thing; so, with the necessary differences, the created intellect and the divine essence become one in the act of understanding [*unum in intelligendo*] when the intellect understands and the divine essence is understood through itself. How it is possible for a separated essence to be joined to the intellect as a form has been shown by the Commentator. Whenever two things are received in something that can receive, and one of them is more perfect than the other, the proportion of what is more perfect to that which is less perfect is like the proportion of a form to what it perfects—just as light is the perfection of color when both are received in a transparent medium. Consequently, since a created intellect, because present in a created substance, is less perfect than the divine essence, the divine essence bears to it in some way the relation of a form

Hoye interprets Aquinas's argument aptly thus: "Because the blessed are joined to God immediately and not by means of an intelligible species, God united Himself to them not just as an object existing in its own right outside of their intellects but as the actualizer of the operation by which they reach their object."[17] He observes that according to Aquinas "the mode in which God specially unites Himself to the blessed consists of the authentic union of His divine essence itself, that is, God's *quid est*, to their intellects. The divine substance causes itself genuinely to inform their intellects. Only because God's essence and substance are His act of being, is He able to give His whole Self to a human knower, seeing that His intelligibility envelops His total substance."[18]

Because God's essence (*quid est* or *quidditas*) cannot be known in this life, there cannot be a proper definition of God's essence either. But because God is the transcendent first cause of everything that is and because being (*ens*) is revealed in each reality as an analogous notion, from knowledge of creatures we can reach analogous knowledge of God: knowledge of God's existence, knowledge of God's names or attributes, and knowledge of the relation of finite beings to God.[19] This analogous knowledge of God, moving from finite being to Being itself, culminates in an approximating nominal definition of God (*ipsum esse subsistens*; *ST* I, q. 4, a. 2). This divine name accounts for the fact that God's essence and substance are his act of being. The subsistent act of existing itself transcends all the categories of being. Because the divine essence completely escapes

---

[*comparabitur divina essentia ad illum intellectum quodammodo ut forma*] as long as it exists in it. We can find some sort of example of this among natural things. A self-subsistent thing cannot be the form of any matter if it contains matter itself. For example, a stone cannot be the form of any matter. A self-subsistent thing lacking matter, however, can be the form of matter, as is clear in the case of the soul. Similarly and in some way or other, and even though it is pure act [*actus purus*] and has an act of being [*esse*] entirely distinct from the intellect, the divine essence becomes related to the intellect as its form in the act of understanding" (*De ver.*, q. 8, a. 1; *Truth*, 1:313).

17. Hoye, *Actualitas Omnium Actuum*, 154–55.

18. Ibid., 284–85.

19. *ST* I, q. 2, a. 2, ad 3: "From every effect the existence of the cause can be clearly demonstrated, and so we can demonstrate the existence of God from His effects; though from them we cannot perfectly know God as He is in His essence." See chap. 10 in my *Dust Bound for Heaven*.

God—Man's Beatitude 401

the direct human conceptual grasp, "the beatific vision demands not just that [the human being] becomes the divine essence *intentionally* (as would be the case in regard to knowledge *per essentiam* of a pure intelligence, that is, of an angel) but that he becomes the divine essence *really*."[20]

But how is the created finite intellect able to receive the uncreated infinite divine essence as cognitive object by way of a formal medium "through which" (*quo*) that is uncreated and infinite? The formal medium *quo* can obviously not become finite. Nor can the human intellect become infinite in its substance. If it did, it would cease to be the faculty of a created rational soul, which is the spiritual but finite substantial form of a created and finite body. It is for these reasons, Aquinas argues, that the created faculty of the human intellect must be elevated or strengthened by God to the point that the created and finite human intellect becomes capable of cognizing the uncreated and infinite divine essence.

Aquinas's argument turns on the following metaphysical principle formulated crisply in the prologue to his commentary on Aristotle's *Metaphysics*: "The intellect and the intelligible object must be proportionate to each other and must belong to the same genus, since the intellect and the intelligible object are one in act."[21] Simply relying on the power of the active intellect, humans are incapable of effecting the beatific vision. Hence, the human intellect must be elevated, ennobled so that God can somehow become the form of the intellect.[22] In short, the human being stands in need of a disposition

---

20. Hoye, *Actualitas Omnium Actuum*, 274.

21. *In duodecim libros Metaphysicorum Aristotelis expositio*, prooemium: "Intelligibile enim et intellectum oportet proportionata esse, et unius generis, cum intellectus et intelligibile in actu sint unum."

22. SCG III.53.3: "Nothing is receptive of a more sublime form unless it be elevated by means of a disposition to the capacity for this form, for a proper act is produced in a proper potency. Now, the divine essence is a higher form than any created intellect. So, in order that the divine essence may become the intelligible species for a created intellect, which is needed in order that the divine substance may be seen, it is necessary for the created intellect to be elevated for this purpose by a more sublime disposition." SCG III.53.2: "So, it is impossible for this essence to become the intelligible form of a created intellect unless by virtue of the fact that the created intellect participates in the divine likeness. Therefore, this participation in the divine likeness is necessary so that the substance of God may be seen."

to become the divine essence *intentionally* as well as *really*. This created supernatural disposition is the light of glory (*lumen gloriae*). In natural cognition, the active intellect (*intellectus agens*) abstracts the intelligible species from the sensible phantasms (*ST* I, q. 79, aa. 3–5) and thus provides the needed intellectual light whereby the intellect cognizes the intelligible species. In the beatific vision, analogically, God provides the supernatural light of glory whereby (*sub quo*) the intellect cognizes the divine essence that itself becomes the intelligible form of the intellect. Aquinas states:

> Everything which is raised up to what exceeds its nature, must be prepared by some disposition above its nature.... But *when any created intellect sees the essence of God, the essence of God itself becomes the intelligible form of the intellect* [*Ipsa essentia divina fit forma intelligibilis intellectus*]. Hence it is necessary that some supernatural disposition [*dispositio supernaturalis*] should be added to the intellect in order that it may be raised up to such a great and sublime height. Now since the natural power of the created intellect does not avail to enable it to see the essence of God ... it is necessary that the power of understanding [*virtus intelligendi*] should be added by divine grace. Now this increase of the intellectual powers is called the illumination of the intellect [*illuminatio intellectus*], as we also call the intelligible object itself by the name of light of illumination. And this is the light spoken of in the Apocalypse (Apoc. 21:23): "The glory of God hath enlightened it"—viz. the society of the blessed who see God. By this light the blessed are made "deiform"—i.e. like to God [*deiformes, id est Deo similes*], according to the saying: "When He shall appear we shall be like to Him, and we shall see Him as He is" (1 Jn. 2:2).[23]

---

23. *ST* I, q. 12, a. 5 (emphasis added). See also Aquinas's quite similar argument in chap. 105 of his *Compendium*: "Previous discussion has brought out the fact that no creature is associated with God in genus. Hence the essence of God cannot be known through any created species whatever, whether sensible or intelligible. Accordingly, *if God is to be known as He is, in His essence, God Himself must become the form of the intellect knowing Him and must be joined to that intellect, not indeed so as to constitute a single nature with it, but in the way an intelligible species is joined to the intelligence.* For God, who is His own being, is also His own truth, and truth is the form of the intellect. Whatever receives a form, must first acquire the disposition requisite to the reception of that form. Our intellect is not equipped by its nature with the ultimate disposition looking to that form which is truth; otherwise it would be in possession of truth from the beginning. Consequently, *when it does finally attain to truth, it must be elevated by some disposition newly conferred on it*. And this we call the light of glory, whereby our intellect is perfected by God, who alone by His very nature has this form properly as His own.... This is the light that is spoken of in Psalm 35:10: 'In Your light we shall see light'" (*Comp. theol.*, c. 105; emphasis added).

God—Man's Beatitude

Nota bene: The light of glory is not to be confused with the formal medium "through which" (*quo*) of the vision, the divine essence itself. Unlike the uncreated divine essence, the light of glory is something created by God in the finite intellect, a supernatural disposition or *habitus* that perfects the intellect's act of *intelligere*. It is crucial not to mistake the light of glory for a similitude or a medium "in which" (*in quo*) the divine essence is seen. Aquinas emphasizes that

> this light is required to see the divine essence, not as a similitude in which God is seen, but as a perfection of the intellect [*perfectio quaedam intellectus*], strengthening it to see God. Therefore it may be said that this light is to be described not as a medium in which [*in quo*] God is seen, but as one by which [*sub quo*] He is seen; and such a medium does not take away the immediate vision of God. (*ST* I, q. 12, a. 5, ad 2)

The distinction between *sub quo* and *in quo* might strike the hasty reader as Scholastic hairsplitting that is impossible to translate into clear English. Yet Aquinas's point is important. A medium *in quo* is a medium between the intellect and the object that engages it. Such a medium would obviously compromise the immediate vision of God. The light of glory, conceived of as a medium *sub quo*, is an infused created perfection (*habitus*) that intrinsically informs the act of the intellect (*intelligere*) itself. Such a perfection of the intellect's own act in no way compromises the immediate vision of God. I shall designate in the following the created perfective *medium sub quo* as medium "whereby" in order to distinguish it linguistically from the uncreated formal medium "through which" (*quo*).

Elevated by the light of glory, the medium "whereby" (*sub quo*), the human intellect can become united with the divine essence, the medium "through which" (*quo*) and thus cognize the divine essence (*obiectum quod*). In article 5 of question 12, Aquinas introduces the important term, *deiformitas*. The light of glory has the effect of making the *comprehensor*'s intellect "deiform," capable of receiving the quasi-form of the medium "through which" (*quo*) of the divine essence. The divinization that begins with the life of grace (see chapter 5) thus reaches its consummation in the beatific vision. The light of glory is the indispensable causal condition for that formal union to come about.

Yet if the light of glory has such an elevating and strengthening effect on the finite human intellect that through the formal union with the infinite divine essence an intellectual vision of the selfsame divine essence comes about, how is it that the finite human intellect can receive such an elevation without being transformed into something else? In the response to the third objection of article 4, Aquinas offers an argument why the intellect is naturally open to the elevation or strengthening by the light of glory:

> The sense of sight, as being altogether material, cannot be raised up to immateriality. But *our intellect ... inasmuch as it is elevated above matter in its own nature, can be raised up above its own nature to a higher level by grace.* The proof is, that sight cannot in any way know abstractly what it knows concretely; for in no way can it perceive a nature except as this one particular nature; whereas our intellect is able to consider abstractly what it knows concretely. Now although it knows things which have a form residing in matter, still it resolves the composite into both of these elements; and it considers the form separately by itself. (*ST* I, q. 12, a. 4, ad 3; emphasis added)

Matter restricts to one determinate mode; things that are material can only be what they determinately are. Immaterial beings that are intellectual by nature are, by contrast, unrestricted. In his *On the Soul*, Aristotle characterizes the rational soul as "somehow all things" because by cognizing and understanding all things it has the capacity to become all things intentionally.[24] Aquinas takes the unique ontological constitution of the human intellect to be its fundamental openness to all being (*ens commune*). It is this openness to being that accounts for the intellect's natural potency to be elevated by God

24. Aristotle, *De anima* III.8, 431b20–21. Consider Aquinas's interpretation of Aristotle's analysis of the intrinsic immateriality of sensation and intellection: "In the lower terrestrial natures there are two degrees of immateriality. There is the perfect immateriality of intelligible being; for in the intellect things exist not only without matter, but even without their individuating material conditions, and also apart from any material organ. Then there is the half-way state of sensible being. For as things exist in sensation they are free indeed from matter, but are not without their individuating material conditions, nor apart from a bodily organ. For sensation is of objects in the particular, but intellection of objects universally. It is with reference to these two modes of existence that the philosopher will say, in Book III, that the soul is somehow all things." Thomas Aquinas, *Commentary on Aristotle's De Anima*, trans. Kenelm Foster, OP, and Sylvester Humphries, OP (New Haven, Conn.: Yale University Press, 1951), §284.

beyond its natural capacity: "Since therefore the created intellect is naturally capable of apprehending the concrete form, and the concrete being abstractedly, by way of a kind of resolution of parts; it can by grace be raised up to know separate subsisting substance, and separate subsisting existence [*esse separatum subsistens*]" (*ST* I, q. 12, a. 4, ad 3). Hence, the human intellect is naturally *capax Dei*. The subjective disposition of the light of glory, the medium "whereby" (*sub quo*), suffices to realize that capacity. As Hoye explains: "Its arrival is tantamount to the effectuation of the whole actuality of the beatific vision."[25] In the beatific vision, the human intellect remains itself unaltered, because the light of glory functions like a facility to act, like a *habitus*: "The created light is necessary to see the essence of God, not in order to make the essence of God intelligible, which is of itself intelligible, but in order to enable the intellect to understand in the same way as a habit makes a power more able to act" (*ST* I, q. 12, a. 5, ad 1). What exactly does the light of glory actually effect? Aquinas offers a succinct answer:

> The agent intellect makes things actually intelligible, just as light in a way makes things actually visible. Therefore, this disposition whereby the created intellect is raised to the intellectual vision of divine substance is fittingly called the light of glory; not because it makes some object actually intelligible, as does the light of the agent intellect, but because it makes the intellect actually powerful enough to understand [*sed per hoc quod facit intellectum potentem actu intelligere*]. (*SCG* III.53.6)

In the beatific vision the created light of glory, like a *habitus*, allows the active intellect to do its proper job, to understand (*intelligere*) the essence of God—nothing more and nothing less.

One of the important implications of the formal union between the human intellect and the divine essence in the beatific vision is that, being the surpassing actualization of the intellect, the beatific vision does not exclude other operations and objects. As Hoye explains, "*because the intellect can somehow become all things, the intellectual union with God includes the richest possible experience*, since all things exist in God."[26] Hence, "all other operations and things in-

---

25. Hoye, *Actualitas Omnium Actuum*, 277.
26. Ibid., 155 (emphasis added).

volved in [the human being's] heavenly life with God emanate from the total intellectual act and are related to it as accidents are related to their substance, for all operations and things are nothing other than modes of being. *The three fundamental dynamisms in human nature, namely knowledge, love, and joy, are contained within the intellect's horizon.*"[27] Because in heaven the blessed attain the supreme good, which is necessarily the universal good, every possible desire, no matter how negligible and inconsequential, will necessarily be fulfilled. In heavenly beatitude therefore, all desires that paradise would satiate are necessarily and surpassingly fulfilled.

After having explicated the full entailment of the Latin position, Aquinas finally returns to the Greek position to do full justice to the eschatological *agnosia* that the Greek Fathers were pressing. What was briefly acknowledged in the response to the first objection in article 1 of question 12 receives now a full treatment in article 7 of the same question: "Can any created intellect comprehend the divine essence?" Aquinas affirms the metaphysical principle that underlies the position of the Greek Fathers: "The infinite cannot be comprehended by the finite" (*ST* III, q. 10, a. 1). Indeed there is a fundamental incommensurability between a finite intellect and an infinitely knowable subject. Because every created intellect is necessarily finite, every created intellect is essentially incapable of comprehending the uncreated infinity of the divine essence. Everything turns, of course, on the exact meaning of the term "comprehension." In the lexicon of the Greek Fathers, as Aquinas understands it, "comprehension" means a consummate and exhaustive knowledge of a truth to the highest degree of its intrinsic intelligibility. Given this most rigorous understanding of perfect intellectual comprehension, in the beatific vision the one whom the tradition designates as a *comprehensor* does indeed have a genuine immediate vision of, but does not comprehend, the divine essence. In order to do justice to the Greek *agnosia* of the infinite divine essence as well as to the traditional Latin designation of the blessed as *comprehensor*, Aquinas distinguishes between comprehension in the strict sense of the term, on the one hand, and, on the other hand, comprehension as signifying merely

27. Ibid. (emphasis added).

the state of arrival at the designation of the beatific vision and the *comprehensor*'s beholding—that is, in a certain way possessing—what the wayfarer (*viator*) hopes eventually to behold and possess.²⁸

Aquinas adduces another distinction in order to elucidate the difference between the *comprehensor*'s comprehension, that is, comprehension in the sense of beholding and possessing the infinite divine essence in an interminable formal union, and the divine self-comprehension, that is, comprehension in the strict and perfective sense of a comprehensive act of understanding the infinite divine essence. In the beatific vision, in virtue of the light of glory the blessed see the whole (*totus*) of God because they are formally united with the divine essence. Yet even in the beatific vision the blessed cannot comprehend the uncreated infinity of the divine essence wholly (*totaliter*) because their intellect, despite its elevation, remains a creaturely finite faculty.²⁹ Hoye draws out the implications of Aquinas's argument in a lucid way: "Without altering [the human

---

28. Aquinas states: "'Comprehension' is twofold: In one sense it is taken strictly and properly, according as something is included in the one comprehending; and thus in no way is God comprehended either by intellect, or in any other way; forasmuch as He is infinite and cannot be included in any finite being; so that no finite being can contain Him infinitely, in the degree of His own infinity. In this sense we now take comprehension. But in another sense 'comprehension' is taken more largely as opposed to 'non-attainment'; for he who attains to anyone is said to comprehend him when he attains to him. And in this sense God is comprehended by the blessed, according to the words, 'I held him, and I will not let him go' (Cant 3:4); in this sense also are to be understood the words quoted from the Apostle concerning comprehension. And in this way 'comprehension' is one of the three prerogatives of the soul, responding to hope, as vision responds to faith, and fruition responds to charity. For even among ourselves not everything seen is held or possessed, forasmuch as things either appear sometimes afar off, or they are not in our power of attainment. Neither, again, do we always enjoy what we possess; either because we find no pleasure in them, or because such things are not the ultimate end of our desire, so as to satisfy and quell it. But the blessed possess these three things in God; because they see Him, and in seeing Him, possess Him as present, having the power to see Him always; and possessing Him, they enjoy Him as the ultimate fulfilment of desire" (*ST* I, q. 12, a. 7, ad 1).

29. "The word 'wholly' [*totaliter*] denotes a mode of the object; not that the whole [*totus*] object does not come under knowledge, but that the mode of the object is not the mode of the one who knows. Therefore he who sees God's essence, sees in Him that He exists infinitely, and is infinitely knowable; nevertheless, this infinite mode does not extend to enable the knower to know infinitely; thus, for instance, a person can have a probable opinion that a proposition is demonstrable, although he himself does not know it as demonstrated" (*ST* I, q. 12, a. 7, ad 3).

being's] natural limitation to material objects, God can nevertheless unite Himself *per essentiam* to a human intellect, for He gives Himself as pure act. Thus He is truly seen in His totality even though His substance is not fully embraced in a *species expressa* or *impressa* nor His actuality fully realized in the act of the beatified intellect."[30]

In sum, because the vision of God is a formal union with the consummate good that is most desirable (see chapters 1 and 2), it presupposes and entails the rectitude of the will (see chapter 6), such that what is most lovable is also loved rightly (that is, with the love of friendship, charity; see chapter 5). The beatific vision is essentially an immediate union of knowledge and love. This union must be understood therefore as a *real* experience of the *comprehensor* and not just as the interminably ongoing instantiation of a mere *notional* apprehension of God (to use Newman's helpful distinction from his *Grammar of Assent*). Furthermore, because knowledge and love are features characteristic of persons, this intimate union of knowledge and love must be understood as an exceedingly *personal* experience comprising the whole existential range of the blessed as human persons and not only their intellect and will. Aquinas considers creatures as effects of God and therefore as manifestations of particular modes of the divine universal transcendent being. Hence, the vision of the consummate good is equivalent to the vision of all that is a good.[31] It is therefore perfectly consistent to assert that (1) God comprises the whole substance of heaven and that (2) the blessed experience other rational creatures in heaven. All of human beatitude arises from the vision of the divine essence and yet this beatitude extends to and includes other rational creatures as well as their own bodies and their operations of knowing, loving, and delighting. Most modern theologians, however, maintain that there is more to heaven than God and the immediate vision of God. They take the vision of God to be just one component among others of what is first and foremost conceived of as a paradisiacal happiness. By making this claim these theologians betray a conception of God that is fun-

---

30. Hoye, *Actualitas Omnium Actuum*, 292.
31. *De Potentia Dei*, q. 5, a. 1, ad 15: "The goods, the accumulation of which makes the state of beatitude perfect, have their source in the creature's union with its cause: since the beatitude of the rational creature consists in enjoying God."

damentally different from the one that informs Aquinas's theology of the beatific vision and of eternal life. We will now turn to a typical and influential representative of this deeply problematic view.

THE SINGLE ULTIMATE END

As discussed in the prologue and chapter 1, Aquinas's vision of the *viator*'s sojourn to beatitude is informed by a central philosophical conclusion he puts thus: "Just as of all [human beings] there is naturally one last end [*unus finis ultimus*], so the will of an individual [human being] must be fixed on one last end [*in uno ultimo fine*]" (*ST* I-II, q. 1, a. 5). While adopted by many theologians, Aquinas's conclusion has also proven controversial, first and foremost among contemporary moral philosophers and theologians. The most persistent objections against this conclusion are raised by representatives of the New Natural Law theory, most especially by the noted moral philosopher Germain Grisez who advances two substantive lines of criticism against Aquinas's teaching on beatitude. Grisez's first line of criticism is directed against Aquinas's thesis that "the true ultimate end of human beings is God alone, attained by the beatific vision."[32] He thinks that "Thomas is mistaken in concluding that at any one time a person's will must be directed to a single ultimate end in willing whatever it wills" and proposes instead a number of basic goods that may function as genuine final ends for human action.[33] His second line of criticism pertains to Aquinas's thesis that the beatific vision satisfies all desires.

Let us take up Grisez's first line of criticism and consider immediately the particular problem that drives his critique of Aquinas's thesis: "Thomas holds that, when people who have taken God as their ultimate end commit mortal sin, they thereby take something else as their ultimate end, while those who commit only venial sins, even deliberate ones, still intend God as their ultimate end. That position raises a question that Thomas never directly addresses: What

---

32. Germain Grisez, "The Ultimate End of Human Beings: The Kingdom, Not God Alone," *Theological Studies* 69, no. 1 (2008): 38. For penetrating critiques of Grisez's construal, see Ashley, "Integral Human Fulfillment according to Germain Grisez," 225–69.
33. Ibid., 44.

ultimate end do those living in grace intend in choosing to commit deliberate venial sins?"[34] If it turns out that Aquinas is unable to offer a coherent answer to this question based on his thesis that there obtains only one single ultimate end "to which a person's will must be directed at any one time in willing whatever it wills," to use Grisez's own words, Aquinas's thesis would be unsustainable.

It indeed seems to be the case that Aquinas never directly addresses explicitly the question of what ultimate end a person living in the state of grace intends when he or she chooses to commit deliberately a venial sin. But he offers the necessary elements for a response to Grisez's objection when he treats of the distinction between mortal and venial sin. First he offers a description of the difference between mortal and venial sin that is of immediate relevance for the present discussion:

Disorders in things referred to the end, are repaired through the end, even as an error about conclusions can be repaired through the truth of the principles. Hence the defect of order to the last end [*defectus ordinis ultimi finis*] cannot be repaired through something else as a higher principle, as neither can an error about principles. Wherefore such sins are called mortal, as being irreparable [*mortalia, quasi irreparabilia*]. On the other hand, *sins which imply a disorder* [*inordinatio*] *in things referred to the end, the order to the end itself being preserved*, are reparable. These sins are called venial [*venialia*]: because a sin receives its acquittal [*veniam*] when the debt of punishment is taken away, and this ceases when the sin ceases. (*ST* I-II, q. 88, a. 1; emphasis added)

The key phrase here is "a disorder [*inordinatio*] in things referred to the end" and the key principle is this: "Disorder in things referred to the end, are repaired through the end." In his answer to the third objection, Aquinas specifies further: "He that sins venially, cleaves to temporal good, not as enjoying it, because he does not fix his end in it, but as using it, by referring it to God, not actually but *habitually* [*non actu, sed habitu*]" (*ST* I-II, q. 88, a. 1, ad 3; emphasis added). The key term here is "habitually." And in Aquinas's response in article 2 of the same question, a key term already mentioned reappears—"inordinateness" (*inordinatio*). "Sometimes ... the sinner's

---

34. Ibid.

will is directed to a thing containing a certain *inordinateness* [*inordinatio*], but which is not contrary to the love of God and one's neighbor, e.g. an idle word, excessive laughter, and so forth: and *such sins are venial by reason of their genus*" (*ST* I-II, q. 88, a. 2; emphasis added). And the distinguishing property of the genus of venial sin is that such sins do not contradict the love of God and of one's neighbor. When referred to the ultimate end, who is God, not expressly but habitually through charity, venial sins are reparable precisely on account of the charity that obtains between God and the *viator*. In Aquinas's direct treatment of venial sin in question 89, the key term appears again: "Venial sin occurs in us ... through some *inordinateness* [*inordinatio*] in respect of things referred to the end, the due order to the end being safeguarded" (*ST* I-II, q. 89, a. 3; emphasis added). The passages in which he uses these terms are characteristically dense and require some unpacking.

First, it is necessary to clarify the limited but still intentional use Aquinas makes of Augustine's distinction between the use (*uti*) and the enjoyment (*frui*) of something in his discussion of venial sin. Aquinas states that a person who sins venially clings to a temporal good by using (*uti*) it. The *uti/frui* distinction was widely in use among Western medieval theologians. It appears for the first time in the familiar form in the first book of Augustine's *On Christian Doctrine*, where he considers the relationship between love of God and love of neighbor and uses both terms for the first time together. In book 1, chapter 4, Augustine offers a definition of the terms *uti* and *frui*, a definition that also guides Aquinas's use of these terms: "To enjoy [*frui*] a thing is to rest with satisfaction in it for its own sake. To use [*uti*], on the other hand, is to employ whatever means are at one's disposal to obtain what one desires, if it is a proper object of desire; for an unlawful use ought rather to be called an abuse."[35] After having introduced the distinction, Augustine immediately em-

---

35. Augustine, *On Christian Doctrine*, trans. J. F. Shaw, in *Nicene and Post-Nicene Fathers*, vol. 2: *Augustine: City of God, Christian Doctrine*, ed. Philip Schaff (Peabody, Mass.: Hendrickson, 1995), 523. For an instructive discussion of the reception of Augustine's distinction, see the article "The Uti/Frui Distinction," in *The Oxford Guide to the Historical Reception of Augustine*, 3 vols., ed. Karla Pollmann and Willemien Otten (Oxford: Oxford University Press, 2013).

ploys it in what he takes to be its normative theological context: "We have wandered far from God; and if we wish to return to our Father's home, this world must be used, not enjoyed, that so the invisible things of God may be clearly seen, being understood by the things that are made,—that is, that by means of what is material and temporary we may lay hold upon that which is spiritual and eternal."[36]

In the modern context there exists the grave danger of profoundly misunderstanding the *uti/frui* distinction when one intentionally or unintentionally places it into the conceptual framework of Kant's categorical imperative: "So act that you treat humanity, whether in your own person or in the person of any other, always at the same time as an end, never merely as a means."[37] Read through the lens of the Kantian "mere means principle," the Augustinian "use" (*uti*) looks all too much like the immoral use of another person merely as a means to an end and seems to suggest the following: only God, the ultimate end, is to be enjoyed (*frui*) for God's own sake; everything else is to be used (*uti*) in relationship to the ultimate end. Unsurprisingly, most modern persons find such a principle morally repelling, and rightly so. And such moral repulsion would be shared by Aquinas, for read through the lens of the Kantian "mere means principle," Aquinas's use of the *uti/frui* distinction is not properly understood, but rather severely distorted. The reason is this: for Aquinas the *uti/frui* distinction does not signify the distinction between those inclinations of the will that fall into the orbit of the theological virtue of charity (purportedly *frui*) and those inclinations of the will that remain excluded from it (purportedly *uti*). Rather, the *uti/frui* distinction obtains *within* the order of charity in which everything is referred to the ultimate end, God, for the sake of the love of God, charity. Hence, in the order of charity, every instance of "use" (*uti*) is completely qualified by the theological virtue of charity and signifies the referral of every good that is not God to God, the highest good and ultimate end.[38]

---

36. Augustine, *On Christian Doctrine*, 523.

37. Immanuel Kant, *Groundwork of the Metaphysics of Morals*, in *Immanuel Kant: Practical Philosophy*, trans. Mary Gregor (Cambridge: Cambridge University Press, 1996), 429.

38. Consider Aquinas's argumentation regarding the order of charity in *ST* II-II, q. 26, a. 1: "Wherever there is a principle, there must needs be also order of some kind. But it has been said above [q. 23, a. 1; q. 25, a. 12] that the love of charity tends to God

Only the ultimate end itself does not undergo a referral and hence is to be enjoyed for its own sake (*frui*).

In the modern Kantian sense of the "mere means principle," to use a person merely as a means to an end is immoral. In Aquinas's usage of the *uti/frui* distinction, on the contrary, the potential moral problem does not lie at all with *uti*—as long as it is understood as referred to the ultimate end within the order of charity. Rather, for Aquinas, what constitutes the real moral failure, and in the case of the Christian a mortal sin, is misplaced "enjoyment" (*frui*), that is, taking as one's ultimate end to which all of one's actions are referred, anything other than God. Consider this example: for a Christian to enjoy (*frui*) his homeland or nation (*patria*), and to refer all other goods and actions to the nation as the highest good and the ultimate end, is to commit the mortal sin of idolatrous patriotism or jingoism ("my country first and above everything else"). Alternatively, for a Christian to refer (*uti*) the unquestionable good of homeland to the highest good and the ultimate end, God, is an example of the virtue of piety, which charity commands.[39] Hence, the proper referral

---

as to the principle of happiness [*principium beatitudinis*], on the fellowship of which the friendship of charity is based. Consequently there must needs be some order in things loved out of charity [*dilectio caritatis*], which order is in reference to the first principle of that love [*dilectio*], which is God." And in reply to the first objection he states: "Charity tends towards the last end considered as last end: and this does not apply to any other virtue, as stated above [II-II, q. 23, a. 6]. Now the end has the character of principle in matters of appetite and action, as was shown above [II-II, q. 23, a. 7, ad 2; I-II, q. 13, a. 3; q. 34, a. 4, ad 1]. Wherefore charity, above all, implies relation to the First Principle, and consequently, in charity above all, we find an order in reference to the First Principle."

39. Consider Aquinas's characterization of the virtue of piety (*pietas*) in *ST* II-II, q. 101, a. 1: "[A human being] becomes a debtor to other [human beings] in various ways, according to their various excellence and the various benefits received from them. On both counts God holds first place, for He is supremely excellent, and is for us the first principle of being and government. In the second place, the principles of our being and government are our parents and our country, that have given us birth and nourishment. Consequently, [a human being] is debtor chiefly to his parents and his country, after God. Wherefore just as it belongs to religion to give worship to God [*cultum Deo exhibere*], so does it belong to piety, in the second place, to give worship to one's parents and one's country [*exhibere cultum parentibus et patriae*]. The worship due to our parents [*cultus parentum*] includes the worship given to all our kindred [*cultus omnium consanguineorum*], since our kinsfolk are those who descend from the same parents, according to the Philosopher (Ethic. viii, 12). The worship given to our country [*cultus patriae*] includes homage to all our fellow-citizens [*cultus concivium et omnium patriae amicorum*] and to all the friends of our country. Therefore piety extends chiefly to these."

to the ultimate end, God, of the good of homeland and the actions of the virtue of piety within the order of charity does not preclude love of country. Rather, pious acts, informed by charity, constitute the appropriate Christian exercise of love of homeland. In short, in Aquinas's usage of the *uti/frui* distinction within the order of charity, "use" is always the referral of a subordinate good to the highest good and ultimate end, God, for the sake of the love of God and friendship with God, charity.

And so, when Aquinas states that a person who sins venially clings to a temporal good by "using" it, to "use" a temporal good means here to refer it habitually to God, that is, to refer it to God on account of the infused virtue of charity. The *viator*'s clinging to a temporal good manifests a certain inordinateness (*inordinatio*). But this clinging to a temporal good does not contradict the love of God and of one's neighbor. And so the sin is reparable by the ultimate end, God, because of the love of friendship that obtains between God and the *viator*.

Now we can address Grisez's question regarding how such "inordinateness in respect of things referred to the end" should be accounted for in a person in a state of grace and charity, who lives in friendship with and love of God. For Aquinas, the inordinateness of venial sin results from failing to consider the ultimate end explicitly; the temporal good to which the person clings is referred to God only habitually and not in a considered way. In his lucid description of Aquinas's analysis of the genealogy of evil acts, Jacques Maritain calls this failure "the non-consideration of the rule."[40] Let us first consider the relevant passage in Aquinas's *De Malo*:

> In all things of which one ought to be the rule and measure of another, good results in what is regulated and measured from the fact that it is regulated and conformed to the rule and measure, while evil results from the fact that it is not being ruled or measured. Therefore, suppose there is a carpenter who ought to cut a piece of wood straight by using a ruler; if he does not cut straight, which is to make a bad cut, the bad cutting will be due to his failure to use the ruler or measuring bar. Likewise, pleasure and everything else in human affairs should be measured and regulated by the rule

---

40. Jacques Maritain, *Existence and the Existent* (New York: Pantheon, 1948), 91.

of reason and God's law. And so the nonuse of the rule of reason and God's law is presupposed in the will before the will made its disordered choice.[41]

Consider now Maritain's cogent presentation of Aquinas's theory. Because of its importance, I shall cite the relevant passage in full:

> In one of his most difficult and most original theses, Thomas Aquinas explains on this point that the emergence of a free and evil act resolves into two moments—distinct, not according to the priority of time, but according to ontological priority. At a first moment, there is in the will, by the fact of its very liberty, an absence or a nihilation which is not yet a *privation* or an evil, but a mere lacuna; the existent *does not* consider the norm of the *thou shouldst* upon which the ruling of the act depends. At a second moment the will produces its free act affected by the privation of its due ruling and wounded with the nothingness which results from this lack of consideration.
>
> It is at this second moment that there is moral evil or sin. At the first moment there had not yet been moral fault or sin, but only the fissure through which evil introduces itself into the free decision about to come forth from the person, the vacuum or lacuna through which sin will take form in the free will before being launched into the arteries of the subject and of the world. This vacuum or lacuna, which St. Thomas calls non-consideration of the rule, is not an evil or a privation, but a mere lack, a mere nothingness of consideration. For, of itself, it is not a duty for the will to consider the rule; that duty arises only at the moment of action, or production of being, at which time the will begets the free decision in which it makes its choice. Non-consideration of the rule becomes an evil, or becomes the privation of a good that is due, only at the second of the two moments we have distinguished—at the moment when the will produces some act or some being; at the moment when it causes the choice to irrupt; at the moment when the free act is posited, with the wound or deformity of that non-consideration.[42]

One might immediately think of the nonconsideration of the ultimate end as intimately related to the nonconsideration of the rule. The *viator* when desiring something particular might not always be thinking explicitly at that moment of the ultimate end. And, in fact, in Aquinas's own formulation one may easily observe that he takes this familiar phenomenon to be a version of the nonculpable nonconsideration of the rule:

---

41. Thomas Aquinas, *De malo*, q. 1, a. 3 (trans. Davis, 87).
42. Maritain, *Existence and the Existent*, 90–91.

> One need not always be thinking of the last end, whenever one desires or does something: but the virtue of the first intention, which was in respect of the last end, remains in every desire directed to any object whatever, even though one's thoughts be not actually directed to the last end. Thus while walking along the road one need not be thinking of the end at every step. (*ST* I-II, q. 1, a. 6, ad 3)

The ultimate end does not need to be—indeed, cannot be—constantly considered, just as the rule of reason and God's law need not nor can be constantly considered. But the nonconsideration of the ultimate end gives rise to venial sin as soon as the *viator* in a state of grace and charity "cleaves to temporal good ... as *using* it, by referring it to God not actually but *habitually*" (*ST* I-II, q. 88, a. 1, ad 3; emphasis added). The habitual referral of the temporal good to God occurs because "the virtue of the first intention, which was in respect of the last end, remains in every desire directed to any object whatever, even though one's thoughts be not actually directed to the last end" (*ST* I-II, q. 1, a. 6, ad 3). To stay with Aquinas's own example: while walking along the road, the *viator* does not need to be thinking of the destination at every step of her sojourn. It is one thing for the *viator* to decide spontaneously, that is, deliberately—while at the same time omitting to consider explicitly the destination—to take a detour that promises a good night's sleep in a comfortable bed after a sumptuous meal with old friends. This detour entails a considerable delay, but no change of the destination. It is quite another thing for the *viator* to choose a direction or a route that leads to a different final destination.

Now let us turn to the very heart of Grisez's objection:

> Something loved habitually can function as a human agent's end only if, although not brought to mind, it is the real reason why that agent chooses to act for a proximate end. But since even a venial sin, insofar as it is a sin, is evil, divine goodness cannot in any way be promoted or attained by deliberately committing a venial sin; so God cannot be the real reason for pursuing any proximate end by choosing to commit a venial sin.[43]

It is clear that Grisez implicitly rejects the Augustinian *uti/frui* distinction upon which Aquinas's response turns. For Aquinas, as dis-

---

43. Grisez, "The Ultimate End of Human Beings," 45.

cussed above, the person is committing a venial sin by being inordinately attached to a temporal good. Yet such a person "uses" this good, that is, refers it to God habitually on account of the virtue of the first intention that keeps it within the order of charity.

Guided by his dismissal of the *uti/frui* distinction as applied to venial sin, Grisez construes the matter quite differently. According to him, the person who sins venially, is moved by an end he *loves* habitually without any referral of this end to the ultimate end, God. Grisez thus simply supposes what Aquinas explicitly denies. On Grisez's supposition it is indeed not possible to claim what Aquinas claims: "In technical language, if one has a single ultimate end, it must be the per se final cause of everything one does. God loved habitually cannot be the per se final cause of sinning—cannot be one's real reason for choosing to do anything sinful."[44] According to Grisez, the final cause for sinning venially must be something other than the purportedly single ultimate end, something loved by the person as an end. This final end, however, cannot replace the ultimate end, God (otherwise it would be a mortal sin). It must, rather, be a final end compatible with God as the ultimate end. Grisez has posited that there are a certain number of incommensurable basic goods that serve as irreducible and independent final ends for integral human flourishing. In the case of venial sin, one of these basic goods is taken as an ultimate end *next* to the ultimate end, God.[45]

Aquinas, however, does not need to admit more than one formal and material ultimate end, and this for two reasons. First, because of the theory of the nonconsideration of the rule. The cause of any sin is never a genuine good, but a deficiency in the moral agent, initially a nonculpable limitation of the finite creature that becomes culpable as soon as the agent moves to an action under the condition of

44. Ibid.
45. Grisez develops this argument in an important and influential essay: Germain Grisez et al., "Practical Principles, Moral Truth, and Ultimate Ends," *American Journal of Jurisprudence* 32 (1987): 99–151. For astute descriptions and analyses of the problems in the position advanced in the essay, see Jean Porter, "Basic Goods and the Human Good in Recent Catholic Moral Theology," *The Thomist* 57 (1993): 27–49; and Peter Simpson, "Grisez on Aristotle and Human Goods," *American Journal of Jurisprudence* 46 (2001): 75–89. For penetrating critiques of Grisez's construal, see also Steven A. Long, "Fundamental Errors of the New Natural Law Theory," *The National Catholic Bioethics Quarterly* 13, no. 1 (2013): 105–32, esp. 111–17.

this deficiency.[46] Second, Aquinas assumes that preconversion habits (*habitus*) characterized by a certain inordinateness typical of the incontinent person may linger on in the *viator*. Attachments to temporal goods previously in line with an alternative ultimate end—for example, bodily flourishing or comprehensive "wellness"—continue to linger on in the form of an attachment to some good—for example, good food—even after the reception of the gift of sanctifying grace and the gifts of the Holy Spirit. But this good is now habitually referred to God as "food for the journey." The *viator* does not consider the ultimate end while he is cleaving to a temporal good due to an acquired *habitus* not yet properly reformed (the person still diets and does not know yet how to fast). The extant *habitus* is stimulated by exposure to a temporal good that in turn becomes a sense object and as such engages the sense appetite. The respective sense conveys the object to the *habitus* of the corresponding appetite. Right reason, the proper interaction between intellect and will in the consideration of the rule and in the determination and execution of what is due, does not intervene, because the ultimate end is not explicitly considered. But he "uses" the temporal good rather than "enjoying" it, on account of charity; the actions of the still unreformed *habitus* are already habitually referred to the ultimate end, God. How so?

Because "the virtue of the first intention, which was in respect of the last end" (*ST* I-II, q. 1, a. 6, ad 3) remains habitually in the desire that elicits actions of this still unreformed *habitus*, the action commanded by the *habitus* is referred by charity *qua* infused *habitus* to the single material ultimate end, God. The *per se* final cause of the action is thus indeed the ultimate end, God and the love of God. The

---

46. Jacques Maritain offers a lucid explanation of Aquinas's metaphysical account of evil that guides his thinking on this point: "*Ens et bonum convertuntur.* The good is being, and plenitude or completion of being. When we reason in the line of good, we reason in the line of being, of that which exercises being or bears being to its accomplishment. Evil, on the contrary, of itself or insofar as evil, is absence of being, *privation* of being and of good. It is a nothingness which corrodes being. When we reason in the line of evil, we reason in the line of non-being, for evil is in nowise being; evil is only a vacuum or a lack of being, a nothingness or privation. It follows, then, with absolute necessity that there will be a dissymmetry between our manner of looking at and explaining things in the perspective of good and our manner of looking at and explaining things in the perspective of evil." Jacques Maritain, *God and the Permission of Evil*, trans. Joseph W. Evans (Milwaukee, Wis.: Bruce Publishing, 1966), 9.

action, however, is also inordinate because commanded by the unreformed *habitus* without the due consideration of the rule and of the end. A distinct inordinateness diminishes the moral quality of such an action.

Consider the person that gives thanks to God for the good of food he deliberately overindulges in. The temporal good to which the person is attached does not constitute an alternative ultimate end, but is rather referred by the person to the ultimate end. The person uses (*uti*) the temporal good instead of enjoying it for its own sake (*frui*). Could we say that he "loves" the food? Yes, of course, but he loves it only in a certain respect (*secundum quid*). This love is not the love characteristic of *frui*. Because of the culpable nonconsideration of the rule and because of the fact that the *habitus* is insufficiently re-formed, it is an inordinate action and therefore a sin. But because the inordinateness does not contradict the love of God and of one's neighbor, the sin is venial. It is reparable by the very end to which the action is referred, God and God's own love, charity. An action of such an unreformed *habitus* is *qua* human action, of course, intentional and, in this precise sense, deliberate. Yet, if it occurs within the order of charity—and this is what Aquinas presupposes—such an action is still, on account of the infused habitus of charity, referred to the single ultimate end, God. The *per se* final cause of such an action, *qua* action, is the ultimate end. What makes the action a sin is the culpable nonconsideration of the rule and of the end; and what makes the action a venial sin is its reparability by the love of and friendship with God to whom the action is still referred.

In sum, Aquinas successfully accounts on his own terms for deliberate venial sins under the supposition of a single ultimate end that is the *per se* final cause of everything one does. Hence, the first prong of Grisez's objection does not defeat Aquinas's thesis that "just as for all [human beings] there is naturally one last end, so the will of an individual [human being] must be fixed on one last end" (*ST* I-II, q. 1, a. 5).

While the first prong of Grisez's critique aims at a central question of moral philosophy and theology and thereby relates only tangentially to Aquinas's substantive doctrine of beatitude, the second prong of his critique aims at the very heart of it. Grisez claims flatly: "Christians are mistaken if they expect the beatific vision to satisfy all their desires."[47] Grisez ups the ante by pitting his understanding of the Catholic faith against Aquinas's: "Thomas maintains that it is *contrary to the faith* to hold that human beings' ultimate end is to be found in something other than God.... But I hold it to be *a truth of faith* that human beings' true ultimate end is the kingdom of God, not God alone."[48] In the following, I shall not consider how magisterial determinations have shaped the Catholic faith in regard to the issue under dispute. Ezra Sullivan, OP, has advanced what I take to be a conclusive demonstration that the cumulative magisterial determinations promulgated in the centuries after Pope Benedict XII's 1336 *Benedictus Deus* consistently move into a direction that clearly favors Aquinas's teaching over against Grisez's contrary position.[49]

Recall Aquinas's definition of beatitude: "Beatitude is the perfect good of an intellectual nature" (*ST* I, q. 26, a. 1). Recall also the consequence of this definition for divine beatitude: "Beatitude is a certain perfection. But the divine perfection embraces [*complectitur*] all other perfections.... Therefore the divine beatitude embraces [*complectitur*] all other beatitudes" (*ST* I, q. 26, a. 4, s.c.). Hence, the promise of a participation in the divine beatitude entails the proper perfection of integral human happiness in a mode that surpasses our present understanding but does entail the perfect realization of all true good of body, soul, and conviviality (that is, every mode of perfection characteristic of human nature) humans desire in order to attain happiness. Every genuine created good (in con-

---

47. Grisez, "The Ultimate End of Human Beings," 46.
48. Ibid., 61n69.
49. See Ezra Sullivan, OP, "Seek First the Kingdom: A Reply to Germain Grisez's Account of Man's Ultimate End," *Nova et Vetera* (English edition) 8, no. 4 (2010): 959–95. He concludes his extensive analysis thus: "In 2008, Germain Grisez wrote, 'I hold it to be a truth of faith that human beings' true ultimate end is the kingdom of God, not God alone' (61, n. 69). In contrast to previous discussions of Grisez's thought, this article has examined Grisez's faith-claim primarily in light of the faith as taught by the Catholic Magisterium. We have seen that, though Grisez's citations of Magisterial authority seem to verify his faith-claim, Catholic Tradition as a whole teaches otherwise. Vatican I, Leo XIII, Pius X, Pius XI, Pius XII, Vatican II, John Paul II, and Benedict XVI, when read within their proper context, clearly affirm that God in Himself, apart from all creatures, is man's supreme ultimate end" (993–94).

trast to a merely apparent good) the attainment of which is genuine happiness (in contrast to a merely apparent happiness) is entailed in divine beatitude, the possession of the perfect good. According to Aquinas, therefore, all conceivable human desires that are conformable to the will's rectitude and to the love of charity will indeed be fulfilled in the beatific vision, first for the *comprehensor*'s separated soul *qua* intellectual principle before the resurrection of the body and, after the resurrection of the body, for the *comprehensor*'s whole embodied person.

It is difficult if not impossible for Grisez to adopt this view because of an antecedent philosophical commitment he holds. In a characteristically modern way, Grisez conceives of the human being as a rational animal without *intellectus*.[50] As became clear in chapter 1, according to Aquinas, only *intellectus* can account for the overarching finality of human nature, a hierarchy of ends at the top of which stands the contemplation of the first truth. And as also already observed in chapter 1, Grisez's desire to expunge completely the alleged "other-worldliness" of classical Catholic moral theology leads him to deny such a teleological hierarchy and with it the ontological structure of *intellectus* to obtain in the human being. Yet a creature that is not *capax Dei* is arguably also not *capax beatitudinis*, for if, as Aquinas holds, beatitude is "the perfect good of an intellectual nature" (*ST* I, q. 26, a. 1), without *intellectus*, there cannot obtain any proportionality whatsoever between the finality of human nature and its surpassing supernatural fulfillment. Grisez's rational animal, conceived under all too modern rationalistic strictures as a living being equipped with an advanced computational and discursive rationality and the capacity for practical judgments, is not truly *capax Dei*. It is important to realize, however, that this does not mean that Grisez would deny some kind of vision of the triune God to occur in the "gratuitous fulfillment in Jesus." On the contrary. He states:

What about the beatific vision? It is neither an act a human person can choose to do, nor a good that human persons can bring about. It is entirely

---

50. See his *The Way of the Lord Jesus Christ*, esp. 809–10, and "A Critique of Russell Hittinger's Book, *A Critique of the New Natural Law Theory*," *The New Scholasticism* 62, no. 4 (1988): 438–65, esp. 459–60.

a gift of the Father, Son, and Spirit—a sharing, somehow, in their own joy. Nevertheless, the beatific vision will fulfill human persons. Integral communal fulfillment includes human persons' harmony with God, a fundamental good of human persons that can be realized less and more.[51]

According to Grisez, the vision is some kind of gift that is somehow accepted. But it remains unclear what this vision actually is (even if only analogically conceived); what exactly the gift consists in; how it actually can be accepted by the human being, who, according to Grisez, is radically disproportionate to it and lacks any capacity to receive it; and, finally, what difference this gift actually makes if, as Grisez claims, the blessed equipped with this gift "will continue to desire, act, and be increasingly fulfilled."[52]

While Grisez's proposed gratuitous "eschatological fulfillment in Jesus" includes everlasting perfect integral human well-being and even comprises some gratuitous vision of the Trinity, a vision that is somehow passively received (that is, without a human act of intellection), his account actually excludes the beatific vision in any meaningful sense of the term: a formal union between the human intellect and the divine essence. While happiness might increase considerably or even "ever more" in the "eschatological fulfillment in Jesus," as Grisez indeed supposes, the definitive formal attainment of the consummate good, God, can and will never occur. Thus, according to Grisez's proposal, those who enjoy the eschatological fulfillment in Jesus will never be *comprehensores* in the precise sense of the term, but only *viatores* of a higher kind, for the blessed "will continue to desire, act, and be increasingly fulfilled, so that the heavenly wedding feast will never end and will always grow still more joyful."[53] On Aquinas's terms, Grisez's "eschatological kingdom of God" would resemble all too much paradise regained but heaven denied.[54] Hence, from a Thomist perspective, the real issue is not that "Christians are mistaken if they expect the beatific vision to satisfy

---

51. Grisez, "The Ultimate End of Human Beings," 59.
52. Ibid., 61.
53. Ibid.
54. This is not a problem unique to Grisez but rather one encountered widely in contemporary Protestant, and especially Evangelical theology. For an instructive example, see Wright, *Surprised by Hope*.

all their desires,"⁵⁵ but rather that Grisez's anthropology makes it inherently impossible to embrace the spiritual and ontological depth and all-encompassing nature of the beatific vision that necessarily includes the perfect satisfaction of all of the *comprehensor*'s desires.⁵⁶ If one were to conceive of the beatific vision merely as the paradisiacal sight of the glorified human nature of the risen Christ alone, many other desires would indeed need to be satisfied additionally in what Grisez calls the "eschatological fulfillment in Jesus." But such an eschatological scenario would, as already stated, resemble at best paradise regained and improved upon by the paradisiacal sight of the glorified human nature of the risen Lord. Yet it would emphatically not be heaven in the precise sense of the participated eternity of the vision of God, the deifying and hence unitive and perfective participation in the divine essence, life, and beatitude. As shown in the first section of this epilogue, and as will become clear in the next section, according to Aquinas, the beatific vision always already entails whatever paradise has to offer for the *comprehensor* (depending on his state before or after the resurrection of the body). Hence, Aquinas is fully able to ward off the second prong of Grisez's critique.

But it should be mentioned that, at least from a Thomist perspective, Grisez's construal gives rise to grave theological concerns. As heaven cannot be additively conjoined to paradise, the blessed according to Grisez's account—who "will continue to desire, act, and be increasingly fulfilled"—will never become genuine *comprehensores* and, while their joy might ever increase, will nevertheless fail to attain perfect happiness, beatitude. Despite all that they receive continuously and increasingly in all eternity—even, as Grisez claims, a gratuitous sharing in the joy of the Father, the Son, and the Holy Spirit⁵⁷—Aquinas could rightly hold that the last phrase of Psalm 94 would still be said of the blessed: "They shall not enter into my rest" (*Non introibunt in requiem meam*). Entering defin-

---

55. Grisez, "The Ultimate End of Human Beings," 46.
56. For the way how Aquinas differentiates between the state of the separate soul in the beatific vision before the resurrection of the body and the integral embodied person in the resurrection life the source and summit of which is still the beatific vision, in short, how he spells out the principle *beatitudo in omnibus modis*, see the following section of the epilogue.
57. Grisez, "The Ultimate End of Human Beings," 59.

itively and perfectly into God's own rest requires all three elements of perfect happiness: "Vision, which is perfect knowledge of the intelligible end; comprehension, which implies presence of the end; and delight or enjoyment, which implies repose of the lover in the object beloved" (*ST* I-II, q. 4, a. 3). From a Thomist perspective, the blessed according to Grisez's proposal will forever remain *viatores* in paradise and never arrive in heaven proper. Despite an everlasting increase in happiness, these blessed will forever be deprived of vision, comprehension, and delight, and hence from the very perfection characteristic of beatitude proper. They will never enter into God's rest.

Furthermore, because God is the *ipsum esse subsistens* (or *esse* as *actus purus*), the formal participation of the *comprehensor* in the divine essence and the divine beatitude is far from static (as Grisez imputes). Rather, in virtue of its participation in the divine perfection of the *actus purus*, human beatitude is surpassingly dynamic, *ek-static*, yet simultaneously perfectly at rest. In reference to the beatitude attained in the beatific vision, the qualification "static" necessarily connotes a distinct imperfection; it falls short of the perfection that human participation in divine beatitude entails. For the divine life of beatitude is anything but static; it is, rather, absolutely dynamic and perfectly at rest. Therefore the real participation of the human in divine beatitude is characterized by the perfect actualization of the intellect and will, and therefore a most dynamic realization of human beatitude and simultaneously the perfect rest of the intellect in the first truth (*visio*) and of the will in the highest good (*comprehensio*). From a Thomist perspective an everlasting dynamic increase of paradisiacal happiness denotes a distinct imperfection that falls short of the perfection beatitude entails; for the dynamic increase Grisez envisions is never in possession of perfect beatitude. Rather, this dynamic enlargement of happiness, as Grisez emphasizes, is a purely passive reception. Yet such a purportedly neverending increase in happiness is actually meaningless, because it lacks the *telos* of a genuine perfection. Due to this lack, Grisez's "eschatological fulfillment in Jesus" denotes an in principle nonperfectible increase. From a Thomist perspective, this everlasting a-teleological condition of a passive increase in happiness, bereft of its possible perfection, lacks what is ontologically necessary for a qualitative increase. Rather, this purportedly neverending increase resembles what is characteristic of mere quantitative augmentation, that is, of additions of discrete quantities of creaturely well-being. While quantitatively dynamic in a computational sense, this paradisiacal happiness bereft of its surpassing perfection, unitive participation in the divine beatitude, remains essentially imperfect and hence qualitatively static.

In summary, Grisez's alternative eschatological proposal creates overall more problems theologically than it solves in regard to the supposed philosophical problems he imputes to Aquinas. Therefore, the second prong of Grisez's objection fails to drive home its critical thrust. It seems rather to expose the critic's own position to a necessary theological interrogation and critique.

THE RESURRECTION OF THE BODY

Let us now turn to a concern voiced by a variety of theologians, especially in the second half of the twentieth century: how can the resurrection of the body be truly integrated in a beatitude construed around the beatific vision? Is the resurrection body for Aquinas merely an extrinsic accidental addition to the *comprehensor*'s bliss? Could the resurrection body actually be dispensed with, without loss for Aquinas's account of beatitude? Such a theological move would take away significant pressure to justify the Christian faith in a modern intellectual context in which Christ's bodily resurrection from the dead and the promise of the bodily resurrection of all human beings at the end of history is considered the most difficult part of the Christian faith to embrace and conceive of intellectually—especially for those held captive by a world picture informed by a strictly materialist interpretation of modern cosmology. Yet every theological strategy of accommodation and adaptation—in the modern period they are legion—is at best a pyrrhic victory, for such strategies compromise the very heart of the Christian faith to which belongs centrally and indispensably the bodily resurrection of Christ from the dead and the promise of the general bodily resurrection at the end of history.

On the other hand, if theological positions (as, for instance, the theory of the "resurrection in death")[58] that aim at an accommodation to the presently dominant world picture must be rejected on interpretive as well as substantial theological grounds and if therefore the resurrection body is an integral component of beatitude both in reality and in Aquinas's thought, how can the blessed attain perfect happiness in the beatific vision before the resurrection of the body? Will not their beatitude increase when the souls of the blessed receive their imperishable resurrection bodies? Is not the reconstitution of full embodied personhood an increase in perfection and hence, necessarily, in beatitude? And if there indeed occurs such an increase in perfection and in beatitude, would not the beatitude of the blessed continue to increase in the company of the glorified humanity of Christ, the Virgin Mary, and all the other saints, not to mention the hosts of angels? Would beatitude not have to be conceived, as Grisez among others maintains, as increasing everlastingly in proportion to all that is added to the initial bliss of the separated soul?[59]

Across all his writings, Aquinas unequivocally affirms and defends the first and fundamental point: the beatitude of the blessed in its full integrity does not simply pertain to the blessed *qua* separated souls but to the blessed *qua* human beings. Embodiment is natural to human beings; hence, also in resurrection life, the human soul remains ordered to inform and enliven a body; for the human being is essentially an embodied being. While the formal principle, the ra-

---

58. The theory of the "resurrection in death" is a theological position according to which the individual resurrection occurs at the moment of death. The magisterium of the Catholic church addressed this problematic theory in a "Letter on Certain Questions Concerning Eschatology," issued on May 17, 1979, by the Congregation of the Doctrine of the Faith. See the prologue, above, 54n53.

59. For the best recent studies of this complex matter, see Brian Kromholtz, OP, "La perfection de la nature: la doctrine de saint Thomas d'Aquin sur la resurrection du corps, sa reception et son developpement," *Revue Thomiste* 116, no. 1 (2016): 57–70; Markus Schulze, SAC, *Leibhaft und Unsterblich. Zur Schau der Seele in der Anthropologie und Theologie des Hl. Thomas von Aquin* (Freiburg: Universitätsverlag Freiburg Schweiz, 1992); and Carlo Leget, *Living with God: Thomas Aquinas on the Relation between Life on Earth and "Life" after Death* (Leuven: Peeters, 1997). I have also profited greatly from reading the study by John Joseph Williams, "The Participation of the Resurrected Body in the Beatitude of Man," STD diss., Facultés Catholiques de Toulouse, 1977.

tional soul, continues to subsist after death, this subsistent soul—even in the beatific vision—is not the complete human person. In fact, for Aquinas, the hylomorphic constitution of the human being is one of the strongest arguments for the rational intelligibility and defensibility of the revealed truth of the resurrection of the body. In short, for Aquinas, the resurrection life in the beatific vision is the life of a complete human being, the life of a hylomorphic body-soul composite. The resurrection of the body belongs to the full integrity of the beatitude of the blessed *qua* human beings.

On the question of whether the beatitude of the *comprehensores* increases after they are united with their resurrection bodies, Aquinas's position changes. Aquinas's early position can be found in an appendix (*supplementum*) to the *Summa Theologiae* that his students put together from the relevant sections of his early *Sentences* commentary after Aquinas's death. Consider, for example: "Whether the happiness of the saints will be greater after the judgment than before?" (*ST* III, q. 93, a. 1, suppl.). The response the supplement provides states this: "It is manifest that the happiness of the saints will increase in extent after the resurrection, because their happiness will then be not only in the soul but also in the body. Moreover, the soul's happiness also will increase in extent, seeing that the soul will rejoice not only in its own good, but also in that of the body. We may also say that the soul's happiness will increase in intensity." According to his early position, the *comprehensor's* beatitude grows *extensively* as well as *intensively* with the soul's reunion to its body.[60]

---

60. Aquinas offers the following argument for the intensive growth of beatitude: "A [human being's] body may be considered in two ways: first, as being dependent on the soul for its completion; secondly, as containing something that hampers the soul in its operations, through the soul not perfectly completing the body. As regards the first way of considering the body, its union with the soul adds a certain perfection to the soul, since every part is imperfect, and is completed in its whole; wherefore the whole is to the part as form to matter. Consequently the soul is more perfect in its natural being, when it is in the whole—namely, man who results from the union of soul and body—than when it is a separate part. But as regards the second consideration the union of the body hampers the perfection of the soul, wherefore it is written (Wis. 9:15) that 'the corruptible body is a load upon the soul.' If, then, there be removed from the body all those things wherein it hampers the soul's action, the soul will be simply more perfect while existing in such a body than when separated therefrom. Now the more perfect a thing is in being, the more perfectly is it able to operate: wherefore the operation of the soul united to such a body will be more perfect than the operation of the separated soul. But the glorified

After a more exacting consideration of the beatific vision in *ST* I, q. 12, and of the precise correlation of the body to the rational soul, in the hylomorphic constitution of the human being in *ST* I, qq. 75–76, Aquinas's position changes. He takes the body's contribution to beatitude to be only an extension of beatitude; for, crucially, the soul's perfect rest is attained in virtue of its union with the proper object of the intellect, the first truth, and the proper object of the will, the highest good:

> The desire of the separated soul is entirely at rest, as regards the thing desired; since, to wit, it has that which suffices its appetite. But it is not wholly at rest, as regards the desirer, since it does not possess that good in every way that it would wish to possess it. Consequently, after the body has been resumed, happiness [*beatitudo*] increases not in intensity, but in extent [*beatitudo crescit non intensive, sed extensive*]. (*ST* I-II, q. 4, a. 5, ad 5)

The resurrection body perfects beatitude, not intensively, by contributing to the depth or intensity of beatitude, but rather extensively, contributing to beatitude's extension into the resurrection life of the *comprehensor* and thereby expanding beatitude to the embodied mode of existence and bringing about well-being (*bene esse*). Instead of contributing to the soul's beatitude (which the body actually cannot do, as the rational soul's beatitude arises completely from the perfect union with its proper object), the resurrection body becomes, so to speak, the "sounding board" for the soul's beatitude "carrying over," expanding, or extending the soul's beatitude into the resurrection body.

The strength of the distinction between an intensive and an extensive beatitude rests on the hylomorphic unity of soul and body as the two constitutive but asymmetrical causal principles of the human substance. This is, of course, not the place to enter into a full-fledged discussion of the hylomorphic constitution of the human

---

body will be a body of this description, being altogether subject to the spirit. Therefore, since beatitude consists in an operation [see *ST* I-II, q. 3, a. 2], the soul's happiness after its reunion with the body will be more perfect than before. For just as the soul separated from a corruptible body is able to operate more perfectly than when united thereto, so after it has been united to a glorified body, its operation will be more perfect than while it was separated" (*ST* III, q. 93, a. 1, suppl.).

being according to Aquinas. Attending to its most central and salient elements will have to suffice.

The Ontology of the Rational Soul as Form of a Body

One of the fundamental principles of Aquinas's anthropology is that the living human being is composed of soul and body.[61] Neither the soul by itself nor the body by itself is a human being. Only the integral whole, the soul as the single substantial form, informing the body, is a living human person (*SCG* II.89.17). Yet after death, after the separation of the soul from the body, the rational soul continues to subsist because it is a simple intellectual form that cannot decompose or disintegrate into more basic causal principles (*ST* I, q. 75, a. 2; *SCG* II.87.3). But unlike the intellectual form that subsists as a separate substance, that is, the angel, the human separate soul is a substantial form ordered to incarnate a body: its essence is "form of a body." Hence, when a soul does not inform its body, it does not exist as a fully realized substance and is, therefore, in a certain way incomplete. In order to become complete, in order for its essence to be fully realized, the human soul must inform its body.[62] Therefore, the human rational soul without the body is in an unnatural state. This includes, importantly, the soul of the *comprehensor* before the general resurrection of the body. The human soul, separated from the body (*anima separata*), is not a substance and hence not a human person in the strict and full sense—although, crucially, the separate soul is still capable in certain ways of intellection and volition, acts of *intelligere* and *velle*.[63]

Consider now the argument that Aquinas advances in *SCG* IV.79

---

61. *ST* III, q. 75, a. 1, ad 3, suppl.: "Ipse homo compositus ex anima et corpora."
62. *ST* I, q. 76, a. 1, ad 6; *Quaestiones de anima* [hereafter "*Q. de an.*"], a. 1, ad 1.
63. *ST* I, q. 89, a. 5. Significantly, in *ST* I, q. 89, a. 8, Aquinas argues that the separated human souls are capable of the care of those who still live on earth (*cura de rebus viventium*) and with whom they were and still are united in charity. All of this seems to entail that while the integrity of the human person is not fully regained before the resurrection of the body, the separated human soul is very well capable of certain actions characteristic of a human person. See Kromholtz, "La perfection de la nature," 60, and in greater detail, John Wippel, "Thomas Aquinas on the Separated Soul's Natural Knowledge," in *Thomas Aquinas—Approaches to Truth: The Aquinas Lectures at Maynooth, 1996–2001*, ed. James McEvoy and Michael Dunne (Dublin: Four Courts, 2002), 114–40.

in support of the fundamental reasonableness of the inspired biblical witness to the resurrection of the body:

> To establish that there will be a resurrection of the flesh there is an evident supporting argument which is based on the points made earlier. For we showed in Book II that the souls of [human beings] are immortal. They persist, then, after their bodies, released from their bodies. It is also clear from what was said in Book II that the soul is naturally united to the body, for in its essence it is the form of the body. It is, then, contrary to the nature of the soul to be without the body. But nothing which is contrary to nature can be perpetual. Perpetually, then, the soul will not be without the body. Since, then, it persists perpetually, it must once again be united to the body; and this is to rise again. Therefore, the immortality of souls seems to demand a future resurrection of bodies. (*SCG* IV.79.10)

The rational soul is the single substantial form that actualizes the body.[64] The essence of the rational soul is therefore "form of a body." The body belongs to the definition of the species "rational animal." The integral human being, the human person, is a composite of soul and body and the death of the human being is the separation of the soul from its body. With death, the body, bereft of its substantial form, turns into a corpse and the rational soul ceases to realize its essence; the "form of a body" continues to exist, yet in a way contrary to its proper nature. For this very reason, the separate soul has an inclination toward the resurrection and an aptitude to inform anew, in virtue of the resurrection, its body. Eventually, the rational soul will be reunited with its body, because nothing that is unnatural can be perpetual.[65] Hence, the very immortality of the rational soul itself calls for the resurrection of the body.

It is not my concern here to defend the soundness of all the premises that inform Aquinas's argument. What is clear, however, as an entailment of this argument, is that Aquinas regards the resurrection body—precisely because of the essence of the rational soul as form of a body—as an indispensable feature of full resurrection life: the state of the separated rational soul is not the full realization of its

---

64. For Aquinas's defense of the unicity of the substantial form, see *ST* I, q. 76, aa. 3–4; *Quod.* I, q. 4, a. 1; *Q. de an.*, a. 11.

65. See *Super I Epistolam ad Corinthios*, c. 15, lect. 2 (v. 19).

essence. Yet what does this mean for the beatitude of the separated soul? Here is Aquinas's answer:

> Furthermore, there was shown in Book III the natural desire of [the human being] to tend to happiness. But ultimate happiness is the perfection of the happy one. Therefore, anyone to whom some perfection is wanting does not yet have perfect happiness, because his desire is not entirely at rest, for every imperfect thing naturally desires to achieve its perfection. But the soul separated from the body is in a way imperfect, as is every part existing outside of its whole, for the soul is naturally a part of human nature. Therefore, [the human being] cannot achieve his ultimate happiness unless the soul be once again united to the body, especially since it was shown that in this life man cannot arrive at his ultimate happiness. (*SCG* IV.79.11)

Aquinas's robust argument in the *Summa contra Gentiles* for the intrinsic reasonableness and fittingness of the resurrection of the body seems to contradict his later teaching on beatitude in *ST* I-II, qq. 1–5. The problem seems to be the following: ultimate happiness is the perfection of the happy one. The human soul separated from its body is in a way imperfect because its essence—form of a body—is not realized. The separated soul is not yet perfectly at rest because it still desires union with the body. Ultimate happiness entails the resurrection of the body and the union of the soul with its body. And this seems to entail that until the resurrection of the body occurs, the human soul—while in the beatific vision—is not yet perfectly happy, has not yet attained beatitude *simpliciter*. But this conclusion contradicts Aquinas's emphatic insistence in the treatise on beatitude that the *comprehensor* before the resurrection of the body has attained beatitude, perfect happiness.

Aquinas's considered mature position may be put briefly thus: the soul's reunion with its body after the resurrection augments the soul's beatitude by extension (*extensive*) but not beatitude's intensity (*intensive*). The body is not essential for the soul's beatitude *qua* soul, but contributes to its *bene esse*.[66] In the beatific vision, the *com-*

---

66. Numerous Thomist commentators have introduced at this point a pair of terms that remain vulnerable to considerable misunderstanding: "essential" beatitude and "accidental" beatitude: Sylvester of Ferrara, Domingo de Soto, Domingo Bañez, and much later, Réginald Garrigou-Lagrange and Santiago Ramirez. As Brian Kromholtz rightly argues, this terminology, while not wrong, nevertheless does occlude a central aspect of

prehensor's soul is perfectly united with its *object*, the first truth and the highest good and hence perfectly at rest in the beatific vision. Because of the perfection of the *object* and the perfection of the rational soul's union with it, the beatitude of the rational soul *qua* intellectual form cannot increase intensively.

Yet the *subject* of beatitude, the separated soul, *qua* substantial form of the body, is still imperfect in the beatific vision before the resurrection of the body because its essence remains unrealized. In this regard it is necessary to recall the distinction that is at work in Aquinas's considerations in *ST* I-II, q. 4, a. 5—the distinction between the *comprehensor qua* rational soul before the resurrection of the body and the *comprehensor qua* integral whole in its hylomorphic integrity and hence perfection, in short *qua* human being after the resurrection of the body. While the body is not essential to the beatitude of the *comprehensor qua* separate soul, the body is essential to the beatitude of the *comprehensor qua* human being in the resurrection life.

Let us turn to Aquinas's highly condensed treatment of this matter in *ST* I-II, q. 4, a. 5: "Whether the body is necessary for human beatitude?" He continues: "Happiness [*beatitudo*] is the perfection of [the human being]. But the soul, without the body, is not [the human being]. Therefore, happiness cannot be in the soul separated from the body" (obj. 3). Now consider Aquinas's response to this objection: "Happiness belongs to [the human being] in respect of his intellect: and, therefore, since the intellect remains, it can have happiness" (ad 3). In his response to the objection, Aquinas specifies what he states more generally already in the body of his response:

The intellect needs not the body for its operation, save on account of the phantasms, wherein it looks on the intelligible truth [*veritas intelligibilis*], as stated in the First Part [*ST* I, q. 84, a. 7]. Now it is evident that the Divine Essence cannot be seen by means of phantasms, as stated in the First

---

Aquinas's teaching. Interestingly, Cajetan in his commentary on the *Summa Theologiae* remains closer to Aquinas's terminology. Cajetan characterizes the absence of the body from the separated soul as the defect of a perfection in its extension. Thomas de Vio [Cajetan], *Commentaria in Summam theologiae*, In Iam Iae, q. 4, a. 5, Leonine edition, vol. 6 (Rome: S. C. de Propaganda Fide, 1891), 43–44. See Kromholtz, "La perfection de la nature," 59–61.

Part [*ST* I, q. 12, a. 3]. Wherefore, since [the human being's] perfect happiness consists in the vision of the Divine Essence, it does not depend on the body. Consequently, without the body the soul can be happy [*Unde sine corpore potest anima esse beata*]. (*ST* I-II, q. 4, a. 5)

With the resurrection of the body nothing is added to the formal beatitude of the *comprehensor*'s soul *qua intellectus*. Its intensive beatitude is absolutely perfect. Yet because the soul of the *comprehensor* is not fully realized as to its essence, the *subject* of beatitude remains still imperfect. But as soon as the soul *qua* substantial form is reunited with the body, the soul's beatitude "flows over," "spills over" into the body; for as the rational soul *qua* substantial form realizes the body, so does the soul's beatitude necessarily extend itself into the body. Thus, after the resurrection of the body the *comprehensor*'s beatitude increases *extensive*. Now the whole human being is in beatitude "in every manner" (*secundum omnem modum*; *ST* I-II, q. 4, a. 5, ad 5). Perfect intensive beatitude pertains to the perfection of the *object* of beatitude and the rational soul's perfect union with its object, the first truth and the highest good. Perfect beatitude *extensive* pertains to the extension of beatitude "in every manner" (*secundum omnem modum*) and thereby to the perfection of the *subject* of beatitude.

The "Ontological" Desire of the Comprehensor's Separated Soul for Union with Its Body

But if we grant that the subject of beatitude is imperfect until it is united with the resurrection body, would not the *comprehensor*'s soul in the beatific vision desire to be united with its body? And would such a desire not entail that not all desires of the *comprehensor* are fulfilled before the general resurrection? Should one not conclude that while the desire for the vision of God is fulfilled, the desire for a created good, the body is still unfulfilled and therefore perfect integral beatitude not yet attained?

The concern behind the question is that in the beatific vision the *comprehensor* is aware of and indeed experiences a definite subjective deficiency that would necessarily diminish the overall experience of beatitude. Behind this concern is, first, the modern conception of "subject" and "object." Second, there is a tacit assumption built on this modern understanding: the *comprehensor* (before the resurrection of the body) has self-consciousness, which entails an awareness of the *comprehensor*'s imperfection. For the above concern to make sense, the *comprehensor* must be conceived of as a modern subject one of whose essential characteristics is self-awareness. Yet as soon as one understands *object* (*obiectum*) in Aquinas's precise sense[67] and understands the object of the beatific vision to be the first truth and the highest good with whom the *comprehensor*'s intellect is formally united, such a supposed self-awareness either does not obtain at all in the beatific vision, or if it indeed does obtain, the imperfection is already overcome by the warranted anticipation of the state of perfection.[68]

Recall: to be in the beatific vision means to be united with God. The *viator*'s faith has been perfected in the intellectual sight of the beatific vision; the *viator*'s hope has been perfected in comprehension, that is, in the secure possession of the ultimate human end; only the *viator*'s charity remains as the charity of the *comprehensor*. The prayers of the blessed are an expression of their charity (love of God and through it love of neighbor in God)[69] by which they participate in the ongoing unfolding of divine providence.[70] Further-

---

67. "The term [*obiectum*] 'object' stands for the reality, thing or person, that engages an act." O'Brien, "Appendix 1," 178. See chapter 4 for a more extensive discussion of these matters.

68. This point entails assumptions about (1) human self-knowledge in the beatific vision and (2) the knowledge of contingent futures by intellectual creatures in the vision of God through a participation in God's eternity. It would transcend the scope of this epilogue to enter into the worthy consideration of (1). The first step in this direction would be a serious reconsideration of self-knowledge according to Aquinas. Therese Scarpelli Cory has undertaken this step in her excellent study *Aquinas on Human Self-Knowledge* (Cambridge: Cambridge University Press, 2014). Regarding (2), it will have to suffice to point to Carl J. Peter's study *Participated Eternity in the Vision of God* (Rome: Gregorian University Press, 1964), 49–71.

69. See above, chapter 5.

70. *ST* II-II, q. 83, a. 2: "We pray not that we may change the Divine disposition, but that we may impetrate that which God has disposed to be fulfilled by our prayers, in other words 'that by asking, men may deserve to receive what Almighty God from eternity has disposed to give,' as Gregory says (Dial. i, 8)." For a lucid metaphysical analysis of Aquinas's position in comparison to two modern accounts, see Stephen Brock, "On the Causality of the Prayer of Petition: C.S. Lewis, Peter Geach, and Thomas Aquinas," *Acta Philosophica* 23, no. 1 (2014): 79–87.

more, the blessed before the resurrection of their bodies do not exist in the interim state of disembodied ghostlike beings simply waiting (consciously or unconsciously) for their embodiment in some kind of neutral holding-pattern (the "sleep of the soul"). Rather, the separated souls already exist in the full and perfect ecstasy of the beatific vision and in the beatific vision they participate in the divine knowledge and hence have the certain knowledge that they will eventually be reunited with their bodies. Hence, the desire of the blessed to be reunited with their bodies must be understood as an implicit "ontological desire" that characterizes the separated soul that is still configured ontologically to inform a body in contrast with an elicited actual desire of the will of the *comprehensor*'s soul. The separated soul in the beatific vision already anticipates with certitude the fulfillment of the ontological desire in the beatific knowledge of the glorious humanity of the risen Christ and of the full resurrection life, soul and body, of the Virgin Mary. To suppose an elicited actual desire of the will for the soul's union with its body is to misunderstand or to deny the unitive nature and ecstatic reality of the beatific vision itself.

When Grisez takes Aquinas's beatitude to be "static,"[71] it is the modern concept of "subject" (a rational animal with computational and discursive capabilities but without *intellectus*) which he presupposes that is responsible for this serious misconception. The way Aquinas conceives of the state of perfection—rest in the first truth and highest good—must appear to Grisez as static because he conceives of the subject as an essentially finite creature. Under the conditions of created finitude, for Grisez "rest" can only be "static," an imperfect state of immobility and uneventfulness—and therefore essentially a state of death. In order to avoid such rightly disconcerting consequences, Grisez supposes an everlasting dynamic that adds ever new created goods to the experience of the vision of the risen Lord in the glory of his resurrection body and of the Virgin Mary that continue to increase the person's happiness in paradise. Beatitude can only be kept from becoming "static" by a continuous and interminable flow of goods. Grisez's central concern betrays a profound misunderstanding of Aquinas's account of beatitude. Accord-

---

71. Grisez, "The Ultimate End of Human Beings," 52.

ing to Aquinas, the perfection and hence the beatitude of the *subiectum* in the beatific vision is completely determined by the *obiectum* with which it is united, the divine essence, the *ipsum esse subsistens*. The created substantial form that has the very capacity to be elevated to such a union is *intellectus*, the human rational soul. In light of a modern rationalistic anthropology, which Grisez seems to presuppose, for which reason is a computational and discursive faculty bereft of the ontological status of *intellectus*, Aquinas's beatitude must appear static. It is seen as the non-unitive completion of a finite rational subject *in se* instead of being seen as the unitive perfection of *intellectus capax Dei* with its proper object, the first truth and the highest good. The ontological result of this formal union of the created finite rational soul with its uncreated infinite *obiectum* can only be a surpassing everlasting created and finite *ek-stasis* in the eternal now of the divine subsistent act of existing itself. The created participation in the uncreated divine essence takes the form of a mode of perfect ecstatic creaturely activity—the acts of glory.[72] *Ek-stasis* is the opposite of a static condition. To mistake the *ek-stasis* of the formal union for a static satiation would mean that (1) the comprehensor's vision is an exhaustive comprehension, which Aquinas shows is impossible for the finite creature to obtain, and (2) that the subsisting act of existing itself is static—which is patently absurd. In virtue of the *intellectus* that is *capax Dei* and by way of its finite participation in the infinite *actus purus*, the *comprehensor*'s beatitude is attained in a perfection of intensity that is qualified by the very essence of its object, *actus purus*, and is therefore surpassingly dynamic.

In sum, because the rational soul is the constitutive principle of the human body, the lack of the body does not diminish the perfection of the constitutive principle *qua* principle, that is, the perfection of the rational soul's beatitude *qua* intellectual principle. Yet because the rational soul's essence is "form of a body," the rational soul's beatitude is not yet the beatitude of the human person *qua* embodied and *qua* social being. The latter is only realized in every manner (*secundum omnem modum*) after the resurrection of the body and in the full conviviality of the heavenly *societas* of angels and humans.[73]

---

72. See Peter, *Participated Eternity in the Vision of God*, 35–71.

73. But must there not necessarily be sorrow in heaven? And does such sorrow not

THE COMMUNAL CHARACTER OF HEAVENLY BEATITUDE

It is not at all uncommon among modern theologians who attend to the challenging topic of eschatology, the "last things," to emphasize the inherently social, interactive, and in a certain way even political character of Christian eschatology. The anthropocentric focus of these accounts yields the predictable result of a redeemed politics of paradise. The Eschaton is conceived of usually as a new creation, now of interminable duration and equipped with inexhaustible resources of goods, a plenitude that requires ongoing social and political interaction among the redeemed in order to assure full participation of all in the common good of the new creation. Configured as a restored and expanded paradise, the new creation is the setting in which redeemed humanity resumes its original role as the steward of creation. Not only in this present economy of salvation is God conceived to stand, so to speak, "behind" the redeemed faithful, sending them into the world before them to do God's work there; but also in the new creation this directionality from God to the world remains. The theological premise that leads to the conclusion that God stands behind the world is that the human being, while created by God, is created and then redeemed not for God but rather for a communal paradisiacal existence in a new creation. Differently put, humanity is created for paradise but not for the participated eternity of heaven, for union with God.[74]

If Aquinas's eschatology is considered at all in these profoundly anthropocentric modern social or political eschatologies, it is most

---

necessarily diminish the beatitude of the blessed? On the supposition of irresistable universal salvation (Bulgakov), or on the supposition of Christian hope that hell might exist, but that it is not occupied by any human being (Hans Urs von Balthasar), or on the supposition that the act of being is withdrawn (annihilation) from all the unjust (Paul J. Griffiths), the question does not arise. Only on the supposition of the theological *lectio difficilior* (which rests on the witness of scripture, the dominical words of warning, the virtually unanimous position of the magisterial tradition, affirmed by successive magisterially approved private revelations, most notably Fatima) does this question arise. For a recent recapitulation of Aquinas's position that is as astute as it is accessible, see Reimers, *Hell and the Mercy of God*, 229–38.

74. Wright's *Surprised by Hope* is a theologically instructive example of an account popular especially in Evangelical theological circles.

often misread as a neo-Platonic "*solus cum solo* eschatology." All the blessed, like monads, are filled with the divine glory and beatitude, in full possession of the consummate good, as if each *comprehensor* were the only extant creature. In possession of the consummate good, the *comprehensor*'s soul is in a state of ecstasy that makes the world of the new creation and all other blessed fall away into utter insignificance and oblivion. God and the disembodied soul, suffused by God's glory and beatitude, is all there is—God and the soul, all in all.

A cursory reading of Aquinas's treatise on happiness in *ST* I-II might very well give rise to such an erroneous impression, especially if the hasty reader's gaze comes to rest on a passage like the one already cited earlier: "If there were but one soul enjoying God, it would be happy, though having no neighbor to love" (*ST* I-II, q. 4, a. 8, ad 3). Read in isolation from its proper context in Aquinas's argument, a passage like this seems to confirm that Aquinas betrays the profoundly communal character, indeed the very *communio*-character, of Christian eschatology by committing the unforgivable sin of introducing a neo-Platonically inspired and hence deeply distortive *solus cum solo* beatitude.

My reading of Aquinas's treatise on beatitude in the prologue and of his treatment of the resurrection of the body in the previous section of the epilogue, however, make it quite clear that he does not at all entertain such a *solus cum solo* eschatology and, furthermore, that in the above passage he is emphasizing merely the complete sufficiency of God, the consummate good, for the *comprehensor*'s beatitude. If God is indeed the consummate good and if the *comprehensor* is indeed in possession of it in virtue of the intellect's formal union with the divine essence, it follows necessarily that the *comprehensor* needs no one and nothing in addition in order to achieve beatitude. Yet Aquinas significantly adds the following statement: "But supposing one neighbor to be there [*sed supposito proximo*], love of him results from perfect love of God. Consequently, friendship is, as it were, concomitant [*quasi concomitanter*] with perfect Happiness" (*ST* I-II, q. 4, a. 8, ad 3). The truth of the intrinsic relation between the consummate good, its perfect possession by an intellect, and the intellect's beatitude constitutes the metaphysical backdrop of the fundamentally theocentric orientation of Aquinas's eschatological vision. The added supposition of other humans (one suffices to make the point) present in the participated eternity of heaven, like the supposition of the resurrection of the body, is a definitive truth of divine revelation held by divine faith.

The organizing principle that integrates both truths into the one comprehensive horizon of sacred theology is the principle that grace does not destroy but perfects nature (*ST* I, q. 1, a. 8, ad 2). Applying this principle to the beatific vision, Aquinas posits a continuity between the natural and the supernatural life of the human being. The supernatural life does not "build" onto human nature by adding something inherently alien on top of it. Rather, the supernatural life extends the very capacity of human nature by elevating its faculties along the lines of their natural finality so that humans can indeed become "deiform" and thus fully realize the likeness for which we are created and toward which we are ordered (*ST* I, q. 93).[75] The participated eternity of heavenly life is thus indeed not the abrogation or even annihilation but rather the sublimation and fulfillment of earthly life in its very transformation into the *deiformitas* that the light of glory effects and that in turn affords the immediate vision of God.

Yet if the participated eternity of heavenly life is indeed not the abrogation or annihilation but rather the sublimation and fulfillment of earthly life, a particular question does arise for many—especially in sociocultural contexts in which subjective sovereignty has become the normative ideal self-image and in which orgiastic experiences are regarded as a great and sometimes even as the highest good: will there be sex in heaven? Those who entertain a merely paradisiacal and indeed anthropocentric eschatology (which along with the Christian theologians discussed above is also the prevalent conception in Islam and Mormonism), quite consistently posit that in the Eschaton there indeed will be sex. On the supposition of a theocentric participated eternity in the vision of God, however, the assumption that there will be sex in heaven is simply misguided. Aquinas does not mince his words:

---

75. See chapters 1 and 5. The best study on this topic is still Merriell, *To the Image of the Trinity*.

It seems ridiculous to search for bodily pleasures which the brute animals share with us there where the loftiest pleasures which we share with the angels are expected—the pleasures in the vision of God which will be common to us and the angels.... Unless, perhaps, someone wants to say that the beatitude of the angels is imperfect because the angels lack the pleasures of the brutes—which is completely absurd. Pertinent to this is our Lord's saying in Matthew (22:30), that "in the resurrection they shall neither marry nor be married, but shall be as the angels of God." (*SCG* IV.83.13)

As absurd as it would be to assume that a theoretical physicist at the very moment of conceptual breakthrough to the mathematical formula she has been searching for would stop to have marital intercourse with her husband; and as absurd as it would be to assume that a mystic in the state of ecstasy of infused contemplation would be tempted by the longing for venereal pleasure—just as absurd would it be to posit sex in heaven. Those who do so simply do not understand the proper meaning of heaven—participated eternity in the vision of God—and replace it *de facto* with paradise—a state of natural, or even preternatural perfection, that is, absent all natural and moral evils (suffering, sickness, death, sin, and wickedness) but also absent the beatific vision. Participated eternity and the acts of glory in the vision of God that make up the beatific existence of the *comprehensor* perfect and therefore surpass the *ek-static* delight concomitant with the infused contemplation of the mystic. This is the basic supposition in light of which the question of bodily delights characteristic of the present life will need to be understood. All bodily delights are completely enfolded in and surpassed by the *ek-static* delight concomitant with beatitude. In the acts of glory, the *comprehensor* in virtue of the quasi-formal union "through which" (*quo*) with the divine essence surpasses the very conditions of creatureliness. The duration of the acts of glory become indeed identical with the everlasting instant of the "divine now." In Carl Peter's apt formulation, "for Thomas Aquinas the creature in the Vision of God is assimilated to the divine Now so that all it can know and love in immediate union with the divine essence, it does, in an instant that lasts forever immutably."[76] Yet this immutability is the immutabili-

---

76. Peter, *Participated Eternity in the Vision of God*, 71.

ty of absolute actuality, because in virtue of the quasi-formal union "through which" (*quo*) with the divine essence, the *ipsum esse subsistens*, the *comprehensor* participates in the divine perfection of *esse*, that is, in absolute immutable actuality. Aquinas states: "The entire power of the creature will be applied to seeing and loving God."[77] This is the very principle that accounts for the essentially communal character of heavenly beatitude. In the participated eternity of the vision of God in virtue of the light of glory, the blessed exist in a perfect community of charity, that is, friendship with God and friendship with each other.

The perfection in charity does not entail, however, some abstract quasi-quantitative equality of the amount of charity received and enacted. Such a misguided notion has as its determinative point of reference an abstract egalitarian collective. The perfection in charity Aquinas proposes has as its determinative point of reference the concrete *comprehensor* whose particularity corresponds to that person's individual degree of cooperation with sanctifying grace as a *viator*. The *viator*'s cooperation with sanctifying grace issues in interior as well as exterior acts of the theological virtue of charity that in turn merit an increased infusion of charity.[78] Hence, the perfection of charity takes the form of a differentiated gradation that reflects in each *comprehensor* the *viator*'s personal sojourn toward, with, and in charity.

Charity, the love of friendship with God, is the cause of the love of friendship with the neighbor, that is, all the other blessed. What begins in the life of the *viator* by sanctifying grace, is completed in the eternal life of the *comprehensor* by the light of glory:

77. *De caritate*, a. 10, ad 5: "Totum posse creaturae applicabitur ad videndum et diligendum Deum."
78. See chapter 5 and also *ST* I, q. 12, a. 6: "Of those who see the essence of God, one sees Him more perfectly than another. This ... will take place because one intellect will have a greater power or faculty to see God than another. The faculty of seeing God, however, does not belong to the created intellect naturally, but is given to it by the light of glory, which establishes the intellect in a kind of 'deiformity'.... Hence the intellect which has more of the light of glory will see God the more perfectly; and he will have a fuller participation of the light of glory who has more charity; because where there is the greater charity, there is the more desire; and desire in a certain degree makes the one desiring apt and prepared to receive the object desired. Hence he who possesses the more charity, will see God the more perfectly, and will be the more beatified." See also *ST* I-II, q. 114, aa. 4 and 8, and for a lucid analysis the study by Wawrykow, *God's Grace and Human Action*.

Charity signifies not only the love of God [*amorem Dei*], but also a certain friendship with Him [*amicitiam quandam ad ipsum*]; which implies, besides love, a certain mutual return of love, together with mutual communion [*cum quadam mutua communicatione*], as stated in Ethic. viii, 2. That this belongs to charity is evident from 1 Jn. 4:16: "He that abideth in charity, abideth in God, and God in him," and from 1 Cor. 1:9, where it is written: "God is faithful, by Whom you are called unto the fellowship of His Son." Now this fellowship of [the human] with God, which consists in a certain familiar colloquy with Him [*quaedam familiaris conversatio cum ipso*], is begun here, in this life, by grace, but will be perfected in the future life, by glory. (*ST* I-II, q. 65, a. 5)[79]

The *communicatio* or *conversio* constitutive of the heavenly friendship ceaselessly flows in the beatific vision from the life of the triune God that is charity to the blessed and returns as charity to the triune God, including in the return the charity shared among the heavenly *communio* of the blessed. Like the resurrection body, the companionship of friends does not increase beatitude, but rather extends beatitude into the fully embodied and comprehensively communal existence of all the blessed. As with the body, there occurs a constant, interminable, and irrepressible "flowing over" of the soul's beatitude into the resurrection body and into the fellowship of the blessed. Aquinas draws upon Augustine to illustrate his argument:

If we speak of perfect Happiness [*perfecta beatitudo*] which will be in our heavenly Fatherland [*patria*], the fellowship of friends is not essential to Happiness; since [the human being] has the entire fullness of his perfection in God. But the fellowship of friends conduces to the well-being of Happiness [*ad bene esse beatitudinis*]. Hence Augustine says (Gen. ad lit. viii, 25) that "the spiritual creatures receive no other interior [*intrinsecus*]

---

79. Aquinas offers a similar line of argumentation in his extended treatment of the theological virtue of charity in the *Summa*: "[The human being's] life is twofold. There is his outward life in respect of his sensitive and corporeal nature: and with regard to this life there is no communication or fellowship [*communicatio vel conversatio*] between us and God or the angels. The other is [the human being's] spiritual life in respect of his mind, and with regard to this life there is fellowship [*conversatio*] between us and both God and the angels, imperfectly indeed in this present state of life, wherefore it is written (Phl 3:20): 'Our conversation is in heaven.' But this 'conversation' [*conversatio*] will be perfected in heaven [*in patria*], when 'His servants shall serve Him, and they shall see His face' (Apoc 22:3,4). Therefore charity is imperfect here, but will be perfected in heaven" (*ST* II-II, q. 23, a. 1, ad 1).

aid to happiness than the eternity, truth, and charity of the Creator. But if they can be said to be helped from without [*extrinsecus*], perhaps it is only by this that they see one another and rejoice in God [*gaudent in Deo*], at their fellowship." (*ST* I-II, q. 4, a. 8)

The rejoicing of the blessed at their fellowship as friends occurs in God (*in Deo*), because their respective ontologically and soteriologically prior friendship with God, the *communicatio* of charity between God and each *comprehensor* is the cause of their mutual friendship. The friendship among the blessed is an extension of their friendship with God. The blessed are aware of the fact that God's friendship with each one of them brings about their fellowship as friends and—in God—they praise God for it. The friendship among the blessed is most intimate because they know each other in God, in the beatific vision, see each other as God sees them, and love each other with the charity that flows from God in virtue of their formal union with God and returns from them by acts of charity and religion to God while they are all the time in God. It is a most perfect communion perfectly dynamic in the *ek-stasis* of the acts of glory and simultaneously perfectly at rest in the possession of the consummate good in the divine now.

Because this fellowship is a supernatural communion of grace—of sanctifying grace in this life and of the light of glory in the next—and because this grace is merited by the passion of the incarnate Lord, it is a Christologically configured communion: "The Church, on earth, is the congregation of the faithful [*congregatio fidelium*]; but, in heaven, it is the congregation of comprehensors [*congregatio comprehendentium*]. Now Christ was not merely a wayfarer, but a comprehensor. And therefore He is the Head not merely of the faithful, but of comprehensors, as having grace and glory most fully" (*ST* III, q. 8, a. 4, ad 2). Christ is the head, the Church is his body. Grace flows from the head into the body (*ST* III, q. 8). This fundamental structure is not superseded in heaven. What is true for the *viatores* is also true for the *comprehensores*. Together they are the body whose head is Christ. And therefore the friendship of the blessed is nothing but the perfection and fulfillment of what obtains now already for the wayfarers: "I have called you friends, because I have made known to you everything that I have heard from my Father" (Jn 15:15). Hence, the *conversatio* of participated eternity is Christologically configured. It is, in Augustinian terms, the *totus Christus*, the head and body of Christ. For this very reason and in this very sense—but for this reason and in this sense only—is it true to say: *Ecclesia finis omnium*, the church is the end of all things.[80]

At a certain point even the analogical language of theological discourse will break down. We have reached this point in this study some time ago. The heavenly communication or fellowship (*communicatio vel conversatio*) between the triune God, the blessed, and the angels that Aquinas gestures toward at the very limits of the discourse to which sacred theology is committed, calls for an appeal to the imagination, an imagination elevated by sanctifying grace, informed by faith, strengthened by hope, and inflamed by charity. Perfectly consonant with Aquinas's teaching, Dante Alighieri in his immortal poem, the *Divine Comedy*, makes such an appeal to the imagination. In canto 31 of *Paradiso*, Dante depicts the "secure and joyful kingdom" of the blessed and the angels who are directing their gaze and their love to the triune God, and in and through this shared vision and love of God are enjoying the most perfect heavenly communion with the unforgettable image of the celestial rose, the *rosa candida*:

> So now, displayed before me as a rose
> Of snow-white purity, the sacred might
> I saw, whom with His blood Christ made His spouse.
>
> But the other, winging ever in His sight,
> Chants praises to the glory it adores,
> Its Maker's good extolling in delight.
>
> As bees ply back and forth, now in the flowers
> Busying themselves, and now intent to wend
> Where all their toil is turned to sweetest stores,
>
> So did the host of Angels now descend
> Amid the Flowers of the countless leaves,
> Now rise to where their love dwells without end.

---

80. This crucial aspect of the finality of the universe as well as of the economy of salvation is the theme of the comprehensive and profound study by François Daguet, *Théologie du dessein divin chez Thomas d'Aquin: Finis omnium Ecclesia* (Paris: Vrin, 2003).

Their glowing faces were as fire that gives
Forth flame, golden their wings; the purest snow
The whiteness of their raiment ne'er achieves.

Down floating to the Flower, from row to row,
Each ministered the peace and burning love
They gathered in their waftings to and fro.

Between the Flower and that which blazed above
The volant concourse interposed no screen
To dim the splendour and the sight thereof;

For God's rays penetrate with shafts so keen
Through all the universe, in due degree,
There's naught can parry them or intervene.

Drawn from the new age and antiquity,
This realm of saints, whose joy no dangers mar,
Gazed on one sign in love and unity.

O trinal light, which shining as one star
It fills them with delight to gaze on there,
Look down on us, storm-driven as we are![81]

81. *The Comedy of Dante Alighieri the Florentine. Cantica III: Paradise (Il Paradiso)*, trans. Dorothy L. Sayers (New York: Basic Books, 1962), 327–28. Since every translation is at its best only an approximation to, and often unavoidably a betrayal of, the original (or, as the saying goes, *traduttore, traditore*), especially in the case of the *Divine Comedy*, I regard it as indispensable to include the early fourteenth-century Florentine tongue of Dante's original, which is taken from Alighieri, *Paradiso* (trans. Singleton), 346–49:

In forma dunque di candida rosa
mi si mostrava la milizia santa
che nel suo sangue Cristo fece sposa;

ma l'altra, che volando vede e canta
la gloria di colui che la 'nnamora
e la bontà che la fece cotanta,

sì come schiera d'ape che s'infiora
una fïata e una si ritorna
là dove suo laboro s'insapora,

nel gran fior discendeva che s'addorna
di tante foglie, e quindi risaliva
là dove 'l sü̈o amor sempre soggiorna.

Le facce tutte avean di fiamma viva
e l'ali d'oro, e l'altro tanto bianco,
che nulla neve a quel termine arriva.

Quando scendean nel fior, di banco in banco
porgevan de la pace e de l'ardore
ch'elli acquistavan ventilando il fianco.

Né l'interporsi tra 'l disopra e 'l fiore
di tanta moltitudine volante
impediva la vista e lo splendore:

ché la luce divina è penetrante
per l'universo secondo ch'è degno,
sì che nulla le puote essere ostante.

Questo sicuro e gaudïoso regno,
frequente in gente antica e in novella,
viso e amore avea tutto ad un segno.

Oh trina luce che 'n unica stella
scintillando a lor vista, sì li appaga!
guarda qua giuso a la nostra procella!

Selected Bibliography

WORKS BY THOMAS AQUINAS

Compendium theologiae ad fratrem Reginaldum socium suum carissimum. In *Sancti Thomae Aquinatis opera omnia,* vol. 42. Leonine Edition. Rome: Editori di San Tommaso, 1979.

De caritate. In *Quaestiones disputatae,* edited by Raymund M. Spiazzi, OP, 2:753–91. Rome: Marietti, 1965.

De ente et essentia. In *Opuscula Philosophica,* edited by Raymund M. Spiazzi, OP, 1–18. Rome: Marietti, 1954.

De malo. In *Sancti Thomae Aquinatis opera omnia,* vol. 23. Leonine Edition. Rome: Editori di San Tommaso, 1982.

De potentia Dei. Edited by Pauli M. Pession, OP. In *Quaestiones disputatae,* vol. 2, edited by Raymund M. Spiazzi, OP. Rome: Marietti, 1965.

De veritate. In *Sancti Thomae Aquinatis opera omnia,* vol. 22. Leonine Edition. Rome: Editori di San Tommaso, 1975–76.

De virtutibus cardinalibus. In *Quaestiones disputatae,* edited by Raymund M. Spiazzi, OP, 2:813–28. Rome: Marietti, 1965.

De virtutibus in communi. In *Quaestiones disputatae,* edited by Raymund M. Spiazzi, OP, 2:707–51. Rome: Marietti, 1965.

Expositio super Iob ad litteram. In *Sancti Thomae Aquinatis opera omnia,* vol. 26. Leonine Edition. Rome: Editori di San Tommaso, 1965.

Expositio super primam et secundam Decretalem ad Archidiaconum Tudertinum. In *Opuscula Theologica,* edited by Raymund M. Spiazzi, OP, 1:415–31. Rome: Marietti, 1954.

In Aristotelis libros Peri Hermeneias et Posteriorum Analyticorum expositio. Edited by Raymund M. Spiazzi, OP. Rome: Marietti, 1955.

In decem libros Ethicorum Aristotelis ad Nicomachum expositio. Edited by Raymund M. Spiazzi, OP. 3rd ed. Rome: Marietti, 1964.

In duodecim libros Metaphysicorum Aristotelis expositio. Edited by M. R. Cathala, OP, and R. M. Spiazzi, OP. Rome: Marietti, 1964.

In librum beati Dionysii de divinis nominibus expositio. Edited by Ceslaus Pera, OP. Rome: Marietti, 1950.
In librum Boetii de Trinitate expositio. In *Opuscula Theologica*, edited by Raymund M. Spiazzi, OP, 2:313–89. Rome: Marietti, 1954.
In octo libros Physicorum Aristotelis commentarium. Edited by P. M. Maggiolo, OP. Rome: Marietti, 1954.
In quattuor libros Sententiarum. In *S. Thomae Aquinatis Opera Omnia*, vol. 1, edited by R. Busa, SJ. Stuttgart-Bad Cannstatt: Frommann, 1980.
In salutationem angelicam Vulgo "Ave Maria" expositio. In *Opuscula Theologica*, edited by Raymund M. Spiazzi, OP, 2:239–41. Rome: Marietti, 1954.
Quaestiones disputatae. Edited by P. Bazzi, OP, M. Calcaterra, OP, T. S. Centi, OP, E. Odetto, OP, and M. Pession, OP. 2 vols. Rome: Marietti, 1965.
Quaestiones disputatae de anima. Edited by B. C. Bazan. In *Sancti Thomae Aquinatis opera omnia*, vol. 24.1. Leonine Edition. Paris: Cerf, 1996. See also *Quaestio disputata de anima*. Edited by J. H. Robb. Toronto: Pontifical Institute of Mediaeval Studies, 1968.
Quaestiones quodlibetales. Edited by Raymund M. Spiazzi, OP. Rome: Marietti, 1949.
Sentencia libri De Anima. In *Sancti Thomae Aquinatis opera omnia*, vol. 45.1. Leonine Edition. Paris: Vrin, 1984.
Sententia libri Ethicorum. In *Sancti Thomae Aquinatis opera omnia*, vol. 47.1–2. Leonine Edition. Rome: Editori di San Tommaso, 1969.
Summa contra Gentiles. In *Sancti Thomae Aquinatis* opera omnia, vols. 13–15. Leonine Edition. Rome: R. Garroni, 1918–30.
Summa contra Gentiles. 3 vols. Rome: Marietti, 1961.
Summa theologiae. In *Sancti Thomae Aquinatis opera omnia*, vols. 4–12. Leonine Edition. Rome: R. Garroni, 1886–1906.
Summa theologiae. 3rd ed. Turin: Edizioni San Paolo, 1999.
Super Epistolas Sancti Pauli Lectura. Edited by P. Raphaelis Cai, OP. 2 vols. Rome: Marietti, 1953.
Super Evangelium S. Ioannis Lectura. Edited by P. Raphaelis Cai, OP. Rome: Marietti, 1952.

TRANSLATIONS OF WORKS BY THOMAS AQUINAS

The Angelic Salutation. Translated by Joseph B. Collins. New York: Wagner, 1939.
The Aquinas Prayer Book: The Prayers and Hymns of St. Thomas Aquinas. Latin-English. Edited by Robert Anderson and Johann Moser. Manchester, N.H.: Sophia Institute Press, 2000.
Aristotle: On Interpretation. Commentary by St. Thomas and Cajetan (Peri Hermeneias). Translated from the Latin with Introduction by Jean T. Oesterle. Milwaukee, Wis.: Marquette University Press, 1962.
Commentary on Aristotle's De Anima. Translated by Kenelm Foster, OP, and Sylvester Humphries, OP. New Haven, Conn.: Yale University Press, 1951.
Commentary on Aristotle's Metaphysics. Translated by John P. Rowan. Notre Dame, Ind.: Dumb Ox Books, 1995.

Selected Bibliography

Commentary on Aristotle's Nicomachean Ethics. Translated by C. I. Litzinger, OP. Notre Dame, Ind.: Dumb Ox Books, 1993.
Commentary on Aristotle's Physics. Translated by Richard J. Blackwell, Richard J. Spath, and W. Edmund Thirkel. Notre Dame, Ind.: Dumb Ox Books, 1999.
Commentary on Aristotle's Posterior Analytics. Translated by Richard Berquist. Notre Dame, Ind.: Dumb Ox Books, 2007.
Commentary on Colossians. Edited by Daniel A. Keating and translated by Fabian Larcher, OP. Naples, Fla.: Sapientia Press, 2006.
Commentary on the Gospel of John, Part II. Translated by James A. Weisheipl and Fabian R. Larcher. Petersham: St. Bede's Publications, 1980.
Commentary on the Letter of Saint Paul to the Romans. Edited by J. Mortensen and E. Alarcón. Translated by F. R. Larcher, OP. Latin-English Edition of the Works of St. Thomas Aquinas 37. Lander, Wyo.: The Aquinas Institute for the Study of Sacred Doctrine, 2012.
The De Malo of Thomas Aquinas. Latin-English. Edited by Brian Davies. Translated by Richard Regan. Oxford: Oxford University Press, 2001.
Disputed Questions on the Virtues. Edited by E. M. Atkins and Thomas Williams. Translated by E. M. Atkins. Cambridge: Cambridge University Press, 2005.
Faith, Reason, and Theology: Questions I-IV of his Commentary on the De Trinitate *of Boethius*. Translated by Armand Maurer. Toronto: Pontifical Institute of Mediaeval Studies, 1987.
La Somma Teologica, vol. 18. Translated by Tito Sante Centi, OP. Siena: Salani, 1967.
Light of Faith: The Compendium of Theology. Translated by Cyril Vollert, SJ. Manchester, N.H.: Sophia Institute Press, 1993.
The Literal Exposition on Job: A Scriptural Commentary Concerning Providence. Translated by Anthony Damico. Atlanta: Scholars Press, 1989.
On Charity: De caritate. Translated by Lottie H. Kendzierski. Milwaukee, Wis.: Marquette University Press, 1960.
On the Power of God (Quaestiones disputatae de potentia Dei). Translated by the English Dominican Fathers. Westminster, Md.: Newman Press, 1952 (1932).
Quodlibetal Questions 1 and 2. Translated by Sandra Edwards. Toronto: Pontifical Institute of Mediaeval Studies, 1983.
Somme Théologique: La Béatitude. Edited by Servais Pinckairs, OP. Nouvelle Édition de La Revue des jeunes. Paris: Cerf, 2001.
Somme Théologique. Le Verbe Incarné en ses mystères. Tome 1, L'entrée du Christ en ce monde. Edited by Jean-Pierre Torrell, OP. Nouvelle Édition de La Revue des jeunes. Paris: Cerf, 2003.
Summa contra Gentiles. Book One: God. Translated by Anton C. Pegis, FRSC. Notre Dame, Ind.: University of Notre Dame Press, 1975.
Summa contra Gentiles. Book Two: Creation. Translated by James F. Anderson. Notre Dame, Ind.: University of Notre Dame Press, 1975.
Summa contra Gentiles. Book Three: Providence. Part I. Translated by Vernon J. Bourke. Notre Dame, Ind.: University of Notre Dame Press, 1975.
Summa contra Gentiles. Book Three: Providence. Part II. Translated by Vernon J. Bourke. Notre Dame, Ind.: University of Notre Dame Press, 1975.

Summa contra Gentiles. Book Four: Salvation. Translated by Charles O'Neil. Notre Dame, Ind.: University of Notre Dame Press, 1975.
Summa Theologiae. Translated by the Fathers of the English Dominican Province. New York: Benziger Bros., 1948.
Summa Theologiae, vol. 16: *(1a2ae. 1–5), Purpose and Happiness.* Edited by Thomas Gilby, OP. New York / London: Blackfriars and McGraw-Hill Book Company / Eyre and Spottiswoode, 1969.
Summa Theologiae, vol. 39: *(2a2ae. 80–91), Religion and Worship.* Edited by Kevin D. O'Rourke, OP. New York / London: Blackfriars and McGraw-Hill Book Company / Eyre and Spottiswoode, 1964.
Summa Theologica: Deutsch-lateinische Ausgabe (Die Deutsche Thomas-Ausgabe), vol. 12: *Die Sünde.* Commentary by Otto Herman Pesch. Vienna: Styria, 2004.
Summa Theologica: Deutsch-lateinische Ausgabe (Die Deutsche Thomas-Ausgabe), vol. 21: *Tapferkeit, Masshaltung* (1. Teil). Commentary by Josef Fulko Groner, OP. Heidelberg: F. H. Kehrle, 1961.
Summa Theologica: Deutsch-lateinische Ausgabe, vol. 36: *Die letzten Dinge.* Commentary by Adolf Hoffmann, OP. Heidelberg/Graz. F. H. Kehrle/Styria, 1961.
Truth, vol. 1: *Questions 1–9.* Translated by Robert W. Mulligan, SJ. Indianapolis, Ind.: Hackett, 1994.
Truth, vol. 2: *Questions 10–20.* Translated by James V. McGlynn, SJ. Indianapolis, Ind.: Hackett, 1994.
Truth, vol. 3: *Questions 21–29.* Translated by Robert W. Schmidt, SJ. Indianapolis, Ind.: Hackett, 1994.

THOMIST COMMENTATORS AND CLASSICAL THOMIST INTERPRETERS

Báñez, Domingo, OP. *Comentarios inéditos a la prima secundae de Santo Tomás,* vol. 1: *De fine ultimo et de actibus humanis (qq. 1–18).* Edited by R. P. Vicente Beltran de Heredia, OP. Salamanca: Imprenta de Aldecoa, 1942.

Bobik, Joseph. *Aquinas on Being and Essence: A Translation and Interpretation.* Notre Dame, Ind.: University of Notre Dame Press, 1965.

———. *Aquinas on Matter and Form and the Elements: A Translation and Interpretation of the* De Principiis Naturae *and the* De Mixtione Elementorum *of St. Thomas Aquinas.* Notre Dame, Ind.: University of Notre Dame Press, 1998.

Cajetan, Tommaso de Vio Gaetani. *Commentaria in Summam Theologiae Sancti Thomae Aquinatis* (1507–22). In *Sancti Thomae Aquinatis Doctoris Angelici Opera Omnia iussu impensaque Leonis XIII P.M edita,* vols. 4–12. Rome: Leonine Commission, 1886–1906.

Garrigou-Lagrange, Réginald, OP. *De Eucharistia accedunt De Paenitentia quaestiones dogmaticae Commentarius in Summam theologicam S. Thomae.* Rome: Marietti, 1943.

———. *De Beatitudine, de Actibus Humanis et de Habitibus: Commentarius in Summam Theologicam S. Thomae Ia–IIae qq. 1–54.* Turin: R. Berruti, 1951.

———. *Beatitude: A Commentary on St. Thomas's Summa, $I^a\ II^{ae}$, qq. 1–54.* Translated by Patrick Cummins, OSB. St. Louis, Mo.: Herder, 1956.

Gredt, Joseph, OSB. *Logica: Philosophia Naturalis*. Freiburg: Herder, 1956.
Horvath, Alexander M., OP. *Annotationes ad II-II Quaest. 81–91 De Virtute Religionis (Pro Manuscripto) Pontificum Institutum Internationale "Angelicum."* Rome: Tipografia Agostiniana, 1929.
John of St. Thomas, OP. *Cursus philosophicus thomisticus secundum exactam, veram, genuinam Aristotelis et Doctoris Angelici mentem*. 3 vols. Paris: Vivès, 1883.
Labourdette, Marie-Michel, OP. *Cours de Théologie Morale*, vol. 1: *La fin dernière de la vie humaine (Ia–IIae, Q. 1–5)*. Unpublished manuscript. Toulouse, December 1961.

———. *Cours de Théologie Morale*, vol. 1: *La fin dernière de la vie humaine (La Béatitude) Ia–IIae, Qu. 1–5*. Nouvelle édition entièrement refondue. Unpublished manuscript, Toulouse, March 1990.

———. *Cours de Théologie Morale*, vol. 15: *La vie sexuelle: La chasteté*. Unpublished manuscript, Toulouse.

Lugo, Juan de, SJ. *De virtute fidei divinae*. Lyon, 1646.
Ramirez, Jacobus M., OP. *De Hominis Beatitudine*, vols. I–V. In *Opera Omnia*. Edited by Victorino Rodríguez, OP. Madrid: Instituto de Filosofía "Luis Vives," 1972.
Smith, Elwood F., OP, and Louis A. Ryan, OP. *Preface to Happiness*, vol. 2 of *A Guidebook to the Summa (Corresponding to the* Summa Theologiae, *I-II)*. New York: Benziger, 1950.
Suárez, Francisco, SJ. *Opera Omnia*. Paris: Vivès, 1855–78.
Sylvester of Ferrara, Francis, OP. *Commentaria in libros quatuor contra gentiles sancti Thomae de Aquino*. In *Sancti Thomae Aquinatis Doctoris Angelici Opera Omnia iussu edita Leonis XIII P.M.*, vols. XIII–XV. Rome: Commissio Leonina, 1918–26.

CLASSICAL, PATRISTIC, AND MEDIEVAL WORKS

Aristotle. *Categories. On Interpretation. Prior Analytics*. Translated by H. P. Cooke and Hugh Tredennick. Loeb Classical Library 325. Cambridge, Mass.: Harvard University Press, 1938.

———. *Metaphysics Books X–XIV. Oeconomica. Magna Moralia*. Translated by Hugh Tredennick and C. Cyril Armstrong. Loeb Classical Library 28. Cambridge, Mass.: Harvard University Press, 1935.

———. *Nicomachean Ethics*. Translated by H. Rackham. Loeb Classical Library 73. New York: G. P. Putnam's Sons, 1926.

———. *On Sophistical Refutations. On Coming-to-be and Passing Away. On the Cosmos*. Translated by E. S. Forster and D. J. Furley. Loeb Classical Library 400. Cambridge, Mass.: Harvard University Press, 1955.

———. *On the Soul. Parva Naturalia. On Breath*. Translated by W. S. Hett. Loeb Classical Library 288. Cambridge, Mass.: Harvard University Press, 1957.

———. *Physics, or Natural Hearing*. Translated by Glen Coughlin. William of Moerbeke Translation Series. South Bend, Ind.: St. Augustine's Press, 2004.

———. *Posterior Analytics. Topica*. Translated by Hugh Tredennick and E. S. Forster. Loeb Classical Library 391. Cambridge, Mass.: Harvard University Press, 1960.

---. *The Works of Aristotle*. Translated under the editorship of W. D. Ross and J. A. Smith. Oxford: Clarendon Press, 1910–31.

Augustine. *City of God*, vol. I: *Books 1–3*. Translated by George E. McCracken. Loeb Classical Library 411. Cambridge, Mass.: Harvard University Press, 1957.

---. *City of God*, vol. II: *Books 4–7*. Translated by William M. Green. Loeb Classical Library 412. Cambridge, Mass.: Harvard University Press, 1963.

---. *City of God*, vol. III: *Books 8–11*. Translated by David S. Wiesen. Loeb Classical Library 413. Cambridge, Mass.: Harvard University Press, 1968.

---. *City of God*, vol. IV: *Books 12–15*. Translated by Philip Levine. Loeb Classical Library 414. Cambridge, Mass.: Harvard University Press, 1966.

---. *City of God*, vol. V: *Books 16–18.35*. Translated by Eva M. Sanford and William M. Green. Loeb Classical Library 415. Cambridge, Mass.: Harvard University Press, 1965.

---. *City of God*, vol. VI: *Books 18.36–20*. Translated by William Chase Green. Loeb Classical Library 416. Cambridge, Mass.: Harvard University Press, 1960.

---. *City of God*, vol. VII: *Books 21–22*. Translated by William M. Green. Loeb Classical Library 417. Cambridge, Mass.: Harvard University Press, 1972.

---. *The Confessions*. Translated by Maria Boulding, OSB, in *The Works of St. Augustine: A Translation for the 21st Century*, 1.1. Hyde Park, N.Y.: New City Press, 1997.

---. *De Genesi ad litteram libri duodecim. La génèse au sens littéral en douze livres* (I–VII). Bibliothèque Augustinienne 48. Turnhout: Brepols, 1972.

---. *De Genesi ad litteram libri duodecim. La génèse au sens littéral en douze livres* (VIII–XII). Bibliothèque Augustinienne 49. Turnhout: Brepols, 1972.

---. *Epistula CXLVII* (*Liber ad Paulinam de videndo Dei*). In *CSEL* 44, *S. Aureli Augustini Operum Sectio II: S. Augustini Epistulae*, 274–331. Leipzig: Freytag, 1904.

---. *Homilies on the First Epistle of John* (*Tractatus in Epistolam Joannis ad Parthos*). In *The Works of St. Augustine: A Translation for the 21st Century*, translated by Boniface Ramsey, 3.14. Hyde Park, N.Y.: New City Press, 2008.

---. *On Christian Doctrine*. Translated by J. F. Shaw. In *Nicene and Post-Nicene Fathers*, vol. 2: *Augustine: City of God, Christian Doctrine*, edited by Philip Schaff. Peabody, Mass.: Hendrickson Publishers, 1995.

---. *Sermo 169*. In *PL* 38:915–26.

---. *Tractatus in Joannis Evangelium CXXIV*. 2 vols. Edited with commentary by H. Hurter, SJ. Paris: Lethielleux, 1884.

---. *True Religion* (*De vera religione*). Translated by Edmund Hill, OP. In *The Works of St. Augustine: A Translation for the 21st Century*, 1.8. Hyde Park, N.Y.: New City Press, 2005.

Boethius. *Tractates. The Consolation of Philosophy*. Translated by H. F. Stewart, E. K. Rand, and S. J. Tester. Loeb Classical Library 74. Cambridge, Mass.: Harvard University Press, 1973.

Chrysostom, John. *Homilies on Matthew*. In *PG* 57.

Dante Alighieri. *The Comedy of Dante Alighieri the Florentine. Cantica III: Paradise* (*Il Paradiso*). Translated by Dorothy L. Sayers. New York: Basic Books, 1962.

———. *The Divine Comedy. Inferno 1: Text and Translation.* Translated by Charles S. Singleton. Princeton, N.J.: Princeton University Press, 1970.
———. *The Divine Comedy. Purgatorio 1: Text and Translation.* Translated by Charles S. Singleton. Princeton, N.J.: Princeton University Press, 1973.
———. *The Divine Comedy. Paradiso 1: Italian Text and Translation.* Translated by Charles S. Singleton. Princeton, N.J.: Princeton University Press, 1975.
Frachet, Gérard de. *Vitae Fratrum Ordinis Praedicatorum* (1260). Monumenta Ordinis Fratrum Praedicatorum Historica. Edited by Benedictus Maria Reichert, OP. Louvain: Charpentier and Schoonjans, 1896.
Gregory the Great. *Sancti Gregorii Magni Moralia in Job.* Edited by Marc Adriaen. Turnhout: Brepols, 1985.
———. *Morals on the Book of Job.* Translated by James Bliss. Oxford: John Henry Parker, 1844–50.
Lombard, Peter. *Libri IV sententiarum.* Studio et cura PP. Collegii S. Bonaventurae in lucem editi. Secunda editio ad fidem antiquiorum codicum mss. iterum recognita. Ad Claras Aquas: Typographia Collegii S. Bonaventurae, 1916.
———. *The Sentences*, Book 1: *The Mystery of the Trinity.* Translated by Giulio Silano. Toronto: Pontifical Institute of Mediaeval Studies, 2007.
———. *The Sentences*, Book 2: *On Creation.* Translated by Giulio Silano. Toronto: Pontifical Institute of Mediaeval Studies, 2008.
———. *The Sentences*, Book 3: *On the Incarnation of the Word.* Translated by Giulio Silano. Toronto: Pontifical Institute of Mediaeval Studies, 2008.
———. *The Sentences*, Book 4: *On the Doctrine of Signs.* Translated by Giulio Silano. Toronto: Pontifical Institute of Mediaeval Studies, 2010.
Plato. *The Republic*, vol. 1: *Books I–V.* Translated by Paul Shorey. Loeb Classical Library 237. Cambridge, Mass.: Harvard University Press, 1930.
———. *The Republic*, vol. 2: *Books VI–X.* Translated by Paul Shorey. Loeb Classical Library 276. Cambridge, Mass.: Harvard University Press, 1935.

PAPAL, CONCILIAR, AND MAGISTERIALLY INVITED DOCUMENTS, AS WELL AS PAPAL WRITINGS

All papal pronouncements from Leo XIII onward can be found online at vatican.va or papalencyclicals.net.

Benedict XVI, Pope. *Letter of His Holiness Benedict XVI to the Participants of the Plenary Session of the Congregation for the Causes of Saints.* April 24, 2006.
———. *Address at Regensburg (Regensburg Lecture)* on "Faith, Reason and the University. Memories and Reflections." University of Regensburg. September 12, 2006.
———. *Sacramentum Caritatis.* Post-Synodal Apostolic Exhortation. February 22, 2007.
———. *Angelus.* Saint Peter's Square, Rome. March 25, 2007.
———. *Spe Salvi.* Encyclical Letter. November 30, 2007.
———. *General Audience.* Papal Summer Residence, Castel Gandolfo. August 11, 2010.

———. *Porta Fidei*. Apostolic Letter. October 11, 2011.
Benedict XVI, Pope (as Joseph Ratzinger). *Jesus of Nazareth: From the Baptism in the Jordan to the Transfiguration*. New York: Doubleday, 2007.
———. *Jesus of Nazareth: Holy Week: From the Entrance into Jerusalem to the Resurrection*. San Francisco, Calif.: Ignatius Press, 2011.
———. *Jesus of Nazareth: The Infancy Narratives*. New York: Image Books, 2012.
Catechism of the Catholic Church. Second Edition Revised in Accordance with the Official Latin Text Promulgated by Pope John Paul II. Vatican City: Libreria Editrice Vaticana, 1997.
Congregation for the Doctrine of the Faith. *Letter on Certain Questions Concerning Eschatology*. May 17, 1979.
———. *Doctrinal Commentary on the Concluding Formula of the* Professio Fidei. June 29, 1998.
Daily Roman Missal. Edited by James Socias. 7th ed. Woodridge, Ill.: Midwest Theological Forum, 2012.
Decrees of the Ecumenical Councils. 2 vols. Edited by Norman P. Tanner, SJ. London / Washington, D.C.: Sheed and Ward / Georgetown University Press, 1990.
Denzinger, Heinrich. *Enchiridion symbolorum definitionum et declarationum de rebus fidei et morum. Kompendium der Glaubensbekenntnisse und kirchlichen Lehrentscheidungen*. Edited by Peter Hünermann. 40th ed. Freiburg: Herder, 2005.
———. *Compendium of Creeds, Definitions, and Declarations on Matters of Faith and Morals*. Revised, enlarged, and, in collaboration with Helmut Hoping, edited by Peter Hünermann, Robert Fastiggi, and Anne Englund Nash. 43rd ed. San Francisco, Calif.: Ignatius Press, 2012.
Finn, Robert W. *Blessed Are the Pure of Heart: A Pastoral Letter on the Dignity of the Human Person and the Dangers of Pornography*. Available at issuu.com/knightsofcolumbus/docs/323.
Francis, Pope. *Address of the Holy Father, Meeting for Religious Liberty with the Hispanic Community and Other Immigrants*. Independence Mall, Philadelphia. September 26, 2015.
———. *Lumen Fidei*. Encyclical Letter. June 29, 2013.
International Theological Commission. *The Interpretation of Dogma*. 1990.
John Paul II, Pope. *Veritatis Splendor*. Encyclical Letter. August 6, 1993.
———. *Fides et Ratio*. Encyclical Letter. September 14, 1998.
———. *Theotokos—Woman, Mother, Disciple: A Catechesis on Mary, Mother of God*. Boston: Pauline Books and Media, 2000.
———. *Ecclesia de Eucharistia*. Encyclical Letter. April 17, 2003.
———. *Man and Woman He Created Them: A Theology of the Body*. Translated and introduced by Michael Waldstein. Boston: Pauline Books and Media, 2006.
Lambertini, Cardinal Prosper (Pope Benedict XIV). *De servorum Dei beatificatione et beatorum canonizatione*, vol. 3. Rome: Excudebant Nicolaus et Marcus Palearini, 1748.
Leo XIII, Pope. *Mirae Caritatis*. Encyclical Letter. May 28, 1902.
Paul VI, Pope. *Mysterium Fidei*. Encyclical Letter. September 3, 1965.

Selected Bibliography 455

———. Address during the Last General Meeting of the Second Vatican Council. December 7, 1965.
———. *Solemni Hac Liturgia* (*Credo of the People of God*). June 30, 1968.
Pius X, Pope. *Ad Diem Illum Laetissimum*. Encyclical Letter. February 2, 1904.
Pius XII, Pope. *Mediator Dei*. Encyclical Letter. November 20, 1947.
———. *Munificentissimus Deus*. Apostolic Constitution. November 1, 1950.
Saint Dominic Missal. Latin–English. New York, N.Y.: Saint Dominic Missal, 1959.
Second Extraordinary General Assembly of the Synod of Bishops. *The Extraordinary Synod—1985: Message to the People of God*. Boston: St. Paul Editions, 1985.
Vatican Council II. *Gaudium et Spes*. December 7, 1965.

MODERN WORKS

Akkara, Anto. "Newly Beatified Indian Lay Martyr Praised for Refusing to Reject Faith." *Catholic News Service*, December 4, 2012. Available at catholicnew.com/data/stories/cns/1205075.htm.
Alfaro, Juan, SJ. "Supernaturalitas fidei iuxta S. Thomam." *Gregorianum* 44 (1963): 501–42 and 731–87.
Allen, John L., Jr. "Don Pino: The Most Important Beatification of the Early 21st Century." *National Catholic Reporter*, May 10, 2013. Available at ncronline.org/blogs/allthings-catholic/don-pino-most-important-beatification-early-21st-century.
Anderson, Gary A. *Sin: A History*. New Haven, Conn.: Yale University Press, 2009.
Angelic Warfare Confraternity. Available at angelicwarfare.org.
Anscombe, G. E. M. *Intention*. 2nd ed. Ithaca, N.Y.: Cornell University Press, 1963.
Arintero, John G., OP. *The Mystical Evolution in the Development and Vitality of the Church*. 2 vols. Translated by Jordan Aumann, OP. St. Louis, Mo.: Herder, 1949.
Ashley, Benedict M., OP. "Integral Human Fulfillment according to Germain Grisez." In his *The Ashley Reader: Redeeming Reason*, 225–69. Naples, Fla.: Sapientia Press, 2006.
———. *The Way toward Wisdom: An Interdisciplinary and Intercultural Introduction to Metaphysics*. Notre Dame, Ind.: University of Notre Dame Press, 2006.
Aubert, Roger. *Le problème de l'acte de foi: Données traditionelles et résultats des controverses récentes*. Louvain: E. Warny, 1958.
Austriaco, Nicanor Pier Giorgio, OP. *Biomedicine and Beatitude: An Introduction to Catholic Bioethics*. Washington, D.C.: The Catholic University of America Press, 2011.
Banks, Russell. *Lost Memory of Skin*. New York: HarperCollins, 2011.
Balthasar, Hans Urs von. "Human Religion and the Religion of Jesus Christ." In *New Elucidations*, translated by Sr. Mary Theresilde Skerry, 74–87. San Francisco, Calif.: Ignatius Press, 1986.
———. *Dare We Hope "That All Men Be Saved"?: With a Short Discourse on Hell*. Translated by David Kipp and Lothar Krauth. San Francisco, Calif.: Ignatius Press, 1988.
———. *Apokalypse der deutschen Seele: Studien zu einer Lehre von letzten Haltungen*. 3 vols. 3rd ed. Freiburg: Johannes Verlag Einsiedeln, 1998.

Barth, Karl. "Gottes Offenbarung als Aufhebung der Religion." In *Kirchliche Dogmatik* I/2, §17, 304–97. Zürich: Theologischer Verlag Zürich, 1940.

———. *On Religion: The Revelation of God as the Sublimation of Religion*. Translated by Garrett Green. New York: T and T Clark, 2006.

Bartmann, Peter. *Das Gebot und die Tugend der Liebe: Über den Umgang mit konfliktbezogenen Affekten*. Stuttgart: Kohlhammer, 1998.

Bauckham, Richard. *Jesus and the Eyewitnesses: The Gospels as Eyewitness Testimony*. 2nd ed. Grand Rapids, Mich.: Eerdmans, 2017.

Beck, Heinrich. *Der Akt-Charakter des Seins: Eine spekulative Weiterführung der Seinslehre Thomas v. Aquins aus einer Anregung durch das dialektische Prinzip Hegels*. Munich: Max Hueber, 1965.

Bellah, Robert N. *Religion in Human Evolution: From the Paleolithic to the Axial Age*. Cambridge, Mass.: Belknap Press, 2011.

Bentley, G. E., Jr. *The Stranger from Paradise: A Biography of William Blake*. New Haven, Conn.: Yale University Press, 2001.

Berning, Vincent. *Martin Honecker (1888–1941): Auf dem Wege von der Logik zur Metaphysik—Die Grundzüge seines kritisch-realistischen Denkens*. Weilheim: Gustav-Siewert-Akademie, 2003.

Bethke, Jefferson. "Why I Hate Religion, But Love Jesus." Available at youtube.com/watch?v=1IAhDGYlpqY.

Betz, John. "Review Essay: Paul J. Griffiths and Reinhard Hütter, editors, *Reason and the Reasons of Faith*." *Pro Ecclesia* 16, no. 2 (2007): 218–30.

Bilokapić, Ante. "Die Erbsünde in der Lehre des Matthias Flacius Illyricus." In *Matthias Flacius Illyricus—Leben & Werk*, Internationales Symposium, Mannheim, 1991, edited by Josip Matešić, 43–52. Munich: Südosteuropa-Gesellschaft, 1993.

Blanchette, Oliva. *The Perfection of the Universe according to Aquinas: A Teleological Cosmology*. University Park: Pennsylvania State University Press, 1992.

———. *Philosophy of Being: A Reconstructive Essay in Metaphysics*. Washington, D.C.: The Catholic University of America Press, 2003.

Blankenhorn, Bernard, OP. *The Mystery of Union with God: Dionysian Mysticism in Albert the Great and Thomas Aquinas*. Washington, D.C.: The Catholic University of America Press, 2015.

Blumenberg, Hans. *The Legitimacy of the Modern Age*. Translated by Robert M. Wallace. Cambridge, Mass.: MIT Press, 1983.

Böckenförde, Ernst-Wolfgang. *State, Society and Liberty: Studies in Political Theory and Constitutional Law*. Translated by J. A. Underwood. New York: Berg Publications, 1991.

Boeve, Lieven. *Interrupting Tradition: An Essay on Christian Faith in a Postmodern Context*. Leuven: Peeters, 2003.

Bonino, Serge-Thomas, OP. *Angels and Demons: A Catholic Introduction*. Translated by Michael J. Miller. Washington, D.C.: The Catholic University of America Press, 2016.

The Book of Concord: The Confessions of the Evangelical Lutheran Church. Translated and edited by Theodore Tappert in collaboration with Jaroslav Pelikan, Robert H. Fischer, and Arthur C. Piepkorn. Philadephia: Fortress, 1959.

Bourke, Vernon J. "The Role of *Habitus* in the Thomistic Metaphysics of Potency

and Act." In *Essays in Thomism*, edited by Robert E. Brennan, OP, 101–10 and 370–73. New York: Sheed and Ward, 1942.
Bouyer, Louis. *The Seat of Wisdom: An Essay on the Place of the Virgin Mary in Christian Theology*. Translated by A. V. Littledale. New York: Pantheon, 1962.
Bowler, Kate. *Blessed: A History of the American Prosperity Gospel*. Oxford: Oxford University Press, 2013.
Boyle, Leonard E. *The Setting of the "Summa Theologiae" of Saint Thomas Aquinas*. Toronto: Pontifical Institute of Mediaeval Studies, 1982.
Bradley, Denis J. M. *Aquinas on the Twofold Human Good: Reason and Human Happiness in Aquinas's Moral Science*. Washington, D.C.: The Catholic University of America Press, 1997.
Braine, David. *The Human Person: Animal and Spirit*. Notre Dame, Ind.: University of Notre Dame Press, 1992.
———. "The Debate between Henri de Lubac and His Critics." *Nova et Vetera* (English edition) 6, no. 3 (2008): 543–90.
———. *Language and Human Understanding: The Roots of Creativity in Speech and Thought*. Washington, D.C.: The Catholic University of America Press, 2014.
Brock, Stephen L. *Action and Conduct: Thomas Aquinas and the Theory of Action*. Edinburgh: T and T Clark, 1998.
———. "Intentional Being, Natural Being, and the First-person Perspective in Thomas Aquinas." *The Thomist* 77, no. 1 (2013): 103–33.
———. "On the Causality of the Prayer of Petition: C. S. Lewis, Peter Geach, and Thomas Aquinas." *Acta Philosophica* 23, no. 1 (2014): 79–87.
———. *The Philosophy of Saint Thomas Aquinas: A Sketch*. Eugene, Ore.: Cascade Books, 2015.
Bulgakov, Sergius. "On the Question of the Apocatastasis of the Fallen Spirits (In Connection with the Doctrine of S. Gregory of Nyssa)." In *Apocatastasis and Transfiguration*, translated by Boris Jakim, 7–30. New Haven, Conn.: Variable Press, 1995.
———. *The Bride of the Lamb*. Translated by Boris Jakim. Grand Rapids, Mich.: Eerdmans, 2002.
Caputo, John, and Gianni Vattimo. *After the Death of God*. Edited by Jeffrey W. Robbins. New York: Columbia University Press, 2007.
Carlo, William E. *The Ultimate Reducibility of Essence to Existence in Existential Metaphysics*. The Hague: Martinus Nijhoff, 1966.
Cavanaugh, William T. *The Myth of Religious Violence: Secular Ideology and the Roots of Modern Conflict*. New York: Oxford University Press, 2009.
Cessario, Romanus, OP. *The Godly Image: Christ and Salvation in Catholic Thought from Anselm to Aquinas*. Petersham: St. Bede's Publications, 1990.
———. *Christian Faith and the Theological Life*. Washington, D.C.: The Catholic University of America Press, 1996.
———. "Duplex Ordo Cognitionis." In *Reason and the Reasons of Faith*, edited by Paul J. Griffiths and Reinhard Hütter, 327–38. New York: T and T Clark International, 2005.

———. *The Moral Virtues and Theological Ethics*. 2nd ed. Notre Dame, Ind.: University of Notre Dame Press, 2009.

———. "Sonship, Sacrifice, and Satisfaction: The Divine Friendship in Aquinas and the Renewal of Christian Anthropology." In Romanus Cessario, OP, *Theology and Sanctity*, ed. Cajetan Cuddy, OP, 69–98. Ave Maria, Fla.: Sapientia Press of Ave Maria, 2014.

Chenu, Marie-Dominique, OP. "Pro supernaturalitate fidei illustranda." In *Xenia Thomistica*, edited by Sadoc Szabo, 3:297–307. Rome: Polyglottis Vaticanis, 1925.

———. *La théologie comme science au XIIIe siècle*. 3rd ed. Paris: Vrin, 1957.

Christoph, Markus, SJM. "Justice as an Infused Virtue in the *Secunda Secundae* and Its Implications for Our Understanding of the Moral Life." STD diss., University of Fribourg, 2011.

Clark, Patrick M. *Perfection in Death: The Christological Dimension of Courage in Aquinas*. Washington, D.C.: The Catholic University of America Press, 2015.

Coerver, Robert Florent. *The Quality of Facility in the Moral Virtues*. Washington, D.C.: The Catholic University of America Press, 1946.

Cole, Basil, OP. *The Hidden Enemies of the Priesthood: The Contributions of St. Thomas Aquinas*. Staten Island, N.Y.: Society of St. Paul, 2007.

Congar, Yves M.-J., OP. *Tradition and Traditions: A Historical Essay and a Theological Essay*. Translated by Michael Naseby and Thomas Rainborough. New York: Macmillan, 1967.

Cory, Therese Scarpelli. *Aquinas on Human Self-Knowledge*. Cambridge: Cambridge University Press, 2014.

Cunningham, Francis L. B., OP. *The Indwelling of the Trinity: A Historico-Doctrinal Study of the Theory of St. Thomas Aquinas*. Dubuque, Iowa: Priory Press, 1955.

Daguet, François, OP. *Théologie du dessein divin chez Thomas d'Aquin: Finis o mnium Ecclesia*. Foreword by Cardinal Christoph Schönborn. Paris: Vrin, 2003.

Dahm, Brandon. "Distinguishing Desire and Parts of Happiness: A Response to Germain Grisez." *American Catholic Philosophical Quarterly* 89, no. 1 (2015): 97–114.

Day, Dorothy. *All the Way to Heaven: The Selected Letters of Dorothy Day*. Edited by Robert Ellsberg. New York: Image Books, 2010.

Decosimo, David. *Ethics as a Work of Charity: Thomas Aquinas and Pagan Virtue*. Stanford, Calif.: Stanford University Press, 2014.

Dedmon, Jonathan. "Is the Internet Bad for Your Marriage? Online Affairs, Pornographic Sites Playing Greater Role in Divorces." Press release from American Academy of Matrimonial Lawyers, 2002. Available at prnewswire.com/news-releases/is-the-internet-bad-for-your-marriage-online-affairs-porno graphic-sites-playing-greater-role-in-divorces-76826727.html.

De Koninck, Charles. *The Writings of Charles de Koninck*. 2 vols. Edited and translated by Ralph McInerny. Notre Dame, Ind.: University of Notre Dame Press, 2008–9.

Dewan, Lawrence, OP. "Truth and Happiness." *Proceedings of the American Catholic Philosophical Association* 67 (1993): 1–20.

———. *Form and Being: Studies in Thomistic Metaphysics*. Washington, D.C.: The Catholic University of America Press, 2006.

———. "'Objectum': Notes on the Invention of a Word." In his *Wisdom, Law, and Virtue: Essays in Thomistic Ethics*, 403–43. New York: Fordham University Press, 2007.

DeYoung, Rebecca Konyndyk. "Resistance to the Demands of Love: Aquinas on the Vice of *Acedia*." *The Thomist* 68, no. 2 (2004): 173–204.

———. *Glittering Vices: A New Look at the Seven Deadly Sins and Their Remedies*. Grand Rapids, Mich.: Brazos, 2009.

———. "Aquinas on the Vice of Sloth: Three Interpretive Issues." *The Thomist* 75, no. 1 (2011): 43–64.

DeYoung, Rebecca Konyndyk, Colleen McCluskey, and Christina Van Dyke. *Aquinas's Ethics: Metaphysical Foundations, Moral Theory, and Theological Context*. Notre Dame, Ind.: University of Notre Dame Press, 2009.

Divry, Édouard, OP. *La transfiguration selon l'orient et l'occident: Grégoire Palamas–Thomas d'Aquin: vers un dénouement oecuménique*. Paris: Téqui, 2009.

Doidge, Norman. *The Brain that Changes Itself: Stories of Personal Triumph from the Frontiers of Brain Science*. New York: Vintage, 2007.

Dondaine, Hyacinthe-François, OP. "L'objet et le 'medium' de la vision béatifique chez les théologiens du XIIIe siècle." *Recherches de théologie ancienne et médiévale* 19 (1952): 60–130.

Dörnemann, Holger. *Freundschaft als Paradigma der Erlösung*. Würzburg: Echter, 1997.

Dostoyevsky, Fyodor. *Demons*. Translated by Richard Pevear and Larissa Volokhonsky. New York: Vintage, 1995.

Dulles, Avery, SJ. *The Assurance of Things Hoped For: A Theology of Christian Faith*. New York: Oxford University Press, 1994.

Dümpelmann, Leo. *Kreation als ontisch-ontologisches Verhältnis: Zur Metaphysik der Schöpfungstheologie des Thomas von Aquin*. Freiburg: Karl Alber, 1969.

Dunnington, Kent. *Addiction and Virtue: Beyond the Models of Disease and Choice*. Downers Grove, Ill.: Intervarsity Press, 2011.

Dupré, Louis. *Passage to Modernity: An Essay in the Hermeneutics of Nature and Culture*. New Haven, Conn.: Yale University Press, 1993.

Eliade, Mircea. *The Sacred and the Profane: The Nature of Religion*. New York: Harcourt, Brace and Co., 1959.

"Enough is Enough: Making the Internet Safer for Children and Families." Available at *enough.org/stats_porn_industry*.

Eschweiler, Karl. *Die zwei Wege der neueren Theologie: Georg Hermes—Matth. Jos. Scheeben. Eine kritische Untersuchung des Problems der theologischen Erkenntnis*. Augsburg: Filser, 1926.

Eubank, Nathan. *Wages of Cross-Bearing and Debt of Sin: The Economy of Heaven in Matthew's Gospel*. Berlin: Walter de Gruyter, 2013.

Fabro, Cornelio, CPS. *Participation et Causalité selon S. Thomas d'Aquin*. Foreword by L. de Raeymaeker. Louvain / Paris: Publications Universitaires de Louvain / Éditions Béatrice-Nauwelaerts, 1961.

———. *God in Exile: Modern Atheism: A Study of the Internal Dynamic of Modern*

Atheism, from Its Roots in the Cartesian Cogito to the Present Day. Edited and translated by Arthur Gibson. New York: Newman Press, 1968.

———. "The Intensive Hermeneutics of Thomistic Philosophy: The Notion of Participation." *Review of Metaphysics* 27, no. 3 (1974): 449–91.

———. *La nozione metafisica di partecipazione secondo San Tommaso d'Aquino.* Opere Complete 3. Segni: Editrice del Verbo Incarnato, 2005.

———. *La svolta antropologica di Karl Rahner.* Opere Complete 25. Segni: Editrice del Verbo Incarnato, 2011.

———. *Introduzione all' ateismo moderno.* Opere Complete 21. Segni: Editrice del Verbo Incarnato, 2013.

———. *God: An Introduction to the Problems in Theology.* In *Selected Works of Cornelio Fabro,* vol. 9, translated by Joseph T. Papa and edited by Nathaniel Dreyer. Chillium: IVE Press, 2017.

Falanga, Anthony J., CM. *Charity the Form of the Virtues According to Saint Thomas.* Washington, D.C.: The Catholic University of America Press, 1948.

Farrow, Douglas. *Desiring a Better Country: Forays in Political Theology.* Montreal: McGill-Queens University Press, 2015.

Feingold, Lawrence. *The Natural Desire to See God According to St. Thomas Aquinas and His Interpreters.* 2nd ed. Naples, Fla.: Sapientia Press, 2010.

Feser, Edward. *The Last Superstition: A Refutation of the New Atheism.* South Bend, Ind.: St. Augustine's Press, 2010.

———. *Scholastic Metaphysics: A Contemporary Introduction.* Heusenstamm: Editiones Scholasticae, 2014.

———. *Five Proofs of the Existence of God: Aristotle, Plotinus, Augustine, Aquinas, Leibniz.* San Francisco, Calif.: Ignatius Press, 2017.

Feuerbach, Ludwig. *The Essence of Christianity.* Translated by George Eliot. Westminster: Penguin Random House, 1989.

Fields, Stephen M., SJ. *Analogies of Transcendence: An Essay on Nature, Grace, and Modernity.* Washington, D.C.: The Catholic University of America Press, 2016.

Flacius Illyricus, Matthias, and Victorinus Strigel. *Disputatio de originali peccato et libero arbitrio, inter Matthiam Flacium Illyricum et Victorinum Strigelium, publice Vinariae per integram hebdomadam, praesentibus Illustriss. Saxoniae Principus, Anno 1560. Initio Mensis Augusti.* Weimar, 1562.

Flanagan, Owen. *The Bodhisattva's Brain: Buddhism Naturalized.* Cambridge, Mass.: MIT Press, 2011.

Flynn, Gabriel, Paul D. Murray, and Patricia Kelly, eds. *Ressourcement: A Movement of Renewal in Twentieth-Century Catholic Thought.* Oxford: Oxford University Press, 2011.

Forster, Karl. *Die Verteidigung der Lehre des heiligen Thomas von der Gottesschau durch Johannes Capreolus.* Munich: Karl Zink Verlag, 1955.

Foucault, Michel. *The Order of Things: An Archaeology of the Human Sciences.* Translated by Alan Sheridan. New York: Random House, 1970.

———. *The Archaeology of Knowledge & The Discourse on Language.* Translated by A. M. Sheridan Smith. New York: Pantheon Books, 1972.

———. *Discipline and Punish: The Birth of the Prison.* Translated by Alan Sheridan. New York: Pantheon Books, 1978.

Froget, Barthélemy, OP. *The Indwelling of the Holy Spirit in the Souls of the Just According to the Teaching of St. Thomas Aquinas*. Translated by Sydney A. Raemers. Westminster, Md.: Newman Press, 1952.

Gaine, Simon Francis, OP. *Did the Saviour See the Father? Christ, Salvation, and the Vision of God*. London: Bloomsbury T and T Clark, 2015.

Gardeil, Ambroise, OP. *Le Donné révélé et la théologie*. 2nd ed. Paris: Cerf, 1932.

Garrigou-Lagrange, Réginald, OP. *Le Réalisme du Principe de Finalité*. Paris: Desclee de Brouwer et Cie, 1932. German translation: *Der Realismus der Finalität*, translated by Joachim Volkmann. Heusenstamm: Editiones Scholasticae, 2011.

———. *God, His Existence and His Nature: A Thomistic Solution of Certain Agnostic Antinomies*. 2 vols. Translated by Bede Rose, OSB. St. Louis: Herder, 1934.

———. *The Mother of the Saviour and Our Interior Life*. Translated by Bernard J. Kelly, CSSP. Dublin: Golden Eagle, 1949.

———. *The Sense of Mystery: Clarity and Obscurity in the Intellectual Life*. Translated by Matthew K. Minerd. Steubenville, Ohio: Emmaus Academic, 2017.

Geiger, Louis-Bertrand, OP. *La participation dans la philosophie de s. Thomas d'Aquin*. Paris: Vrin, 1942.

George, Francis Cardinal, OMI. "The Wrong Side of History." *The Cardinal's Column, Catholic New World. Newspaper for the Archdiocese of Chicago*, October 21–November 3, 2012.

Gilson, Étienne. *The Christian Philosophy of St. Thomas Aquinas*. Translated by L. K. Shook, CSB. Notre Dame, Ind.: University of Notre Dame Press, 1994.

———. "Sur la problématique thomiste de la vision béatifique." *Archives d'histoire doctrinale et littéraire du moyen âge* 31 (1964): 67–88.

———. *Thomist Realism and the Critique of Knowledge*. Translated by Mark A. Wauck. San Francisco, Calif.: Ignatius Press, 1986.

———. *From Aristotle to Darwin and Back Again: A Journey in Final Causality, Species, and Evolution*. Translated by John Lyon. San Francisco, Calif.: Ignatius Press, 2009.

Grabmann, Martin. *Die theologische Erkenntnis- und Einleitungslehre des hl. Thomas von Aquin auf Grund seiner Schrift "In Böethium de Trinitate." Im Zusammenhang der Scholastik des 13. und beginnenden 14. Jahrhunderts dargestellt*. Fribourg: Paulusverlag, 1948.

Grabowski, John S. *Sex and Virtue: An Introduction to Sexual Ethics*. Washington, D.C.: The Catholic University of America Press, 2003.

Gradl, Stefan. *Deus beatitudo hominis: Eine evangelische Annäherung an die Glückslehre des Thomas von Aquin*. Leuven: Peeters, 2004.

Gregory, Brad S. *The Unintended Reformation: How a Religious Revolution Secularized Society*. Cambridge, Mass.: Belknap Press, 2012.

Greschat, Katharina. *Die Moralia in Job Gregor des Großen: Ein christologisch-ekklesiologischer Kommentar*. Tübingen: Mohr Siebeck, 2005.

Griffiths, Paul J. *Intellectual Appetite: A Theological Grammar*. Washington, D.C.: The Catholic University of America Press, 2009.

———. "In the Red." *Commonweal* 137, no. 2 (January 29, 2010): 25–26.

———. "Impossible Pluralism: Choosing between Universal Academic History and

Christian Faith." *First Things* (June 2013), available at firstthings.com/article/2013/06/impossible-pluralism.
———. *Decreation: The Last Things of All Creatures*. Waco, Tex.: Baylor University Press, 2014.
Grisez, Germain. *The Way of the Lord Jesus Christ: Christian Moral Principles*. Chicago: Franciscan Herald Press, 1983.
———. "A Critique of Russell Hittinger's Book, *A Critique of the New Natural Law Theory*." *The New Scholasticism* 62, no. 4 (1988): 438–65.
———. "The True Ultimate End of Human Beings: The Kingdom, Not God Alone." *Theological Studies* 69, no. 1 (2008): 38–61.
Grisez, Germain, et al. "Practical Principles, Moral Truth, and Ultimate Ends." *American Journal of Jurisprudence* 32 (1987): 99–151.
Grudzen, Corita R., et al. "Comparison of the Mental Health of Female Adult Film Performers and Other Young Women in California." *Psychiatric Services* 62 (2011): 639–45.
Guindon, Roger. *Béatitude et théologie morale chez Saint Thomas d'Aquin: Origines, interpretation*. Ottawa: Éditions de l'Université, 1956.
Habermas, Jürgen. *A Theory of Communicative Action*. 2 vols. Translated by Thomas McCarthy. Boston: Beacon, 1985.
———. *The Philosophical Discourse of Modernity: Twelve Lectures*. Translated by Frederic G. Lawrence. Cambridge, Mass.: MIT Press, 1987.
———. "Reconciliation through the Public Use of Reason: Remarks on John Rawls' Political Liberalism." *Journal of Philosophy* 92, no. 3 (1995): 109–31.
———. *Religion and Rationality: Essays on Reason, God, and Modernity*. Edited by Eduardo Mendieta. Cambridge, Mass.: MIT Press, 2002.
———. *Between Naturalism and Religion: Philosophical Essays*. Translated by Ciaran Cronin. Cambridge: Polity Press, 2008.
———. *Nachmetaphysisches Denken 2*. Frankfurt: Suhrkamp, 2012.
Habermas, Jürgen, and Joseph Ratzinger. *The Dialectics of Secularization: On Reason and Religion*. Edited with a foreword by Florian Schuller. Translated by Brian McNeil, CRV. San Francisco, Calif.: Ignatius Press, 2006.
Habermas, Jürgen, and Charles Taylor. "Dialogue: Jürgen Habermas and Charles Taylor." In *The Power of Religion in the Public Sphere: Judith Butler, Jürgen Habermas, Charles Taylor, Cornel West*, edited and introduced by Eduardo Mendieta and Jonathan VanAntwerpen, 60–69. New York: Columbia University Press, 2011.
Hain, Raymond F., IV. "Practical Virtues: Instrumental Practical Reason and the Virtues." PhD diss., University of Notre Dame, 2009.
———. "*Consilium* and the Foundations of Ethics." *The Thomist* 79, no. 1 (2015): 43–74.
Hald, Gert Martin, et al. "Pornography and Attitudes Supporting Violence against Women: Revisiting the Relationship in Nonexperimental Studies." *Aggressive Behavior* 36 (2010): 14–20.
Hald, Gert Martin, and Neil M. Malamuth. "Self-perceived Effects of Pornography Consumption." *Archives of Sexual Behaviour* 37 (2008): 614–25.

Selected Bibliography 463

Hanby, Michael. *No God, No Science? Theology, Cosmology, Biology*. Oxford: Wiley Blackwell, 2013.

Hart, David Bentley. *Atheist Delusions: The Christian Revolution and Its Fashionable Enemies*. New Haven, Conn.: Yale University Press, 2010.

———. *The Experience of God: Being, Consciousness, Bliss*. New Haven, Conn.: Yale University Press, 2013.

———. *The Hidden and the Manifest: Essays in Theology and Metaphysics*. Grand Rapids, Mich.: Eerdmans, 2017.

Hauerwas, Stanley. *With the Grain of the Universe: The Church's Witness and Natural Theology*. Grand Rapids, Mich.: Brazos, 2001.

Healy, Nicholas J. "Henri de Lubac on Nature and Grace: A Note on Some Recent Contributions to the Debate." *Communio* 35, no. 4 (2008): 535–64.

Hefner, Philip J. *The Human Factor: Evolution, Culture, and Religion*. Minneapolis, Minn.: Augsburg Fortress, 2000.

———. *Technology and Human Becoming*. Minneapolis, Minn.: Augsburg Fortress, 2003.

Heidegger, Martin. *Sein und Zeit*. 16th ed. Tübingen: Max Niemeyer Verlag, 1986 (1927). English translation: *Being and Time*, translated by John Macquarrie and Edward Robinson. New York: Harper and Row, 1962.

———. *Die Grundbegriffe der Metaphysik: Welt—Endlichkeit—Einsamkeit. Freiburger Vorlesung 1929/30*. Edited by Friedrich-Wilhelm von Herrmann. Frankfurt a.M.: Vittorio Klostermann, 1983. English translation: *The Fundamental Concepts of Metaphysics: World, Finitude, Solitude*, translated by William McNeill and Nicholas Walker. Bloomington: Indiana University Press, 1995.

Hendel, Kurt K. "Johannes Bugenhagen: A Retrospect on His 500th Birthday." *Currents in Theology and Mission* 12 (1985): 277–89.

———. "The Care of the Poor: An Evangelical Perspective." *Currents in Theology and Mission* 15 (1988): 526–32.

Herdt, Jennifer A. *Putting On Virtue: The Legacy of the Splendid Vices*. Chicago: University of Chicago Press, 2008.

Hildebrand, Dietrich von. *Christian Ethics*. New York: David McKay, 1953.

Hill, Christopher. *The World Turned Upside Down: Radical Ideas During the English Revolution*. New York: Viking Press, 1972.

Hinnebusch, William A., OP. *The History of the Dominican Order*, vol. 2: *Intellectual and Cultural Life to 1500*. New York: Alba House, 1973.

Hoeres, Walter. *Gradatio entis: Sein als Teilhabe bei Duns Scotus und Franz Suárez*. Heusenstamm: Editiones Scholasticae, 2012.

Hölderlin, Friedrich. *Selected Poems and Fragments*. Translated by Michael Hamburger. Edited by Jeremy Adler. London: Penguin, 1998.

Honnefelder, Ludger. *Scientia transcendens: Die formale Bestimmung der Seiendheit und Realität in der Metaphysik des Mittelalters und der Neuzeit (Duns Scotus, Suárez, Wolff, Kant, Peirce)*. Hamburg: Meiner, 1990.

Horkheimer, Max, and Theodor W. Adorno. *Dialectic of Enlightenment: Philosophical Fragments*. Edited by Gunzelin Schmid Noerr. Translated by Edmund Jephcott. Stanford, Calif.: Stanford University Press, 2002.

Hoye, William J. *Actualitas Omnium Actuum: Man's Beatific Vision of God as Apprehended by Thomas Aquinas*. Meisenheim am Glan: Hain, 1975.
Hudson, É. William Donald, ed. *The Is-Ought Question*. London: Macmillan, 1969.
Hugon, Édouard, OP. *Principes de philosophie: Les vingtquatre thèses thomistes*. Paris: P. Tequi, 1922.
Hume, David. *Treatise of Human Nature*. Edited by P. H. Nidditch. Second Edition. Oxford: Clarendon, 1973.
———. *Dialogues and Natural History of Religion*. Edited by J. C. A. Gaskin. Oxford: Oxford University Press, 1993.
Hütter, Reinhard. *Suffering Divine Things: Theology as Church Practice*. Translated by Doug Stott. Grand Rapids, Mich.: Eerdmans, 2000.
———. "*Desiderium Naturale Visionis Dei—Est autem duplex hominis beatitudo sive felicitas*: Some Observations about Lawrence Feingold's and John Milbank's Recent Interventions in the Debate over the Natural Desire to See God." *Nova et Vetera* (English edition) 5, no. 1 (2007): 81–131.
———. "Relinquishing the Principle of Private Judgment in Matters of Divine Truth: A Protestant Theologian's Journey into the Catholic Church." *Nova et Vetera* (English edition) 9, no. 4 (2011): 865–81.
———. *Dust Bound for Heaven: Explorations in the Theology of Thomas Aquinas*. Grand Rapids, Mich.: Eerdmans, 2012.
———. "Enlightenment: Reflections on Pope Francis' Encyclical Letter Lumen Fidei." *Nova et Vetera* (English edition) 12, no. 1 (2014): 1–10.
———. "Human Sexuality in a Fallen World: An Economy of Mercy and Grace." *Nova et Vetera* (English edition) 15, no. 2 (2017): 433–64.
Jenkins, John I., CSC. *Knowledge and Faith in Thomas Aquinas*. Cambridge: Cambridge University Press, 1997.
Jenson, Robert W. *On Thinking the Human: Resolutions of Difficult Notions*. Grand Rapids, Mich.: Eerdmans, 2003.
Journet, Charles. *L'Église du verbe incarné: Essai de théologie spéculative*. 5 vols. Saint-Maurice: Editions Saint-Augustin, 1998-2005.
Jüngel, Eberhard. *Death: The Riddle and the Mystery*. Translated by Iain and Ute Nicol. Philadelphia: Westminster, 1975.
Kant, Immanuel. *Grundlegung zur Metaphysik der Sitten*. Edited by Karl Vorländer. Leipzig: Meiner, 1920. English translation: *Groundwork of the Metaphysic of Morals*, translated and analysed by H. J. Paton. London: Routledge, 1991.
———. *Practical Philosophy*. Translated and edited by Mary Gregor. Cambridge: Cambridge University Press, 1996.
———. *Kritik der reinen Vernunft*. Edited by Raymund Schmidt. Hamburg: Meiner, 1956. English translation: *Critique of Pure Reason*, translated and edited by Paul Guyer and Allen W. Wood. Cambridge: Cambridge University Press, 1997.
———. "The End of All Things." In *Religion within the Boundaries of Mere Reason and Other Writings*, translated and edited by Allen Wood and George Di Giovanni, 193–205. Cambridge: Cambridge University Press, 1998.
Kantorowicz, Ernst H. *The King's Two Bodies: A Study in Medieval Political Theology*. Princeton, N.J.: Princeton University Press, 1957.

Kato, Testsuo-Marcel (Fabrice Hadjadj). *Traité de Bouddhisme Zen à l'usage du bourgeois d'Occident*. Paris: Éditions du Parc, 1998.
Kelsey, David. *Eccentric Existence: A Theological Anthropology*. Louisville, Ky.: Westminster John Knox, 2009.
Kerr, Gaven. *Aquinas's Way to God: The Proof in* De Ente et Essentia. Oxford: Oxford University Press, 2015.
Klubertanz, George P., SJ. *The Discursive Power: Sources and Doctrine of the Vis Cogitiva According to St. Thomas Aquinas*. St. Louis, Mo.: The Modern Schoolman, 1952.
———. *Habits and Virtues*. New York: Appleton-Century-Crofts, 1965.
Knobel, Angela McKay. "The Infused and Acquired Virtues in Aquinas' Moral Philosophy." PhD diss., University of Notre Dame, 2004.
———. "Can the Infused and Acquired Virtues Coexist in the Christian Life?" *Studies in Christian Ethics* 23, no. 4 (2010): 381–96.
———. "Two Theories of Christian Virtue." *American Catholic Philosophical Quarterly* 84, no. 3 (2010): 600–618.
Komonchak, Joseph A. "Theology and Culture at Mid-Century: The Example of Henri de Lubac." *Theological Studies* 51 (1990): 579–602.
Kors, J.-B., OP. *La Justice primitive et le Péché originel d'après s. Thomas. Les Sources. La Doctrine*. Paris: Vrien, 1930.
Kretzmann, Norman. *The Metaphysics of Theism: Aquinas's Natural Theology in* Summa contra gentiles *I-II*. 2 vols. Oxford: Clarendon Press, 1997–99.
Kromholtz, Brian, OP. *On the Last Day: The Time of the Resurrection of the Dead according to Thomas Aquinas*. Fribourg: Academic Press Fribourg, 2010.
———. "La perfection de la nature: la doctrine de saint Thomas d'Aquin sur la resurrection du corps, sa reception et son developpement." *Revue Thomiste* 116, no. 1 (2016): 57–70.
Kuhn, Johann Evangelist von. *Katholische Dogmatik*, vol. 1: *Einleitung in die katholische Dogmatik*. 2nd ed. Tübingen: Verlag der H. Laupp'schen Buchhandlung, 1859.
Lakebrink, Bernhard. *Klassische Metaphysik: Eine Auseinandersetzung mit der existentialen Anthropozentrik*. Freiburg: Rombach, 1967.
Lambert, Nathaniel M., et al. "A Love That Doesn't Last: Pornography Consumption and Weakened Commitment to One's Romantic Partner." *Journal of Social and Clinical Psychology* 31 (2012): 410–38.
Layard, Richard. *Happiness: Lessons from a New Science*. London: Penguin, 2005.
Layden, Mary Anne. Testimony given at the hearing on "The Brain Science behind Pornography Addiction." Subcommittee on Science, Technology, and Space, United States Senate, Washington, D.C., November 18, 2004. Available at ccv.org/wp-content/uploads/2010/04/Judith_Reisman_Senate_Testimony-2004.11.18.pdf.
Le Guillou, Marie-Joseph, OP. "Surnaturel." *Revue des sciences philosophiques et theologiques* 34 (1950): 226–43.
Leget, Carlo. *Living with God: Thomas Aquinas on the Relation between Life on Earth and "Life" after Death*. Leuven: Peeters, 1997.

Leonhardt, Rochus. *Glück als Vollendung des Menschseins: Die Beatitudo-Lehre des Thomas von Aquin im Horizont des Eudämonismus-Problems.* Berlin: de Gruyter, 1998.

Leuba, James Henry. *A Psychological Study of Religion: Its Origin, Function, and Future.* New York: Macmillan, 1912.

Levering, Matthew. "Sloth and the Joy of the Resurrection." In his *The Betrayal of Charity: The Sins that Sabotage Divine Love*, 41–62. Waco, Tex.: Baylor University Press, 2011.

———. *Mary's Bodily Assumption.* Notre Dame, Ind.: University of Notre Dame Press, 2014.

Lévy, Antione, OP. *Le créé et l'incréé: Maxime le confesseur et Thomas d'Aquin: aux sources de la querelle palamienne.* Paris: Vrin, 2006.

Lewis, C. S. *The Abolition of Man.* San Francisco, Calif.: HarperOne, 2001.

Lichacz, Piotr. "Did St. Thomas Aquinas Justify the Transition from 'Is' to 'Ought'?" STD diss., University of Fribourg, 2008.

Lisska, Anthony J. *Aquinas's Theory of Perception: An Analytic Reconstruction.* Oxford: Oxford University Press, 2016.

Locke, John. *Four Letters on Toleration.* London: Ward, Lock, and Tyler, 1876.

Loisy, Alfred [as A. Firmin]. "La définition de la religion." *Revue du clergé français* 18 (1899): 193–209.

——— [as A. Firmin]. "L'idée de la révélation." *Revue du clergé français* 21 (1900): 250–71.

———. *Autour d'un petit livre.* Paris: Alphonse Picard et fils, Éditeurs, 1903.

Lombardo, Nicholas E., OP. *The Logic of Desire: Aquinas on Emotion.* Washington, D.C.: The Catholic University of America Press, 2010.

———. "Boredom and Modern Culture." *Logos: A Journal of Catholic Thought and Culture* 20, no. 2 (2017): 36–59.

Lonergan, Bernard, SJ. "Theology and Understanding." *Gregorianum* 35 (1954): 630–48.

———. *Collected Works of Bernard Lonergan*, vol. 1: *Grace and Freedom: Operative Grace in the Thought of St. Thomas Aquinas.* Edited by Frederick E. Crowe and Robert M. Doran. Toronto: University of Toronto Press, 2000.

Long, Steven A. *The Teleological Grammar of the Moral Act.* Naples, Fla.: Sapientia Press, 2007.

———. *Natura Pura: On the Recovery of Nature in the Doctrine of Grace.* New York: Fordham University Press, 2010.

———. "Speculative Foundations of Moral Theology and the Causality of Grace." *Studies in Christian Ethics* 23, no. 4 (2010): 397–414.

———. "Fundamental Errors of the New Natural Law Theory." *National Catholic Bioethics Quarterly* 13, no. 1 (2013): 105–32.

———. "The Gifts of the Holy Spirit and Their Indispensability for the Christian Moral Life: Grace as *Motus*." *Nova et Vetera* (English edition) 11, no. 2 (2013): 357–73.

Lossky, Vladimir. *The Vision of God.* Translated by Asheleigh Moorhouse. Yonkers, N.Y.: St. Vladimir's Seminary Press, 1983.

Lubac, Henri de. *A Brief Catechesis on Nature and Grace*. Translated by Richard Arnandez, FSC. San Francisco, Calif.: Ignatius Press, 1984.
———. *Surnaturel: Études historiques. Nouvelle édition avec la traduction intégrale des citations latines et grecques*. Paris: Desclée de Brouwer, 1991.
———. "The Mystery of the Supernatural." In *Theology and History*, translated by Anne Englund Nash, 281–316. San Francisco, Calif.: Ignatius Press, 1996.
———. *The Mystery of the Supernatural*. Translated by Rosemary Sheed. New York: Crossroad, 1998.
———. *Augustinianism and Modern Theology*. Translated by Lancelot Sheppard. New York: Crossroad, 2000.
Lukács, Georg. *The Destruction of Reason*. Translated by Peter R. Palmer. London: Merlin Press: 1980.
Luther, Martin. *De servo arbitrio*. In *D. Martin Luthers Werke. Kritische Gesamtausgabe*, 18:600–787. Weimar: Hermann Böhlau und Nachfolger, 1883–2009. English translation: *On the Bondage of the Will*, translated by J. I. Packer and O. R. Johnston. Grand Rapids, Mich.: Baker Academic, 2012.
———. *Vorlesungen über den Römerbrief* (1515/16). Vol. 56 of *D. Martin Luthers Werke. Kritische Gesamtausgabe*. Weimar: Hermann Böhlau und Nachfolger: 1883–2009.
Lynch, Reginald M., OP. *The Cleansing of the Heart: The Sacraments as Instrumental Causes in the Thomist Tradition*. Washington, D.C.: The Catholic University of America Press, 2017.
MacDonald, Paul A. *Knowledge and the Transcendent: An Inquiry into the Mind's Relationship with God*. Washington, D.C.: The Catholic University of America Press, 2009.
Machuga, Ric. *In Defense of the Soul: What It Means to Be Human*. Grand Rapids, Mich.: Brazos, 2002.
MacIntyre, Alasdair. "The Intelligibility of Action." In *Rationality, Relativism, and Human Sciences*, edited by J. Margolis, M. Krausz, and R. M. Burian, 63–80. Dordrecht: Nijhoff, 1986.
———. *First Principles, Final Ends, and Contemporary Philosophical Issues*. Milwaukee, Wis.: Marquette University Press, 1990.
———. *Three Rival Versions of Moral Inquiry: Encyclopaedia, Genealogy, and Tradition*. Notre Dame, Ind.: University of Notre Dame Press, 1990.
———. *After Virtue*. 3rd ed. Notre Dame, Ind.: University of Notre Dame Press, 2007.
———. *Ethics in the Conflicts of Modernity: An Essay on Desire, Practical Reasoning, and Narrative*. Cambridge: Cambridge University Press, 2016.
Madden, James D. *Mind, Matter, and Nature: A Thomistic Proposal for the Philosophy of Mind*. Washington, D.C.: The Catholic University of America Press, 2013.
Malloy, Christopher J. "De Lubac on Natural Desire: Difficulties and Antitheses." *Nova et Vetera* (English edition) 9, no. 3 (2011): 567–624.
Manning, Jill C. Hearing on "The Impact of Internet Pornography on Marriage and the Family." Subcommittee on the Constitution, Civil Rights and Prop-

erty, Committee on Judiciary, United States Senate, Washington, D.C., August 2005. Available at s3.amazonaws.com/thf_media/2010/pdf/ManningTST.pdf.
Mansini, Guy, OSB. "The Abiding Theological Significance of Henri de Lubac's *Surnaturel.*" *The Thomist* 73, no. 4 (2009): 593–619.
Maritain, Jacques. *Existence and the Existent*. Translated by Lewis Galantiere and Gerald B. Phelan. New York: Pantheon, 1948.
———. *The Degrees of Knowledge* (*Distinguish to Unite*). Translated from the 4th French edition under the supervision of Gerald B. Phelan. New York: Scribner's Sons, 1959.
———. *God and the Permission of Evil*. Translated by Joseph W. Evans. Milwaukee, Wis.: Bruce Publishing, 1966.
Marschler, Thomas. *Karl Eschweiler (1886–1936): Theologische Erkenntnislehre und nationalsozialistische Ideologie*. Würzburg: Pustet, 2011.
Marshall, Bruce D. "*Quod Scit Una Uetela*: Aquinas on the Nature of Theology." In *The Theology of Thomas Aquinas*, edited by Rik van Nieuwenhove and Joseph Wawrykow, 1–35. Notre Dame, Ind.: University of Notre Dame Press, 2005.
———. "Treasures in Heaven," *First Things* 199 (January 2010): 23–26.
Martin, Regis. *The Last Things: Death, Judgment, Hell, and Heaven*. Charlotte, N.C.: TAN Books, 2014.
Mattison, William C., III. *The Sermon on the Mount and Moral Theology: A Virtue Perspective*. Cambridge: Cambridge University Press, 2017.
Mattiussi, Guido, SJ. *Les points fondamentaux de la philosophie thomiste: Commentaire des vingt-quatre thèses approuvées par la S. Congrégation des Etudes*. Translated by J. Levillain. Turin: Marietti, 1926.
McInerny, Ralph. "Prudence and Conscience." *The Thomist* 38, no. 2 (1974): 291–305.
———. *Aquinas Against the Averroists: On There Being Only One Intellect*. West Lafayette, Ind.: Purdue University Press, 1993.
———. *Characters in Search of Their Author: The Gifford Lectures Glasgow 1999–2000*. Notre Dame, Ind.: University of Notre Dame Press, 2001.
———. *Praeambula Fidei: Thomism and the God of the Philosophers*. Washington, D.C.: The Catholic University of America Press, 2006.
———. "Ethics and Metaphysics." In his *Aquinas on Human Action: A Theory of Practice*. Washington, D.C.: The Catholic University of America Press, 2012.
McKirahan, Richard. *Posterior Analytics, Principles and Proofs: Aristotle's Theory of Demonstrative Science*. Princeton, N.J.: Princeton University Press, 1992.
Merriell, D. Juvenal. *To the Image of the Trinity: A Study in the Development of Aquinas's Teaching*. Toronto: Pontifical Institute of Mediaeval Studies, 1990.
Metz, Johannes Baptist. *Christliche Anthropozentrik. Über die Denkform des Thomas von Aquin*. Munich: Kösel, 1962.
Milbank, John. *The Suspended Middle: Henri de Lubac and the Debate Concerning the Supernatural*. Grand Rapids, Mich.: Eerdmans, 2005.
Miner, Robert. *Thomas Aquinas on the Passions: A Study of Summa Theologiae 1a2ae 22–48*. Cambridge: Cambridge University Press, 2009.
Möhler, Johann Adam. *Symbolik, oder Darstellung der dogmatischen Gegensätze der Katholiken und Protestanten nach ihren Bekenntnisschriften*. Mainz: F. Kupfer-

berg, 1832. English translation: *Symbolism: Exposition of the Doctrinal Differences Between Catholics and Protestants as Evidenced by Their Symbolical Writings*, translated by James Burton Robertson. New York: Crossroad, 1997.

Moore, G. E. *Principia Ethica*. Cambridge: Cambridge University Press, 1903.

Morality in Media (National Center on Sexual Exploitation). Available at moralityinmedia.org.

Mulcahy, Bernard, OP. *Aquinas's Notion of Pure Nature and the Christian Integralism of Henri de Lubac*. New York: Peter Lang, 2011.

Mulchahey, M. Michèle. *"First the Bow is Bent in Study": Dominican Education before 1350*. Toronto: Pontifical Institute of Mediaeval Studies, 1998.

Mullady, Brian T., OP. *The Angelic Warfare Confraternity*. 4th ed. New Hope, Ky.: St. Martin de Porres Lay Dominicans, 2006.

Mullaney, T. A., OP. "Mary Immaculate in the Writings of St. Thomas." *The Thomist* 17 (1954): 433–68.

Newman, John Henry Cardinal. "The Influence of Natural and Revealed Religion Respectively." In his *Fifteen Sermons Preached before the University of Oxford between A.D. 1826 and 1843*, 16–36. Notre Dame, Ind.: University of Notre Dame Press, 1997.

———. *Certain Difficulties Felt by Anglicans in Catholic Teaching*, vol. II. London: Longmans, Green, and Co., 1888. Westminster, Md.: Christian Classics, 1969.

———. *An Essay in Aid of a Grammar of Assent*. Notre Dame, Ind.: University of Notre Dame Press, 1979 (1870).

———. "The Infidelity of the Future. Opening of St. Bernard's Seminary, 2nd October 1873." In his *Faith and Prejudice and Other Unpublished Sermons of Cardinal Newman*, edited by The Birmingham Oratory. New York: Sheed and Ward, 1956.

Nichols, Aidan, OP. "The Mariology of St. Thomas." In *Aquinas on Doctrine: A Critical Introduction*, edited by Thomas G. Weinandy, Daniel A. Keating, and John P. Yocum, 241–60. London: T and T Clark, 2004.

———. *Romance and System: The Theological Synthesis of Matthias Joseph Scheeben*. Denver, Colo.: Augustine Institute Press, 2010.

Nicolas, Jean-Hervé, OP. *Les Profondeurs de la Grâce*. Paris: Beauchesne, 1969.

———. *Synthèse dogmatique*. 2 vols. Paris: Editions Beauchesne, 1985–93.

Nietzsche, Friedrich. *Thus Spoke Zarathustra*. Edited by Adrian Del Caro and Robert B. Pippin. Translated by Adrian Del Caro. Cambridge: Cambridge University Press, 2006.

O'Brien, T. C., OP. "Appendix 1: Objects and Virtues." In Thomas Aquinas, *Summa theologiae*, vol. 31: *Faith (2a2ae 1–7)*. Edited and translated by T. C. O'Brien, OP, 178–85. Cambridge: Cambridge University Press, 2006.

O'Rourke, Fran. *Pseudo-Dionysius and the Metaphysics of Aquinas*. 2nd ed. Notre Dame, Ind.: University of Notre Dame Press, 2005.

Oakes, Edward T., SJ. "The Paradox of Nature and Grace: On John Milbank's *The Suspended Middle: Henri de Lubac and the Debate Concerning the Supernatural*." *Nova et Vetera* (English edition) 4, no. 3 (2006): 667–96.

———. "The *Surnaturel* Controversy: A Survey and a Response." *Nova et Vetera* (English edition) 9, no. 3 (2011): 625–56.

———. "Scheeben the Reconciler: Resolving the Nature-Grace Debate." *Nova et Vetera* (English edition) 11, no. 2 (2013): 435–53.

Oberman, Heiko. *The Harvest of Medieval Theology: Gabriel Biel and Late Medieval Nominalism*. Grand Rapids, Mich.: Baker Academic, 2001.

Oliver, Simon. *Philosophy, God, and Motion*. London: Routledge, 2005.

Ols, Daniel, OP. "La Bienheureuse Vierge Marie selon saint Thomas." In *Littera Sensus Sententia: Studi in onore del Prof. Clemente J. Vansteenkiste, O.P.*, edited by Abelardo Lobato, OP, 435–53. Milan: Massimo, 1991.

Osborne, Thomas M., Jr. "Perfect and Imperfect Virtues in Aquinas." *The Thomist* 71, no. 1 (2007): 39–64.

Otto, Rudolf. *Das Heilige. Über das Irrationale in der Idee des Göttlichen und sein Verhältnis zum Rationalen*. Breslau: Trewendt, 1917. English translation: *The Idea of the Holy: An Inquiry into the Non-Rational Factor in the Idea of the Divine and Its Relation to the Rational*, translated by John W. Harvey. London: Oxford University Press, 1950.

Overmyer, Sheryl. *Two Guides for the Journey: Thomas Aquinas and William Langland on the Virtues*. Eugene, Ore.: Cascade, 2016.

Peifer, John Frederick. *The Mystery of Knowledge*. Albany, N.Y.: Magi Books, 1964.

Pelster, Franz. "Das Wachstum der Seligkeit nach der Auferstehung. Um die Auslegung von S.th. 1, 2 q. 4 a. 5 ad 5." *Scholastik* 27 (1952): 561–63.

Pennington, Jonathan T. *The Sermon on the Mount and Human Flourishing: A Theological Commentary*. Grand Rapids, Mich.: Baker Academic, 2017.

Pesch, Otto Herman. *Die Theologie der Rechtfertigung bei Martin Luther und Thomas von Aquin: Versuch eines systematisch-theologischen Dialogs*. Mainz: Grünewald, 1967.

———. "Das Streben nach der *beatitudo* bei Thomas von Aquin im Kontext seiner Theologie. Historische und systematische Fragen." *Freiburger Zeitschrift für Philosophie und Theologie* 52, no. 3 (2005): 427–53.

Peter, Carl J. *Participated Eternity in the Vision of God: A Study of the Opinion of Thomas Aquinas and his Commentators on the Duration of the Acts of Glory*. Rome: Gregorian University Press, 1964.

Peterson, Erik. *Ausgewählte Schriften*, vol. 1: *Theologische Traktate*. Würzburg: Echter, 1994. English translation: *Theological Tractates*, edited and translated by Michael J. Hollerich. Stanford, Calif.: Stanford University Press, 2011.

Petry, R. C. "The Social Character of Heavenly Beatitude According to St. Thomas Aquinas." *The Thomist* 7 (1944): 65–79.

Pfau, Thomas. *Minding the Modern: Human Agency, Intellectual Traditions, and Responsible Knowledge*. Notre Dame, Ind.: University of Notre Dame Press, 2013.

Pieper, Josef. *Zucht und Mass: Über die vierte Kardinaltugend*. Leipzig: Hegner, 1939.

———. "Sur l'espérance des martyrs." In *Espoir humain et espérance chrétienne: Semaine des intellectuels catholiques, 24 au 31 mai 1951, Centre catholique des intellectuels francais*, 76–84. Paris: P. Horay (Etampes, Impr. la Semeuse), 1951.

———. *The Four Cardinal Virtues: Prudence, Justice, Fortitude, Temperance*. Notre Dame, Ind.: University of Notre Dame Press, 1966.

———. *Living the Truth: Reality and the Good*. Translated by Lothar Krauth. San Francisco, Calif.: Ignatius Press, 1989.
———. *Living the Truth: The Truth of All Things*. Translated by Stella Lange. San Francisco, Calif.: Ignatius Press, 1989.
———. *Happiness and Contemplation*. Translated by Richard and Clara Winston. South Bend, Ind.: St. Augustine's Press, 1998.
———. *Leisure: The Basis of Culture* and *Happiness and Contemplation*. Translated by Gerald Malsbary. South Bend, Ind.: St. Augustine's Press, 1998.
Pilsner, Joseph. *The Specification of Human Actions in St. Thomas Aquinas*. Oxford: Oxford University Press, 2006.
Pinckaers, Servais, OP. *The Sources of Christian Ethics*. Translated by Sr. Mary Thomas Noble, OP. Washington, D.C.: The Catholic University of America Press, 1995.
———. *Morality: The Catholic View*. Translated by Michael Sherwin, OP. South Bend, Ind.: St. Augustine's Press, 2001.
———. "Notes." In S. Thomas D'Aquin, *Somme Théologique: La Béatitude*. Éditions de La Revue des jeunes. Paris: Cerf, 2001.
———. *The Spirituality of Martyrdom: To the Limits of Love*. Translated by Patrick M. Clark. Washington, D.C.: The Catholic University of America Press, 2016.
Plantinga, Alvin. *Where the Conflict Really Lies: Science, Religion, and Naturalism*. Oxford: Oxford University Press, 2011.
Plé, Albert, OP. *Chastity and the Affective Life*. Translated by Marie-Claude Thompson. New York: Herder and Herder, 1966.
Plested, Marcus. *Orthodox Readings of Aquinas*. Oxford: Oxford University Press, 2012.
Pollmann, Karla, Willemien Otten, et al. *The Oxford Guide to the Historical Reception of Augustine*. 3 vols. Oxford: Oxford University Press, 2013.
Pope, Stephen J., ed. *The Ethics of Aquinas*. Washington, D.C.: Georgetown University Press, 2002.
Portalié, Eugène. "'Dogma and History': Part 3 of 'Autour des fondements de la foi,' (1904)." In *Defending the Faith: An Anti-Modernist Anthology*, edited and translated by William M. Marshner, 121–85. Washington, D.C.: The Catholic University of America Press, 2017.
Porter, Jean. "Basic Goods and the Human Good in Recent Catholic Moral Theology." *The Thomist* 57 (1993): 27–49.
Possenti, Vittorio. *Nihilism and Metaphysics: The Third Voyage*. Translated by Daniel B. Gallagher. Albany: State University of New York Press, 2014.
Raeymaeker, Louis de. *The Philosophy of Being: A Synthesis of Metaphysics*. Translated by Edmund H. Ziegelmeyer. St. Louis, Mo.: Herder, 1954; reprinted in Heusenstamm: Editiones Scholasticae, 2015.
Rahner, Hugo, SJ. *Our Lady and the Church*. Translated by Sebastian Bullough, OP. Bethesda, Md.: Zaccheus Press, 2004.
Rahner, Karl, SJ. *Geist in Welt: Zur Metaphysik der endlichen Erkenntnis bei Thomas von Aquin*. Munich: Kösel, 1957. English translation: *Spirit in the World*, translated by William Dych. New York: Herder and Herder, 1968.

———. *Hörer des Wortes: Zur Grundlegung einer Religionsphilosophie.* Edited by Johannes B. Metz. Munich: Kösel, 1963. First published in 1941. The original 1941 edition and the 1963 edition, prepared and significantly edited by Metz are available in: *Hörer des Wortes: Schriften zur Religionsphilosophie und zur Grundlegung der Theologie.* Sämtliche Werke 4. Solothurn / Freiburg: Benziger / Herder, 1997. English translation: *Hearer of the Word: Laying the Foundation for a Philosophy of Religion,* translated by Michael Richards. New York: Herder and Herder, 1969.

———. "Theology and Anthropology." In *Theological Investigations,* vol. 9, translated by Graham Harrison, 28–45. New York: Herder and Herder, 1972.

———. "Yesterday's History of Dogma and Theology for Tomorrow." In *Theological Investigations,* vol. 18, translated by Edward Quinn, 3–34. New York: Crossroad, 1983.

———. *Maria, Mutter des Herrn: Mariologische Studien.* Sämtliche Werke 9. Erster Teilband. Solothurn / Freiburg: Benziger / Herder, 2004.

Rawls, John. *A Theory of Justice.* Revised edition. Cambridge, Mass.: Harvard University Press, 1999.

———. *Political Liberalism.* Expanded edition. New York: Columbia University Press, 2005.

Reese, Philip Neri, OP. "Theology, Faith, Universities: From Specialization to Specification in Theology." *New Blackfriars* 92, no. 1042 (2011): 691–704.

Reimers, Adrian J. *The Soul of the Person: A Contemporary Philosophical Psychology.* Washington, D.C.: The Catholic University of America Press, 2006.

———. *Hell and the Mercy of God.* Washington, D.C.: The Catholic University of America Press, 2017.

Reinders, Hans S. *Receiving the Gift of Friendship: Profound Disability, Theological Anthropology, and Ethics.* Grand Rapids, Mich.: Eerdmans, 2008.

Richardson, William J., SJ. *Heidegger: Through Phenomenology to Thought.* Dordrecht: Martinus Nijhoff, 1963.

Rilke, Rainer Maria. *Duino Elegies & The Sonnets of Orpheus: A Dual-Language Edition.* Translated by Stephen Mitchell. New York: Vintage, 2009.

Rolnick, Philip A. *Origins: God, Evolution, and the Question of the Cosmos.* Waco, Tex.: Baylor University Press, 2017.

Romero, Miguel J. "Aquinas on the *Corporis Infirmitas*: Broken Flesh and the Grammar of Grace." In *Disability in the Christian Tradition: A Reader,* edited by Brian Brock and John Swinton, 101–51. Grand Rapids, Mich.: Eerdmans, 2012.

———. "St. Thomas Aquinas on Disability & Profound Cognitive Impairment." ThD diss., Duke University, 2012.

———. "Cognitive Impairment, Moral Virtue, and Our Life in Christ: Can My Brother Live a Happy and Holy Life?" *Church Life* 4, no. 4 (2014): 79–94.

———. "The Happiness of 'Those Who Lack the Use of Reason.'" *The Thomist* 80, no. 1 (2016): 49–96.

———. "To Think Theologically About Disability: The Contemporary Challenge and a Proposal." *Culture e Fede (Pontificium Consilium de Cultura)* 24, no. 3 (2016): 203–4.

———. "The Goodness and Beauty of Our Fragile Flesh: Moral Theologians and our Engagement with 'Disability.'" *Journal of Moral Theology* 6, no. 2 (Special Issue) (2017): 206–53.
Root, Michael. "Aquinas, Merit, and Reformation Theology after the *Joint Declaration on the Doctrine of Justification*." *Modern Theology* 20, no. 1 (2004): 5–22.
Rose, Matthew. "Tayloring Christianity: Charles Taylor is a Theologian of the Secular Status Quo." *First Things* (December 2014), available at firstthings.com/article/2014/12/tayloring-christianity.
Rosen, Stanley. *The Question of Being: A Reversal of Heidegger*. New Haven, Conn.: Yale University Press, 1993.
Ross, James. *Thought and World: The Hidden Necessities*. Notre Dame, Ind.: University of Notre Dame Press, 2008.
Rziha, John. *Perfecting Human Actions: St. Thomas Aquinas on Human Participation in Eternal Law*. Washington, D.C.: The Catholic University of America Press, 2009.
Salkin, Allen. "No Sympathy for the Sex Addict." *The New York Times*, September 7, 2008. Available at topics.nytimes.com/topics/reference/timestopics/subjects/s/sexual_addiction/index.htm.
Sánchez Sorondo, Marcello. *La gracia como participación de la naturaleza divina según Santo Tomás de Aquino*. Salamanca: Universidad Pontificia, 1979.
———. "La grazia come partecipazione della natura divina: implicazioni antropologiche dei misteri della fede Cristiana." In *Doctor Communis: Credere, amare, e vivere la verità*, Proceedings of the XIII Plenary Session of the Pontifical Academy of Saint Thomas Aquinas in the Year of Faith, 21–23 June 2013, 83–93. Vatican City: Libreria Editrice Vaticana, 2014.
Scheeben, Matthias Joseph. "Glaube." In *Wetzer und Welte's Kirchenlexikon, oder Encyclopädie der katholischen Theologie und ihrer humanen Hilfswissenschaften*, 5:616–74. Freiburg: Herder, 1888.
———. *Handbuch der katholischen Dogmatik*, vol. 1: *Theologische Erkenntnislehre*. 2nd ed. Freiburg: Herder, 1948.
———. *Gesammelte Schriften*. 8 vols. Edited by Josef Höfer et al. Freiburg: Herder, 1949-67.
———. *The Mysteries of Christianity*. Translated by Cyril Vollert, SJ. St. Louis, Mo.: Herder, 1951.
———. *Nature and Grace*. Translated by Cyril Vollert, SJ. St. Louis, Mo.: Herder, 1954.
Scheler, Max. *Über Ressentiment und moralisches Werturteil*. Leipzig: Wilhelm Engelmann, 1912. English translation: *Ressentiment*, edited by Lewis A. Coser, translated by William W. Holdheim. New York: Cronwell-Collier, 1961.
Schleiermacher, Friedrich. *On Religion: Speeches to Its Cultured Despisers*. Translated by John Oman. Louisville, Ky.: Westminster John Knox Press, 1994.
Schmid, Aloys. *Untersuchungen über den letzten Gewißheitsgrund des Offenbarungsglaubens*. Munich: Ernst Stahl, 1879.
Schneewind, J. B. *The Invention of Autonomy: A History of Modern Moral Philosophy*. Cambridge: Cambridge University Press, 1998.
Schubeck, Thomas, SJ. "Salvadoran Martyrs: A Love that Does Justice." *Horizons* 28 (2001): 7–29.

Schulze, Markus, SAC. *Leibhaft und Unsterblich. Zur Schau der Seele in der Anthropologie und Theologie des Hl. Thomas von Aquin*. Freiburg: Universitätsverlag Freiburg Schweiz, 1992.
Seckler, Max. *Instinkt und Glaubenswille nach Thomas von Aquin*. Mainz: Grünewald, 1961.
Sherwin, Michael S., OP. *By Knowledge and by Love: Charity and Knowledge in the Moral Theology of St. Thomas Aquinas*. Washington, D.C.: The Catholic University of America Press, 2005.
———. "Infused Virtue and the Effects of Acquired Vice: A Test Case for the Thomistic Theory of Infused Cardinal Virtues." *The Thomist* 73, no. 1 (2009): 29–52.
———. "Happiness and Its Discontents." *Logos: A Journal of Catholic Thought and Culture* 13, no. 4 (2010): 35–59.
Siewerth, Gustav. *Das Schicksal der Metaphysik von Thomas zu Heidegger*. 3rd ed. Freiburg: Johannes Verlag Einsiedeln, 2003.
Simon, Yves R. *An Introduction to Metaphysics of Knowledge*. Translated by Vukan Kuic and Richard J. Thompson. New York: Fordham University Press, 1990.
Simpson, Peter. "Grisez on Aristotle and Human Goods." *American Journal of Jurisprudence* 46 (2001): 75–89.
Smith, Christopher. "*Surnaturel* Revisited: Henri de Lubac's Theology of the Supernatural in Contemporary Theology." STD diss., University of Navarra, 2014.
Smith, Steven D. *The Disenchantment of Secular Discourse*. Cambridge, Mass.: Harvard University Press, 2010.
Snell, R. J. *Acedia and Its Discontents: Metaphysical Boredom in an Empire of Desire*. Kettering, Ohio: Angelico Press, 2015.
Spaemann, Robert, and Reinhard Löw. *Natürliche Ziele: Geschichte und Wiederentdeckung des teleologischen Denkens*. Stuttgart: Klett-Cotta, 2005.
Speer, Andreas. "Das Glück des Menschen." In *Thomas von Aquin: Die Summa theologiae (Werkinterpretationen)*, edited by Andreas Speer, 141–66. Berlin: de Gruyter, 2005.
Spezzano, Daria. *The Glory of God's Grace: Deification According to St. Thomas Aquinas*. Ave Maria, Fla.: Sapientia Press, 2015.
———. "'Be Imitators of God' (Eph. 5:1): Aquinas on Charity and Satisfaction." *Nova et Vetera* (English edition) 15, no. 2 (2017): 615–51.
Spicq, Ceslas, OP. *Théologie morale du Nouveau Testament*. 2 vols. Paris: Lecoffre, 1965.
Staudt, Robert Jared. "Religion as a Virtue: Thomas Aquinas on Worship through Justice, Law, and Charity." PhD diss., Ave Maria University, 2008.
Stout, Jeffrey. *The Flight from Authority: Religion, Morality, and the Quest for Autonomy*. Notre Dame, Ind.: University of Notre Dame Press, 1981.
Stump, Eleonore. *Aquinas*. New York: Routledge, 2003.
Sullivan, Ezra, OP. "Seek First the Kingdom: A Reply to Germain Grisez's Account of Man's Ultimate End." *Nova et Vetera* (English edition) 8, no. 4 (2010): 959–95.
Swafford, Andrew Dean. *Nature and Grace: A New Approach to Thomistic Ressourcement*. Eugene, Ore.: Pickwick Publications, 2014.

Selected Bibliography 475

Tanner, Kathryn. *Christ the Key*. Cambridge: Cambridge University Press, 2010.
Taylor, Charles. *A Secular Age*. Cambridge, Mass.: Belknap Press, 2007.
te Velde, Rudi. *Participation and Substantiality in Thomas Aquinas*. Leiden: Brill, 1995.
———. *Aquinas on God: The 'Divine Science' of the* Summa Theologiae. Burlington, Vt.: Ashgate, 2006.
Thompson, E. P. *Witness against the Beast: William Blake and the Moral Law*. New York: New Press, 1993.
Tilley, Terrence W. *Inventing Catholic Tradition*. Maryknoll, N.Y.: Orbis, 2000.
———. *Faith: What It Is and What It Isn't*. Maryknoll, N.Y.: Orbis, 2010.
Titus, Craig Steven. *Resilience and the Virtue of Fortitude: Aquinas in Dialogue with the Psychosocial Sciences*. Washington, D.C.: The Catholic University of America Press, 2006.
Tolksdorf, Wilhelm. *Analysis fidei: John Henry Newmans Beitrag zur Entdeckung des Subjektes beim Glaubensakt im theologiegeschichtlichen Kontext*. Frankfurt: Peter Lang, 2000.
Tomberg, Markus. *Glaubensgewißheit als Freiheitsgeschehen: Eine Relecture des Traktats 'De analysi fidei.'* Regensburg: Pustet, 2002.
Torchia, Joseph, OP. *Restless Mind: Curiositas & the Scope of Inquiry in St. Augustine's Psychology*. Milwaukee, Wis.: Marquette University Press, 2013.
Torrance, Alan J. *Persons in Communion: An Essay on Trinitarian Description and Human Participation, with special reference to Volume One of Karl Barth's Church Dogmatics*. Edinburgh: T and T Clark, 1996.
———. "*Auditum Fidei*: Where and How Does God Speak? Faith, Reason, and the Question of Criteria." In *Reason and the Reasons of Faith*, edited by Paul J. Griffiths and Reinhard Hütter, 27–52. New York: T and T Clark International, 2005.
Torrell, Jean-Pierre, OP. *Recherches thomasiennes: Études revues et augmentées*. Paris: Vrin, 2000.
———. "Notes." In Saint Thomas d'Aquin, *Somme Théologique (3a, qq. 27–34). Le Verbe Incarné en ses mystères. Tome 1, L'entrée du Christ en ce monde*. Paris: Cerf, 2003.
———. "Nature and Grace in Thomas Aquinas." In *Surnaturel: A Controversy at the Heart of Twentieth-Century Thomistic Thought*, edited by Serge-Thomas Bonino, OP, translated by Robert Williams, and revised by Matthew Levering, 155–88. Ave Maria, Fla.: Sapientia Press, 2009.
Trueman, Patrick A. "The Pornography Pandemic." *Columbia* (November 2011): 24.
Tschipke, Theophil, OP. *Die Menschheit Christi als Heilsorgan der Gottheit unter besonderer Berücksichtigung der Lehre des heiligen Thomas von Aquin*. Freiburg: Herder, 1940. French translation: *L'humanité du Christ comme instrument de salut de la divinité*, translated by Philibert Secretan. Fribourg: Academic Press, 2003.
Tugwell, Simon. *Human Immortality and the Redemption of Death*. Springfield, Ill.: Templegate, 1990.
Turner, Denys. *Faith, Reason, and the Existence of God*. Cambridge: Cambridge University Press, 2004.
Týn, Tomáš, OP. *Metafisica della sostanza. Partecipazione e analogia entis*. Edited by Giovanni Cavalcoli, OP. Verona: Fede e Cultura, 2009.

Ulrich, Ferdinand. *Homo Abyssus: Das Wagnis der Seinsfrage*. 2nd ed. Freiburg: Johannes Verlag Einsiedeln, 1998. English translation: *Homo Abyssus: The Drama of the Question of Being*, translated by David C. Schindler. Washington, D.C.: Humanum Academic Press, 2018.

Vattimo, Gianni. *Farewell to Truth*. Translated by William McCuaig. New York: Columbia University Press, 2007.

Verschuuren, Gerard M. *Aquinas and Modern Science: A New Synthesis of Faith and Reason*. Kettering, Ohio: Angelico Press, 2016.

Vogel, Heinrich J. "The Flacian Controversy on Original Sin." In *No Other Gospel: Essays in Commemoration of the 400th Anniversary of the Formula of Concord 1580–1980*, edited by Arnold J. Koelpin, 1–15. Milwaukee, Wis.: Northwestern Publishing House, 1980.

Waldstein, Michael Maria. "Dietrich von Hildebrand and St. Thomas Aquinas on Goodness and Happiness." *Nova et Vetera* (English edition) 1, no. 2 (2003): 403–64.

———. *Glory of the Logos in the Flesh: Saint John Paul's Theology of the Body*. Ave Maria, Fla.: Sapientia Press, 2019.

Ward, Graham. "The Commodification of Religion or the Consummation of Capitalism." *The Hedgehog Review* 5, no. 2 (2003): 50–65.

Ward, Keith. *In Defense of the Soul*. London: Oneworld Publications, 1998.

Wawrykow, Joseph P. *God's Grace and Human Action: "Merit" in the Theology of Thomas Aquinas*. Notre Dame, Ind.: University of Notre Dame Press, 1995.

Wenzel, Siegfried. *The Sin of Sloth: Acedia in Medieval Thought and Literature*. Chapel Hill: University of North Carolina Press, 1967.

Westberg, Daniel. *Right Practical Reason: Aristotle, Action, and Prudence in Aquinas*. Oxford: Clarendon Press, 1994.

Wetter, Friedrich. *Die Lehre Benedikts XII. vom intensiven Wachstum der Gottesschau*. Rome: Gregorian University, 1958.

Wetterneck, Chad T., et al. "The Role of Sexual Compulsiveness, Impulsivity, and Experiential Avoidance in Internet Pornography Use." *The Psychological Record* 62 (2012): 3–18.

Whelan, Matthew. "The Land of the Savior: Oscar Romero and the Reform of Agriculture." PhD diss., Duke University, 2016.

White, Thomas Joseph, OP. *Wisdom in the Face of Modernity: A Study in Thomistic Natural Theology*. Ave Maria, Fla.: Sapientia Press, 2009.

———. "The 'Pure Nature' of Christology: Human Nature and *Gaudium et Spes* 22." *Nova et Vetera* (English edition) 8, no. 2 (2010): 283–322.

———. "Good Extrinsicism: Matthias Scheeben and the Ideal Paradigm of Nature-Grace Orthodoxy." *Nova et Vetera* (English edition) 11, no. 2 (2013): 537–63.

———. "Sociology as Theology: Robert Bellah's Book Renews the Liberal Protestant Project." *First Things* (June 2013), available at firstthings.com/article/2013/06/sociology-as-theology.

———. "The Virgin Mary and the Church: The Marian Exemplarity of Ecclesial Faith." *Nova et Vetera* (English edition) 11, no. 2 (2013): 375–405.

———. "Imperfect Happiness and the Final End of Man: Thomas Aquinas and the Paradigm of Nature-Grace Orthodoxy." *The Thomist* 78, no. 2 (2014): 1–43.

———. "Monotheistic Rationality and Divine Names: Why Aquinas's Analogy Theory Transcends both Theoretical Agnosticism and Conceptual Anthropomorphism." In *God: Reason and Reality*, edited by Anselm Ramelov, OP, 37–79. Munich: Philosophia, 2014.

———. *The Incarnate Lord: A Thomistic Study in Christology*. Washington, D.C.: The Catholic University of America Press, 2016.

———. "Gaudium et Spes." In *The Reception of Vatican II*, edited by Matthew L. Lamb and Matthew Levering, 113–46. New York: Oxford University Press, 2017.

———. *The Light of Christ: An Introduction to Catholicism*. Washington, D.C.: The Catholic University of America Press, 2017.

Wicki, Nikolaus. *Die Lehre von der himmlischen Seligkeit in der mittelalterlichen Scholastik von Petrus Lombardus bis Thomas von Aquin*. Fribourg: Universitätsverlag, 1954.

Williams, A. N. *The Ground of Union: Deification in Aquinas and Palamas*. Oxford: Oxford University Press, 1999.

Williams, John Joseph. "The Participation of the Resurrected Body in the Beatitude of Man." STD diss., Facultés Catholiques de Toulouse, 1977.

Wippel, John F. *The Metaphysical Thought of Thomas Aquinas: From Finite Being to Uncreated Being*. Washington, D.C.: The Catholic University of America Press, 2000.

———. "Thomas Aquinas on the Separated Soul's Natural Knowledge." In *Thomas Aquinas—Approaches to Truth: The Aquinas Lectures at Maynooth, 1996–2001*, edited by James McEvoy and Michael Dunne, 114–40. Dublin: Four Courts, 2002.

———. *Metaphysical Themes in Thomas Aquinas*, vol. II. Washington, D.C.: The Catholic University of America Press, 2007.

———. "Thomas Aquinas on Philosophy and the Preambles of Faith." In *The Science of Being as Being: Metaphysical Investigations*, edited by Gregory Doolan, 196–220. Washington, D.C.: The Catholic University of America Press, 2012.

———. "Aquinas on Creation and Preambles of Faith." *The Thomist* 78, no. 1 (2014): 1–36.

Wojtyła, Karol (Pope John Paul II). *Love and Responsibility*. Translated by H. T. Willetts. New York: Farrar, Straus and Giroux, 1981.

Wright, N. T. *Surprised by Hope: Rethinking Heaven, the Resurrection, and the Mission of the Church*. New York: HarperOne, 2008.

Wuellner, Bernard, SJ. *Summary of Scholastic Principles*. Chicago: Loyola University Press, 1956.

Wyser, Paul, OP. *Theologie als Wisssenschaft: Ein Beitrag zur theologischen Erkenntnislehre*. Salzburg: Pustet, 1938.

Yearly, Lee H. *Mencius and Aquinas: Theories of Virtue and Conceptions of Courage*. Albany: State University of New York Press, 1990.

Zychlinski, Alexander von. "Die species impressa und expressa beim beseligenden Schauakt nach der Lehre des hl. Thomas von Aquin. Eine thomistische Studie." ThD diss., University of Breslau, 1918.

Index of Names

Adorno, Theodor W., 65n63
Akkara, Anto, 299n5
Albert the Great, 100, 233n11, 394
Alfaro, Juan, 209n32
Allen, John L., Jr., 299n6
Althaus, Paul, 54n53
Ambrose, 375n13, 383
Anderson, Gary A., 176–78
Anscombe, G. E. M., 15n17, 172
Arintero, John G., 188n17
Aristotle, 4n4, 11, 15n17, 18n18, 19–20, 22n26, 30–32, 34n34, 37–39, 44–45, 48, 61, 65n63, 72, 87, 89n4, 92, 110–12, 115–16, 118, 123, 166, 193, 205, 247–48, 276–77, 279–80, 336n11, 341, 397, 401, 404
Ashley, Benedict M., 89, 116, 132n57, 132n59, 140, 409n32
Aubert, Roger, 199n15
Augustine, 22n26, 32, 34n34, 45–46, 50–51, 100, 106, 186n15, 187, 192, 196, 210, 240, 253, 260, 264–65, 274, 276–77, 278n40, 279–80, 297, 347–48, 350, 355n50, 356–57, 375n13, 393, 411–12, 442, 444
Auriol, Peter, 394n12
Austriaco, Nicanor Pier Giorgio, 24n28
Avicenna, 100

Baius, Michael, 135
Balthasar, Hans Urs von, 88n2, 135n63, 199, 391n7, 436n73
Bañez, Domingo, 108, 431n66

Banks, Russell, 353n44
Barth, Karl, 54n53, 145–46, 264, 265n18, 289
Bartmann, Peter, 55n54
Bauckham, Richard, 5n7
Bautain, Louis Eugène, 199n14
Bellah, Robert N., 262n14
Benedict XII, Pope, 43n42, 51n50, 420
Benedict XIV, Pope, 301n10, 320, 321n39, 321n41
Benedict XVI, Pope, 108n30, 201–3, 301n10, 323nn42–43, 325, 327, 369n2, 420n49. See also Ratzinger, Joseph
Bentley, G. E., Jr., 261n10
Bergson, Henri, 99
Berning, Vincent, 221n59
Bethke, Jefferson, 261n11
Biel, Gabriel, 51n49
Bilokapić, Ante, 52n51
Blake, William, 261
Blanchette, Oliva, 89, 100, 122n46, 229n6
Blankenhorn, Bernard, 241n25
Blondel, Maurice, 99, 135n63
Blumenberg, Hans, 65n63
Bobik, Joseph, 112n37
Böckenförde, Ernst-Wolfgang, 285–86
Boethius, 13, 31, 106
Boeve, Lieven, 98n15
Bonaventure, 233n11
Bonino, Serge-Thomas, 97n14
Boulding, Maria, 357
Bourke, Vernon J., 342n22

479

Index of Names

Bouyer, Louis, 372, 381–83
Bowler, Kate, 7
Boyle, Leonard E., 113n38
Bradley, Denis J. M., 22n25, 38, 272n29, 277n38
Braine, David, 58n56, 135n63
Braun, Herbert, 54n53
Brock, Stephen L., 131n56, 398n14, 434n70
Bugenhagen, Johannes, 177
Bulgakov, Sergius, 125, 145, 436n73
Bultmann, Rudolf, 54n53
Buridan, Jean, 111

Cajetan, 42, 431n66
Calvin, Jean, 51, 264
Capreolus, John, 394n12
Caputo, John, 99n17
Catherine of Siena, 5, 287
Cavanaugh, William T., 258n5
Centi, Tito, 265n19
Cessario, Romanus, 177n3, 212, 218n53, 303n13, 334n7, 342n22, 352n43
Chenu, Marie-Dominique, 93n9, 205
Christoph, Markus, 277n38, 304n15, 306
Cicero, Marcus Tullius, 265
Clark, Patrick M., 300n9
Coerver, Robert Florent, 277n38
Cole, Basil, 351n40
Congar, Yves, 69n66, 98n15
Conrad-Martius, Hedwig, 89, 100
Cory, Therese Scarpelli, 434n68
Cullmann, Oscar, 54n53
Cunningham, Francis L. B., 233n11

Daguet, François, 444n80
Dante Alighieri, 64, 251, 294n63, 444, 445n81
Darwin, Charles, 56
Dawkins, Richard, 56
Day, Dorothy, 5n8
Decosimo, David, 55n54, 277
Dedmon, Jonathan, 349n38
De Koninck, Charles, 58n56, 89, 100, 159n9, 229n6, 317n35
Dennett, Daniel, 56
Descartes, René, 207, 226
De Soto, Domingo, 431n66
Dewan, Lawrence, 89, 206

DeYoung, Rebecca Konyndyk, 55n54, 351n40
D'Holbach, Baron, 56
Dilthey, Wilhelm, 197n6
Dionysius. *See* Pseudo-Dionysius
Divry, Édouard, 393n9
Doidge, Norman, 358n55
Dondaine, Hyacinthe-François, 394n11
Dörnemann, Holger, 248n33
Dostoyevsky, Fyodor, 155n2
Dulles, Avery, 198nn10–11, 199n15, 211n36, 213n42, 218n54
Dunnington, Kent, 348n34, 353n44, 361n59
Duns Scotus, John, 51n50, 394n12
Dupré, Louis, 65n63
Durandus of Saint-Pourçain, 394n12

Elert, Werner, 54n53
Eliade, Mircea, 264n17
Eschweiler, Karl, 197n6, 222n60
Eubank, Nathan, 176n1
Evagrius of Pontus, 350

Fabro, Cornelio, 58n56, 89, 100, 222n60, 228, 291n57, 388n2
Falanga, Anthony J., 277n38
Farrow, Douglas, 285n51
Feingold, Laurence, 134n62
Feser, Edward, 58n56, 111n35
Feuerbach, Ludwig, 56, 264
Fichte, Johann Gottlieb, 169n33
Fields, Stephen M., 135n63
Finn, Robert W., 331n2
Fisher, John, 323
Flacius Illyricus, Matthias, 52
Flanagan, Owen, 149n78
Forster, Karl, 394n12
Foucault, Michel, 65n63
Francis, Pope, 201n18, 255, 260, 285, 295, 323n42, 327
Frederick II, Emperor, 318n36
Freud, Sigmund, 56
Froget, Barthélemy, 233n11

Gaine, Simon Francis, 97n14
Gardeil, Ambroise, 98n15
Garrigou-Lagrange, Réginald, 58n56,

102n22, 110n31, 118n41, 374n10, 375n13, 380n17, 431n66
Geiger, Louis-Bertrand, 89, 100, 228n4
George, Francis, Cardinal, 326
Gérard de Frachet, 318n36
Gilson, Étienne, 58n56, 89, 100, 110n31, 207n27, 398n15
Godfrey of Fontaines, 394n12
Grabmann, Martin, 96n13
Grabowski, John S., 332, 338n16
Gradl, Stefan, 55n54
Gregory of Valentia, 197
Gregory Palamas, 393n9
Gregory the Great, 325n44, 350, 355, 393, 434n70
Gregory, Brad S., 261n12, 294n62
Greschat, Katherina, 355n50
Griffiths, Paul J., 176n1, 262n14, 356n51, 436n73
Grisez, Germain, 143–44, 388, 409–10, 414, 416–26, 435–36
Grudzen, Corita R., 331n3
Guindon, Roger, 22n26

Habermas, Jürgen, 65n63, 259–60
Hadjadj, Fabrice, 149n78
Hain, Raymond F., IV, 166n30
Hald, Gert Martin, 331n3, 349n36
Hanby, Michael, 56n55
Harris, Sam, 56
Hart, David Bentley, 58n56, 89n4
Hauerwas, Stanley, 55n54, 146n74
Healy, Nicholas J., 136n65
Hefner, Philip J., 149n77
Hegel, G. W. F., 65n63, 99, 125, 145, 259
Heidegger, Martin, 54n53, 58n56, 60n57, 65n63, 88–89, 100, 220–21, 351n41, 391n6
Hendel, Kurt K., 177n2
Henry of Ghent, 394n12
Herdt, Jennifer A., 55n54
Hermes, Georg, 199n13
Hildebrand, Dietrich von, 49n46
Hill, Christopher, 261n10
Hinnebusch, William A., 318n36
Hitchens, Christopher, 56
Hobbes, Thomas, 56
Hoeres, Walter, 89n4, 100n18

Hölderlin, Friedrich, 390–91
Holl, Karl, 53
Honecker, Martin, 221n59
Honnefelder, Ludger, 100n18
Horkheimer, Max, 65n63
Horvath, Alexander M., 267, 268n24
Hoye, William J., 390, 400, 401n20, 405, 407, 408n30
Hugon, Édouard, 99n16
Hume, David, 56, 161, 226, 263n15
Husserl, Edmund, 99–100, 157

Innocent IV, Pope, 318n36
Isidore of Seville, 265, 341
Iwand, Hans Joachim, 53

Jenkins, John I., 92n8, 195n4
Jenson, Robert W., 52n51
John Cassian, 350
John Chrysostom, 357, 393, 396
John of Damascus, 112, 380n17, 393
John of the Cross, 108
John Paul II, Pope, 68–71, 86–87, 92, 97, 101, 108n30, 299n4, 323n42, 324, 365n66, 380n17, 420n49. See also Wojtyła, Karol
Journet, Charles, 97n14
Jüngel, Eberhard, 54n53

Kant, Immanuel, 58n56, 89, 99, 131, 149n77, 157, 207, 220–21, 226, 259, 412–13
Kantorowicz, Ernst H., 320n38
Kato, Testsuo-Marcel. See Hadjadj, Fabrice
Kelsey, David, 147–48
Kerr, Gaven, 58n56
Kierkegaard, Søren, 145
Kinghorn, Warren, 331n3
Kleutgen, Joseph, 199, 213, 216n48
Klubertanz, George P., 342n22, 397n13
Knobel, Angela McKay, 277n38
Komonchak, Joseph A., 135n63
Kretzmann, Norman, 58n56
Kromholtz, Brian, 426n59, 429n63, 431n66
Kroner, Richard, 131
Kuhn, Johann Evangelist von, 198n11
Kupfer, David, 347n32

Labourdette, Michel, 344n26
Lakebrink, Bernhard, 221n59
Lambert, Nathaniel M., 331n3
Lambertini, Prosper, Cardinal. *See* Benedict XIV, Pope
Langland, William, 10n12
Layard, Richard, 7
Layden, Mary Anne, 331n2
Leget, Carlo, 426n59
Le Guillou, Marie-Joseph, 137
Leonhardt, Rochus, 55n54
Leo XIII, Pope, 260, 420n49
Leuba, James Henry, 257n4
Levering, Matthew, 351n40, 371n6
Lévy, Antione, 393n9
Lewis, C. S., 354n47
Lichacz, Piotr, 161n16
Lisska, Anthony J., 397n13
Locke, John, 286n54, 398
Loisy, Alfred, 263n16
Lombard, Peter, 22n26, 206, 242, 246, 319
Lombardo, Nicholas E., 336n10, 353n44
Lonergan, Bernard, 97n14, 235n14, 236, 238n22, 240n24
Long, Steven A., 24n28, 131n56, 136n64, 142n68, 311n30, 417n45
Lossky, Vladimir, 393n9
Loux, Michael, 100
Löw, Reinhard, 26n30, 110n31, 111
Lubac, Henri de, 134n62, 135–36, 142, 243n29
Lugo, Juan de, 198, 216n48
Lukács, Georg, 65n63
Luther Martin, 50–52, 177
Lynch, Reginald M., 187n16, 270n26

MacDonald, Paul A., 195n2, 207n27
Machuga, Ric, 58n56
MacIntyre, Alasdair, 7, 15n17, 65n63, 88, 92n8, 172–73, 354n47
Madden, James D., 58n56
Malamuth, Neil M., 349n36
Malloy, Christopher J., 136n64
Manning, Jill C., 349
Mansini, Guy, 136n65
Maréchal, Joseph, 135n63
Maritain, Jacques, 58n56, 89, 100, 207n27, 397n13, 414–15, 418n46

Marschler, Thomas, 197n6
Marshall, Bruce D., 102n23, 176n11
Marx, Karl, 56, 65n63
Mattison, William C., III, 4n5
Mattiussi, Guido, 98n16
Maximus the Confessor, 393n9
McCluskey, Colleen, 55n54, 351n40
McInerny, Ralph, 88–89, 94n10, 100n19, 130n52, 136n64
McKirahan, Richard, 92n8
Merriell, D. Juvenal, 231n9, 439n75
Metz, Johannes Baptist, 388n2
Meyer, Regina Pacis, 370n4
Milbank, John, 135n63
Mill, John Stuart, 259
Miner, Robert, 336n10
Möhler, Johann Adam, 198n11
Moore, G. E., 161
More, Thomas, 322
Mulcahy, Bernard, 136n64
Mulchahey, M. Michèle, 113n38
Mullady, Brian T., 363n63
Mullaney, T. A., 372n9
Mumford, Stephen, 100

Newman, John Henry, 59, 170n34, 195n2, 198n11, 200n17, 217n51, 290–91, 408
Nichols, Aidan, 214, 372n9
Nicolas, Jean-Hervé, 97n14
Nietzsche, Friedrich, 56, 59–61, 65n63, 89, 149–50, 292
Nygren, Anders, 53

Oakes, Edward T., 135n63, 136n65
Oberman, Heiko, 51n49
O'Brien, T. C., 205n23, 207, 211n34, 434n67
O'Callaghan, John P., 11n14
Ockham, William, 111
Oliver, Simon, 111n36
Ols, Daniel, 372n9
Origen, 54n53, 107, 145
O'Rourke, Kevin D., 266n22, 283n50
Osborne, Thomas M., Jr., 277n38
Otto, Rudolf, 264
Overmyer, Sheryl, 10n12

Index of Names

Paul VI, Pope, 75–76, 287, 292
Peifer, John Frederick, 397n13
Pennington, Jonathan T., 4n5
Peter, Carl J., 434n68, 436n72, 440
Peterson, Erik, 297
Pfau, Thomas, 26n31, 65n63, 286n54
Pieper, Josef, 19n20, 130–31, 155n3, 160n12, 164n23, 165, 227n3, 277n38, 326n46, 338
Pilsner, Joseph, 24n28
Pinckaers, Servais, 161n14, 163n20, 300n9, 334n5
Pius IX, Pope, 373
Pius X, Pope, 211n35, 375n13, 420n49
Pius XI, Pope, 420n49
Pius XII, Pope, 371, 420n49
Plantinga, Alvin, 56n55
Plato, 34n34, 65n63, 89, 110n31, 111, 267n23
Plé, Albert, 338n16
Portalié, Eugène, 263n16
Porter, Jean, 417n45
Possenti, Vittorio, 60n57, 61, 89, 100
Prenter, Regin, 53
Przywara, Erich, 89
Pseudo-Dionysius, 100, 127, 237n19, 339n18, 375n11, 393, 396

Raeymaeker, Louis de, 89, 100
Rahner, Hugo, 367, 385
Rahner, Karl, 88n2, 135n63, 220–21, 370, 385, 388n2
Ramirez, Jacobus M., 134n62, 334n5
Ratzinger, Joseph, 259n7
Rawls, John, 259–60
Reese, Philip Neri, 96n12
Regan, Richard, 351n40
Reimers, Adrian J., 5n6, 10n13, 33n33, 58n56, 436n73
Reinders, Hans S., 62n59
Richardson, William J., 391n6
Rilke, Rainer Maria, 390–91
Rolnick, Philip A., 56n55
Romero, Miguel J., 50n47, 62n60
Root, Michael, 47n45, 274n31
Rose, Matthew, 255n2
Rosen, Stanley, 89n4
Ross, James, 207n28
Ross, W. D., 100

Rousselot, Pierre, 199
Rziha, John, 159nn10–11, 161n15, 230n7, 334n7

Salkin, Allen, 347n32
Sánchez Sorondo, Marcello, 228n4, 241n25
Scheeben, Matthias Joseph, 97n14, 121n44, 194, 198n11, 199, 204, 212–17, 219–20, 222, 242
Scheler, Max, 354
Schelling, Friedrich Wilhelm Joseph, 125
Schleiermacher, Friedrich, 263
Schmid, Aloys, 198n10
Schneewind, J. B., 162n17
Schubeck, Thomas, 323n42
Schulze, Markus, 426n59
Seckler, Max, 135n63, 236n16
Severus of Antioch, 380n17
Sherwin, Michael S., 211n34, 236n16, 277n38, 346n30
Siewerth, Gustav, 89, 100
Simon, Yves R., 89, 317n35, 397n13
Simpson, Peter, 417n45
Singleton, Charles S., 251n35
Smith, Christopher, 136n65
Smith, Steven D., 260n9
Snell, R. J., 351n41
Spaemann, Robert, 26n30, 110n31, 111
Speer, Andreas, 22n26
Spezzano, Daria, 177n3, 241n25
Spinoza, Benedict, 149
Staudt, Robert Jared, 275n36
Steenberghen, Fernand van, 89, 100
Stein, Edith, 89, 100
Stout, Jeffrey, 65n63
Strigel, Victorinus, 52n52
Stump, Eleonore, 183n10
Suárez, Francisco, 142n69, 197–98
Sullivan, Ezra, 420
Swafford, Andrew Dean, 136n65
Sylvester of Ferrara, 431n66

Tanner, Kathryn, 146–47
Taylor, Charles, 2, 65n63, 105, 255n2, 260
Teresa of Avila, 108
te Velde, Rudi, 104n24, 105, 228n4
Thompson, E. P., 261n10

Tilley, Terrence W., 98n15, 200n16
Titus, Craig Steven, 360n56, 361
Tolksdorf, Wilhelm, 200n17
Tomberg, Markus, 200n16
Torchia, Joseph, 356n51
Torrance, Alan J., 146n74
Torrell, Jean-Pierre, 318n36, 334n6, 372n9
Trueman, Patrick A., 350n39
Tschipke, Theophil, 186n14
Tugwell, Simon, 43n42
Turner, Denys, 58n56, 105n26
Týn, Tomáš, 89, 100

Ulrich, Ferdinand, 89, 100

Van Dyke, Christina, 55n54, 351n40
Vattimo, Gianni, 98n17
Verschuuren, Gerard M., 56n55, 58n56
Vogel, Heinrich J., 52n51

Waldstein, Michael Maria, 49n46, 365n66
Ward, Graham, 262n13
Ward, Keith, 58n56
Watson, Philip S., 53
Wawrykow, Joseph P., 47n45, 247n31, 274n31, 441n78

Wenzel, Siegfried, 351n40
Westberg, Daniel, 277n38
Wetter, Friedrich, 43n42
Wetterneck, Chad T., 347n32
Whelan, Matthew, 323n42
White, Thomas Joseph, 58n56, 67n65, 89n4, 97n14, 104n25, 133n61, 136n65, 221n59, 243n29, 262n14, 287n55, 381n18, 387, 392n8
Wicki, Nikolaus, 22n26, 394n11
William of Auvergne, 393–94
Williams, A. N., 393n9
Williams, John Joseph, 426n59
Wippel, John F., 94n10, 218n52, 228n4, 429n63
Wittgenstein, Ludwig, 145–46
Wojtyła, Karol, 329, 345, 354, 364
Wright, N. T., 149n77, 422n54, 437n74
Wuellner, Bernard, 99n16
Wyser, Paul, 96n13

Yearly, Lee H., 304n16

Zychlinski, Alexander von, 398n15

General Index

acedia, 293, 333, 350–59, 363n62, 365; boredom (*ennui*), 351, 353–54, 359, 361; *ressentiment*, 351, 353–55, 359; spiritual remedy for, 358–65; wandering of the mind (*pervagatio mentis*), 351, 355–56
addiction, 347–48, 353n44, 356, 363n62
adoptionism, 377
adoration, acts of, 256, 265n19, 266, 267n23, 283
almsgiving, 176–78, 190–91
analogy of being: analogical apprehension of divine essence, attributes, 11–12, 392, 400
analysis fidei, 197–99, 200n17, 201, 213n42
Angelic Warfare Confraternity, 363–64
angelism-animalism polarity, 27, 154, 226–27, 251
angels, 9, 32–33, 77, 85, 132n57, 141, 231, 273, 374–77, 383, 394, 396, 399, 429, 436, 440, 442n79, 444
annihilationism. *See* total-death theory
anthropocentric turn, 152–56, 162, 165, 169, 172–73, 194, 196–204, 207, 219–22, 224–29, 251–52, 284, 291, 388, 390n3
apophatic discourse on God, 12
Apostles' Creed, 371
appetites, sensory: irascible and concupiscible, 129n51, 132, 359–60
appetitive powers: as passive potencies, 206–7
apprehensive powers: as passive potencies, 206–7

Aristotle: account of scientific knowledge, 92–94; on beatitude, 4n4, 30–31, 38; on finality, 110–11, 116, 123; metaphysics of, 100; objective vs. subjective end, 18; on perfect friendship, 247–48; semantic triangle (*res-ratio-nomen*), 11; virtue ethics of, 276–77, 279–80
articles of faith, 96, 105, 194, 195n4, 218
atheism, modern, 56, 58n56, 59
Augustine: theology of beatific vision, 393–94, 396; theology of sin and grace, 276–77, 279–80
auxilia: preternatural, 142; supernatural, 142

Baianism, 134, 136, 141
baptism, 43n42, 63, 80, 178, 185, 187–89, 191, 247, 270, 280–81, 289; as incorporation into Christ's passion and death, 188–89; sacramental character of, 247, 270, 280–81
beatific vision, 2, 5, 13–14, 19–21, 33–37, 39–48, 71, 74–75, 94, 106, 133, 137–41, 143, 145n72, 147–48, 192, 209n32, 210, 216, 219, 222, 224, 231n8, 232, 234, 252, 256, 271, 272n29, 273, 294, 308n26, 329, 380n17, 382, 387, 389–409, 420–28, 431–36, 438–44; attainment prior to resurrection, 42–44, 426–28, 431–36; degrees of intensity, 46–47, 441n78; essential vs. accidental, 431n66; human capacity for, 13–14, 21, 22n25, 37, 46–47,

485

beatific vision, human capacity for (*cont.*) 137–41, 143, 249, 272n29, 392, 404–5, 421–22, 436; loss of, 47; as non-comprehensive, 396–97, 406–7, 436; object of as theophany or God's essence, 392–408; possibility of intensive growth in, 43n42, 427–28, 431–33; possibility of *visio* known only by faith, 272n29. *See also* Thomas Aquinas

beatitude: as central theme of medieval theology, 22n26; conditions for human happiness, 40–45; definition of, 3–4, 8–10; intrinsically communal character of, 74–75, 408, 437–45; modern distortions of, 6–8; as occurring in the theoretical intellect, 32; as perfection of human happiness, 24, 29–30, 37–38, 40; role of body in, 42–45, 74–75, 421, 423, 425–36, 439–40, 442; role of friends in relation to, 45; role of senses in, 31–32, 42

Benedictus Deus (Benedict XII), 43n42, 420

bios praktikos, 19, 37, 45, 72, 193

bios theoretikos, 20, 21n23, 37, 45, 72, 193

categorical imperative (Kant), 412–13

causality: divine transcendental causality, 236–38; *per se* series of causes, 124; priority of final cause, 123; secondary, 236

certitude. *See* faith

character, sacramental, 247, 270, 280

charity, virtue of, 5–6, 17, 20–21, 37, 39, 40n40, 46–48, 60–61, 63, 72–73, 174, 176, 178, 183–92, 197, 207, 210, 211n34, 219–20, 222, 224–25, 229, 231–33, 242–52, 254, 269, 273, 276, 278–83, 288, 290, 293, 295, 298–99, 302–6, 308–16, 318–19, 321–23, 331n4, 338, 340, 344–45, 351–52, 359, 362–64, 388, 407n28, 408, 411–14, 416–19, 421, 429n63, 434, 441–44; as bringing about inchoate union with God, 6, 20, 61, 184, 186, 188, 192, 197, 233, 247, 250, 269, 273, 281–82, 290, 295, 304, 352; as commanding other virtues, 73, 246, 254, 281, 283, 288, 293, 310, 314, 413; connaturality, 225, 250; as created *habitus*, 246; as determinate

for intensity of beatific vision, 46–47; as form of faith, 20, 186, 210, 211n34, 219–20, 232, 313–14; as form of the virtues, 73, 276, 282–83, 290, 305–6, 308, 310n27, 314, 319

chastity, 72–74, 329–35, 337–38, 340–41, 344, 350, 354n48, 355, 358–59, 362–65, 367; sins against, 340–41; "spiritual chastity," 362–65

church: indefectibility of, 82; as necessary for salvation, 82; as visible, 287

communion of the saints, 74

concupiscence, 132, 170, 179n4, 315, 335, 345, 347–48, 356, 358–59; as "germ of sin," 345

confession, exterior act of, 309–10, 313

conscience, 57, 61, 69, 71, 152, 162–72, 227, 267n23; binding character of dictates of, 168; counterfeit of, 152–53, 167–72; disappearance in light of evolutionary naturalism, 57, 227; erroneous, 153, 167–71; examination of, 170; proper formation of, 61, 170

consequentialism, 173

contemplation: as conforming the human to God, 32; of first cause, 20, 133; infused, 17, 140, 440; of separate substances, 33

contractarianism, 173

contrition, 365

conversion, 234–41

cosmos: eternity of, 118

courage, virtue of, 72–74, 278n40, 288, 297–98, 304n14, 338–39, 359–61, 367

creation, 9, 109; gratuity of, 109

"Credo of the People of God" (Paul VI), 3, 75–85

cultus: counterfeit, 292–94. *See also* religion, virtue of

curiosity, 355–57. *See also* acedia

De analysi fidei. See analysis fidei

death of God, 56–57

debitum naturae, 138–39

Decalogue, 294

deification. *See* divinization

Dei Filius (Vatican I), 199, 202–3, 205, 213, 215

General Index 487

Dei Verbum (Vatican II), 108n30, 211
deontology, 173
Deus sive natura (Spinoza), 149
Devasahayam Pillai: martyrdom of, 299, 311, 325
devotion, interior acts of, 265n19, 266, 282–83, 285, 296, 316–17
Disability Studies: beatitude in light of, 61–65
divinization, 9, 21–22, 37, 72–73, 109, 127–28, 147–48, 176, 223–24, 231–33, 235, 241n25, 242n26, 243–44, 246n30, 251–52, 377, 403, 423, 439
doctrine-praxis relation, 67

emotivism, 354
endurance, act of, 306, 311, 314
eschatology: inner-worldly realization of, 148–49
essence-existence distinction, 18, 105, 112
esse reale-esse intentionale distinction, 157, 398, 401–2
eternal law. *See* law
Eucharist, 63, 82–83, 178, 187, 189, 191, 289, 371n7, 383; as sacrifice, 82–83, 187–89, 371n7; satisfactory power of, 189
eudaimonian ethics, 22n26, 53
evil: as privation of good, 179; question of as unanswerable to philosophy, 33n33
evolutionary naturalism, 56–58
exegesis, biblical, 98, 108; spiritual exegesis of, 56n55, 108
experiential expressivism, 263, 288

face-to-face vision of God. *See* beatific vision
faith, virtue of, 5, 17, 20, 37, 39, 41, 49, 51, 60, 63, 72, 77, 95–96, 98, 102–3, 174, 186, 193–225, 231–32, 242–45, 269, 280–81, 289, 298, 302, 304, 306, 308–11, 312–16, 322–23, 351, 362, 368–73, 377, 381, 386, 390, 407n28, 439; anthropocentric vs. theocentric, 194–203, 219–22; authority faith (Scheeben), 214–16; as blind faith, 121; certitude of, 196–97, 200, 202, 217, 369; definition of, 201–3; as divine, 22n25, 95–96, 98, 103, 194, 197, 199, 202–3, 209n32, 215–17, 219–20, 245, 298, 306, 316, 322, 369–73, 377, 381, 386, 390, 439; formal object of assent, 203, 207–8, 210–18, 219, 308; as formed, 211, 219–20, 232, 313–14; as inchoate beatitude, 72, 193, 195, 197, 199, 202–5, 211–12, 216–17, 219, 222–23, 369, 390; as infused supernatural habit, 95, 102, 204–5, 207, 209n32, 211–12, 214, 216–17, 219; lifeless, 186; material object of, 208, 210–12, 217–18; as necessary to rightly direct humans to beatitude, 49, 195; nonthematic, 368, 386; *obiectum formale quo* vs. *obiectum formale quod*, 211–17; obscurity of, 77; as opposed to private judgment, 369, 386; as rational faith, 199; vs. vision, 209, 217
faith-reason relationship, 91
Fall, the, 50–53, 121, 268, 290, 334, 340, 379–80; as devastating creation, 50–53, 121
fideism, 107, 150, 198–99, 212; dialectic formed with naturalist rationalism, 199, 212
Fidelis of Sigmaringen: martyrdom of, 315
Fides et Ratio (John Paul II), 68–71, 86–87, 92, 99, 101
fides quaerens intellectum, 196
final end of human being: attained by human action, 151; disagreement as to nature of, 16–17, 18n19, 25, 27–33, 59–60; material and formal aspects of, 16–18, 25–26; means of ordering humans to, 15–16, 69, 175–76; objective and subjective distinction in, 18, 25, 30, 37, 40–41, 46, 60, 71, 75, 252, 271; singular ultimate end, 15–16, 25, 36, 74, 132, 139, 172, 333, 388–89, 409–25. *See also* beatific vision
finality, principle of. *See* teleology
final perseverance. *See* grace
First Vatican Council, 199, 202–3, 209, 213, 420n49
Formula of Concord (1577), 52n52
fortitude, virtue of, 166, 301–12, 315, 319, 323, 325, 359; acquired vs. infused, 304–6, 319; acts of, 303, 305, 307–19, 339n18; civic, 278, 305; virtues annexed to, 303
freedom, human: 69, 161, 226n2, 230, 240n24, 375, 414–15; emergence of evil

from misuse of, 414–15; *liberum arbitrium*, 236, 238n22, 239, 323n43, 348
friendship, 247–51
fruits of the Spirit, 171n37, 295; charity, 295n64; faithfulness, 295n64; generosity, 295n64; gentleness, 295n64; goodness, 295n64; joy, 295; kindness, 295n64; modesty, 295n64; patience, 295n64; peace, 295n64; self-control, 295n64. *See also* chastity

Gaudium et Spes (Vatican II), 66–67
gifts of the Holy Spirit, 63, 102n22, 232, 243n29, 246, 269–70, 274, 312, 418; counsel, 171n37; piety, 269–70, 281; wisdom, 102n22, 171n37, 232
gluttony, vice of, 330, 342
God: attributes as identical with essence, 11–12; beatitude or happiness of, 2, 4–14, 38, 46, 248, 389, 420, 424–25; as common good, 36, 120, 140, 182; as Demiurge, 122; denial of the existence of, 56–57; essence of, 10–13, 39, 77, 105, 137, 156n4, 209, 228n5, 246n30, 390, 392–97, 399–405, 407–8, 422–24, 432–33, 436, 438, 440–41; as first cause, 18, 20, 56, 120, 122, 124, 132n59, 137, 271n28, 292, 400; as first truth, 21, 33–37, 59, 95–96, 104, 132–34, 140–41, 143, 171, 197, 208–10, 217–19, 252, 308, 421, 424, 428, 432–35; goodness of, 9, 12, 20, 39, 77, 120, 122, 124–25, 127–28, 144, 230, 242, 249, 274; as *ipsum esse subsistens*, 18, 89n4, 156, 158, 229, 390, 400, 424, 436, 441; noncompetitive sovereignty of, 156; no proper definition of, 105; omnipotence of, 77, 141, 362, 372; omniscience of, 77; oneness of, 8, 77; providence of, 9, 47, 77, 103, 110–11, 119–21, 127, 160, 256, 291, 363–64; as pure act, 111, 395, 408, 424, 436; relation of justice to mercy in, 180–81, 185; righteousness of, 9; subjugation to the principle of finality, 125; transcendence of, 392, 400
grace, 4–5, 10, 19, 21, 30, 36–37, 39–40, 46, 49–50, 52, 63, 71, 73, 77, 80–81, 84, 102–3, 105, 127, 134, 139–42, 145–47, 150, 180, 183–85, 224–25, 228n4, 229, 232–47, 250–51, 269–70, 273–74, 277, 280, 289–90, 294, 305, 312, 323, 333–34, 340, 348, 352, 359, 361–64, 372, 375, 379–80, 382, 392, 402–5, 410, 414, 416, 418, 439, 441–44; as accident, 242, 244; actual, 225, 233–41, 247; as analogical notion, 233; capital, 289; cooperating, 234, 237–40, 246; as distinct from theological virtues, 242–43; of final perseverance, 240; gratuitous, 127; gratuity of, 138–39, 144–47; as habitual, 233–34, 238–39, 247; as healing, 276, 280, 362; operating, 234–35, 237–40, 244, 372; as perfecting nature, 102–3, 140–41, 150, 244, 269, 333, 439; preserving, 52; prevenient, 135n63; sanctifying, 19, 37, 39–40, 63, 73, 135n63, 139, 141–42, 183–85, 225, 229, 232–34, 240–45, 247, 269–70, 274, 289–90, 305, 340, 352, 359, 361–62, 379–80, 382, 392, 418, 441, 443–44; state of, 134, 184, 246n30, 277n38, 410, 414, 416; supernatural character of, 225, 232–33; as supernature, 242n28, 243n29; uncreated, 146

habitus: on increase and diminishment in, 342n22, 346n30
happiness. *See* beatitude
Heidegger, Martin: critique of metaphysics of, 89, 100
hell, 45n44, 436n73; as empty, 45n44, 436n73; occupied hell as producing sorrow in heaven, 45n44, 436n73
Hellenism: intrusion into the Gospel, 54
historicism, 68, 88, 97
Holy Orders. *See* Orders, sacrament of
Holy Spirit: eternal spiration of, 9, 78; indwelling of, 246n30, 248, 250, 290; love as proper name of, 245; as *vinculum caritatis*, 245
hope, virtue of, 5, 17, 20, 37, 39, 41, 60, 63, 72, 174, 201, 207, 222, 242–44, 269, 280–81, 302, 304, 311, 351–52, 361–62, 407, 444
human action: *actiones humanae* vs. *actiones hominis*, 23, 336; irreducibly moral quality of, 24, 131; no infinite regress of ends possible, 25; ordering of penulti-

mate ends to final end, 25; reasons for deficiency in, 24n28

human being: dignity of, 331, 365; as image of God, 13, 112–13, 141, 251–52, 274, 286; natural liability to corruption, 379; paradoxical character of, 48; proportionate end of, 10, 15–16, 19–21, 36–37, 53, 109, 137–46, 149, 279, 334; as rational animal, 26, 143, 336, 421, 430, 435; supernatural end of, 9–10, 22n25, 36–37, 63, 138–40, 148, 219, 232, 237–38, 240n24, 245, 256, 274, 278–79, 294, 295, 304–6, 333–34; as super-primate, 27, 57, 154, 226–27; as wounded by original sin, 107, 179, 268, 276, 279–80, 305, 308

humanism. *See* secular humanism

hylomorphism. *See* rational soul

Hypnopsychites, 54n53

ideas, divine, 54–55, 157

image of God. *See* human being

imitation: conformity of creatures to God by means of, 125–28

imperfect happiness, 19, 20–21, 28, 31, 35, 37–40, 42, 44–45, 47, 61, 72, 138, 193, 271, 334

impetuosity, sin of, 346

Ineffabilis Deus (Pius IX), 373

initium fidei, 234–41, 244

instinctus fidei, 135n63, 236

intellect: active, 397n13, 398n15, 401–2, 405; as epiphenomenon of neurological processes, 154, 227; finality of, 8, 19, 86, 91, 128–46, 148, 150; possible, 20, 398n15; practical, 32, 130–31, 160, 161n13, 162, 164–65, 166n29, 172, 174; proper object of, 29, 33, 35, 129, 140, 307n23; theoretical, 32, 65, 130–31, 160, 165

intellectus fidei, 69–70, 86, 106

intelligent design, 122

intemperance, vice of, 340–43, 349n36, 358

internet use, 73, 329–30, 345, 347–49, 357, 361n58, 366. *See also* pornography

Jägerstätter, Franz: martyrdom of, 323n42

James the Apostle: martyrdom of, 299–300, 324

Jansenism, 121, 134, 136, 141

Jesus Christ: as agent who helps humans achieve beatitude, 48–49; ascension of, 43n42, 78–79, 371, 383–84; humanity as instrument of divinity, 186–87; as incarnate God, 5, 66, 78–79, 94, 103, 146–47, 173–74, 178, 209, 215, 267n23, 289, 291, 298, 371, 381, 443; merits of, 74, 79, 272, 368, 378–79, 384, 443; Paschal Mystery of, 69, 81, 379; Passion of, 43n42, 72, 74, 80, 176, 178, 182–88, 192, 281, 291, 334, 374n10, 443; priesthood of, 178, 184–87; resurrection of, 5n7, 78–79, 81, 247, 367, 371, 380, 384; satisfaction of, 72, 178, 182–88, 192

John of Cologne: martyrdom of, 315

John the Baptist: martyrdom of, 299–300, 313, 315n34, 324, 327

John, Gospel of: composed by eyewitness, 5n7

judgment: general, 43n42

justice, virtue of, 72, 126, 166, 253–54, 266–67, 275, 278n40, 284, 288–89, 303, 304n14, 308–9, 312n31, 316, 331n4, 337–40, 343, 359; virtues annexed to, 254, 266–67, 275, 284, 308, 316

justification, 72, 127, 175, 224, 235, 239–40, 305

just war. *See* war, just

Kantian critical idealism, 99, 130–31, 157, 207, 220–21, 226

Kolbe, Maximilian Mary: martyrdom of, 323n42

law: divine, 274–75, 281n44, 294, 300, 306, 313, 316–17, 322–23; eternal, 71, 152, 158–61, 230, 334, 336n11; human, 275, 281n44, 294; moral, 69; natural, 71, 126, 152, 158–59, 161, 163, 170–74, 268, 274, 334n7, 337n13, 348

liberum arbitrium. *See* freedom

light of faith, 137, 216

light of glory, 20, 33, 36–37, 141, 217, 245, 247, 252, 394, 402–5, 407, 441, 443

Locke, John: epistemology of, 398

Lord's Day: keeping of, 353n44; neglect of, 294n62

love of God, natural: inability of fallen man to perform act of, 276, 279–80
lumen fidei. See light of faith
Lumen Fidei (Pope Francis), 201n18, 327
lumen gloriae. See light of glory
lust, vice of, 330, 332–33, 336, 340n20, 341–44, 348, 349n36, 357–59, 365; as giving rise to illicit, culturally accepted sexual practices, 348–49; inordinate vs. disordered, 343; spiritual remedy for, 358–65
Luther Martin: one-side reading of Augustine on grace, 50; pessimistic anthropology of, 50–53, 121

macula peccati. See sin
Maria Goretti: martyrdom of, 316
marriage: indissolubility of, 337n13; threefold good of, 337
martyrdom, act of, 72–73, 297–301, 304–25, 328; canonical criteria for determining, 301n10, 320–21; for the faith, 299n7, 300–301, 312, 315, 317, 321n40, 323n42, 324; question of death suffered for *res publica*, 317–22; for virtue and truth, 300–1, 312–19, 321n40, 322–23, 324–27
Mary, 65n62, 74, 78–79, 84, 363–64, 367–86, 435; bodily assumption of, 65n62, 74, 79, 367–68, 370–74, 377–78, 380–81, 383–86; divine motherhood of, 372–74, 377, 382–83, 385; as ever-virgin, 79, 371, 378; exemplary character of life, 74; fullness of grace, 372–75, 377–80, 382; Immaculate Conception of, 79, 373–74; as mediatrix of grace, 375n13; as mother of all believers, 74, 368, 384–85; as New Eve, 79; question of death of, 378n15, 380; sinlessness of, 378–79; superiority over angels, 375–77; as type of the church, 383, 385
Mass. *See* Eucharist
materialism, 8, 149
merit, 46–48, 138, 234, 239, 245, 247, 273, 274n31, 293, 375n13; condign, 247, 375n13; congruous, 247, 375n13
metaphysics: as "divine science," 94, 101; formal object of, 101, 103; of the good (metaphysics of morals), 152–53, 171, 173; Kantian restrictions on, 89, 99; nature of, 90; as ontology, 101; as theology's privileged instrument, 2, 70–71, 87–88, 90–91, 103–8, 150. *See also* Aristotle; Thomas Aquinas
mind. *See* intellect
missions, temporal, 245, 248
Modernism, Catholic, 263, 377
modernity: formation of, 65n63; rejection of teleology as characteristic of, 26, 110
Monoenergism, 121n44
Monotheletism, 121n44
Munificentissimus Deus (Pius XII), 371

natural desire: as conditional, 35, 133; as elicited, 132; to know causes, 132–33; as unconditional, 36; under *ratio* of first cause, 21n24, 35–36, 133, 137; for vision of God, 34–37, 71, 87, 90–91, 109, 133–34, 136–37
naturalistic fallacy, 161–62
natural law. *See* law
natural theology, 58n56, 87, 145, 220, 264, 267n23
nature: finality as intrinsic to, 121–22, 150
nature-grace distinction, 86–87, 90, 109, 133–34, 141–50, 334, 359; grace-extrinsicism, 90–91, 136, 141–44, 147–48, 150; grace-integralism, 90–91, 135, 141–42, 146–47; as paradigmatic example of role of metaphysics in relation to theology, 91
New Atheists, 56, 58n56
New Natural Law, 143–44, 409
Nicene Creed, 76, 371
nihilism, 60n57, 150
nominalism, 51, 121

obediential potency: general, 140–41, 147–48; specific, 140–41, 251
obiectum: Western Scholastic understanding of, 205–8, 210
oblation, acts of, 256, 266, 268, 283
observance, virtue of, 266
ontotheological naturalism, 144–45
Orders, sacrament of, 82
original righteousness, 50, 63, 134, 142,

General Index 491

179n4, 183, 340, 379–80, 382; loss of, 50, 179n4, 340, 380
original sin. *See* sin

paradise, 406, 422–23, 435, 437, 439–40
patience, virtue of, 303, 308, 314
Pelagianism, 52, 54, 134, 243n29, 264
penance, 188
penance, sacrament of, 185, 365
perseverance, virtue of, 303, 308, 315
personalist ethics, 49n46
phenomenology, 99, 157; of belief, 200n17
philosophia perennis, 65n63, 99–100, 150, 207; Scotist-Suárezian strand of, 100n18
piety, virtue of, 266, 413–14
pope: infallibility of, 81, 371n7
pornography, 73, 329–33, 343–50, 353, 356–59, 361, 363, 365; spiritual remedy for, 358–65; statistics on use of, 330n1
positive theology, 98
posthumanism, 154
postmodernism, 67
potency-act division, 101, 111–12, 117
potentia oboedientialis. *See* obediential potency
poverty, holy, 127
praeambula fidei, 94, 102n23, 106
Pragmatism, 130–31
praxis. *See* doctrine-praxis relation
prayer, interior acts of, 239, 265n19, 266–67, 283, 285, 290, 296, 363–64; communal, 363–64; discipline of, 363–64
preambles of faith. *See praeambula fidei*
predestination, 363, 378
pride, vice of, 9, 61
primordial conscience. *See synderesis*
principle of noncontradiction, 160, 171
private judgment, 217n51
process theology, 125
Prosperity Gospel, 7
Protestant Reformation, 22n26, 50–55, 176, 194, 246; classical Protestant biblicism, 56n55; fundamentalism, 56n55; liberal Protestantism, 262n14, 263–64, 377; North American Protestantism, 260–61, 286–87
proofs for God's existence, 58n56; Aquinas's fifth way, 118–19

providence. *See* God
prudence, virtue of, 71–72, 152–53, 164–67, 173, 278n40, 303–4, 308, 316, 336n11, 338–40, 342, 346n29, 358, 360–61, 365–66; in relation to conscience, 153, 164–67; three acts of, 166
public sphere, secular, 258–59
Puglisi, Giuseppe: martyrdom of, 299–300, 321–22, 325
pure act. *See* God
pure nature, state of, 139, 142–43; as identical with fallen nature, 142
purgatory, 43n42, 84, 188, 384–85

rational soul, 13–14, 21–22, 29–30, 37, 44, 54–57, 58n56, 62–63, 77, 128n50, 132, 139, 271–72, 371n7, 399n16, 426–27, 429–36; as *forma corporis*, 13, 22, 29, 37, 44, 62, 128n50, 132n57, 139, 271–72, 399n16, 426–27, 429–36; immortality of, 44, 54–57, 77, 371n7, 391, 427, 429–30
rational vs. nonrational agency, 23–24
reatus poenae. *See* sin
Regensburg address (Benedict XVI), 51n50
religion, virtue of, 61, 72–74, 152, 244, 253–57, 265–71, 275–76, 279–96, 316–17, 367, 443; acquired vs. infused, 269, 276, 279–82, 284–85, 290–91, 413n39; acts of, 73, 256, 266–68, 282–85, 293–94, 296; *cultus* as formal object of, 268, 270, 280, 282, 285; as means to end of beatitude, 256; natural vs. revealed, 290–91; *Religionswissenschaft* view of, 262–64, 284, 288; vs. relationship, 261, 286–87; vs. "religion" in contemporary parlance, 257–65, 283–93; vs. revelation, 264–65, 289
religion-science conflict, 56n55
religious freedom, 258
Renaissance humanism, 143, 196, 197n6, 201
resurrection, 31, 45, 51–52, 74–75, 84–85, 421, 423, 425, 427, 429–31, 433–36, 439; general, 31, 75, 84, 425, 429, 433
resurrection body, 24, 42, 44–45, 74–75, 252, 384, 389, 425–26, 428, 433, 442

resurrection-in-death theories, 54n53, 426
Romanticism, German, 391
Romero, Oscar: martyrdom of, 323n42

Sabbath. *See* Lord's Day
sacra doctrina. *See* sacred theology
sacraments, 63, 81, 183, 270, 280, 289, 311, 365, 371n7; efficacious nature of, 63, 371n7; as instrumental causes of grace, 187n16. *See also* character, sacramental
sacred theology, 68–71, 87, 92–99, 102–9, 113, 134, 136, 150, 174, 195–96, 386, 439, 444; articles of faith as providing first principles, 96, 105, 195n4; definition of, 94–98; *obiectum formale quo* of, 95, 96n12, 103; *obiectum formale quod* of, 95, 96n12, 103; material object of, 95, 96n12, 104; modern dissolution of, 68, 88, 90; relation of metaphysics to, 102–9; as *scientia argumentativa*, 96, 97n14, 103, 107–8, 113; scriptural interpretation as soul of, 108; as speculative, dogmatic theology, 70, 92, 97–98; as subordinate science, 94, 96n13, 97n14, 103, 105, 195n4; superior to alternative models of theology, 93, 97–98
sacrifice: acts of, 256, 265n19, 266, 267n23, 283, 290; meaning of, 184
saints: communion of, 368, 383; intercession of, 363–64
sanctification, 72, 175, 224, 244
sanctifying grace. *See* grace
Satan, 145
satisfaction: need for arising from post-baptismal sin, 187–88; as performed for another, 183–84; possibility of forgiveness without, 181–82; as removing debt of punishment, 181–83, 191
science, Aristotelian, 92–94; definition of 92; subordinate sciences, 93. *See also* Aristotle
science, modern natural, 148, 154
science of conclusions, 97. *See also* sacred theology
Second Vatican Council, 66–67, 108, 135, 200, 380n17, 383, 420n49
secular humanism, 28, 222, 292

semantic triangle. *See* Aristotle
Semipelagianism, 246
separate substances, 101
sexuality, human, 335–38, 355, 439–40; pejorative views of, 338; question of sex in heaven, 439–40
sin: actual, 9, 38, 53, 179–81, 233; debt of punishment for (*debitum poenae*), 176–83, 185, 188, 191–92; four wounds resulting from, 179–80, 188; liability of punishment for (*reatus poenae*), 179–80; mortal, 63, 246n30, 247, 377, 379, 409–11, 413, 417; original, 9, 38, 50, 52–53, 63, 80, 107, 179, 183, 235, 264, 289, 340, 344n26, 345–46, 353, 362, 371n7, 377, 379, 380n17; stain of (*macula peccati*), 179–82, 185, 188; venial, 340, 344n27, 345, 353, 377, 379, 409–11, 414, 416–17, 419
sloth, spiritual. *See* acedia
Son of God: eternal generation of, 9, 78
sophiology (Bulgakov), 145
soul. *See* rational soul
soul sleep, 384, 435
sovereign self. *See* subjective sovereignty
Spe Salvi (Benedict XVI), 201–5, 219, 223, 369n2, 386
Stephen the Deacon: martyrdom of, 299–300, 324
subjective sovereignty, 6, 26, 144, 152–56, 162, 165, 172–74, 194, 226–27, 251, 257, 288, 291, 293, 326–27, 439
supernatural existential, 135n63
supernature. *See* grace
synderesis, 152–53, 157, 160–64, 167–68, 170–74; as containing first principle and first precept of practical reason, 160–61, 172; definition of, 160
Synod of Bishops (1985), 67

teleology: analogical applications of, 118–120, 122, 126, 128; chance as intelligible only in light of, 116–17; crisis produced by rejection of, 26; fault as presupposing natural finality, 117; natural vs. rational agency, 128–29; as necessary for theology, 2, 71, 86–87, 109, 387; principle of finality, 109–34, 141; universal

applicability of, 23–26, 57, 71, 109–11, 114–22, 127, 144, 150, 152, 161–62; voluntarist evacuation of intrinsic finality, 111, 121
temperance, virtue of, 72, 166, 278n40, 288, 303–4, 307, 338–42, 346, 358, 365
Teresa Benedicta a Cruce: martyrdom of, 323n42
Thnetopsychites, 54n53
Thomas Aquinas: on analogy, 11–12, 392n8; on beatific vision, 2–3, 6, 8–21, 33–34, 42–44, 46–49, 74, 389–409; on body in beatitude, 389, 425–36; as common doctor, 1, 87–88, 92, 204, 222; epistemology of, 397–99, 402; on faith in ST II-II, 204–212; on human happiness in ST I-II, 22–49, 438; on Immaculate Conception, 373–74, 379; impediments to reception of his teaching on happiness, 50–65, 152; late twentieth-century neglect of, 87; magisterial recommendations of thought of, 91, 99; meditation on Angelic Salutation to Mary, 368, 372–80; on merit, 47n45; metaphysics of, 100–108; metaphysics of participation, 225, 228–33, 236, 251; three premises of metaphysics of being of, 156–58; on virtue of religion, 265–71
tithes, 256, 265n19, 266, 283
tradition, sacred, 108, 231
transcendence: counterfeit notions of in Romanticism, 390–91
transubstantiation, 83
Trent, Council of, 80, 87–88
total-death theory, 54–55, 436n73
total depravity, 55
transhumanism, 26, 109, 154
Trinity, 8–9, 20, 36–37, 39, 49, 69–70, 77–78, 92, 97, 103, 106, 134, 140, 144, 212, 216, 219, 222, 231, 233, 245, 247–48, 251–52, 267n23, 270, 280, 285–86, 291, 334, 352, 360, 377, 386, 388, 390, 421–22, 442, 444; of subsistent relations, 231
truthfulness (*veracitas*), virtue of, 308–9, 317

turn to the subject. *See* anthropocentric turn
Twenty-four Thomistic theses, 99

ubiquity of Christ's body: Lutheran theory of, 384
ultimate end of human being. *See* final end of man
universalism, salvific, 145, 436n73
uti-frui distinction, 411–14, 416–17, 419

Vatican Councils. *See* First Vatican Council; Second Vatican Council
Veritatis Splendor (John Paul II), 87n1, 324
vice: capital, 343, 351
virtue: acquired moral, 274, 276, 277nn37–38, 278–80, 306n21, 310; cardinal, 301–3, 304n14, 305, 338–39; "co-existence theory" of acquired and infused moral virtue, 277n38, 283, 304n15, 306n21, 361; infused moral, 232, 243, 274, 276, 277nn37–38, 278, 280, 282, 289, 302, 306n21, 310, 314, 352; intellectual, 302n11; moral, 253, 265, 279, 282–83, 290, 302n11, 304n11, 310, 313, 316, 339; pagan, 276; theological, 141, 174, 207–8, 229, 232, 243–44, 265n19, 269, 274, 278, 302–3, 314, 317, 352, 362
voluntarism, 32, 51, 111, 121
voluntas ordinata, 51n50
vows, 256, 265n19, 266, 283

war, just, 317
weakness, sin of, 346
will: as first principle of sin, 235; incurvature toward self-love, 50, 53; interior vs. exterior actions, 238–39; nonexistence of, 61; as ordered to happiness, 19, 26–27; proper object of, 23, 29, 35, 113–14, 120, 129, 211n34; rightly ordered will as indispensable for beatitude, 152; will as nature (*voluntas ut natura*), 26; willing end vs. means, 238, 240

ALSO IN THE
THOMISTIC RESSOURCEMENT SERIES

———◆———

Series Editors: Matthew Levering
Thomas Joseph White, OP

Analogy after Aquinas
Logical Problems, Thomistic Answers
Domenic D'Ettore

The Metaphysical Foundations of Love
Aquinas on Participation, Unity, and Union
Anthony T. Flood

The Cleansing of the Heart
The Sacraments as Instrumental Causes in the Thomistic Tradition
Reginald M. Lynch, OP

The Ideal Bishop
Aquinas's Commentaries on the Pastoral Epistles
Michael G. Sirilla

Aquinas and the Theology of the Body
The Thomistic Foundations of John Paul II's Anthropology
Thomas Petri, OP

Angels and Demons
A Catholic Introduction
Serge-Thomas Bonino, OP
Translated by Michael J. Miller

www.ingramcontent.com/pod-product-compliance
Lightning Source LLC
Chambersburg PA
CBHW020312010526
44107CB00054B/1813